Charlatans or Saviours?

Charlatans or Saviours?

Economists and the British economy
from Marshall to Meade

Roger Middleton

*Reader in the History of Political Economy,
University of Bristol, UK*

Edward Elgar
Cheltenham, UK • Northampton, MA, USA

Published by
Edward Elgar Publishing Limited
8 Lansdown Place
Cheltenham
Glos GL50 2HU
UK

Edward Elgar Publishing, Inc.
6 Market Street
Northampton
Massachusetts 01060
USA

A catalogue record for this book
is available from the British Library

Library of Congress Cataloguing in Publication Data

Middleton, Roger, 1955–
    Charlatans or saviours? : economists and the British economy from
    Marshall to Meade / Roger Middleton
      Includes index.
      1. Economists—Great Britain. 2. Economics—Great Britain–
    –History. 3. Great Britain—Economic policy.   I. Title.
    HB103.A2M53   1998
    330'.094—dc21   98–21065
                                                            CIP

ISBN 1 85898 904 3 (cased)

Printed and bound in Great Britain by
Biddles Ltd, Guildford and King's Lynn

The activities of economists – what they do and how and why they do it – are of at least as much interest and importance as the activities of the people economists themselves study . . .   (Hutchison 1955, p. 1)

we economists in recent years have done vast harm – to society at large and to our profession in particular – by claiming more than we can deliver. We have thereby encouraged politicians to make extravagant promises, inculcate unrealistic expectations in the public at large, and promote discontent with reasonably satisfactory results because they fall short of the economists' promised land.

(Friedman 1972, pp. 12, 17–18)

a country's economic progress is in inverse proportion to the distinction of its economists!   (Allen 1979, pp. 18–19)

Contents

List of figures and tables

FIGURES

TABLES

Abbreviations

AEA	American Economic Association
AER	*American Economic Review*
AES	Alternative economic strategy
AFEE	Association for Evolutionary Economics
APTE	Association of Polytechnic Teachers of Economics
ASI	Adam Smith Institute
AUT	Association of University Teachers
AUTE	Association of University Teachers of Economics
BAAS	British Association for the Advancement of Science
BEA	British Economic Association
BPP	British Parliamentary Papers
CBA	Cost–benefit analysis
CBI	Confederation of British Industry
CEA	Council of Economic Advisers
CEI	Committee on Economic Information
CEIS	Central Economic Information Service
CEPR	Centre for Economic Policy Research
CEPS	Central Economic Planning Staff
CHUDE	Conference of Heads of University Departments of Economics
CNAA	Council for National Academic Awards
CPRS	Central Policy Review Staff
CPS	Centre for Policy Studies
CSE	Conference of Socialist Economists
CSO	Central Statistical Office
DAE	Department of Applied Economics, Cambridge
DEA	Department of Economic Affairs
DIYE	Do-it-yourself-economics
EAC	Economic Advisory Council
EC	European Community
EEC	European Economic Community
EJ	*Economic Journal*
EMU	European monetary union
ERM	Exchange rate mechanism

ES	Economic Section
ESRC	Economic and Social Research Council
EU	European Union
FBI	Federation of British Industries
GDFCF	Gross domestic fixed capital formation
GDP	Gross domestic product
GES	Government Economic Service
GFCF	Gross fixed capital formation
HEFC	Higher Education Funding Councils
HMG	Her/His Majesty's Government
HMSO	Her/His Majesty's Stationery Office
IBRD	International Bank for Reconstruction and Development (World Bank)
ICBH	Institute of Contemporary British History
IEA	Institute of Economic Affairs
IFS	Institute for Fiscal Studies
ILO	International Labour Organization
JEL	*Journal of Economic Literature*
JMK	Collected writings of John Maynard Keynes
JPE	*Journal of Political Economy*
JRSS	*Journal of the Royal Statistical Society*
LBS	London Business School.
LCES	London and Cambridge Economic Service
LSE	London School of Economics
MPC	Monetary Policy Committee
MS	*Manchester School of Economic and Social Studies*
MSRP	Methodology of scientific research programmes
MTFS	Medium-term financial strategy
NAIRU	Non-accelerating-inflation rate of unemployment
NCM	New classical macroeconomics
NCS	Neo-classical synthesis
NEDC	National Economic Development Council
NEDO	National Economic Development Office
NIER	*National Institute Economic Review*
NIESR	National Institute of Economic and Social Research
OECD	Organization for Economic Cooperation and Development
OEP	*Oxford Economic Papers*
OERG	Oxford Economists' Research Group
ONS	Office for National Statistics
OPCS	Office of Population Censuses and Surveys
PACE	Public authorities' current expenditure on goods and services
PEP	Political and Economic Planning

PPE	Philosophy, politics and economics
PPP	Purchasing power parity
PRO	Public Record Office
PSBR	Public sector borrowing requirement
QJE	*Quarterly Journal of Economics*
RAE	Research assessment exercise
RES	Royal Economic Society
REStud	Review of Economic Studies
SBE	Society of Business Economists
SJPE	*Scottish Journal of Political Economy*
SMF	Social Market Foundation
SSCI	Social Science Citation Index
SSR	Student:staff ratio
SSRC	Social Science Research Council
TCSC	House of Commons Treasury and Civil Service Committee
TFI	Total factor inputs
TFP	Total factor productivity
TPE	Total public expenditure
UCL	University College London
URPE	Union for Radical Political Economists

Preface

This study marks a return to an earlier preoccupation, that of the relationship between economists and economic policy. This was the focus of my 1981 Cambridge Ph.D. dissertation on Keynes and fiscal policy in Britain in the 1930s, subsequently rewritten and published as *Towards the managed economy* (Middleton 1985). It was also an element in my most recent book, *Government versus the market* (1996), which, as the title indicates, was concerned with what Wolf (1993) terms the 'cardinal choice' faced by all economic systems: that of the appropriate balance between government and the market. As Okun (1975, p. 119) has noted, 'the market needs a place, and the market needs to be kept in its place'. The question is what is the correct balance; and how, and why, has it changed over time? *Government versus the market* addressed these issues within the context of the long-run decline of the British economy. However, whilst it was concerned with a century of debate rather than a decade, with economic performance as well as policy, and with the role of ideas – ones which many would see as constituting the core of economics as an academic discipline as well as its more commercial applications – the publisher's brief offered no scope to deal in any detail with individual policy episodes or with the role of economists. It is to remedy this neglect of the development of economic ideas, of the policy process, and in particular of the contribution made by economists towards redressing Britain's relative economic decline, that this book is directed.

Its style, argument and focus derive from a number of influences and seek a variety of audiences. First and foremost, this book is the product of having taught on and around these topics for over twenty years, though in very particular circumstances. Thus my principal audience have been senior economics undergraduates who were mainly refugees from applied econometrics or accountancy – such are the limited choices in modern economics degrees – whilst I was employed in an economic history or history department. As a consequence, my teaching has had a very particular focus, one which might not be shared by a historian (economist) teaching history (economics) students in-house, and this is reflected in the current study. Without undue characterisation, my refugees have been, in their economics, technically very able but curiously reluctant to apply their theory to historical data and episodes; almost wholly innocent of the practical operation of economies and of their structure; unable, that is those few that have taken a history of economic thought course, to make the connection between developments in theory and the parallel economic and political histories; largely uninformed, and frequently ill-informed, about British history and politics, even for the very recent past; easy victims to *post hoc propter hoc* arguments along with all the other variants of amateurish historical interpretation; too ready to make assumptions about what constitutes rationality at any particular point in time or space; prone to overestimate the breadth of the policy space and the role of economists, by which they typically mean professional economists; and cynical about politics and politicians yet, strangely, still liable to impute to government some greater authority in problem-solving. The above list is by no means exhaustive but it does provide at least a minimum specification of ills which this book seeks to address. This said, in preparing this study the first group that I wish to thank are all those students who, first in Durham and now in Bristol, have taken my courses on the British economy.

The second motivation for this study is to provide a counterweight to much of the existing literature where, typically, the story of British economic policy is told as a series of episodes, often disconnected from underlying economic performance and with none of the longer-term consistency of policy problems highlighted. The long-term roots to relative economic decline, the recurrent nature of economic policy problems and responses and the distinctiveness of the policy process will all feature heavily in what follows.

Thirdly, and probably because economics – as distinct from its parent, political economy – is still in its infancy as a separate academic discipline, economists have neglected the history of their subject. There exists no history of the Royal Economic Society (RES), though a very useful volume was published to mark the society's centenary (Hey and Winch 1990); indeed no comprehensive study of the growth of the economics profession in Britain, save that much useful material has been collected by Bob Coats (1981a; 1991a; 1992a; 1993) and **Sir Alec Cairncross** (1986; 1989b; 1992; Cairncross and Watts 1989)[1] and that Alon Kadish and Keith Tribe are actively researching the topic, though their publications to-date are confined mainly to the early years of professional economics (Kadish 1982; 1989; Tribe 1992; 1997; Kadish and Tribe 1993a). In short, I suspect, the majority of practitioners in Britain have little sense of how economics came to occupy

---

[1] The careers of those whose names are emboldened in the text are detailed in the dramatis personae (appendix I).

the influence – or perhaps lack of it – that it does today. This book will, therefore, try to sketch a history of the profession: of its aims, its leading lights and how and why they came to exercise influence, both as policy insiders and outsiders in government. Inevitably, this means much attention will be devoted to Keynes, but as will be shown the real significance of economics lay with less glamorous spirits and more with the lowlands of the market's operation than with the uplands of macroeconomic theory.

From this follows the fourth motivation for this book: that of providing some historical perspective to the claims current that economics is in crisis; that economists are unable to explain and then provide solutions for even basic economic phenomena such as unemployment or low growth; and that academic economists have lost their authority with politicians and policy-makers. There is actually nothing new about such criticisms of orthodox economics, but it would again be helpful to have a historical context against which to measure the achievements and failings of economics and economists. Much of the story that will unfold concerns how and why economic issues came to prominence in twentieth-century British politics, indeed how relative economic decline became the central issue of political debate. As **Joan Robinson** (1962a, p. 1) observed, economics 'has always been partly a vehicle for the ruling ideology of each period as well as partly a method of scientific investigation', though as we shall see the balance between ideology and science was always fluid. This was to reach ridiculous extremes when, for example, **Margaret Thatcher** could claim in an interview 'that I really am the true Keynesian, when I'm taken as a whole' (cited in R. Middleton 1989, p. 36), this at a time when she and her chancellor had just subjected the British economy to the deepest and most sustained depression since 1920–21. Economists, academic and other, made a substantial contribution to the change in policy which brought about that depression. Then, as before, the question arises of whether economics and economists have been culpable in the decline of Britain's economy or whether they have been largely innocent victims of the political market place. Or something in-between? Once more the unique British circumstances of paranoia about relative decline, and the unusually high influence of financial interests in the economic debate, will need to be incorporated into any evaluation. Without entirely giving away the conclusion at this early stage, it will be argued that the distinct ethical concerns of British economics made it especially vulnerable to the difficulties engendered by politics and politicians. Around this theme we will then be able to make sense of the public's eventual disenchantment with economics and economists' attempts to distance themselves from the hubbub of policy issues.

It was originally intended that this book would update Winch's classic study, *Economics and policy*. There is certainly a case for such a revision as Winch (1969) was published just as the new thirty year rule for official records came into operation and, with the release of these records through the Public Record Office (PRO), we now know far more about the policy process. Moreover, Winch's study was a product of its times in another important sense: written at the zenith of the Keynesian era its modelling of the policy process accorded a privileged position to professional economists – the 'hidden' policy-makers – and to economic theory which are no longer accepted as realistic within public policy studies. Politics matters much more than hitherto accepted, the role of Keynes has been somewhat overstated and, as recent work has shown, there were strong autonomous forces making for an enlargement of the economic role of the state.

As this project took shape, however, I came to the conclusion that there was sufficient recent, easily available literature to remedy most of the shortcomings of Winch's account, and to bring the end of the story from the 1960s to the 1990s, and that there was a more pressing need for a companion volume to the existing textbooks on twentieth-century British economic policy and performance. Thus, rather as Jim Tomlinson (1981b) sought to achieve in his *Problems of British economic policy*, a study which explores economic policy by considering why an issue becomes a problem for policy in the first place, *Charlatans or saviours?* is intended as a supplement not as a competitor to existing texts. The interaction of history, politics and economics required for this study will hopefully make this book more approachable to a non-technical audience, though readers should be forewarned that this is most assuredly not a textbook and indeed it assumes that the reader has a working knowledge of the main trends and themes in British economic policy and performance over the last century. For those for whom this may not be the case, or who wish to deepen their knowledge in these and other areas, a guide to further reading is provided.

Acknowledgements

First, for access to copyright material and permission to quote from it, I am grateful to the Controller of HMSO (Crown Copyright) and to the following for allowing me to cite unpublished or forthcoming papers: Roger Backhouse, Alec Cairncross, Bob Coats, Fred Lee, Alan Peacock, George Peden and Keith Tribe. I apologise to any holder of copyright whom I have failed to contact or trace.

Secondly, and more than ever before with my research, I am beholden to the many friends, old and new, who read the manuscript in whole or in part, who saved me from error, provided references, data, encouragement when needed and discouragement when probably appropriate. Amongst my customary network of economic historians I particularly thank my former colleagues, George Peden and Steve Rosevear, who read the whole of the manuscript. I thank also Alec Cairncross, who not only read all of the chapters in draft but, as Britain's most senior economic adviser, was an invaluable resource for the contemporary historian.

Thirdly, in preparing this study I have benefited greatly from many new contacts made within the history of economic thought community. Foremost here have been Bob Coats, Roger Backhouse and Keith Tribe. As the list of Bob's entries in the bibliography attests he has been the most productive of economist-watchers over the years, but he has also in the context of this project been quite extraordinarily generous with his time, saving me from error over and over again, providing encouragement and – in the best possible sense – education of one who to begin with was so deeply ignorant of so many parts of the story of the professionalisation of British economics. I thank Roger and Keith also, not only for reading the whole work in draft but for still being able to contemplate future joint writing projects beyond our paper to the 1997 History of Economic Thought conference, this also a vehicle to market test some of the ideas in the present study (Backhouse *et al.* 1997). Tom Wilson also read many of the chapters and provided freely of his time in putting me right on the LSE in the 1930s and on Oxford in the 1940s and 1950s, with additional help on the latter from Walter Eltis and Ian Little. I thank also Bernard Alford, Mark Blaug, Tony Brewer, Alan Budd, Samuel Brittan, Maria Fourcade-Gourinchas, Phil Hobbs, Terrence

Hutchison, Fred Lee, Rodney Lowe, Andy Marrison, Oliver Westall, Mark Wickham-Jones, Donald Winch and Warren Young for references and for helpful conversations and criticisms. Any remaining errors of fact, analysis or interpretation are, of course, my own.

Fourthly, I thank Alan Armstrong for his generosity in filling in the gaps in my collection of postwar *EJs*, the raw material for much of this study; Eleanor Burke and Kathy Crocker of the RES, and Jonathan Whitehead of the AUT, for providing data; Astrid Ringe for help in the PRO; and Dymphna Evans, Julie Leppard and Barbara Slater, indeed all on the team at Edward Elgar, for making as painless as possible the final stages of preparing this study for publication. The staff of my university library have, as ever, provided an excellent service in increasingly difficult circumstances, and I thank them, as I do also acknowledge financial assistance from the University of Bristol Research and Conference Funds and the very great benefit provided by a University Research Fellowship which ensured a year largely free of teaching and almost wholly unencumbered by administration in which to undertake this project.

Finally, I thank Sharon Leftley, for love and support, and, in reading the whole manuscript, bringing to bear her expertise in theological disputes amongst early sixteenth-century Italian monks, thereby providing an unorthodox but none the less useful mirror with which to reflect upon my equally disputatious twentieth-century economists.

1. Introduction

Economics is the only field in which two people can get a Nobel Prize for saying exactly the opposite thing.

A party of economists was climbing in the Alps. After several hours they became hopelessly lost. One of them studied the map for some time, turning it up and down, sighting on distant landmarks, consulting his compass and eventually the sun. Finally he said, 'OK see that big mountain over there?' 'Yes', answered the others eagerly. 'Well, according to the map, we're standing on top of it.'

'Murphy's law of economic policy': Economists have the least influence on policy where they know the most and are most agreed; they have the most influence on policy where they know the least and disagree most vehemently.[1]

1.1 THE BIRTH OF MODERN BRITISH ECONOMICS

In November 1890, a few days after the climax of the first Baring crisis, a graphic demonstration of the perils of unregulated capitalism and a milestone in the emergence of modern central banking, there occurred another event in London, somewhat less dramatic but nonetheless of long-term economic significance and an appropriate beginning for this study. This was a meeting at University College London (UCL), chaired by the Chancellor of the Exchequer (**Goschen**) and attended by some two hundred persons representing Britain's nascent economics profession. From this emerged the British Economic Association (BEA), the precursor of today's RES which is the nearest Britain's economists come to a professional body and the publisher of Britain's leading academic journal devoted to economics, the *Economic Journal* (or, amongst economists, the *EJ*). For **Maynard Keynes** (1940b, p. 855), writing on the occasion of the society's jubilee, 1890 marked the beginning of the 'modern age of British economics', with the foundation of the society coinciding with the publication of **Marshall's** *Principles of economics* (1890) and the

---

[1]   A selection of jokes about economics and economists, with the last attributed to Alan S. Blinder, compiled by Pasi Kuoppamäki and available on the world-wide-web (hereafter all URLs emboldened in text) at <**http://www.etla.fi/pkm/joke.html**> (mirrored, for Britain, at <**http://netec.mcc.ac.uk/JokEc.html**>).

1

compilation of Palgrave's *Dictionary of political economy* (1894–1908), the former *de facto* the first modern British textbook of economics and the latter the first substantive English language encyclopaedia of economics.

It is a commonplace that the origins of an organisation are important for its future development; that the intentions of the creators at the moment of creation can endure long after their passing; and that the style, structure and aspirations of an organisation once set are difficult to reform. In all of these respects, the BEA (granted a royal charter in 1902 and renamed the RES) is no exception.[2] Its creation was the product of a number of pressures and influences which were to have very significant implications for the future. Foremost amongst these were Alfred Marshall's efforts to professionalise British economics, an objective which he was uniquely qualified to pursue. His tenure of Cambridge's chair in political economy since 1885, achieved after a distinguished earlier career there as a junior lecturer and his subsequent appointment as the first Principal of University College, Bristol, together with the much-awaited publication of the massive and authoritative *Principles*, made Marshall the doyen of British economics. Hitherto, section F (Economics and Statistics) of the British Association for the Advancement of Science (BAAS) had been the closest approximation to a national forum for economics and economists,[3] but this body suffered from major limitations. It met but annually and as **Sidgwick**, Marshall's colleague and co-founder of the Cambridge school of economics, put it: 'Despite some good papers, it seemed impossible to have a good discussion owing to time limits and the presence of certain familiar bores' (cited in Smyth 1971, p. 168).

Marshall's election as president of section F in 1890 provided an opportunity to break free of these constraints, and it was he who, after much consultation and characteristic hesitation, issued the circular proposing the establishment of an English Economic Association which was to be discussed at the November meeting. The BEA that resulted was consciously modelled on the AEA, founded five years previously, but adopted a 'more cautious and restricted policy than its transatlantic counterpart' where many

---

[2]   The foundation of the BEA is well-documented, beginning with **Edgeworth's** (1891) contemporary account, Keynes (1940b) and Groenewegen (1995, pp. 464–8). Coats (1968b), the unofficial historian of the RES and American Economic Association (AEA), contains the most detailed account of this meeting and of the early history of the BEA/RES; see also his allied studies (Coats 1964; 1967; 1980; Coats and Coats 1970; 1973); and the contributions by Winch (1990a), Kadish and Freeman (1990) and Maloney (1990) to the RES's centenary volume (Hey and Winch 1990). Finally, the speeches given at the centenary dinner on 20 November 1990 at UCL are reported in *RES Newsletter*, no. 73 (March 1991), pp. 6–13.

[3]   See Smyth (1971) for a history of Section F which was also instrumental in the foundation of the London Statistical Society (granted a royal charter in 1887 and thenceforth the Royal Statistical Society, RSS). Since the 1960s the proceedings of Section F have routinely been published in volumes edited by each year's president, as for example in Deane (1990a).

of its most prominent members – not least one of its notorious founding fathers, Richard Ely, an ardent Christian Socialist – were engaged in vigorous public controversy over methodological and policy issues (Coats 1987a, p. 129; 1987b, p. 227). The 'fear of disclosing the substantial divisions within the ranks' of economists was important in Marshall's mission for professionalisation; it probably also influenced the practice – again contra the AEA – of selecting prominent non-academics as presidents (and hence the choice of Goschen for the inaugural meeting). We will deal more fully in chapter 4 with what has been termed Marshall's mission, but here we follow Maloney's (1985, p. 2) excellent study in which he observes that Marshall's:

> objectives for Cambridge economics were also his objectives when he turned his thoughts to the national scene. First, he wanted economists to be trained in a body of theory which – without excessive grief – he recognised would be inaccessible to laymen. Secondly, he sought, via the development of welfare economics, to give the economist a specialist voice in the art of policy-making. Third, he wanted to enhance the scientific authority of his subject by keeping it clear of political partisanship.

1.2 OBJECTIVES AND STRUCTURE OF STUDY

Marshall's mission for the professionalisation of British economics thus entailed three elements: an attribute (specialist knowledge), an attitude (freedom from political partisanship) and a consequent reward (privileges in policy-making). The central objective of this study is to map out subsequent events, the realisation of this mission, and more particularly to:

- explain the extent to which British economic policy has been conditioned by changes in economic thought, making clear whether it was professional economists or others claiming expert economic knowledge who played a central role;
- explore the relationship between economic policy and economic performance, with a focus on the various remedies proposed by economists for reversing relative economic decline and why they have been of such limited success; and
- provide a brief history of academic economics in Britain and of its changing mission from the early days of Marshall, through the heyday of the Keynesian era and professional economists, to more recent times when there are once more many competing sources of economic advice.

Hitherto, in so far as the economics profession have been studied it has been largely in terms of the development of economic theory. This study seeks to redress the balance slightly by investigating why economists adopt the policy positions they do, in other words to acknowledge strong normative influences. It gives room for economists to recount in their own words their ethics as well as their economics, and highlights leading personalities and institutions in the evolution of the discipline. It also keeps to the forefront the electoral and broader political realities that governments and bureaucracies work with and how these invariably determine the policy space; moreover, how they have changed over time, such that there has been no settled terrain over which economists operate. In the process it is hoped that a number of myths can be punctured, in particular concerning the rationalist fallacy: that of the primacy of economic theory in the determination of policy with, as Tomlinson (1981b, p. 3) rightly identifies, 'its implications of a history of economic policy seen as a reflection, presumably with lags, of a history of economic thought.'

The rationalist fallacy creates quite unrealistic expectations amongst both the users and producers of economic knowledge. Indeed, it may well be uniquely unhelpful in the British case where very particular circumstances determined the incorporation of expertise of all sorts into government and policy-making. In what follows unceasing emphasis is placed upon the real world, where economic policies are but one aspect of governmental activity, and much use will be made of the writings of those economists who have been active in advising and/or observing government. Foremost here for the postwar period is Alec Cairncross, whose long experience led him to conclude that 'The aims of policy are generally obscure, in conflict and inconsistent', with political forces so dominant that few issues can be labelled technical and economic. Thus:

> Governments may be inhibited from using particular instruments of policy such as bank rate by ideological considerations or by force of popular feeling which they have stirred up earlier when in opposition. They may commit themselves publicly to doctrines about how the economy should be run that rest on little more than assertion and then find it impossible to retract when the doctrines are put to the test. Persuasion becomes not merely an act of political leadership but an economic weapon; and skill in managing the economy begins to rest more heavily on proficiency in economic psychiatry than on insight into econometric relationships.   (Cairncross 1970c, pp. 20–21)

Further, he warned (1970d, p. 5) that 'Those who have never served in a large Government department are inclined to take too exalted a view of the rationality of the process of decision-making', giving the following 'insider's' description which should council caution in using the surviving documentary record to interpret contemporary and, in particular, past policy decisions:

what is not always understood is that bureaucracies even in normal times are usually slightly mad and in moments of crisis easily become crazy. What survives on paper may appear to be almost uniformly articulate and logical; but the atmosphere of a large Government department is frequently almost indistinguishable from that of the [sic] looney bin. I use the term in no pejorative sense; it is simply one of the facts of official life.

The representation of 'economists as supermen able to transform the economy by technical wizardry and rendering administrators and ministers alike redundant', might now seem laughable but was a not altogether unfair caricature at the height of the Keynesian hegemony. But here too Cairncross (1970a, p. 203) cautioned:

Anyone who talks in these terms has never been present at the kind of discussion between economists, administrators and ministers at which it is by no means uncommon for the economist to talk politics, the administrators to talk economics, and ministers to discuss administrative complications. An outsider might have great difficulty in deciding who, among those present, was a professional economist and would be very unlikely to conclude that an economist, as such, was in a particularly powerful position in debating most issues of economic policy.

Having introduced our broad approach and sympathies we can now proceed to some matters of organisation and structure in this study which is divided into two main parts. The first consists of this and the following two chapters which, in turn, survey the first century of British professional economics, from Marshall to **Meade**; explore the various ways in which the policy process, and the role of economists therein, has been modelled; and then proceeds to survey long-run trends in the market for economic advice. The second part (chapters 4–7) then proceeds chronologically with one chapter devoted apiece to the prewar and interwar periods and two to the years since the Second World War, the divide made to coincide with the collapse of Keynesian hegemony. These chapters discuss the main theoretical and policy issues in each period and then pursue a limited number of case studies to illustrate our major themes and in particular the contribution of economists to the relative decline debate. Finally, there is a short concluding chapter which discusses the current health of the discipline and offers some reflections on the possibilities for retrieving that combination of rigorous intellectuality and immense moral authority which was the hallmark of the best of British economics from Marshall to Meade.

1.3   FROM MARSHALL TO MEADE: THE FIRST CENTURY OF BRITISH PROFESSIONAL ECONOMICS

The *Economic Journal*

We can approach subsequent events, indeed the whole of the first century of professional British economics, by systematic analysis of the *EJ* which became, in effect, the *raison d'être* of the new BEA. The journal was launched in 1891, being in fact just pipped at the post by the *Economic Review*, the product of Oxford economists with strong Christian Socialist leanings and a further illustration of the intermingling of ethics and economics in contemporary perceptions of political economy.[4] Nonetheless, the *EJ* quickly established itself as the premier British scholarly journal in economics, indeed as a major world authority in economics until at least the Second World War when, as with the real economy, Britain's decline relative to America became impossible to ignore. While economics is now dominated by American journals and American academics, the *EJ* remains the foremost British journal by the conventional test of citations.[5] Moreover, although not the oldest English-language economics periodical, a title held by the *Quarterly Journal of Economics* (*QJE*) launched in 1886,[6] the *EJ* has a substantially longer history than the *American Economic Review* (*AER*), the AEA's journal which began publication in 1911 and which now has the highest circulation of any economics periodical.[7]

Given the well-established role that economics journals play in the communication, scrutiny and acceptance of new ideas (Stigler 1964; Coats 1971), and the much longer history of the involvement of British economists in public policy and controversy, we might expect that the *EJ* and other British journals[8] would have been extensively investigated by economists

[4]   Coats (1968b, p. 355). It ceased publication in 1914.
[5]   Bibliometric research on citations (with impact adjusted citations in parenthesis) ranked the *EJ* 11th (12th) in 1970, 17th (19th) in 1980 and 29th (28th) in 1990, with the top rated UK journal being *Economica* in 1970 at 9th (9th) and the *Journal of the Royal Statistical Society* (*JRSS*) in 1980 at 16th (78th) and in 1990 at 17th (68th) (Laband and Piette 1994, tables 1–2). In terms of academic prestige, however, American economists ranked the *EJ* 5th, the top ranking UK journal, with *Economica* 7th, the *Review of Economic Studies* (*REStud*) 9th and *Oxford Economic Papers* (*OEP*) 12th. The *AER* was ranked first (Hawkins *et al.* 1973, table 1).
[6]   The *Journal of Political Economy* (*JPE*), the house journal of the Chicago school, was launched in December 1892.
[7]   There were 26,949 total AEA members and *AER* subscribers at end 1995 as against 6,437 for the RES and *EJ* – *AER* vol. 86 (2) (May 1996), p. 477; and information provided by the RES.
[8]   For example, and in order of seniority (with current journal name, *JEL* journal abbreviation, first launch date and institutional affiliation – where not obvious – in parenthesis) there are the following British general interest journals: *Economica* (1921, LSE), the *Manchester School of Economic and Social Studies* (*Manchester Sch. Econ. Soc. Stud.*, 1930), the *Review of*

and historians interested in the development of economic thought and the economics profession.[9] In fact, it is the dearth of literature that is most conspicuous, especially in respect of the RES and the *EJ*. Admittedly, there have been Coats's various studies, now collected together (Coats 1993) and a recent centennial volume by Hey and Winch (1990). But, with two exceptions (Jha 1973 and Tribe 1992), and some mentions in passing in other work, the society and its journal have never been subject to serious empirical scrutiny, a somewhat curious omission given the well-known proclivity of economists to enumerate. Unfortunately, the two exceptions are restricted in their coverage: Jha to the first quarter-century and Tribe to the first half-century of the *EJ's* existence, while the recent centenary volume does not venture beyond casual empiricism about the *EJ's* authors and subjects.[10] An opportunity has thus been missed to use the RES and its journal as the basic raw material for a history of the British economics profession and of its concerns, and in the following we begin with three snapshots of the *EJ* at fifty years intervals to introduce the broad issues and to provide necessary background from which our story can unfold.

Our discussion draws upon some initial results derived from DISMAL,[11] a machine-readable database of *EJ* papers and their authors which takes its name from the so-called dismal science. In particular, DISMAL allows us to address some basic questions about the characteristics of economists (gender, whether professionals or amateurs, and, if the former, their institutional affiliation) and their writings, both in terms of subject matters within the discipline (as measured by the 1983 *Journal of Economic Literature's* (*JEL*) classification schema)[12] and styles of writing economics,

---

Economic Studies (*Rev. Econ. Stud.*, 1933), *Oxford Economic Papers* (*Oxford Econ. Pap.*, 1938), the *Bulletin of the Oxford University Institute of Statistics* (now *Oxford Bulletin of Economics and Statistics, Oxford Bull. Econ. Statist.*, 1940), the *Yorkshire Bulletin of Economic and Social Research* (now *Bulletin of Economic Research, Bull. Econ. Res.*, 1948), the *Scottish Journal of Political Economy* (*Scottish J. Polit. Economy*, 1954) and the *Cambridge Journal of Economics* (*Camb. J. Econ.*, 1977).

[9] The most recent work on the *EJ* is Backhouse (1997a) and Oswald (1991a), with the former concentrating on the postwar period and the latter limited to the use of microeconomic data in *EJ* papers and to the period 1959–90.

[10] See, for example, Winch (1990a, pp. 17–18) and Kadish and Freeman (1990, p. 38); see also Friedman's (1991) retrospective on the first volume of the *EJ* and progress since. For more considered empirical analysis of recent issues, see Morgan (1988); and, for earlier issues, Coats (1969, p. 61 n. 12) and Collard (1990, pp. 172–4).

[11] This database, implemented in ACCESS v2.0, is in the first stages of development and currently consists of all papers (defined in Table 1.1 note a) and their authors for 1891, 1900 and thereafter for the first year of each decade through to 1990 (a one in ten sample).

[12] The 1983 classification (superseded in 1991) was used because the RES had already coded all papers between 1931–80 in the cumulative index for those years (RES 1983). Strictly speaking, the *JEL* classification is actually that of the AEA and was first introduced in the 1960s. For details of the *JEL* 1991 schema, and a table translating the old and new categories, see *JEL*, vol. 29 (1) (March 1991), pp. v–xxviii.

Table 1.1   Economic Journal: *basic statistics, 1891, 1940 and 1990*

	1891	1940	1990
1. Total pages	840	592	1,458
2. Total number of articles[a]	59	31	91
3. Total number of books reviewed	51	81	133
4. Total number of book notes[b]	0	0	343
5. Editors[c]	F.Y. Edgeworth (Oxford)	J.M. Keynes (Cambridge) E.A.G. Robinson (Cambridge)	J.D. Hey (York) M.J. Artis (Manchester) D.G.M. Newbery (Cambridge) S.J. Nickell (Oxford) M.A.M. Smith (Sussex)
6. Number of identified authors[d]	39	31	136
7. Females as percentage of identified authors	2.6	3.2	8.1
8. Academics as percentage of identified authors[e]	35.9	77.4	100.0

Notes

[a] Defined as articles, notes/memoranda and contributions to the policy forum and controversy sections.
[b] The *EJ*'s designation for short book reviews.
[c] Managing first, then Assistant Editors (affiliations in parenthesis).
[d] Of single- and multi-authored papers, excluding anonymous unsigned contributions. Authors identified from: *DNB*, *Who was who?* and RES directories.
[e] As having or as having had an academic post, defined to include non-partisan research organisations and government economic service (incl. Bank of England).

8

which we have in deference to the campaign launched by McCloskey (1983) against the scientific pretentiousness of economics termed rhetorical style. Thus Table 1.1 provides some basic statistics about the *EJ* and its authors; Table 1.2 a classification of rhetorical styles (according to a very simple schema); and Figure 1.1 the distribution of papers as between the ten first order (one-digit) categories in the *JEL's* 1983 classification.

Table 1.2 Economic Journal: *classification of papers by rhetoric type (% of total) and mode (Y=presence of style; N=absence), 1891, 1940 and 1990*

Year	Alg-ebra	Cal-culus	Dia-grams	Econo-metrics	Stat-istics	Wholly literary
1891						
Total (%)	1.7	0.0	1.7	0.0	33.9	64.4
Mode (64.4%)	N	N	N	N	N	
1940						
Total (%)	22.7	13.0	9.7	0.0	38.7	38.7
Mode (38.7%)	N	N	N	N	N	
Mode (38.7%)	N	N	N	N	Y	
1990						
Total (%)	72.6	68.2	20.9	47.3	52.8	17.6
Mode (30.8%)	Y	Y	N	Y	Y	

Note: Component parts do not sum to 100 per cent because each *EJ* paper can exhibit more than one style.

Taking each in turn, Table 1.1 details a number of characteristics of the *EJ* as a journal and of its contributor economists for its first year of publication, jubilee and centennial volumes. It might be objected that 1940, as a war year, is unrepresentative. Certainly, the total number of pages was less than in 1939 (794 pages), but there were no substantive differences in the topics covered or in the characteristics of their authors. Moreover, as we shall see, war has been very important for the development of economics, the influence of economists on policy in particular; it has played a central role in the relative decline of the British economy; and, by virtue of its possession of an empire, a very substantial military–industrial sector and its being a leading player in world trade, the British state has had very distinctive characteristics by European and American standards. Thus war – whether as current hostilities, preparation for future conflicts, or recovery from past belligerency – has been the central fact of the twentieth century.

Figure 1.1 Economic Journal: *papers by Journal of Economic Literature (1983) classification, 1891, 1940 and 1990*

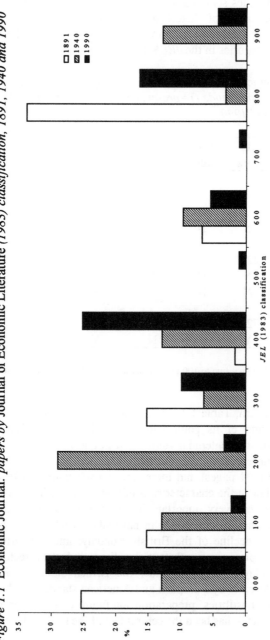

Note: JEL (1983) classification: **000** General Economics; Theory; History; Systems; **100** Economic Growth; Development; Planning; Fluctuations; **200** Quantitative Economic Methods and Data; **300** Domestic Monetary and Fiscal Theory and Institutions; **400** International Economics; **500** Administration; Business Finance; Marketing; Accounting; **600** Industrial Organisation; Technological Change; Industry Studies; **700** Agriculture; Natural Resources; **800** Manpower; Labour; Population; **900** Welfare Programmes; Consumer Economics; Urban and Regional Economics

The long-term increase in the size of the *EJ* and in the number of articles published stands out clearly over the first century of the RES. The increase in the number of books reviewed is even more striking, especially as such has been the explosion in the volume of books published that the *EJ* was by 1990 reviewing but a small part of the total (around 2,250 per annum), and this very heavily biased towards English-language works. In 1891 a professional economist could hope to keep abreast with the totality of economics, while an interested amateur could hold his or her own. By 1990 such was the immense volume, and its distribution across so many different specialisms, some of them technically (mathematically) very demanding, that this position no longer held. And there was no hope for the interested amateur whatsoever by this later date. Table 1.1 also shows that the *EJ*, like other journals, has evolved from being edited by a single individual to more collective efforts, such that by 1990 the managing editor was supported by no less than four assistants, all of professorial rank. One further editorial characteristic is also noteworthy: that of the shift from Oxbridge – in particular Cambridge – dominance in the management of the *EJ* to a much more diffuse position incorporating newer centres of economics as well as traditional authorities. Even so, the period of Cambridge's pre-eminence was long and important, beginning with Keynes's appointment as editor in 1911 (a position held until 1945) and stretching through the tenures of **Austin Robinson** (1934–70), Charles Carter (1961–70), Brian Reddaway, David Champernowne and Phyllis Deane (1971–7).[13]

Table 1.1 also provides the basis to draw three further important conclusions about our sample of economists. First, economics, like the natural sciences from which it draws much of its inspiration and professional models (especially from physics, on which see Mirowski 1989), has become increasingly a team effort, with the construction of economic knowledge being a social activity undertaken by a distinctive economic community (Weintraub 1991, p. 6). Neither in 1891 nor in 1940 were there any multi-authored papers, whereas in 1990 no less than 46 per cent of papers had two or more authors. The gender balance, however, was much slower to change, with economics remaining overwhelmingly a male profession, a characteristic which many contend has had deleterious effects on the discipline's methodology, focus and, consequentially, its policy influence (May 1996). Finally, we can use this data to make some comments about the professionalisation of economics, which, as measured by the proportion of authors identified as having or having had an academic post, was complete by 1990 but still maintaining an important role for the non-

---

[13] The most notable omission here is, of course, **Roy Harrod** (1945–61). For complete details of *EJ* editors and other RES officers, see Robinson (1990a, pp. 189–91).

specialist in 1940 and with the majority of authors in 1891 not being academic economists. Thus in 1891 authors were drawn from the civil service (the Board of Trade and the Postmaster General's office) and included journalists, barristers and bankers.

The professionalisation of economics

Using the literature on the sociology of professions, and writing from the standpoint of Marshall's central role in British economics, Maloney (1985, pp. 3, 57) identifies three relevant criteria for assessing the process of professionalisation: first, that the economist must be 'trained in a specialised body of knowledge'; second, that the economist 'has an effective monopoly of a defined specialist function or functions', thereby imbuing the economist with an 'authoritative voice in policy discussions'; and, third, that the economist 'observes professional ethics which either institutional sanctions or the force of colleagues' opinions impel him to maintain'. In short, 'Economics becomes a profession when "who chooses economics?" becomes a less important question than "who does economics choose?"' This approach is very different from that of the earlier tradition of writings on professionalisation, where for example Stigler (1964, pp. 37–8) argued that the 'specialized writer on economics, with a professional base, was dominant by 1900'. Specialisation is clearly of great importance, and it is highly relevant that as the twentieth century progressed few economists – unlike their nineteenth-century predecessors – were equipped or inclined to maintain a publishing presence in such disciplines as philosophy, politics or statistics, themselves mainly or in part the product of the fragmentation of political economy which produced economics as a separate discipline.

For Marshall the task for economics was no less that the new discipline attain escape velocity from its earlier subordination to other literary or scholarly pursuits, typically moral philosophy; that there be initiated a new age of 'scientific' economics, one which left sufficient scope for a strong moral (normative) component; and that professional authority (and thus policy influence) could only be achieved through self-discipline and a distancing of economists proper from the cranks, pamphleteers and propagandists who had done so much to give economics its reputation as the dismal science. Indeed, it is no exaggeration that the transmission of economic ideas into the political realm in the nineteenth-century came largely from 'journalists and popular writers who preached an over-simplified version of classical political economy from which the qualifications and subtleties had been removed' (Holmes 1976, p. 681). Such had been the low esteem of economics that during the 1870s, a period when the presidents of section F of the BAAS tended to be politicians, it was seriously proposed that the discipline be excluded from the association (Deane 1990b, pp. 1–2). Even as late as 1895 no less an authority than Goschen, former Chancellor and first president of the BEA, complained that economics 'was not treated with the respect accorded to other sciences' and 'received scant courtesy at the hands of politicians and of the practical man, who never reads, never writes, and seldom thinks'. He also took particular exception to the Foreign Office's decision to replace political economy with shorthand in its entrance examinations (Anon 1895, p. 301). The storm was weathered but with at least two important consequences for the immediate direction of economics and of the professionalisation sought by its leading practitioners. The first was that what we would now call macroeconomics – a term not invented until the 1930s – received almost no attention for a generation; and the second concerns the role of authority in economics, authority in the sense used by Coats (1964, p. 87) as the 'power to influence action, opinion, belief' and not as 'power to enforce authority'. From this would stem the conditions under which economists should and should not become embroiled in public debate.

Our starting point for the former proposition is with the application to economics of Lakatos's Methodology of Scientific Research Programmes (MSRP), this a vibrant and thoroughly esoteric debate about how economists justify their theories, how they interpret the real world and why they prefer one theory over another.[14] Here the preoccupation is less with a single theory or with an individual's theories *per se*, than with a programme of research embodying a hard core of provisionally accepted assumptions, ones treated as irrefutable so long as the programme endures; a protective belt of auxiliary hypotheses which defends the hard core by accommodating anomalies; and a positive heuristic, a problem-solving apparatus. In this representation of economic science a special role is played by the protective belt in allowing a programme to survive falsification, that is empirical evidence which appears to invalidate current theory, until a better programme emerges. The notion of a better, a superior programme relates to Lakatos's distinction between degenerating and progressive programmes, with the latter existing where, when confronted with anomalies, the auxiliary hypotheses are able to be modified in ways which predict novel, hitherto unexpected facts, which are confirmed and which provide a

---

[14] The literature on the methodology of economics is enormous, but Blaug (1992a) provides a masterly introduction; c.f. the methodological pluralism proposed by Caldwell (1982). See also Backhouse (1985, ch. 1) for a gentle introduction to Lakatos and to Popper and Kuhn, two earlier philosophers of science who have contributed most to economists' understanding of what they do, and McCloskey's (1994, esp. ch. 7) rejection of Lakatos and other rationalist approaches. The variety of new directions in economic methodology is indicated in Backhouse's (1994) collection of edited papers, while De Marchi and Blaug (1991) evaluate the utility of the MSRP in economics.

forward-looking research strategy. If, however, the research programme is only able to accommodate new facts through perpetual *ad hoc* adjustments it is classified as degenerating. This may all seem rather arcane, overly-complicating for a study of the relationship between economic policy and theory, especially where non-experts (Treasury officials and politicians) and not professionals exercise the key roles, but in fact the element of change in economics, the capacity to ignore or refute anomalies, the striving for originality, especially through mathematics, will all be central to what follows. So also will economics and economists as a research community with their own language, their rhetoric, their norms and values. Above all the notions of crisis, of revolutions and of progress have all acted as powerful aphrodisiacs to economists, with for its greatest practitioners – from Marshall, through Keynes, to Meade – the escape from orthodoxy being both the prize and the destination.

Not surprisingly there are different views about Marshall, his contribution and his legacy in terms of research programme (see chapter 4). Indeed, with so complex and central a figure we should expect no definitive view. There should, however, be no disagreement that Marshall belonged to the marginalist epoch, was not the inventor of marginalist analysis – a distinction usually divided between Jevons, Menger and Walras – but the economist who honed it into powerful tools in the economists' kitbag. Maloney's (1985, pp. 22, 234) portrayal of the professionalisation of economics, and of Marshall's central role, makes the useful distinction between the marginal idea and the people it attracted into professional economics. Thus marginal utility analysis was quickly taken up by academics, but it also provided an attraction for a different kind of recruit into academic economics – those whose background was in logic and mathematics – such as Marshall. More particularly, as Maloney (1985, p. 35) further argues, 'By deriving from marginal utility theory the concept of consumer's and producer's surplus, Marshall hoped to make economics a basis for policy without compromising scientific standards and ideological neutrality.'

The constructs of consumer's and producer's surplus kept economics preoccupied with microeconomic phenomena; they focused professional and thus popular attention on the impersonal theory of market exchange, and allowed the nascent profession to:

> distinguish between what they called an art of political economy (which could absorb criticisms provoked by the debatable political and ethical implications of their results) and a positive science of economics (which could draw methodological and conceptual analogies from the natural sciences and develop quantitative and/or mathematical techniques of analysis).   (Deane 1990b, p. 2)

Thus did the professionalisation of economics entail a significant retreat from the breadth of the classical economists' agenda. The payoff, it was hoped, would be in an indefinitely progressive research programme which would raise the profession's internal morale and its external standing. However, 'For Marshall, economists ... not only have to explain their world, they have an unambiguous duty to assist in changing it for the better' (Groenewegen 1995, p. 761). The vital role played by the social philosophy of the dominant members of the new profession, and of the interpretation of social market failure that Marshall and others developed before the First World War, is explored more deeply in chapter 4. At this stage we should note the intention that economics, in Viner's (1941, p. 233) delicious phrase, should become 'a serviceable instrument of human betterment', and that analytically and pragmatically this led to Marshall's (1885, p. 159) credo that economics 'is not a body of concrete truth but an engine for the discovery of concrete truth'. This tenet long endured, resonating loudly and clearly in the Cambridge Economic Handbooks, launched in 1922 and extremely influential in providing up-to-date treatments for a lay audience of specialist topics which were not always covered in the then textbooks. The series was edited by Keynes whose general introduction is worth quoting at some length:[15]

> The Theory of Economics does not furnish a body of settled conclusions immediately applicable to policy. It is a method rather than a doctrine, an apparatus of the mind, a technique of thinking, which helps its possessor to draw correct conclusions. It is not difficult in the sense in which mathematical and scientific techniques are difficult; but the fact that its modes of expression are much less precise than these, renders decidedly difficult the task of conveying it correctly to the minds of the learners.
> . . .
> The main task of the professional economist now consists, either in obtaining a wide knowledge of *relevant* facts and exercising skill in the application of economic principles to them, or in expounding the elements of his method in a lucid, accurate and illuminating way, so that, through his instruction, the number of those who can think for themselves may be increased.
> This Series is directed towards the latter aim.

Marshall's *Principles* (1890, p. 1), even in its final (eighth) edition, opens with a definition of economics which is in part a manifesto:

> Political Economy or Economics is a study of mankind in the ordinary business of life. . . .

---

[15] This is taken from Keynes's contribution to the first volume in the series, **Hubert Henderson's** minor classic, *Supply and demand* (1922), which 'for thousands of English students during the following 30 years was their first introduction to economics' (Robinson 1987, p. 639).

Thus it is on the one side a study of wealth; and on the other, and more important side, a part of the study of man. For man's character has been moulded by his every-day work, and the material resources which he thereby procures, more than by any other influence unless it be that of his religious ideals; and the two great forming agencies of the world's history have been the religious and the economic.

The quest for autonomy for the new discipline most certainly did not entail that economics be separated from ethics or other emerging academic disciplines capable of illuminating human behaviour in the round. Foremost here was psychology, a subject which much interested Marshall, indeed so much so that earlier in his career it nearly commanded his attention in preference to economics (Reisman 1990, p. 7). Of relevance also was history, with much scholarly attention having been given to how, in creating the economics tripos at Cambridge, which was enormously influential for economics education elsewhere, Marshall had the practical effect of distancing economics from economic history, to the detriment of both (Coleman 1987; Kadish 1989). Authority and ambition for the new subject became fused as one with ethics in the closing lines of Marshall's (1885, pp. 173–4) inaugural lecture:

Why should it be left for impetuous socialists and ignorant orators to cry aloud that none ought to be shut out by the want of material means from the opportunity of leading a life that is worthy of man? Of those who throw their whole souls into the discussion of this problem, the greater part put forth hastily conceived plans which would often increase the evils that they desire to remedy: because they have not had a training which is most rare in the world and plentiful only in Cambridge. . . .

. . .

It will be my most cherished ambition, my highest endeavour, to do what with my poor ability and my limited strength I may, to increase the numbers of those, whom Cambridge, the great mother of strong men, sends out into the world with cool heads but warm hearts, willing to give some at least of their best powers to grappling with the social suffering around them; resolved not to rest content till they have done what in them lies to discover how far it is possible to open up to all the material means of a refined and noble life.

The phrase 'cool heads and warm hearts' encapsulates Marshall's mission: that economics must aspire to the highest scholarly standards but without sacrificing the vision of a more humane capitalist system. What was sought was a professionalisation of economics which would produce a market for economic ideas dominated by the new professionals. For example, and again in Marshall's (1897a, p. 296) own words:

Never again will a Mrs Trimmer, a Mrs Marcet, or a Miss Martineau earn a goodly reputation by throwing them [general economic principles] into the form of a catechism or of simple tales, by aid of which any intelligent governess might make clear to the children nestling around her where lies economic truth, and might send them forth ready to instruct statesmen and merchants how to choose the right path in economic policy, and to avoid the wrong.

These references to nineteenth-century propagandists of crude laissez-faire might be thought to rather trivialise the problem, but Martineau's *Illustrations of political economy* attained sales of 10,000 or so per month at their peak; it represented 'the whole doctrine of laissez-faire, bag and baggage: the perfection of the competitive system; the harmony of interests that reigns within a society so organized; the illegitimacy and perverse consequences of government interference'; above all the 'promise [of] eternal progress – if only the laws of nature are allowed to work' (Gordon 1971, p. 196). Between these crude apologies for capitalism, which by denying the possibility of market failure gave no role to government and thus made economics impotent, and the equally uninformed claims made for socialism in the more popular quarters, ones which downgraded economics to the mere servant of politics, there lay a middle ground but one in which the integrity of economics, like democracy, required eternal vigilance.

Marshall's concern to control the supply of economic knowledge, indeed the very definition of legitimate economic expertise itself, was not universally shared and was, in any case, confronted by the stark realities of establishing the BEA as a viable organisation at a time when there existed but a handful of academic economists. An association so confined in membership would have been stillborn in terms of public influence (Coats 1964, p. 96). Thus, at the November 1890 meeting, it was agreed that the new body be 'open to all schools and parties [with] no person ... excluded because of his opinions', and with no minimum technical qualification for membership. It was further agreed that the *EJ* 'be conducted in a similar spirit of toleration', that is 'open to writers of different schools' where 'The most opposite of doctrines may meet here on a fair field' with no 'attempt .. to prescribe the method, any more than the result, of scientific investigation.' From this it was hoped that in the long-run a consensus would emerge, or as Edgeworth (1891, p. 2), the *EJ's* first editor, put it: 'What Milton had hoped for theology in the seventeenth century may prove true of political economy in the nineteenth.'

Such expectations have never been fulfilled, though many would agree that economists' disputes might be likened to those of warring theologians in earlier ages. Academic economists have never secured even a near monopoly of advice in the market for economic knowledge, unlike for example, physicians or lawyers who have obtained legal rights in their markets (Peden 1996). Nearly a century after the formation of the BEA one prominent British economist (**David Henderson** 1986, p. 3), with much international experience of government service, lamented that:

> There is no doubt that the policies of government have been, and still are, strongly influenced by economic ideas. But contrary to what Keynes assumed, these have not necessarily been the ideas of economists. Over wide areas of policy the judgements of politicians and their officials, as also of public opinion in general, have been and still are guided to a large extent by beliefs and perceptions about the working of the economic system, and about national interests and the welfare of the community, which owe little or nothing to the economics profession. In so far as the world is indeed ruled by economic ideas, these are often the intuitive ideas of lay people, rather than the more elaborate systems of thought which occupy the minds of trained economists. The history of national economic policies down the years bears witness not only to the influence of economists, whether defunct or alive, but also to the power of what I call '*do-it-yourself economics*'.

Do-it-yourself economics (DIYE) will feature heavily in our account of British economic policies over the last century. Before embarking upon that story we complete our introduction to the professionalisation of British economics by considering some further results drawn from DISMAL (Figure 1.1 and Table 1.2). Looking first at the papers published in the journal we see an enormous shift in focus even when measured by the crude one-digit *JEL* classification schema. Thus in 1891 there are no publications in quantitative economic methods and data (class 200), administration (500) or, perhaps less explicable, agriculture (700). The leading classes were manpower (800), some 34 per cent of the total, and general economics (000), some 25 per cent (with classes 100 and 300 each having 15 per cent of papers). Examining the papers more closely we cannot but agree with Jha (1973, p. 199) that 'The most conspicuous feature of the contributions ... is the interest of the British economists in contemporary economic problems' of all types, and in particular in their preoccupation with 'projects for economic and social reform', in which they cast their net widely to report on pertinent developments in other advanced capitalist countries. The dominant issue of the day, indeed of the whole period through to the outbreak of the First World War, was what contemporaries called the labour question. We discuss this more fully in chapter 4 but here we note that this involved a complex of economic, political and social phenomena: the promotion of industrial peace, measures to alleviate poverty, ill-health, low educational attainments and, in the background, a perception of relative economic decline which knitted together these elements.

Discussions of the labour question necessarily blended administrative issues with economic analysis and resulted in the *EJ* being very readable. This is clear from Table 1.2 on rhetorical style where the dominant style was entirely literary, entailing none of the devices we have identified as now dominating the economics literature. Austin Robinson (1990a, pp. 185, 188), one of the longest serving RES council members, and a former *EJ* editor who knew many of the founding fathers of the association, characterised the RES as beginning life as 'an alliance of the working economist and the academic economist', an alliance maintained throughout Keynes and then Harrod's editorship. Thus in the 1930s the RES was concerned with the 'total profession of economists'; by the 1970s, however, university economists came to predominate on the RES council and the 'alliance between the two sectors of the profession ... almost disappeared, not ... by intention but by inadvertence.' Simultaneously, the *EJ* 'progressively changed from being, as it had been under Keynes and Harrod, reading matter for those interested in modern applied political economy, to being reading matter for those who enjoy mathematical models, to the benefit of the latter but the slight regret of the former.'

Leontief's complaint

These changes are clear from Figure 1.1 and Table 1.2. Thus in its jubilee year the dominant class of papers was no longer 800 but 200 (29 per cent of total papers), clear evidence of the growing preoccupation with quantitative issues (with classes 000, 100, 400 and 900 all represented at 13 per cent each). Yet there has been very little shift in the modal rhetoric type with the literary style still dominant. Thus the 1940 issue was, as it had been in 1891, easily accessible to the general reader and full of papers with immediate policy relevance. Algebra, calculus and statistics (but not econometrics) were all more evident in 1940 than 1891 but as yet the mathematical model-builders had not made an appearance (although the 1940 volume does contain the famous Tinbergen-Keynes exchange on the utility of econometrics). Thirty years later, however, Wassily Leontief (1971), who received the 1973 Nobel prize for his contribution to input-output analysis,[16] a necessarily highly quantitative and mathematical topic, was to devote his presidential address to the AEA to a condemnation of economics for its lack of relevance, its shaky empirical foundations and its obsession with mathematical prowess. He repeated his concerns (Leontief 1982, p. 104) about economics' dominance by mathematical model-builders in a letter to the journal *Science* in which, after conducting a content analysis of the *AER* between 1972–81, he lamented:

Page after page of professional economic journals are filled with mathematical formulas leading the reader from sets of more or less plausible but entirely arbitrary assumptions to precisely stated but irrelevant theoretical conclusions.

---

[16] See appendix II for a full listing of Nobel economics laureates.

The growing incidence of mathematical models with no data is clear from Table 1.2, although it is also apparent that the purely literary style had not been altogether eclipsed by 1990. Further shifts in the profession's focus are also revealed in Figure 1.1 with the 500 and 700 class making an entrance for the first time and international economic issues (the 400 class) also acquiring a strong following. It is no exaggeration that the 1990 volume of the *EJ* would not be recognisable to the majority of the readership of the 1891 volume. It is certainly difficult to imagine what a career Treasury civil servant would make, for example, of Kotlikoff *et al's* 'A strategic altruism model in which Ricardian equivalence does not hold'.

Leontief's (1971) concerns were mirrored in Britain by the presidential addresses of that year to section F and to the RES. In the former, Worswick (1972a, p. 83) complained that 'Too much of what goes on in economic and econometric theory is of little or no relevance to serious economic science', while in the latter **Phelps Brown** (1972, p. 6), in a measured but spirited tirade against much contemporary economics and economists, spoke of the 'divergence between the increasing power of economists to elaborate trains of subtle and rigorous reasoning and build complex models, on the one hand, and on the other the slow advance of their power to diagnose and prescribe for the problems of our day.' The question arises of whether there was anything particularly new or significant about these examples of self-questioning and self-criticism within the discipline. We will observe in later chapters that economics has actually thrived on crises, revolutions and counter-revolutions (see Coats 1977 and Hutchison 1984 for necessary historical perspective). It is also the case, as Heller (1975) identified in one of the few optimistic presidential address of this period,[17] that the disparagement of economics often provides a convenient smokescreen for those claiming the superiority of one brand of economics over another.

We will survey in later chapters the extent to which there were genuine – in the methodological sense – crises in economics in the prewar, interwar and postwar periods.[18] So far as the 1970s are concerned the crisis certainly felt real for contemporaries, and in retrospect it does indeed appear to have been a watershed in the influence of academic economics. Coats (1988, p. 219) refers to the 'collective "self-flagellation"' of these years, a reflection of 'professional and public concern following the ending of the Keynesian hegemony (c.1945–1965), and ... a reaction from the collective hubris and exaggerated claims of that era.' The crisis embraced theoretical controversies which were symbolised in the public mind by the conflict

---

[17]	For the AEA; see also **MacDougall's** (1974) RES presidential address.

[18]	These terms are used throughout and the reader should note that prewar means before the First World War, the late-Victorian and Edwardian era, whereas postwar refers to the period after the Second World War.

between Keynesians and monetarists, but actually also involved a revival of interest in the market, new classical writings on business cycles and the first stirrings of the supply-siders. Above all the crisis coincided with, or was caused according to taste, by the ending of the golden age of capitalism, the period of super growth for the OECD economies which began around 1950 and was terminated by the first oil price shock (OPEC I) in 1973. Hitherto economists generally believed themselves to have made a central contribution to economic welfare, in particular that super growth and full employment were, to an important extent, attainable because of greater economic knowledge. The appearance of stagflation made disciplinary introspection inevitable, especially as economists had become increasingly prominent in public affairs on both sides of the Atlantic. However, a broader disillusionment with economists was developing some time before the ending of the golden age.

Postan's plague of economists

The opening shots in Britain came outside of professional economics and were actually fired by an economic historian, albeit one with substantial experience of government service (in the Ministry of Economic Warfare). Writing in *Encounter* in 1968, Michael Postan (1968, pp. 42, 47) began with a blunt question for economists: 'Have they with their models, measurements and forecasts, helped the economic recovery, or have they, on the contrary, aggravated Britain's predicament by misdirecting the attention of the government and the public?'; indeed would 'Britain's economy ... have been healthier and Britain a happier country to live in had its economists been less influential than they are?' Postan's concern was not with the quality of British economics as measured by professional standards, but with the professional standards themselves: 'the qualifications and attitudes which the economist bring, and are expected to bring, to their governmental and journalistic jobs.' His concern was that 'the very quality of post-war economics, the greater sophistication of its theoretical constructions, its much refined statistical and econometric methods, have put it out of touch with real economic situations.'

Postan's case against contemporary economics and economists is worth reporting in some detail, as is one of the responses – by **Harry Johnson** – it generated in subsequent issues of *Encounter*.[19] Postan took special exception to the prevailing aggregate view of the economy ('Keynesian *par*

---

[19] In addition to Johnson's defence of economists, there were responses by Michael Stewart ('A plague of politicians', May 1968, pp. 54–6) and Peter Wiles ('Are the economists to blame?', July 1968, pp. 56–9) and a riposte from Postan ('The uses and abuses of economics', September 1968, pp. 85–90).

excellence'), an over-preoccupation with macro- to the neglect of microeconomic phenomena which resulted in the raw material for economists – national totals or averages – being artefacts which were unhelpful in framing policies appropriate to Britain's real (structural) economic difficulties. Thus macroeconomic indicators (the savings ratio) or policy instruments (interest rates) were 'generalised holistic concepts, detached from their local and specific circumstances' which lead to economic policies which were similarly generalised, or systemic, operating on the whole economy without finesse or regard for the localised, specific nature of Britain's economic difficulties. Stop-Go policies were the clear target here:

> All the painful dilemmas of the economy – whether to inflate or to deflate, whether to reduce comparative costs by devaluation or by universal wage freeze, whether to stimulate national investment by tax concessions or by curbs on alternative uses of savings – are posed and debated as if they affect in equal measure and in the same way all and every branch of the economy.
>
> (Postan 1968, p. 43)

The complaint was not just that the aggregate view led to macroeconomic policies which were inappropriate for Britain's actual economic problems, a solution to which required microeconomic understanding and policy instruments, but that macroeconomic policies had unintended effects which were deleterious to sectors of the economy hitherto in good health. We will explore more fully in chapter 6 the case against Stop-Go policies, but here we note that the reservations about macroeconomics have a long tradition in British public policy. They were an essential part of the interwar Treasury's case against the Keynesian solution for mass unemployment, whilst the existence and significance of unintended policy effects were to force much work on policy evaluation but not before contributing to the reaction against discretionary economic management in the 1970s.

Johnson's (1968) response is of interest as part defence of contemporary economics and as part condemnation of British economists, a theme he went on to develop – via his controversial critique of the Keynesian revolution (Johnson 1971b) – into his five propositions, or defining characteristics, of British economics (Johnson 1975b). Taking first the 1968 critique, Johnson's defence of the macroeconomic perspective of contemporary economics – as both scientific and efficient in the sense of minimising the costs of forecasting the effects of policy actions – broke no new ground; it was the next stage of the argument that was significant, that it was:

> a great mistake, though a common one, to assume that governmental economic policy is really made in accordance with, or even much influenced by, the best that economic science has to offer. Instead, the government economist is more

frequently a barrister making the best case for his client's behaviour that he can
. . . This is true not only in England, but in the contemporary homeland of
scientific (as contrasted with forensic) economics, the United States. The
difference is that in the United States a pluralistic university system based on
competition in academic excellence . . . provides incentives for economists to
base their careers on scientific accomplishment rather than political usefulness,
to challenge forensic nonsense on scientific grounds rather than accept and repeat
it out of a sense of responsibility to and personal participation in the power
structure, and to relate themselves to government for the most part as
scientifically qualified expert consultants rather than employees or general policy
advisers.   (Johnson 1968, p. 52)

In short the problem lay not with the shortcomings of contemporary
economics, but with the deficiencies of British economists. The inferences
are clear, and the charge serious: British economists were both a product
and a cause of the British disease, that shorthand term for the economic
decline of Britain which encompasses a dysfunctional body politic, due in no
small part to Oxbridge dominance and characterised by an obsession with
class and with the cult of the amateur; successive economic policy mistakes;
a contempt for production, science and technology and so on (Allen 1979).
More specifically, Johnson charged British economics with being
amateurish, in the sense of lacking a proper graduate programme of
economics education and, as a consequence, unable to develop firm
traditions of scientific progress. Particular ire was reserved for Oxbridge and
the civil service, the former for its undue influence on British academe and
the political classes; and the latter, together with the honours system, for its
corrupting influences:

The result is that academic economists are too easily bought, either as public and
ostensibly impartial defenders of party and government policies or as expert
advisers to and servants of government, willing to allow their reputations to
sanction policies adopted contrary to their advice or to the prescriptions of their
science in return for the opportunity to exercise some residual influence in some
areas of policy-making. That residual influence, in turn, is frequently exercised,
not by demonstrating superior competence in problem analysis, but by
demonstrating superior ability to invent politically appealing economic policy
gimmicks.   (Johnson 1968, p.52)

Harry Johnson and the British economics establishment

Subsequently, Johnson (1975b, pp. 222–5) developed his five propositions of
British establishment economics, 'all of them connected with the career and
the writings of ... Keynes – by which is meant, not what Keynes actually
wrote and thought, but what Keynes is believed or construed to have thought
(or would have thought, if he had understood his own theory) by his

modern-day successors':[20]

1. 'all economics in the main tradition of scientific economics is mere "orthodoxy", and as such is to be despised and turned on its head by the clever economists,' one implication of which was the 'assumption that the more startling "unorthodox" a new proposition is, the more true it must be.'
2. 'money cannot possibly matter – because Keynes triumphantly established this point against the barbarous forces of orthodoxy, and demolished the quantity theory once and for all.'
3. '"full employment" is an exclusive definition of social well-being, and as such to be pursued at virtually any cost.'
4. 'workers ought to be so grateful for the efforts of their intellectual and political superiors to give them the benefits of full employment that they will refrain from embarrassingly inflationary wage demands.'
5. 'faster economic growth is the panacea for all England's economic (and for that matter political) problems and that faster growth can easily be achieved by a combination of generally inflationary demand-management policies and politically appealing fiscal gimmickry.'

It might be objected that Harry Johnson's strictures should not be taken too seriously, that they were the product of his very particular experiences with the British economics establishment in the three attempts he, a Canadian by birth but cosmopolitan by nature, made to settle first in Cambridge, then Manchester and, finally, the LSE.[21] Further defences might be sought in Johnson's 'colourful' personality, his uncompromising independence from all intellectual fashions and his never having directly advised governments, so that his economics remained unsullied by politics. However, the opposite case could be put with equal conviction: that it was the nature of these experiences, his cosmopolitanism and, above all, his standing in the profession which made him uniquely qualified to pass such judgements: 'a scholar with a rare breadth of knowledge and with broad scientific and historical perspectives', a verdict with which few could disagree (Frenkel 1987, p. 1023); or, a colossus bestriding the profession, such that for economists the third quarter of this century should be known as the age of Johnson, the opinion of the 1981 Nobel prize winner in

[20] See Peacock (1989, pp. 3–8) and **Hahn** (1990, p. 539) for alternative specifications.
[21] We still lack a biography of this most important of the postwar generation, but see Tobin's (1978) affectionate memoir, Frenkel's (1987) brief guide to his writings, the November 1978 special issue of the *Canadian Journal of Economics* (vol. 11 (4)), and the 1984 issue of the *JPE* (vol. 92 (4), pp. 565–711) which contains a number of papers surveying his contribution to economics, especially Laidler (1984). This issue of the *JPE* also contains a listing of Johnson's writings which does not claim to be complete (and is not) but none the less runs to 53 pages.

economics (Tobin 1978, p. 443). Johnson will eventually form a fertile topic for historians of economic thought, not least because few economists, and particularly one who died so young (aged 53), have left such an immense body of work.

Johnson's verdict on the British economics establishment, and on the dominance of forensic as against scientific economics, cannot be dismissed as mere caricature. Not only was he at the frontiers of theoretical economics, making important contributions in monetary and international trade theory, but of his generation he was one of the few to give serious thought to the sociology and production of knowledge. Moreover, he had a unique Anglo-American perspective. All of this comes to fruition in his analysis of the Keynesian revolution and the monetarist counter-revolution, the subject of his controversial Ely lecture to the AEA (Johnson 1971b). In a connected, but much less cited paper, Johnson (1970, pp. 82–4) contrasted the highly centralised British economics establishment with its extremely decentralised American counterpart, this with obvious implications for the ability of Keynes and the Keynesians to become dominant in the former but much less so in the latter:

> In Britain, Keynesianism was successful in virtually sweeping the intellectual board, and becoming the dominant orthodoxy. Those of the older generation who did not accept the new Keynesian orthodoxy had either to shut up and divert their intellectual efforts to another field, or become pitiful and pitied voices crying in the wilderness. . . .
>
> In the United States, on the other hand, the diversity and competition of the academic world meant that Keynesianism never succeeded in sweeping the intellectual board. It conquered Harvard and the eastern seaboard, and secured its outposts in the west; and this enabled it to dominate so long as the Democrats were in power. But it could not prevent the academic survival of the pre-Keynesian tradition. Moreover, in the United States, in contrast to Britain, it is possible to be both intellectually and academically respectable and, at the same time, a conservative with significant political influence. Hence an anti-Keynesian school . . . could flourish; and it could be (and inevitably would be) based on institutional and geographical rivalries between men in the same age group rather than on the mechanics of the generation gap as has been necessary in Britain. The intellectual rivalry between Paul Samuelson, as leader of the Keynesians, and Milton Friedman, as leader of the quantity theorists, is a rivalry between generational, intellectual and institutional equals, a very different kind of rivalry than the conflict in Britain between the older generation in command of Oxford and Cambridge and the younger generation in the provincial universities (which term now includes the London School of Economics).

The divergence of the American economics profession from its British counterpart, of course, long predates Keynes and the Keynesians (Coats 1980; 1981c) and relates to the broader story of different national trends in the growth of the professions and the universities and their relations with the state (Winch 1990b). Viewed as a scientific research programme, economics has characteristics which have long transcended national boundaries, although it is arguable that the extent to which there might be a global agenda is a very new phenomenon and one very much dominated by the US (Portes 1987; Frey and Eichenberger 1993). The different market conditions facing American and British, indeed European, economists is explored further in chapter 3 but here we raise the central question whether there is substance in the claim that in Britain the relationship between academic economics and government is different from that prevailing elsewhere, and whether as a consequence there have been costs for both the reputation of economics and the performance of the British economy. Johnson (1973a, pp. 70, 71) was in no doubt that this was the case, arguing in a subsequent paper that the discipline had been converted 'from a scientific subject into a species of political necromancy' in which economists became prized for their 'cleverness in making forensic use of other people's research for political purposes.'

Such claims provide an obvious benchmark for us to examine a number of propositions in this study; it provides one possible destination with which to look back to Marshall's mission for the professionalisation of economics and what then transpired; it aids sideways glances to simultaneous developments in America and Europe; and it supplies a ready-made bridge linking economic theory and economists to economic policy and economic performance. We will, in fact, reject much of Johnson's case for the prosecution but in compiling the economists' defence we will necessarily have to steer a course between the forces identified as particularly dysfunctional in Britain and the more general, global problems affecting the discipline. Accordingly, we complete this section of our introduction by surveying subsequent events, thereby bringing the story up to date, and identifying the full range of issues which will occupy us in later chapters.

Disciplinary disarray and the 1970s crisis in economics

We recommence the story thus with the early 1970s as a combination of deteriorating economic performance, a crumbling Keynesian theoretical paradigm, political instability and the growing power of financial markets began to change the nature of the economic debate, both in terms of its dominant participants and arenas of conflict. However, even before the crisis of Keynesianism reached a crescendo, British economists were adjudged to have shot themselves in the foot in their inability to present a common front on the potential benefits/disbenefits of Britain becoming a member of the then European Economic Community (EEC), now in much enlarged form, the European Union (EU). Thus during the critical parliamentary debate on membership there was the unedifying sight of *The Times* letters page carrying two lists of economists side-by-side and under the banner 'How the economists divide',[22] there being 153 signatories who 'believe[d] that the economic effects of joining the Common Market, taking both short and long-term effects into account, [were] more likely to be unfavourable than favourable to Britain', and 140 who took the contrary view.[23] The public's perception of the propensity of economists to disagree was thereby reinforced, a perception which long predates Keynes but finds its most expressive form in the interwar aphorism that 'Where five economists are gathered together there will be six conflicting opinions and two of them will be held by Keynes!'.[24] It is now widely accepted that the debate preceding EEC membership was neither illuminating, balanced nor well-informed. Nevin (1972, p. 54), one of the signatories to the letter supporting membership, was later to lament the lack of substantive contribution from professional economists to the debate and the 'schizophrenic letter to *The Times* in which the only measurable evidence appeared to be the relative length of academic names.'

This point accepted, Nevin might also usefully have commented on the authority and status of the departmental divide on this issue and what it revealed about the state of contemporary British economics. Thus analysis of the institutional affiliations of the signatories reveals that of the pro-membership lobby only two departments with international research reputations (Glasgow and York) exhibited strong support (defined as a ratio of at least 2:1 in favour) for the motion, with the majority of Britain's leading departments being in the anti-membership lobby (Bristol, Cambridge, Manchester, Oxford, Southampton, Sussex, UCL and Warwick). The one exception from this list is the LSE which on balance just favoured membership. Moreover, there is a broader point which has also not received comment, namely the possible dissonance between the lack of agreement between economists in *The Times* letter and the findings of a contemporaneous survey into economists' opinions in which the potential benefits/disbenefits of EEC membership was one of the few questions considered amenable to purely professional – as against private –

---

[22] *The Times*, 22 October 1971, p. 13.

[23] The letters derived from a questionnaire inspired by **Kaldor** which was jointly sponsored by Harry Johnson and distributed through the Association of University Teachers of Economics (AUTE). In an assessment of the responses, Khan and Johnson's (1972, p. 316) arithmetic yielded 154 signatories against entry and 142 for entry in the published letters, with figures of 196 and 222 respectively for total respondents, actually a majority in favour of entry. In addition there were 99 respondents who were undecided. The large difference between the published and total tallies reflected a number of late responses but more significantly the large number of economists who did not want to signal their disagreements in such a public manner.

[24] As reported by Jones (1954, p. 19).

judgement.[25] Between the widespread public expectation that economists ought to agree on largely technical issues and the perception of their appearing to disagree openly about all issues lies fertile territory for exploration in this study.

The orthodox division of economics into positive and normative does not really capture the essence of the problem and in the following we will make much use of a third category, the 'art of economics' which derives from **J.N. Keynes's** *Scope and method of political economy* (1891), this the standard text on economic method for the new Cambridge school produced by one of Marshall's favoured pupils and, of course, father to the more famous son. The 'art of economics' has recently been revived by Colander (1994, p. 35) in the form of applied policy economics which 'relates the insights learned in positive economics to the goals determined in normative economics,' a sort of engineering branch of economics. Art is not here juxtaposed to science; what is sought, rather as McCloskey has attempted in his methodological excursions, is to create a usable middle ground free from the sterility of the perpetual conflict between rigour and relevance in economics. The 'art of economics' provides different methodological rules because, being concerned not with the testing of general theories, the preoccupation of positive economics, but with the application of the insights of theory to specific policy cases, it has different objectives. Accordingly, greater allowance is possible for real-world institutions and constraints, those typically abstracted from in pure theory; and there is greater clarity in distinguishing normative goals from positive theory.

The typical defence for what Samuelson (1959, p. 192) called the 'babel of voices' within economics is that all economic decisions require a view on the future, by definition uncertain, and 'involve ethical ends that transcend positive science.' The latter claim, of course, is particularly contentious for, in effect, it denies the possibility of a positive economics. We discuss this point further in chapter 2 in relation to **Friedman**'s (1953) case for positive economics, but here our concern is that Samuelson and others miss a prior point: why did there arise expectations that there ought to be agreement amongst economists and that, if on the contrary disagreement pertains, economists should have but limited influence on policy? Objectively, surveys of economists' opinions in Britain, as in the US, reveal very much more agreement than the public or politicians might anticipate. In one of the first

---

[25] This research was organised by **Samuel Brittan** and conducted by the Esmée Fairbairn Economics Research Centre using a sample of 250 economists A response rate of 46.8 per cent was recorded (N=117), with the respondents in four categories: 44 academic economists, 37 government economists, 21 business economists and 15 others. The question on EEC membership was in part B of the questionnaire, that deliberately designed to be in the realm of positive rather than normative economics. Participants were asked 'Whether real income *per capita* in Britain would rise if Britain joined the Common Market' (Brittan 1973, p. 102).

of such surveys, one based on a random sample of 600 US-based economists in 1976, Kearl *et al.* (1979, p. 36) concluded that the perception of widespread disagreement within the discipline was quite 'simply wrong', although 'Consensus tends to center on micro-economic issues involving the price mechanism while the major areas of disagreement involve macro-economic and normative issues.' A follow-up survey, again of US-based economists but this time with more than double the sample size (1,350), broadly confirmed the results of the earlier survey on the extent of a consensus on basic economic propositions as well as introducing evidence to the effect that degree vintage, defined as the decade in which an economist gained his or her highest degree, was an important explanatory variable (Alston *et al.* 1992, p. 208). The suggestion that 'during the course of graduate study, some economists form economic convictions which they preserve for decades' should come as no surprise; it should also reinforce pre-existing reservations about the 'scientific' status of economics.

The available evidence for Britain would not contradict these findings. Indeed, the original 1971 survey results in many ways surprised its instigator, especially the finding that the degree of agreement amongst economists was not just substantial but uncorrelated with the types of questions asked, whether politically charged and highly controversial (part A) or more technical in nature (part B). In respect of part A of the questionnaire, a control group of Labour and Conservative MPs were used, and analysis of the results suggested that on average the differences between economists were very much less than the differences between economists as a group and politicians. This reinforces our earlier observation about economics being a social activity; it also led Brittan (1973, p. 28) to a significant conclusion:

> The differences between them [the politicians] and the economists may reflect inadequate knowledge on the part of either side, different value judgements or more subtle differences in the concepts with which the world is viewed. These differences lead to striking contrasts in diagnosis and policy conclusions. To the extent that they reflect different value judgements, this too is interesting. For value judgements do not arrive from heaven; and the kind of learning experience accumulated by a politician tends to produce a different outlook on 'ought' [normative] questions from that accumulated by the typical economist. Another factor, however, may be that those who stick to economics as a career may tend from the outset to have different value judgements from those who are more attracted to – or more liable to be successful in – politics.

Whereas Brittan's survey focused on the extent of agreement amongst British economists, subsequent studies have been as interested in the extent of disagreement. Thus Ricketts and Shoesmith's (1990; 1992) survey, which was based on a much larger sample (981) than in 1971, abandoned the original questionnaire and instead adapted for UK conditions the questions used by Kearl and his colleagues. This allowed international comparisons to be made and, to a limited extent, some sense of how economists' opinions might have changed over time. In respect of the former, Ricketts and Shoesmith suggested that British economists were more Keynesian and more in favour of the redistributive role of government than their American and continental European counterparts. One reference point here was Frey *et al.* (1984) which, based on a sample of 2,072 economists, found distinctive national characteristics: of the Americans, Germans and Swiss tending to support more strongly the market than government as social decision-making mechanisms than their French and Austrian counterparts who took a more favourable line towards government than the market. Table 1.3 summarises some of this cross-sectional data, amply demonstrating the existence of national differences in questions classified as both positive (anticipated policy effects) and normative (desirable policy objectives).

Frey and Eichenberger (1993, p. 185) put it starkly: 'America and Europe differ with regard to what economics is understood to be, how it is practised, and how professional academic economists behave', attributing these differences to dissimilarities in market conditions as between America and Europe. We explore these in chapters 3, 6 and 7 and here note that there are stronger incentives in Europe for its economists to become involved in public policy than in America, where the routes to professional prestige are more narrowly defined. The question naturally arises whether British economics and British economists more closely resemble the discipline and peer group in continental European or, as with much else with the British economy and society, America. The disproportionate number of Nobel prizes in economics awarded to British citizens (7 out of 41) suggests that, judged by peer review, British economics is closer to the American than to the European model. However, we should observe that until Mirrlees's award in 1996, all three of the laureates who had spent their professional lives in Britain (**Hicks**, Meade and **Stone**), as against those who had considerable professional experience elsewhere (**von Hayek**, Lewis and Coase), have a direct association with Keynes and Cambridge economics in the 1930s. Until 1996, no prize had been awarded to one of the later generation of British economists. This pattern is entirely consistent with British economists having world leadership until the Second World War, and an important presence thereafter at the research frontiers in some fields where local conditions gave a comparative advantage in existing areas or, as with British experience of privatisation, created new centres of expertise in public economics (Portes 1987, p. 1333). We should, however, ask one further important question at this point: does this loss of leadership matter? After all, the German, French, Italian and Japanese economies all did extremely

Table 1.3 International comparisons of economic opinion, selected countries, 1970s and 1980s

No.	Proposition		US (1979)	Austria (1984)	France (1984)	Germany (1984)	Canada (1988)	UK (1989)
1	A minimum wage increases unemployment among young and unskilled workers	Agree	88	64	38	69	85	76
		Disagree	10	35	60	30	15	24
2	A ceiling on rents reduces the quantity and quality of housing available	Agree	96	89	52	93	95	85
		Disagree	2	11	44	6	5	14
20	Consumer protection laws generally reduce economic efficiency	Agree	50	29	22	35	46	23
		Disagree	46	70	77	65	52	77
27	Tariffs and import quotas reduce general economic welfare	Agree	95	86	70	94	96	84
		Disagree	3	13	27	6	4	15
30	Wage-price controls should be used to control inflation	Agree	28	47	54	7	26	39
		Disagree	71	52	43	92	73	60
35	The redistribution of income in the developed industrial nations is a legitimate task for government	Agree	78	88	88	79	84	91
		Disagree	19	11	11	21	15	8

Source: Ricketts and Shoesmith (1990, table 3).

well after the Second World War without the benefit of economics professions which, apart from a limited number of individuals, were world-class, not at least according to prevailing American definitions. Might there then be some substance to Allen's (1979, pp. 18–19) proposition, which heads this study, that 'a country's economic progress is in inverse proportion to the distinction of its economists!'

Continuing with our narrative, we should highlight the profession's failure to predict the oil price shock, the productivity slowdown and all of the other characteristics of economic life after the golden age of super-growth as a major factor in the loss of credibility of economics and of its practitioners over the last quarter century. That economics became associated with forecasting was in no sense part of Marshall's mission or, indeed, Keynes's (1930b, p. 332) aspiration 'If economists could manage to get themselves thought of as humble, competent people, on a level with dentists, that would be splendid!' In no small part, disillusionment with economics resulted from the public having accepted the image that economists sought to present of their discipline as a positive science advancing theories with high predictive power and open to testing and falsification. We will, however, need to take account of the attempt by alternative sources of expertise to wrest power and influence from academic economists in the 1970s, and, as we enter the 1980s, a return of a certain sort of anti-intellectualism here immortalised in another one of Thatcher's famous sayings: 'What have educated people ever done for this country?' (cited in Walden 1996, p. 199).

Disciplinary self-examination has been a recurrent theme since the early 1970s, but it has usually been confined to presidential addresses to the RES and the AEA and to conference volumes which have not attracted much attention (for example, Wiles and Routh 1984). There are, however, some notable exceptions: a special issue of *Public Interest* in 1980 devoted to the crisis in economic theory and attracting some leading names – for example, Arrow and Hahn – on both sides of the Atlantic (reissued as Bell and Kristol 1981); **Balogh's** *The irrelevance of conventional economics* (1982); Thurow's *Dangerous currents* (1983); Eichner's *Why economics is not yet a science* (1983); Henderson's (1986) Reith lectures which formalise the concept of DIYE; Malabre's 'insider' history of economists, *Lost prophets* (1994); Paul Ormerod's *The death of economics* (1994) which made it to the book clubs; Krugman's *Peddling prosperity* (1994), a powerful attack on the misuse of economics for political and sectional advantage; Heilbroner and Milberg's *The crisis of vision in modern economic thought* (1995); and, most recently, Perelman's *The end of economics* (1996). As an antidote to such seriousness there have even been light-hearted attempts to provoke the reform of economics, as for example in Covick's (1974) hilarious parody of the Keynesian-monetarists debate in terms of a restatement of the quantity theory of drink, entailing such equilibrium devices as the PISS point (the paralytically incapable stationary state) and Eddie Maynard Waring's *General theory*. Evocative also was Leijonhufvud's (1973) spoof on life among the Econ, a lonely tribe inhabiting the northern territories whose:

> land appear bleak and dismal to the outsider, and travelling through it makes for rough sledding; but the Econ, through a long period of adaptation, have learned to wrest a living of sorts from it. They are not without some genuine and sometimes even fierce attachment to their ancestral grounds, and their young are brought up to feel contempt for the softer living in the warmer lands of their neighbours, such as the Polscis and the Sociogs. Despite a common genetical heritage, relations with these tribes are strained – the distrust and contempt that the average Econ feels for these neighbours has been heartily reciprocated by the latter – and social intercourse with them is inhibited by numerous taboos. The extreme clannishness, not to say xenophobia, of the Econ makes life among them difficult and perhaps even somewhat dangerous for the outsider.

In Britain, morale amongst academic economists reached a definite lowpoint in the early 1980s. Here for example, and not entirely tongue-in-cheek, was the advice given by Alan Prest (1983, pp. 130–31), at that time Britain's most distinguished public finance economist, to a young (male) economist seeking a career path that would maximise his chances of professional and political rewards:

> You will, I am sure, not fall into the trap of thinking there is any mileage nowadays in being a disinterested and dispassionate searcher after truth in important economic matters, or in adding a morsel to the knowledge accumulated since Adam Smith's time in the tradition of the great 19th or earlier 20th century economists. The scholar who works on his own with a grasp of the historical context of his subject, humble about his own work, and innately suspicious of the Johnny-come-lately with the hot line to God, will soon be dead as a dodo.
> . . .
> The suggested PhD thesis title "n solutions to n-1 problems" is a very promising theme for an academic career devoted to High Theory. Nowadays this is the super-highway to eminence and professional acclaim. And you will very quickly discover that your standing and stature will rise in geometrical proportion to the irrelevance and obscurity of what you say and write.
> . . .
> The other alternative for an academic is to embrace quantitative work. . . . What you must do is cook up elaborate relationships between whatever economic series you can lay your hands on without a moment's thought on whether the data bear any relationship to reality. And, of course, you must never dream of comparing any forecasts from your equations with the actual outcome. At the very least, such sacrilegious activities would cast doubts on your fitness for the priesthood, and might even lead to unfrocking.
> The disadvantage of such work is that people cannot be quite so sure of its unimportance as with High Theory, so you are guaranteed permanent second-

class status. There is also the ever-present danger that you might be seduced into doing something useful, though I suspect you could resist any such satanic temptation.

The 364 economists

We can be even more precise in dating this lowpoint for professional economics and economists in Britain, to March 1981 and to the letter signed by 364 university economists:[26]

> We, who are all present or retired members of the economics staffs of British universities, are convinced that:
> a There is no basis in economic theory or supporting evidence for the government's belief that by deflating demand they will bring inflation permanently under control and thereby induce an automatic recovery in output and employment;
> b present policies will deepen the depression, erode the industrial base of our economy and threaten its social and political stability;
> c there are alternative policies;
> d the time has come to reject monetarist policies and consider urgently which alternative offers the best hope of sustained economic recovery.

This round robin was prompted by **Howe's** budget earlier that month which, amidst the deepest depression since 1920–21, confounded (Keynesian) conventional wisdom by a further tightening of fiscal policy. Organised by two Cambridge professors, Frank Hahn and **Robert Neild**, on the premise that 'a large number of economists in British universities, whatever their politics, think the Government's present economic policies to be wrong and that, for the sake of the country – and the profession – it is time we all spoke up', their efforts secured not just sheer quantity of opposition, but quality and stature. Thus the signatories included four former Chief Economic Advisers to the Government (**Robert Hall**, Sir Alec Cairncross, **Sir Bryan Hopkin** and **Sir Fred Atkinson**), 76 professors, past and present senior officers of the RES; in short, what the *Financial Times* called 'a who's who of the post-war British economics establishment' (cited in Wickham-Jones 1992, p. 176). Moreover, it is almost certain that more names could have been acquired, not least if the search had extended into the then polytechnics, now the 1992 universities. In the event probably between one quarter and one third of all university economists signed the letter, though the missing economist, the 365th, the one who would have

---

[26] Published in *The Times* and other broadsheets on 30 March. For an academic assessment of this episode, see Wickham-Jones (1992); for retrospective political assessments by the three central characters, respectively the PM, Chancellor and Financial Secretary to the Treasury, see Thatcher (1993, pp. 132–9), Howe (1991) and **Lawson** (1992, ch. 9).

then allowed an economist (and no doubt their opinion) for every day of the year, proved elusive but a staple subject for senior common rooms and the less elevated sections of the British press.

We will consider the detail of the economists' theoretical critique in chapter 7, but here we concentrate on the reception it received and the implications of this for the profession's standing. The immediate response was a Treasury counterblast that there were legitimate theoretical underpinnings for the monetary and fiscal deflation being undertaken, while in any case economic recovery was already underway. That the letter did, in fact, coincide with the lower turning-point of the business cycle, proved 'exquisite' timing. As Lawson (1992, p. 98) later crowed, it was the 'prelude to eight years of uninterrupted growth [which] ... left our economic critics bewildered and discredited', such that 'In the course of time the 1981 Budget came to be seen almost as a political equivalent of the Battle of Britain: the Thatcher Government's finest hour; its most widely acknowledged success and a turning point in its political fortunes.' The ability of a determined government to foster the line that an association between variables is equivalent to a relationship between variables in which the direction of causation follows from commonsense will prove a recurrent theme in this study, albeit one entering a new chapter in the 1970s as economic policy become the main battleground between political parties.

The reaction to the economists' 1981 letter also illustrates another theme of great relevance. Thus, for example, Thatcher's first counterblast proceeded along the lines that since the policies of the 364 had already been tried and failed 'the 364 did themselves more damage than anyone else' (Hansard 1981, col. 152). To this condemnation for past misdoings was the sin of omission; that the economists' letter was entirely in the negative, failing to make clear what alternative policies there were, this being inevitable because economists could never agree anyway. That the economics profession were outmanoeuvred by an infinitely more astute and powerful political machine should not surprise, but it should have suggested that economists in future give more attention to the presentation of their views: to the mechanics of persuasion, to the appeal of the message and the coherence of the messenger. One of the letter's organisers was later to argue that the economists' intervention forced the government to rethink, or at least to refine, its policy stance (Hahn and Weale 1988). This remains debatable, not least because the economists may not have been sufficiently attuned to the conjuring trick being attempted by the first Thatcher government: that of a severe budget to provide a smokescreen for the relaxation of monetary policy, this at least being the view of certain leading financial journalists who understood the importance of policy credibility (Wickham-Jones 1992, p. 181).

The British economics profession today

It is probable that the greater significance of the 364 economists is that after 1981 academic economists have had a much lower public profile than at any time since the First World War. University economists have not so much been evicted from the body politic, for they still operate within Whitehall as insiders, both generalists and specialists, and as outsiders in the Keynesian tradition as policy advisers, the Treasury Panel of Independent Forecasters (the Chancellor's 'panel of wise men') being a recent incarnation, but the evening TV news and the morning paper economics column now rarely feature their expertise. Instead, it is the chief economist of this or that bank, or a newspaper's in-house financial expert, that has captured this important segment of the market for economic advice, that which gives the electorate their perception of economic issues and politicians the ground upon which debate will be conducted. However, this outcome was not just the product of interest group competition and of changes in the nature of the political process. We will thus need to view the economists' condition within the broader context of post-modern challenges: to established authority, ones eroding the monopoly of the universities as the primary locus of knowledge production and reproduction; and to the inevitable adjustments to economic science now that the natural sciences have, via chaos theory and other developments, lost much of the certainties that underpinned their disciplines.

As economists contemplate the second century of their project it is axiomatic that the world of the 1990s is very different from that of the 1890s, and particularly so in Britain where relative economic decline has forced momentous changes which reverberate throughout the whole of Britain's society to dominate its politics. British economists, like the British economy, face a future which is perceived as much more uncertain, risk-prone and less amenable to the product economists have to offer than that the situation Marshall and his contemporaries contemplated a century earlier. Whether economics is still in 'crisis' remains a moot point, although the occasion of the RES's centenary, and the various publications that ensued, can be used as a measure of the discipline's mood. In particular, the January 1991 issue of the *EJ* carried a number of pieces, drawn from an invited subset of distinguished members of the society, reflecting on what the coming century might have in store for economics and the economy. Being economists it was perhaps de rigueur that the result was a little like the curate's egg. Some denied the existence of a crisis. Thus Hahn (1991), Britain's most senior authority on general equilibrium analysis, provided an extremely upbeat contribution which made a virtue of the current preoccupation with pure theory and charted one route towards an economics which, in its attempts to answer the really interesting questions, would be led back to its Marshallian affinities to biology and evolution. Others lamented the likelihood that economics would continue to be stronger on analysis than prescription, with the consequence that it had but a limited contribution to make towards alleviating the most pressing problems, such as Third World poverty (Stiglitz 1991).

Widening our sample somewhat, the early 1990s saw a number of survey articles which were distinctly more optimistic in tone than had been characteristic during the 1970s and 1980s when disputes between competing camps had been theological in their intensity and about as useful. Thus, for example, Bleaney's (1996, p. 1) introduction to a major overview of the state of economics identified a 'cooling of controversy and gradual re-establishment of some form of consensus in the profession for the first time since the mid-1960s' with the prevailing mood being 'more placid, more assured and more reminiscent of recovery from trauma than of trauma itself.' Cobham (1984) has argued that there occurred a significant realignment in British macroeconomics in the decade after OPEC I, one entailing a convergence between so-called Keynesians and monetarists, a development we explore more fully in chapter 7. However, for many such macroeconomic issues pale into insignificance compared with the collapse of the centrally planned economies in 1989–90, events producing momentous, as yet unknown, implications for geo-political alignments, the cardinal choice between government and the market and the future of economics. Thus Buchanan's (1991) contribution to the crystal ball exercise reported in the *EJ* took as its starting point that, with economists newly liberated from what Hayek called the 'fatal conceit' of socialism, a convergence of economists' normative attitudes was at last now possible. Whether the twenty-first century proves to be post-socialist is, as yet, unknowable. Nor should the failure of collectivism at the end of this century be allowed to obscure the very real difficulties still facing economics and economists.

Some indication of continuing difficulties is provided by Table 1.4, part of the results of a detailed survey of opinions amongst postgraduate economics students at America's elite research universities about the prerequisites for professional success. They make chilling reading, especially when it is acknowledged that those polled include the future movers and shakers of the profession at a world level. The finding that only 3 per cent of the profession's future leaders considered a thorough knowledge of the economy as very important for career success, and 68 per cent as quite unimportant, attracted particular attention (Hutchison 1992, pp. 24–9; McCloskey 1994, pp. 173–4). For example, for Blaug (1992a, p. xxiii) the observation that 'American graduate students ... correctly perceived that nothing succeeds in economics like mathematical

*Table 1.4   Colander and Klamer: survey results of the perceptions of
             career success amongst American economics postgraduates*

	Very important	Moderately important	Un-important	Don't know
1. Being smart in the sense of being good at problem-solving	65	32	3	1
2. Excellence in mathematics	57	41	2	0
3. Being very knowledgeable about one particular field	37	42	19	2
4. Ability to make connections with prominent professors	26	50	16	9
5. Being interested in, and good at, empirical research	16	60	23	1
6. Having a broad knowledge of the economics literature	10	41	43	5
7. Having a thorough knowledge of the economy	3	22	68	7

Note: Questionnaire distributed to the six top-ranking postgraduate economics programmes:
           Chicago, Columbia, Harvard, MIT, Stanford and Yale.
Source: Colander and Klamer (1987, table 3).

pyrotechnics, supplemented on occasion by some fancy econometrics', was 'simply a reflection of the empty formalism that has come increasingly to characterize the whole of modern economics.' And he asked the question whether this mattered; should it cause concern? His answer is representative of the anxiety felt by many, both producers and users of economic knowledge, about the discipline. First, formalism acts as a deterrent to the acquisition of knowledge about how the economy actually operates, thereby weakening curiosity about economic phenomena – the reason why students and the public come to the subject in the first place. Secondly, formalism threatened to divert economics from its historical mission of influencing economic policy for the improvement of human welfare.

The case for economic science having as its central aim prediction and not just understanding follows naturally from Blaug's position as one of the foremost proponents of falsification in the methodology debate. This is fiercely contested in a number of quarters and especially since McCloskey (1983) launched his attack on the scientific pretensions of economics. The importance of policy relevance and policy enlightenment is also a common thread in Hutchison's writings, another (qualified) proponent of falsification and an economist whose long career and deep knowledge of the British economy and of the history of economic thought makes him well-qualified to pass comment. For Hutchison (1992, p. 99) economics' malaise could be likened to the condition exposed in Bloom's *The closing of the American mind* (1987), of mass culture, mass higher education and the Balkanisation of the social sciences leading to 'the draining from the minds of those undergoing graduate education in the subject, of their initial interest in real-world policy-making, while, at the same time, the historical dimension of the subject is largely eliminated, and a knowledge of economic literature, beyond some recent or current articles, is dismissed as unimportant.' What **Lionel Robbins** (1952, pp. 1–2) called 'provincialism in time', an 'indifference to the intellectual past' such that we 'cannot hope to understand the problems of our own day if we do not know the problems and policies out of which they grew', had therefore returned with a vengeance.

Colander and Klamer's (1987, p. 95) survey was prompted by the disquiet that 'departments of economics are graduating a generation of *idiots savants* brilliant at esoteric mathematics yet innocent of actual economic life'. Out of the discussions this engendered came an AEA decision to appoint a commission on graduate education in economics, this to address a somewhat limited subset of the misgivings about economics which had been gathering pace (Krueger *et al.* 1991). The commission was unmoved by accusations that there was an excessive use of mathematics in economics, but agreed that the linkages between tools in the economists' kitbag and real-world problems could be improved as could the communication skills of these apprentice economists. In short, there was nothing drastically wrong with postgraduate education and much that was good, a predictable outcome given the commission's brief and membership, and one in fact predicted by Klamer and Colander (1990, p. 200).

No such enquiry has been undertaken in Britain, although there were economists who by the 1980s were deeply unhappy about economics education. Thus, for example, David Simpson (1988, p. 11), who vacated an economics chair in Scotland to become chief economist at a life assurance company, contributed a swansong paper proposing the following reforms:

1. A greater proportion of the curriculum should be devoted to political economy at the expense of formal analytical methods.
2. There should be more attention to institutional economics rather than to macroeconomics, and more emphasis on evolutionary rather than optimisation perspectives.
3. Students of economics should be made aware of developments in other social sciences. They should be required to take a course in economic history.

4. The principles of statistical theory should be taught in place of applied statistics. Emphasis should be placed on the evaluation and interpretation of data.
5. Greater use should be made of case study material as a means of teaching students how to apply economic theories to practical problems.

The RES did in fact commission in 1987 an enquiry into the current state of the economics profession in Britain, with Towse and Blaug (1988) producing a report which was greeted with far from universal approval.[27] However, the proximate reason for the enquiry was much less the methodological issues surveyed above, or even concern about the influence of the profession on policy, than a local preoccupation with the impact of cuts in public expenditure on higher education. Nonetheless, in the letters section of the *RES Newsletter* a debate of sorts was conducted which touched on much of the ground covered in America and reveals much of interest for our purposes. The ball was set rolling by Austin Robinson who took exception to the Towse-Blaug report's definition of an economist, as someone with at least a second degree in the subject, for excluding 'almost the whole of the very professional and very competent government economic service and the majority of economists working in the business world'.[28] We noted earlier that this definition of economics as the preserve of academic economists, and of this group as the prime audience of the *EJ*, troubled Robinson who was concerned that the *EJ* had become far too specialised and technically too demanding. Appealing to the greats, he gently chided: 'Were both Marshall and Keynes wrong in saying that what could be thought clearly could be said clearly? I have been reading with much profit the latest volume of James Meade's papers. He was able, when he wished, to communicate very complex ideas in language that enabled the general working economist to understand the issues and to apply the reasoning to his own special case.'

The Towse-Blaug report had little to say specifically on the curriculum, but did pass on representations from employers that economics education was excessively theoretical. A complementary study for the RES, conducted in the winter of 1988-9 (Lawson 1990), investigated undergraduate economics training much more fully, yielding results that indicated a high degree of realism on the part of academics about the use their students would make of their economics training. It also confirmed the shortfall in practical skills identified by Towse and Blaug, but was optimistic that departments were sufficiently flexible to remedy these shortcomings. In the

---

[27]   An abbreviated version of the report was published in the *EJ* (Towse and Blaug 1990) alongside an alternative analysis by Dolton and Makepeace (1990).
[28]   *RES Newsletter*, no. 69 (March 1990), pp. 16-19.

main, in Britain, concerns about higher education funding dominated and there was little public discussion about the content and purpose of the curriculum, although Cairncross's (1989a, p. 184) Tawney lecture continued to press the case for the inclusion of economic history 'as preparation for an uncertain world and [as an] antidote to the certainties of theory'. The nature and purpose of the Ph.D., by now the qualification required to become an academic economist, also came under scrutiny, although here the agenda was set less by economists than by the Economic and Social Research Council (ESRC), the funding agency for social science research in Britain.[29]

It would be understandable to draw the conclusion from all of this that, while many British economists were concerned about the state of the discipline, far less debate and action ensued than in America. This would actually be gravely misleading for the centenary of the RES acted as a spur to a re-examination of the society's objectives and practices, from which has resulted a reinvigoration of its activities and a number of strategic developments. But, in typically British fashion, all of this occurred behind the scenes and without apparent fuss or drama. Thus David Hendry, the society's outgoing president, recorded in 1995 that recent RES activities were all directed at 'confront[ing] ... the many dangers facing the profession and our Society':

> These dangers centre around the public perception of the irrelevance and disputative nature of economics and economists, claimed policy and forecasting failures, and the apparently growing problems facing society . . . The long-term solution is to increase the power and comprehensiveness of economic analysis, and its comprehension by both the public and politicians.[30]

Four areas for action emerged from RES deliberations: that there be efforts to assist new entrants to the profession; greater liaison with key institutions; an enhancement of the benefits of membership of the RES; and the raising of the profile of economists more generally. In seeking to secure these objectives there have been a number of notable developments. The *EJ* has now expanded in size and scope with its policy forum and controversies sections, but as yet has no supplementary publication like the AEA's *Journal of Economic Perspectives* which attempts to fill the gap between the general interest press and most other academic economics journals, one function of which is to provide a forum for largely non-technical economic analyses of public policy issues. Considerable energies have been devoted to greater networking, providing press briefings and a media consultant has

---

[29] *RES Newsletter*, no. 72 (December 1990), pp. 11–14; no. 73 (March 1991), pp. 4–6; no. 75 (October 1991), pp. 4–5.
[30] *RES Newsletter*, no. 89 (April 1995), p. 2.

even been appointed, one jointly shared with the ESRC and based at the Centre for Economic Policy Research (CEPR), itself an agency which has done much to sponsor applied research and to communicate it in ways that are relevant and accessible to policy-makers.[31] Noteworthy also was the much higher profile of the RES annual conference which, through its absorption of the conferences held by the then separate bodies representing teachers of economics in old (i.e. pre-1992) and new (1992) universities (the former polytechnics),[32] at last resulted in a single body representing the profession as other agencies had long achieved in the social sciences (namely, the Political Studies Association and the British Sociological Association).[33] All of this may seem rather mundane for a study professing to be about economic policy and performance, but as was made clear at the start of this chapter, professional societies matter for what their disciplines can achieve.

What goes largely unrecorded in RES documents made public, though it is hinted at in a number of places,[34] is that change only really became possible once the society became a more democratic body with nominations to its council and the elections of its president through universal suffrage. This had to await near completion of the first century of its existence, for the greater part of which the society, mirroring British economics, was dominated by a small number of very influential figures. For example, what other world class journal only had two editors in its first fifty five years (Edgeworth and Keynes); founding fathers, born in the mid-nineteenth century but still active in RES affairs as late as the 1930s (Bonar and Higgs); or a council member serving for fifty nine years (Austin Robinson), however distinguished? These points are offered less as a criticism of Britain's economic establishment than as an observation that an organisation founded in 1890 might reasonably experience considerable difficulties in reforming its constitution and mission. Indeed, the history of the RES might, like other market and non-market structures, have something in common with the diagnoses of Britain's relative economic decline identified by what has become known as the institutional rigidity school, namely that:

Britain's distinctiveness derived less from the conservatism of its cultural values

---

[31] Ibid., pp. 2–3; no. 93 (April 1996), p. 7.
[32] The former, the AUTE has a long history, having been formed in 1925 to cater for a need not provided for by the RES, that of annual conference for those providing undergraduate economics education (*EJ*, 35 (March 1925), pp. 153–5; Winch 1990a, p. 19). The Association of Polytechnic Teachers of Economics (APTE) was in existence between 1972–92 (*RES Newsletter*, no. 77 (April 1992), p. 1).
[33] *RES Newsletter*, no. 77 (April 1992), p. 1.
[34] For example, *RES Newsletter*, no. 78 (July 1992), p. 1; no. 89 (April 1995), p. 3.

per se than from a matrix of rigid institutional structures that reinforced these values and obstructed individualistic as well as collective efforts at economic renovation.   (Elbaum and Lazonick 1986b, p. 2)

In this sense British economics and the British economy may share a common history. It remains, of course, highly contestable whether recent years have seen something of a renaissance in the latter; and too early no doubt to judge whether contemporaneous developments in the economics profession will transform what Galbraith has aptly called 'economists' special commitment to obscurity' into something more closely resembling the mission set forth by Marshall and his contemporaries over a century ago. Some further thoughts on the future of economics are reserved for the concluding chapter. Here we note that having examined in some detail the beginning and the end of the first century of British professional economics, with the intervening years left largely untouched, we have acquired a number of reference points with which to evaluate how we got from Marshall to Meade.

2. Economics, economists and policy

[T]he ideas of economists and political philosophers, both when they are right and when they are wrong, are more powerful than is commonly understood. Indeed the world is ruled by little else. Practical men, who believe themselves to be quite exempt from any intellectual influences, are usually the slaves of some defunct economist. Madmen in authority, who hear voices in the air, are distilling their frenzy from some academic scribbler of a few years back. I am sure that the power of vested interests is vastly exaggerated compared with the gradual encroachment of ideas. Not, indeed, immediately, but after a certain interval; for in the field of economic and political philosophy there are not many who are influenced by new theories after they are twenty-five or thirty years of age, so that the ideas which civil servants and politicians and even agitators apply to current events are not likely to be the newest. But, soon or late, it is ideas, not vested interests, which are dangerous for good or evil.   (Keynes 1936, pp. 383–4)

2.1 INTRODUCTION

This famous passage from the closing paragraph of Keynes's *General theory* was, not surprisingly, taken to heart by a self-interested economics profession. Its representation of the policy process as – in the long-run – driven by the triumph of ideas over vested interests remained true to the traditions of nineteenth-century British idealistic philosophy, but sought also to further the authority of academic economics, by securing privileges for economists in policy-making. Truly was Keynes a product of Cambridge economics, the embodiment of Marshall's mission. Yet, and notwithstanding that this passage from the *General theory* has been much analysed, it is of significance as much for what is absent as for what is observable in Keynes's conception of the policy process. Thus, neither in the *General theory* nor elsewhere within his extensive writings (the RES-sponsored edition of Keynes's collected works amounts to 30 volumes) is there a real consideration of the nature of the relationship between the expert and the madmen in authority, no acknowledgement of what we would now call government failure, the counterpoise to market failure. As Skidelsky (1996, p. 75) observes 'Keynes's reliance on expertise as a *deus ex machina* ... gave him an exaggerated view of the state's problem-solving capacity.' The respective capabilities of economists and governments, the latter here

44

defined as a composite of politicians and civil servants, thus provides the key to a modelling of the policy process. We will argue that criticisms of the politics of Keynes's economics have been somewhat overdone, but amidst this critical literature the recent attempts to rehabilitate Keynes as a 'liberal' economist have shed new light on a number of issues pertinent to our discussion (R. Middleton 1989).

First and foremost, whilst Keynes and the *General theory* are often portrayed as anti-capitalist in intent and effect, he was in actuality a lifelong liberal, an 'individualist to the finger-tips' according to his first biographer (Harrod 1951, p. 191). The *General theory* was part of his broader attempt to reconstruct liberalism via deliberate but limited state action which reformed capitalism into a more efficient and humane economic system. Thus the *General theory* was attempting to steer a mid-course between the twin peaks of Marxism, for which capitalism was incapable of reform, and fascism, where capitalism was capable of infinite corruption for totalitarian purposes. The phrase 'soon or late, it is ideas, not vested interests, which are dangerous for good or evil', says Skidelsky (1992, p. 570) in his life of Keynes, was written as a 'double condemnation' in which Stalin, Neville Chamberlain, Marx and the classical economists were all implicated.

Secondly, the scrutiny to which Keynes's assumptions about political and bureaucratic behaviour have been subject has resulted in renewed interest in what Harrod (1951, pp. 183, 192–3) called, after Keynes's birthplace in Cambridge, the 'presuppositions of Harvey Road'. At one level these are definable as a mindset which assumed 'a stable British Empire and assured material progress' and at another as 'the idea that the government of Britain was and would continue to be in the hands of an intellectual aristocracy using the method of persuasion.' Here we emphasise the element of persuasion, upon which Keynes's gravest and perhaps, in the long-run, most effective critic von Hayek (1966, pp. 103–4) observed: 'although he liked to pose as a Cassandra whose dire predictions were not listened to, he was really supremely confident of his powers of persuasion and believed that he could play on public opinion as a virtuoso plays on his instrument.'

If economics as a discipline be thought of as the study of optimising behaviour exercised through markets, and politics as the pursuit of power mediated through groups and institutions, persuasion lies dead centre in influencing the parameters of what is economically rational and politically possible. Economic policy is by definition a fusion of economics and politics, but with the precise balance indeterminate *a priori*. Clearly, the state of the market for economic advice will be one determinant of this fusion at any particular time, and it is of considerable relevance that as the twentieth century has progressed the realm of the private has been progressively squeezed by the public domain, of government over market. Indeed, the conduct of government itself has become more and more dominated by economic issues as politicians have responded to voter preferences, the latter themselves much influenced by politicians' claims about their ability to manage the economy and to deliver affluence. **Harold Wilson's** dictum, that 'all political history shows that the standing of a Government and its ability to hold the confidence of the electorate at a General Election, depends upon the success of its economic policy', might provide a useful guide were it not for the ahistoricism of the 'all'. Thus the conditions under which economic performance came to determine political popularity, and the role economists played in this process, forms a central issue for this study.

In seeking to understand this long-term process, indeed the wider relationship between economics and politics, we are both aided and hindered by the literature on the theory and practice of public policy, in particular that on economic policy-making. Although there are a number of works – theoretical and applied, both historical and contemporary – of real quality,[1] there is much that is indifferent or unhelpful within the huge literature. Moreover, the greater part concerns the postwar period and is characterised by the distinct and separate disciplinary traditions of economics, political science, public administration, history (of various persuasions) and sociology. Thus the potential benefits of interdisciplinary social scientific understanding, a case often preached but rarely practised, have not been realised. As a consequence any attempt to model the policy process runs the risk of being acceptable to few and objectionable to the many. Accordingly, the following is not intended to be anything other than an indication of the possible approaches to the problem, with their potentiality and pitfalls indicated. The focus is how and why the producers and consumers of economic knowledge typically entertain quite different views of the world, from which we can glean much about the propagation of economic ideas and the reasons why economists disagree. The remainder of this chapter divides into two parts: beginning with a consideration of the possible causal connections between economic ideas and economic events in section 2 the discussion then proceeds in section 3 to the broader issue of the formulation of economic policy.

---

[1]   See Parsons (1995) for a recent, reliable and comprehensive exposition of the broad field of public policy studies by a social scientist combining catholic interests with an adequate grounding in economics. Of relevance also is what Americans call public choice theory, and the British more usually the economics of politics. This is also a substantial literature, superbly summarised in Mueller (1989), and with Buchanan *et al.* (1978), IEA (1978) and **Peacock** (1992a) all pertinent to the British case. Dixit's (1996) transaction-costs approach to economic policy-making should also be consulted.

2.2 MODELLING THE POLICY PROCESS

Textbook expositions

Students of economics, undergoing initiation into the discipline at school or university, are typically presented with a textbook exposition of economic policy as entailing essentially technical choices. In such a world ends are the concern of politics, means the preserve of economics. Thus governments have certain objectives (for example, economic growth and price stability), attainable by matching assigned policy instruments, and it is the responsibility of politicians to interpret society's (utility) welfare function to determine which objectives are to be pursued, and where there are trade-offs between these objectives (as in economic growth and price stability), how much of one will be sacrificed for the achievement of the other. It then becomes the task of economists to calculate the magnitudes entailed in such a trade-off, and to advise on other matters concerning economic facts and behaviours.

Our point here is not that economists do not grow out of these textbook exercises, but that they often mistake a Weberian ideal type for something more durable and that such a characterisation encourages false expectations about what politicians might require and economists can deliver. To illustrate this we need first to distinguish between three different levels of economic ideas which are fed into the policy process (adapted from Coats 1987c, p. 51):

1. The ultimate objectives of economic policy: the security of the nation state, the maximisation of national output.
2. The intermediate objectives or ends, such as a stable exchange rate or favourable trade balance, which are in turn means to achieve the ends incorporated in (1) above.
3. The more technical, lower-level discussion of the means to achieve (2) above: the nitty-gritty of policy instruments, both macro- and microeconomic, and between those having big effects (through, for example, changes in income tax and exchange rates) and more subtle changes (to incentives, relative prices etc.).

On the basis of such a schema, and assuming that the ultimate objectives are given, economic policy then becomes a function of understanding about how the economic system works and the relationship between means and ends. Both, in turn, pose the question at what point expert knowledge of the economy is required, while in addition we must accommodate Tomlinson's (1981b, p. 1) criticism that too much of the policy literature assumes the existence of economic problems without 'discussing for whom these problems exist, how they came to exist, and what the conditions of existence of such policy objectives are.'

Why economists disagree

We have also to consider why economists disagree amongst themselves, notwithstanding the evidence reported in chapter 1 that such disagreements have been overplayed in the popular mind. Indeed, the reasons why economists disagree forms a convenient entry point to the relationship between economic ideas and economic policy.

Typically, economists' disagreements derive from one or more of the following four sources.[2] First, we have matters of formal logic, more particularly the properties of abstract economic models. The scrutiny to which models and theory are subject forms the centrepiece of economics' claim to be a science; paradoxically, of course, the domination of economics by mathematical model-builders, ones who appear untroubled by real world concerns, has undermined public confidence in economics and, to a lesser extent, created disquiet within the profession (Leontief's complaint).

Secondly, we have the interpretation of empirical evidence, from which – together with scrutiny of formal logic – follows the possibility of verification or at least falsification. The ability to withstand empirical testing is certainly seen in popular terms as economics' Achilles heel, but within the profession the debate is altogether more complicated. In an important methodological essay, Milton Friedman (1953, pp. 5, 7) argued that the ultimate goal of economics as a positive science is the development of theory capable of producing predictions of phenomena not yet observed.[3] Asserting the possibility of positive economics, free from ethics and normative positions, the task of economics – and thus its appeal to policy-makers – was to generate robust generalisations which allowed predictions of the consequences of one course of action rather than another. So far so good, but what caused real consternation was the next stage of the argument, what Samuelson later called the F-twist: 'the notion', here in Blaug's (1992a, p. 91) words, 'that conformity of the assumptions of a theory with reality provides a test of validity different from, or additional to, the test of its predictions.' With all predictions by definition deriving from positive economics, 'differences about economic policy among disinterested citizens derive predominantly from different predictions about the economic consequences of taking action – differences in principle that can be

[2]   Adapted from Ricketts and Shoesmith (1990, pp. 20–22).
[3]   See Caldwell (1982, ch. 8) and Blaug (1992a, pp. 90–105) for assessments of this classic work.

eliminated by the progress of positive economics – rather than from fundamental differences in basic values, differences about which men can ultimately only fight.'

However, in economics the observer is not independent of the process being observed, and as we now know even the 'hard' sciences have not proved immune to normative influences or lapses in scholarly standards. The ability to replicate the empirical results of other researchers is an essential part of scientific progress. Yet, in practice it is not often attempted in economics where the profession's incentive structure encourages new work, not the verification of existing results. In any case, where such attempts have been made they reveal that economics is prone to inadvertent errors, if not fraud. Thus, for example, Dewald *et al.* (1986), the results of a major project which for obvious reasons have not been much communicated outside the profession, encountered very serious difficulties in replicating the calculations reported in the majority of papers published in the *Journal of Money, Credit and Banking* between 1980–84 for which they were able to obtain data from their authors. To these difficulties we should add more recent concerns about the error-proneness of modern econometric software packages (Lovell and Selover 1994), and the tendency of the modern economist to use off-the-shelf datasets supplied by others, thereby insulating themselves from the all-important stage of data collection, from which much can be learnt about a research topic and many errors avoided.[4]

Thirdly, the issue of disinterestedness, of vested interests, rears its head. Without necessarily claiming that economists are hired guns, representing their own particular interests, either functionally (as industrial or financial economists) or sectionally (monetarists, Keynesians, Marxists, etc.), the scientific impartiality of economists is frequently impugned, providing ready-made justifications for economists' disagreements.

Fourthly and finally, and once more connected to the Friedmanite case for a positive economics, it is contended that divisions between economists derive from differing ethical judgements. Thus many economists question whether economic advice can ever be relieved of ethical precepts, Samuelson for one as we have seen. Many would doubt the desirability of such a stance even were it possible, and given what we know about the advent of professional economics in Britain we should expect ethical standpoints to play an important role. Indeed, they do but as we shall see in chapter 7 the Marshallian project, and its assumptions, were challenged in the 1970s by economists who were either influenced by Friedman or who subscribed to very different ethical positions.

---

[4]   Klamer and Colander (1990, pp. 195–6); see also Mayer (1993, pp. 70–74, 140–42) on the problems of data-mining.

Before broadening our account a final comment is appropriate here about Friedman's methodological instrumentalism. Were economic theory to be nothing more than an instrument for generating predictions (what will be the value of money GDP in twelve months' time? the RPI?), economics would be without the greater part of its heuristic; it would lack explanatory power (how might the path of money GDP be influenced? pressures on prices contained?) and would be consequently of limited utility to policy-makers. This is not to deny that prediction has come to play an important role in economics, one in part conditioned by the explosion in demand for forecasts, but to assert that the policy process is much richer and more involved, more an art than a science in the creative processes that are valued by those demanding and those supplying economic expertise.

The suppliers of economic expertise

The market for economic advice is considered more fully in chapter 3, but here it is appropriate to indicate the various forms of economic knowledge available to policy-makers. Peden (1996, pp. 171–2) distinguishes between:

1. Information: which may derive from government agencies, either departments (for example, the Board of Inland Revenue) or specialist data collectors (the Office for National Statistics, ONS); private agencⁱ. (the Confederation of British Industry, CBI); or bodies such as parliamentary enquiries and royal commissions.
2. Practical experience: foremost here is the expertise provided by those at the heart of the City of London, knowledge that is sought and proffered on more than just financial issues. In addition, and according to the ideology of the ruling party, whether peace or wartime, and the pressing economic problems of the moment, representatives from industry and the trade unions may also be incorporated into the policy process, with expertise sought and available at both national and regional levels.
3. Economic theory: now the domain of academic economists, but before the Second World War there was room for those not holding a university post (most notably **Ralph Hawtrey**, a Treasury official and a leading expert on monetary theory, discussed at pp. 69, 154, 199) and, since the 1970s, with something of a revival of non-academic economists as a conduit for new ideas.
4. Informed opinion: providing something of an overlap with (2) above, but a category which seeks to capture the wide policy network in Britain, thereby embracing contributions from leading financial journalists, Oxbridge senior common rooms, the church, parliamentary lobbies etc. This category might be said to embody much of the inner, but particularly

the outer, circles of the 'establishment', that amorphous group which social critics of the 1950s and 1960s identified as the true rulers of Britain (Thomas 1959). However labelled, this group has an especial significance if the related critique be accepted, that a central element of the British disease has been the cult of the amateur, a persistent belief in the merits of leaving high policy to an Oxbridge educated elite, trained in the classics and ignorant of science, technology – and economics (Allen 1979, p. 42). If so, we should expect 'informed opinion' to harbour much DIYE.

5. Realities of political economy: a residual category which captures the 'art of the possible in economic affairs', and more particularly gives to the higher civil service the role as guardians of past experience and mediators of perceived present constraints and possibilities.

Policy paradigms: the interaction of events and ideas

The availability of such disparate sources of economic expertise enormously complicates the task of modelling the policy process, as does the very different approaches historians and economists adopt in representing human behaviour. We can illustrate this by Figures 2.1 and 2.2. The former is designed to represent the interconnections between economic ideas and events, and is adapted from a model of the policy process constructed to understand seventeenth and eighteenth-century mercantilism, an era in which debate over the appropriate economic functions of the state, and the role of economic ideas in that debate, provides many parallels with more recent concerns. The approach is thus explicitly historical, with our revisions being mainly at the institutional level in recognition of particular late twentieth-century concerns, more specially international and supra-national constraints and obligations. The second approach, which is divided into two parts which conceptualise the conventional and more recent economic models, is far less informed by, though not ignorant of, the history of economic thought and is drawn from the work of a recently retired British economist with experience of government service and a specialism in public finance and, more latterly, public choice theory.

The reader is not here being asked to choose between these models. They are not competitors but complementary. The former deliberately uses non-technical language to model the policy process as a loop, an iterative social activity in which there is the possibility of learning (through feedback effects); there exist leakages (between policy actions and policy implementation), in which the state's capacity to successfully deliver policy outputs depends upon expertise and the power to enforce its will; and economists play multiple roles, initiating ideas, acting as policy

Figure 2.1 Interaction of economic ideas and events

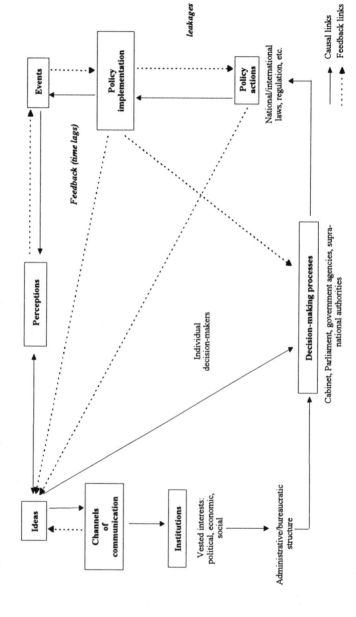

Sourec: Adapted from Coats (1987c, figure 2).

52

Figure 2.2 Policy paradigms

A. Conventional theory of economic policy

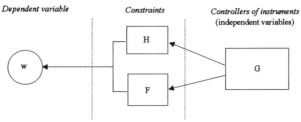

w = welfare function of government; G = government (collective welfare maximiser); F = firms (profit maximisers); H = households (utility maximisers)

B. Public choice theory of economic policy

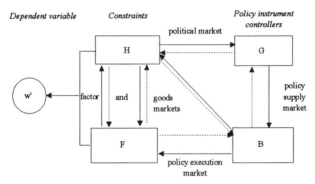

w' = policy outcomes (as reflected in objectives, e.g. rate of inflation, employment, etc.); G = government (vote maximiser); B = bureaucracy (output maximiser? budget maximiser?); H = households/voters (utility maximisers); F = firms (profit maximisers).

Source: Adapted from Peacock (1992a, figure 1).

entrepreneurs and as administrators of agreed policies.

By contrast, the language of the second model is much more technical and explicitly economic, involving as it does agents (government, bureaucrats, firms and households), markets (economic, political and policy), welfare functions (utility and other forms of maximisation), dependent and independent variables. This is the economist's conception of the world *par excellence*, but there are important differences between the conventional theory portrayed in panel A and the public choice model of panel B.

The conventional theory of economic policy, which first began to take shape in the 1950s and derives from the work of two Dutch economists (Tinbergen and Theil), treats government as the independent variable and as amenable to economic analysis in the manner of the twin agents of households and firms. Typically, government is modelled as having a welfare function comprising several quantifiable economic objectives which are traded off against one another. This function is then maximised subject to prevailing constraints, themselves a function of the economy's structure, the known behaviour of firms and households and the extent to which the economy is open and thus externally constrained. Given the Keynesian foundations of this approach it should come as no surprise that such exercises generally yielded evidence of market failure requiring remedial action by government, typically acting on aggregate demand. In this characterisation economic policy is an optimising process conducted by rational actors, from which it follows that policy-making is almost exclusively a technocratic process, one providing a clear-cut and substantial role for the economist (Peacock 1979, p. 7). However, the conventional theory rests on some very strong assumptions: that government is a unitary authority with a stable welfare function; that it has discretionary control over policy instruments; and that, so far as adjustments to private sector demand are required, it can dominate decision-making by firms and households. In retrospect, it was an approach very much the product of time and place: of 'golden age' growth for the western economies, of a dominant hydraulic (Keynesian) version of the economy's operation, of confidence in econometrics and of certain (naive) assumptions about the extent to which government was an agency of the public good as against having its own political reaction function.

The public choice approach by contrast, one version of which is represented in panel B, takes a more realistic – if, perhaps, still narrow – stance on both economics and politics. As befits a blending of the subject matter of political science (the non-market activities of voting, party politics and bureaucracy) with the analytic tools of economics (human behaviour as egoistic, rational and utility maximising), public choice provides rich insights into the economic policy process. Recognition of the shortcomings of the conventional theory leads us to model no dominant decision-maker. Rather, economic policy is the product of bargaining between government, bureaucracy, firms and households operating through economic and political/policy markets. Feedback mechanisms also feature strongly. Indeed, it is the essence of the public choice approach that governmental attempts to manage the economy generate concomitant protective institutions (interest groups) and behaviours in the private sector. Thus firms and households are not passive adjusters to the opportunity sets forced on them by governments; indeed, if the Lucas critique of macroeconomic policy is brought to bear (see p. 293), the very opposite is the case and government must operate in an environment in which the same policy instruments can have very different effects according to time and place. Such models also distinguish between government and bureaucracy. The former is usually represented as a vote maximiser, the analogy being with a firm and profit maximisation, whilst the latter is accorded a new presence in policy, thereby recognising the possibility of its enjoying an independent welfare function. Finally, and here the bureaucracy plays a major role requiring explanation, public choice models such as this distinguish between a policy supply market, in which bureaucrats supply economic policy packages which compete for the favours of politicians, and policy execution markets in which firms and households trade their cooperation with government policies in return (rent-seeking, the profit motive by another name) for services provided by government (subsidies, tax breaks etc.).

As we now turn our attention to a more formalised exposition of the formulation of economic policy we note the very different approaches adopted by historians and economists. The former might be considered unduly *ad hoc*; the latter as yet further evidence of economics' imperialist mission to explain every aspect of human behaviour through rational calculation models, most notably *Homo economicus*. This construct, rational economic man, now integral to the theory of consumer choice and of the firm, was for a large part of the twentieth century something of an embarrassment to economists seeking to understand individual – as against representative or aggregative – human behaviours. As Rosenberg (1979, p. 509) puts it: 'The idea that human action, economic or otherwise, was strictly determined by the maximization of utility or preference subject to the constraint of beliefs about available alternatives, was considered so implausible, that even in economics ... its explanatory pretensions were systematically pruned to the barest minima.' Yet, beginning in the 1960s, rational calculation models returned with a vengeance, and nowhere more so than in economics and politics, as for example in Tullock's work on bureaucracy and voting and Becker on the family and aspects of individual behaviour such as addiction. The juggernaut of rational economic man has not, however, driven all before it. Resistance continues from those who highlight the poverty of economics' psychological understanding. Indeed, there exists a vibrant sub-discipline of the social psychology of economics and important interdisciplinary work which reassesses the psychological premises of market behaviour.[5]

There exist further misgivings about contemporary economics and the capacity of rational calculation models to explain decision-making. There is, of course, the ahistoricism of much of the literature on policy-making and the limited time frame with which today's economists appear to operate. Many, including some very eminent professional economists, would contend

---

[5]   For example, see Lewis *et al.* (1995) for the former and Lane (1991) for the latter.

that economists are increasingly unable to explain real world economic problems, and thus give good policy advice, because their training does not encourage them to think of problems as the product of long-run, dynamic path-dependent processes. There have been many attempts this century to recreate a more historical economics, to repair the breach between the two disciplines which Marshall inadvertently encouraged, but currently the efforts of Paul David are particularly prominent. Mindful of McCloskey's dictum that economists needed to persuade, and that the manner of the storytelling determines persuasiveness, David (1993, p. 29) picked an apparently frivolous example, that of why the seemingly irrational layout of the QWERTY keyboard has endured despite there being technically superior alternatives, to illustrate how a 'particular sequence of events in the past is capable of exerting persisting effects upon current conditions; of how adventitious, seemingly transient actions may become so magnified as to exercise a controlling (and sometimes pernicious) influence over matters of far greater economic and social significance.' Path-dependency is particularly appealing for those seeking to understand Britain's economic predicament, for 'systems possessing this property cannot shake off the effects of past events' and this limits their future possibilities, unless the system is subject to severe shocks.

A final comment is also appropriate here about public choice. In essence an American creation, great caution is required in the application of public choice theory to British public policy. An initial obstacle is 'the open hostility to the public sector of most of the authors using a public choice framework' (Heald 1983, p. 308), a consequence largely of its origins and of the political agenda of the agencies responsible for popularising public choice in Britain, in particular the Institute of Economic Affairs (IEA). In such stories government invariably features as a malevolent Leviathan rather than as benevolent public goods provider. However, there is more to public choice theory than the vision provided by Buchanan and his followers. Thus too often the case presented for the market rests on an idealised version of its operation contrasted with the real world failings of government. The very different political systems, constitutional arrangements and balances between the government and the market in America and Britain need also to be taken into account. In different hands public choice can provide more realistic assessments of the capabilities of both government and the market (for example, Self 1993), and in the following our assessment of the role of economics and economists in the policy process is grounded within this broader debate.

2.3 ECONOMISTS AND THE FORMULATION OF POLICY

Such has been the influence of Keynes and the Keynesians in Britain that, almost without exception, from the end of the Second World War until the early 1980s historians of economic policy broadly conceived of the policy process within an essentially Keynesian framework, that is one in which developments in theory determined, after a lag, the direction and detail of policy. Michael Stewart's *Keynes and after* (1972, pp. 296–7), a hugely popular text with economics undergraduates, epitomised this approach with his confident prediction that because of the Keynesian revolution 'It seems safe to predict that unemployment will never again be more than a fraction of the amount suffered between the wars.' The collapse of the Keynesian hegemony of the 1970s, the return of mass unemployment and the methodological crises within economics, has led both economists with contemporary concerns and students of the history of economic policy to rethink their position. To begin with Tomlinson (1981b), after contrasting the strengths and weaknesses of the Keynesian model in relation to the Marxist and public choice approaches, both in essence representing in very different ways the triumph of vested interests over ideas, proposed an eclectic approach because only this could capture the role of institutions and the historical contingency of economic objectives. New conceptual approaches and schematic characterisations of economic policy, however, soon developed and in what follows we explore some of these which have the most relevance to our historical purpose.[6]

State-centric models

We begin with state-centric approaches which model economic policy as a vector diagram in which pluralistic pressures are applied to the state (defined variously as the nation's executive, legislative and judicial apparatus) which then responds according to the strength of such pressures but within the context that it also has an independent impact upon public policy. State-centric theories, originally developed by neo-Marxists to explain the durability of capitalism, now come in many guises. What they share in common is a framework for understanding economic policy much less as the product of economic theory than as a process determined by the capacity of institutions to incorporate economic ideas into policy. The state thus has interests and policy preferences of its own, and the adoption of a 'new' economic idea might be said to have to pass four market tests:

---

[6] See pp. 383–5 for a guide to further reading on the role of economists in economic policy.

1. A preliminary, screening process of peer group assessment which
   provides entry qualifications (the intellectual market);
2. A reality check in which the idea is tested for its goodness of fit with the
   perception of the economic circumstances then existing (the economic
   market);
3. An assessment of the net political advantage for the governing party (the
   political market); and
4. A judgement of its administrative feasibility (the bureaucratic market).

The attraction of such an approach lies in its capacity to explain why
economic ideas shape policy in different ways in different countries at
different times. Foremost amongst the representatives of this approach, and
a major channel for its application to the British case, has been the political
scientist, Peter Hall. Both in his re-examination of the adoption of
Keynesian ideas across nations and his comparative analysis of the decline
of the British economy, Hall (1986a; b; 1989b; 1993) has developed a much
more conceptually robust means of modelling policy and of capturing what
is historically distinctive about the British case than has been provided by
the Keynesian, Marxist, public choice or other approaches. For Hall (1992a,
p. 85) 'politicians draw upon a reservoir of ideas to formulate and justify the
policies they devise' so that 'the nature of the ideas in the reservoir will
affect the character of policy', with economists occupying a central role by
providing a 'rich vocabulary of principles on which politicians, like all
human beings, must draw to confer meaning on their action'. However, 'the
large size of the reservoir still leaves policy-makers considerable room for
manoeuvre in response to other influences', and in particular provides ample
scope for DIYE (see also Winch 1990b). Moreover, if it be accepted that
economists have their own political preferences, preferring certain
theoretical systems because of the channels through which policy operates,
with implications for the distribution of income and the role of government
(Coughlin 1989, p. 205), we have an additional justification for the ways in
which politicians might use economists and economic ideas.

Accordingly, this approach places great emphasis on the institutional
setting within which economic policies are conducted, with Hall (1986b, p.
279) arguing that 'British policy was different from the policies of other
capitalist democracies in large part because of the institutional peculiarities
of the British environment.' Four aspects of the structural setting are
identified as of relevance:

> the position of Britain within the international system, the organizational
> configuration of British society, the institutional structure of the state itself, and
> the nature of the wider political system, understood as the network of political
> parties and interest intermediaries that seek to influence policy.

with:

> Each of these variables affect[ing] the likelihood that the government would be willing to formulate a particular policy or the chances that they would be able to influence such a policy. Together, they pushed policy-makers in a particular direction by altering the balance of perceived costs and benefits that accrued to any one policy. Sometimes the variable acted on policy-makers' perceptions; as often, they exacted real costs.

The British policy space

We are led, therefore, towards the important suggestion that the institutional setting in Britain severely limits the policy space, the parameters of what is possible. The policy space is a useful concept designed to capture the interplay of past policies, choices and inherited institutional structures and the way in which they influence the definition of current problems, the perception of the range and efficacy of potential policy instruments and the resulting space for manoeuvre (Hogwood and Gunn 1984, p. 13). This is path-dependency dressed up in different (political) clothing. Thus, for Hall, Marquand (1988), Gamble (1994a) and many other writers sympathetic to the institutional rigidity school interpretation of economic decline (pp. 42–3), Britain's political system was shaped, as was its economy, by the formative influences of early industrialisation and empire. Presented in this manner we have a powerful instrument with which to explore dysfunctions within and between the twin areas of economic performance and policy.

This approach does need, however, to be supplemented by some further general and historical findings from the policy studies literature. First, there are well-established national differences in policy styles. In Britain, and notwithstanding the almost universal charge of institutional conservatism, the state has exhibited very considerable institutional and ideological flexibility, particularly in respect of accommodating the challenges posed by organised labour and the demand for full democratic rights. The imperative of flexibility, upon which the continuance of the nation state rested, led to a British policy style of consultation and a bias against policy actions which challenged well-entrenched interests. Radical change was, thereby, precluded and policy tended to be reactive rather than initiatory (Jordan and Richardson 1982). Secondly, there is a distinctive policy community which initially generated and now sustains this policy style, a nexus of interests whereby cooperation flows from a sense of mutual advantage, assisted no doubt by politicians and civil servants having attended the same public schools followed by an Oxbridge education (Heclo and Wildavsky 1981).

Thirdly, as has long been recognised, in advanced industrial economies, characterised by mature welfare systems and broadly consensual economic policy objectives, policy may well have its own causes rather than being due to policy evaluation or new problems. Rose and Karran (1984, p. 44) put it starkly: 'Governing today is not so much about making fresh choices; it is principally about living with the consequences of past choices. Most activities of government do not reflect today's decisions, but decisions made yesterday.' Inertia thus limits the policy space, while the unintended effects of policy, particularly in respect of fiscal instruments and their consequences for incentives and resource allocation, are typically as important as the intended effects. Fourthly, if there are few opportunities to start afresh in policy terms it might be argued that the policy space was nonetheless very wide at the beginning of the century because government was small, there was a widespread expectation about the possibility of beneficial economic and social reform and entropy had not yet the opportunity to establish itself at the institutional level. We shall see, however, that the laissez-faire, minimalist state provided no such clean slate.

Social learning

The concept of social learning is also relevant, that is politics as a process of social learning – of puzzlement about what to do – exercised through policy. This is usually represented as incorporating three main properties (current policy as a function of previous policies; experts as the guiding force in the learning process; and the state as exercising a strong measure of autonomy) operating, in turn, on three central variables (the intermediate objectives of policy; the policy instruments used to attain those objectives; and the precise settings of those instruments). This concept does not, in fact, require that the state be autonomous and when used by Hall (1993) to explore the British case provides a demonstration of policy which privileges expertise, albeit bounded by social bargaining, and models big changes in terms of paradigm shifts, a concept with which economists – through Kuhn – are accustomed. From these foundations three types of change can then be distinguished, ones which will prove immensely useful for our purposes:

1. First-order: alterations to the settings of policy instruments (e.g. movements in interest rates);
2. Second-order: shifts in the hierarchy of policy instruments (e.g. the introduction of cash limits in 1976 to provide improved control over public expenditure in response to the perceived breakdown of the old control system) without major adjustment to the hierarchy of policy objectives; and
3. Third-order: dramatic shifts in the hierarchy of policy objectives (e.g. the displacement of the full employment by the price stability objective in

1979–80) such as to constitute a transformation of the policy regime or paradigm (represented as the eclipse of Keynesianism by monetarism).

In subsequent chapters we will encounter policy shifts mainly of the first-order, less frequently of the second-order and only twice of the third-order. Such a schema provides useful benchmarks for assessing the magnitude of change, its significance and the extent to which expertise inside the state (for first- and second-order change) as against politicians and agents outside of the state (for third-order change) dominate the learning process. It also brings us back to the role of ideas in politics and to a certain symmetry between policy and economics in the sense of dominant paradigms which are able, to a certain degree, to accommodate anomalies but when these become too numerous the conditions are laid for dramatic, even revolutionary shifts.

The spread of economic ideas

To conclude this section we consider Coats and Colander's (1989) three models of the spread of economic ideas, models which are at least in part complementary and which are capable of sustaining both historical and current concerns. Their first model likens ideas to an infectious disease and includes such elements as carriers (the propagators of new ideas), channels for infection (journal articles, the media) and susceptible populations (perhaps the young). By contrast, their second model, that of the marketplace for ideas, views the propagation process in terms of competition between the sellers and buyers of ideas. We explore the market for economic advice in chapter 3 and here merely raise the point that there may be market imperfections which limit the policy space in some countries. Thirdly, they suggest that the spread of ideas might be understood in terms of information theory. Here the focus is on the transmission and reception of ideas, the bandwidth, signal strength and mechanisms for feedback. In such a world:

> The economist's job is to think up ideas that may be useful to society and encode them so that they can be efficiently transmitted through the institutions. The job of the transmission institutions is to send out the ideas with an optimal amount of noise and to decode them so that the policymaker can use them to improve society. (Coats and Colander 1989, p. 15)

For Coats and Colander each one of these three models provides a springboard from which to ask penetrating questions about the propagation of ideas, but with the processes through which ideas spread so numerous and diverse there can be no general theory. Certainly, echoes of each can be found in the writings of those who have been economic advisers where market analogies abound and comments are frequently made that, as Cairncross (1981, p. 5) puts it, 'Policy makers, as a rule, are slightly deaf: there is too much noise.' While the infectious disease model does not feature prominently it has unconscious overtones in much of the writings on shifts in policy paradigms, as for example in Galbraith's (1975a) account of how the Keynesian revolution came to America and Cockett's (1994) reconstruction of the reaction against Keynesianism by Thatcher and the neo-liberal strand of the Conservative Party. The propensity of economists to participate in theory-driven fads (for example, currently the application of game theory to every level of economic process) provides another manifestation of the infectious enthusiasms to which the discipline has become increasingly subject.

2.4 CONCLUSIONS

An eclectic approach to a modelling of the policy process provides escape from the rather sterile rationalist preoccupation of ideas versus vested interests, as if the latter could ever be bereft of the former (Gamble 1989). Politicians and economists both have political/ethical standpoints; the former do not have operational autonomy in economic policy and the latter lack a monopoly over the supply of economic advice. Economics and politics cannot be usefully separated when analysing economic policy, and thus economists need an understanding of the policy process if they are to be effective in influencing public policy (Nelson 1987; Portes 1990). But this presupposes that economists want to shape policy and, if so, to take a stand on the methodology of economics.

For Harry Johnson (1974b, p. 214), the proper function of economics 'is to arrive at a set of principles for understanding and interpreting the economy that are both scientifically "robust" and sufficiently simple to be communicable to successive generations of students and to policy-makers and the general public – not to establish a politically coerced consensus on a package of national economic policies'. As we shall see, for many British economists this is a highly restrictive and thus contentious job description. Moreover, the proper function of economists is in practice determined as much outside as inside the discipline. Thus, study of the market for economic advice is inextricably connected with political questions:

> Where would economic offices be placed organizationally within the government? How would economic experts succeed in communicating with political leaders who typically had little or no background in economics and often found economic reasoning difficult to follow? What would happen when an economist reached a conclusion that was politically damaging to current

leadership? In general, what would be the nature of the role that economic experts would assume in the process of governing?   (Nelson 1989, pp. 1–2)

If government policies towards, for example, education, the law or the family do not privilege educationalists, lawyers or sociologists why alone of the social sciences has economics attained a privileged position in policy-making? In part, the explanation is quite straightforward: economics concerns resource allocation, that is problems of choice which are, in effect, the central preoccupation of politics. Economics also provides a 'causal nexus' which, combining a facility for social accounts with an encompassing body of social theory, appears to make sense of disparate social phenomena. In short, for politicians, economics is more immediately useful than sociology. But, as we now turn to examine the market for economic advice, we should conclude this part of the discussion with the observation that the case for economics and economists is variable, strongly contingent upon time, place and, very frequently, personality.

3. The market for economic advice

Economic policy making is an activity like any other activity which involves producers competing to supply a market and consumers hoping to find their wants supplied. Economists may produce ideas and their ideas may be drawn upon at the official or the ministerial level. But what guides policy may have very little to do with the ideas that economists put forward. It may be dominated by non-economic considerations or by the views of non-economists or by doctrines refuted long ago or in widespread disrepute. What economists have to say may be neglected because its bearing on policy is obscure, contested, ambiguous, or insufficiently precise; because economists' conclusions rest on mistaken or inappropriate assumptions; because they are not adapted to the needs of the policy maker; or because, for that or any other reason, they simply fail to get a hearing. Policy makers, as a rule, are slightly deaf: there is too much noise.

(Cairncross 1981, p. 5)

3.1 INTRODUCTION

Those possessing or claiming economic knowledge have long provided advice for governments, be they monarchs or, more recently, career politicians. Thus, in the century preceding Marshall and the beginnings of this study, we have the celebrated examples of Smith, Ricardo and J.S. Mill, all economists who exercised great influence during and after their lifetimes. Nevertheless, before the First World War, if not a little later, the fundamental preconditions for a developed market in advice were absent. The very definition of what constituted an economist and, indeed, economics remained fluid, yet to be determined; there was as yet little government demand for expertise of any sort beyond that available within the military, the civil service, the broader political elite and/or key personnel in the City of London; and the potential supply of advice specifically economic in nature had yet to really distinguish itself from the broader currents of ideas and interests operating upon the political system.

For a market in advice to emerge political economy had to be transformed into economic science, from which an economics profession could develop with a clear identity and functions. This was, of course, Marshall's mission for the professionalisation of British economics which sought, on the supply side, to augment the quantity and, above all, the quality of university-trained economists. The objective was thus a new scientific authority for the discipline, one freed from political partisanship and, true to the spirit of Say's Law, with these supply-side reforms creating their own demand from government and other grateful recipients of specialist economic advice. We explore Marshall's mission more fully in chapter 4 but here introduce the important observation that, in terms of the market for economists and economic advice, Marshall and his contemporaries were involved in a supply-side push which was initially unmatched by demand.

In this chapter we explore the upshot of Marshall's mission in terms of the developing market for economic advice. Beginning with the supply schedule for advice in section 2 and progressing to demand factors in section 3 we survey a century of change, paying particular attention on the demand side to the years of the Second World War and to certain institutional developments – what we might call the infrastructure for economic advice. Some preliminary conclusions are then drawn in section 4. The expansion of the public sector and the growth and fluctuations of the British economy were, of course, important determinants of these demand and supply schedules in the market for advice, as well as providing the backdrop to the economic policy debate. British economic policy and performance since the 1890s has proved intensely controversial, with core concerns about economic decline connecting to much else in political, economic and social conflict. However, since they were also the central concerns of my previous book, *Government versus the market* (Middleton 1996), and there exists a rich and accessible literature on them,[1] we do not here incorporate any discussion of these topics beyond that absolutely essential to understand the various policy episodes considered in later chapters.

3.2 THE SUPPLY OF ECONOMISTS AND THE SOURCES OF POLICY ADVICE

Defining an economist

We start with the thorny problem of how to define an economist, a precondition for calculating the numbers who might be included under this heading. Since there is no generally agreed definition in our own time, no internationally recognised qualifications and standards for professional competence (Coats 1981b, p. 343), we inevitably encounter serious problems in attempting a definition which might be historically durable. We have also a cultural problem in that there has been less concern for professionalisation

---

[1]   See pp. 382–5 for a guide to further reading.

in Britain than in America, a reflection of very different development paths for higher education, which in turn created distinct national styles in economic research (Johnson 1973a), although the AEA, like the RES, has never imposed a membership qualification (Coats 1980). If, as Jacob Viner defined it, economics is what economists do, can we avoid circularity in defining economists themselves?

A useful starting point is with Tolles's (1968) typology. This was developed from responses received by the US National Science Foundation to questionnaires sent to 443,000 professional persons in the US in 1964, including AEA members. Respondents (N=223,900) were allocated to one of twelve professions according to the speciality in which each claimed their greatest interest, with each subject being defined in terms of a number (59 in the case of economics) of specialities from which respondents ranked the four most appropriate to their education and employment. From this, and in descending order, Tolles constructed the following definitions: possession of some speciality in economics (A); a degree in economics (B), current employment as an economist (C), greatest competence in some economics speciality (D), membership of a professional economic association (E), self-identification as an economist (F), possession of all specialities in economics (G) and those teaching and/or conducting research in economics (H). On this basis Tolles estimated the parameters for the supply of economists as between 4,939 (H), in effect the core academic community, and 16,727 (A), the profession at its very broadest.

There exist no comparable semi-official estimates for Britain at that time, nor historical series for either country. Since the 1960s the AEA has regularly surveyed its members, and, as was noted earlier, the RES did so in the late 1980s. This data can be supplemented by the qualified manpower surveys (based on 10 per cent samples) produced in Britain as part of the population censuses, with the most recent (1991) indicating that there were approximately 55,000 residents in Great Britain possessing an economics qualification above 'A' level, of whom some 6,100 or so were employed within the standard occupational classification (group 252) of actuaries, economists and statisticians.[2] None of this is very satisfactory for our purposes, and in particular lacking an equivalent of the US National Register of Scientific and Technical Personnel, where an economist can be defined by self-identification, we have no means of estimating the population of people claiming professional competence in economics. In their report for the RES, where an economist was defined as someone possessing at least a higher degree in the subject, Towse and Blaug (1988, p. 7; 1990, p. 228) estimated a total stock of economists in Britain of about

---

[2]　HMSO (1994, vol. 1, pp. 2–3 and table 6; vol. 2, table 14D).

3,500, with approximately three-quarters employed in higher education (cf. Dolton and Makepeace 1990).

If precision is not possible in the present, it is quite unrealisable for the past. Fortunately, we have Booth and Coats's (1978) pioneering survey of the market for economists between 1945–75, but for the earlier periods the available evidence is as yet largely unexplored in published work.[3] Indeed, the lack of attention devoted to the market for economists before the Second World War is particularly surprising in light of interest by both sociologists and historians in the role played by elite groups in the rise of professional society.[4] Even amongst those who have studied long-term occupational change, economists are absent from the narrative; nor do they feature in the major studies of the growth of the universities and the academic professions.[5] Strangely, in terms of the overall supply of economists, we actually know rather more about the prewar than the interwar years. Thus there is nothing comparable to Kadish and Tribe (1993a) for the interwar period, though the years between the wars have been more intensively researched in terms of the demand for and supply of policy advice, and we have a number of useful economists' memoirs on economics education.[6] There are a number of aspects to our difficulties.

First, we have to take account of the extraordinary heterogeneity of the early members of the RES. With no effective conditions guarding entry, beyond payment of a nominal annual subscription, membership of the RES was hardly synonymous with being an economist. Yet within its ranks were almost all of those who might make such a claim. Of the 1891 membership, which totalled 710, Coats and Coats (1970, table 1) have been able to identify the occupations of 501 individuals who were resident in the UK (an additional 115 were overseas residents, leaving 94 about whom nothing substantive is known). The most highly represented group were those in business (22.5 per cent) with academics ranked second (17 per cent), lawyers third (10 per cent) and civil servants fourth (9 per cent). At the beginning of our period a strong interest in economics, as measured by the

---

[3] Fortunately, the published record will be much enriched when Keith Tribe completes his study of the British economics profession between 1860–1970, research which *inter alia* draws upon an analysis of the university records for economics graduates.

[4] For example, Perkin (1989; 1996) or, more narrowly, Hargrove (1972).

[5] For example, Halsey and Trow (1971) and Halsey (1992), but see also Sanderson (1972).

[6] For example, Cairncross (1992) on interwar Glasgow and Cambridge; Lionel Robbins (1971, ch. IV) on the LSE in the early 1920s and Arthur Brown (1987) on Oxford in the mid-1930s, which gives an undergraduate's perspective on the publication of Keynes's *General theory*; see also Collard (1990) on Cambridge after Marshall; Young and Lee (1993) on Oxford and the establishment of the Philosophy, Politics and Economics (PPE) degree; and Robinson (1988) and Jones (1988) on the efforts to found a British equivalent of the Brookings Institute, this eventually taking shape in the National Institute of Economic and Social Research (NIESR), established in 1938; and Tribe's (1997) collection of interviews with leading British economists.

propensity to be a RES member, was thus widely diffused.

Secondly, even amongst the academic community, which continued to rank second to business as late as 1960 in terms of RES membership (Coats and Coats 1973, table IV), the educational qualifications necessary to practise as an economist were only a first degree and this not necessarily in economics. Thus, for example, Maynard Keynes's qualifications were principally in mathematics, with his initial training in economics at best described as an extended summer vacation's worth of directed reading (supervised by Marshall). Graduating in 1905, Keynes was none the less considered suitably qualified by 1908 to be appointed to a lectureship in economics in Cambridge and by 1911 to the editorship of the *EJ* (Skidelsky 1983, pp. 206–7). Of the next generation, and indeed Keynes's successor at the *EJ*, we might also mention Roy Harrod who after a first degree in Literae Humaniores and then modern history was, on his appointment as an Oxford fellow and lecturer, given two terms' leave to mug up on economics – which he did initially at Cambridge with Keynes – so that he could teach for the new PPE degree, which remains today the only means for an Oxford student to study economics at first degree level.[7]

Thirdly, just as the creation of a government department can be taken as institutionalising a commitment to state action in that policy area, the appointment of an official economic adviser constitutes recognition of knowledge that is specifically economic and of the state having need of such knowledge. In Britain, however, the appointment of government economic advisers was not synonymous with the penetration of British government by professional economists, although early appointments were not unpromising (Chester 1982, p. 132). Consider, for example, the post of Chief Economic Adviser to HMG. The first appointment was made in 1919, and the first incumbent, **Llewellyn Smith**, was by contemporary standards well-equipped to perform such a function, having a long history of involvement in progressive social issues, especially the labour problem, and a reputation for applied work in economics, beginning with his being awarded the Cobden prize for an essay on the economics of state socialism whilst he was reading for an Oxford mathematics degree (Davidson 1985, pp. 113–16). He was also an active RES member. However, his appointment owed as much to internal politics, being a sidewise move from the Board of Trade where he was permanent secretary, and the new post was designed to deal with

---

[7]   Phelps Brown (1980b, pp. 7–8). Seven years later, in 1930, Meade also spent time in Cambridge (with **Dennis Robertson**) between his first degree (PPE) and taking up his Oxford Fellowship so that he could learn his subject before being asked to teach it. From this followed Meade's membership of 'the Circus' of younger economists (principally **Richard Kahn**, **Sraffa**, the Robinsons, Tarshis, Plumptre and Gifford) which met to discuss Keynes's *Treatise on money* (1930a) and which was so influential in the transition to the *General theory* (Moggridge 1992, ch. 21).

external economic issues, principally multilateral economic negotiations. The second postholder (**Sydney Chapman**, in post 1927–32), a former professor of economics, was indeed an economist by any academic definition, whereas the third appointment (**Leith-Ross**, who served 1932–46), most decidedly was not, describing the title in his memoirs (1968, p. 145) as a misnomer, and with duties almost wholly concerned with external non-economic issues. Moreover, there have been a number of suggestions that his appointment owed more to internal Treasury politics than to any particular claims to expertise (for example, Clarke 1988, p. 30). We have also the case of Hawtrey, a self-taught economist who made original contributions to monetary theory and who, as Director of Financial Enquiries, was the nearest the Treasury actually came to an in-house economist between the wars. We consider his career and contribution in chapter 5, but here record that he played but only an intermittent part in the policy debates on domestic issues within the department, such that when Churchill was Chancellor (1924–9) he was prone, according to one of his Treasury colleagues, to 'demand ... from time to time that the learned man be released from the dungeon in which we were said to have immured him, have his chains struck off and the straw brushed from his hair and clothes and be admitted to the light and warmth of an argument in the Treasury board room' (Grigg 1948, p. 82).

Fourthly, in a study of the British profession there are problems associated with applying definitions which seek to identify economists on the basis of their publications. Thus, for example, in their biographical dictionary of major economists who lived between 1700 and 1981, Blaug and Sturges (1983, pp. vii–viii) define 'an economist as one who published more or less regularly in one of the hundreds of learned journals of economics' and with 'major' evaluated on the basis of citation counts which, for all of their well-known flaws, are taken as the best proxy for peer group recognition. Acknowledging that their criteria for who's who is 'unfair' in certain respects, to dedicated teachers who published little, to those in international agencies, much of whose published work necessarily remains anonymous, they add 'a sprinkling of other names whose works may be rarely cited but whose achievements in advice to policy-makers in business and government are generally recognised by their peers'. No indication is given of the number of economists who are so added, but one may infer that is small relative to the 1,071 economists enumerated.[8] With its emphasis thus upon academic economics, and with the 1,071 dominated by American

---

[8] Of which 674 were living, about 5 per cent of the world's total stock of living economists on the basis of their definition, thereby ensuring that 'the editors of this biographical dictionary . . . have made twenty times as many enemies as friends!' (p. ix). Indeed, so contentious was their criteria that in the second edition (1986) the 'sprinkling of other names' were removed.

born or American resident economists, we label this the American definition of economics. It is too restrictive for our purposes.

We are led inevitably, therefore, towards an evolving definition of an economist. For the postwar period we follow Coats's (1981c, p. 373) definition of 'a person with a recognised academic qualification in the subject and a job title which acknowledges the specialisation.' This translates into a combination of Tolles's categories B and C, which in numerical terms would give a broad definition. However, as Coats acknowledges, his definition is perhaps more appropriate from the standpoint of the professionalisation of economics than in terms of the potential supply of economic advice, especially in the British context where:

> for most of the post-war period the bulk of official economic work, from low-level routine functions to high-level economic decisionmaking, has been undertaken by non-economists . . . [with] the majority of key decisionmakers in post-war Britain, including ministers, Governors of the Bank of England, and heads of the nationalised industries, hav[ing] no formal training in economics.

Throughout the twentieth century there has been an anti-specialist ethos amongst the elite grade of the British civil service, the Administrative Class, part of a British political tradition which accords much greater weight to knowledge as accumulated experience than as academic study. Accordingly, even when entrants to this elite did start to possess economics degrees, something which became more common from the 1960s, they soon lost touch with their academic background, soon came to terms with an incentive structure which valued general problem-solving skills and on-the-job achievements rather than academic prowess (Hargrove 1972, pp. 57–61). In any case, as Coats (1981c, p. 373) reminds us, 'there is no conclusive evidence that trained economists necessarily make the best economic decision-makers!' We arrive, therefore, at a minimalist definition for the postwar period, one which also permits backward projection. Thus an economist is here defined as fulfilling a minimum of either:

- self-identification as an economist; and/or
- possession of expertise, whether validated within the peer group (academic qualification and/or publication) and/or revealed demand for their knowledge, which is recognised as both economic and expert.

The production of economists

Working from this definition we can now consider changes in the production of economists, beginning with the producer group itself: academic economists. Table 3.1 provides some very approximate estimates

Table 3.1 The supply of economists, selected years, 1891–1993

	(1)[a]	(2)[b]	
A. Academic posts			
1891	20		
1915	85		
1918/20	141		
1925	180		
1939	286		
1947	166		
1950	446		
1951	254		
1960	679	367	
1969	1,802	814	
1974	1,031		
1980/1	1,310		
1983/4	1,152		
1992/3	1,319		
	(1)[c]	(2)[d]	(3)[e]
B. Degrees awarded			
1928–9	164		
1938–9	309		
1949–50	894	529	
1959–60	1,120	999	
1969–70		1,420	426
1974/5		1,859	606
1980		2,117	631
1990		2,453	1,003
1993		2,565	1,415

Notes:

[a] Academic posts in economics and related subjects.

[b] University teaching posts in economics. The Booth-Coats dataset excludes polytechnic (now 1992 university) lecturers. The 1992/3 estimate assumes that economics staff constitute the same ratio of Administrative, Business and Social Studies as in 1983/4, the last year for which subject detail is available.

[c] First degrees awarded in economics and related subjects, including PPE.

[d] First degrees (single/joint honours) in economics, including PPE.

[e] Higher degrees in economics.

Sources: (1) Coats (1975, table I); (2–3) Booth and Coats (1978, tables 1, 4) supplemented by *Universities' Statistical Record* for later years.

of the number of university teaching staff in economics since the late nineteenth century and the annual output of first degrees in economics (or a closely related subject for the earlier part of the period). For both producers and product,[9] we should stress the poor quality of the data, its incompleteness and sensitivity to definitional changes.[10] Nonetheless, the broad trends are clear. Thus before the Second World War, although both producers and product were rising, there was a very high ratio of academic economists to the number of graduates produced. The longer-term statistical record thus confirms Kadish and Tribe's (1993b) hypothesis that economics as we now know it originated in a supply-side push, initially unmatched by demand. Booth and Coats (1978, p. 440) felt so uneasy about the available postwar data that they do not press the claim for any substantive expansion before the mid-1950s, with trend growth thereafter and, in particular, two spurts associated first with the Robbins report in the 1960s and then with the decision of the late 1980s to move towards a mass higher education system.

The initial high ratio of academics to undergraduate economists seems to have been typical of the developing British elite higher education system, one dominated by Oxbridge and with great emphasis placed on undergraduate teaching to the detriment, as Harry Johnson (1973a) highlighted for economics, of rigorous programmes of postgraduate study. Economics before the Second World War, and indeed for many years after in Oxbridge and elsewhere, was supremely a social activity, one dominated by interlocking networks. In such circumstances, in economics as in other disciplines, graduate work, when it did eventually develop, took the form of supervised study with a distinguished professor rather than registration for a full postgraduate programme of research training. Thus when Alec Cairncross (1992, p. 6) arrived in Cambridge in 1932, after completing a first degree in economics at Glasgow, there were no students registered for the Ph.D. degree, no staff in residence possessing a Ph.D. and when he was awarded his four years later it was only the third ever in the faculty. Nonetheless, as bountiful evidence on 1930s Cambridge attests, there was a vibrant group of postgraduates and young research staff in the faculty throughout the decade.[11]

---

[9]   The production function construct can be extended to the supply of economic knowledge. If this is measurable as a stock, variously defined as the cumulative stock of journal articles, AEA/RES members and Ph.D.s, analysis suggests exponential growth since the late nineteenth century with economics exhibiting similar characteristics to the sciences (Lovell 1973).

[10]   For example, working from broadly similar sources, Booth and Coats obtain significantly higher estimates than Sanderson (1972, p. 271) for the output of economics degrees between the wars. More generally, there are problems interpreting the economic content of the London B.Sc. (Econ.), the PPE degree and even the Cambridge economics tripos.

[11]   Cairncross (1981, p. 7) further recollects that on the eve of the First World War there was only one economist in Britain with a doctorate (**Arthur Bowley**), although it is probable that he would have self-identified more as a statistician. In fact, Cairncross has forgotten about one of

Postgraduate education in economics remains almost wholly a development since the Second World War, indeed since the 1960s in any systematic manner. Thus contemporary labour market definitions of an economist, such as that employed by Towse and Blaug, are not historically durable. As with the estimates reported in Table 3.1 for economists and first degrees awarded, the available data on higher degrees is of poor quality. Booth and Coats (1978, table 2) give estimates of 93 such degrees awarded in 1963/4 and 579 a decade later. Growth then slackened for the remainder of the 1970s, before resuming in the mid-1980s and then accelerating with the transition to a mass higher education system. In 1993 over 1,400 higher degrees in economics were awarded, broadly equivalent to the annual output of first degrees a quarter of a century earlier, with the balance between taught masters and Ph.D.s continuing to favour the former by a ratio of approximately seven to one. This was both a response to overall labour market trends and, in relation to academic career paths, recognition that by the late 1960s the pace of theoretical advance in economics was such that a first degree was no longer a sufficient foundation for university employment.

Economics is also taught in many lower-level educational institutions and as part of professional training for many commercial occupations. Indeed, that economics should be made intelligible to the intelligent layman was an integral part of Marshall's mission for the professionalisation of British economics: the 'cool heads but warm hearts' of his inaugural lecture (1885). Thus, before the First World War sub-degree economics teaching was the principal channel for promoting greater economic literacy, and whilst this influence has waned with the subsequent development of the universities it has been far from extinguished. Indeed, at the school level economics become a popular subject[12] and as a consequence the stock of human capital imbued with at least basic economic competency grows yearly.[13] In 1997 the number of candidates sitting GCSE and 'A' level examinations in economics were 9,600 and 20,873 respectively, as against 115,498 and 33,359 for business studies, increasingly its competitor at both school- and

Britain's most distinguished Marxist economists, Maurice Dobb, who was appointed to a university lectureship in economics in 1925 after receiving his doctorate from the LSE (see Dobb 1978, p. 117). On interwar Cambridge, see also Robinson's (1947, pp. 26–7) account of Keynes's Political Economy Club to which undergraduates and young researchers gave papers: 'in those days researchers in economics were few, their distinction from undergraduates unimportant, and the Ph.D. unknown.'

[12] A number of economists, however, consider the opportunity cost of studying economics in schools as a preparation for degree-level economics to be too high (Peacock 1989, p. 3), a view which is gaining ground as the technical (mathematical) barriers to entry rise.

[13] Currently, the principal organisation for sub-degree economics education is the Economics Association which publishes *Economics*; see also the *Economic Review*, a journal which caters for the beginning economics student, whether 'A' level or first-year university, and specifically targets contemporary economic problems in an accessible manner.

university-level, and 16,264 and 6,451 for the classics, the traditional elite subject.[14] The inclusion of classics in this listing might seem surprising, but for many of the RES's founders the hope was entertained that economics, by insisting upon the intellectual rigour and hard work that was the hallmark of a good classical education, could supplant the classics to become the preferred discipline of study for the educated and, above all, for the policy-making elite. What Marshall (1901) sought was an antidote to 'the narrowness of that dilettante education which looks only backwards, and does not prepare the mind for strong constructive work in its own age.'

The transmission of economic ideas

The financial press, other print and communications media and the market for popular economic works also deserve mention in terms of the prospects for fulfilment of Marshall's broader mission for a growing stock of human capital possessing basic economic competency. As yet there has been little systematic research into these areas, and it is to be hoped that our growing perception that the way in which economic events are reported in the media has an enormous impact on the public's understanding (or not!) of economics will eventually translate into an interest in the history of economic news and its popularisation.[15] One fruitful line of research concerns the use of language and metaphor in economics, with for example Emmison (1983), after a content analysis of newspapers and magazines (including *The Times* and the *Economist*), demonstrating that since the early nineteenth century the use of the word 'economy' has been quite transformed. Until the 1920s 'economy' was used in the formal sense of economising, but with the 1930s and the Second World War, the beginnings of explicit economic management, it acquires its modern meaning. However, initially its metaphorical use was passive – things were done to the economy – but this later developed into much more active metaphors and anthropomorphism (Lewis *et al.* 1995, p. 286). Thus, the process whereby economic knowledge is diffused to a broader audience is of importance, not least for politicians, who in responding to voter preferences must do so knowing that they are formed by the public's understanding of economic issues which may bear no relation to the realities of the situation.

In understanding the interaction of ideas and events at this level, and of the supply of economic advice more generally in terms of Peden's (1996) five forms of economic knowledge, we are fortunate in having a rich literature on the financial press. Foremost here is Parsons's (1989)

---

[14] *Guardian*, 14 August 1997, p. 9; 21 August 1997, p. 11.
[15] For example, Corner (1996); see also Henderson *et al.* (1993).

comparative study of the power of the financial press to influence economic opinion in Britain and America, although he has little to say on the years before the 1929 Wall Street crash. We have also useful histories of the *Financial Times* and the *Economist*, whilst the history of *The Times* project continues, with the most recent volume covering the Thompson years, the period in which Rees-Mogg as editor and **Peter Jay** as economics editor were influential in undermining the Keynesian hegemony.[16]

Unfortunately, no one has as yet made much use of the rich store of economists' and others' writings in the journals that, until the financial stringency of the 1980s, used to be published by the clearing banks and which were widely read by City opinion-formers.[17] These were a particularly useful avenue for academic economists to write on current policy issues and for the general reader to be made aware of economics at its best, in service of society. For example, in the 1970s the *Lloyds Bank Review* hosted some of the early snipings between Cambridge economists and Milton Friedman (Kaldor 1970a; b; Friedman 1970b), in the 1980s it provided space for debate over the existence of a Laffer curve and, over a long period, carried articles on Britain and European integration. The bank reviews even provided a forum for groups of economists to contribute to the policy debate, as for example in the CLARE group who were published in the *Midland Bank Review* between 1977 and the journal's demise.[18] The significance for policy-makers of such outlets for economists to write on current problems is attested by the frequency with which cuttings from the bank reviews, together with those from the *Financial Times*, *Economist* and *The Times*, are found in Treasury and other economic departments' files in the PRO.

Beyond 'informed opinion' there exists a much larger, more popular market for works which synthesise the writings of economists and apply them to greater or lesser effect to contemporary economic problems. Very recent examples of this genre include **Will Hutton's** *The state we're in* (1995) and Christopher Johnson's *In with the Euro* (1996), but there is a much longer and distinguished history here which has not been investigated. We know a little about the crankier ends of this market, especially monetary cranks and the underconsumptionists who continue to generate scholarly interest. But we know very little about the broad swath of writers and popularisers, mainly but not exclusively financial journalists, between

[16] Kynaston (1988), Edwards (1993) and Grigg (1993).
[17] Hutchison (1968) is a rare exception. Bank reviews were published by all of the major London/Scottish clearing banks under a number of titles as bank amalgamations took effect and with interruptions for wars, with Roberts (1995) providing an initial assessment of their significance, both contemporary and historical.
[18] In origin, a discussion group convened by Robin Matthews which evolved from the London and Cambridge Economic Service (LCES, discussed at p. 159). It now publishes less frequently in the *National Institute Economic Review* (*NIER*).

Bagehot's *Lombard Street* (1873) and say **Andrew Shonfield**, author of a number of widely read works on the postwar British economy (1958; 1965). This largely unexplored territory includes some very significant names. For example, before the First World War we would identify **F.W. Hirst** and **Hartley Withers**, successive editors at the *Economist*, 1907–21, and between the wars (and after), **Paul Einzig** and **Oscar Hobson** who in long and varied careers were attached *inter alia* to the *Financial News*, later amalgamated with the *Financial Times*. The predecessors of such distinguished postwar financial journalists as **Geoffrey Crowther** (another *Economist* editor), **Graham Hutton**, **Harold Wincott** and Samuel Brittan need to be reintegrated into our history if we are to fully understand the transmission of economic ideas and the ultimate role played by economists.[19]

The century or so from Hartley Withers (b. 1867) to Will Hutton (b. 1950) marks a transformation in financial and economic reporting, from the arid, technical and dull 'City notes' of the late nineteenth century through to modern financial journalism which, whilst now market-focused once more, makes clear the broader economic and political interconnections of financial activity. The careers of Crowther and Shonfield exemplify a – perhaps – particularly British process of acquiring influence and status in economic affairs on the basis of at most a first degree in economics (or no higher education at all in the case of Wincott). Thus there was much more to their careers, as with many of the others here discussed, than is indicated by the occupational label of financial journalist. While both wrote on economic subjects, of the two Shonfield was the more prolific and committed to academe such that he eventually left financial journalism, going first to the Royal Institute of International Affairs and then to the European University Institute. Crowther (1940) published a theoretical text on money which was quickly popular with students and the public, and was still in print twenty years later, but he is most remembered for his time at the *Economist*. Under his long editorship the magazine was transformed, its circulation rising from 10,000 to 55,000, making it one of the world's most influential economic publications, and there were important new departures such as the creation of the Economic Intelligence Unit which is now a major research and consultancy organisation.

---

[19] Of these key opinion formers, we have a series of broadly autobiographical essays from Hirst (1947) and a full autobiography from Einzig (1960), two very different characters. Of the two Hirst, author of ten books or more, including a biography of Gladstone and works on the economics of war and public finance, was much more of an establishment figure than Einzig, a Transylvanian refuge who wrote over 50 books on a wide range of domestic and international economic issues. Hobson also wrote a number of popular works, including one on the city (1938), as did Withers, whose works included *The meaning of money* (1909). Both Graham Hutton and Wincott were also involved in the early days of the IEA (Cockett 1994, pp. 119, 128, 132, 142–3, 169, 185).

Beyond these well-known financial journalists, whose jobs required to varying degrees that they maintain contacts with those leading academic economists who sought a public stage, there has long existed a much broader demand for, and supply of, popular economic works. The market for such literature has a long but largely unexplored history, but any full account of the transmission of economic ideas to the general public must include the products of the Home University Library, established in 1911 whose early authors included Hirst on the stock exchange, the Left Book Club between the wars and Allen Lane and Penguin Books since, the latter not least as the UK publisher of Galbraith's many works, probably the most widely read economist in the world today. Thus, and without exaggeration, this extends almost indefinitely the potential supply of economic advice, as Chancellors know full well from their mailbags in the run up to budget day as many DIYE-minded citizens peddle their favourite nostrum.

After his experiences in government service, as both insider (at the Department of Trade and Industry, DTI)[20] and outsider (a member of significant government committees), Alan Peacock (1991, p. 723) considered that 'the supply of economic advice is very inelastic with respect to money price and the position of the supply curve is such that a very large quantity of it will be supplied free.' Our historical survey confirms this. Whether, as Harry Johnson and many within the public choice tradition maintain, the lure of government service is potentially corrupting for economists, resulting in inefficiencies or even failure in the policy market, remains for us to examine. But first we look at the demand side, including the broader apparatus and infrastructure for economic policy advice.

3.3 THE DEMAND FOR ECONOMISTS AND THE FORMALISATION OF POLICY ADVICE

The demand for economists

With the exception of wartime the greatest demand for economists has been by universities, such that approximately three quarters of the current stock of

---

[20] Although Peacock was appointed by Howe, he also spent an interesting year during which Benn was Secretary of State for Industry (1974–5), the latter then being moved to Energy where there was less risk of him being able to implement socialist economic policies. Such a marriage of minister and adviser was not made in heaven, with Benn (1989, p. 152) recording in his diary that 'Professor Peacock is utterly wedded to laissez-faire, and it is extremely difficult to operate with that sort of advice coming to you. I just have to think of ways of out-flanking them' (see also p. 191). For Peacock's judgement upon Benn see his 'Giving advice in difficult times' (1977a); see also Peacock (1994) for some tantalising comments on the division of labour between himself and Francis Cripps, Benn's personal economic adviser.

professional economists – by the Towse-Blaug definition – are so employed in teaching and/or research. The demand for economists is, of course, derived and – as with supply – through time difficult to measure, especially for the early years. We complete this part of the discussion by considering the demand side of the market for economic advice, this necessarily leading us to encroach also upon the issue of economists' influence on policy.

Before the First World War there was little revealed commercial, financial or industrial demand and only a trickle of university posts while the needs of government for expert economic advice were intermittent, infrequent and informal. Sanderson (1972, p. 184), after studying the development of economics/commerce degrees at the three leading prewar universities producing such graduates (Birmingham, Cambridge and the LSE), concluded that the 'relevance of the output of students from such courses to industry was as yet only modest.' Thus it is estimated that between 1902–20 only 13 per cent of LSE B.Sc. (Econ.) graduates – that is all graduates, not just economists – went into business, with the great bulk obtaining employment as teachers, researchers and in government posts, although the real value of the LSE and many other higher education institutions for business continued to be in the sub-degrees courses offered, as for example in the 'vastly attended' Gilbart banking lectures at King's College, London (Sanderson 1972, p. 210). Kadish and Tribe's (1993b, p. 8) more recent and comprehensive work confirms this overall picture: 'Significant "demand" in Britain for graduates with a background in commerce and economics first developed in the context of teaching, public administration and business in the 1920s, and not before.' The British case illustrates that supply does not necessarily create its own demand.

What of the prewar demand from government for economic advice? Given the small size of the public sector and the limited ambitions of government in respect of economic policy before the First World War we would not expect any striking developments, although as we shall see the Liberal administration elected in 1906 lay the foundations for modern big government. The core of the central government in Britain, the higher civil service, amounted to only 200 or so by the eve of the war, with the Treasury having no more than 33 administrative grade officials.[21] Looking back at the market for economists as it had existed in 1911, Cairncross (1981, pp. 7, 8) described the situation thus: 'no government or government department had ever knowingly hired a professional economist', while 'in general the few economists who took an interest in policy had to content themselves with a letter to *The Times* if they wanted to bring their views to the public.' Less visible, although probably more important, was the expert testimony of

---

[21] Burk (1982b, p. 85) and Peden (1999, ch. 2).

economists before royal commissions and government enquiries, a professional activity which absorbed much of Marshall's time and energies. Yet less visible, but commensurably significant, economists occasionally provided confidential advice to the Chancellor, as for example in 1903 when Marshall's view were solicited on the tariff question, which had erupted into the leading issue of the time.

Coats (1975, pp. 282–3) has described the next part of the story, from the early 1900s to the Second World War, as 'significant, but unspectacular', with the demand for economists by commerce, industry and government rising but slowly in comparison with developments in the US.[22] For Coats, as for many others at that time, there could be no significant change in the demand schedule until there occurred striking proof of economists' utility, this being provided by the publication of Keynes's *General theory* which 'demonstrated the relevance of academic economics to public policy-making, and laid the foundations for the wartime and postwar employment of economists in government.' Access to much more of the official record concerning the so-called Keynesian revolution than was the case in the 1970s, together with greater historical perspective on the fate of Keynesianism, leads us to argue that Coats greatly understates the significance of this period by being overly preoccupied with Keynes's *General theory*. We now know how slowly Keynes's ideas were diffused in the context of postwar economic management; that the *General theory* was far less a landmark in terms of policy than of theory; and that there were forces making for an increased public sector, and a greater economic role for the state, which were quite independent of the contemporaneous debates which reached eventual fruition in the Keynesian revolution, if indeed that term can still be applied to Britain after the doubts raised by recent work.

It is arguable also that Coats, by focusing on the professionalisation of economics, misses much of the story of economists influencing policy (and hence our minimalist definition of p. 70 which seeks to capture important activities before the Second World War). Further, those who emphasise Keynes typically understate the significance of the First World War, both in terms of the demand for economic expertise it generated during the conflict and thereafter, especially in respect of external economic problems concerning reparations, war debts, tariffs and currency/exchange rate stabilisation. Finally, the First World War had an important displacement effect on the public sector. With an expenditure ratio of 25 per cent of GDP, and a greatly enlarged national debt, government now had a macroeconomic impact whether it desired it or not. Budgetary and monetary policy would thus never be the same again, while there had occurred a profound shift in

---

[22] See Norton (1969) and, for other OECD states, the contributions to Coats (1981a).

the balance between government and market (Middleton 1996, pp. 89, 110, 310). An increase in the demand for economic advice was a natural concomitant, with the important question for this period being from where such advice would be solicited and from where provided – whether the new professionals or the traditional City-dominated networks?

At this juncture the demand for economic advice has to be placed within the broader setting of the growth of government and of its requirement for expertise in all fields. Historians no longer label the nineteenth century as laissez-faire and instead talk in terms of a steady accretion of responsibilities in economic and social affairs since at least mid-century, of individualism and collectivism clashing as rival ideologies but also advancing in tandem as the changing needs of the market required collectivist responses, particularly in social affairs when the market destroyed the stable communities and intermediate agencies upon which individualism had depended (Harris 1990a, p. 113). One manifestation of this process of government growth was the increasing use of experts who acquired authority by virtue of the presumption of their possessing rational knowledge, and with a *modus vivendi* which privileged policy results over the policy process. Such developments were greatly accelerated by the First World War, such that by the early 1920s 'Specialists, no longer glamorous, had become a governing assumption, taken for granted, [but] mistrusted by public, politicians and scholars alike' (MacLeod 1988b, pp. 1–2). Thus dependency upon the expert did not, has never, translated into a liking for the technocrat or a permanent acceptance of expert authority; rather, the expert in Britain has always had to tread a very fine line between the traditional antipathy towards the highly educated and the growing intolerance of risk and uncertainty which generates the demand for expertise (Reddy 1996).

The minimalist British state of the nineteenth century had always lacked the means to enforce such limited policies as it had attempted, and had thereby relied on interest groups (professional and trade organisations, trade unions, friendly societies) to increase its capacity. In this sense economics conformed with the general pattern, with such demand as there was for economic expertise met by outside suppliers, more particularly Bank of England-City networks (Green 1992). However, during the interwar period, such was the volume, complexity, frequency and day-to-day nature of the economic problems confronting government that the old *ad hoc*, customary systems and networks were no longer sufficient. For example, in 1918 and 1919 alone there were government enquiries into the machinery of government, commercial and industrial policy, income tax, land values, currency and foreign exchanges, financial facilities, agricultural policy, anti-dumping, trusts, transport, industrial unrest, and much else. Economists sat on a number of these, including **Stamp** and **Pigou** on the royal commission on the income tax; Pigou (again) and Cassel on the Cunliffe committee on currency and foreign exchanges, which was instrumental in the eventual return to the gold standard in 1925, and gave evidence to many more.

There were some like Haldane, a senior Liberal politician, who appreciated the need for a much more technocratic civil service capable of managing the intellectual problems caused by rapid change (Turner 1988, p. 204), but the First World War did not bring forth such reforms. Instead, public administration between the wars remained the epitome of muddling through. None the less, the interwar period does see the beginnings of systematic full-time employment of professional economists in the civil service, save that their expertise was not in the economics of unemployment but of farms. That the professionalisation of economic advice began with the agricultural economists, with the Ministry of Agriculture's appointment of an 'economic student and investigator' in 1924 (retitled Economic Investigator by 1929, and having three assistants by 1933), well-illustrates our argument about the particular nature of the demand for economists and the competing sources of supply. The process 'occurred first in agriculture because the government adopted a more active and detailed interventionist policy in that sector than elsewhere' (Coats 1976, p. 384; 1981c, pp. 367–8). Quite simply, the market for agricultural economics expertise was less contestable than that for economics proper, and more particularly in the fields of public finance, money and banking, the central preoccupations of the Treasury where there were established Bank-City networks supplying advice. Moreover, in terms of the leverage exercised by interest groups, neither industry nor the unemployed ever came close to the financial and regulatory benefits captured by the agricultural lobby between the wars (Middleton 1996, pp. 365, 392).

The preoccupation with Keynes and macroeconomic issues has long obscured important developments in government's economic role and public sector growth between the wars, and whilst it is undoubtedly the case that there was no operational acceptance of the Keynesian solution for unemployment before 1939, there was none the less a significant shift in the government demand schedule for economists and advice some years before the outbreak of war. In part this was a process associated with the activities of the Economic Advisory Council (EAC), of which Keynes was a leading member, and of its effective successor sub-committee, the Committee on Economic Information (CEI). However, so far as the influence of economists were concerned, this was a doubled-edged instrument. As Leith-Ross (1968, p. 147), the Treasury representative on the CEI, put it:

> The discussions at the meetings were lively and often controversial, but I do not
> think that any of the reports produced gave a clear and unqualified guidance to
> Ministers in regard to economic policy. The secretary . . . worked like a slave to

secure agreement between the irreconcilable views of the members on the recommendations to be made.

Howson and Winch (1977, pp. 156–64) dispute this verdict as at variance with the textual record of the meetings where – with one glaring exception, in which it was Treasury officials not the economists, who clashed – it was the convergence of views which predominated, while in any case the record 'shows that disagreements among economists did not prevent them from making definite policy recommendations.' Moreover, they suggest that 'The airing of differences of viewpoint in front of the Treasury members may even have been beneficial in changing the theoretical basis of the Treasury's views'. Thus proximity to debate created the possibility of social learning for civil servants as they became 'more aware of the issues at stake'. It also resulted, Howson and Winch contend, in Dennis Robertson becoming a more influential adviser than Hubert Henderson, his old Cambridge teacher, because the former was able and willing to engage with Keynes at a theoretical level whereas the latter, after his brief period in Whitehall, had grown increasingly disillusioned by the potential of economic theory to guide policy and practice. Indeed, the case of Henderson illustrates how an essentially radical and optimistic spirit can be broken by experience of government service, though within the Treasury he later provided sterling war service as the 'eternal critic, with a duty to ensure that no one should ever overlook any possible difficulties of any proposed source of action' (Robinson 1987, p. 639).

It should be evident that Howson and Winch were working with an (implicit) model of the role of economic theory in policy, one which led them to conclude firmly on the side of Keynes's influence on interwar policy-makers. Whilst their boldest claims for Keynes's influence have not survived critical scrutiny, the general point is accepted that Treasury officials such as **Hopkins** and **Phillips**, the latter a CEI member, were an important conduit for the diffusion of new ideas, and that they were much more receptive to economists and theoretical developments than the previous generation of Treasury mandarins, such as **Niemeyer**. However, Treasury officials remained implacably opposed to a shift in the existing balance between civil service and professional economic advice in the formulation of policy. This was not just self-interest, but, as Hopkins explained:

> it seems useless to endeavour to follow professional economic teaching, for there is no criterion for determining the proper economists to follow, and whoever one chooses, one is apt to find oneself led into actions which are either repugnant to commonsense or incapable of practical achievement.
>
> It is for reasons such as these that the layman is entitled to have his say.
>
> (PRO 1932, p. 2)

The demand for expert economic advice

The history of the EAC and CEI suggests the need to distinguish between: first, the actions of soliciting advice from economists and others claiming economic expertise; secondly, the bureaucratic incorporation of economists into the policy process, either externally in separate agencies such as the EAC/CEI or internally at the heart of departments; and, thirdly, the extent to which the policy recommendations of economists actually prove decisive. What Howson and Winch demonstrated, as did a host of other studies of the time, was a growing demand under the first head, some institutional innovation under the second, although principally externally positioned, and very little of the latter. Moreover, the demand for economic advice can be either positive, in the sense of motivated by social learning, or negative, borne of political defensiveness about existing policies and/or bureaucratic self-preservation. Interwar developments accorded more closely to the latter, with an eventual weakening of Treasury opposition to professional economists within Whitehall lest ministers look for advice outside of the civil service (for example, the Bank appointed its first professional economist as adviser to the governor in 1927). Thus we can observe politicians and Treasury officials being forced to react to policy failures such as the restored gold standard, which did much to discredit the Bank and the traditional policy networks whose advice had been accepted in 1924–5; the debacle of the original official specification of the 'Treasury view' on deficit-finance in 1929; Keynes's mauling of Montagu Norman before the Macmillan committee in 1930; newspaper campaigns, such as that launched by *The Times* in 1934 on the depressed areas which led to the beginnings of modern regional policy; and above all the pretty constant flak generated by Keynes and other academic economists through *Times* letters, syndicated newspapers articles, pamphlets and radio broadcasts.

What the Treasury ultimately came to see in economists was a means of sharing or diluting responsibility for economic management, in a world now stripped of Victorian certainties, but without endangering its intellectual authority and bureaucratic pre-eminence. Changes in the economy's behaviour compounded upon shifts in voter preferences and the transformation of political competition would no doubt have brought such a result in any case, but in Britain Keynes's voice was decisive. Here at last was a figure who was both of the establishment and a relentless critic of the establishment. Here also was a self-publicist, possessing all of Marshall's analytical powers, but none of his reticence. As successive interwar government battled with the aftermath of one war, prepared for the next and tried to manoeuvre in the limited policy space remaining the important question became less whether professional economists would be more fully

involved in policy than how they would be so used. The Second World War
was to be decisive in settling this, but before turning to that we complete our
account of interwar developments by considering the private sector's
demand for economists.

Between the wars a few private sector companies recruited economists
and, as we saw in Table 3.1, the number of academic posts did increase,
perhaps doubling. We can infer from the published company histories of the
clearing banks and other financial institutions that a few economists were
now being employed within the City,[23] a process which began before 1914.
However, they very rarely if at all exercised what we would see as their
modern advisory function and instead were part of the broader
administrative and executive organisation. So far as industry is concerned,
Hannah (1983, p. 89), with due acknowledgement to Burke, has observed
that by the 1930s 'sophisters, economists and calculators were coming into
the large decentralized corporations to supplement and partially to succeed
the more inchoate signals and discipline of the market.' But, as is well-
known, the 'visible hand' was slow to develop in British businesses, and it
was not until 1953 that a Society of Business Economists (SBE) was
established in recognition of there being a demand for such expertise outside
of government or the universities (Alexander *et al.* 1967). If a senior Bank
of England official in the 1930s could sustain the opinion, 'I am inclined to
expect people to be spoilt for our purposes by three or four years at the
University' (cited in Anon 1976, p. 442), we should not expect much of a
demand for economists elsewhere. Such opinions may just represent the
sorts of prejudice against graduates beloved by advocates of the British
disease, but it might also suggest that there was a problem with the
attributes of graduates. Thus while more universities launched commerce/
economics degrees between the wars, including Oxford with the PPE,
employers remained wary of their products. Even in Cambridge survey
evidence indicated that while firms were actually more prepared to employ
those with arts than those with science/technology degrees 'they did not
want such arts men trained in commerce or even in the Cambridge
Economics Tripos which they regarded as too theoretical' (Sanderson 1972,
pp. 270, 272). Back at the LSE, where 13 per cent of the B.Sc. (Econ.) had
gone into business between 1902–20, the figure rose slightly to 16.4 per cent
between 1920–32, with a number of 'keen and repeated employers',
including the Bank of England, the London clearing banks but also the
GWR, ICI and Lever Brothers, and with statistical functions the most
frequently cited for those for whom first employment destinations are

---

[23]   The growth of economic expertise within the financial sector remains quite unexplored, but it is
known that when Barclays announced the formation of an economic intelligence department in
1918 such departments were becoming commonplace (Roberts 1995, p. 47).

known. Elsewhere, the evidence suggests that the majority of those graduating with economics degrees took employment as schoolteachers. Sanderson (1972, p. 273) concludes:

> the early claims of economists such as Ashley and Marshall that economics was going to prove especially suitable as a university training for industry proved . . . to be largely unfounded. The large numbers still going into teaching suggest that it had not proved itself as distinctively different from any other non-vocational arts subject as its pioneers would have wished.

The Second World War

We observe, therefore, that by 1939 Marshall's mission for economics had yet to achieve a critical mass so far as demand from commerce, finance and industry were concerned. The turning-point for all categories of demand came with the Second World War, and within government with the Stamp Survey, appointed in June 1939 to 'undertake a review of the plans and proposals prepared by the various Departments for the purpose of keeping the country going during the war' which, once war was declared, concentrated increasingly on the formulation and coordination of economic policy to avoid major dislocations in the transition stage (Howson and Winch 1977, p. 151). Stamp, expert in public finance, pioneer national income statistician, businessman and now civil servant, a 'kind of economic Pooh-Bah, sought after by ... [and] acceptable to all', promptly recruited two professional economists, Henderson and **Henry Clay**, and whilst he and his survey had little staff, 'no executive authority, and no integral connection with any powerful administrative department' he 'enjoyed access to confidential data and departmental experience, ... and ... free[dom] to take a central and comprehensive view of the proposals it considered, undeterred by the administrative or political difficulties they might present' (Cairncross and Watts 1989, pp. 13–14).

From these perhaps unpromising, but very British, beginnings emerged two new major bodies: the Central Statistical Office (CSO) and the Economic Section of the War Cabinet (ES, transferred to the Treasury in 1953), the latter comprising the first group of professional economists to operate at the centre of government in Britain. The journey from the Stamp Survey, via the interim Central Economic Information Service (CEIS), from which the CSO and ES were formed in January 1941, makes fascinating reading but is beyond our remit. What is important, however, is that it quickly became apparent that professional economists had something distinct to offer the war effort. Thus, in late 1939-early 1940, Stamp's original team were augmented by the arrival of **John Jewkes**, later the first Director of ES, Austin Robinson and **Harry Campion**, another Manchester economist and later the first Director of the CSO. With the ending of the phoney war and the formation of Churchill's new Cabinet the recruitment of economists from the universities then began in earnest. Accordingly, within a year the CEIS/ES acquired amongst others: Lionel Robbins, Norman Chester, Stanley Dennison, **Ely Devons**, **Evan Durbin**, Alec Cairncross, Harold Wilson, Richard Stone and James Meade, the latter two future Nobel prize winners and Meade, the architect of much of the 1944 employment policy white paper (HMSO 1944), only obtained after some drama involving a desperate journey across Europe (from his post with the League of Nations in Geneva) with his young family in flight from the advancing Nazi armies. Cairncross (1994, p. 20) estimates that over the course of the Second World War some fifty officials served in Whitehall who had at one time or another been academic economists, whereas in the First World War there had only been Keynes and three others (Henry Clay, Hubert Henderson and **Walter Layton**) together with a handful of others such as **Beveridge** who were self-taught economists but fit our definition in terms of supplying economic advice.

Meanwhile, Churchill had set up his own Prime Minister's Statistical Branch which was headed by Lindemann his scientific adviser (the 'Prof'), and this recruited Harrod, MacDougall, Bryan Hopkin and Bensusan-Butt amongst others.[24] Existing and new wartime departments were also active in recruitment, with – amongst many others – Kahn, Reddaway and Tout going to the Board of Trade; **Gaitskell** and the economic historians Eileen Power and her husband, Michael Postan to the Ministry of Economic Warfare; Robert Hall and **Douglas Jay** to the Ministry of Supply; and **Frank Paish**, David Champernowne and Brian Tew to the Ministry of Aircraft Production (now led by Jewkes and accompanied by Devons and Cairncross who had all transferred from the ES and CSO).[25] To this influx of new blood were added a few of those, possessing economic expertise if not all the label 'economist', who had entered Whitehall temporarily during the First World War. Here we would include the 'Old Dogs' (Lydia Keynes's delightful label for): Layton (formerly Ministry of Munitions), **Arthur Salter** (Allied Maritime Transport Council) and Beveridge (Munitions and Food), the last of whom was desperate to acquire a wartime niche which, after some delay, he achieved by taking charge of a manpower survey which he then used as a springboard for the more famous Beveridge report on social insurance.[26]

---

[24] On the ES, see the insider history by Cairncross and Watts (1989); on Lindemann and the Statistical Branch, the insider accounts by MacDougall (1951) and Wilson (1995); on economists and the war, Booth (1985; 1986; 1989); and Booth and Coats (1980).

[25] The history of this ministry is related in Cairncross (1991b), but see also the various essays in Chester (1951a) and Devons (1970), the latter of which includes much additional material on economic planning, policy and the role of advisers.

[26] See Harris (1977, ch. 15) and Moggridge (1992, p. 628).

We have also, of course, Keynes who, although now recovered from his first heart attack, initially had no desire to return to public service. Yet, his November 1939 *Times* articles on *How to pay for the war*, rewritten as a pamphlet (1940a), once more propelled him on to the stage. The proposal for forced saving eventually obtained the support of both the political left and right, even ending the long estrangement with Norman at the Bank. But above all, *How to pay for the war* came as close as one might expect in British public policy to a blueprint for the financial conduct of the war. Indeed, incorporated as it was to be in Kingsley Wood's path-breaking 1941 budget, which for the first time used national income statistics (compiled by Stone and Meade in the new CSO) to calculate excess demand *ex ante* and *ex post*, the Keynesian approach to budgetary policy was to influence not just the war but to provide clear pointers for the possibility of peacetime demand management. Indeed, for many this was the first ever Keynesian budget, while the white paper containing the estimates of national income and expenditure that accompanied it is an important historical document in its own right.[27] Serving first on the Chancellor's Consultative Council, announced on 1 July 1940, Keynes acquired a room in the Treasury by 12 August and thereafter was quickly back in harness, having a roving commission, membership of various key committees and day-to-day access to both papers and officials (Moggridge 1992, pp. 633, 636–8).

Subsequently, Keynes devoted the greater part of his energies to problems of external economic policy, most famously of course the Bretton Woods agreement of 1944 and the dollar loan of 1945–6. Whilst maintaining some involvement in the discussions surrounding the 1944 employment policy white paper, so often taken as the 'formal recognition of the Keynesian revolution in Britain' (Winch 1969, p. 269), it is arguable that the real test of the economists' mettle was at a much lower level, with the routine administration of the war economy. Thus whilst a few economists 'advised', the greater number managed, compiled and analysed statistics, employing at most their first year economic theory (opportunity cost, demand theory)[28] to guide the deployment of scarce resources between competing users, both

---

[27] Sayers (1956, pp. 23, 33, 58–9); on national income accounting, see Hancock and Gowing (1949, p. 222), Stone (1951), Cairncross (1988) and Ward and Doggett (1991, chs III–IV).

[28] See Alexander and Kemp (1967, table 36) for the results of a survey of business economists in 1965 in which they reported on the usefulness of economic concepts in their working lives. The five most cited as having frequent practical application were opportunity cost, price and income elasticity of demand, value added and marginal revenue product; the least cited, liquidity preference, trade creation/diversion, the speculative motive, multiplier and production function. See also Allen (1977, p. 50) who, on the basis of interviews with leading postwar American economists, stressed that government economists on the whole worked with basic economic concepts, having little time for technical refinements, being 'quick-draw specialists, shooting from the hip: gathering a few data and prepare a memo by tomorrow morning – if not by this afternoon.' This impression is confirmed by Nelson (1987) and many other studies.

civilian and military. Economic theory and economists gave clarity to priorities, the establishment of which was the central political and military challenge. Such a comment is not intended to belittle the economists' contribution, far from it. Rather, we have to explain how by 'the end of the war, academic economists were in demand and their stock (though not their pay) was high. What they had to say commanded attention and respect' (Cairncross 1989b, p. 43).

A useful starting point is with Keynes's (1924b, pp. 173–4) conception of the necessary intellectual equipment of a good economist:

> The study of economics does not seem to require any specialised gifts of an unusually high order. Is it not, intellectually regarded, a very easy subject compared with the higher branches of philosophy and pure science? Yet good, or even competent, economists are the rarest of birds. An easy subject, at which few excel! The paradox finds its explanation, perhaps, in that the master-economist must possess a rare *combination* of gifts. He must reach a high standard in several different directions and must combine talents not often found together. He must be a mathematician, historian, statesman, philosopher – in some degree. He must understand symbols and speak in words. He must contemplate the particular in terms of the general, and touch abstract and concrete in the same flight of thought. He must study the present in the light of the past for the purposes of the future. No part of man's nature or his institutions must lie entirely outside his regard. He must be purposeful and disinterested in a simultaneous mood; as aloof and incorruptible as an artist, yet sometimes as near the earth as a politician.

A reading of the various contemporary accounts and later memoirs of the economists, a listing of which is equivalent to who's who of the British economics profession,[29] provides a very clear sense of how the 'irregulars', a term not then current but invented later by Brittan to describe these most temporary of civil servants, had to adapt to Whitehall if they were to be of service to the war effort and to have a longer-term impact on governmental perceptions of the worth of academic economists as insiders. As Robbins (1971, pp. 183–4) recorded in his memoirs, while 'Few episodes in my career have given me more satisfaction than our success ... in this introduction of professional economic advice into the centre of the administrative system', it must be emphasised 'that any success that we had was due partly to our willingness to become part of the machine and accept its logic rather than pretend to some special status, partly to the willingness with which the best elements among the permanent civil servants were prepared to co-operate.'

This stance was continued by Meade when he succeeded Robbins as director of the ES, and indeed by the next incumbent, Robert Hall who, if

---

[29] Cairncross and Watts (1989, app.) list 33 staff who served in the ES between 1939–45.

anything, underplayed the case for professional economists, as against economically informed advice, within Whitehall (Coats 1981c, p. 382). Viewing the demand for economic advice from a slightly different angle, we should observe that the circumstances of war in many ways simplified the task confronting the economists. Churchill had decreed that this was a war to be won whatever the cost, from which followed clarity in the ultimate economic purpose. For Robinson (1951, p. 34) 'The economic direction of a nation at war must be judged by one relatively simple criterion – the concentration of the nation's maximum effort against the enemy, so as to bring the fullest possible force to bear upon him at the appropriate moments within the period of hostilities.' The economic problem of war might also be described as entailing flexibility in resource allocation, to match changing strategic priorities; the satisfaction of minimum civilian consumption needs, not least for purposes of morale (upon which the maximisation of production partially depends); and some attention to the minimisation of future difficulties, particularly in respect of the level of debt finance and the maintenance of peacetime export markets; and perhaps some eye to the future (minimisation of borrowing, some safeguarding of export markets).

With the construction of the war economy government eventually came to control some two-thirds of GDP and, in effect, the whole of the working population. With the market system thereby suspended, resource allocation decisions became largely 'choices by the Government of the way that resources can best be used by itself to achieve its own objectives' (Robinson 1951, p. 35). Following Sayers's (1956, p. 21) well-known conclusion that, 'In the sense that financial obstacles were never allowed to obstruct the war effort, British policy in the Second World War was undoubtedly successful', we can identify the economists' chief influence as on the real economy, and with the greater part of their activities concerning microeconomic issues. Cairncross and Watts (1989, pp. 56–7) characterised those within the ES as 'brokers in ideas and information: assembling and clarifying them and then making them circulate where they were in demand,' with their advantages as economists twofold:

> the perspective which a training in economics gave to our ideas and the superior information, especially statistical information, which we assembled. Our training gave us a bird's-eye view of the economy, with all the actions and reactions between its component parts. We were, in a sense, at home in a war economy while others were not, and we could judge where it was most essential to engage in a concentrated effort of planning and co-ordination.

Underlying these central activities was a bi-directional exchange of staff and ideas within and between the departments, one fuelled by the creation and dissemination of statistical information. Indeed, in the official history of the war economy much is made of the creation of the CSO and of its first fruits, two series of statistical digests (A and B, the latter the precursor of the *Monthly Digest of Statistics* which continues to be published) which 'for the first time assembled the main heads of information necessary for keeping under continuous review the economic problems of the war'.[30] As MacDougall (1987, pp. 23–4) was to find in the PM's Statistical Branch, where Churchill was something of a connoisseur of numbers if displayed in a visually appealing manner, there were considerable benefits to be reaped in terms of decision-making from the investment in collecting and disseminating data of all sorts.

To this perhaps rather mundane facet of the war we should add other factors which gave the economists a unique influence. First and foremost, *pace* the problem that economic policy is by definition a fusion of economics and politics, in wartime the more partisan aspects of politics are in abeyance for the duration, with economists and other advisers one of the main beneficiaries. Secondly, the war years demonstrate how much can be achieved by bureaucrats, whether irregulars or established civil servants, who enjoy the backing of a strong minister of unquestioned authority, a condition satisfied after January 1941 when John Anderson, recently appointed as Lord President, took charge of the ES. Thirdly, the position of economists within Whitehall is in inverse relation to the standing of the Treasury. For most of the war the Chancellor was not a member of the War Cabinet and financial issues were largely subordinated to management of the real economy. The waning of ES influence between 1945–7, as the Treasury reasserted its authority as the central economic department, bears out such a conclusion.[31] The period of **Dalton's** Chancellorship also suggests that having a former academic economist in this post would be to the detriment of the ES, or indeed economists generally. Thus Meade experienced a rather unhappy and frustrating year and a half as Director of the ES,[32] during which time the separation of financial and economic functions handicapped the coordination of economic policies and, in so far as Dalton sought advice, he looked elsewhere in the civil service (**Bridges**, Hopkins, Eady) or to bankers, especially Catto and Cobbold at the Bank (Pimlott 1985, pp. 469–72). As his former pupil (Robbins 1971, p. 211) later put it, Dalton's 'infatuation with politics had by then long outlasted any great interest in, or perception of, the problems of economic policy.' This leads to the fourth consideration, that of personalities, which are so-important in Whitehall. It

---

[30] Hancock and Gowing (1949, p. 221); see also Ward and Doggett (1991, pp. 34, 56).

[31] See Meade's diary entry for 5 November 1944 (Howson and Moggridge 1990b, pp. 1–2).

[32] Formally, his appointment began on 1 January 1946 but, with Robbins absent in Washington, he was in effective charge from autumn 1945 through to his resignation on grounds of ill-health in April 1947.

was quite critical for the ES's wartime operations and later role that Robbins had got on so well with Anderson, enjoying his complete trust, and had generally excellent relations with the Treasury (Cairncross and Watts 1989, p. 54). As has been found in other countries and in other periods (Nelson 1987) the most successful economists in government service are often those with the most developed interpersonal skills, a persuasiveness born of character and willingness to compromise as well as technical prowess.

Before leaving the war years, this most exciting of periods for professional economists, we need briefly to return to Keynes and to the influence of economic theory on policy. Our starting point is Chester's (1951b, p. 15) observation, from his own experience in the ES, 'that Ministers and the administrative class gained immeasurably by having in Whitehall a number of "temporaries" whose approach to the process of policy formation was wider, less orthodox and less concerned with the practical difficulties involved.' Social learning for the irregulars and the established civil servants was a two-way street, though not all encounters were as high-brow as is suggested in the following report by one of Keynes's wartime Treasury colleagues:

> Conferences in Keynes' room at the Treasury were seminar classes in adult education and his new, but middle-aged, pupils at the Treasury experienced something of the same sense of excitement as the younger men who had worked with Keynes when he was a teacher at Cambridge.(cited in Robinson 1947, p. 53)

That Keynes raised the intellectual tone in the Treasury is well-attested. **Otto Clarke**, for example, on hearing of Keynes's death, wrote in his diary: 'it will be interesting to see whether the Treasury [now] lapses into habitual slovenliness and complacency or whether some new man is found for providing stimulus' (cited in Hubback 1988, p. 19). We know that many senior Treasury officials became greatly influenced by Keynes, even those who had staunchly opposed him between the wars. Thus Hopkins, who had defended the 'Treasury view' in face of challenging questions from Keynes in 1930, read the *General theory* twice during the war, even using quotations from it in writing the report which laid the foundations for postwar monetary policy (Howson and Winch 1977, p. 152). Keynes also, of course, acquired an establishment respectability (a peerage, even election to the court of the Bank), from which emanated a greatly enhanced reputation for economics which many economists were to enjoy in the years to come.

However, as we now turn to postwar developments we need to ask to what extent the irregulars had by their war service a permanent impact on the Treasury. The following entry from Meade's diary should limit our expectations:

Had a long conversation with Keynes . . . [who was] inveighing against the Treasury officials who (with the exception of Hoppy [Sir Richard Hopkins]) he said were utterly incapable and incompetent to deal with technical economic matters. How have they the face to write long documents on economic matters! He (Keynes) would not take it upon himself to write a treatise on electricity. Economics was not yet taken as a serious subject. Hoppy, who understood the issues, was now too old and tired to do more than give his love and good wishes. All this was *à propos* of the report of the official committee on the future of the public utilities and of the electricity industry, in which – he said – they did not even show themselves aware of the economic problems of pricing which Marcus Fleming and I discussed in our symposium in the current *EJ*. He said that he had just written such a stinker on this subject that Sir Alan Barlow had spent the whole morning trying to get hold of a copy of the *Economic Journal*.[33]

Economists and the prospect of normal politics

On the face of it at the end of the war the economists' standing in Whitehall gave grounds for optimism about their future role. In particular, the 1944 employment policy white paper (HMSO 1944, pp. 1, 26), which opened with the famous pledge 'The Government accept as one of their primary aims and responsibilities the maintenance of a high and stable level of employment after the war', signalled the establishment 'on a permanent basis [of] a small central staff qualified to measure and analyse economic trends and submit appreciations of them to the Ministers concerned.' It was also quite explicit that 'the Government recognise that they are entering a field where theory can be applied to practical issues with confidence and certainty only as experience accumulates and experiment extends over untried ground.'

Historians now take a much less elevated view of this white paper, viewing it much more as a compromise between conflicting views of the administrative, economic and political constraints that would face postwar governments than evidence of an official conversion to Keynesian theory (Tomlinson 1987, ch. 3). In fact, the white paper contained no sanction for Keynesian deficit-financing were a postwar slump to materialise, as was widely feared and as had happened in 1920–21. Thus 'None of the main proposals contained in this Paper involve deliberately planning for a deficit in the National Budget in years of sub-normal trade activity', and instead there was to be reliance on the counter-cyclical use of public investment and, 'when settled conditions return', variations in national insurance contributions, a form of automatic stabilisation (HMSO 1944, pp. 21–4). The proposal for an element of automatic stabilisation, which derived from Meade's prior work in this area, and especially his proto-Keynesian textbook

[33] Meade diary, 7 January 1945 (Howson and Moggridge 1990b, p. 26). The symposium on 'Price and output policy of state enterprises' was in the December 1944 issue (pp. 321–39). J.M. Fleming was in the ES, 1943–5 while Barlow was Joint Second Secretary, Treasury, 1938–48.

(1936), was never to be implemented. Moreover, on the basis of the official records now available in the PRO, we now know that fiscal policy as an instrument of demand management came to be implemented after 1947 to control inflation and excess demand and that at no point before at least 1954 was a budget deficit on stabilisation grounds countenanced within the Treasury. Indeed, the first explicit use of the budget in a Keynesian manner to stimulate employment was as late as 1959 (Middleton 1996, pp. 540–43) and there are strong grounds for arguing that even during the period of Keynesian hegemony maintenance of full employment was always subordinate to balance of payments and other considerations.

These are important revisions to our understanding of postwar British economic history which for too long took an overly optimistic (and simplistic) view of the diffusion of Keynesian ideas into the Treasury and of their translation into macroeconomic policy. We are not here denying that Keynes and the Keynesians like Meade had influence; that there were concrete and lasting achievements from the war years. The incorporation of the Keynesian income-expenditure model into Treasury thinking about the budget and the development of national income statistics and forecasting are all testimony to the durability of wartime developments. But with the war over, party political and bureaucratic competition re-established there were strong pressures operating within the market for economic advice which led it to revert to interwar policy networks and priorities. Pre-Keynesian attitudes endured, not least that many interwar officials who had to a greater or lesser extent opposed Keynes in the 1930s (Barlow, Brittain, Eady, Gilbert, but not Bridges) continued in post until the 1950s. As Meade confided to his diary in January 1945: 'How bleak the prospect for the post-Keynes Treasury is' (Howson and Moggridge 1990b, p. 28).

With the end of the war in sight the thoughts of Meade and the majority of economists, whether within the ES or attached to the departments, quite naturally turned to the attractions of returning to academic life. The majority in fact did so within months of the armistice, but notwithstanding Meade's misgivings about the post-Keynes Treasury he viewed with grave alarm the prospect that the ES 'might come to grief not because Whitehall, but because the economists, were unwilling to continue it' (Howson and Moggridge 1990b, p. 1). He thus accepted the Directorship, and, as we indicated above, the subsequent transitional period (1946–7) for the ES was neither a satisfactory experience for the economists who stayed, nor in retrospect as constructive for British economic policy as it might have been. Cairncross and Watts (1989, pp. 130–31) muse on what might have transpired if Cripps had become Chancellor at an earlier point.

Long before the end of the war, as part of the process of planning for postwar reconstruction, a number of decisions were made about the future employment of economists in government service which were to have enduring effects. These were to emerge from the deliberations of the 1943 official committee on the machinery of government, 'the first and only time in British history, an official committee prepared a report on "The role of the economist in the machinery of government".'[34] In his evidence Robbins (PRO 1943, pp. 6–7) ventured four guiding principles for any future ES:

1. It 'should be an official organisation' not an advisory body composed of part-time outsiders.
2. It 'must be composed, at least in part, of men or women with full professional training in economics,' for otherwise economic policy will suffer 'the incredible muddles which continually emerge from lay discussion.'
3. Something 'more than an interdepartmental committee of high officials, or even departmental economists, is necessary.' What was needed was continuous study of problems of economic policy as a whole from a comprehensive not a departmental point of view.
4. The organisation must be attached to a 'powerful Minister'; if not, it would be little better than a research group.

The key questions were thus: should economists be located at the centre of government (Cabinet Office or Treasury) or be scattered throughout the departments?; how should they be recruited?; what should be their terms of service and remuneration?; and what freedoms should they enjoy in respect of participating in the academic community from whence they derived. Whilst the committee was to recommend the retention of the ES at the centre of Whitehall, it is clear from the evidence presented before it that the ES and economists generally would not have the influence they had enjoyed during wartime. Thus the Chief Economic Adviser to HMG, Leith-Ross the Treasury official, opposed the retention of the ES. As Cairncross and Watts (1989, p. 44) record; he saw 'The role of economist ... [as] simply to explain the economic consequences of the government's policy; and this did not require a separate central unit which would be likely to overemphasize the academic aspects of policy-making and create friction with heads of departments. For the co-ordination of advice on economic matters it would be better to rely on the economic advisers at the Treasury and the Board of Trade, who could take the lead in any departmental enquiry.' This view was not accepted, and indeed apart from the ES, the Treasury and the Board of Trade, very few departments recruited economists until the mid-1960s. Thus, for example, David Henderson (1961, pp. 7–8), who had just

---

[34] Cairncross and Watts (1989, pp. 40–49), Booth and Coats (1980) and Cairncross (1994).

completed a short spell in the ES, found it astonishing that in 1960 there was not one economist in the Inland Revenue, the Board of Trade or the Ministries of Labour, Transport, Housing and Local Government. Similarly, Cairncross (1968, p. 3) reports: 'when I entered the Treasury in 1961 I doubt if there was a single professional economist anywhere in Whitehall who was engaged on a full-time basis in analysing the problems posed by the need to manage the public sector.'

Booth and Coats (1978, table 5) estimate that there were 10 professional economists in government service in 1945, 18 in 1953 when the ES was transferred from the Cabinet to the Treasury and 19 a decade later (25 if agricultural economists are included). To this establishment we need to add a number recorded as statisticians, especially in the CSO, who would have been undertaking economic duties. However, even when these are included it is clear that for nearly twenty years after the war government demand for economists was very low. But if demand was small, so also was the potential supply of academic economists who were prepared to offer themselves up to the unfavourable terms and conditions of service and relatively low salaries which the Treasury had imposed. In his evidence to the official committee Keynes had warned that academics would find government service uncongenial if economists were not allowed to write books and to contribute to the academic journals and if salary levels were not set according to the economist's opportunity cost, while in any case those recruited would 'only be useful if they had in fact developed dangerous powers of self-expression.' The subsequent difficulties of Hall and then Cairncross in recruiting economists of sufficient calibre are a testimony to the long-term effects of Treasury establishment policies (Cairncross 1994, p. 29; 1995). The result was that the typical economist in Whitehall in the late 1940s and 1950s was comparatively junior, quite often Australian – a reflection of Hall's origins – and not planning on staying in post very long, not least because with the rapid changes in academic economics it could be difficult to escape back to academe for, as another distinguished economist who had spent time as Deputy-Director of the ES (1953–5) put it, 'no one can remain an up-to-date professional economist for very long in Whitehall' (Little 1957, p. 37).

The buoyant state of the British and world economies certainly provides some explanation for the generally low level of government demand for economists and economic advice, and it should also be noted here that recent revisionist writings on the adoption of Keynesianism in postwar Britain stress that its attraction and acceptability to both organised capital and labour was that, relative to the alternatives, it entailed less detailed intervention by government in the market economy. It is also the case that whatever the size and influence of the ES, and of the few departmentally-based economists, there were many other channels whereby economists provided advice. Thus, for example, Harold Macmillan, who in the 1930s had shared many progressive economic views in common with Keynes, was advised if not influenced by Roy Harrod, while the Bank continued to have an enduring influence. None the less, as the 1950s progressed there was certainly no shortage of voices claiming that deficiencies in Britain's economic performance stemmed from policy failures, themselves originating in government's unwillingness to improve its economic policy-making machinery.

Brittan (1964, p. 288), in his enormously influential assessment of the Treasury during the thirteen years of Tory rule, referred to 'bad tactics, intellectual misunderstandings, and failures of timing' combining with an obsession with sterling which caused the Treasury to behave 'like a simple Pavlovian dog responding to two main stimuli: One is a "run on the reserves" and the other is "500,000 unemployed".' Others were even more scathing, in particular the economists waiting in the wings for the long years of Tory rule to end, for the white heat of the technological revolution to begin. Foremost here was Tommy Balogh's (1959, esp. pp. 102–12) fierce denunciation of Treasury dilettantism which, he claimed, had on more than one occasion brought the country close to ruin in recent years. Balogh was also a leading spirit in a Fabian working party which met in the winter of 1963 to advise on the scope for any future Labour government to establish a second central economics department as a counterweight to the Treasury, from which of course emerged the Department of Economic Affairs (DEA) which was intended to champion the real economy as against traditional Treasury preoccupations.[35]

The challenge to Treasury authority reached up to the highest level within the Labour shadow Cabinet, including Harold Wilson who 'had a career-long animus' against the institution (Hennessy 1990, p. 180). He was also, of course, the first Prime Minister in waiting who had been a practising economist, first as Beveridge's research assistant, then in the ES and then elsewhere in Whitehall, before embarking upon a political career after refusing a permanent post with the Treasury at the end of the war. Important reforms were in fact already taking place at the Treasury during the early 1960s. Thus the Plowden report resulted in a new system (PESC) for public expenditure control; there was an administrative reorganisation in 1961–2; a new permanent secretary, **William Armstrong**, and a different generation of Treasury officials now in senior posts, most notably Otto Clarke, who were

---

[35] In addition to Michael Shanks (1970, p. 244), author of another influential Penguin book *The stagnant society* (1962), the working party included Tony Crosland, Shirley Williams, Robert Neild, David Henderson and John Grieve-Smith. See also **Eric Roll's** (1985, pp. 149–50) memoirs on events leading up to the creation of the DEA, on how he became the Permanent Secretary in waiting of a department which did not yet exist.

far more receptive to new ideas; while, upon Hall's retirement, Cairncross's appointment to the post of Chief Economic Adviser to HMG led him to launch a recruitment drive some time before the October 1964 election. Meanwhile, on the wider front, the growing preoccupation with Britain's relative economic decline led the Macmillan government to create the National Economic Development Office and Council (NEDO and NEDC) in 1962 which, before its first Economic Director (MacDougall) and half of its economists decamped to the new DEA in 1964, became the second largest government employer of economists (MacDougall 1987, ch. 7).

The irregulars

All of this then brings us to the exciting events of 1964, the watershed in terms of the employment of economists within British government, at least numerically if not in terms of enduring influence. First, a broad outline of the numbers. From the previous base of 19 professional economists in government service in 1963, Booth and Coats estimate that there were 21.5 in post in 1964, 42 in 1965, 76.5 in 1966 and, as exponential growth gave way to more moderate expansion, a rise through to 236 by 1970. In six years the numbers employed has increased elevenfold, and in fact rather more if the agricultural economists and statisticians are included (Coats 1981c, table 1). As Anthony Sampson (1965, p. 310), whose earlier *Anatomy of Britain* (1962) did so much to change the climate of opinion against the Conservatives, put it 'with the new government of 1964 the economists suddenly and dramatically entered their kingdom in Whitehall.'

Expectations were high amongst the newcomers (for example, Samuel Brittan and Wilfred Beckerman to the DEA and Andrew Graham to work with Balogh at the Cabinet Office) and even amongst those returning to government service (Roger Opie and Michael Stewart),[36] while there was much press interest in the newly established DEA and the personalities of some of the high-level advisers, most particularly the appointments as special advisers of Balogh (notionally on overseas development issues, but effectively adviser to Wilson personally) and Kaldor (on taxation, with an

---

[36] See Brittan (1969; 1971, ch. 8) for an account of his subsequent disappointments; and for the others: Opie (1968a) and Stewart (1977). Unfortunately, Neild did not publish an account of his years as an adviser, and we still await a history of the DEA (but see Clifford and McMillan 1997) We do have a fascinating account by Graham (1992) of Balogh's life, including the period in which Graham served in the *de facto* policy unit Balogh operated in 10 Downing Street. Kaldor's years as an adviser are detailed in Thirlwall (1989), with Wass (1987) providing a glowing Treasury assessment, one quite at variance with the public perception of Kaldor. See also Beckerman (1972) for an assessment of the 1964–70 economic record by economists who were irregulars during the period (cf. Henderson 1966, a volume which shared many of the contributors with the Beckerman collection and provides a reference point in terms of the economists' expectations).

office in the Treasury and reporting to the Chancellor). Completing the trio was Robert Neild who went to the Treasury, and for a brief period looked as if he might be used to push Alec Cairncross out of the Treasury. After some heavyweight politics,[37] Cairncross survived the abolition of the title of Chief Economic Adviser to HMG and became the first head of the newly created Government Economic Service (GES). He records:

> Not that I was left free to carry out these duties. Ministers appointed private armies of economists without reference to me and frequently without notifying me. Salaries were fixed without regard to the position of long-serving members of the Economic Section. Dr Balogh took it upon himself to recruit independently, denounce appointments already made and generally do his best to take over the job and make a nuisance of himself. (Cairncross 1996, pp. 102–3)

In such circumstances it is inevitable that the subsequent economic record of the Wilson government, and of the role played by the new irregulars in the policy process, remains highly controversial. Whilst, amongst historians, there have been recent attempts to rehabilitate the Wilson governments of 1964–70 (Coopey *et al.* 1993), even Wilson himself (Pimlott 1992), it remains the case that economists and economic policy advice were politicised as never before. Extravagant claims had been made in the 1964 general election campaign about the capacity of economic expertise, once properly harnessed in a modernised, technocratic government machine, to deliver higher and sustainable economic growth. Indeed, in the sense of economics dominating the campaign this was the first modern general election. Having made such promises the new government had to make good, and were it to fail to do so the politicians would pay the penalty at the ballot box whilst the economists' credibility would be no less damaged. But, for the latter, the loss of prestige applied to all, not just those economists who served between 1964–70 or in other ways supported Labour. Here are the origins of the crisis of Keynesian economics, ones long predating OPEC I or indeed the breakdown of the Phillips curve.

The politicisation of economic advice was most evident in the appointment of Balogh and Kaldor, who 'had for years been favourite bogeymen for the right, and although rivals and often at loggerheads, they had been associated firmly together, and nicknamed "Buda" and "Pest", a reference to their both being refugees in the 1920s from the Hungarian capital (Sampson 1965, p. 311). To have introduced such legendary figures into Whitehall was, at least in retrospect and for many at the time, a risky strategy but one worthwhile if what was intended was a radical shake-up of Britain's policy-making machinery, and its economic policies in particular.

---

[37] See Cairncross's (1997) recently published diary for 1964–9.

However, this was never genuinely on the cards and it is certainly not what transpired. There is abundant evidence that the DEA, the figurehead of the economic strategy, was a device to mollify George Brown who had only just missed election to the leadership in 1963 and when it was already widely agreed that the Chancellorship would go to Jim Callaghan who secured third place in the ballot.[38] The DEA in its short life secured little; the scuttling of its National Plan damaging the reputation of all associated with the enterprise; and by 1970, when Labour left office, little had been secured by way of reform in either the Treasury or the civil service who had pretty successfully seen off the threat posed by the Fulton commission (Fry 1993, ch. 8).

The economists as a group were thus in part pawns in a political game, one many participants enjoyed but also a source of disillusionment for others who, having little or no prior experience of Whitehall, had not understood what was at stake. In any case, the impotence of academic economics, and the limitations of the economists to actually influence the course of high policy, were determined in the first weekend of the new administration. Thus, as is argued in our case study in chapter 6, the demand- and supply-side strategies of the new government were fatally compromised at the outset by the decision, against the majority advice of the five senior economic advisers, not to immediately devalue sterling. Political calculation dominated over economic reasoning, an experience since reproduced in scores of studies. It is also, of course, somewhat ironic that, as with the years before 1964, the majority of members of the GES were not advising ministers at all but were engaged in analytical and statistical work, including the appraisal of trends in key sectors of the economy and economic forecasting. The provision of economic intelligence and economic information continued to dominate the work of the majority of government economists, and while their 'contributions may ultimately form part of the data or findings upon which policy decisions are formulated ... they are required to exercise little or no judgement in their work about what such policy should be.'[39]

The Government Economic Service

The change of government in 1970 had no appreciable effect upon government demand for economists, with the upward trend continuing through to the 1990s. From a GES of 236 in 1970 numbers had risen to 380 by 1980, at which point the Bank was also employing over 100 economists

---

[38] For example, Stewart (1977, pp. 36–7), Callaghan (1987, p. 165) and Pimlott (1992, p. 280).
[39] Chester (1982, p. 140); see also Boyle (1979).

(Chester 1982, p. 139), and on to approximately 500 by 1995, with annual recruitment of 40–50 graduates, typically at Master's degree level.[40] The GES allocates economists to parent departments, including the Treasury, but has an important role in maintaining professional contacts. During the 1970s and 1980s much applied economic research was undertaken by GES economists, but this is now increasingly being contracted out. According to recent promotional literature, GES economists now typically work alongside administrators and other specialist groups in the following types of activities:

- Policy analysis: as members of policy development teams, where their economic expertise provides necessary technical skills and a valuable approach towards policy issues.
- Technical/modelling work: using econometrics, investment appraisal and other techniques to reduce uncertainty and to quantify options.
- Briefing/assessment: both regular and *ad hoc*.
- Scrutiny/challenge role; assessing the opportunity costs of policies/actions, questioning the validity of approaches taken and long-term appraisal of policy effectiveness.

Currently, of the 500 or so GES members nearly 100 are located in the Treasury and employed in macroeconomic modelling, forecasting and policy analysis. Elsewhere in Whitehall, the employment of economists tends to be on more microeconomic problems and policies, with 34 employed at the Department of Transport, 22 at Health and 54 at Trade and Industry. The Ministry of Overseas Development also employs a number of economists directly, and has call upon a substantial network of outside advisers, as indeed had its predecessor department, the Colonial Office, for at least half a century (Ingham 1992). Towse and Blaug (1990, p. 232) reported that the GES seem to encounter few difficulties in recruiting economists but major problems in retaining them as City salaries, presumably post-Big Bang, were so much more attractive. Similar problems were also experienced by the Bank, but in fact there is nothing particularly new about this phenomenon. Thus Dale's (1941, p. 195) study of the interwar higher civil service makes mention of at least five Treasury officials, 'all recognized as men of remarkable capacity', who were lost to City jobs.

So far as the overall balance of the market for economists is concerned there is currently some dispute about whether it is characterised by excess supply or approximate equilibrium. Towse and Blaug thought the former,

---

[40] *RES Newsletter*, no. 88 (January 1995), p. 17; no. 90 (July 1995), p. 4. Little has been published on the GES, but see *Economic Progress Report*, 99 (June 1978), pp. 1–3.

although as was mentioned earlier their definition of an economist is contested. There is also strong evidence on earnings to suggest that, in terms of private rates of return, an economics or related degree can be considered one of the very best investments in human capital, providing investors do not enter academic life where the erosion of salaries has been very pronounced (see pp. 327–9). Whether public service (and the universities) will continue to attract and retain economists of quality at all levels of seniority remains unknown, but after a century of Marshall's mission that there will be a demand for economists in all sectors of the economy and government seems assured.

3.4 CONCLUSIONS

Hitherto our treatment of the market for advice has been exclusively in terms of British developments. Yet, as was explained in chapter 1, the Johnson critique of the British economics establishment derived in part from the failure of the UK market for economists and advice to develop along the same lines as those in the US. Johnson (1973a, pp. 70–71) was especially concerned about the corrupting influence of Whitehall on economists' scientific standards of conduct and, more generally, the polarisation of the profession into 'left wing and right wing which originated in the deep political tensions that rocked the country in the interwar period.' In reality, his critique was somewhat lacking in historical perspective. Oxford and Cambridge had been divided in their approaches towards economics before the First World War, and the Cambridge-LSE cleavage was never robust in terms of economics or politics. In any case, it was not until 1964 that economics became politicised in any enduring sense. Moreover, US academics are not unaffected by ideology, as was so vividly apparent during the Reagan years and earlier with greater or less (McCarthyite) subtlety. The problem is less that economics became politicised in Britain, more why this occurred and with what implications for the present capacity of any set of economic ideas to influence policy for the general good.

It is also the case that the market for economists has changed very considerably since the 1960s. On the supply side there is clear evidence of differences in the output mix of US and European economists, a reflection of different incentives in the professional job markets (Frey and Eichenberger 1993). In this context the British market represents something of a 'mid-Atlantic hybrid' (Baumol 1995), with some academics clearly American in their research orientation and methods, and others approximating more to the European model where economists participate more in local and national life than their American counterparts; are less prone to academic fads; as deeply engaged in applied as in theoretical research; less attached to neo-classical economics and more interested in institutions; and more preoccupied with undergraduate than with graduate education. Some have argued that a process of convergence on the American model is taking place (Portes 1987); others that for strong linguistic and cultural reasons a heterogeneous European economics will long survive and that said barriers will equally maintain the distance between British economists and their European peers (Kolm 1988). Others predict that the growing ideological and methodological disputes within economics make convergence of any sort most unlikely (for example, Peacock 1995), whilst there remain a vocal body of those who look to the EU and the European project, in particular growing labour market integration, as bringing about such an eventual result even if not desired by many of the participants (such as Forte 1995, incidentally an interesting example of a European academic economist who has also been politically active, including being Minister of Finance in the national government, 1983).

On the demand side, since the 1960s the civil service and those few private sector agencies recruiting economists specifically for their economic expertise have typically sought personnel with a much higher level of technical skills, especially in modelling, forecasting and appraisal, than the generalists who entered service during the Second World War and the early postwar years. This shift in the demand schedule lagged the rising technical barriers to entry to undergraduate and postgraduate economics education, which in turn lagged the growing formalisation of economics itself. We have, therefore, another supply-side push by academic economists which, given the minute proportion of economics graduates whose subsequent employment makes use of their degree, is as yet unmatched by demand.

One political manifestation of this supply-side push were the efforts by a group of politically committed economists, prominent in Labour Party circles in the run up to the 1964 election, to educate the Wilson shadow Cabinet on economics in a series of seminars held at Nuffield College, Oxford.[41] This was in reality not much of a departure from economists' activities between the wars, as for example in the involvement of Hubert Henderson, Keynes and Layton in the Liberal Summer Schools of the 1920s, which produced a report widely considered as a blueprint for the managed-mixed economy which emerged in Britain after the Second World War

---

[41] Callaghan (1987, p. 153) records in his memoirs that these were organised by Tony Crosland and included amongst them Kaldor, MacDougall, Kit McMahon and Neild. He also reports: 'But one field of experience was not included among my advisers, namely a first-hand knowledge of how the City of London works [and] ... Like most if not all Chancellors, I did not learn the ways of the City until I had held the post for some time, and consequently made mistakes.'

(Middleton 1996, pp. 306–7). However, with politics more polarised, economists more clearly associated with political parties than ever before, there being parallel developments on the right with agencies such as the IEA, and with disappointments in the sphere of economic performance and policy about to become very much more significant, the stage was set for the modern chapter of economists' influence. As we shall see in later chapters there existed a brief period, between the 1930s and the early 1960s, when academic economists commanded attention and exercised unparalleled influence on policy. We have already identified the Second World War as critical in this respect. It was a formative influence for those subsequently seeking to supply economic advice, who used Keynes as their model of successful persuasion, and for those in government compelled to address economic problems of such complexity and strategic importance that reliance could no longer be made on existing City-based and DIYE networks.

4. Marshall's mission, the prewar permeationist strategy and the professionalisation of economics

If Marshall was *too anxious* to do good, then it would also be true to say that [today's] economists are *not anxious enough*; and that there is no better place for them to turn for intellectual regeneration and spiritual uplift than to the work of an economic moralist who thought big and whose anthropocentric, holistic, multidisciplinary and quintessentially dynamic analysis of the capitalist market economy, developed while anxious to do good, constitutes one of the most stimulating contributions to the literature. (Reisman 1990, p. 2)

4.1 INTRODUCTION

In an unusually forthright and focused chapter of his *Principles of economics* Marshall (1890, p. 42) established that 'The dominant aim of economics in the present generation is to contribute to a solution of social problems', with the core challenge – identified somewhat earlier in his career – being 'How to get rid of the evils of competition while retaining its advantages' (cited in Keynes 1924b, p. 16). The project was thus limited in the sense that no fundamental challenge to the market order was offered by Marshall, or indeed by the greater part of the nascent economics profession. None the less the period from the publication of the *Principles* to the end of the First World War, if not a little beyond, is universally seen as the Age of Marshall, and in certain quarters his ideas are represented as providing 'a theoretical basis for increasing state intervention in [the] economic life of the community in Britain ... [which] helped the Liberal Government ... lay the foundations of a Welfare State' (Jha 1973, p. xv).

Although public sector growth was established by this period, with the principal engine for growth (progressive taxation of incomes) in place by 1909, for many historians the notion that there ever was a welfare state is now highly contentious, and even amongst those that accept the concept, most are dismissive of the notion that its foundations lie with the prewar reforms. Moreover, in so far as any substantive connection between economic theory and economic and social policy can be identified for these years, it was Marshall's favoured pupil and successor in the Cambridge chair, Arthur Pigou, appointed in 1908 at the extraordinarily young age of 30, who was to prove more decisive. Too often remembered for his *Theory of unemployment* (1933), which was used and abused by Keynes in the *General theory* as an example of the inability of classical – more properly neo-classical – economics to furnish a solution to mass unemployment, it is now widely argued that Pigou's more fundamental work, *Wealth and welfare* (1912), constituted 'virtually a blueprint for the welfare state', one which 'elaborated Marshall's invention of the concept of externalities into a general economic theory of government intervention'.[1] As Harry Johnson (1960, p. 153) recorded in an obituary notice unusually sympathetic to a Cambridge economist, 'The remainder of Pigou's long working life can be regarded as largely occupied with strengthening the foundations laid in *Wealth and Welfare* and elaborating the superstructure erected on them.'

In this chapter we explore Marshall's mission for the professionalisation of British economics in section 2 and his ambitions for Britain's economy and society in section 3. In section 4 we then survey very briefly the broader economic policy debate, and the role of economists therein, in the quarter century or so before the First World War before turning our attention to a case study in section 5 on the tariff reform campaign in which Marshall with reluctance, and Pigou and others more enthusiastically, became involved. Some preliminary conclusions are then drawn in section 6.

4.2 MARSHALL'S MISSION

Marshall's mission[2] had the ultimate objective of securing a more humane capitalism in a manner which did not undermine the scholarly detachment and impartiality appropriate for the new learned body (the BEA) representing the infant scientific discipline of economics (as against political

---

[1] Blaug (1992b, p. ix; 1997a, p. 287). *Wealth and welfare* was expanded vastly over the next thirty years, being retitled *The economics of welfare* (1920), achieving a fourth edition by 1932 and along the way, to contain its size, having a number of topics hived off, these eventually becoming *Industrial fluctuations* (1927) and *A study in public finance* (1928). Unfortunately, Pigou has not attracted even one per cent of the biographical attention devoted to his 'master', being 'caught between the shadow of Marshall and the pyrotechnics of Keynes' (Collard 1990, p. 184), see also Collard's (1981b) essay and Robinson's (1968) warm biographical sketch.

[2] This phrase derives from Reisman (1990), the final volume in a trio of studies of Marshall's life and thought. The literature on Marshall is enormous, with Maloney (1985), Whitaker (1990a; 1996) and Groenewegen (1995) particularly recommended. These should be supplemented by Fry (1976) on Marshall and the role of the state; O'Brien (1981a) and Whitaker's (1986) surveys of Marshall's contribution to theory; Coats (1990) on Marshall's ethics; and Hutchison (1953), Winch (1969) and Wood (1983) on contemporary economists and economic thought.

economy). Indeed, both social reform and social science were to be reconciled as 'economic chivalry' was attained. This was Marshall's attempt to steer a middle way between the unregulated capitalism borne of rampant individualism and the alternative of a stifling collectivism deriving from a socialist ideology bereft of economic analyses. Thus, in his own words, 'Economists generally desire increased intensity of State activity for social ameliorations that are not fully within the range of private effort: but they are opposed to that vast extension of State activities which is desired by Collectivists' (1907, p. 333).

The Organon

Marshall's mission comprised three principal elements: that economists should acquire an attribute, that of training in a body of theory which was rigorous and inaccessible to the uninitiated; be imbued with an attitude, an impartiality in politics which was buttressed by the scientific possibilities of applied welfare economics; and seek a consequent reward, that of a privileged position and voice in policy-making. In charting subsequent events our purpose is necessarily limited to an assessment of whether Marshall succeeded in his mission and the extent to which it influenced the development of economic theory and policy. Here we follow Collard's (1990) use of Marshall's Organon, loosely translated as an instrument of thought or research programme in the Lakatosian sense. This had five constituent parts: a core theory, a motivation and style, an aversion to controversy, a quest for 'concrete truth' and a method of propagation.[3]

The core theory derived from the *Principles* which, conceived but never completed as a two-volume study, need to be supplemented by *Industry and Trade* (1919) and *Money Credit and Commerce* (1923) which dealt with some of the material that would have been incorporated in the 'missing' volume, although, as Keynes (1924b, p. 27) lamented, 'time had deprived his ideas of freshness and his exposition of strength and sting.' The vital elements of this core continue to be debated by historians of economic thought, but few would dissent from Winch's (1969, p. 23) judgement that the *Principles* was 'simultaneously an original contribution to knowledge, pointing the way for future research, and a broad exposition of the problems that were, and to some extent still are, of interest to economists.'

Motivation encapsulated the higher moral purpose that should inform the economist's calling and style the stance that good science required that economic theory and policy analysis not be committed to print until

---

[3]   The OED definition is 'An instrument of thought or knowledge; a means by which some process of reasoning, discovery, etc. is carried on; esp. a system of rules or principles of demonstration or investigation; spec. title of the logical writings of Aristotle.'

adjudged definitive. Under Marshall, the requirements of style severely limited the utility of economics to government, for he would not publish his work unless convinced that the logic was impeccable and that the economics served the higher purpose. Neither his professorial successor, Pigou, nor his intellectual child, Maynard Keynes, followed such a dictate, especially the latter who revelled in controversy and used the provisional nature of ideas as the springboard to greater theoretical insights.

The third element was the avoidance of controversy. This was necessary for the economists' professional detachment which, in turn, was a precondition for a growing demand for economists who, having shed their nineteenth-century predisposition to disputatiousness, could be portrayed as engaged in a common journey of scientific discovery.

Fourthly, there was truth: the quest for practical economic knowledge through a creative confrontation between theory and fact. As Keynes (1924b, p. 33) recounted, Marshall 'arrived very early at the point that the bare bones of economic theory are not worth much in themselves and do not carry one far in the direction of useful, practical conclusions' and as a consequence he had a penchant for Blue Books, indeed ravenous appetite for numbers. Marshall had long maintained that economics was 'not a body of concrete truth but an engine for the discovery of concrete truth' (see p. 15), but – and this gives added sense to the elements of style and controversy in the Organon – he became trapped in a vicious circle of 'thwarted ambitions and failed intentions' (Whitaker 1990b, p. 218) in which he could not complete the engine of analysis (volume 2 of the *Principles*) because so little of the prior empirical work had been completed, itself a consequence of there being so few who had been suitably equipped for the task with Marshall's *Principles*. Whilst his energies were often diverted, frequently by duties such as serving on the Labour Commission (1891–4) or the tariff reform issue (1903) which did further his wider mission, Marshall's (1897b, p. 206) own explanation for the delay in completing the second volume is worth citing at some length because it illustrates the enormity of the task he set himself and its dependence upon economic history as much as theory:

> My book makes no progress. The work for it wh I feel I must do before finishing it grows: there is more of it ahead than there was when I finished my first volume. The history of foreign trade seduced me: I thought it exceptionally instructive for modern times: & I spent an incredible time in laboriously producing several chapters about it. And yet, after all, I find they wd.. make the main argument hang so, that I am forced to fall back on the awkward expedient of putting them into an appendix, & making frequent references to them in illustration of my argument. I made the resolve sadly; but at the same time I resolved to read as little history as possible till I had finished my main work. I find that the illustrations wh I want to take from recent events alone will occupy more time than I can spare, & will fill more pages than people will have patience

to read. I must leave economic history to others.

And yet I feel that the absence of any tolerable account of the economic development of England during the last half century & a half is a disgrace to the land, & a grievous hindrance to the right understanding of the economic problems of our time.

One can but wonder how Marshall would have fared a century later in an academic environment of publish or perish, of periodic research assessment exercises (RAEs). It is not surprising that this has been identified as the weakest element of the Organon (Collard 1990, p. 167). However, from the perspective of the 1990s rather than the 1920s, is it still the case that, as Keynes's (1924b, pp. 36–7) put it in an almost throwaway remark in his celebrated obituary, 'Economics all over the world might have progressed much faster and Marshall's authority and influence would have been far greater, if his temperament had been a little different'? Our greater historical perspective reveals Marshall as combining much of the best and much of the worst that the mid-Victorian world had to offer: neurotic and selfish, racked with self doubts but capable of the highest ideals and scholastic devotion, characteristics so well-captured in Groenewegen's (1995) biography. As with Maynard Keynes, and the devotion he was to engender, Marshall's influence transcended his published work and his university to an extraordinary degree.

What Keynes saw as in some sense a dilution of the mission, that Marshall's engine of analysis existed as much as an oral tradition as a text, can thus be seen in a different light. Long before he succeeded in establishing the Cambridge economics tripos, Marshall had built up a network of younger economists who were to populate the new economics departments, the ranks of schoolteachers, even a few into the civil service – the 'cool heads and warm hearts' set forth in his inaugural lecture. Indeed, such had been his activities that **Foxwell** (1887, p. 92) was able to tell an American audience in the 1880s that 'Half the economic chairs in the United Kingdom are occupied by his pupils, and the share taken by them in general economic instruction in England is even larger than this.'

This brings us to the fifth and final element of the Organon: the channels of propagation, principally the Cambridge economics tripos, finally achieved after a long struggle in 1903, and the *EJ*. The latter can be dispatched quickly (it is discussed further in section 4 in connection with DISMAL, our database of *EJ* papers and their authors). Having been a key figure in the establishment of the BEA, Marshall was not then much involved in its activities or in those of the *EJ* which, in any case, developed as an organ for British not Cambridge economics (Tribe 1992, p. 33). This said, he was deeply disturbed by the launching of the *Economic Review* just before that of the *EJ*, seeing it as 'an open public challenge to the hegemony of Cambridge economics' (Coats 1990, p. 167).

Marshall and the Cambridge school

For Marshall, it was the achievement of the tripos which was much more significant: a personal triumph and, for the discipline, a milestone in professionalisation. Yet the number of Cambridge economics graduates produced before the First World War was tiny, albeit comprising a distinguished class list. In any case, events in Cambridge should not detract from the growth of university economics education elsewhere: long-established in Scotland, at Glasgow and Edinburgh (Cairncross 1998); established and enlarging in London (King's and UCL, followed by the LSE); newly established in England's provincial universities (Birmingham, Bristol, Leeds, Liverpool and Manchester); and in existence at Oxford, where it had yet to escape from the yoke of modern history teaching.

Economics in prewar Oxford was particularly significant in offering an alternative research programme based upon a very different conception of the discipline from that promulgated by Marshall (Kadish 1982). This was much influenced by the German historical school's promotion of inductive over deductive reasoning, from which followed an emphasis upon circumstance and history which denied the validity of general theories. The Marshallian vision of economics (and marginal utility theory) were thus rejected by many Oxford economists as being too remote from real-world policy concerns (Ashley 1907, p. 481). This historical-evolutionary approach to the study of social phenomena endured as a major competitor to Marshallian analysis, one which was largely unaffected by Edgeworth's appointment to the Drummond chair. As the foremost contemporary practitioner of mathematical economics he 'was too far ahead of his contemporaries to exert much immediate influence, despite his originality' (Coats 1967, p. 715). Indeed, so far ahead was he in technique that if DISMAL is stripped of his (and Pigou's) contributions the prewar dominance of non-quantitative, non-symbolic rhetorical style is complete.

The academic institutionalisation of economics, however, was but one channel for the diffusion of economic thought, for as Tribe (1993, p. 184) concluded from his study of the northern universities 'Political economy was in later nineteenth-century England more a subject of discussion than a subject for teaching.' Thus, as Kadish and Tribe (1993b) hypothesise, economics as we now know it originated in a supply-side push, initially unmatched by demand. The nature of the offering must be part of the explanation for the paucity of demand. Certainly, **Ashley**, professor at Birmingham, the major prewar rival to Cambridge, and an adversary of Marshall in the tariff reform campaign, thought so. In a series of *EJ* articles reviewing the current state of economics he drew unfavourable comparisons between economics education in Britain and that in North America, of which he had considerable experience, and in particular echoed the business community's complaint that university economics took insufficient account of their requirements. In a deliberately coded passage (1908, pp. 184–5) he questioned the achievements of those universities which did not provide economics tuition under the broader umbrella of a commerce degree, the route of course pursued in his own institution with the B.Comm. Since the method of teaching and research advocated by Ashley did not differentiate between the study of past and current economic phenomena the Birmingham B.Comm. not only offered a more practically oriented economics but the promise of a much higher status for economic history, posing an interesting counterfactual given the eventual fate of the latter.[4]

Marshall greatly feared that Ashley's conception of economics, and his close association with the German historical school, would be detrimental to the success of his theoretical and analytical ambitions for economics. Ashley's vision did not prevail, but neither, in its entirety, did Marshall's. Indeed, as Maloney (1985, p. 117) muses, 'If historicism had had its own Marshall, the story might have been different.' Within Cambridge, Marshall's mission was beset with difficulties: the strained relations with Cunningham and his advocacy of a historical economics, which occasionally erupted into print, most notably in the *EJ*; he had to lobby hard to ensure that it was Pigou who succeeded him in the chair, rather than **Cannan**, Foxwell or indeed Ashley (Groenewegen 1995, pp. 622–7); the economics tripos contained much non-Marshallian baggage, left over from the moral science days, until Pigou's ascension (Collard 1990, p. 171); and the numbers enrolling in both parts of the degree were very small and fell well short of Marshall's ambitions, thus limiting the opportunity to introduce advanced theory, in particular monetary topics, with the consequence that before 1914 the tripos comprised 'potted Marshall and sugared sticks of Hartley Withers' (Maloney 1985, p. 232). While not attaining the advanced curriculum or the numbers that he would have wished, Marshall had been successful in quelling methodological disputes, thereby furthering his broader mission and, in particular, the public repute of economics. Indeed, so successful was he in insulating his undergraduates from such disputes that Dennis Robertson (1951, p. 112), who started to read economics at Cambridge in 1910 and in 1944 succeeded Pigou to Marshall's chair, 'recalled an atmosphere of calm that now seems somewhat forced and unnatural as well as characteristically British in its insularity and

---

[4]   Kadish (1991) and Coleman (1987). Marshall's mission for an analytical economics also entailed a disdain for accounting, with important long-run adverse effects for university-level business education and the development of accounting as a separate discipline (Napier 1996b).

complacency' (Coats 1967, p. 708), and that it was Pigou's *Wealth and welfare* which 'compelled us to formulate our ideas a little more sharply'.

We are thus led once more to Pigou who later described himself as the 'liaison officer' between Marshall and the subsequent generations (1953, p. 3). As Maloney (1985, p. 228) observes: 'Pigou stands out for his determination to use advanced analysis for the purpose of policy recommendation', with his 'unabashed use of mathematics and graphical methods [giving] him a theoretical sophistication which in the early years of his professorship was unchallenged in or out of Cambridge.' Having come to economics from mathematics (and much else) Marshall was better equipped than most to appreciate its potential in economics. However, as Viner (1941, p. 231) recounts 'he had grave mistrust of the consequences of unrestrained employment of formal mathematics in economic analysis'. In speculating upon why this might be so, Viner describes a syndrome which might resonate for more recent addicts to formalist methods:

Mathematics, and especially graphs, were Marshall's fleshpots, and if he frequently succumbed to their lure it was not without struggle with his conscience. It can also be said for Marshall that when he did succumb he not only frequently warned his readers not to take his mathematical adventures too seriously but shielded them from the young and the susceptible by confining them to footnotes and appendices where, as he rightly anticipated, only the hardened sinners already beyond further corruption would prolongedly gaze. Marshall also was anxious for a wide audience, and the fact that the bulk of his potential readers were both unable and unwilling to read economics in mathematical form no doubt was an additional consideration.

To further the mission through Pigou, Marshall had thus to restrain his distrust of mathematics. Indeed, he had to contain his reservations about Pigou's *Wealth and welfare*, so much so that he did not disclose his consternation that his concept of externalities as a justification for government intervention was being developed beyond that he had ever intended or thought defensible (Bharadwaj 1972). Not too much should be made of this, although it can be taken in conjunction with the clear evidence that the manoeuvring to secure Pigou as his successor was motivated, at least in part, by a perception of the fragility of what had been achieved in Cambridge and elsewhere (Groenewegen 1995, p. 625). By augmenting Edgeworth's long-standing formalism with the youthful energies and mathematical capacity of Pigou, the price of the succession was thus the beginnings of the erosion of the dominant literary style in the rhetoric of British economics. Marshall's creation, the Cambridge school of economics was to be brought to maturity under Pigou, later aided by Keynes. Both shared the aspirations of their 'master' for a relevant economics, and for the position of economists in policy-making (although Pigou grew increasingly uncomfortable in his public role), but under their stewardship economics was increasingly conducted in ways which posed barriers to entry to the 'cool heads and warm hearts'. Admittedly, Keynes was the pamphleteer *par excellence*, but the analytical equipment that was to be required to understand the new microeconomics of Joan Robinson (1933) or the macroeconomics of the *General theory* was of an altogether different order from that prevailing prewar.

Amongst historians of economic thought Marshall is now valued as much for the strength of his vision for economics than for his development of a scientific research programme for economic theory in any pure methodological sense (for example, Whitaker 1986, pp. 185–6). As we have now seen the vision remained contested, and the mission had always to be pursued in face of considerable obstacles both within and beyond Cambridge. Whilst there was undoubtedly a Cambridge school of economics by the eve of the First World War many of the claims made for it by Keynes, Pigou and other students of Marshall now appear exaggerated, the product of the competitive process between rival centres for economics – especially with the LSE – that was to characterise the interwar years and, eventually, of Keynes's 'long struggle of escape ... from habitual modes of thought and expression' which produced the *General theory* (1936, p. xxiii).

4.3 MARSHALL AND ECONOMIC CHIVALRY

Marshall and ethics

For all of his intellectual authority, his detailed knowledge of economic conditions (an unusual attribute for an academic economist even at this time)[5] and the diagnostic potential of the engine of analysis there was nothing particularly profound or original about Marshall's view of the British economy and of the tasks facing government. Indeed, that was partly his strength, for what was distinctive about Marshall was the combination of attributes and of his high public standing. As Winch puts it:

> Nor was it simply as an economist in the pure sense that Marshall impressed his stamp on British economics before 1914. As a representative figure, sharing

---

[5] For example, according to Maloney (1985, p. 62), the high regard in which J.N. Keynes was held by Marshall, and the role that was envisaged for him in Marshall's mission, was precisely because of Keynes's commitment to theory over empiricism, one which resulted in an 'exceptional lack of interest in public affairs', with his diaries (a major source for all interested in prewar British economics) characterised by 'an uninterrupted indifference to events outside Cambridge' (at least before 1914) and the sparse entries on economic events being such that 'no one [would] guess that an economist, or former economist, was writing.'

many of the strengths, weaknesses, prejudices and beliefs of other late Victorian students of society, he imparted a brand of middle-class moral earnestness and helped to restore a feeling of public respectability and relevance to the subject. In this respect, Marshall's contribution was to bring economics into closer contact with the major social questions of the day, and the progressive intellectual tendencies of his day – just as John Stuart Mill had done before him and Keynes was to do later. (1969, pp. 23–4)

It would be convenient at this point to establish the dominant economic questions of the day and to detail the corresponding economic analyses and policy proposals of Marshall, but history is less tidy than this and instead there was a complex of issues which we would now characterise as concerns about social harmony and relative economic decline but which at the time did not have such clarity: a confusion of *fin de siècle* anxieties of all sorts, preoccupations with the competitive threat of Germany and the US and the eternal presence of the poor, manifest in a range of labour market issues and given new political salience by the rise of the labour movement. In my earlier study, 1890 is represented as a critical turning-point in the nation's history, more particularly in terms of the choice of government versus the market (Middleton 1996, p. 12). Thus, 1890, in addition to its significance for academic economics, coincided with, and in part conditioned, 'that critical inquest into the state of the British economy which has been going on ever since' with much contemporary debate 'intimat[ing] the need for some form of government action or supervision' (Greenleaf 1983, pp. 103–4). Indeed, the first volume of the *EJ* contained two commissioned papers which set forth the individualist and collectivist solutions to Britain's economic and social problems within that policy agenda.

The *EJ* was thus part of this critical inquest, albeit a minor player. Marshall's position, and his influence upon contemporary debates and the enlarged role for the state which resulted, is best understood in terms of his concept of economic chivalry, one incidentally given its fullest expression in an *EJ* article (1907). Starting from the position that economics was an ethical undertaking, Marshall defined the mission as not just the relief of poverty and suffering but the raising of the 'quality of life',[6] and conceived of economic reality as a complex evolutionary process in which 'the pursuit of broadly-conceived self-interest was far from operating frictionlessly or on the basis of theoretically-complete information or fixed preferences' (Whitaker 1986, p. 182). Human behaviour was thus much richer in reality and in potentiality than was suggested by the theoretical dictates of pecuniary maximisation while there was widespread evidence of imperfect

---

[6] While most writers stress the role of ethics in Marshall's economics, few explore why he was reluctant to explicate his ethical beliefs, but see Coats (1990).

optimisation, as manifest by the conspicuous consumption of the rich and the cheap but unhealthy diversions of the poor, amounting Marshall (1907, pp. 324–5) thought to £400–500 million per year of 'socially wasteful' expenditures, some 25 per cent of GDP.

For Marshall there could be no 'noble life' without physical and moral improvement, and this required a shift in the balance between market and government, capital and labour. However, the extent of Marshall's critique of the market was very limited: he did not challenge private enterprise in the production of wealth, nor question the general superiority of the market as an allocative device, with the exception of natural monopolies associated with economies of scale, though even here we should note that the Marshallian – as against Walrasian – notion of competition was firmly grounded in the real world where such characteristics 'were an inherent part of the system to be analysed, not just a tiresome imperfection' (Collard 1996, p. 923). The development of the modern theory of market failure, of market power, externalities, the (im)possibility of general equilibrium and miscellaneous failings such as improvidence, all feature in Marshall's writings but his principal criticism of laissez-faire related more to what we would now call social market rather than technical market failure: to the social justice of market outcomes and to the equity-efficiency trade-off in the cardinal choice between government and market. Groenewegen (1995, pp. 592, 611) labels Marshall a small 's' socialist, with his 'support for some state enterprises and municipal socialism; tax and social welfare policy for redressing social inequality and poverty; profit sharing and cooperation, as more satisfactory forms of working-class organisation than the new trade unionism.' The category of social democrat might be more appropriate, for his 'socialism' was more symbolic than operational: a belief in 'the potential for human perfectibility and of the possibilities for the improvement of human character'. Moreover, while Marshall maintained a studious non-partisanship in public it is clear that he never sought escape from the tenets of classical liberalism. Indeed, he 'never revealed any doubt that it [poverty] could be substantially resolved within the limits of British parliamentary democracy and of a free enterprise economy' (Viner 1941, p. 227).

In such circumstances it was hardly surprising that Marshall was often attacked as an apologist for the rich. On the one hand, as he had hoped, marginal utility analysis was a powerful instrument for promoting the professionalisation of economics, but on the other, by its continued sanction of the market and free enterprise, it was condemned as bourgeois economics by more radical opinion. The continued antipathy to much political/bureaucratic activity for its inherent inefficiency relative to market agents also limited Marshall's appeal. Thus Marshall had little influence amongst the Fabians, the dominant left-of-centre intellectual current, while the New

Liberalism that was to underpin the reforming Liberal governments of 1906-14 owed more to T.H. Green, the Oxford philosopher, than to Marshall and the nascent economics profession.[7] Contemporaneously, Marshall's mission was frustrated by the numbers and noise created by 'impetuous socialists and ignorant orators', upon whom he had poured such scorn in his inaugural lecture, and 'heretics' such as the underconsumptionist **J.A. Hobson** who had a large following.[8] While Hobson was eventually partially rehabilitated by Maynard Keynes (1936, pp. 364–71) as an important figure in the derivation of the concept of aggregate demand, before the First World War Edgeworth ensured that he remained forever on the fringes of academic life, never offered an academic post or invited to contribute to the *EJ*. The BEA's liberal charter, that it be 'open to all schools and parties' with 'no person excluded because of his opinions' (Edgeworth 1891, p. 2), thus did not extend to Hobson, nor indeed to many others. Marshall was, in fact, not unsympathetic to much of Hobson's work, though he considered him analytically lightweight ; what perturbed him was the threat to the mission for professionalisation at a time when DIYE continued to predominate and there was the widespread belief outside of the universities, not least from commercial sponsors, that the study of economics encouraged socialism.[9]

Marshall and national efficiency

For Marshall, as for most of his academic colleagues, there was no easy – nor desirable – separation between economic and social reform. The possibilities of economic chivalry bound them together; they also limited the need for greater government capacity, at least in terms of overriding the market's allocative functions. The ambitions entertained for more educated and enlightened captains of industry to untap the possibilities of economic chivalry now seem wildly idealistic, as does Marshall's view that the Indian Civil Service's devotion and professional ethics demonstrated that the public good could motivate a bureaucracy. Indeed, it is all too easy to dismiss him as "'mid-Victorian morality seasoned by Benthamism,' much of which the present generation finds almost intolerably tiresome', this being

[7] Maloney (1985, p. 204) and Thompson (1996, p. 16).
[8] See Freeden (1990) for a series of reappraisals of Hobson, especially the chapters by Backhouse on his macroeconomics and Clarke on the similarities between Hobson and Keynes as economic heretics. Surprisingly, given his treatment, Hobson's (1938) memoirs make no mention of Edgeworth or Marshall, though he did record (p. 194) Keynes's tribute to him in the *General theory* and, in the section detailing the publication of his first heretical work (*The physiology of industry* 1889, co-authored with A.F. Mummery the mountaineer and businessman), he referred to the subsequent refusal of the London Extension Board to allow him to lecture on political economy because of 'the intervention of an economics Professor who had read my book and considered it as equivalent in rationality to an attempt to prove the flatness of the earth' (p. 30).
[9] Whitaker (1996, vol. II, pp. 279, 335); Sanderson (1972, pp. 209–11).

Guillebaud's complaint (his nephew, cited in Coats 1990, pp. 168–9), and
thereby miss the significance of Marshall's mission for the future of British
economics and economic policy. Schumpeter (1954, p. 129) had Marshall
very much in mind when he wrote of the 'tendency of the social philosopher
to exalt his own schema of life's values into an ethical norm from which to
judge the habits and tastes of all other men' and with 'this conception ...
shaped on the model of the typical life of a Cambridge professor.'

True to his evolutionary model of economic change Marshall (1907)
argued that the temporary suspension of the law of diminishing returns
provided a unique opportunity for social reform. Retrospectively, we see that
the extremely low marginal tax rates and the heavily skewed income
distribution of the late nineteenth century, combined with the potentiality of
the concept of consumers' surplus as an instrument for applied welfare
analysis, for the first time provided both the opportunity and the means for
government growth sanctioned not on grounds of the distributional struggle
but economic theory. It would be understandable if this preoccupation with
social reform was conceptualised as a redefinition of the politically
acceptable equity-efficiency trade-off, but this would be a misspecification
which missed what Marshall and many of his contemporaries were
attempting: both greater economic efficiency and equity.

The diagnosis that Britain's economic difficulties derived in part from
productive inefficiencies created by social inequalities of education, health,
housing and income was to find its fullest exposition in the national
efficiency movement. The quest for national efficiency was borne of
Edwardian anxieties about competitiveness and possible national decline
(militarily, socially and morally as well as economically); it provided an
organising theme for a variety of intellectual movements and, in the field of
public policy, drove the agenda for reform in education, science,
manufacturing industry, trade, monetary and fiscal policy, defence and
public health; indeed few areas were untouched by it. Marshall's stance in
these debates combined the idealism of economic chivalry, the normative
positions generated by his ethical concerns and the positive conclusions
deriving from his essentially classical conception of economic growth. Thus,
in terms of factor supply in growth, he argued for policies which, by
improving the health of the industrial population, would increase its
efficiency; and for greater investment in human capital, notably industrial
education for the workforce and business/scientific education for the
entrepreneurial class, which again would raise efficiency and allow the
realisation of the potential of technical progress. The importance of capital
accumulation, investment as a vehicle for new technology, institutional
incentives to support private savings, new forms of business organisation all
also receive attention and are seen as integral to the growth process.

Viewed retrospectively Marshall's growth theory is recognisably modern to a very great extent (O'Brien 1981a, pp. 51–5). However, much of his thinking about growth remained unpublished, and is only now coming to light with the efforts of Whitaker and others. His contemporary significance lay more in the fact that he lent authority, however qualified by his chronic reticence to become involved, to the burgeoning critique of the market that characterised prewar public debate: that markets were neither self-equilibrating nor producing distributional results whi h were supportable on grounds of social justice or economic efficiency. By contemporary standards this is a very moderate version of the case against the market being developed by progressive, let alone socialist, opinion. None the less, Marshall and his professional colleagues provided hard analysis for concerns which hitherto had been largely couched in moral terms. Unemployment and poverty, the technical failings of British industry and import penetration of German manufactured goods were now being made comprehensible within a single system of thought. This did not mean that economists were speaking with a single voice; far from it as we are about to see. But at least part of Marshall's mission for professionalisation was being attained: that systematic, scientific analytical economics and economists provided insights into contemporary problems which were both rigorous and relevant.

Marshall and economic policy

Before turning our attention to the role of the broader economics profession in the policy debate and the activities of government we complete this section by summarising Marshall's stance on the major policy issues, This is very deliberately couched in terms of what John Williamson (1994b) has called the 'Washington consensus', an agreed set of measures which had, following the defeat of communism in Europe and the global triumph of the market in the late 1980s, emerged as the consensual view of the US (and to a large extent) British policy community (see pp. 344–7). Clearly, this might be viewed as anachronistic and/or teleological, and well it ought if taken to extremes. But, when used with discretion, it is a convenient device with which to establish a benchmark for later developments. It provides continuity, for the questions that economists ask have changed little over the century, this also being the case with the major policy issues. Marshall's economic policy positions can be summarised thus:

- fiscal disciplines: followed the classical economists that budgets should always be balanced on current account, with borrowing justified for capital works on economic grounds and during wartime. There was no sanction for deficit-financing as a remedy for cyclical unemployment and the balanced budget rule was justified as much on political (opposing rent-seeking) as economic grounds (crowding-out).

- Public expenditure priorities: supported a rebalancing of priorities towards greater expenditure on education, public health, housing and other functions which would contribute towards greater social welfare and economic efficiency.
- Taxation policy: a limited increase in the tax burden to finance the reordering of expenditure priorities, with strong support for progressivity in income and wealth taxation subject to the limitations of incentives and risks to the entrepreneurial dynamic.
- State enterprise: a general preference for the market on grounds of its superiority as an allocative device and for reasons of dynamic and X-efficiency.
- Government regulation: limited in product markets, to preventing monopoly abuse and maintaining competitive disciplines; but more substantial in labour markets where social market failure was endemic.
- Monetary policy: favoured the status quo of an independent central bank exercising regulatory and supervisory responsibilities within the context of a liberal financial system.
- Exchange rate and international finance: maintenance of the gold standard and of the City of London as the world's financial centre through unhindered capital mobility.
- Trade: qualified approval for free trade.
- Property rights: the legal system should provide secure property rights at low costs and with reform necessary in certain areas, especially company accounts.

Translating these categories into prewar policy instruments and objectives we first conclude that Marshall's economics posed no significant challenge to the core defences of the minimalist laissez-faire state: that of the gold standard, which in theory placed monetary policy in the hands of a politically neutral Bank of England; the minimal balanced budget rule, which imposed a supply-side taxation constraint on public expenditure growth; and free trade, which *inter alia* kept industry and agriculture at arm's length from government. Admittedly the strong support for progressive taxation and social reform, together with the predisposition towards greater intervention at the microeconomic level, qualifies this somewhat but the essential picture remains: Marshall was not pressing for a stabilisation function for government and there was no challenge to free enterprise. What was sought was a controlled and marginal shift in the balance of government and market.

4.4 ECONOMICS, ECONOMISTS, POLICY AND THE CHALLENGE TO LAISSEZ-FAIRE

An examination of the major economic trends for the late-Victorian and Edwardian period reveals unstable economic growth around a trend figure between one half and two-thirds of that experienced by competitor economies who were enjoying the benefits of the catch-up bonus. Accordingly, there was substance to contemporary concerns about the loss of industrial hegemony, but economic decline was always relative and living standards on average continued to rise through to 1914, albeit at a much reduced rate in the 1900s as a consequence of slower productivity growth. The current account balance of payments was in substantial surplus throughout the prewar period, but only because of the enormous positive balance on invisibles. With such a huge deficit on visible account it is not difficult to see why some contemporaries argued that tariff protection was required to stem economic decline. Prices were on trend broadly stable, with the price falls of the 1890s slightly more than matched by rising prices in the new century. Unemployment, however, was far from stable although on average moderate compared with that of the interwar period.

Contemporary economic statistics

It cannot be overstressed that this representation of the prewar economy entails a conception of a macroeconomy alien to the age and is based upon data unavailable to contemporaries.[10] For example, in the labour market the word unemployment was only just about to enter into common usage,[11] there were no continuous, reliable official statistics of unemployment before 1888 and the central characteristic of the interaction of labour demand and supply was casual employment and short-term working rather than the pattern of cyclical unemployment we now experience (Harris 1972, ch. 1). Although the nineteenth century had seen considerable progress in the collection of statistics in all branches of knowledge, and their growing use in public debate, in the economic sphere there was as yet little systematic data collection and no expectation that decision-making should routinely proceed

---

[10] We lack a history of the development of official statistics in Britain. Cairncross (1988) provides an outline of the story, Hutchison (1953, pp. 426–7) a brief assessment of prewar developments and Kendrick (1970) a comparative history. See also Garside (1980) and Davidson (1985) on labour statistics; Stamp (1916) and Bowley (1921) on the overall position by 1914; and MacKenzie (1981) and Porter (1986) on the 'statistical movement' of the nineteenth century.

[11] According to Garside (1980, p. 1) the word unemployment entered the lexicon of political economy in 1888 and was in common use by 1895, the year in which Hobson provided the first modern definition – that of involuntary idleness of the able-bodied – in a series of articles in the *Contemporary Review* (see also Harris 1972, p. 4).

on the basis of data analysis. As Phelps Brown (1959, p. 336) summarised it: 'By present standards it was an age of statistical darkness.' Indeed, any one reading the prewar (and, indeed, interwar) Treasury files in the PRO is immediately struck by the absence of statistical material and the infrequency with which data analysis features in the decision-making process (see Peden 1999, ch. 2). Within the policy studies literature it is generally accepted that the ways in which problems are defined and analysed influences decisions and outcomes, and with some authorities invoking the rhetoric of persuasion in their accounts of the policy process in a manner which has similarities to McCloskey's argumentative approach in economics (Parsons 1995, pp. 32, 153). The essentially literary tradition of the prewar Treasury apparently even extended to one of its Joint Permanent Secretaries, **Bradbury**, who, possessing a double first in classics and history, was so bad as arithmetic that all his budget calculations had to be checked by a subordinate (McFadyean 1964, p. 45). More seriously, the Treasury's limited analytical capacity resulted in its control of public expenditure being restricted to the cash input side of the process to the detriment of efficiency of output and the quantification of policy outcomes (Middleton 1996, p. 240).

In so far as we can detect the incorporation of a more empirical approach in decision-making it is to the Board of Trade that we must look. A departmental statistical section had been founded as long ago as 1833, but the modern phase of its activities began in 1876 when **Robert Giffen**, in a career shift from financial journalism, became head of this department. This was the key appointment in terms of the production of official (especially labour) statistics and of the creation of a culture in which data might become integral to the policy process. Giffen, a founder member of the BEA, was also able to make an important contribution to economics, pioneering national income accounting and cross-country comparisons. In addition, having negotiated an extraordinary dispensation upon joining the civil service, whereby he was allowed to promote his own views on economic and social reform as if he were not an official, he was also active in a number of public debates, especially tariff reform where his privileged access to economic intelligence worked initially to great advantage to the free trade case, although he eventually committed a volte-face in a *Times* letter on the eve of the January 1910 general election as he came to fear the socialism of the Liberals more than the tariffs of the Conservatives. Moreover, not only was Giffen able to operate in this highly unusual manner, but also as the official responsible for compiling the official trade statistics it was his choice how they were presented (Mason 1996, p. 172, 186–7).

In surveying the relationship between the statistical movement and social policy, Harris (1990b, pp. 387–8) notes that 'Many of the great heroes of modern social reform', from Edwin Chadwick through to Beveridge and the

Webbs, 'held highly ambitious views about the ultimate possibility of formulating scientific laws (and thereby solving social and administrative problems) through a process of collecting and sifting empirical social and economic data', in which 'precise, positivistic, scientific knowledge [was] the only rational basis for social action, and rigorous inductionism as the only basis for that knowledge.' Clearly, however, Marshall and his disciples were somewhat more ambivalent about what was possible through the inductive method, but the point that needs to be made here is that the influence of social and economic statistics on the policy process is frequently to reinforce the existing policy agenda (in this case minimal government under siege from progressive opinion) as to buttress the case for reform.

The agenda for reform before the First World War, being predominantly social, did not generate the conditions under which systematic collection of economic data, other than for labour and foreign trade, became politically necessary. There were frequent calls for a much bigger effort in respect of economic intelligence: for example, in 1888 a deputation to the Chancellor of the Exchequer and the President of the Local Government Board by Marshall, then president of the RSS and others campaigning for an occupational census (Higgs 1988, p. 81); and somewhat later a call for the establishment of a central statistical office by Bowley, one of Marshall's progeny and another pioneer of national income accounting. There was a recognition that British official statistics lagged developments in the US, and it is certainly the case that Giffen used such a disadvantage to further the cause of labour statistics in the Board of Trade. But, with the case for greater economic intelligence as yet unrecognised in most private sector organisations, and the Treasury unwilling to support the Labour Department's activities without major battles over expenditure, what we might call the statistical infrastructure for economic policy-making remained wholly underdeveloped. Indeed, as Davidson (1993, p. 258) demonstrates: 'the Treasury imposed a catch-22 situation' on prewar social administrators. It expected Whitehall to demonstrate the cost-effectiveness of its measures, but resisted the deployment of resources by means of which both short- and long-term policy options and objectives might be evaluated and the social and economic repercussions of decision making monitored.'

Admittedly, a census of production was eventually carried out in 1907, population census having been undertaken since 1801, but prewar policy-makers continued to operate without any systematic indicators of cyclical and trend behaviour, although the Board of Trade was producing a quarterly survey of economic trends for the Cabinet by 1910 (Offer 1983, p. 125). The unemployment statistics, initially deriving from trade union returns and then supplemented in 1912 by the national insurance scheme, covered but part of the labour force and were unrepresentative. There were no official national income statistics, although very crude proxies existed for business activity such as the weekly returns of railway traffic and the monthly balance sheets of the London clearing banks. As yet there were no share price indices, with the first *Financial Times* index – the FT 30 share equity – compiled as late as 1935 and, incidentally, by a future Treasury official, Otto Clarke, at that time one of the paper's leader writers (Hubback 1988, p. 21). The situation was somewhat better with price trends in goods: the Board of Trade had been publishing wholesale price indices in its *Journal* since 1871 and the *Labour Gazette* from 1893; the Saurerbeck-*Statist* index became available from 1886; and the first official cost-of-living-index was established at the outset of the First World War, albeit that it was based on a family budget study of 1904. The Bank of England did not interpret its role as requiring the publication of monetary or any other statistics, though what was available, particularly bond prices, interest rates and the volume of bank clearings, were an integral part of the *Economist's* activities, the one financial journal which also provided economic commentary and some economic data at a time when most financial journalists had yet to broaden their approach (Parsons 1989, ch. 1).

The most developed class of official economic statistics were those of foreign trade, published monthly in the *Board of Trade Journal* and, in more detail, in the *Accounts relating to trade and navigation of the United Kingdom*. These had been produced on a broadly comparable basis since the middle of the nineteenth century but they related only to merchandise trade; tradable services were not enumerated; and there were no published estimates of the current account balance of payments. The capital account was similarly unknown.[12] Our knowledge of what was officially unmeasured derives entirely from private enquiries. Thus for data on Britain's overseas investments one has to turn to **George Paish's** regular publications in the *JRSS* and the *Statist*, the latter periodical – which was established by Giffen in 1878 with the aim of combining up-to-date financial commentary with a scientific and statistical approach – an important prewar vehicle for social reformers participating in the policy debate increasingly on the basis of the results of empirical research. Moreover, such trade data as was in the official domain was adjudged by a committee of experts, including Bowley, Giffen and Sydney Chapman, to contain serious internal inconsistencies, such that they 'could find no case where the values registered of country X of goods imported from country Y corresponded at all closely with the values registered by Y as exported to X' (Platt 1989, p. 5).

It is the absence of official statistics which explains why such a large

---

[12]   The first official prewar current account balance estimates were made retrospectively by the Board of Trade in 1923 (Sayers 1976, vol. III, app. 32).

proportion of the *EJ's* (and the *JRSS's*) contents before the First World War, indeed before the late 1920s, were devoted to economic intelligence. In explaining why official statistics were slow to develop in the economic sphere we need to consider the market for economic advice, the nature of the policy process and the limits to state authority. Whilst there was a long tradition of social investigations in Britain, which in essence delve into the lives of the poor and the politically marginal, there was enormous resistance to any intrusion into the affairs of wealthy individuals or businesses. This is evident in the initial design and subsequent administration of the restored Peel income tax, where the state had to tread with great care in acquiring information about income and assets; in the difficulties encountered in enforcing health and safety legislation and in compiling the first census of production. The opposition of the business community to requests for any information which might possibly be deemed commercially sensitive were to delay the publication of official national income statistics in Britain until the Second World War, even to the extent that an official exercise of 1929 remained unpublished and indeed publicly unacknowledged (Stone 1977).

The limited agenda of those seeking to augment the economic functions of the state before the First World War set clear limits to the demand for an expansion of official statistics. Even amongst those who campaigned for a primitive stabilisation function, such as the Webbs with their counter-cyclical public works proposals in the 1909 minority report of the royal commission on the poor law, were not much preoccupied with deficiencies in what we would now label macroeconomic statistics. Moreover, examination of such official statistics as were published on a monthly basis shows clearly that the content and presentation were directed as much to informing private sector decision-making as other elements of the bureaucracy. The Board of Trade's *Labour Gazette*, for example, had evolved greatly by the eve of the First World War, carrying articles each month summarising labour market trends (wages, prices, employment, unemployment and industrial disputes) together with periodic items on overseas developments, especially in the empire, and with a high proportion that was statistical in content. That rational deliberateness which Marshall identified as increasingly characteristic of modern economic life (Winch 1990b, p. 53) was thus being furthered within certain parts of the civil service. But progress towards rational, statistically-informed debate continued to be hindered by the activities of policy entrepreneurs who were not part of Marshall's mission, who used 'doubtful numbers to advance a strongly-felt case' (Platt 1989, p. 5), as for example in Mulhall's *Dictionary of statistics* (1899), a widely read compendium which reflected the author's ardent free trade views.

Economists, the *EJ* and the policy debate

Whilst it is difficult to date the beginnings of the concern for economic decline it is generally agreed that the final report of the royal commission on the depression of trade and industry did much to focus attention on the new competitive challenge of Germany and the US. This, in turn, initiated debate: initially, on the wisdom of free trade; and then on broader issues concerning the entrepreneurial spirit, industrial structure and the efficiency and justice of the market's operations. Contemporary debate decomposed Britain's economic difficulties into sets of internal and external arguments, which have dominated discussions of economic decline ever since (Supple 1990). The former stressed deficiencies internal to the fabric of Britain's economy and society, including entrepreneurial failure, weaknesses in education and much else that related to Marshall's concept of economic chivalry; the latter was principally concerned with the costs of maintaining free trade in face of the tariff barriers erected by Germany and the US. Our search for economists' activity and influence encompasses output measures (both academic and more popular publications); political recognition of expertise in the form of membership of royal commissions and other government bodies, together with evidence to such agencies; privileged participation in policy networks; examples of group lobbying (such as letters to *The Times*); indirect effects through teaching and lecturing; and, most importantly, evidence for the lack of influence in the sense of a continuity in policy-making, of the continued predominance of a generalist civil service advising ministers who, when their DIYE was patently inadequate for the task, had recourse to established City experts.

Taking output measures first, we report in Figure 4.1 and Table 4.1 some results from DISMAL. Comparing the 1910 with the 1891 volume of the *EJ* we observe a broad continuity in the subjects upon which economists were writing, save that the *JEL* (1983) 900 class had expanded absolutely and relatively. This reflected the pronounced contemporary interest in social reform, which is also manifest in the strong showing for the 800 class where the bulk of papers related to labour markets and policy. These results support Jha's (1973) earlier quantitative work on the *EJ*[13] and Davidson's (1985, table 2.1) content analysis on the extent of articles on the labour problem in leading periodicals and *Times* editorials.[14] In contrast to the sorts

---

[13] See, however, Tribe's (1992, p. 42) considerable reservations about Jha's quantitative results and their interpretation, especially in connection with Jha's category of 'labour problems' where he did not separate labour market issues from those of policy.

[14] Davidson's dataset did not include the *EJ* or the *Economic Review* but was compiled from *The Times*, the *Economist*, *Contemporary Review*, *Edinburgh Review*, *Fortnightly Review*, *Nineteenth Century*, *Quarterly Review* and the *Spectator*.

Figure 4.1 Economic Journal: *papers by* Journal of Economic Literature *(1983) classification, 1891, 1900 and 1910*

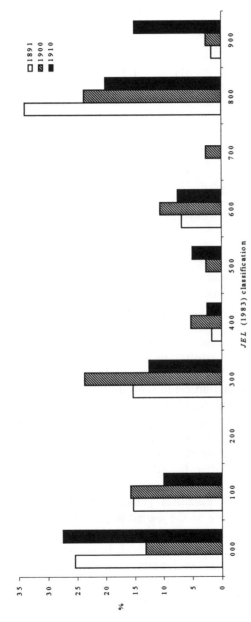

Note: *JEL* (1983) classification: **000** General Economics; Theory; History; Systems; **100** Economic Growth; Development; Planning; Fluctuations; **200** Quantitative Economic Methods and Data; **300** Domestic Monetary and Fiscal Theory and Institutions; **400** International Economics; **500** Administration; Business Finance; Marketing; Accounting; **600** Industrial Organisation; Technological Change; Industry Studies; **700** Agriculture; Natural Resources; **800** Manpower; Labour; Population; **900** Welfare Programmes; Consumer Economics; Urban and Regional Economics

Charlatans or saviours?

Table 4.1 Economic Journal: *classification of papers by rhetoric type (% of total) and mode (Y=presence of style; N=absence), 1891, 1900 and 1910*

Year	Alg-ebra	Cal-culus	Dia-grams	Econo-metrics	Stat-istics	Wholly literary
1891						
Total (%)	1.7	0.0	1.7	0.0	33.9	64.4
Mode (64.4%)	N	N	N	N	N	
1900						
Total (%)	0.0	0.0	0.0	0.0	23.7	76.3
Mode (76.3%)	N	N	N	N	N	
1910						
Total (%)	17.5	12.5	7.5	0.0	32.5	62.5
Mode (62.5%)	N	N	N	N	N	

Note: Component parts do not sum to 100 per cent because each *EJ* paper can exhibit more than one style.

of criticisms levelled against economics and economists today, economic writing before 1914 was thoroughly grounded in social reality. The modal rhetorical style continued to be entirely literary, with the presence of statistics and/or graphs and tables having a secondary presence. More formalistic and mathematical representations were, however, becoming evident in the 1910 volume although five out of the seven papers which included more than statistics in their rhetoric type were provided by Edgeworth, Pigou and Stanley Chapman. Here in embryonic form was the modern style of journal article in economics, replete with tables, diagrams and equations, although the pioneer in this respect was less Edgeworth and Pigou than Irving Fisher, the leading US mathematical economist and one of the founding fathers of the Econometric Society.

These contributions apart, in general before the First World War, and indeed for some time after, the *EJ* 'was devoted to descriptive accounts of economic issues, or engaged with issues of public interest such as socialism, trade and tariffs, and bimetallism' (Tribe 1992, p. 39). A direct Cambridge or Marshallian influence on the journal before it moved to Cambridge with Keynes's assumption of the editorship in 1912 is not readily detectable, and Collard's (1990, p. 172) verdict on its contents appears at first sight about right: 'it was very slow to develop and remained what must seem to modern eyes a dull and second-rate quarterly', giving the appearance of a 'profession marking time' (Maloney 1985, p. 229) and with little to indicate that it would become the leading academic journal by the 1920s. But, as Tribe (1992) reminds us, the dullness was a product of the stress on topicality and the inclusion of much economic intelligence not reported elsewhere, whilst the style of the *EJ* also reflected that of its editor, Edgeworth: 'incisive but not divisive, conciliatory and not confrontational' (Reisman 1990, p. 193). In any case there were other journals in which to publish, books (both textbooks and monographs), pamphlets and popular journalism. Some basic cohort analysis reveals the range of economists' activity.

Table 4.2 details the principal professional activities of the twenty four economists contained in Maloney's (1985) dramatis personae who were still alive by 1914. Whilst these constitute only between a quarter and a third of the total stock of economists in Britain on the eve of the First World War (Table 3.1), they were in effect the key players in the sense of public visibility, notwithstanding that some were far from being 'professional'.[15]

---

[15] Given our earlier definition of an economist there are a number of obvious omissions. First, using the 'manifesto of the fourteen professors' as our guide, we should also include E.C.K. Gonner, one of Marshall's students and eventually Professor of Economic Science at Liverpool; L.H. Courtney, formerly Professor of Political Economy, UCL and then a MP, 1876–1900; Arthur Bowley; Lancelot Phelps, President, Oriel College, Oxford and editor of the *Economic Review*; Charles Sanger, Lecturer in Political Economy, UCL; W.R. Scott, Lecturer in Political Economy at St. Andrews (appointed to the Adam Smith chair in political economy in Glasgow in 1915); C.R. Fay, who after a period as a research student at the LSE returned to Cambridge as a college lecturer, mainly but not exclusively in economic history; and George Armitage-Smith, author of *The Free-trade movement and its results* (1898), an extension lecturer in economics, later Principal of Birkbeck College (not later a Treasury official, as Groenewegen (1995, p. 385) contends, who mistakes son Sydney Armitage for the father). Beyond these we should include Clara Collet, one of the founding members of the BEA and since 1892 an official in the Labour Department of the Board of Trade; Beveridge, then also a Board of Trade official and whose 1909 book on unemployment defined the field; Layton, at that time a Cambridge economics lecturer and author of two monographs *An introduction to the study of prices* (1912) and *The relations of labour and capital* (1913) as well as one of the few economists to have ever published in the *EJ* whilst still an undergraduate (a first-year no less); the economic statisticians Leak and Stamp; H.O. Meredith, who succeeded Pigou as Girdler's Lecturer in Cambridge (1908–11) before becoming Professor of Economics, Queen's University, Belfast, 1911–45; A.W. Flux, one of Marshall's pupils, a prolific *EJ* author who, after a period teaching economics in Manchester and then Montreal, returned to UK to join the Board of Trade; D.H. Macgregor, another prolific *EJ* author and Marshall student who was Professor of Economics at Leeds, and eventually Drummond Professor at Oxford on Edgeworth's retirement, and assistant editor of the *EJ*, 1926–34; Hawtrey, the Treasury official whose work on the monetary theory of the trade cycle was just beginning to appear (1913); D.H. Robertson whose study of the trade cycle (1915) was about to be published; Frederick Lavington, one of Keynes's first students who, after service in the Board of Trade, returned to Cambridge in 1918 as a Lecturer in Economics; H.W. Macrosty, who, along with Macgregor, was an expert on the growth of monopolistic combinations; and T.E. Gregory who, in 1913, had just begun his academic career at the LSE. Finally, our listing also excludes the major financial journalists, such as F.W. Hirst and Hartley Withers; self-acknowledged amateur economists such as H.H. Cunynghame, another Marshall acolyte, soldier, civil servant and polymath whose *Geometrical political economy* (1904) attracted some professional approval; MPs such as Chiozza Money and Charles Mallet, the former of whom laid much of the statistical foundations for the attack on income/wealth inequality; and civil servants such as Llewellyn Smith and Arthur Salter.

Table 4.2 The British economics profession: key persons, 1914

Name	Age	Employment	Mono-graph	Text-book	Policy advocacy	Policy advice	Journ-alism	Extension movement
Ashley, William J.	54	Prof. of Commerce, Birmingham		Yes	Yes[a]			
Bastable, Charles F.	59	Prof. of Political Economy, Trinity College, Dublin	Yes		Yes[a]		Yes	
Bonar, James	62	Royal Mint, Ottawa	Yes					Yes
Cannan, Edwin	53	Prof. of Economics, LSE	Yes	Yes				
Chapman, Stanley J.	43	Prof. of Economics, Manchester	Yes	Yes	Yes[a]	Yes[b]	Yes	
Clapham, John H.	41	Fellow, Cambridge	Yes					
Crozier, J.B.	65	Doctor of medicine	Yes				Yes	
Cunningham, W.	65	Church		Yes	Yes[a]			Yes
Edgeworth, F.Y.	69	Prof. of Political Economy, Oxford	Yes					Yes
Foxwell, Herbert S.	65	Fellow, Cambridge; Prof. of Political Economy, UCL	Yes					Yes
Hewins, W.A.S.	49	MP		Yes	Yes[a]	Yes[e]	Yes	Yes
Higgs, Henry	50	H.M. Treasury		Yes			Yes	Yes
Hobson, John A.	56	Author and lecturer	Yes		Yes		Yes	Yes
Keynes, J. Maynard	31	Lecturer in Economics, Cambridge	Yes			Yes[c]	Yes	
Keynes, John N.	62	Fellow, Cambridge	Yes					

Marshall, Alfred	72	Emeritus Prof. of Political Economy, Cambridge	Yes	Yes	Yes[a]	Yes[c, d]	Yes
Nicholson, J.Shields	64	Prof. of Political Economy, Edinburgh	Yes	Yes	Yes[a]		Yes
Palgrave, R.H.I.	87	Financial journalist	Yes			Yes[c]	Yes
Pigou, Arthur C.	37	Prof. of Political Economy, Cambridge	Yes		Yes[a]		Yes
Price, Langford L.F.R.	52	Reader in Economic History, Oxford	Yes		Yes		Yes
Smart, William	61	Prof. of Political Economy, Glasgow	Yes		Yes[a]	Yes[c]	Yes
Ward, James	71	Prof. of Philosophy, Cambridge,					
Webb, Sidney	55	Prof. of Public Administration, LSE	Yes		Yes (with B. Webb)	Yes (with B. Webb)[c]	Yes
Wicksteed, P.H.	70	Author and lecturer	Yes	Yes	Yes		Yes

Notes:

[a] Tariff reform.
[b] Chairman, Royal commission or equivalent.
[c] Member, Royal commission or equivalent.
[d] Evidence to Royal commission or equivalent.
[e] Tariff Commission.

Sources: Maloney (1985, pp. 238-41) supplemented by Eatwell *et al.* (1987), *DNB* and *Who was who*.

Indeed, the inclusion of figures such as Crozier, a medical doctor who published a highly idiosyncratic textbook at his publisher's prompting, 'a magnificently bad economist' is evidence of 'how far the professionalisation of economics had still to go in 1907' (Maloney 1985, pp. 133, 137). Table 4.2 provides neither a full record of publications – journal articles are excluded which were the favoured channel of output for some, e.g. Edgeworth – nor of professional activities,[16] but it does illustrate that some economists did very little beyond their university teaching duties (J.N. Keynes) and that one was quite patently not an economist (Ward); that one third produced textbooks but that almost all had at least one specialist work to their credit. We observe further that the majority were policy advocates, some very much so and with the non-university economists the most active (Hobson and Webb); that a lesser number served as policy advisers,[17] with Marshall the most active; that less than one half and one third were active in the extension movement and journalism respectively; and that no economist features in all areas of professional activity.

Marshall's position as the doyen of British economics stands out clearly from Table 4.2, with his public position in sharp contrast to that of Edgeworth whose highly abstract and mathematical technique, combined with a lack of interest in undergraduate teaching and a personality which was even more retiring than that of the master, did nothing for Oxford economics in the policy debate.[18] There was nothing novel about economists sitting on, or giving evidence to, the great public enquiries into economic and social questions of the day. The activities of Ricardo (the bullion controversy) and Nassau Senior (poor law reform) come instantly to mind for an earlier generation,[19] but, as Harris (1990b, pp. 383–4) observes, 'Later, in the Victorian period and in the early twentieth century, however, economists were more often than not conspicuous by their absence.' A number of very significant royal commissions and other official enquiries contained no economic expert amongst their members, and, perhaps more importantly, 'when economic experts did sit on or submit evidence to social policy inquiries, it was often not qua economists but because they were deemed to possess some other kind of relevant administrative or

---

[16] Evidence for policy advice is much more visible than that for involvement in journalism and the extension movement where reliance has been placed upon the *DNB* and *Who was who* entries.

[17] With the war at least three would soon serve as official policy advisers, at least one as an outsider (Ashley) and two as irregulars (Clapham and Pigou in the Board of Trade). The former also gave advice privately to the Conservative Party before the war (Harris 1990b, pp. 385–6). In addition, Chapman entered the established civil service in 1915, never returning to academic life while Giffen, only recently deceased, had of course a long second career as an official.

[18] Skidelsky (1992, p. 412) puts the differences thus: 'Edgeworth wished to establish theorems of intellectual and aesthetic interest, Marshall to establish maxims of practical and moral importance.'

[19] See Robbins (1952, pp. 95–8); O'Brien (1975, pp. 148–53).

philanthropic experience.' Thus, for example, the two economists on the royal commission on the poor law (Lancelot Phelps and William Smart) owed their appointment not to their economic expertise but to their experience of local and charitable administration, while Beveridge's claim to give expert testimony to the commission rested not on his academic authority but his being the chairman of the Labour Exchanges Commission.

In respect of this commission, 'often seen as the crucible of Edwardian social reform ideas and a harbinger of subsequent welfare state thought', Harris (1990b, p. 386) records that evidence was not taken from any prominent 'New Liberal' economist and that the commission were uninterested in a memorandum submitted by Pigou which, in embryonic form, contained many of the ideas which would reach maturity in *Wealth and welfare*. Here then was an attempt to introduce scientific, objective benchmarks into the welfare debate; and it came to naught.[20] The absence of economists in the policy process is particularly significant for at heart this was a debate about the future of the public finances, and whether funding should be by national insurance, which retained some residue of the benefit theory of taxation, or by progressive taxation on the ability-to-pay principle (the furtherance of which can be ascribed to Edgeworth's equal marginal sacrifice rule), one which culminated in the constitutional crisis of 1910. Thus, and again on the basis of Harris's (1990b, p. 384) research, we know that such vital topics as the economics of poverty, the distribution of income/ wealth and taxable capacity all remained the preserve of civil servants when it came to the communication of ideas to ministers.

We can generalise from matters of social reform to the broader economic stage and the role played by the new professional economists. Taking the Treasury first, while Peden (1999, ch. 2) shows how, under pressure from the Liberal welfare reforms, Treasury officials adopted a broader conception of the economy and of their responsibilities than that simply of being guardians of the public finances, he does not identify an enhanced role for expertise. Similarly, Sayers's (1976, vol. I, p. 64) history of the Bank portrays an institution jealously guarding its independence from politics and politicians to the extent that,[21] acting on the unofficial advice of George Paish, and officially briefed by Bradbury, Lloyd George in early 1914 was considering a commission to review the Bank's role in regulating credit in which 'it would be well to introduce into its composition a strong leaven of

---

[20] Not all bodies were quite so dismissive of economics expertise. Harris (1990b, p. 385 n. 18) records that, with Bowley's tutorage, the House of Commons select committee on the income tax gave serious consideration to contemporary economic opinion and even attempted to understand Pareto optimality.

[21] The Bank had complete discretion in fixing Bank rate, with it being normal practice not to give prior notice, or not more than an hour or so, to the Chancellor of any rate change.

officials and scientific economists to keep the banking element in check.'

It will be recollected that Bradbury entered our account earlier as the numerically challenged Treasury permanent secretary. However, on the basis of assessments by his colleagues,[22] he should perhaps be remembered for having an unusually highly-developed grasp of economics for a civil servant, and it is certainly the case that over the next fifteen years or so he was to be a major figure in providing policy advice, the more so after he left the civil service. The Treasury, much more so then than now, considered itself administratively and intellectually pre-eminent in Whitehall. It had taken everyone who had passed top in the civil service examinations since 1906, in which economics was now a compulsory element. This had nearly included Maynard Keynes, but his worst marks were in economics and mathematics and the coveted place in the Treasury went to Niemeyer – a future adversary in the conflict over the 'Treasury view' – whilst Keynes went to the India Office.[23] The situation by 1914 can be summarised thus in terms of Marshall's permeationist strategy. Within Whitehall there was a perception that economics had not yet matured into a discrete area of expertise, but Bradbury's case illustrates that, true to the traditions of the Trevelyan-Northcote civil service reforms of mid-century, it was now expected that all members of the administrative grade have a basic familiarity with economic concepts and economic debate, with freedom and opportunity to develop this to a considerable extent on the basis of personal initiative.

The relatively relaxed working lives of prewar civil servants and politicians, together with cultural norms of an elite where broad intellectual interests were expected, resulted in the wide diffusion of basic economic literacy. It also, of course, in effect sanctioned DIYE, and resulted in economic discussions amongst generalists which were largely ignorant of the progress of economic science. In this sense, there was a non-partisan conservatism or orthodoxy to debate in which the core activities of professional economists were, then as now, unknown by policy-makers. Truly were 'the ideas which civil servants and politicians and even agitators apply to current events ... not likely to be the newest', and there is no doubt that the marginalist revolution and the earliest stirrings of welfare economics passed quietly unnoticed within Whitehall.

There was a durability to long-standing economic ideas, expressed in particular during the tariff reform debate, but no stasis. Whether Marshall,

---

[22] See McFadyean (1964, p. 45) and Leith-Ross (1968, p. 22),
[23] Roseveare (1969, p. 232) and Burk (1982b, p. 85). On Keynes, Skidelsky's (1983, p. 175) account is uncharacteristically bland. Salter's (1967, p. 3) memoirs, however, provide colour and comment with the report that Keynes blamed the result on his knowing more on the subject than the examiners, with his poor showing in economics a testimony to a culture where 'an examination designed to pick those best qualified for administrative responsibility should prefer orthodox ability to innovating genius.'

representing the professionals, or Hobson, the freelance partisans, be studied all were part of a political debate over government versus the market. The subordination of economics, and of economic ideas, to politics cannot be overstressed. Admittedly, on occasions, technical expertise could be used to very great effect, as for example in the empirical evidence on national income and factor shares presented by Giffen and Bowley to the royal commission on the poor law as justifications for enhanced welfare provisions (Harris 1990b, p. 392). It is also the case that Lloyd George, when Chancellor, was prepared to solicit advice beyond traditional Bank-City networks when the necessary expertise was either not available or unhelpful, with George Paish exercising influence behind the scenes from at least early 1913 onwards.[24] Disliking and mistrusting his permanent secretaries (first Murray and then Chalmers) he was well used to seeking advice elsewhere and thus something of an exception, so much so that according to one Treasury official 'there is only one man who has ever made the Treasury do what it didn't want to do. That was Lloyd George.'[25] Finally, in searching for economists' influence we must keep to the forefront the essentials of the British policy style and the characteristic that government growth came in a series of piecemeal reforms which predated collectivist theories, sufficiently coherent and commanding of majority approval, which might in other institutional contexts have underpinned such developments. In this sense, Harris's (1972, p. 362) conclusions about government and the labour problem provides a suitable epitaph: 'there was little conscious theory in the Liberal reforms; and in tracing the evolution of a national unemployment policy it is difficult to point to the decisive influence of any single set of reforming ideas or to discover any logical sequence of institutional change.'

4.5 THE TARIFF REFORM CAMPAIGN

An opportunity for influence?

The tariff reform campaign launched in May 1903 by Joseph Chamberlain, Colonial Secretary in Balfour's Conservative administration, brought economists and economic debate to a new prominence. Indeed, no other event before the First World War offered the same public opportunities for economists to seek to influence the course of events. None the less, we use it here to illustrate the limited success of Marshall's mission in the policy

---

[24] Sayers (1976, vol. I, p. 64) introduces Paish into the account at early 1914; Peden (1999, ch. 2) has him advising Lloyd George in the setting of the 1913 budget, while Offer (1983, p. 126) documents Lloyd George soliciting advice from him as early as 1910.

[25] P.J. Grigg cited in Peden (1999, ch. 2).

sphere and to identify certain inherent problems associated with economists' activities which continue today to undermine their authority with public and politicians alike. With its implications for industrial performance, the public finances, the economic role of the state, the tariff reform campaign – which had been gathering pace for some time – suddenly erupted:

> into a fiercely burning political issue. The result was the first major debate on an economic issue since the battle over the Corn Laws, and the first electoral contest on an economic issue in the new age of mass democracy. In this it can be represented as the most significant single step in the transition towards a twentieth-century politics dominated by continual conflict over economic policy.
>
> (Marrison 1996, p. 25)

This campaign is widely represented as the 'first major political response to the problem of British decline, the first major attempt to change the course of British policy' (Gamble 1994a, p. 162).[26] Ostensibly an economic debate about whether Britain should reverse its historic commitment to international economic liberalism, the campaign had in fact diverse origins and many strands which connected to the social policy debate and to anxieties about Britain's geo-political position which were as much military and imperial as economic. Thus, for Chamberlain as for many others, tariff reform appealed because of the possibilities it offered to strengthen imperial connections, to construct a Greater Britain as a federation of Anglo-Saxon settler states, an economic bloc of potentially unparalleled and unassailable economic and political weight. The reform campaign thus derived from the same sorts of anxieties that produced the national efficiency movement; it did, however, result in pioneering analyses of Britain's objective industrial position which added greatly to contemporary understanding of what economic decline actually meant. These were a by-product of the Tariff Commission appointed by Chamberlain to devise a 'scientific tariff' and whose secretary, **Hewins**, gave academic credibility to the project since he was a professional economist and first director of the LSE, such that 'in its early years [it was] one of the most theoretically innovative business groups that Britain has ever seen' (Marrison 1996, p. 434). Chamberlain's campaign was to fail, and quite spectacularly so (unless one counts it as a family enterprise, since free trade in peacetime was finally abandoned when his son become Chancellor in 1931). It split the Conservative Party, and contributed to three successive electoral defeats which appeared to consign

---

[26] The core secondary literature on the tariff reform campaign now runs to many hundreds of items, but see Marrison's (1996) magnum opus. For a shorter political and economic introduction, see Cain (1979); on Marshall and the manifesto issued by the 'economics professors', see Coats (1964, pp. 100–3; 1968a) and Groenewegen (1995, pp. 376–89); and for the latest historical research on tariffs and economic performance, see Capie (1994).

the party to the political wilderness. Equally important, for our purposes, was what that failure illustrates for the conduct of economic debate and the British attachment to dogmas born of earlier economic circumstance.

There were many variants of the case for tariff reform. In the more sophisticated, the argument deployed went beyond that of changing the relative prices of domestically-produced and imported goods, to the potential of protection to increase domestic competition and to promote structural change by virtue of the higher expected rates of return which would follow from the economies of scale made possible by an enlarged home market; a line of argument which has a resonance in current 'new' trade theory (Capie 1994, pp. 15–17). Yet, even amongst professional economists, public debate – as opposed to private correspondence – was rarely on this level. In general, free traders continued to rest their case on the demonstrable welfare maximisation of pursuing comparative advantage, and, more particularly, to avoid raising subtleties of analysis and developments in economic thought since Ricardo. Thus, for example, Marshall was reluctant to introduce increasing returns into the argument, lest it be used to justify protection of infant industries, a strategy which did not go unnoticed by the professional economists who backed Chamberlain's campaign (Marrison 1996, p. 26).

For the economists the debate lagged that of the politicians by a month or so, and was initiated by a series of anonymous articles on 'The fiscal policy of the Empire' in *The Times* which were published under the by-line 'by an Economist' and which, we now know, were written by Hewins. Under his leadership, and with the Webbs' patronage, economics at the LSE had become a viable 'dissenters' alternative' to Marshall's Cambridge, not least because Hewins, impressed by the role that professional economists had secured in policy formulation in Germany, had ambitions for the LSE – not Cambridge – to become the main source for the economists who would transform British economic policy (Koot 1987, pp. 160, 174–5). Such wider ambitions, combined with existing political networks and his leanings towards the German historical school, led naturally to Hewins becoming Chamberlain's chief economic adviser. Professing his ignorance of economics, and telling Hewins 'I do not pretend to be an economic expert. I once read Mill and tried to read Marshall. You must supply the economic arguments' (cited in Coats 1968a, p. 188), the stage was set for competing authorities to slug it out in the correspondence columns of *The Times*, a pattern not unknown from the nineteenth century but one about to become much more familiar and to be the basis of the public's perception of disputatious economists hungry for the ear of politicians.

In total Hewins wrote sixteen articles for *The Times* between June and September 1903, with the public response of those economists – always the majority – who supported the status quo taking some time to organise whilst, in addition, there were important developments occurring out of public view. Taking the latter first, in early July the Chancellor of the Exchequer's private secretary wrote Marshall soliciting his views on the controversy. In his first response, Marshall apologised that 'the rather long time w^h.. I have given to International Trade has not resulted in much print as yet', although 'The problems now in the air occupy a large space in that part of my Vol. II w^h.. is nearly ready for press'.[27] Fortunately, Ritchie was not about to become another casualty of the missing volume of the *Principles*, and in the next few days Marshall began work on a 'Memorandum on fiscal policy of international trade' which, after long delays, much rewriting and, finally, prompting from Lloyd George when he became Chancellor – who discovered the memorandum languishing in the Treasury files – was eventually published in 1908 as a House of Commons paper.[28]

Marshall's memorandum has been described as 'surely one of the finest policy documents ever written by an academic economist' (Hutchison 1978b, p. 114), and whilst it certainly demonstrated what was possible when the 'engine of analysis' was brought to bear upon a topic of great policy relevance, this episode also illustrates how ill-suited was Marshall to the role of high policy adviser. Thus the six week interval between the Treasury's initial request for advice and Marshall's delivery of a first draft, whilst evidence of great diligence on his part, also demonstrates a disregard for the politician's timescale (even when due allowance is made for the vagaries of the postal service and the holiday season). Consider the alacrity with which Maynard Keynes would have responded to such an opportunity. Keynes would also never have produced a first draft which, as Marshall said of his offering, was 'horribly confused & out of proportion' (Groenewegen 1996, p. 304). Five years later, when consenting to the memorandum's publication, Marshall made clear how limited was his commitment to policy advice:[29]

> I have always acted on the principle that a professional economist should as a rule abstain from controversy ... In exceptional cases he may be fitted, as Professor Fawcett was, for an active part in political conflict. But more generally he should, I think, give his attention almost exclusively to those difficulties for which time can seldom be found in the hurry & pressure of political life: he should avoid rather than seek those particular issues of the day as to which it is not easy even for a private citizen to preserve a wholly unbiased judgement.

[27] The correspondence is contained in Whitaker (1996, vol. III, pp. 31–3).

[28] It is reproduced in Keynes's (1926a, pp. 367–420) collection of Marshall's official papers produced for the RES; see also Groenewegen (1996, pp. 299–356) for additional background and a discussion of a Treasury document drawn up in 1903, which was informed by Marshall's memorandum, but which – contrary to a claim by J.C. Wood – was not written by Marshall.

[29] Whitaker (1996, vol. III, p. 195). Henry Fawcett (1833–84), Marshall's predecessor in the Cambridge chair, had combined his professional appointment with being a Liberal MP, even serving as Postmaster General from 1880 to his death.

Unfortunately, we are altogether lacking in evidence for the influence of this memorandum within the Treasury. It is known that certain senior Treasury officials (notably Hamilton and Mowatt) were ardent free-traders, resulting perhaps more in advocacy than in advice to the Chancellor. This posed no real problem for Ritchie, a leading free trader, but when he was replaced by Austen Chamberlain, elder son of Joseph, the position of the two Treasury permanent secretaries was less tenable and the subject of much press speculation (Coats 1968a, pp. 185–7). Hamilton, once described by Beatrice Webb as 'a flashy fast Treasury clerk', was known for his Liberal Party sympathies, while Mowatt's adherence to sound Gladstonian principles of public finance and trade policy was no secret. Both, argues Roseveare (1969, pp. 220–22), 'transgressed the normal limits of official impartiality'. Whether, as he further suggests (p. 223), part of Hamilton's motivation was not just to defeat the tariff reform movement but to guard against a rise in government spending on welfare programmes, this an integral element of Chamberlain's social imperialism, still remains largely unexplored. Whatever the case, in so far as the tariff reform campaign prompted the Liberal Party, long in disarray since Gladstone split the party over Irish home rule, to reorganise itself in defence of free trade such an ulterior purpose was to be lost in the repackaging of the case for, and possible financing of, social reform that occurred after the Liberals were elected in January 1906.

Trial by *Times* correspondence column

Returning to the more visible elements of the economists' participation in this debate we now examine their response to Hewins's *Times* articles. This was organised by Edgeworth and took the form of a letter to *The Times*,[30] known as the 'manifesto of the fourteen professors'. In fact, there were only six professors (with Bastable, Gonner, **Nicholson** and Smart joining Edgeworth and Marshall), one former professor turned politician (Courtney) and seven 'teachers' of economics (Bowley, Cannan, Phelps, Pigou, Sanger, Scott and Armitage Smith),[31] but the choice of language, of 'manifesto' and 'professors', captures the contemporary appeal to authority for the scientific conclusions of the economics profession. Indeed, their letter begins that the object of the exercise was to 'express our opinions on certain matters of a more or less technical character connected with the fiscal proposals which now occupy the attention of the country', and later it is made clear that the authors were motivated in this by the 'prevalence of certain erroneous

---

[30] Published on 15 August 1903, the letter is reproduced in the *EJ*, vol. 13 (September 1903), pp. 446–8, together with the full list of 14 signatories and their institutional affiliations.

[31] See p. 127 n.15 for career details of many of these.

opinions'. As Coats's (1964, pp. 100–1) researches have made clear, in the month that followed *The Times* published some thirty letters and several editorial comments on the professors' manifesto. One effect of the former was to make clear just how divided the economics profession actually was. Support for the fourteen came only from Sydney Chapman and J.H. Clapham, whilst Chamberlain's supporters were able to amass: Foxwell, Palgrave, Price, Venn and Yule (two Cambridge statisticians) and, of course, Hewins. The behaviour of Langford Price, a former Marshall student, was particularly damaging, for not only had he declined to sign the professors' manifesto but he wrote *The Times* with his reasons why, these being published immediately below the manifesto. As J.N. Keynes had confided to his diary, 'I think the issue of the Manifesto unwise and likely to injure the authority of professed economists' (cited in Groenewegen 1995, p. 383).

The subsequent trial by correspondence column which occupied *The Times* for much of the remainder of that summer, with its appeal to authority (Smith and Ricardo) and counter-authority (contemporary British, European and US economists who were pro-protection), not surprisingly horrified Marshall, reinforcing his initial reluctance to get involved but no doubt also vindicating his decision not to take up *The Times's* offer to directly reply to the Hewins articles (Coats 1968a, p. 220). The fourteen were accused of trying to stifle debate, while the editor of *The Times* derided:

> The spectacle of these fourteen dervishes emerging from their caves and chanting in solemn procession their venerable incantations . . . it is quite certain that the day has gone by when the professors of political economy can impose opinions upon the country by the weight of authority . . . A more scientific conception of their own science, which pretends to be, but never is, an experimental science, would save professors from the painful discovery that they convince nobody who stands in need of conviction.   (cited in Coats 1964, p. 101)

Such was the opprobrium that the fourteen attracted that, according to such partisan (pro-protection) authority as L.S. Amery, 'in subsequent controversy a reference to the fourteen professors only evoked hilarity' (cited in Coats 1968a, p. 22). This episode was a rite of passage for the economists and a grave blow to Marshall's mission, although strangely it does not feature in Maloney's (1985) assessment of the progress made towards professionalisation by 1914. Maloney does, however, highlight Pigou's participation in the debate. *The riddle of the tariff* (1903) 'was a harbinger of Pigou's life-long readiness to go into battle over policy questions', and 'represent[ed] a return to the traditional norm, a reassertion that the economist was, and should be, involved in the issues of the day' (pp. 226–7). Once more, therefore, for the future of economics it was Pigou and not Marshall's inheritance which endured.

Twelve propositions of the British economic policy debate

From this episode, and from the subsequent course of the tariff reform campaign, we can draw certain broader conclusions about economists' participation in public debate and of the treatment of economic ideas by politicians and public. These are presented in the form of twelve propositions, with further support for each offered in later chapters where the policy episodes of the interwar and postwar periods are dissected.

1. Economic policy debates are recurrent and, as Balfour remarked, 'Popular disputations insist on labels and likes its labels old' (cited in Coats 1968a, p. 183).
2. Debates frequently sustain a basic contradiction which act not to cut short but to prolong controversy; for example, how could a tariff designed to protect industry also act as a major revenue earner?
3. As Cain (1979, p. 41) notes, 'some defenders of the existing system, including learned ones, did show an alarming propensity to assume that free trade was a kind of natural law to question which implied either crassness or blasphemy,' a position we will find repeated with respect to the two additional core defences of the minimalist laissez-faire: the gold standard and the balanced budget rule.
4. The vulnerability of an argument to the business cycle, with confusion and conflation of trend and cyclical behaviours. Thus the initiation of Chamberlain's campaign owed much to the business cycle downturn following the end of the Boer War, whilst its eventual rejection coincided with the subsequent sharp upturn later that decade.
5. The British economic policy debate is prone to pseudo syllogisms, in this case: the economies of Germany and the US were growing more rapidly than that of Britain; Germany and the US had tariffs and Britain a commitment to free trade; therefore, protection in Britain would allow growth to equal that of these competitors.
6. The potential of some proposals to widen (tariff protection, floating exchange rates and deficit finance) and others to narrow (free trade, the gold standard and budgetary orthodoxy) the policy space, less because of the policy instruments thereby made available or denied, and more in terms of the opportunities for politicians to lay claim to favourable economic developments and to deny responsibility for adverse trends.
7. The capacity of those supporting a policy proposal to nonetheless have a deleterious effect on its political prospects, as in the protectionist sentiments of some businessmen being dismissed as mere self-interest and tariffs being widely viewed within the working class as a device by which the rich might avoid income redistribution (Cain 1979, p. 59), not

to mention a concealed real wage cut.

8. Debates which require, as did tariff reform, the interpretation of quantitative information are incapable of majority resolution and generate behaviours amongst the public which demonstrate the popular appeal of self-evident, self-validating premises when data appears to invalidate common sense. Thus, for example, in 1903 there was an exchange reported in *The Times* between Joseph Chamberlain, who claimed that statistics showing an increase in manufactured imports demonstrated Britain's competitive weakness, and Giffen who denied such an inference from data subject to margins of error of approximately 70 per cent, all of which resulted in one correspondent protesting at the unwelcome complications introduced by the statistician (Coats 1968a, p. 207).

9. Hutchison (1992, p. 71) observes a similarity between the 1903 debate and that preceding the repeal of the Corn Laws in 1846, for in both the economists 'based their arguments on largely non-quantified predictive judgements which were highly imprecise, not simply quantitatively, but with regard to the policy objectives aimed at.' But, in the former debate the claims made for the authority of the 'laws' of political economy were very much more robust than the situation prevailing by 1903 when 'the classical "laws" had been much reduced (notably by Alfred Marshall) to rather imprecise and highly conditional statements of "tendencies"'.

10. In British elite culture *The Times* correspondence column occupies a pivotal position, but notwithstanding its attractions as a national stage it is an unsuitable medium for conveying complex ideas, economic or otherwise. The British attachment to fair play allows all to have their say and indiscriminately so; it, like the House of Commons debating chamber, is best avoided by all but the most robust and where the cause requires little subtlety.

11. There have been few shifts in policy regime which have not had the support of senior Treasury officials.

12. If professional economists agree, they have no influence for they are not relevant; if they disagree, some have temporary influence but at the expense of the profession's standing with the public.

In general, economic historians now doubt that free trade made much difference to the performance of the nineteenth-century economy or that tariff reform offered an economically appropriate solution to relative economic decline at the beginning of the twentieth century. Some revision of this latter assessment has recently been attempted by Marrison (1996), but it remains the case that, as Cain (1979, p. 35) has concluded, 'the political successes and failures of tariff reform before 1914 often had very little to do with any objective assessment of Britain's needs as a great industrial power.'

Tariff reform was rejected decisively by the electorate on three occasions. The newly enfranchised working-class were not persuaded by Chamberlain's call for imperial economic unity and national social reform, and were mindful that a major part of the Conservative Party remained wedded to free trade whilst the party leader occupied an uncomfortable middle ground for the sake of party unity. But the tariff reform campaign did allow the Liberal Party to recover from the home rule debacle; in reunifying to defend free trade it then launched itself into an intensive phase of reform which, by the eve of the First World War, had so challenged the prevailing laissez-faire philosophy of government that Britain had the second widest coverage of social welfare programmes in Europe (Middleton 1996, p. 225).

4.6 CONCLUSIONS

To what extent, therefore, can we judge Marshall as having been successful in his mission for the professionalisation of British economics? And to what extent had the permeationist strategy resulted in a scientific economics becoming an integral element in the rational deliberateness that many see as the zeitgeist of late-Victorian and Edwardian Britain (Winch 1990b, p. 53)? Some criteria for assessment are naturally provided by the three core elements of the mission: that an economist be someone trained in a body of theory which was rigorous and inaccessible to the uninitiated; that they be impartial, aloof from party politics; and that they have a privileged position and voice in policy-making. Our account of the prewar period offers a number of correctives to the heroic account of the age of Marshall.

First, by temperament Marshall was most unsuited for the mission he set himself, so much so that towards the end of his life he even became disillusioned with a core element of the mission itself: the potential of economic theory to guide policy.[32] Although he exercised a greater influence in his day than any other economist, Coats (1964, p. 96) amongst many has suggested that, by being 'unduly deferential to the great figures of the past, extremely slow to publish his own ideas, and very careful not to exaggerate the novel features of his own writings or those of his contemporaries' he 'may have unintentionally inhibited the progress of theoretical speculation'. Equally, he was decidedly not – in modern parlance – a policy entrepreneur. The reticence was part temperament, but also integral to the ethical dynamic that underlay his economics. Maloney (1985, p. 36) well captures the subtlety of the impediment with his comment that Marshall looked always to

---

[32] This is particularly the case with *Industry and trade* (1919); cf. *Economics of industry* (1879), in which economic 'Laws' feature prominently (O'Brien 1981a, p. 40).

the 'complexity of injustice' and to 'the intellectual subtlety which must be gained before prescribing cures for it and the difficulty of choosing between alternative (and perhaps superficially similar) measures'.

As a policy entrepreneur Marshall's shortcomings were, at least initially, more than counterbalanced by Pigou. Unfortunately, we still have no biography in prospect of this important figure in British economics. But it is clear from what is available that before his experiences during the First World War initiated the process which resulted in him becoming a recluse,[33] Pigou had many of the personal qualities, and all of the academic attributes, that were necessary to gain the ear of policy-makers. Moreover, much more than Marshall, Pigou had a 'brilliant lecturing style' and spoke and wrote on the central policy issues of the day: on tariff reform, unemployment, industrial fluctuations but not international monetary organisation. Whilst deferring to his former teacher, Pigou never practised what the master taught: that the *Principles* had fixed the subject; nor did he exhibit, with the exception of the latter,[34] that 'complacent self-assurance, insularity and deference to authority' which Coats (1980, p. 597) takes as characteristic of Edwardian economics. But, as Johnson (1960, p. 152) observed, 'his intellectual bent, and the chronological drift of his work (in method, at least), was towards a mathematical formalism whose justification is easier to make out in terms of light than of fruit'. The struggle between economics as intellectual puzzle and economics in the service of mankind were thus well set before the First World War. Whilst agreeing with Stigler's (1990, p. 12) broad judgement, that 'One should reckon amongst a scholar's achievements not only what he wrought but also what he prevented', the importance we here ascribe to Pigou would not support his specific conclusion 'that Marshall by his towering prestige delayed the coming of the age of abstract formalism of the Lausanne tradition by at least a generation, and with the aid of his premier student, Keynes, by possibly two generations.'

The emphasis here given to Pigou should also serve as a corrective to the rather personal association given by most historians of economic thought between the professionalisation of economics and Marshall's mission. One consequence of this has been that certain very prominent prewar economists have been almost lost from view. For example, we have the case of Nicholson, a Marshall pupil, one of the earliest to gain a Cambridge doctorate in economics and, elected before his thirtieth birthday, professor of

---

[33] As a conscientious objector he served as a volunteer at the front during university vacations with a Society of Friends ambulance unit (Johnson 1960, p. 57); see also Collard (1981b, p. 108) who reports the judgement of C.R. Fay, his life-long friend and colleague: 'World War I was a shock to him, and he was never the same afterwards'.

[34] It is noteworthy that the extended apologies about becoming involved in controversy which preface successive editions of *The economics of welfare* (1920) do not feature in *Wealth and welfare* (1912).

political economy at Edinburgh from 1880 to 1925. Although Maloney (1985, pp. 75–90) and Koot (1987, pp. 155–9) have done something to rescue him from unwarranted obscurity, it is significant that Nicholson did not figure in the major accounts of Hutchison (1953) or Winch (1969) and that his entry in the New Palgrave dictionary is minute. Yet Nicholson was a prominent figure in British economics, south as well as north of the border, for very nearly half a century. His three volume *Principles of political economy* (1893–1901) was a popular alternative to Marshall's *Principles* amongst undergraduates, and he gained further authority when he published an abridged and highly accessible edition for teaching purposes (1903). Nicholson's *Principles* sought a reconciliation of the mathematical, historical and statistical approaches to economics, with the result that by the 1890s he was firmly established as offering an alternative to Marshall's analytical vision of economic science: one which was historically much richer and gave greater emphasis to the continuity of the classical tradition. In addition, he made important contributions to human capital theory; was frequently published in the *EJ*, including an exchange with Edgeworth in 1894 on utility theory in which the latter did not prevail; indeed was, in publishing terms, one of the most productive economists of the day (Table 4.2); was as active in the tariff reform campaign as Pigou, combining support for the imperial project with a defence of free trade; and was to feature prominently during the First World War and after in his warnings about war finance, loose expenditure controls and the perils of long-run deficit-financing.

Scholarly interest in the professionalisation of British economics, hitherto largely confined to Birmingham, Cambridge, the LSE and Oxford, thus needs to travel north and to become genuinely British in scope.[35] Nicholson has a further significance as one of the few economists who, in furtherance of the mission for professionalisation, targeted financial journalists as of great importance if the quality of public debate was ever to be raised and, perhaps a vain hope, if economics was to be cleansed of much unnecessary political conflict.[36] But Nicholson was also thoroughly typical of this generation. He, like Marshall, Edgeworth and other leading figures such as Foxwell and Wicksteed 'may have been the first generation to professionalise themselves in terms of theory', but as Maloney (1985, pp. 194–5) observes, 'they were also in another sense the last pre-professional generation. None of them was an economist to begin with; but their own influence on the subject made them the last generation who could come to

---

[35] Even Kadish and Tribe (1993a) exclude Scotland, although they do examine the northern English universities and include one chapter on Ireland, while Wales remains unexplored.

[36] In his address to the BEA annual meeting of 1894, reproduced in Nicholson (1896, ch. VIII) and discussed briefly in Maloney (1985, pp. 75–6).

economics relatively late without being at a grave and perhaps life-long professional disadvantage.'

In terms of the first criterion stemming from Marshall's mission, that of the exclusion of the amateur through a body of specialist theory, British economics had by the First World War become dominated by academics, so much so that, were it not for the infelicity of the term, Coats (1980, p. 589) would label the process not professionalisation but academicisation. The leaders in economic science were now almost wholly academics. Less success, however, is evident in terms of the other two criteria: non-partisanship and privileges in policy-making. The tariff reform campaign well-illustrates the inability of the new profession to derive the same policy conclusions when the engine of analysis was applied to one of the most political issues of the day. Similarly, whilst the limited role of government in the economic sphere in turn constrained the ambitions for policy influence that many economists harboured, it is the case that at no time between 1890 and 1914 did any British economist command even a fraction of the authority with politicians enjoyed earlier in the century by James Pennington (1777–1862) or Walter Bagehot (1826–77).

As the First World War approached government was making increasing use of experts of all sorts (MacLeod 1988a), but as we saw in chapter 3 this was less so in economic policy until the war and, more particularly, the peacetime problems it generated provided a demand, limited to begin with, for economic expertise which could not be provided by traditional policy networks. That there was still a very long way to travel before Marshall's mission was realised in terms of policy influence is nowhere given clearer testimony than in the royal commission on the poor law's deliberations and report which make frequent reference to Aristotle as appropriate intellectual authority but ignored Marshall and Pigou (Harris 1990b, p. 395). Thirty years later, it is difficult to conceive of a comparable enquiry which would not have incorporated Keynes, albeit very probably negatively. We conclude, therefore, that the influence of professional economists on policy outcomes was largely indirect before 1914 and that they played an even smaller role in policy formulation. Where there was a coalescence between popular progressive opinion and the economists, as for example was the case with the growing acceptance of the case for progressive taxation, the latter could sway the debate by providing useful additional 'authority' for those seeking to justify change. But, in so far as Marshall's economics remained stronger at analysis than in prescription, there were limits to what was attainable.

5. Five economists and six opinions: economics comes of age between the wars

> Perhaps the chief task of economists at this hour is to distinguish afresh the *Agenda* of government from the *Non-Agenda*; and the companion task of politics is to devise forms of government within a democracy which shall be capable of accomplishing the *Agenda*.   (Keynes 1926b, p. 288)

5.1 INTRODUCTION

Before the First World War the general buoyancy of the British economy, combined with the laissez-faire stance of governments and the small scale of the public sector, provided no case for macroeconomic intervention and little macroeconomic impact from such economic activities as there were. Admittedly, changes in the nature of political competition had produced a social reform agenda which would soon generate significant expenditure commitments, while developments in economic thought were contributing towards governments taking a less passive position on issues such as the trade cycle. This was the background against which Marshall's mission for the professionalisation of economics was set, and, as we saw, in general the adjustments to economic policy sought by the majority of the new profession were marginal and posed no substantive challenge to laissez-faire.

The First World War shattered this equilibrium in economics and politics. Its costs were of such immense magnitude, and had such enduring implications for economic performance and policy thereafter, as to wholly vindicate the classical economists' purely negative conception of war. The national debt rose elevenfold and, even with government expenditure reined back in the immediate aftermath of the conflict, there was still a very substantial displacement effect on the public finances. Thus the expenditure and tax ratios were by the early 1920s over double those of 1913 and were to rise on trend throughout the interwar period under pressure from unemployment, demands for further welfare spending and, eventually, preparations for the next war. The problem of funding and managing this enlarged national debt dominated interwar monetary policy, and with the public sector now exercising significant demand leverage, and with the standard rate of income tax over four times higher than prewar, government thus had a macro- and microeconomic impact whether desired or not.

The dislocation to the real economy was equally serious, although its full long-term significance took longer to appreciate. As we now know, long-run relative economic decline has not proceeded uniformly with respect to time or competitor countries, and this war was significant for opening up the productivity gap with the US. For contemporaries, the preoccupation was not with growth as such but with a complex of issues:

- the transformation of the balance of payments, both on current and capital account;
- the need for a structural readjustment of British industry entailing the rationalisation of the staple sectors to restore competitiveness and the transfer of resources to new sectors with growth and export potential; and
- the emergence of mass unemployment.

Initially, it was possible for policy-makers to reassure themselves that the travails of the British economy lay in the dislocation of the war: to the collapse of world trade and international monetary institutions; to the uncertainties created by war debts and reparations; and to the disorder created by governments not quickly imposing sound financial policies and freeing their domestic markets from the physical controls built up during the war. All of this suggested a return to the old certainties of laissez-faire at home and, in external economic policies, free trade and the gold standard which, by promoting the recovery of the world economy, would stimulate British exports, encourage structural change and thus resolve the unemployment problem. The orthodoxy of this strategy, although clearly in accord with the well-articulated interests of the City of London, derived from a broadly based opinion that there be a return to normalcy, the recreation of the pre-1914 economic order. This extended less to the social order where the political contest, now operating with a full electorate and with powerful expectations of a Land fit for Heroes, produced a social welfare programme which, if it had been implemented in full, would have profoundly shifted the peacetime balance between government and market.

The conflict between economic and social policy that resulted dominated the interwar period. At stake was whether British governments, confronted by an unstable and unpredictable economy and operating within a political contest now transformed by the rise of labour and the advent of democracy, could sustain laissez-faire in the economic sphere. In economic terms, few initially perceived that the liberal world order might not be capable of reconstruction and that the costs of war would not be speedily discharged. Maynard Keynes was a rare exception in this respect, and it is appropriate to introduce him here because what launched him onto a world stage was his devastating critique of the Versailles peace treaty and its underlying economic assumptions. Hitherto largely unknown outside of Cambridge, the Bloomsbury group and latterly the Treasury, Keynes's *The economic consequences of the peace* (1919) established his credentials, if not as an economist in the most technical of senses, than as a political economist with the most persuasive of pens and an unfailing eye for the main issue.

Hereafter, and in sharp contrast to Marshall and his private vision of the Organon, leading academic economists were to have a much higher profile in public debate and to be far less reticent about proffering advice to policy-makers, unsolicited as well as sought. Few went public with the alacrity and frequency which Keynes exhibited, while many fretted that he compromised the dignity and long-run influence of the newly established profession (for example, Pigou 1933, p. v). However, as the initial assessment of the economic situation was shown to be hopelessly optimistic, and as the British economy was subjected to unprecedented exogenous shocks, particularly during the world depression (1929–33), politicians, Treasury officials and even central bankers eventually incorporated economists into the policy process on a routine basis. In this chapter we detail how academic economics came of age; how, in Keynes's description of his own influence in the 1920s, 'the croakings of a Cassandra who could never influence the course of events in time' (1931, p. xvii) were transformed into an enlarged peacetime role for the state in economic and social affairs which, although as yet not 'Keynesian' in any meaningful sense, was massively different from that prevailing before the First World War.

This chapter is organised as follows. We begin with that element of the Organon, Marshall's injunction that controversy be avoided, which provides the sharpest divide between prewar and interwar British economics. We then examine in section 3 the further progress towards professionalisation in economics made between the wars and include an account of the methodological debate initiated by Robbins's *An essay on the nature and significance of economic science* (1932) (hereafter, *Essay*). This is familiar to most economists as the source of a standard means-ends definition of the subject, namely 'Economics [a]s the science which studies human behaviour as a relationship between ends and scarce means which have alternative uses' (p. 16), but it has a further significance as it greatly influenced economists' views about the nature of their discipline which, in turn, affected the perception of professional responsibilities towards economic policy: all core elements of the Organon. We then survey very briefly in section 4 the broader economic policy debate, and the role of economists therein, paying close attention to their views on the two central economic issues of the day, the adjustment crisis facing British industry and mass unemployment. Our case study follows in section 5, and concerns the return to the gold standard in 1925 and subsequent developments. This provides important 'insider' detail on the interactions between economists and policy-makers, and we use this case study to substantiate our earlier claim that, in terms of demonstrating their utility to policy-makers, economists had made the breakthrough sometime before Keynes's *General theory*. Some preliminary conclusions are then drawn in section 6.

5.2 ECONOMICS AND CONTROVERSY

The cost-benefits of controversy

Looking back on the interwar period, and contemplating the future role that economists might play in the managed-mixed economy that would probably emerge from the Second World War, Evan Durbin (1943, p. 257 n. 1), economist and leading exponent of British social democracy, lamented that:

> Economists became discredited in the early thirties through indulging in disputes that became unduly acrimonious. We deprived ourselves, quite unnecessarily, of all influence. And yet the propositions to which all, or very nearly all, economists could have been persuaded to subscribe were, or very soon became, far more important than the scholastic details over which we [sic] quarreled bitterly and, worse still, loudly. Pursuing with passion the by-ways of thought, moved by academic austerity and human vanity, we forgot to state with authority the simpler conclusions that were not in dispute between us. Yet this common doctrine would have brought a flood of light to the harassed politician and public servant. This tragedy of wasted knowledge will be repeated after the war if economists do not give their best energy to stating and enlarging the field of their agreement. The subject is greater than the professor of it.

These observations capture not just the economists' self-assessment of their interwar influence,[1] but the public reputation of the profession, as represented in our chapter title which draws upon the contemporary aphorism on disputatious economists,[2] and Keynes in particular as

---

[1]   See also, and from a very different political standpoint, Hutt (1936).

[2]   Thus the established prewar pattern of rival groups of economists slugging it out in the correspondence columns of *The Times* was repeated on a number of occasions between the wars. See, in particular, the call for reflation made by Macgregor, Pigou, Keynes, Layton, Salter and Stamp (17 October 1932) and the LSE reply by Gregory, Hayek, Plant and Robbins (19 October) which Robbins latterly came to judge as gravely mistaken. Shortly afterwards, in the run-up to the 1933 budget, there occurred a sustained attempt by an even larger proto-Keynesian group to persuade official opinion of the case for reflation (*The Times*, 10 March 1933). Keynes

congenitally unable to limit himself to one opinion. For the latter, flexibility in policy advice was an obvious requirement in a fast-changing world; for many contemporaries, however, and particularly those yearning for the certainties and stability of the prewar era, consistency and consensus were valued above all. For Keynes there were 'few passages in the history of controversy more valuable ... than that which took place amongst economists in the ten years ... before the war.'[3] Others were less certain about this challenge to the Organon.

Keynes and the *General theory*

As is well-known, in writing the *General theory*, Keynes consciously sought a revolution in economic theory and appeared to display scant regard for the reputations and sensitivities of the chosen representatives of neo-classical thought who were to be discarded in the process. As he wrote Harrod in response to comments received on draft chapters: 'I *want*, so to speak, to raise a dust; because it is only out of the controversy that will arise that what I am saying will get understood.' But there was purpose to the barb, a considered rhetorical intent:[4]

> I expect a great deal of what I write to be water off a duck's back. I am certain that it will be . . . unless I am sufficiently strong in my criticism to force the classicals to make rejoinders. . . . If I had left out all the parts you object to about the classical school, you would simply have told me that you were largely in sympathy and liked it. But my attack on the classical school has brought to a head the fact that I have only half shifted you away from it. Your preoccupation with the old beliefs – and much more so in the case of most other people – would prevent you from seeing the half of what I am saying unless I moved to the attack.

An early victim was Dennis Robertson whose friendship and professional collaboration with Keynes did not survive the transition to the *General theory*. As the first British economist to emphasise the role of real factors in business cycles, and as an early exponent of coordinated fiscal and monetary expansion to remedy cyclical unemployment, in policy terms there was little of real substance that separated them, at least initially. But, as the trek to the *General theory* gathered pace, there emerged very important theoretical differences which had also policy implications. With few exceptions and

---

was not a signatory – amongst whom were G.C. Allen, Phelps Brown, Gaitskell, Guillebaud, Hall, Harrod, Macgregor, Meade, the Robinsons, Sargent Florence and Wootton – but the letter was a softening-up exercise for 'The means to prosperity' (1933). Finally the efforts of British economists to influence opinion even extended abroad, as in the letter, signed by leading Oxford economists, pressing the case for public works on Roosevelt in 1933 (see Winch 1969, p. 221).

[3] Keynes to Durbin, 24 October 1942 (cited in Howson and Winch 1977, p. 164).

[4] Keynes to Harrod, 27 August 1935 (in JMK, Vol. XIII, p. 548).

until very recently,[5] the story of the Keynes-Robertson split, which of course caused a fissure at the heart of Cambridge economics and led Robertson to depart temporarily for London, has been largely told from the point of view of the immediate victor. Accordingly, Keynes's vision of the potentiality of fiscal policy to secure full employment triumphed over Robertson's very pertinent reservations about its use in practice and his theoretical insights about the potential trade-offs between full employment and sustained economic growth. But there is another side to the estrangement between these erstwhile colleagues which was of more immediate significance: that of Robertson's abhorrence of Keynes's characterisation of the postulates of classical theory and of the associated attack, through a caricature of Pigou's *Theory of unemployment* (1933), on Marshall.

In Robertson (1936; 1938) and Pigou's (1936) reactions to the *General theory* we observe that Keynes had touched some very raw nerves indeed about authority amongst the older generation. Respect for past masters and the evolutionary, as against revolutionary, character of progress in economic science were a creed amongst the prewar Cambridge faculty, one undiminished by Marshall's passing.[6] That there was a inverse relationship between age and enthusiasm for the new economics has long been known. **Arthur Brown** (1987, p. 18), at that time an Oxford undergraduate, recollects that 4 February 1936 'is the only time I have knowingly gone out to buy a book on the day of publication', while Galbraith (b. 1908), then an assistant professor at the other Cambridge (Harvard), recounts the excitement with which the text was received, especially in Harvard where there was 'a large community of young economists, most of them held there by the shortage of jobs that Keynes sought to cure.' This has a particular resonance since Harvard was also the home for Edward Chamberlin (1933) who shares with Joan Robinson (1933), located in the original Cambridge, the credit for a concurrent revolution in microeconomics, that of the theory of imperfect competition. Galbraith (1975a, pp. 135, 138–9) further observes, and here captures much of the essence of the – in Blaug's (1992a, p. 28) words – '*Gestalt* switch' which occurs in the younger generation when no longer able to accept the anomalies of the theoretical status quo:

> Those who objected to Keynes were also invariably handicapped by the fact that they hadn't (and couldn't) read the book. It was like attacking the original Kama Sutra for obscenity without being able to read Sanskrit.

5   Robertson retains a small but credible following amongst historians of economic thought (for example, Anyadike-Danes 1985 and Presley 1992). That the Keynes-Robertson split continues to divide opinion is illustrated by the difference in length and tone of the recent accounts offered by Skidelsky (1992, pp. 589–93) and Moggridge (1992, p. 567).

6   So much so that Henderson (1936) even went so far as to return to Cambridge to deliver his critique in person before the faculty's Marshall Society.

Samuelson (b. 1915), another early convert to the new economics, and also at that time at Harvard, considered age to be quite crucial in explaining subsequent developments (1946, p. 187):

> I have always considered it a priceless advantage to have been born as an economist prior to 1936 and to have received a thorough grounding in classical economics. . . .
> To have been born an economist before 1936 was a boon – yes. But not to have been born too long before.
> . . .
> The *General Theory* caught most economists under the age of 35 with the unexpected virulence of a disease first attacking and decimating an isolated tribe of south sea islanders. Economists beyond fifty turned out to be quite immune to the ailment. With time, most economists in-between began to run the fever, often without knowing or admitting their condition.

To modern eyes much of the immediate debate surrounding the publication of the *General theory* appears overly personalised. However, it illustrates much about Cambridge economics and about the sociology of professional debate, traits which have endured. We will, for example, see important similarities when we come to examine the Cambridge capital controversies of the 1960s (pp. 227–8). Kaldor, a participant in this later Cambridge controversy, and a colleague of Robertson during his sojourn at the LSE, provides a unique insight into what so distressed him:[7]

> I think the explanation of this passion is that he thought it was the duty of economists to resist easy solutions, to tell politicians that they are the victim of slogans and that they too easily believe in 'cures'. Here comes Keynes – a great economist with a great reputation – putting forward the simple idea that all you have to do is to spend more and lower the rate of interest and firms will invest more. So if the government spends more everything will be in order, and Robertson found this . . . immoral because it is much more complicated than that.

Here once more we have the Marshallian vision of the professional responsibility of the economist clashing with a quite different conception of what economists had to provide for politicians for economics to take its rightful place in policy: adopt the politician's timescale and apply Occam's razor to the economics. The war and the depression of the 1920s, the latter much more important in Britain than the mass unemployment generated by the 'great depression' in other western countries, radically changed the policy environment and the demand schedule for economic policy advice. But what we see here is no simple generational shift. After all Robertson was actually Keynes's student, not Marshall's.

---

[7] Here commenting on Anyadike-Danes (1985) and reproduced in Harcourt (1985, p. 131).

In reflecting on 'Whether Keynes could have achieved a radical rethinking of economics without wounding', Austin Robinson (1968, p. 96) concluded 'that it was a sad but necessary cost of the revolution of thought.' As an unofficial 'economist watcher'[8] Robinson is an unrivalled authority: far from a revolutionary by temperament, indeed always more interested in applying theory than developing theory for its own sake (a 'tool-user' not 'tool-maker'),[9] his conclusion about Keynes and the *General theory* remains the dominant British view. But it is very much a Cambridge (England) view. Moreover, as we shall see, there are important postwar voices of dissent about the necessity for a Keynesian revolution in theory, either as an appropriate policy response to the economic problems of the interwar period), or in light of the inherent stabilising properties of market economies once free of government intervention, a reassertion of the invisible hand which developed as part of the subsequent reaction against Keynesianism.

Keynes, the *General theory* and professionalisation of British economics

The presumption that Keynes was right because he captured professional economists pervades the literature on the interwar period. What have been largely neglected, however, are the implications of this verdict for the professionalisation of economics, and we here complete our discussion of the element of controversy in the Organon by considering Pigou's initial protest against the *General theory* and the conflict that emerged between Cambridge and the LSE. Pigou's outrage at the *General theory*, first publicly expressed in his *Economica* review (1936), is noteworthy not least for its rich store of apposite quotes - as in 'How is it that an author ... whose vividness of phrase has made him a valued contributor to the *Daily Mail*, when he comes to the subject to which he has devoted most attention, is barely intelligible to many ... of his own professional colleagues' (p. 119).

Part of Pigou's irritation with Keynes was that he had tried to refute the *General theory* before it had been published, but his theoretical arguments had simply been ignored. That he was horrified by Keynes's caricature of all who disagreed with him as 'classical' economists, and that he felt slighted personally, is all well-known. Equally, the issues of theoretical substance that really divided them have received much attention, while those who stress the eventual triumph of Keynesianism have also emphasised Pigou's (1950) subsequent and very public change of heart about the *General theory*. What, however, have received less adequate treatment are Pigou's concerns about the rhetorical devices employed by Keynes. This was not just about

---

8 The phrase comes from Coats's (1996) biographical essay.
9 See Cairncross's (1993a) biography of Robinson and the latter's biographical essays and essays on economists (1947; 1990a; b; 1992).

preserving the reputation of Marshall, the master, although that clearly was psychologically important for Pigou; rather, the *Economica* review displays incomprehension that Keynes was pioneering, in modern parlance, a very different type of 'conversation' between economists. Pigou (1936, p. 115) admits as much early on: 'It is not by this manner of writing that his desire to convince his fellow economists ... is best promoted.' Nor was he alone; another erstwhile colleague, Henderson, writing to Harrod on the day he publicly delivered his critique of the *General theory* before Keynes and the assembled ranks of Cambridge economics, admitted that:

> I regard Maynard's book, as I say in my paper, as a farrago of confused sophistication, and I find intensely exasperating the tacit assumption that prevails in certain circles that those who do not accept its general doctrine are to be regarded as intellectually inferior beings.   (cited in Skidelsky 1992, p. 587)

The rise of what McCloskey (1994, p. 117) calls a 'scientistic' style was already well-advanced in economics by the 1920s, with the *EJ* as other economic journals having a increasing proportion of articles written with a technical vocabulary which 'only people socialised within the community of economics can understand'. Keynes was part of this trend, indeed in the vanguard. He was also, as McCloskey (1994, p. 125) reminds us, 'the best writer of English that economics has seen', such that he 'hypnotized three generations of economists and politicians with his graceful fluency in English.' Moreover, and in light of Galbraith's earlier comments about the readability of the *General theory*, we here hypothesise that Keynes understood the shift in the social psychology of the economics community: that had the book been too readily comprehensible, too deferential to established authority, it would have been ignored for it would have offered scant intellectual challenge and insufficient leverage in the generational conflict. In short, we imply that the incentive structure was changing in economics: novelty and technical virtuosity were becoming more highly valued; deference to established authority less so.

There is a further sense in which Robertson, Pigou, Henderson and others of that generation did not understand the way in which economic discourse was being transformed as Keynes, and those we would later label Keynesians, developed forms of communication and networks more suited to the faster pace of theoretical developments and the urgency of policy problems. Foremost here was the, perhaps, unprecedented 'market testing' to which drafts of the *General theory* were subjected by the 'Circus' of younger Cambridge economists led by Richard Kahn, whose 1931 *EJ* paper on the multiplier was an important building block for the emerging new economics. Formed initially to meet weekly to discuss the *Treatise on money* (1930a), the Circus combined many of the rising stars in British economics

(Austin and Joan Robinson, Meade, Shove, Sraffa) as well as an important US-Canadian presence (with graduate students, Tarshis, Plumptre and Gifford); in Kahn it had a facilitator supremely gifted in asking the right questions and reporting back to Keynes possible avenues for theoretical re-evaluation. But most of all, and quite unprecedented in a Cambridge economics still very much dominated by the ghostly presence (manifest in Pigou and Robertson) of Marshall, the circus had permission to dissect, criticise – Schumpeterian creative-destruction at its best. From surviving accounts of its activities (Kahn 1984), and of the way in which Keynes responded, we see in effect a process of creative tension between the young (all, with the exception of Shove, born between 1897–1911) and established authority entering into economics as it had into the natural sciences. The Circus was, in effect, a natural extension of Keynes's long-running Monday night Political Economy Club which brought together promising undergraduate economists, postgraduates and the younger faculty, itself a linear development from the Apostles of his undergraduate days.[10]

To this network, which greatly influenced the eventual analytical tools of the *General theory*, we should add the at times almost daily exchange of written notes with Harrod in Oxford;[11] and even a long-running correspondence with Hawtrey, although this should not be taken as implying that Keynes's ideas were widely and speedily assimilated within the Treasury as Hawtrey remained an isolated figure who delighted in 'huge nit-picking memoranda.'[12] Nonetheless, together with Keynes's activities in the CEI, membership of which included two leading Treasury officials, here was an important channel of communication about the *General theory* which went directly to the heart if not of government, then at least to that part which prided itself on its intellectual capacities (Howson and Winch 1977).

Economic research was coming of age in a number of ways. The presence of north Americans, both graduate students and visiting academics, was becoming a routine part of life at Cambridge and the LSE. We can date what Baumol (1995, p. 187) has characterised as the mid-Atlantic character of British economics – 'a home halfway, culturally, between the European and North American continents' – from the late 1920s. The younger generation, for the first time no longer having to serve a long apprenticeship of observing and deferring to established authority, were important also in establishing this mid-Atlantic character. This had its fullest expression in a new journal, the *Review of Economic Studies* (*REStud*), which was launched in 1933 by a small group of LSE graduate students, a distinct postgraduate

[10]	Robinson (1947, pp. 26–9) and Cairncross (1992, p. 7).
[11]	These are contained in JMK XIII-XIV (1973).
[12]	Skidelsky (1992, p. 586). Hawtrey's critique (PRO T208/195) was circulated within the Treasury and eventually published as chapter VII of his *Capital and employment* (1937).

community itself being a significant new development in professionalisation. Its first issue contained papers by its three managing editors (Abba Lerner, at that point at the LSE), Paul Sweezy (Harvard) and Ursula Webb (soon to be Hicks, Oxford and the LSE) along with Joan Robinson, George Shackle, L.M. Fraser, W.S. Hopkins (Stanford), Kahn and John Hicks. With one eventual Nobel prize winner, Britain's most distinguished woman economist and two leading lights in postwar US economics, few journals can rival such a cast list in their launch issue. Equally, the new journal's constitution requires comment: this was an outlet for the young (Readers and Professors were barred until the 1950s) – indeed within Cambridge it was known as the 'children's magazine' – and at least one member of the editorial board must be resident in the US (Coats 1991b, pp. 95–6). Moreover, relative to the *EJ*, *Economica*, or indeed *The Manchester School* and *Oxford Economic Papers*, the *Review of Economic Studies* positively bristled with diagrams, advanced mathematics, technical language and all the other scholarly apparatus that we associate with the scientistic style. It was also, of course, launched in the same year as *Econometrica*, the first volume of which was dominated by US authors (with Bowley the only British presence).

It's all in Marshall

The belief that 'the work of economic analysis had been practically completed ... by Marshall, and that only the application of that analysis to practical problems remained to be done'; the creed that 'it's all in Marshall, if you'll only take the trouble to dig it out' (Wright 1927, p. 504) did not survive the 1920s for the younger generation. The catalyst was Sraffa, who had been enticed to Cambridge by Keynes, and, according to Austin Robinson (1992, p. 210), whose 'lectures set us free to rethink even the basics of our subject.' As an Italian émigré Sraffa had no prior commitment to Marshall or, indeed, to British academic authority. Moreover, as his later career attests in Cambridge one can acquire deep and enduring influence by publishing little: two *EJ* papers on increasing returns (1926 and 1930), a devastating *EJ* review of Hayek's *Prices and production* and then nothing theoretical until a 1960 book, unorthodox in the extreme but the springboard for a vibrant neo-Ricardian revival which continues today. For Blaug (1985, p. 238), Sraffa's repute is 'surely ... one of the most unpredictable success stories in the entire history of ideas'; for Cambridge economics the assault on neo-classical value theory begun in the 1926 *EJ* paper produced short- and longer-term returns: first for the theory of imperfect competition, with early contributions from Kahn and Joan Robinson; much later in reigniting the fires that were to become the Cambridge capital controversy.

Meantime, as Robinson (1977, p. 29) recollects, Sraffa 'gave Cambridge economics its second wind', not by being a major provider of new ideas but as a critic, as 'an eliminator of mistakes and red-herrings and as a puncturer of other people's over-inflated bright ideas.' Dennis Robertson (1940, p. viii), his Trinity colleague, once put it that amongst the many conversations he had enjoyed with fellow economists 'those with Mr Sraffa stand out in memory as most inevitably ending in theft.' Invoking Harry Johnson's (1977a) concept of the social geography of economics departments, the social relations governing members of the same department, we obtain a very definite sense from the available memoirs, as well as from the many references in the Keynes collected writings, that Sraffa in his own quiet way legitimised the modern form of economists' debate: of small groups working on very distinctive topics, not necessarily of immediate social relevance; communicating with each other and exchanging papers before publication; relishing the provisional nature of research; and substituting mathematics and statistics for literary logic and commentary as the more powerful analytical tool (Johnson 1973a). Contrast this with the keepers of Marshall's mission, especially Pigou. Increasingly reclusive and self-absorbed, Robinson (1977, p. 30) says that he never had a proper economic discussion with him. Equally, late Pigou epitomised Marshallian economics in another important sense: endlessly elaborating and refining earlier works, and while not aspiring to write a volume of principles himself – what need when it was all in Marshall? – none the less operating with a nineteenth-century conception of the subject and of the lonely struggle of the individual scholar.

Challenges to Cambridge hegemony

As the birthplace of the *General theory* the social geography of Cambridge has been deeply mined and, perhaps like the whole Keynes industry, is now experiencing diminishing returns. We thus leave Cambridge for the present and turn first to Oxford and then the LSE,[13] centres where developments may have been less obsessively examined by the participants and by later historians but were none the less critical to the subsequent direction of British economics; so much so that the verdict now in vogue is that 'What went on at the London School in the early thirties appears in retrospect almost as important as what was going on at Cambridge [for] At LSE, the world of Anglo-American economics was being won over from the tradition

[13] On the LSE during the years of Beveridge's directorship, see Dahrendorf's (1995, pt. II) history, Coats's (1982) reconstruction of the LSE economics ethos, McCormick (1992) on Hayek and the accounts of two of the participants: Hayek (1963) and Robbins (1971); on Oxford, see Chester (1986), Young and Lee (1993) and the *OEP*, n.s. vol. 5 (1953) supplement devoted to Henderson. Finally, for a survey of both centres, and of Cambridge, from the perspective of the developing economics of democratic socialism, see Durbin (1985, esp. ch. 5).

of Ricardo and Marshall to modern neo-classical economics' (Leijonhufvud 1984, p. 26). Without undue caricature Oxford economists are typically cast in a supporting role to Keynes and Cambridge, with the LSE the opposite. Indeed, **Colin Clark** (1977, p. 80) has gone so far as to argue that had there not emerged a Cambridge-LSE split, and more particularly a 'violent quarrel' between Keynes and Robbins, 'the subsequent course of history might have been very different' in so far as a failure to agree policies which would produce a recovery from the world depression of 1929–32 heightened the damage caused by the Treaty of Versailles and led Germany inevitably towards war. This is a heavy charge to place upon economists, although it should be noted that by the 1970s Clark had long ago defected from his intellectual roots in Cambridge and the new economics in the 1930s and had gone back to basics – our term for the reaction beginning in the 1970s against government and revival of belief in the potency of the market forces.

Oxford and applied economics

Taking developments in Oxford first, Young and Lee (1993) characterise the research programme developed there in the 1930s as one of 'grounded empiricism'. With the PPE degree established, the foundation for undergraduate education, and following a university wide review of Oxford's activities, attention turned towards developing Oxford as a centre for economic research. From this emerged a number of research centres (the Oxford Institute of Statistics, the Oxford Agricultural Economics Research Institute); a new journal, *Oxford Economic Papers*, which pioneered applied economics and was a forum for the Oxford Economists' Research Group (OERG), a loose grouping of younger economists who, by the standards of their time, let alone their later careers, were world-class (**Andrews**, Harrod, Meade, Marschak, Phelps Brown, Shackle) together with an older generation (Henderson, Macgregor and Salter), many of whom had experience in government service as policy-advisers.

The case for many of these initiatives had earlier been put by Henderson (1931, pp. 78–9), some time before he resigned as the official economist on the EAC to take up a research fellowship at All Soul's in 1934:

> The most conspicuous defect of the present state of economics is the lack of adequate contact between the work of theoretical analysis on the one hand and realistic study on the other. In both compartments there has been a very rapid development in recent years of the work that is being done, and much of the work is characterised by a high degree of thoroughness and intellectual integrity. But the compartments are essentially watertight. . . . The theoretical economist is concerned with the elaboration of a highly complex and abstract logical system. The foundations on which he rears his analysis are not for the most part generalizations of fact, but distinctions between alternative logical possibilities.

... On the other hand, the professional statistician or research institute worker is concerned . . . with the accurate collection, assembly, and presentation of economic facts, and not with their explanation.

Henderson had by this stage become distrustful of pure theory and disillusioned by its potential to guide policy. In part this reflected his experience as an official adviser, but his manifesto for Oxford to become the centre of applied economics also derived from his antipathy towards Cambridge economics and Keynes in particular (Robinson 1987; Skidelsky 1992, pp. 137–8). Thus Henderson, like Robertson, could not stomach Keynes's style of policy entrepreneurship: one which finessed too many practical problems which would bite when it came to policy implementation; one which distilled the economic problem into simple propositions (demand deficiency) and solutions (budget deficits and cheap money). In short, he railed against panaceas, whether they be the Treasury view of the 1920s or the Keynesian solution of the 1930s. His was a longer-run diagnosis of Britain's economic problem: one which accepted cyclical unemployment, but as magnifying an underlying structural condition of uncompetitiveness deriving from low productivity and high real product wages.

Within the dominant (Keynesian) historiography of the interwar period such issues as costs have been viewed almost exclusively in terms of the debate over wage cuts as a solution for unemployment, with the result that broader issues of productivity growth and economic performance have been largely ignored. The cyclical story has thus crowded out the structural condition which preoccupied Henderson and many other prominent economists, for example Henry Clay.[14] His *The post-war unemployment problem* (1929) was widely respected for combining a strong case for industrial rationalisation with a perceptive assessment of labour market operation born of detailed study of the actual behaviour of workers and employers. Later, during the war, when Henderson was back in Whitehall, he continued to press home his concerns about industrial underperformance, opposing both the Beveridge plan on grounds of its huge unsustainable cost for the postwar economy, and the Keynesian proselytising of those ES economists (notably Meade) who were drafting what was to become the 1944 employment policy white paper (Booth 1989, esp. ch. 6). The flame of

---

[14]   Clay is noteworthy for at least one other reason: as an example of successful entryism in the policy advice market. Initially recruited to advise a subsidiary of the Bank of England on industrial issues, he proved his worth as an economic adviser during the 1931 crisis and by 1933 he was Economic Adviser to the Governor (Sayers 1976, vol. II, p. 388). He was also one of the leading figures behind the establishment in 1938 of the NIESR, successfully maintaining its viability during the war by recruiting émigré economists (Balogh, Levy, Rostas, Singer) who the British establishment felt were unsuitable for sensitive war work, notwithstanding that 'most had better reason than any of us to hate Hitler' (Robinson 1988, p. 64).

controversy between Henderson and Keynes thus smouldered on long after the *General theory*, affecting both Oxford economics and the Treasury whose permanent staff were made only too aware during the war that Keynes had far from captured all of the British economics profession.

Cannan, Robbins, Hayek and the LSE

Our starting point is necessarily that from its inception the LSE had consciously sought to develop as a rival centre to Cambridge economics, more particularly to Marshall's limited conception of the responsibilities of the professional economist. Between the wars this institutional rivalry was to be greatly intensified but the drama of the story of Keynes, Robbins and Hayek should not detract from much routine collaboration between Cambridge and London: notably joint seminars for postgraduates (Cairncross 1992, p. 6); but above all the LCES, an initiative by economists from both centres who, responding to the shortcomings of British official statistics, collected and disseminated basic data for their own use, funding this activity by sales to the business sector (Robinson 1978). The wartime migration to Cambridge of LSE students and those staff not required for war service, the formation in effect of a joint institution, is testimony to strong bonds of friendship and common approaches to economics that, many years later, were stressed by Lionel Robbins (1971, pp. 133–5) in his memoirs. Moreover, without the network of economists (centred on a Cambridge-LSE axis, with the expertise in applied economics coming principally from Oxford and Manchester) built up during the interwar period, it is quite inconceivable that the profession would have been able to become so effective in Whitehall during the war.

Controversy, drama and dispute, especially amongst economists, make more exciting copy, however, than the routine of academic cooperation. The preoccupation with dispute naturally focuses on what is considered the main battle (Keynes vs. Robbins-Hayek), thereby missing preliminary skirmishes which determine the subsequent conflict, with this episode no exception. Accordingly, Cannan's role in maintaining the rift begun by Hewins and Marshall, who had crossed swords at the turn of the century as LSE economists consciously sought to differentiate their product, has become eclipsed by later events. Yet Cannan exercised enormous influence over the LSE until his retirement in 1926 (to be succeeded by Robbins after the very brief tenure of Allyn Young); a man of singular views he – contra Marshall – espoused both a historical economics and a 'common sense' economics (Cannan 1927; 1933). Indeed, when RES president, he chose 'The need for a simpler economics' as his theme, put forcefully the argument that 'the almost complete absorption of the younger teachers in making what they rightly or wrongly believe to be important advances in the higher branches of theory is leaving the public at the mercy of quacks'; that 'contentment in neat equations and elegant equilibria' was at the expense of economists performing their proper duty of preventing 'grotesque blunders' in economic logic and action by public and policy-makers alike (1933, pp. 367, 378).[15]

The need for a simpler economics made no mention of Cambridge; it did not need to, and that is not its significance. Rather, by castigating economists for failing to solve the world depression Cannan was appealing to an older, pre-professionalisation, conception of the economists' responsibility; one shared by many of his LSE colleagues: by the Webbs, with their notion of the functional role and status of the expert (Coats 1982, p. 379); and by Laski (1931, p. 14) who was concerned that the need of modern governments for expertise must not be at the expense of democratic accountability; that experts must not become venerated like priests in primitive societies; and that 'deference to the plain man's common sense' must endure. The world depression thus challenged a core element of the professionalisation process for economists, and the significance for controversy and the Cambridge-LSE split was actually to become less Cannan *per se* than the reaction to Cannan produced in his effective successor, Lionel Robbins. We see this almost immediately, with Robbins's (1930, pp. 23–4) inaugural lecture, 'The present position of economic science', which in effect reasserted Marshall's mission:

> the science which will emerge from the developments I have been indicating will not be a body of knowledge accessible to everyone. The days are gone when Political Economy was a fit subject for a gentleman to study in his moments of relaxation. . . .
> . . . the hope that Economics will ever become something which the layman can comprehend without training is doomed for ever to frustration. No doubt economists might be more intelligible than they are. It is true that there is a kind of obscurity which springs from confused thinking. But the main fault is not with economists but with the world they study. The world of economic reality is a complicated thing, and it is not to be expected that as we come to understand it better our generalisations should be less complicated. It is no service to knowledge to make things simpler than they are.

Earlier, in an *EJ* exchange Keynes (1924a, p. 419) had charged Cannan with being 'unsympathetic with nearly everything worth reading ... which has been written on monetary theory in the last ten years', of writing as 'though none of all this existed, as though his own subject were incapable of development and progress'. In Cambridge eyes, LSE economics in the 1920s

---

[15] Hayek's (1963, pp. 64–73) provides a valuable 'outsiders' assessment of Cannan; Gregory and Dalton (1927) an 'insiders' appreciation; for historical perspective, see McCormick (1992).

was sullied by its association with this congenital deflationist, while the antipathy of Beveridge, towards economic theory was also widely known: a hostility so intense that it led eventually to the departure of a number of the LSE's rising stars, including Hicks (to Cambridge in 1935).[16] It is crucial to an understanding of the Cambridge-LSE controversies of the 1930s, the drama and the invective, that on his appointment Robbins was determined to cast off Cannan and the old guard, to make the LSE a centre for theory, one moreover which did not suffer from the insularity of British (by which was meant, Cambridge) economics (Caldwell 1995b, p. 19).

The opportunities came early and frequently thereafter. Beginning in 1930 with a clash between Keynes and Robbins at the newly established EAC over the former's abandonment of free trade and the latter's insistence upon being in a minority of one, an outturn which damaged at an early stage of the world depression the credibility of economists with politicians who were desperate for usable advice, there developed a gulf between the two figures and two institutions in policy terms. This was extended in 1931 when a number of (predominantly LSE) economists,[17] in an about-turn from the institution's position on the prewar tariff reform issue, nailed their colours firmly to the free trade mast, invoking good Marshallian welfare arguments, championing economic internationalism and deprecating short-term expedients which would not address underlying weaknesses in competitiveness. This policy cleavage was widened yet further by Robbins's *The Great depression* (1934), a book – as with Pigou (1933), long pilloried by the Keynesians and later retracted by its author – which developed his arguments before the EAC in 1930, combining a distinctly Austrian business cycle approach with an emphasis on structural factors (excessive public sector growth and government intervention) which underlay the growing rigidity of the British economy and its resultant inability to adjust to demand/supply shocks. As Wright (1989, p. 475) observes: 'For Robbins the choice was free market capitalism or state socialism – the search for an alternative "between" these was a chimera', this, of course, being the very middle way that Keynes was seeking in the 1930s.

As O'Brien (1988) makes clear, for Robbins, as for many of his older economist colleagues, the opposition to Keynes and Cambridge was partially an instinctive distaste for the attempt to subordinate economic policy to

---

[16] McCormick (1992, p. 24) and Dahrendorf (1995, p. 217); cf. Hicks's (1979, pp. 199–200) own account that the LSE's atmosphere remained 'tolerant' and that he moved to Cambridge not because of 'becoming Keynesian (as in a sense I was) . . . [but] in consequence of an invitation from Pigou, and it was because of the friendship I had already formed with Robertson'.

[17] Led by Beveridge the LSE members were F.C. Benham, Bowley, Gregory, Hicks, Plant, Robbins and G.L. Schwartz; the non-faculty, Walter Layton (previously Cambridge, but now editor of *The Economist*) - see McCormick (1992, table 1.1) for a dramatis personae of LSE economists in the 1930s.

liberal, populist sentiments. Admittedly, behind this lay the neo-classical theory of government failure, but this was under siege by Cambridge, albeit indirectly in the sense that the case for market efficiency was being challenged at both the macroeconomic (Keynes) and microeconomic levels (Sraffa and Joan Robinson). Something new was required to reinforce the traditional, neo-classical case against government. Escape was sought through study of the Austrian and Lausanne schools, the Americans (especially Chicago) and the Swedes; the input of visiting economists, but above all by the appointment of Hayek in 1931, described by Skidelsky 1992, p. 456) as 'the LSE's chief weapon in the power struggle with Cambridge', though he may not have appreciated that at the time.

Hayek's *Prices and production* (1931), his inaugural lecture (1933a) and his earlier Austrian work, now available in translation as *Monetary theory and the trade cycle* (1933b), together with the challenge to Marshall's mission in Robbins's *Essay*, provided a research programme for the newly energised department (McCormick 1992, p. 2). '[T]hings began to hum', John Hicks (1973, p. 2) later reflected on Robbins's arrival in October 1929 as head of department. Indeed, with the possible exception of Daniels's department at Manchester, which was more focused on applied economics and on serving the local community, Robbins was the first modern head of a British economics department in a number of senses: he set out to create an international reputation for the LSE, one based as much on its theoretical contribution and postgraduate education as its undergraduate teaching; he established a rival scientific research programme; and in so doing attracted a sizeable group of promising postgraduates and young lecturers (including Roy Allen, Marian Bowley, John and Ursula Hicks, Kaldor, Lerner, Vera Lutz, Sayers and Shackle) who carried through this programme and elevated the LSE to international status in economic theory. (The collegiate Oxford and Cambridge were less able to replicate this which is partially why they developed their own research institutes to supplement the undergraduate teaching staff.) The irony is that Robbins's project was located in an institution broadly antipathetic towards his politics, and that in terms of research output the eventual result was not to stem but to hasten the Keynesian avalanche. Thus both Hicks and Kaldor, initially strongly influenced by Hayek, eventually escaped Robbins's grand design, although were one to take the long-run it could be argued that the much more restricted notion of governmental capacity, and of the appropriate balance between government and market, offered by interwar Robbins and lifelong Hayek came to prevail (Dahrendorf 1995, p. 211).

5.3 PROGRESS WITH PROFESSIONALISATION

Core theory

We have already observed the strong allegiance, almost religious in intensity, to Marshall's *Principles* exhibited by Pigou and many of the older generation, and that for the young (Sraffa and Robinson) and not so young (Shove and Keynes) who did ' escape ... from habitual modes of thought and expression', the phrase used in Keynes's very self-conscious preface to the *General theory* (1936, p. xxiii), Marshall's text was the spur to rebellion. In addressing what then became of core theory we can follow a number of avenues. There is the hermetic approach of Shackle (1967, pp. 5–6, 7), whose label for the interwar period (more precisely 1926–39), 'The years of high theory', has been widely adopted. Thus:

> At the opening of the 1930s economic theory still rested on the assumption of a basically orderly and tranquil world. At their end it had to come to terms with the restless anarchy and disorder of the world of facts.
> . . .
> Until the 1930s, economics was the science of coping with basic scarcity. After the 1930s, it was the account of how men cope with scarcity and uncertainty.

Casting the net wider, and being excessively Cambridge (England) focused, accounts of interwar theoretical developments typically identify four interwar revolutions:[18] in macroeconomics (Keynes); in microeconomics (Joan Robinson, aided by Shove, Sraffa and Kahn); in welfare economics (Pigou); and in statistics and national accounts (Bowley and Colin Clark). Obvious omissions include John Hicks, initially at the LSE, and an important transitional figure in British professionalisation: 'the product of a generation which was the last to produce in abundance all round economic theorists – economists who could turn their minds to almost any theoretical problem' (Bliss 1987, p. 641). The diversity and breadth of his contributions is breathtaking to the modern, highly specialised economist: labour economics; (with Roy Allen) the recasting of demand theory; the marriage of value theory and monetary theory which produced the famous IS-LM apparatus (1937), an exposition of the *General theory* probably more directly influential than the book itself; and, just to complete the interwar work, *Value and capital* (1939) which nowadays in seen largely as a contribution to general equilibrium analysis (and features heavily in the citation accompanying his 1972 Nobel prize,[19] shared with Kenneth Arrow).

---

[18] For example, Johnson (1974a), Patinkin (1976), Robinson (1990b), Cairncross (1992, p. 7).
[19] *Swedish Journal of Economics*, vol. 74 (1972), p. 486; see also appendix II.

Although in many respects now superseded, Shackle's (1967) depiction of the years of high theory as one of a 'landslide of invention' has endured. Moreover, whilst fierce debate continues over the enduring significance of the various theoretical 'revolutions' initiated between the wars, Shackle's account of theoretical advances being prompted by the end of the Marshallian age of 'tranquillity', and of coming of the new age of 'turmoil', remains a thoroughly useful device. The First World War and its aftermath destroyed certainty, rendering obsolete any theoretical edifice founded on the assumption 'that tranquillity and safety were part of the natural order' (p. 289).[20] In macroeconomics, 'full' or 'fullish' employment was no longer automatic; in microeconomics, perfect competition was patently absurd. Admittedly, neo-classical theory provided potential counter-arguments in terms of market frictions produced by government interference, especially when augmented by Hayek and the Austrians. But the advent of democracy, the rise of labour, and the shock to political elites of the 1926 general strike, robbed such arguments – at least temporarily – of their political applicability (Middleton 1996, chs 8–9). The unprecedented amplitude of business cycle fluctuations, the long duration of mass unemployment, the collapse of the liberal world order all provided challenges to core theory.

Motivation and style

For the historian of economic thought, whether a relativist who denies the notion of 'progress' in economic theory, a constructivist who seeks to guard the history of economic thought from teleological corruption, a devotee of the sociology of scientific knowledge, or of older analytical traditions, the interwar period remains rich in possibilities.[21] Viewed in the round, and relative to the lack of interest in contemporary economic problems exhibited by many leading prewar and postwar British economists, what is striking about the interwar challenges to core theory is that almost all the key players appeared motivated by current policy issues and mindful of the policy-makers' time horizon. In this sense the economists' motivation and style becomes especially relevant in appreciating the challenges to core theory. Cannan may have been right about style limiting policy influence, but he was wrong about economists not being interested.

Examination of the *EJ* between the wars reveals the advance of the 'scientistic' style, but as Table 5.1 shows the wholly literary mode (free of algebra, calculus, diagrams, econometrics and statistics) remained dominant

---

[20] For a contemporary perception of this see Pigou's (1939, p. 217) RES presidential address.
[21] See Backhouse (1995) for an exploration of how at least developments in macroeconomics might be represented.

Table 5.1   Economic Journal*: classification of papers by rhetoric type (%
of total) and mode (Y=presence of style; N=absence), 1910,
1920, 1930 and 1940*

Year	Alg-ebra	Cal-culus	Dia-grams	Econo-metrics	Stat-istics	Wholly literary
1910						
Total (%)	17.5	12.5	7.5	0.0	32.5	62.5
Mode (62.5%)	N	N	N	N	N	
1920						
Total (%)	16.2	10.8	5.4	0.0	24.3	64.9
Mode (64.9%)	N	N	N	N	N	
1930						
Total (%)	10.3	5.1	7.7	0.0	25.7	64.1
Mode (64.1%)	N	N	N	N	N	
1940						
Total (%)	22.7	13.0	9.7	0.0	38.7	38.7
Mode (38.7%)	N	N	N	N	N	
Mode (38.7%)	N	N	N	N	Y	

Note: Component parts do not sum to 100 per cent because each *EJ* paper can exhibit more than one style.

until well into the 1930s, and that while the incorporation of statistical material was becoming routine (and very visibly so in 1940) *EJ* articles blended empiricism with theory in a manner entirely familiar to the prewar profession. The modern economics journal paper was not being advanced very much in the *EJ* (nor *Economica, Oxford Economic Papers* or *The Manchester School*); it was, however, in the 'children's magazine', the *Review of Economic Studies*.

Similarly, and again in common with the other British journals, the subjects of *EJ* papers reflected the economists' preoccupation with contemporary problems, international as well as domestic. Thus the 1920 volume carried papers on exchange rates and the international monetary system (Cassel, Siepmann, Pigou), wage determination (Bowley), the economics of Bolshevism (Einzig), the Austro-Hungarian inflation, income tax (a royal commission then in progress, with contributions from Pigou, Knoop, Edgeworth), industrial productivity (an *EJ* debut by Sargant Florence), the capital levy (Gini), income distributions (by a future Chancellor of the Exchequer, Dalton), and much else. In 1930, with the hopes for successful postwar reconstruction now dashed at home and abroad, the *EJ* included papers on the coal bill then being debated (Macgregor) and the agriculture act just passed, unemployment (Cannan, G.C. Allen, Clay), the gold standard (Einzig, Balogh), foreign investment (by an MP, A.M. Samuel, and the usual survey by Kindersley), the economics of the Soviet Union, UK-US comparative productivity (Jewkes) and industrial rationalisation (Gregory, Keynes, Macgregor and John Ryan, managing director of the newly-established Lancashire Cotton Corporation); noteworthy also were the *EJ* debuts by Hicks and Harrod. The famous 'Symposium', however, on increasing returns and the Marshallian representative firm (which is largely, but not exclusively responsible for the high profile of value theory in Figure 5.1) was exclusively preoccupied with pure theory and made no concessions to contemporary industrial circumstances. It provides a foretaste of economics' future, as well as its past as embodied in the efforts to defend/destroy Marshallian authority. Finally, the 1940 *EJ* reflected wartime conditions with papers on: the measurement of national income and the assessment of war economic potential (Keynes, Bowley), the foreign exchanges (Balogh, Shirras, Seymour Harris, Bauer), wages and the cost of living (Tout, Campion), the economics of national socialism (Guillebaud, Singer) and war finance (Pigou). But these were not entirely at the expense of continuing earlier debates on the trade cycle (Kaldor) and the Keynes-Tinbergen exchange on the potential of econometrics, or the celebration of the RES's jubilee (Keynes 1940b).

Following the 1930 'Symposium' the *EJ* became a much more lively journal. It was almost as if the floodgates had opened, with a number of robust exchanges hereafter: between Sraffa and Hayek in 1931–2, following the former's review of *Prices and production*; on decreasing costs and imperfect competition (Joan Robinson, Harrod, Kahn, Pigou, Shove, Roy Allen) in 1932–3; on the elasticity of substitution (Champernowne, Pigou, Kahn) in 1934–5; on the theory of market pricing in a decentralised socialist economy (Lerner, Durbin) in 1936–7; and, of course, on the *General theory*, although good taste, with Keynes being editor, dictated that the primary critical attention occurred elsewhere. Even so, between 1936–9 the *EJ*, in addition to a very full book review by Hicks, carried thirty articles or notes which related directly to the *General theory*; more if one includes the debate prompted by Harrod's *The trade cycle* (1936), the first important application of Keynesian theory; more even if the countless book reviews used as a vehicle to promote or impede the *General theory's* progress are included (for example, Townsend's review of Hawtrey's *Capital and employment* or Kaldor on Alvin Hansen's *Full recovery or stagnation*).

Figure 5.1 Economic Journal: *papers by Journal of Economic Literature (1983) classification, 1910, 1920, 1930 and 1940*

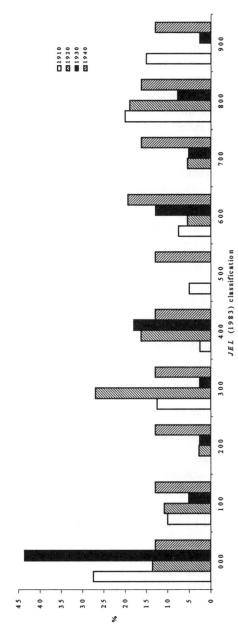

Note: JEL (1983) classification: **000** General Economics; Theory; History; Systems; **100** Economic Growth; Development; Planning; Fluctuations; **200** Quantitative Economic Methods and Data; **300** Domestic Monetary and Fiscal Theory and Institutions; **400** International Economics; **500** Administration; Business Finance; Marketing; Accounting; **600** Industrial Organisation; Technological Change; Industry Studies; **700** Agriculture; Natural Resources; **800** Manpower; Labour; Population; **900** Welfare Programmes; Consumer Economics; Urban and Regional Economics

James Meade

By 1939 the pages of the *EJ* exhibited few signs of the aversion to controversy that had characterised Marshall's mission, and it was now the accepted style for 'good' economic science that theory was always provisional, never definitive. However, this new propensity to argue distressed not just the older generation and the LSE critics of Keynes and Cambridge, but even some amongst those who were in the vanguard of the new economics. Thus, and here is an opportune point to introduce him fully into our story, James Meade never felt comfortable with the emerging professional norm of robust published exchanges between economists. As Harry Johnson (1978, p. 65) described it:

> Meade's style of approach to economics has been one that may be considered typically – or, perhaps more accurately, ideally – British. It may be characterized as that of the single scholar working away in his study, pursuing successive research projects according to a more or less firm lifetime programme, reading carefully the relevant work of other scholars as it comes along, but synthesizing that work into a consistent personal conspectus of the problem or area under research, rather than engaging in detailed controversy with it and acknowledging its contribution to the resulting treatise in comparable detail.

In one sense, therefore, Meade was a pre-modern figure, more Marshall than Keynes perhaps. Here we represent him as a transitional figure between Marshall's mission for professionalisation, which, however well intentioned, in practice was so hidebound as to have limited potential for policy influence, and modern American-style professional economics where the majority of academic economists have little interest in contemporary policy problems, appear devoid of ethical motivations and deficient in the skills of advocacy which would equip them for participation in the policy debate.

Meade, awarded the Nobel prize in 1977 (with Ohlin) for his contribution to international economic theory (1951; 1955a),[22] entered our narrative in chapter 3 with his participation in the 'Circus'. His status as an early Keynesian was then confirmed with his *An introduction to economic analysis and policy* (1936), the first British 'Keynesian' textbook. After a brief period as an international economist-civil servant, he then reappears in our narrative during the Second World War as, in effect, the key author of

---

[22] For academic assessments, see Johnson (1978) and Greenaway (1989); for more personal appreciations, see Cairncross (1993b) and *RES Newsletter*, no. 93 (April 1996), pp. 3–4. Meade's LSE inaugural lecture (1948) makes clear his philosophy that economic theory was the handmaiden of economic policy; see also the updated version of the short autobiographical essay he wrote to accompany his Nobel memorial lecture which is included in the first of four volumes of his collected writings (Howson 1988, pp. 1–5). Meade (1964) provides the best short introduction to his own equity-efficiency trade-off.

the employment policy white paper and, with Dick Stone, as the architect of official national income accounting (Meade and Stone 1941). Were he to have retired from economics on leaving the Economic Section in 1947, were this the sum total of his contribution to economics and policy, he would have been rated as a major British applied economist. But, like many of his generation, he returned to academe and lived for very nearly half a century more, active in economics until the very end (for example, Meade 1995).

His significance for this study lies not just in the breadth and quality of his theoretical contributions, but in the fact of his long life (like that of Austin Robinson), and in his practice of economics which provided a very real link back – through Keynes – to Marshall's Cambridge.[23] Admittedly, Meade was an Oxford graduate and, like Robinson, never met Marshall, but his economics embodied much of Marshall's mission in terms of motivation and style and, after Oxford, the ES and then the LSE, it was to Cambridge that he devoted himself for very nearly the last forty years of his long life, the first ten years of this phase being spent no less occupying Marshall's chair in political economy. 'We owe it to James Meade', argues Cairncross (1993b, p. 4), 'that professional economists remained at the heart of government when the war ended.' Indeed, his influence upon policy remains unsurpassed, at home and abroad, enduring long after his retirement (for example the Meade report – IFS 1978). Beyond this he acted, as Marshall had, as a mentor to many rising stars,[24] establishing important international links (for example, the Australian connection through Corden and Swan) and interdisciplinary connections (for example, his last two major books – Meade 1982; Vines *et al.* 1983 – were collaborations with a younger Cambridge economist and a control engineer).

In many other respects, however, Meade was much closer to Keynes than Marshall, not least in his not being inhibited about going into print. Even so, the personal qualities, and their implications for the economics, also shine through from the master. From his friend of more than half a century, Alec Cairncross (1993b, p. 1), comes the description of Meade as 'a kind of economic missionary or lay preacher: not because of any excess of zeal in pressing his views but because he is so obviously in search of truth for the purpose of human betterment.' Summing up on the style and motivation of his economics, Cairncross writes also of Meade: 'He has been consistent in his efforts to find solutions to economic problems that retain the maximum freedom of enterprise consistent with suppression of restrictive practices and at the same time to provide social security, full employment and greater

[23] Hahn (1993, pp. 251–2) explicitly makes this connection in his discussion of Meade's benevolence and its influence upon his economics.

[24] As attested by the truly international cast gathered together by the other IEA, the International Economic Association, to honour Meade (Atkinson 1993).

equality within limits that would be sustainable and compatible with market freedom' (p. 5). In short, he was the personification of the search for the 'middle way'; itself the epitome of progressive social thought between the wars and the title of a popular work of economics from, at that time, a Conservative dissident but eventually prime minister, Harold Macmillan.

His status as a transitional, intermediate figure in the professionalisation of British economics is confirmed by consideration of the diversity of his economics, of his willingness and ability to address different audiences: the 'intelligent radical', general public (1975a); his peers whose appetites extended beyond journal articles, through a four volume *Principles of political economy* (1965; 1968; 1971a; 1976); even the 'enemy' of Keynes in the shape of the IEA to which he, true to his commitment to a Liberal-Socialist solution, contributed papers and pamphlets (1971b; 1975b). Meade himself (1975a, p. 9) considered that his 'basic economic philosophy ... remained unchanged' from that which had motivated him to become an economist. This, like Marshall's motivation was very British. In Meade, it was manifest in a more benevolent view of the possibilities of welfare-enhancing government action, and thus led him to draw the line between government and market more towards the former than the latter.

But, and here we have the final justification for elevating Meade to a privileged position, he was most assuredly not a member of that group of economists who, according to **Alan Walters** (1978, p. 28), citing Balogh specifically by name and many other leading figures by impute, 'regard all the laws of demand and supply as readily repealed for political purposes.' If postwar British economics was, until at least the 1960s, swamped by the 'presumptions which pervade[d] most of the mainstream literature on the role of government in economic life – the imposed social-welfare function and the myth of omniscient and impartial government', as O'Brien (1981b, p. 64) contends, then Meade stands out as a distinguished figure, avowedly of the political left but always mindful of what could be achieved by government and what must remain the domain of the market. Similarly, combining 'idealism and compassion with hard headed analysis' to the end of his career (Arrow, cited in Atkinson 1993, p. xvii), he never allowed his value system to produce that silence about the fatal flaw in Britain's post-Second World War settlement that characterised so many of his generation, namely the impossibility of sustaining full employment and price stability in the context of Britain's decentralised wage-bargaining system.

Arguably, for Meade's generation the force of contemporary economic problems, the fact that remedial government actions had not yet been attempted, and the glamour of Keynes's challenge to authority provided a ready-made motivation for the younger economists. Indeed, Meade (1983, p. 263) describes himself as being spell-bound by Keynes, 'as a representative of that group of men and women ... who fell under the influence of Keynes because we thought that the mass unemployment of those years was both stupid and wicked and because we found in Keynes someone who inspired us with a hopeful answer to that problem.'[25] The published recollections of others of this generation,[26] the writings of those who made forays into philosophy (Joan Robinson 1962a), all reinforce this image of a very practical ethics underpinning interwar Cambridge economics. Indeed, so strong and enduring was this element of Marshall's mission that Keynes's intellectual journey eventually took him to the point, here taken from a letter of 1941 to the Archbishop of Canterbury, that 'Marshall always used to insist that it was through ethics that he arrived at political economy and I would claim myself in this, as in no other respect, to be a pupil of his' (cited in Skidelsky 1995, p. 89).

The LSE and Robbins's *Essay*

While there was no substantive generational divide in terms of motivation in Cambridge there most certainly was in the LSE. Indeed, the Cambridge value system was increasingly an anathema to Robbins and Hayek. Thus Harris (1977, p. 288) describes the LSE economics department under them 'bec[oming] increasingly deductive and analytical and increasingly hostile to "problem-oriented" research'. Whilst true of these leading figures it was most decidedly not true of the younger economists, who by 1938–9 were swelled by quite significant numbers of postgraduates, almost all of whom had research interests in the new economics, theoretical and applied.[27] Both Robbins and Hayek distrusted government and placed strict limits on its economic capabilities, and this was reflected in their Austrian research programmes. But beyond this was the storm generated by Robbins's *Essay*, not least within the LSE after Cannan's (1932) deeply critical *EJ* review of his former pupil who he considered had attempted a redefinition of economics, which impoverished the economist's task, and in a manner which must prompt any 'common sense' economist to expostulate: 'For

---

[25] Here I hope I will be forgiven for adding a personal note to reinforce this and the earlier point about his generosity to students. As a Cambridge economics graduate student I met Meade in the summer of 1978 to discuss some aspects of my Ph.D. dissertation (which eventually became my 1985 book), our meeting being in the Marshall building, indeed the Keynes seminar room which, appropriately enough, was dominated by a portrait of Keynes. At the time I was struck by the way in which Meade talked of Keynes as if he were present and when, with the meeting over, he rose to leave the room he bowed slightly but noticeably to the portrait.

[26] Robinson (1992); see also Tribe's (1997) series of interviews with economists who started their professional lives in the 1920s and 1930s.

[27] McCormick (1992); conversation with Tom Wilson who was a graduate student between 1938–40, and whose supervisors (Kaldor and Durbin) were deeply involved in applied research and who were leading figures in the LSE graduate seminar (see also Young and Lee 1993, p. 166).

goodness sake give us a reasoned reply without beating about the bush and quoting dozens of foreign economists whom we shall never read' (p. 426).

Robbins's attempted redefinition of the discipline involved a number of propositions critical of the methodological status quo which, in effect, had been established by J.N. Keynes (1891), a Cambridge authority incidentally not cited in the *Essay*. Not all are relevant to our purpose, but three are:

1. The proposition that economic science is value free and can be distinguished from those discussions of economic issues which involve value judgements; that economics can be neutral as to desired ends because there exists no unambiguous concept of welfare-maximisation.
2. The actual redefinition of the discipline in terms of the fact of scarcity rather than as a study of the process of wealth creation.
3. The reassertion that the basic propositions of economics could be logically deduced, thereby rejecting verification or falsification of economic laws.

The first proposition reinforced the growing isolation of economics from the other social sciences (sociology, politics and psychology); the second, with ends given, was interpreted as greatly restricting the economist's remit as regards means and as implying a self-denying ordinance with respect to policy; and the third inhibited the development of econometric testing. The responses came quick and fast and were sustained throughout the decade. Beginning with a highly critical pamphlet from Joan Robinson (1932), debate of Robbins's *Essay* featured regularly in inaugurals and reflective 'state of the subject' essays,[28] culminating in a major debut by Hutchison (1938) who would become Britain's leading economic methodologist, and the populist *Lament for economics* by Barbara Wootton (1938).

The latter jeremiad, produced by one of the first Cambridge women economics graduates who went on to an academic career, was both a call for a reunification of economics with the other social sciences but above all a plea for economists to focus on the pressing social problems and to agree amongst themselves, without which governments would continue to justify their inaction on the basis of their being no expert consensus. Citing her old pupil, Joan Robinson (1933, p. 2) on the 'agonizing sense of shame' suffered by contemporary analytical economists as the subject failed to deliver a practical economic knowledge which would solve real world problems, Wootton (1938, p. 14) tapped into a very raw nerve. Why, at the very time

---

[28] For example, and particularly in relation to the role of the economist, see the following which do not always mention the *Essay* by name but arguably have it mind: Hayek (1933b), Fraser (1938), Durbin (1938) and Harrod (1938), the latter the presidential address to Section F of the BAAS which was devoted to methodology.

when political debate was increasingly conducted in terms of economic issues, why when the world's problems were so evidently economic in nature, why had the economist become 'the stock butt for popular jest'? Instead of being 'among the most influential, and most highly-respected, of all the men of learning' Wootton lamented that 'there can seldom have been an age in which the public at large placed a lower estimate on the usefulness of professional students of economics.'

Wootton's lament not surprisingly did little for her professional standing. There was, however, a surprisingly full review in the *EJ*, testimony to the seriousness with which her charges were taken in terms of their potential to damage the profession. This was undertaken by a leading, but now largely forgotten, methodologist, and in the process there emerges an attempt to take some heat out of the situation by proposing guidelines for the future conduct of economic debate, what we might call a proposed act of settlement for professional economists and their critics (reproduced in Table 5.2). That such a proposal could be seriously put says much about the earnestness of the age and the hopes still entertained for human progress.[29] Touching as this is, what now stands out clearly from the disciplinary introspection of the 1930s is the implicit model of economic policy-making which informed most economists. In a sense the Keynesian conception of policy, one in which developments in theory determine, after a lag, the direction and detail of policy, came to predominate before Keynes's economics.

Professionalisation and the new economics

Recent revisionist work has demonstrated that there were many obstacles to official acceptance of the Keynesian solution between the wars; that the deficiencies in economic theory were but one in a complex of administrative, economic and political constraints; and that the breakthrough, if such there were, is associated more with the war than with a theoretical revolution *per se*. However, for Keynes, at least for Keynes of the *General theory*, it was theory that mattered above all. Thus 'it is my fellow economists, not the general public, whom I must first convince' in the project 'to bring to an issue the deep divergences of opinion between fellow economists which have for the time almost destroyed the practical influence of economic theory, and will, until they are resolved, continue to do so' (1936, p. xxi).

In such manner Keynes made continued progress with professionalisation dependent upon the fate of the new economics. In terms of the Organon two

---

[29] See also Pigou (1941) on how the economics profession was handicapped, and the relevance of its message underappreciated, by the continued practice of the newspapers, *pace* books in the natural sciences where expert reviewers had become routine, to operate on the basis that all economics books be approachable to those blessed with a good general education.

Table 5.2   Fraser's act of settlement for professional economists and their critics

---

1. Economists undertake neither to claim nor in any way to suggest that value theory is the only worth-while branch of economic studies.
2. Economists undertake that when expounding value theory for the benefit of their students or of the general public, they will go out of their way to emphasise that they are aware of the limitations imposed upon their analysis by the facts of economic life.
3. Economists agree not to use the word "science" in any esoteric sense. If they cannot use the word without emotional bias, they undertake not to use it at all.
4. Economists affirm and reiterate their conviction that their subject is a social study, that its purpose is to advance social welfare, and that this purpose can often best be realised by joint research in co-operation with students from other fields of study; provided always that any individual economist who in good faith holds that his own best contribution to truth and social welfare rests in work of a purely economic nature (whether analytical, deductive, or both) shall be entitled to pursue such investigations without vexatious interference.
5. Critics undertake to ascertain what economists are doing and trying to do before formulating or publishing their criticisms.
6. Critics acknowledge the right of economists to define their subject as they please, provided always that: (a) no such definition prevents individual workers from passing outside the area so defined if the workers concerned in good faith hold such conduct to be in the best interests of truth and social welfare; (b) no obstacle is placed in the way of reasonable suggestions by critics (subject to article 5 above) as to the emphasis placed by economists on the various branches of economic studies or as to the desirability of effecting changes in such emphasis.
7. Both parties undertake to discuss their discussions in such a way as not unnecessarily to damage the status of economic studies in the eyes of the public.
8. (Sanctions). Any economist who knowingly and willingly transgresses this agreement shall be deemed to have acted unprofessionally and shall incur the censure of his colleagues. Any critic who knowingly and wilfully transgresses this agreement shall be denounced for ignorance, misrepresentation and obstructionism.

Source: Fraser (1938, pp. 209–10).

observations are relevant here. First, with respect to the quest for concrete truth, the *General theory* remained true to the spirit of Marshall's mission as carried forward in the Cambridge Economic Handbooks. Thus its purpose was 'not to provide a machine or method of blind manifestation, which will furnish an infallible answer, but to provide ourselves with an organised and orderly method of thinking out particular problems' (1936, p. 35). Secondly, as evidenced by the methods of propagation developed between the wars, it was not Cambridge but Oxford and the LSE who were more concerned about professionalisation. Interwar Oxford economics stands out for its commitment to research through both formal institutional structures (the two new research institutes) and informal groupings of economists working on distinctive research programmes. In respect of the former we would highlight what was known as the Hall-Hitch report,[30] the results of a pioneering investigation into business behaviour which produced firm empirical (anti-marginalist) evidence of 'full cost' pricing and, together with related work, cast doubt on the efficacy of the rate of interest as a policy instrument (Meade and Andrews 1938); while the latter is best represented by what Young (1989) calls Harrod's 'growth research programme', this leading eventually to the theory of dynamic economics but which is now seen as much more of a collaborative than an individual achievement (with Meade, once more, a key player). Oxford and the LSE stand out also in terms of the development of the economics doctorate as a growing professional requirement for tenured academic employment.[31] Although this was not as well developed a trend as in the US, the postgraduate research programmes in Britain have an additional significance, as the vehicle for the propagation of the *General theory* (Young and Lee 1993, pp. 166–7).

We need also to mention that some economists took advantage of new media to air their views to a wider audience. Foremost here was Keynes who made at least twenty radio broadcasts,[32] a part of his activities which none of his biographers has given much attention. It seems improbable that Keynes did not quickly recognise the potentiality of the new media to sway opinion. With historical research still very much dominated by study of printed sources it remains unknown the extent to which the broader profession grasped the opportunities offered by the radio, although concerns were expressed by at least one economist, albeit one deeply unfriendly towards the new economics (Hutt 1936, p. 127), that 'there is a most grave danger that disinterested (and hence authoritative) opinion on economic matters will be hidden from the community' unless those controlling the new media were committed to broadcasting unwelcome as well as welcome news.

The propagation of economics through old technologies remained the dominant channel, though here we observe much more entrepreneurial behaviour on the part of certain individuals and groups of economists. With catchy titles, *What everybody wants to know about money*, and by-lines which stressed the institution, 'By nine economists from Oxford' (Cole 1933), topical and authoritative economic commentary increased substantially in volume compared with prewar. Economists became deeply

---

[30] Originally published as Hall and Hitch (1939), this was republished in Wilson and Andrews (1951, ch. III) together with many other of the early *OEP* papers and a series of commissioned interpretative pieces. The first author is Robert Hall, later Head of the ES.

[31] But not without resistance, for at the second annual Conference of Teachers of Economics, from which the AUTE emerged, it was clear from the discussion that the 'Ph.D. degree . . . among economists at least, would seem to have very few friends' (*EJ*, 35 (March 1925), p. 154).

[32] Listed in JMK, Vol. XXX (1989), p. 112.

involved in a number of partisan and politically independent ventures in policy persuasion such as the Liberal Summer Schools, the Liberal Industrial Inquiry and the Next Five Years group.[33] Economists thus made important contributions to, as Marwick (1964) calls it, that 'middle opinion' which lay the groundwork of political and social 'agreement' in the 1930s that would subsequently underpin Britain's managed-mixed economy and welfare state. One agency which was particularly important in this process, and thereafter, was Political and Economic Planning (PEP; later Policy Studies Institute, PSI), a think-tank established in 1931 in which economists were well-represented amongst the panel of experts available to undertake social and economic research. Beyond this, and much more partisan, younger economists, ones particularly but not exclusively associated with Oxford and the LSE (Clark, Cole, Durbin, Gaitskell, Jay and Meade), set about redefining the case for democratic socialism after the debacle of 1931. From this emerged new thinking on economic planning and nationalisation; in short, much of the preparatory work for the postwar Attlee administrations.[34] There was thus much professional activity which was quite independent, though not uninfluenced, by Keynes and the *General theory*. Indeed, Keynes was viewed with some suspicion within the labour movement (Winch 1969, app.), although some of the younger economists – for example, Jay (1937) – were important 'in adapting Keynesianism to socialist goals for the Labour party' (Durbin 1985, p. 113).

We need to reaffirm, however, that all of this activity took place against a background of an economics profession still dominated by 'great intellectual leaders, with extremely small departments and very few students'; that 'Institutions and professional organizations were still embryonic' (Hutchison 1994b, p. 28). Even so, Table 3.1 suggests a doubling of the number of academic posts between the wars, and at minimum a doubling of the number of economics degrees granted. With such progress it is neither appropriate nor possible to repeat the enumeration exercise that was conducted for the prewar profession (Table 4.2). We should report, however, the contemporary evidence that notwithstanding this expansion the supply of economists in Britain, both as a stock and as a flow, was seriously deficient relative to Germany and the US (Sanderson 1972, p. 271). Thus, for example, the *EJ*,

---

[33] Walter Layton chaired the inquiry which produced *Britain's industrial future*, with Henderson and Keynes on the executive committee and, amongst others, Stamp and Robertson as members of the special committees. Layton was also prominent in the Next Five Years group, whose economist members included Geoffrey Crowther, J.A. Hobson and the director of Oxford's Agricultural Economics Research Institute (C.S. Orwin). The group also included a former high-ranking Treasury official, Blackett, who had become persuaded by the new economics.

[34] The New Fabian Research Bureau was particularly prominent in these developments. At various times we would list the following as having been associated with, or sympathetic towards, its activities and its economics: Harrod, Hall, Redvers Opie, Joan Robinson and Shove.

in reporting that Henry Clay had resigned his Manchester chair to take up an appointment as economic adviser at Securities Management Trust, a Bank of England subsidiary, observed 'This appointment, together with those to the staff of the Economic Advisory Council ..., represent a further drain on the straitened supply of well-qualified academic economists into non-academic, though nevertheless research, work of one kind or another.'[35] The shortage of economists was only to become evident, and perhaps important, with the Second World War, but when comparison is made with the US, where the New Deal had led to a huge influx of economists (and lawyers) into government service, it becomes clear the extent to which the supply of economists was dependent upon government demand.[36] This point was made forcefully by the Clapham committee just after the war; critical about a wide range of matters, including, most importantly, the underdevelopment of official statistics, this made the generalised case that under-funding of social science research in Britain was placing the economy at a competitive disadvantage (HMSO 1946).

Finally, lest all of this activity be confused with economists having acquired major influence before the Second World War consider the initial membership of the EAC. This was chaired by the prime minister and consisted of twenty four further members divided between three groups: 4 politicians including the Chancellor, 15 experts chosen 'by virtue of their special knowledge and experience in industry and economics' and a secretariat of 5. This was both an unwieldy body and one in which, in terms of expert members, the economists (Cole, Keynes, Stamp, Tawney) were outnumbered by very nearly four to one by representatives of commercial, financial and industrial knowledge. Only amongst the staff members were the economists (Henderson, H.V. Hodson and Clark) the majority.[37] In size and in composition the EAC perfectly represented Establishment perceptions of the economics community and of the diversity of membership, as well as functional representation, that the first official body charged with proffering economic advice to government ought to embody. This more than confirms that, in the midst of the depression, government considered professional economists but one of many possible sources of economic expertise, evidence we argue which lends support to the earlier hypothesis that official demand for economic advice derives from a strategy of risk- and responsibility-sharing for economic management. Paradoxically, the fact that the economists could not agree in 1930–1, whether it be the Keynes-Robbins clash at the EAC or the disagreements at the Macmillan

---

[35] *EJ*, vol. 40 (March 1930), p. 160.

[36] For a contemporary assessment of comparable US developments see Copeland (1941); for the role of economists in the New Deal, see Norton (1969, esp. ch. 2) and Barber (1996).

[37] *EJ*, 40 (March 1930), pp. 147–50.

committee, actually strengthened the case for bringing economists into the established policy community on a routine basis. Thus, the successor organisation to the EAC, the CEI – formed in the aftermath of the abandonment of gold and the policy reorientation this made possible – was a very much smaller body in which academic economists predominated but under the watchful eye of senior Treasury officials.[38] As we noted earlier, disagreements were prevalent here also but less so, and the new committee served an important function in communicating the real substance of economists' disputes and their policy significance.

5.4 ECONOMICS, ECONOMISTS, POLICY AND CREEPING COLLECTIVISM

Towards the managed economy

All discussions of interwar economic policy should be prefaced by the statement that in 1918 governments did not think of themselves as having an economic policy, not at least in the sense we would understand it today, whereas by 1939 economic events, political responses and changing ideas had compelled them to assemble an armoury of policy instruments, mainly macroeconomic but not exclusively so, which are recognisably modern. Thus the origins of the modern managed economy lie in the interwar period.

Until comparatively recently the history of this period was typically told as a Keynesian fable in which Britain's economic difficulties, initially caused by the war, were compounded by a series of policy failures – notably the gold standard in the 1920s and the refusal to deficit-finance in the 1930s – resulting from the authorities rejecting Keynes and the new economics. Such simple-mindedness was typically combined with extreme pessimism about interwar economic performance. The latter story was being questioned even before the end of the Keynesian era, but the former certainly did not survive the theoretical crisis of the 1970s, especially as it coincided more or less with the opening up of the official papers in the PRO which made possible examination of policy from within. Such has been the revisionist work that our view of economic performance is now much more favourable, indeed at variance with the predominant contemporary perception which was of the economy dominated by the declining staple industries and resulting mass unemployment. Admittedly, the image of a cyclical highly disturbed economy and of unprecedented unemployment has been

---

[38] Howson and Winch (1977). Membership was variable but included Stamp (chairman), Keynes, Henderson, Salter and Robertson and with the Treasury represented by Leith-Ross and Phillips. It was the CEI which, in effect, became the Stamp survey in 1939 (p. 85).

confirmed, but economic growth is now seen as reasonable by historical standards, especially in the 1930s, with relative economic decline much more evident with respect to the US than Europe.

This rewriting of interwar economic performance has been accompanied by a parallel re-evaluation of policy formulation and effectiveness. From this a few have suggested that Keynesian ideas were accepted by official opinion rather earlier than previously thought (Hutchison 1978a), but the majority have reaffirmed that Keynes and the new economics made little headway before the Second World War but that the reasons for this are located not in the obstinacy and anti-intellectualism of Establishment opinion. In the 1920s the Treasury did hold 'firmly to the self-acting model of the economy that minimized its own direct role', but under probing from Keynes and others Treasury officials developed the analytical model underlying their policy advice (Clarke 1990a, p. 203). It was not Keynesian, but with its emphasis upon maintaining the conditions in which British industry could successfully compete, and in its sensitivity to the needs of the City of London operating in a highly uncertain world, and the devastation wrought to the public finances by war, the Treasury's model was not without merit. Treasury critics, above all Keynes, himself an ex-Treasury official, choose to ignore the context within which the institution must operate. Subsequently, many historians have done the same. Indeed, the emphasis upon the role of theory in policy, however long the long-run be, serves to obscure most of the interesting questions about the evolution of British economic policy. Institutional reforms and the growth of the public sector made the interwar Treasury an altogether more powerful agency within Whitehall than it had been before (Burk 1982b), but mutually reinforcing political and economic forces narrowed the available policy space unless there was profound change in political priorities (a privileging of unemployment above all other policy issues) and a substantial accretion of new powers to central government (to make operational the huge public works schemes for which progressive opinion clamoured). Lloyd George campaigned that unemployment must be treated as a policy problem analogous to war; the electorate, by contrast, were more disposed towards Baldwin and safety first.

To summarise the current state of research. Interwar unemployment represented a serious loss of output at the national level, a heavy but variable charge on the public finances and a social catastrophe for a generation of older workers living in outer Britain; the Treasury view was not the product of madmen in authority, but had cogent theoretical reasons for rejecting deficit-finance; and the Keynesian solution, even if administratively feasible, and not resulting in a collapse of confidence and capital flight, would not have generated the volume of employment that was sought by its proponents, not least because current account balance of payments weakness had now generated an external constraint to full employment. In stressing the real-world constraints to adoption of the Keynesian solution we must be mindful, however, that the rehabilitation of the reputation of interwar policy-makers does not proceed to the point of fatalism about the historical possibilities for policy. What is attempted here is to make clear that the policy constraints frequently had little to do with economic theory, that the terrain upon which Keynes was debating, and forced Treasury defences, was often not the decisive element in determining the policy actually pursued. Thus the two sides were often talking past each other.

The challenge of the new economics and the supply of expertise

It is important to stress the continuities of interwar policy with the prewar era which, together with the delayed appreciation of the economic significance of the war, made it so very difficult for the authorities to escape from the laissez-faire policy regime. Thus the gold standard, the minimum balanced budget rule and free trade, the core defences of the prewar minimalist laissez-faire state, formed an interlocking self-acting policy regime which was as much administrative and political as it was economic. Clarke (1990b, p. 169) identifies three facets to this:

1. It 'entrenched the public service ethic against the vulgar pressures of democratic politics', a consideration now even more important with the rise of labour and the electoral reforms of 1918, and one ever present in the stresses to which the public finances were subject between the wars.
2. The 'lack of room for manoeuvre embodied in this system was deceptive because contrived ... enabl[ing] the Treasury and the Bank of England to assure the politicians that there was no alternative – but only on their premises'; and
3. The system, based on the hydraulics, the self-adjusting nature (in theory) of the gold standard, gave it an 'intellectual appeal' with 'The rigour and elegance of this system ... beautifully attuned to strong supple minds schooled in the disciplines of classics and mathematics – the subjects in which virtually all the Treasury mandarins had excelled at Oxford and Cambridge. To them, sound finance spoke with the precision of calculus and the purity of a dead language.'

In short, and as Bradbury put it at the decisive discussion which sealed the fate of the gold standard decision (p. 192), the gold standard 'was knave-proof. It could not be rigged for political or even more unworthy reasons' (Grigg 1948, p. 183). In face of this, the product of administrative experience, political nous and DIYE, it would take more than Keynes's

General theory to convince sceptical Treasury officials, let alone their risk-aversive political masters, that the dangers inherent in deficit-finance were worth the potential rewards. This was only possible with the Second World War and with the groundswell of cross-party opinion that this time the pledge for a Land fit for Heroes had to be redeemed. Admittedly, the sharp recovery of the economy from the slump of 1937–8 once the rearmament programme became debt-financed demonstrated the technical force of the Keynesian solution, but officials continued to maintain that the financial markets would not accept borrowing for peacetime public works. Nor were Treasury officials impressed by the reflationary policy experiments in other countries, in many of which economists were deeply involved (for example, Sweden). Budget deficits were associated with the fascist states and with the US New Deal, the limited recovery of the US economy in the 1930s serving as an object lesson of the dangers of unorthodox economics.[39] In any case, as Leith-Ross complained, a New Deal ill-fitted the British policy style:

> It is becoming the fashion to call for a 'New Deal'. The fashion started in the United States, where gambling holds much the same place in national life as cricket does in ours. Nothing, therefore, is more natural than that the American Government should indulge in a gamble while a British Government has to keep a straight bat . . .   (PRO 1935, p. 1)

That the Keynesian solution was not cricket, that it offended the canons of orthodoxy, was part of its appeal as well as its handicap. In accounts of this challenge to orthodoxy by the progressive wing of the economics profession the focus is typically on their campaign for the state to accept a stabilisation function in addition to its existing (Musgravian) allocative and distributional responsibilities. Yet, because there were forces making for government growth quite independent of the Keynesian policy debate, this focus actually produces a very partial picture of the challenge. Wrapped up within the challenge, and shared to a greater or lesser extent by the growing band of devotees to the new economics, was a very marked shift in the equity-efficiency trade-off. In our earlier account of Marshall's mission we emphasised how limited in practice was the new profession's challenge to the market order, the power of central government, the tax take etc. By contrast, by the 1930s the economists' challenge to small government was much more radical in intent and with deep and enduring implications for all three functions of government. This had a number of aspects.

First and foremost, and relative to prewar, progressive British economists considered the unemployment problem was of such seriousness that long-

---

[39]   See Hall (1989a, ch. 12) for the influence of Keynesian ideas in the Scandinavian countries, and Middleton (1985, pp. 27, 160, 170–1) for official resistance to them in Britain.

standing concerns about governmental efficiency and about politics and politicians must be suspended for the duration. From this derives the third of Harry Johnson's five defining propositions of British economics, that '"full employment" is an exclusive definition of social well-being, and as such to be pursued at virtually any cost' (p. 24). Secondly, the economic case for state ownership had greatly advanced on prewar, being now argued on grounds of both efficiency (allocative, dynamic and X-) and as an aid to macroeconomic stabilisation. The target list of proposed industries varied greatly, as did the preferred method of nationalisation, but the result was to shift the boundaries of government and market for a considerable part of the profession, whether actively engaged in politics or not.

Thirdly, there was widespread support for a more redistributive tax system and an extension of the social wage, this deriving from a complex of influences: a dominant egalitarian ethic, a judgement that organised labour had not increased its functional share of national income through the market place and, in an application of the *General theory*, as a means of raising the average propensity to consume. To judge from the *EJ* and other journals there was little professional concern, at then prevailing tax rates, about the disincentive effects of personal taxation, although there was some interest in the problem of business rates and the possibility of benefit-induced unemployment. While the business community lobbied throughout the period for lower taxation of profits, and of the incomes of the entrepreneurial class, they were somewhat hampered by the negative findings on taxation and incentives by two official committees: Colwyn on the national debt and taxation and Balfour on industry and trade (HMSO 1927; 1929). The former included two economists amongst its members (Stamp and Wootton); the latter was chaired by one of the founding fathers of the RES and a former prime minister and also had economist members (Ashley, Beveridge, Dalton and Llewellyn Smith). Both took evidence from professional economists as a matter of routine, while the latter, which issued no less than seven reports between 1925–7, including one on the factors making for industrial and commercial efficiency, was in effect a study of relative economic decline and of the remedial measures available to government and market.

Continuing with our theme of a shift in the equity-efficiency trade-off we would identify as a fourth development the disdain with which the profit motive came to be held in certain quarters. Keynes's distaste for much of the material motivation of capitalism is well-known, as are his aspirations for the higher moral purpose that capitalism might eventually attain (Moggridge 1992, pp. 454–5). Within the British labour movement there was a long-standing ambivalence towards profits which not infrequently, and especially in the dominant Fabian strand of thought, was manifest as a rejection of competitive activity as wasteful and unjust as well as prone to the growth of monopolies (Thompson 1996, ch. 2). We have already noted that imperfect competition was a very active research field for economists, with much of the case for greater state ownership underpinned by the contemporary evidence on the growth of monopoly, collusion and anti-competitive behaviours. The interwar years marked an important stage in the modern concentration of British industry, the 1920s in particular with rationalisations and mergers (Hannah 1983). But, as is now being suggested by economic historians, competitive pressures were weak in the interwar period, and especially in the 1930s as world trade collapsed with autarky. Pre-existing weaknesses in capital market disciplines, non-existent competition policies and the effects of government-sponsored industrial rationalisation schemes resulted in neither the market nor government acting to eliminate inefficiency (Broadberry and Crafts 1990; 1996).

Such evidence might lead to the charge that between the wars leading economists, no doubt anxious to avoid yet more unemployment as firms shed labour to increase efficiency, did not emphasise the benefits of competition for productivity; similarly, by their silence on the weaknesses of the labour process they allowed weak management and dysfunctional labour processes to endure, all with significant long-term effects. Building upon this it is possible to argue that by the 1930s British governments had developed forms of intervention which, motivated by social rather than technical market failure, underpinned institutional failure, accommodated the social costs of the adjustment crisis without doing very much to improve the market's operation. The extent to which the new economics, by stressing a macroeconomic solution to unemployment, worked to divert intellectual attention from microeconomic and supply-side concerns has not really been investigated. Yet the potential trade-off between macroeconomic policy experimentation and microeconomic efficiency underlay much of Treasury thinking between the wars, and was of course evident in the opposition of Robbins and Hayek to developments in Cambridge economics.

We add two correctives to this interpretation. It was the weakness of the British state in relation to organised capital, itself not very organised with peak associations at this stage, which partially explains this tendency in British policy (Middleton 1996, pp. 409–13), while there were many economists who researched industrial efficiency, industrial relations, foreign trade, labour market failure and the regional problem but they did not enjoy a high standing relative to the theorists. Within such a group we would include Henry Clay (Manchester, then Bank of England), G.C. Allen (Birmingham, then Liverpool), Daniels and his Manchester colleagues (Campion, Dennison and Jewkes), and, of course, Henderson together with countless economists who are now not remembered because their time was not devoted to high theory but to undergraduate teaching and to applied research, much of it of relevance to their localities. Amongst these tool users we would include Ted Allen, H.M. Hallsworth and E.D. McCallum (at what would eventually become Newcastle University), H.O. Meredith (Belfast), P. Ford (Southampton), J.H. Jones and J.H. Richardson (Leeds) and Joseph Sykes (Exeter).[40] Applied macroeconomic research which was national in focus was, of course, proceeding apace in Oxford and, from 1938 onwards, at the NIESR, but there were important developments in the regions which need to be included in a history of professionalisation. Thus, for example, government departments were increasingly contracting-out social research to universities, all part of a broader process in which the Board of Trade and the Ministry of Labour were having recourse to outside expertise as a matter of routine. Finally, on the supply side, and in addition to the economic-financial expertise in the City, a number of industrial sectors had acquired their own economic-statistical experts who operated on a national stage.[41]

The demand for economic expertise

To complete this analysis of the interwar market for economic expertise we should note that, on the demand side, it was not just government which dominated developments. Sanderson (1972, pp. 270, 273, 274) has detected 'a drift of opinion in industry moving slightly more in favour of the economics graduates in the 1930s that was not so discernible in the 1920s', and there seem to have been shortages of statisticians able to interpret economic data. Even so, to judge from the experience of the new departments at Leeds, Newcastle and Southampton, many economics graduates were not able to find employment appropriate to their degree with the majority eventually becoming schoolteachers. As we noted earlier, even by the eve of the Second World War Marshall's aspirations for the profession and of its utility to business was far from being realised, with most commerce-economics graduates having no more career choice than

---

[40] This roll call is taken from the authors to two BAAS section F volumes on Britain in depression and recovery (British Association 1935; 1938) which were produced by a research committee chaired by J.H. Jones and which included, amongst others, Harrod and MacDougall (then at Leeds) amongst their membership. The latter's introduction to the second volume, a study of the British trade cycle 1929–37, shows how interwar economists 'were obliged to piece together the various fragments of information in the days before formally comprehensive statistics of national income and expenditure became available', a process not entirely devoid of benefits because it brought economists close to the data, made them aware of its shortcomings and thus cautious in drawing conclusions (MacDougall 1975, p. viii). MacDougall's (1938) paper was state-of-the-art applied economics without econometrics, and in exactly the sort of style that would become routine for the economists once they entered government service with the war.

[41] For example, contributions to British Association (1938) from L. Isserlis (UK Chamber of Shipping) and L.F. Duval (Motor Manufacturers and Traders Ltd).

their arts-trained peers, at risk of experiencing low job satisfaction but 'quite well remunerated if they stuck to their posts.'

The chief beneficiaries of continued progress in professionalisation thus continued to be that small elite of Oxbridge-London academic economists who were increasingly drawn into the policy community. We have already noted one very visible example of this, with the EAC and its successor organisations, and two examples of economists as members of official committees (Colwyn and Balfour). For economists to be members of official enquiries into economic and social issues did become routine between the wars, as did government establishing such committees in the first place for medium- to long-term policy issues. This is observable across a range of policy issues. Thus, in microeconomics Tawney and Sidney Webb were members of the Samuel commission into the coal industry (1919), Salter and Stamp were chairman and a member respectively of the 1932 rail and road transport conference which considered the thorny problem of the basis of fair competition in goods transportation between these two sectors, while Chapman continued to participate in official enquiries long after his retirement from the Board of Trade (for example, the 1936 Import Duties Advisory Committee report on the steel industry). In what was to become macroeconomics we would highlight Pigou's membership of the Cunliffe committee in 1918–19, which set the framework for the eventual return to gold, and the royal commission on the income tax (1920); and Gregory and Keynes's membership of the Macmillan committee on the finance and industry and trade (1929–31), in effect an official search for a means of escape from the deflationary implications of the gold standard decision. But we should also note that in two of the most sensitive of all economic reports between the wars, those of the Geddes (1921–2) and May committees (1931) on public expenditure, the latter in part responsible for the collapse of the second Labour government, there were no economist members.

It is no exaggeration that in their absence these committees never heard a serious economic analysis of the benefits of public expenditure, this with significant – deflationary – results for the fiscal stance subsequently adopted. However, the omission was not felt for such analyses would have been politically unwelcome. Furthermore, it is arguable that the most appropriate test of whether economists had attained a more significant position within the policy community is whom ministers and senior officials turned to in times of crisis. Here the evidence is somewhat mixed. Thus during and immediately after the 1931 crisis,[42] which resulted in the suspension of the

---

[42] Moggridge (1992, pp. 527–9) records that Keynes and Stamp were brought into Treasury discussions on the day before suspension and that, when in effect offered the opportunity to use his privileged insider information, Keynes did not take financial advantage of this, either in his own affairs or to those institutions he advised.

gold standard, we find the prime minister, always rather prone to panic and indecision, casting far and wide for advice and with Keynes and other economists only too willing to respond. The chancellor and his officials also took soundings from outside, from EAC members and from the Bank-City-business networks.[43] In the Bank of England itself, Sayers's (1976, vol. 2, ch. 17) account of the crisis accords some prominence to the economic advisers: first to Sprague, the official adviser, and then to Clay and to Stamp (a Bank director), especially once gold payments had been suspended and the authorities were extremely anxious about the risk of an uncontrollable depreciation of sterling and the threat of inflation. Yet, for all this the 1931 crisis was widely interpreted at the time as a bankers' ramp in which the Labour government was brought down because the Bank and the financial community so narrowed the policy space that the politicians had no room for manoeuvre and no means of using the independent advice they were receiving from economists and others. Indeed, the 1931 crisis lives on in the collective memory of the Labour Party, being for example invoked during the rather different circumstances of 1976, and it is no accident that the Bank was the first institution to be nationalised in 1946.

For the Bank these events marked the end of its historic, exclusive authority in monetary policy; for government it represented the beginning of quite uncharted territory, that of discretionary economic management; and, for the economists, new and greater opportunities to influence policy now that the foundation of the minimalist state had been shattered. To understand the full significance of this we now turn to consider how and why Britain had returned to gold in the first place and the role that economists and economic ideas had played in that decision.

5.5 KEYNES, THE GOLD STANDARD AND THE QUEST FOR 'FREEDOM OF CHOICE'

The decision to return to the gold standard in 1925 at the prewar parity of $4.86 to the pound, and of its implications for economic performance thereafter, continues to excite controversy.[44] Over seventy years have now

---

[43] Howson (1975, pp. 78–86, app. 4) and Howson and Winch (1977, ch. 4).

[44] On the decision itself Moggridge (1972), supplemented by Howson (1975), remains the key work. This should be supplemented by Pollard's (1970b) polemic (an embryonic version of his 1984 thesis on the Treasury's 'contempt for production'), Sayers's (1960) well-balanced assessment, Tomlinson (1981b, ch. 6) and the important revisionist essay of Boyce (1988). Ham (1981) provides the best example of the potential of the 1925 decision to underpin a longer-term critique of British economic policy as a series of recurring themes and policy failures. Finally, Solomou (1996, ch. 2) provides a rigorous economic assessment of the exchange rate and economic performance in the 1920s.

passed; there have been other equally significant errors in exchange rate policy since (1964, 1990); and episodes in which sterling has appreciated much more under market pressures (25 per cent between 1979–81) than the supposed overvaluation of 10 per cent in 1925; yet, there is something about the decision which continues to fascinate as if it embodies an especial truth about British economic policy and an inherent tendency towards failure.

Johnson's counterfactual

The significance of this policy decision, according to some, is truly momentous. Few have put it as starkly as Harry Johnson (1975a, pp. 110–11) but a variety of counterfactuals do suggest themselves:

> Had the exchange value of the pound been fixed realistically in the 1920s – a prescription fully in accord with orthodox economic theory – there would have been no need for mass unemployment, hence no need for a revolutionary new theory to explain it, and no triggering force for much subsequent British political and economic history. The country would have been worse off than it remembered being before the First World War, due to the inevitable pressures of industrial obsolescence, and the large majority of the assuredly employed or otherwise provided with money income would have been worse off than they actually were, but this would have been more than offset by the gains of those who would have been employed instead of unemployed. With reasonably full employment in the 1920s, moreover, the economic adjustment to industrial obsolescence would probably have been both easier and more effective (involving less concentration on promoting the survival of traditional industries and the preservation of traditional markets for their products – including the Empire) and the political adjustment to Britain's declining importance in the world less crisis-torn and traumatic (for example, Britain might have joined the Common Market at the beginning, or else remained dramatically aloof from it).

At one extreme we thus have the tantalising suggestion that, had the Treasury heeded Keynes's warnings about the gold standard and the prewar parity, there would have been no need for a Keynesian revolution (p. 112). Indeed, in this counterfactual, had there not been the British policy error of 1925, compounded by the Federal Reserve's error of 1929, which transformed an ordinary US cyclical adjustment into a downturn of global force, the 'Great Depression ... would have been nipped in the bud and *The General Theory* either not written, or been received as one eccentric English economist's rationalisation of his local problems ... [but] As it occurred, however, the Great Depression and international monetary collapse set the stage for a view of capitalism and of appropriate government policy to manage it oriented towards the problems of Britain in the 1920s to become the majority view of economists in the Anglo-Saxon countries ever since'.

While this relativist view of progress in economics is contentious, and many would question whether orthodox theory was able fully to explain interwar developments, Johnson was surely right to identify the 1925 decision as the spark which ignited the intellectual quest for national autonomy in macroeconomic policy which culminated in the *General theory*. He was right also in that, had there not been deficient aggregate demand, the adjustment crisis of British industry could have been better handled by both market and government; and, as confirmed by recent research (for example, Eichengreen 1992), substantially correct that the restored gold standard did set the stage for the world depression by heightening the fragility of the international financial system. The suggestion that mass unemployment, which appeared in Britain in the 1920s and in other OECD states in the 1930s, detracted from the appreciation of longer-term economic decline also has some substance, while the notion that interwar unemployment exercised a searing influence over British policy for a quarter of a century after the Second World War is indisputable.

Our concern here is not with the economic impact of the return to gold, for only a minority of economists have since dissented from Keynes's polemical post-mortem on the decision, *The economic consequences of Mr Churchill* (1925): that sterling was overvalued by 10 per cent or so, that this depressed net exports, compelled deflationary monetary policies to support the exchange rate and narrowed the policy space by closing off certain policy options such as a more expansionary (less deflationary) fiscal policy or a greater public works effort. Rather, of more interest is the mechanics of the decision, what it reveals about the evolving relationship between economists and policy-makers, the constraints (real, self-imposed and delusional) under which policy-makers operated and the possibilities, once the gold standard was finally abandoned in 1931, for regaining that 'freedom of choice' after which Keynes (1931, p. xix) and others hankered.

The decision to return

Our account necessarily begins towards the close of the First World War when, with Britain still notionally on the gold standard, there was established the Cunliffe committee on currency and foreign exchanges after the war. Given terms of reference which included 'report[ing] upon the steps required to bring about the restoration of normal conditions in due course', a chairman who was the outgoing Bank of England governor, a membership dominated by City representatives (ten in all), and with senior Treasury officials (Blackett and Bradbury) outnumbering professional economists (Pigou) by two to one, and with the one economist no monetary expert and temperamentally ill-suited to being an official adviser (Collard 1990, p. 188), it is not surprising that, as Moggridge (1972, p. 18) describes it:

The Committee *assumed* that Britain would return to the gold standard at the pre-war par, and members of the Committee and witnesses did not question this assumption by either considering alternative gold standard rates or alternative currency policies.

The committees' two reports (HMSO 1918; 1919) established the policy framework thereafter, dictating – after a lag in which there was a short postwar inflationary boom, which served to reinforce the appeal of the deflationary solution – the interlocking disinflationary monetary, fiscal and debt management policies which were the authorities' response to the economic problems engendered by the war and the means of regaining prewar conditions. The reports were, in Keynes's (1923, p. 153) phrase, the Treasury and Bank of England's 'marching orders'; they were also, as he further argued, flawed in almost every conceivable way: poor examples indeed relative to the long and distinguished British tradition of government-sponsored monetary commissions (Morgan 1970, pp. 7, 9). Thus, the first report, which was the more important, justified its policy recommendation of a speedy return to an effective gold standard at prewar parity, this to be brought about by suitably deflationary fiscal and monetary policies, in terms of an idyllic and wholly ahistorical account of the operation of the prewar gold standard. Indeed, in its stress upon the automatic, hydraulic qualities of the British money supply and balance of payments adjustment mechanism, the committee were guilty of confusing stylised facts with real analysis (Eichengreen 1992, pp. 35–7). From such a weak basis it was perhaps inevitable that the problems of the transition to the lower price level, which would make possible the prewar parity, were finessed, even to the point that the committee spoke not of higher unemployment but of some 'decline in employment'. No quantitative analysis was attempted, a characteristic of official policy-making until a more reasoned and statistically-based policy style was forced upon the authorities in the later 1920s when the Treasury view had publicly to be defended against the onslaught of Keynes and Lloyd George.

The problem of the transition was, in any case, seen largely in terms of how inflationary financial policies had resulted in UK prices diverging from the US level, the sole country comparator; the war's implications for the real economy were largely missed, while contemporaries appeared quite unaware of what we would now identify as one of the most significant developments of this period: the opening up of a huge productivity gap between Britain and the US which, to maintain competitiveness, would have required a substantial devaluation on the prewar parity (Barkai 1993). Append to this the deterioration on the capital account of the balance of payments, which halved the surplus on the invisibles account compared with prewar, and the potential external constraint was magnified yet further. The myopia of the committee can be partially explained by its composition and that its deliberations were completed three months before the armistice, at which point no mature judgement about the war's economic significance was possible, while in any case the gold standard had not yet been formally abandoned (with sterling pegged at $4.76). But, fatally, when it came to submit its final report in December 1919, by which point the heavy cost of foreign exchange support operations had resulted in the abandonment of gold, with sterling trading at a heavy discount (falling to a low of $3.40 by February 1920) and the price level yet further inflated, the committee did not see fit to emphasise how radically different circumstances now were.

The earlier message prevailed because the relevance of its immediate policy recommendation – the deflationary solution – had become politically possible now that politicians, under strong lobbying from the Bank and the Treasury, were re-evaluating the trade-off between unemployment and inflation. In November 1918 the choice had been: either impose the deflationary solution, and risk spiralling unemployment and political upheaval during the demobilisation phase; or delay deflation and risk spiralling inflation but with the pay-off of lower unemployment and – hopefully – lessened political conflict (Middleton 1996, pp. 311, 357). A year later, amidst a wild inflationary boom, and with a wage-price spiral, punctuated by strikes and extremist politics, in progress, delay in adopting the deflationary solution had brought about the very result that politicians had initially sought to avoid. The toughening of the policy stance initiated in December 1919, which eventually brought dear money, credit contraction and an unprecedented fiscal tightening, did more than break the inflationary boom. It had to permanently depress demand, putting downward pressure on wages and prices, if the prewar parity was to be regained.

The lengthy interval between the Cunliffe committee's final report and the actual decision to return to gold at the prewar parity, which was announced by Churchill as the centrepiece of his April 1925 budget, but later deeply regretted as one of the worst decisions of his career, is usually portrayed in terms of the ineluctable course of events driving governments (in sequence coalition, Conservative, minority Labour and then Conservative) towards such a decision as soon as the exchange rate approached parity. The inevitability of the outcome has been questioned, but only occasionally and typically by those whose grasp of the economic fundamentals was in advance of their understanding of political realities (for example, Reddaway 1970). The determination with which the eventual objective was sought, and the acclaim with which Churchill's announcement was greeted, should not, however, blind us to the very real – but imperfectly communicated – dissent from this decision in certain quarters and the uphill struggle faced by the Bank of England and the Treasury in persuading an entirely sceptical Chancellor who, by temperament, would far rather have seen 'Finance less proud and Industry more content.'[45] It is no wonder that, after his exhaustive research into the 1925 decision, Moggridge (1972, p. 234) concluded that 'the decision-making style of the Authorities at the time is one of the most interesting aspects of the return to gold.'

The interwar policy style

From this episode we can identify six characteristics of the policy style which support our broader thesis.

First, the gold standard decision was not the result of thorough, impartial analysis. Neither the condition of the current account balance of payments, nor the relative price implications of $4.86, received consideration. The dominant qualitative mode of analysis mitigated against such questions, as did the underlying (Marshallian) preoccupation with the long-run when considering the transitional phase as the economy adjusted to the gold parity. Moreover, geo-political preoccupations (UK-US relations) appeared to determine the country chosen for comparison, rather than those economies actually preponderant in British trade.

Secondly, there were the difficulties that confront a Chancellor who takes office unconvinced by civil service economic priorities and modes of reasoning. Time and time again Churchill pressed the claim of the unemployed and of the business sector, even invoking Keynes when he lamented that 'The Treasury have never, it seems to me, faced the profound significance of what Mr Keynes calls "the paradox of unemployment amidst dearth"' while 'The Governor shows himself perfectly happy in the spectacle of Britain possessing the finest credit in the world simultaneously with a million and a quarter unemployed' (cited in Moggridge 1972, p. 75). In so doing, Moggridge records, he 'phrased the problems involved in a manner that cried out for analysis, but neither he nor anyone else really demanded it' (p. 234). In this sense, the officials were successful in contriving a limited policy space in which they could assure the Chancellor that there really was no alternative (Clarke 1990b, p. 169).

Thirdly, officials, in confining the terms of the debate to terrain most easily defended, also acted as gatekeepers to potentially dissident opinions which could be represented as academic (Keynes), crankish or both; and exercised great influence over those chosen to advise, as for example in the membership of the Chamberlain-Bradbury committee (additionally, Farrer the banker, Niemeyer and Pigou) which provided the so-called expert

---

[45] Churchill to Niemeyer (22 February 1925), cited in Moggridge (1972, p. 76), one of a series of exchanges in which the Chancellor required his officials to justify their policy advice.

analysis upon which the decision was supposedly based.

Fourthly, there is the majesty of high politics even in circumstances where a decision might be represented as purely technical and economic. Thus at the famous dinner party of 17 March, hosted by Churchill and attended by Niemeyer, Bradbury, McKenna and Keynes, with Grigg (1948, pp. 182–3) as unofficial reporter, the latter reports that after listening to the 'gloomy prognostications of Keynes and McKenna', the only two consistent opponents of return, Churchill turned to McKenna and said: "'But this isn't entirely an economic matter; it is a political decision, for it involves proclaiming that we cannot ... complete the undertaking which we all acclaimed as necessary in 1918 .... You have been a politician; indeed you have been Chancellor of the Exchequer. Given the situation as it is, what decision would you take." McKenna's reply ... was: "There is no escape; you have got to go back; but it will be hell."' The phrase to 'complete the undertaking' was a reference to the strongest element of inevitability in the whole episode, that the Gold and Silver (Export Control) Act, 1920, which gave legal force to the suspension of gold, was due to automatically expire on 31 December 1925. Not to have returned to gold would thus have required fresh legislation and to have invited a storm of criticism, within and outside of Parliament. Moreover, geo-political considerations impinged once more in the form of the sterling area as the southern dominions 'nagged' Britain to return to gold while equally Britain nagged them towards a coordinated return. We find, therefore, a strong element of mutually reinforcing pressures leading to what we might call policy lock-in.

Fifthly, high politics impinged also in the more constitutional sense that senior Treasury officials and the Bank's Governor, the latter according to his critics having made his public lack of interest in the unemployed and the real economy into something of a fetish, continued to practise a style of policy advice as if there had not been the advent of democracy and the rise of labour. This was not mere Establishment disdain for real world developments; on the contrary, it was that they now feared the political market place and its potential to corrupt politicians and thus economic policy. The gold standard and balanced budgets, two of the three traditional defences of the minimalist laissez-faire state, were now more important than ever. It might be objected that, with unemployment already high by historical standards before the decision was made, their actions were wholly unrealistic. But the force of the public service ethic should not be understated, especially as the Treasury had emerged from the war with greatly enhanced powers. It is important also that in the early 1920s the fact of unemployment did not translate automatically into unemployment being the central preoccupation of policy (Tomlinson 1981b, ch. 4), although it was the case that as the 1925 budget approached Niemeyer was beginning to reposition the case for return in terms of it being an employment policy, somewhat ironic given its eventual role in employment destruction.

Sixthly, while the extent of public and interest group agreement with the policy was overstated by its proponents, the case put by the opposition lacked the force that it might have had if it had been better organised. There was persistent criticism of the deflationary stance initiated by the Cunliffe report, and not just from Keynes or from industry, but from within the City itself. Thus 'Keynes might ... be more appropriately regarded as having been, before 1925, in the vanguard of a movement rather than as a voice in the wilderness' (Hume 1963, p. 124). Keynes's heroic role thus needs qualification, while the whole episode illustrates the capacity of establishment opinion to marginalise dissident voices, especially on currency questions where the policy debate can be wrapped up in terms of honour and responsibility, the clarion calls of economic patriotism manifest in the defence of the exchange rate (Boyce 1988). Even so, at the point at which it might have mattered, in giving evidence before the Chamberlain-Bradbury committee, Keynes did not make the best of defences of his managed currency proposal because he, in common with other witnesses, did not appreciate that the committee was actually considering the return to gold. Its title, committee on currency and Bank of England note issue, was unhelpful in this regard, as was its practice of only taking oral evidence which prevented the submission of more considered grounds for opposing the drift of official opinion.[46] Certain weaknesses are also evident in the activities of the Federation of British Industries (FBI), the antecedent (with other employers' associations) of today's CBI. This peak association, which was the only agricultural, industrial or labour organisation to submit evidence to the Chamberlain-Bradbury committee, was still very much in embryonic form and unrepresentative in its membership. It was, however, dominated by the staple, export sectors who could be expected to have a strong interest in exchange rate regimes and rates. But it never put the business case effectively, with its failure to draw together business opinion into one voice a pattern which was to be repeated when it came to the tariff debate of the early 1930s. The immaturity of corporatism in Britain thus helped maintain the dominance of the traditional economic policy community, although we should note in passing that the FBI shortly afterwards appointed an economic adviser – albeit a chemist, turned lawyer, turned economist.[47]

Ultimately, the decision to return to gold was a gamble: on future movements in US prices; on continued money wage flexibility in the UK;

---

[46] For this episode, see Moggridge (1972, pp. 38–51) and, for this particular argument, Reddaway (1970); see also Keynes's *EJ* review (vol. 35 (June 1925), pp. 299–304) of the committee's report in which he did not disguise his outrage at what had occurred.

[47] Roy Glenday (1889–1957); joined the FBI in 1918 and was its Economic Director, 1928–48.

and on potential dissident opinion not disturbing the foreign exchange markets and the upward speculative drift of sterling. Above all it was a gamble, or gigantic delusion according to taste, that the British government and the Bank of England maintained the geo-political presence and economic capacity to lead the world back to an international payments system largely of its design. In this sense also it was an anachronism, the final death throws of a policy style, displaying 'blissful and often aggressive ignorance' (Moggridge 1972, p. 235) which could not endure the political and economic challenges to the minimalist laissez-faire state. In short, the return to gold, and its ignominious but utterly predictable suspension six years later, marked a turning-point in British economic policy. Once the dust had settled from the financial crisis of 1931 British economic policy was, slowly, hesitantly but eventually significantly transformed as politicians and their advisers took advantage of the regained 'freedom of choice'.

Such was the reorientation of policy after 1931 that, even in that citadel of sound finance, **Norman** eventually not only questioned the desirability of resuming the gold standard at some future point but, very probably under the influence of Clay, became a convert to the Keynesian solution of counter-cyclical public works, and so much so that he was to complain of the orthodoxy of the Chancellor in this matter.[48] But here also, in the Treasury, there were to be major changes: with gold gone, exchange rate policy was now directed towards domestic objectives (the cheap money policy) with no return to gold countenanced at some future date; and officials, while maintaining their opposition to the full Keynesian solution, none the less sanctioned the preparation of a counter-cyclical public works programme in 1937–8, though this was rather overtaken by events. Indeed, by the eve of the war, and under the strains imposed by debt-financed rearmament, Treasury officials were consciously managing aggregate demand so as to limit inflationary pressures and maximise the long-term supply capacity of the British economy. These developments, the full significance of which were deliberately shrouded from public view, should not be interpreted as signifying official conversion to Keynesian policies, though from the documents in the PRO it is clear that Treasury officials were working with an implicit Keynesian income-expenditure identity in the way in which they thought of the interaction between financial policy and the real economy. Thus rearmament, whilst making a major contribution towards lessening the

---

[48] Sayers's (1976, vol. II, pp. 462–3) source for this bombshell was the Per Jacobsson dairies, extracts from which had been published by his daughter, Erin E. Jacobsson in 1968 (under the name Erin E. Jucker-Fleetwood). Since then she has published a life of her father which provides both a fuller account of this episode (1979, pp. 109–11) and has done something to rehabilitate Norman as an altogether warmer personality and as a central banker who was receptive to new ideas. Per Jacobsson (1894–1963), a professional economist, was at this time Economic Adviser to the Bank for International Settlements, and later Managing Director of the IMF, 1956–63.

severity of the 1937–8 recession, did not validate the Keynesian solution in peacetime (Middleton 1985, p. 119). Once more it was war, or in this case the preparation for war, which was decisive.

By 1939 we can, therefore, detect demand management in embryonic form, but as an innovation forced upon the authorities and carrying with it no peacetime commitments because of the continued aversion to deficit-finance. But the floating exchange rate regime, cheap money, tariffs (free trade having finally been abandoned in late 1931) and the development of regional and industrial policy instruments all point to a transformation of British economic policy, one which would endure and evidence of what was possible when no longer fettered by gold. The break with gold is decisive, but the pace and significance of subsequent developments cannot be fully understood without an appreciation of the preparatory work undertaken in many quarters. In preparing official opinion for a world without the anchor of gold we particularly highlight the Macmillan committee which reported in July 1931. Whilst its report was to be somewhat overshadowed by the financial crisis of that summer, in the longer-term it was highly significant in the evolution of the managed economy. Amongst its major recommendations was the categorical injunction that 'The monetary system of this country must be a managed system' as 'It is not advisable, or indeed practicable, to regard our monetary system as an automatic system, grinding out the right result by the operation of natural forces aided by a few maxims of general application and some well-worn rules of thumb.' In rejecting – so pithily – the invisible hand and the authorities' practice of DIYE the committee pressed home 'that in the case of our financial, as in the case of our political and social, institutions we may well have reached the stage when an era of conscious and deliberate management must succeed the era of undirected natural evolution'. From this came the first attempt to specify the appropriate objectives of economic policy:

> the maintenance of the parity of the foreign exchanges without unnecessary disturbance to domestic business, the avoidance of the Credit Cycle, and the stability of the price level . . .
> . . .
> The endeavour of domestic management should be to promote the stability of output and of employment at a high level.   (HMSO 1931, paras 9, 280, 282)

In making the case for a managed economy the committee made clear that its realisation was contingent *inter alia* on policy-makers becoming more technically proficient and on being better served by official statistics. Deficiencies in the latter were particularly highlighted and an unfavourable comparison drawn with American developments: 'There can be few worse perversions of the ideal of wise economy than a narrow limitation on what we spend for the improvement of economic knowledge' (para. 406), a reference perhaps to the Treasury's refusal, on the establishment of the EAC, to buy Colin Clark an adding machine.[49] While the committee saw responsibility for the managed currency as residing with the politically-independent Bank of England there was a clear imputation about the appropriate level of technical expertise required for the modern world: 'To put on a more scientific basis our acquaintance with the fundamental facts and trends of our economic life, and to replace empiricism by ordered knowledge, might prove to be the greatest step forward that it lies within our power to take towards raising the economic well-being of our country to the level which the technique of production would allow' (paras 280, 425). This reaffirmation of rational deliberateness derived more from the severity of Britain's economic circumstances and less from a regard for the achievements of professional economists in guiding the committee towards its conclusions. Indeed, in the preface to the report one detects some disappointment about what the professionals could practically offer because of their propensity to disputation (paras 5–6). It is, of course, supremely ironic that just as the Macmillan committee was calling time for the amateur in economic policy, Warren Fisher, the Treasury's permanent secretary, was actually promoting the cult of the amateur to new heights by his stress upon the generalist in the higher civil service (Peden 1999, ch. 5).

5.6 CONCLUSIONS

British economics came of age between the wars in two very distinct senses: as an increasingly self-confident, research-driven academic community with a heightened public profile, if not always repute; and, for a few leading lights within the profession, as a significant supplier of expertise in the marketplace for economic ideas upon which politicians and their officials increasingly came to rely, if only to reject their advice as part of risk-sharing and damage limitation exercises. For Harry Johnson the period stretching from the late 1920s through the mid-1950s was a 'second golden age of British economics', one in which, 'at least in the historical short run, the publication and reception of *The General Theory* gave British economics a prestige in the outside world that it had possessed up to and including the heyday of Marshall but which had been waning ever since, the publication of Joan Robinson's *Economics of Imperfect Competition* constituting the major exception to this generalisation' (1972b, p. 835; 1975a, p. 116). Table 5.3

---

[49] Howson and Winch (1977, p. 25) further observe: 'Given the tradition of Treasury control, the development of national income estimates in 1940 was no doubt facilitated by the fact that Richard Stone bought his own machine.'

Table 5.3   *Economists cited most frequently in a 1948 AEA survey of*
             contemporary economics

Rank	Name	No of citations
1	Keynes, J.M.	70
2	Hicks, J.R.	34
3	Lange, O.	28
4	Marshall, A.	24
5	Pigou, A.C.	23
6	Lerner, A.P.	22
7	Samuelson, P.A.	20
8	Chamberlin, E.H.	19
9=	Hansen, A.H./Kuznets, S./Schumpeter, J.A.	18
10	Clark, J.M.	17
11	Machlup, F.	16
12=	Haberler, G./Robinson, J.	15
13=	Fellner, W./Robertson, D.H.	14
14=	Hart, A.G./Ohlin, B.	13
15=	Pareto, V./Stigler, G.J.	12

Source: Stigler (1949, table 1).

more than confirms this in terms of the economists' preferred indicator of prestige, the rankings here being taken from a major AEA survey of contemporary economics (Ellis 1948). The dominance of Keynes by this measure is so significant that those uncomfortable with the notion of a Keynesian revolution in theory should pause for thought. We should note also the prominent position attained by Hicks at this early point in the postwar period; conversely, that Marshall and his favourite pupil were not quickly ejected from the league tables.

Our account of the process of professionalisation stressed that in certain respects significant progress was made with Marshall's mission but that there were also developments which he would probably have abhorred. The doubling of university economists and of the number of undergraduates would have been welcomed, the continued difficulties in placing the new graduates in employment appropriate to their degree would, however, have disappointed, as would the limited progress towards economic chivalry. No doubt the growth in numbers – if not systematic training – of postgraduates, and of the greater specialisation in research, would also have found approval; that much of the spur to research rested on a rejection of the authority of the past masters, and that much of the published output was of a scientistic style that was no longer accessible to the intelligent businessman, would have disappointed. We have particularly stressed the part played by the younger economists in the developing interwar research programme and of how Keynes provided a role model for those for whom, as Shackle (1967, p. 291) puts it, the war had been a 'psychic release', giving renewed ethical purpose to economics and unshackling the young from the imperative to defer to established authority if they were to attain professional advance. In this sense British economics, in common with much interwar intellectual activity, benefited from a youthful rebelliousness born of the traumas of the First World War and of the disappointments with postwar reconstruction.

For all of these advances in the variety, quality and volume of economics research in Britain serious deficiencies remained in terms of the infrastructure for research, especially with respect to America. No progress had been made in securing regular state funding for economics research, or indeed for any social research, whereas in the US a Social Science Research Council had been established in 1924. The US was also the home to a growing number of independent research organisations which provided employment for economists and agencies for applied economics of a high standard: foremost here being the National Bureau of Economic Research (founded 1920), the Brookings Institution (1927, though with origins in 1916) and the Cowles Commission for Research in Economics (1932) which was funded specifically to undertake econometric research and with *Econometrica* as the in-house journal. Fortunately, the largess of American charitable foundations stretched to involvement in British projects designed to create comparable institutions, in particular the Rockefeller Foundation which aided the foundation of the Oxford Institute of Economics and Statistics in 1935 and the NIESR in 1938.[50]

There also remains Durbin's charge that the very public disputes between economists undermined the profession's standing between the wars. Whilst any verdict upon this hinges on attitudes towards Keynes's achievements, and whether he revolutionised economic theory, it is also the case that within Whitehall the disputatiousness of economists was used, genuinely or otherwise, as a justification for limiting any substantive role that they might play in policy formulation. Thus Leith-Ross's 1928 comment which Clarke (1988, p. 49) cites, that 'I am sorry to see that Keynes is renewing the Press propaganda which has done him little credit as a politician and considerable harm as an economist', and Hopkins's 1932 complaint about economists which we cited earlier (p. 82), can be read two ways: one of which being a relief by hard-pressed civil servants grappling with problems that they barely understood and in which in their confusion they were clearly not alone.

---

[50]   Morgan (1990, pp. 44, 55), Backhouse (1997a, p. 34) and Jones (1988, p. 37).

Alternatively, as Galbraith (1975a, p. 133) has found from experience: 'Public officials do not always admire men who say what the right policy should be'. We should note also that, as occurred later in the 1970s with the monetarists and Keynesians, economists' disputes were greatly overstated by those with more 'practical', market-based economic knowledge who were anxious to limit the influence of academic economists.

The value for the Treasury of Keynes's onslaught is typically omitted from assessments of the interwar policy debate or acknowledged purely in terms of the progress made by 1939 in converting official opinion to the Keynesian cause. Yet, more than anything else it was external censure which forced the Treasury to modernise itself and to take seriously academic economics and economists. The savage onslaught to which the Baldwin government's defence of the Treasury view was subjected in 1929, the humiliation of Norman by Keynes when the Governor gave evidence before the Macmillan committee in 1930, and even Hopkins's discomfiture under close questioning when appearing before that committee,[51] all made a deep impression on Treasury officials. Hitherto, although Hawtrey, the Treasury's one economist, had played some part in the preparation of Treasury arguments used on public occasions, even providing the earliest academic defence for the Treasury view on the futility of public works, as a self-taught economist his major influence was if anything to convince his generalist colleagues that economic theory posed no great intellectual challenge nor had any real relevance to the administrative tasks facing the department. Moreover, given Hawtrey's diagnosis – much of it made public in his many books and journal articles[52] – that Britain's difficulties in the second half of the 1920s stemmed from the high interest rates forced by the return to gold, it is not difficult to see that he would not be a key player in the education and professionalisation of the Treasury that was increasingly forced upon them. Rather, with Niemeyer dispatched to the Bank and Leith-Ross detained on largely external economic matters, it was Hopkins, brought by Fisher from Inland Revenue, Phillips, of whom Keynes had the highest regard, and some younger officials (for example, Bridges) who together, quietly and without fuss transformed the Treasury in the 1930s. While outwardly still at loggerheads with Keynes, and still seriously handicapped by the weaknesses of official statistics, in attitude and policy capability the Treasury by 1939 was very different from that of twenty years earlier. In no

---

[51] On Hopkins, one of the two key interwar Treasury figures, see Peden (1983).

[52] For example, Hawtrey (1927; 1931). Even by the standards of this time, Hawtrey was a prolific writer for a full-time civil servant, so much so that in the 1920s his work in macroeconomics was cited more frequently than Keynes's. Deutscher's (1990, pp. 269–71) incomplete listing of his works includes ten books and ten journal articles/comments published between the wars. Our *EJ* database has 11 articles/notes and memoranda and 26 book reviews in that journal alone between 1920–39.

small measure the economists' challenge to orthodoxy contributed towards this outcome.

While the market for economic advice remained highly contestable between the wars the disputes between economists stemmed not just from differing theoretical and policy positions but from a cleavage between rival camps about the appropriate role of the economist in proffering advice. On the one hand there were those, exemplified by Pigou's conduct during the Cunliffe and Chamberlain-Bradbury committees, who saw the adviser's role as to operate within the constraints laid down by policy-makers (to go back to gold, but when?), and those who followed Keynes and rejected this passivity, thereby interpreting the economist's responsibility as more fundamental and open-ended (should there be a return to gold, and if so at what rate?). This was hardly a new tension at the heart of economics, but the stakes were altogether higher which is why Cambridge economics reacted so negatively to Robbins and the *Essay* which they interpreted as an objection to economists' participation in policy whereas his intention was that economists' advice would acquire greater authority once presented as genuine, value-free science.

We have already shown the decisive role played by the gold standard in propelling Keynes towards a form of policy advocacy and theoretical reappraisal with momentous consequences for British economics and economic policy. We conclude our interwar discussion by emphasising two such consequences which, arguably, proved particularly durable and deleterious to the long-term influence of academic economists. First, in so limiting the authorities' room for manoeuvre the gold standard forced its most severe critics to great ingenuity in circumventing its worst excesses, as they saw them. For Keynes, ever ingenious, the challenge of economic policy became that of designing elegant means of escape from the self-imposed constraints of policy-makers. This inevitably made economic policy appear as much political as technical, compelled a flexibility with attendant risk that he be accused of policy inconstancy and, perhaps unavoidably, resulted in little attention being devoted to the fate of Keynesian policy solutions in a future world which did not share the presuppositions of Harvey Road (p. 45). Secondly, the gold standard era led Keynes and the greater number, but not all, of his associates to focus on aggregate demand and macroeconomics, this to the detriment of a fuller understanding of the supply-side of the economy, in particular to an earlier appreciation of the deep-seated problems of industrial inefficiency which underlay the relative economic decline of the British economy.

6. Economists triumphant? The Keynesian era and golden age growth

American economists are fundamentally more serious about their subject than we are; and the result of this is that they are better economists, but less useful ones.
(Sargent 1963, pp. 1–2)

The descent in reputation of British economics – a science in which we led the world 25 years ago – . . . [is] just one small illustration of this country's decline in its past two insular decades.
(Anon 1971, p. 12)

6.1 INTRODUCTION

For a profession whose reputation, indeed self-esteem, had been so battered by its inability to agree a (Keynesian) solution to the mass unemployment of the 1920s and 1930s the Second World War provided an unparalleled opportunity for redemption; for entryism; even for the fulfilment of those ambitions for enduring influence which had initially motivated Marshall's mission. Here at last was a project of such moment that the profession could demonstrate to public and policy-makers alike that not only did they possess valuable, expert knowledge but that, in time of emergency, the application of this knowledge could be critical to the nation's survival.

As we saw in chapter 3, the subsequent verdict on the contribution made by those economists recruited to Whitehall for war service has, almost without exception, been highly favourable. For the most part playing a 'modest and unobtrusive role' (Booth 1986, p. 673), the fifty or so, mostly quite junior, economists who became 'irregulars' not only did much to rebuild the reputation and public standing of the profession but created the possibility of a durable, enhanced peacetime role at or close to the centre of government. Some, of course, went far beyond a modest and unobtrusive role. Indeed, the massive contributions of Keynes and Beveridge towards what has become known as the postwar settlement conveyed the impression to the public that, at last, ideas had triumphed over vested interests and that the expert had ascended to their rightful place in government.

In this and the following chapter we chart the shifting fortunes of economics and economists since the Second World War, with the divide drawn at 1973 with Britain's membership of the European Community (EC) and OPEC I: the former initiating a process which – together with globalisation – would eventually erode national autonomy in economic policy, while the latter signalled both the end of the golden age of economic growth and the period in which economists might take some credit for economic achievements. In this first chapter we explore the extent to which the British profession was able to build upon its wartime success to achieve an enduring role in policy formulation and with what consequences for economic policy and performance. The case for economists triumphant might be put thus:

- economics was diffused into the schools and consolidated its position in the universities, indeed became the premier social science;
- by all output measures (undergraduate and postgraduate enrolments and publications) the discipline flourished;
- within the labour market, an economics degree becoming the qualification of choice for a significant number of the new managerial and technocratic classes;
- with the arrival of the 1964 Wilson administration offering a radical, modernising vision of Britain, the economists appeared to achieve a major breakthrough in terms of government service; and
- economists might, above all, claim some responsibility for the achievement of full employment since the war and for the unparalleled affluence enjoyed if not by all then – relative to post-1973 economic growth – at least by the many.

Solid reasons can thus be presented for why, by the middle 1960s, the economists' stock was high and their prospects good. Alternatively, these years can be represented very differently. Indeed, we have a choice of negative spins which can be developed from our earlier (pp. 21–3) discussion of:

- Postan's plague of economists: that the US-inspired quest for greater formalism and mathematical sophistication robbed economics of its policy relevance and, combined with local difficulties and policy mistakes, brought British economics to its knees by the middle 1970s to the extent that, from the serious press to alehouse banter, it was widely reported that the most robust empirical relationship for the British economy was that of the inverse correlation between its position in the growth league tables and the number of economists employed in the GES (Hennessy 1975).

* the Harry Johnson critique: that the problem was not the shortcomings of economics but the deficiencies of British economists who had not professionalised in the American sense of becoming an independent scientific community proffering expert advice. For Johnson (1973a, p. 70) British economics had become corrupted, 'converted from a scientific subject into a species of political necromancy'; its practitioners no longer politically independent but, because of class, Oxbridge dominance and much else that was socially dysfunctional, 'intelligent parrot[s], concerned either with maintaining that [their] country is still as great as it used to be – or could be if only it followed [their] advice – or with asserting that if it would only follow some policy adopted by the dominant countries it could restore its greatness.' In this view of the world after Keynes, leadership in economics was not so much wrestled from Britain as passed by default to the US. Thus, save Harrod's extension of Keynes's work to growth theory, with his *Towards a dynamic economics* (1948), and Meade's 'monumental though tedious-to-read' *Theory of international economic policy* (1951; 1955a), British economics produced little of interest and much that was sterile (Johnson 1975a, p. 117), the Cambridge capital controversy typifying the latter.

The fate of British economics after Keynes might be likened to that of Britain's economic performance during the golden age: whilst attaining its fastest rate of growth of output in historical terms, and maintaining some leading-edge world companies, the overall picture was nonetheless one of relative decline. However, unlike the stylised facts of relative economic decline, whereby after the Second World War Britain lost ground to Japan and Europe more than to the US, in terms of economics we can argue that by output measures and prestige Britain maintained its position with respect to all of the OECD save the US. This was, of course, the characteristic of the first stage of the relative decline of the British economy, and we here explain this as a consequence of the British delaying mass higher education and thus maintaining a research effort in the social sciences which was atypical of the non-North American OECD states. It also makes more explicable such decline as did take place for, given the disparities in resources between the US and UK, British economics did not enjoy the potentiality for specialisation and division of labour that was possible across the Atlantic. Thus, with two British economists in the top ten by citations (Kaldor and Little), but eight in the top twenty five,[1] the question becomes not why

---

[1] Data for 1945–68 taken from Bordo and Landau's (1979, tables 3–4) analysis of the most cited journal papers and economists. Kaldor and Little ranked seventh and tenth respectively, with the six additional 'UK' economists (defined on a residence qualification of significant professional activity) being Goodwin, Hahn, J.R. Hicks, Morishima, Phillips and J. Robinson.

Britain lost its world lead in economics but why it was able to maintain a position of such prominence for so long.

For policy-makers and the public, however, the worth of economics and the repute of economists was more associated with the performance of the British economy and their contribution, real and imagined, to the policies pursued by successive governments who became increasingly desperate in their search for a solution to relative economic decline. All of this would eventually culminate in a crisis for economics and demands that economists put their house in order. Indeed, as we shall see, from such recriminations came a disciplinary self-examination which, eventually, produced important modifications to the professional agenda and, arguably, a new theoretical synthesis. However, this crisis was international, not just British, and so we must search for common threads. Moreover, as all considered analyses agree, the decline of the British economy has been overstated, at least for the golden age. Official and public concern about economic performance became a national obsession for reasons infinitely more complex than is suggested by the actual statistical record of Britain's situation.

This chapter is organised similarly to our earlier accounts of prewar and interwar developments. Thus, in sections 2 and 3 we resume the story of the expansion and professionalisation of British economics. We then progress in section 4 to the economic policy debate and provide an explanation for why it was not until 1964 that there occurred a significant expansion in the number of economists employed in government. Our case study in section 5 is also set in 1964 and concerns the decision made by the incoming Wilson government not to devalue sterling, an act which critics argue fatally compromised its modernising strategy for the British economy. Some preliminary conclusions then follow in section 6.

6.2   BRITISH ECONOMICS AFTER KEYNES

The age of Keynes

For almost all British and the greater number of American economists the years from the end of the Second World War to OPEC I were truly the age of Keynes. In economic theory, as in policy, the assimilation, development and refinement of Keynes's *General theory* provided the central preoccupation of the economics profession. 'We're all Keynesians now' was the popular refrain on both sides of the Atlantic, one reflecting pride in the triumph of ideas and satisfaction from the material achievements for which Keynes's disciples might claim credit. Whether there was a Keynesian revolution in the sense of a 'scientific' revolution in theory, and whether economic policy, particularly in Britain, was Keynesian in any meaningful manner, remain however acutely controversial. We touch upon these matters shortly, but here stress that in terms of political economy and policy culture the age of Keynes was very real, manifest not least when politicians believed there was advantage in invoking Keynes and other economists to justify their actions.

The other side to the age of Keynes, however, could not be less triumphant.[2] Thus in one short generation Keynes's public reputation was transformed from being the saviour of capitalism and liberal democracy, whose new economics promised full employment and much else, to the charlatan who, as the economy drifted into stagflation and political instability in the wake of OPEC I, had provided the instruments for economists and politicians alike to cripple the market economy and corrupt the political process. From the acme of economic wisdom Keynesianism had become the underlying malady of western political economy, the demonstration *par excellence* that, as Hayek had predicted in *The road to serfdom* (1944), there was no sustainable middle way between collectivism and libertarianism. It should be remembered, however, that this descent into ignominy was compressed into the very last phase of the Keynesian era as those who have never succumbed to the Keynesian embrace, principally Chicago and its satellites, but also important centres in Britain, were able to use the death-throes of the golden age to launch a sustained campaign for a back to basics in theory and policy. The Keynesian old guard would later complain that anti-Keynesianism was 'among the fastest growth industries in the world' (Balogh 1979, p. 67); yet, only a decade earlier, as the crisis had gathered pace, Harrod (1969, p. 808) was predicting that 'Keynes's place in the history of fundamental economic theory is quite secure ... I would suppose that his influence in ten or twenty years from now will be *greater* than it is at present.'

The intensity of the eventual reaction against Keynesianism stemmed from the profession's failure to live up to the implied promises of previous decades. In Britain, more than elsewhere in Europe or, arguably, America, this crisis was widely ascribed to the economics discipline having lost its direction: to a surfeit of abstract economic theory and to a dearth of good predictions and policy relevance. In this verdict, one put forcefully by 'ultra-empiricists' such as Hutchison (1968; 1977b), this was an era not of economists triumphant but of the '*déformation professionelle*' of economics

---

[2]   The label the age of Keynes was coined by Lekachman who later refined it to make clear that the dominance of Keynesian doctrine owed much to the multiple variants of Keynes's message, thereby appealing to conservative, liberal and radical opinion (Lekachman 1977). For a flavour of the high-water mark of Keynesian optimism in Britain, see Roll's (1968a) enthusiastic assessment of the world after Keynes and Stewart's (1972) panegyric on Keynes.

(1993, p. 284). To understand the crisis, therefore, we must explore why a mismatch developed between what the suppliers of economic knowledge were motivated to provide and what was sought by the consumers of such knowledge. If academic economists came to supply the wrong product in Britain, or at best inappropriate product range, why was this? We thus resume our account of the professionalisation of economics in the knowledge, so-to-speak, that the stakes were higher for all concerned than at any time since Marshall initiated his mission.

Samuelson and the neo-classical synthesis

Whereas for the prewar period we were able with ease to identify Marshall's *Principles* as the accepted core theory, and, for the years between the wars, to argue that it was the absence of such a core that was significant, for the early postwar period it would buttress the case that there was a Keynesian revolution if once more a single volume could be invoked as representative of the age and a testimony to disciplinary agreement about the fundamentals of theory, if not policy. Were economists to agree on the work to be chosen that in itself would also be significant. And they do, with the work in question being Paul Samuelson's *Economics: an introductory analysis*, first published in 1948 and still in print with worldwide sales exceeding four millions and translation into forty one languages (Skousen 1997).

Whilst, in Britain, there would be rival undergraduate textbooks (most notably, Lipsey's *An introduction to positive economics*, first published in 1963 and also still in print), none had the influence or stature of Samuelson, even to the extent of prompting an *Anti-Samuelson* (Linder and Sensat 1977) volume as an antidote to the 'Complacent Establishment Economics' that Samuelson epitomised for those outside the mainstream.[3] He – still rarely she at this stage – who determines the education of the economist shapes the future of economics itself, and in this the Americans set the course for the postwar period. Indeed, many have argued that 'Keynesianism' was properly and primarily an American (Samuelsonian) phenomenon,[4] while few would disagree with Hicks's (1963, p. 312) judgement that the period just after the end of the war marked the effective transference of world leadership in economics from Britain to America as the neo-classicals finally triumphed over the American institutionalists. Samuelson is, of course, the second most cited economist of this period and the Nobel laureate for 1970, 'for the scientific work through which he ... developed static and dynamic economic theory and actively contributed to

---

[3]   Taken from the clarion call for radical economics, made in the US in the late 1960s, and
        discussed in Bronfenbrenner (1970, p. 747).
[4]   For example, Leijonhufvud (1968) and Weintraub (1975, p. 547).

raising the level of analysis in economic science' (appendix II).

With world-class contributions to consumer theory, welfare economics, capital theory, dynamics and general equilibrium, international trade, finance and macroeconomics, few economists could rival Samuelson's range or, indeed, output. 'It is almost impossible to work in any area of central economic theory today without having to study very carefully one or several works by Paul Samuelson' – such was the verdict of the committee which awarded the 1970 Nobel prize (Lindbeck 1970, pp. 342–3). Samuelson's *Economics* followed hard on the heels of his pathbreaking *Foundations of economic analysis* (1947) which more than any other single work transformed the discipline from its pre-scientistic style, one of a dominant text supported by diagrammatic modes of analysis, into the formalistic and mathematical style which has prevailed for the last four decades. If *Economics* was the vehicle whereby core theory was communicated to students it was the *Foundations* volume which set the path for the elaboration and rhetoric of contemporary economic theory. In a sense they returned authority to economics, as in Arrow's (1967, p. 730) observation that 'The graduate student is disciplined to our trade by study of the *Foundations* (1947) and two dozen assorted papers of Samuelson.'

Backhouse (1985, pp. 288–9) identifies three important strands to this contribution. First, Samuelson applied the concept of equilibrium with great effect to diverse problems in the behaviour of individuals and firms, thereby illuminating an underlying unifying framework of economic behaviour (constrained maximisation) and making possible predictions as a routine procedure. Secondly, he argued that the task of economics was to derive operationally meaningful theorems capable of empirical testing. Thirdly, there was an insistence that economic stability be understood in terms of dynamic processes, which in turn drew inspiration from the natural sciences.

As the chief exponent of the application of the analytical techniques of physics to economics, Samuelson occupies centre stage in the hall of infamy constructed by those who decry the transformation of modern economics into a form of social mathematics, in which rigour is everything and relevance nothing. Lauded as the Einstein of economics by some; derided as a bad case of physics envy by others (Mirowski 1989, ch. 7), McCloskey (1996, p. 17) has recently ranked Samuelson alongside two other architects of postwar economics, the pioneering econometricians Jan Tinbergen and Lawrence Klein (Nobel laureates 1969 and 1980), as responsible for the 'vices' (defined as 'bad intellectual habits') that have come to infect contemporary economics:

- First, the Kleinian belief that "statistical significance", using the phrase in its technical sense, is the same as scientific significance.
- Second, the Samuelson belief that blackboard "proofs of existence" are

scientific.
- And, third and most important for practical affairs, and justifying the other two, the Tinbergean belief that these first and second pieces of pseudo-science . . . can be applied to the making of economic policy, in a sort of social engineering.

There is, of course, nothing new in the charge that economics has been incapacitated as a social science by the pursuit of futile blackboard exercises. We observed a similar complaint in the 1930s, with Cannan's plea for 'commonsense' economics. We should also note that, whatever his status and influence as a theorist, Samuelson, like Keynes, acquired a high public profile by the frequency with which he abandoned the blackboard to indulge in popular journalism (especially his *Newsweek* column), congressional committees etc. (Lindbeck 1970, p. 353). Moreover, from the perspective of 1950 or even 1965 it all looked so different, so much more promising for economics than was the case by the 1980s and 1990s. We refer particularly to Samuelson's role as the initiator and exponent of what has become known as the neo-classical synthesis (NCS), the dominant research paradigm or core theory of the golden age years. In retrospect, this was a concoction of neo-classical microeconomics and Keynesian macroeconomics. Its microeconomics was based on highly abbreviated and monolithic constructs (consumers, firms and government) operating in equilibrium states on the basis of symmetrical information while its macroeconomics embodied some basic contradictions and anomalies which would eventually be its undoing at the hands of the new classical macroeconomics (NCM) in the 1970s and 1980s.[5] But, at the time, the NCS constituted an organising framework in which most mainstream macroeconomists felt sufficiently comfortable with the microfoundations of macroeconomics that continued theoretical progress with the latter was possible (Weintraub 1979). Thus we might delineate the synthesis as combining the premise of rationality of individuals and firms, thereby making possible the application of standard microeconomic theory, with the operational assumption that markets did not always function efficiently (imperfect competition) and/or were unable to clear through wage-price adjustments.

The NCS and British economics

From these theoretical characteristics followed strong implications for the research agenda and for policy. First and foremost, aggregate demand was crucial in the short-run determination of economic activity, with the supply-

---

[5] See pp. 288–91. For two very different perspectives on the NCS, see Tobin's (1983) positive appraisal of Samuelson's contribution and Lucas and Sargent's (1978) clarion call for a NCM.

side only really relevant in the longer-run. Secondly, because prices and wages did not adjust quickly enough to clear markets, demand management policies were required to keep the economy close to full employment. In these fiscal policy should take the lead, with the relative standing of monetary policy being somewhat in dispute as the ambiguities of Keynes's own position in the *General theory* provided fertile soil for continuing debate, not least because in Britain more than elsewhere there was much preoccupation with what Keynes actually said, what he really meant when he said it or even, as one has playfully put it, 'what, according to various guardians of the purity of his thought, he was really trying to say and is only now succeeding in saying through them' (Coddington 1983, p. 1). With Keynesianism a UK export product, and synthesis suggestive of something less than a revolutionary contribution by Keynes, the status of core theory was always going to be more problematic in Britain than elsewhere. The question arises, therefore, of the extent to which the following claim, made by Samuelson in successive editions of his textbook, can also be applied to Britain:[6]

> In recent years 90 per cent of American economists have stopped being "Keynesian economists" or "anti-Keynesian economists." Instead they have worked towards a synthesis of whatever is valuable in older economics and in modern theories . . . The result . . . is accepted in its broad outlines by all but a few extreme left-wing and right-wing writers.

In stressing the American nature of the NCS we are not denying the contribution of British economists to postwar core theory (for example, Hicks who could rival Samuelson in range, and whose version of Keynesianism came to prevail, or indeed perhaps Meade), but instead raising a prior question of the extent to which core theory might have been different in Britain. This, in turn, leads us back to the thorny issue of what exactly constituted the Keynesian revolution so far as theory and policy were concerned in Britain. Was there something specific to the British case which then influenced its economics profession and, directly and indirectly, those government economic policies which invoked Keynes and the Keynesians? Certainly, Harry Johnson thought so and we cite his conclusion here in full so as to provide a charge sheet against which to examine both the British economics profession and British governments:

> All in all, it is difficult to avoid the conclusion that Britain has paid a heavy long-run price for the transient glory of the Keynesian Revolution, in terms both of the corruption of standards of scientific work in economics and encouragement to the indulgence of the belief in the political process that economic policy can

---

[6] From the 3rd edn. (1955, p. 212) through the 5th edn. (1961, pp. 241–2).

transcend the laws of economics with the aid of sufficient economic cleverness, in the sense of being able to satisfy all demands for security of economic tenure without balance-of-payments problems, or less obvious sacrifice of efficiency and economic growth potentialities. A good case could even be made to the effect that Keynes was too expensive a luxury for a country inexorably declining in world economic and political importance and obliged to scramble for dignified survival, to be able to afford.   (Johnson 1975a, p. 122)

We shall cut through the debate over whether there was a Keynesian revolution in Britain by making two statements which allow us to progress without hindrance with the matters that concern us here. (Both are easily defensible and would be supported by the greater number of social scientists were they to have opened themselves up to the full range of analytical writings on Keynesianism): [7]

- the greater part of the economics profession believed in the existence of a Keynesian revolution in theory and responded accordingly in the sense that their behaviours were consistent with there being, in the Lakatosian model (pp. 13–14), a progressive scientific research programme;
- economic policy was fundamentally different after the war, with Keynes and the Keynesians invoked as its underlying theoretical rationale whenever the need arose to claim the authority of economists.

With respect to the former, both outside observers of the British scene, and those British economists not part of the Cambridge circle, have echoed the Johnson complaint about the personalisation of postwar British economics and of its dominance by Cambridge and Keynes's disciples until well into the 1960s. Given this characteristic, and given the representation of the *General theory* as a heroic triumph over the forces of orthodoxy (Robinson 1962a), we would expect the notion of a revolution in economics and policy to assume a much greater significance in Britain than in the US. American economics was already much larger in scale, not least from having received a major boost from the arrival of eminent refugees from Hitler, and had a broader geographical distribution of research talent (Johnson 1973a), although that didn't stop American complaints about Harvard's dominance. American universities also contained fewer figures who could – or who would want to – claim a personal stake in the genesis of the *General theory*. Above all, and here we return to the reactive motivation of economists, in America after 1933 government had displayed a policy

---

[7] On this, as much else, the potential for disagreement (agreement) is maximised (minimised) by each social science maintaining its own literature with little overlap or exchange between them. With this caveat, see, from the perspective of the history of economic thought, Blaug (1991); from economic history, Tomlinson (1987); and from political science, Hall (1989a).

activism, if not effectiveness, with the New Deal which was in complete contrast to the dogged commitment, or so it seemed, to economic orthodoxy displayed by successive British governments.

None of this is intended to suggest that economic debate in postwar America was more detached, more 'scientific', that is above matters of personality. Both Reder (1982) and Patinkin's (1981) essays on the oral and written traditions of the postwar Chicago school reveal many lively exchanges and animosities within the department, while Samuelson (1972) and many others have documented the personal elements in conflicts between departments and particularly on the Harvard-MIT-Chicago axis. Our point here is that it mattered more in Britain because of the position of Cambridge in British economics which, as Marshall's influence had waned, was granted renewed authority by Keynes and his disciples; its continued administration of the RES and the *EJ* , including a disproportionate share of journal space;[8] and its Establishment links to Whitehall, both as part of the policy community and as a major producer of future civil servants and politicians. We here leave it to an LSE economist, an observer of Cambridge economics for thirty years or more, to capture the essence of the problem:

> Doing economics at Cambridge is like being a Christian during the English Civil War; you can't just be a Christian. You have to identify yourself as to what sect, what party, what faction you belong to. Your views on the non-substitution theorem are as important as a marker for the rest of your world-view, on everything from beer to sherry to the stance on Vietnam, as your views on transubstantiation were in seventeenth-century England.   (Desai 1997, p. xvii)

Philip Andrews (1914–71)

Such extreme factionalism was most decidedly not the case elsewhere, although attempts to impose professional authority against perceived theoretical heresy have been reported in a number of institutions,[9] most notably in early postwar Oxford with the case of Philip Andrews and his theory of normal-cost pricing (1949; 1964) which, in terms of the Lakatosian MSRP, attacked all three elements of neo-classical economics.

---

[8]   From DISMAL we calculate that of the known institutional affiliations Cambridge contributed 30.8 per cent of authors in 1940, 26.7 per cent in 1950, 6.1 per cent in 1960 and 19.6 per cent in 1970. Whilst the percentage of non-Cambridge authors rose, and in particular the journal was internationalised with a growing proportion of US authors (39.3 per cent by 1970 as against 15.4 per cent in 1940), the *EJ*'s editors acknowledged that the ratio of acceptances to submissions of articles was nearly twice as high for UK as for US economists (Champernowne *et al.* 1973, table IV).

[9]   However, Britain was, of course, spared the havoc wrought by McCarthyism which did such damage to the careers (and civil liberties) of many American economists, touching even a few who would not now be considered remotely politically radical, not least Samuelson.

Of course, for Johnson, factionalism was one reason why truth and progress were more elusive in British economics. However, as in the natural sciences, it is not uncommon for the reception of challenges to core theory to be invariant to the scientific value of the ideas being advanced. Indeed, Earl (1983, p. 90; 1993), using Andrews as one example, has developed a behavioural theory of economists' behaviour, the main conclusion of which 'is that ideas find academic acceptance not necessarily because of their intrinsic scientific worth ... but rather because they are [sic] salable as tools which enable their users more easily to reach their goals'. Whatever the scientific merits of Andrews's theoretical challenge (now all but forgotten by the mainstream, but still evident today as a building block in post-Keynesian price theory and/or as a precursor of contestable market theory),[10] his is certainly an interesting case study of economic heresy and of the transitional stage through which mainstream British economics was then progressing.

In his study of Andrews and eight other 'economic heretics' King (1988, pp. 16–17) ascribes resistance to heterodoxy as the product of one or more sources: defence of scientific rigour, wounded professional pride, professional conservatism and political, especially, class interests. Andrews is an instructive case because he fell victim to all four, including, perhaps surprisingly, and contrary to King's (1988, p. 235) assessment, that of wounding professional pride because important members of his peer group did not rate his scholarly pedigree as an economist, not least because contrary to emerging professional norms he continued to insist that economics be inductive and that economists have actual working knowledge of business activity (Lee 1993, p. 7 n.9).[11] He was also a natural victim for the group of left-wing Keynesians who, with origins in the wartime Oxford Institute of Statistics, and particularly associated with Kalecki, Steindl and Balogh, developed a radical version of Keynesian macroeconomics which combined demand management, the redistribution of income/wealth, nationalisation and detailed microeconomic intervention (Young and Lee 1993, p. 204). The result was a zeitgeist, stronger in Oxford and Cambridge (centring on Joan Robinson) than amongst the London economists, that market failure was endemic at both a micro- and a macroeconomic level. 'Andrews was swimming against this powerful tide', vulnerable to the obvious charge that he had abandoned the socialism of his youth to become in middle age the mouthpiece of business (King 1988, p. 205).

We draw one further conclusion from this case study: that by the early postwar years there already existed a well-defined hierarchy of prestige in

---

[10] For a cryptic insider's account of Andrews's difficulties, see Harrod (1971a); for sympathetic later assessments, see Eichner (1978), Lee and Irving-Lessmann (1992) and Lee (1993).

[11] Desai (1991, p. 61) goes further to argue that he was 'beyond heresy, whereas a Kalecki or Sraffa is seen indulgently as starting but a family quarrel.'

economic research. Although we cannot directly measure this for the late 1940s it is generally accepted that twenty years later the following division, in descending order, prevailed:

A Microtheory, macrotheory, econometrics.
B International trade, money and banking, public finance.
C Industrial organization, labor, economic history.
D Economic development, history of economic thought, comparative economic systems.   (Ward 1972, p. 10)

Andrews's challenge was dismissable as industrial organization, a category C field which was sullied by requiring field work, as against pure theorising, exposure to the work of non-economists and, in the late 1940s, still capable of being pursued within a pre-scientistic style which lacked the formalism and research procedures of class A theory. This latter point, however, should not be overstated. As is clear from Table 6.1 the pre-scientistic style was still dominant in the *EJ* until the 1960s, although in this respect the *EJ* was lagging the key US journals (*AER, JPE* and *QJE* – Backhouse 1999b).

Table 6.1 Economic Journal: *classification of papers by rhetoric type (% of total) and mode (Y=presence of style; N=absence), 1940, 1950, 1960 and 1970*

Year	Alg-ebra	Cal-culus	Dia-grams	Econo-metrics	Stat-istics	Wholly literary
1940						
Total (%)	22.7	13.0	9.7	0.0	38.7	38.7
Mode (38.7%)	N	N	N	N	N	
Mode (38.7%)	N	N	N	N	Y	
1950						
Total (%)	36.6	24.4	19.5	4.9	19.5	41.5
Mode (41.5%)	N	N	N	N	N	
1960						
Total (%)	51.7	30.0	35.0	13.3	25.0	33.3
Mode (33.3%)	N	N	N	N	N	
1970						
Total (%)	66.7	33.3	26.7	11.1	35.6	11.1
Mode (15.6%)	Y	Y	N	N	N	

Note: Component parts do not sum to 100 per cent because each *EJ* paper can exhibit more than one style.

Ethics and the motivation of economists

While, in terms of rhetorical style, the *EJ* was until the 1960s a thoroughly 'traditional' journal, displaying as yet little of the formalism and mathematisation of economics that was to be the hallmark of American-style professional economics, there were other aspects of professionalisation which were closer to the American model. Of these, the profession's lessened introspection about motivation was particularly significant, not least because it might be expected that economists would maintain their interest in 'practical ethics', the hallmark of Marshall, Pigou and then Keynes (Tutton 1976, p. 160), after Little (1950) had demonstrated that the 'new welfare economics' was unable to deal with redistribution of income without value judgements (necessarily formed outside of economics).[12]

The profession's lack of interest in ethics is striking relative to the interwar years. Indeed, it was so much the case that Harrod (1963, pp. 419–20), one of the few postwar economists to have kept up an interest in moral philosophy (Eltis *et al.* 1970, chs 2–4), warned that it was leading the profession, especially those becoming involved in development issues, to confuse economic growth with enhanced human welfare. In part this concern can be linked to the growing scepticism about growth which produced such widely read and disparate works as Galbraith's *The affluent society* (1958), Mishan's *The costs of economic growth* (1967) and the first of the Club of Rome reports on the predicament of mankind (Meadows *et al.* 1972).[13] However, it is probable that Harrod's complaint related more to the younger generation of economists. Thus many of those who had begun their careers between the wars did not abandon their interest in practical ethics as determining the ends of economic policy, with James Meade, of course, the outstanding example here.

Two reasons suggest themselves why many of the postwar generation did not dwell much upon ethics and their motivation as economists. First, now that economists believed themselves to have finally gained influence and a foothold in Whitehall there were fewer incentives for introspection about motivation. Economists were thus being incorporated into policy-making not

---

[12] This project, initiated by Hicks and Kaldor in the *EJ* in 1939, was in part a further response to Robbins's *Essay* (see pp. 147, 171–3). This quest for a 'scientific' welfare economics, which abandoned Pigou and instead applied the concept of Pareto improvement (any change which would make no individual worse off and at least one better off), thus sought to rescue the authority of economics and economists in assessments of the effects of policy on welfare. However, Little demonstrated that there were a myriad of Pareto optima, each corresponding to different income distributions, with the result that 'If the utility of the deprived cannot be raised without cutting into the utility of the rich, the situation can be Pareto optimal but truly awful' (Sen 1985, p. 10). For assessments of this episode and later developments, see Chipman and Moore (1978) and Cooter and Rappoport (1984).

[13] See Arndt (1978, ch. 8) for a review of these early critics of economic growth.

as social reformers but as technocrats. Econometrics, linear programming and CBA all enhanced their aura as scientists, while the Paretian apparatus, if still entailing ethics, could nonetheless be employed as if they had scientific expertise in evaluating competing normative propositions. While some argued that 'value-judgements made by economists are, by and large, better than those made by non-economists' (Turvey 1963, p. 96), this was a minority position. Outside of government service continued progress with professionalisation then acted to enhance these trends. Johnson (1972c, p. 11) was less tactful: 'the modern economist is a middle-class professional man rather than a detached [nineteenth-century] social philosopher, which is one reason why relics of the 1930s revolutionary fervour rail so vehemently against modern "scientific" economics, especially as practised in the United States.' Secondly, at a very basic level, the achievement of full employment, when combined with growing affluence, was seen widely as having solved the social questions that had motivated British economists since Marshall. However, two consequences followed from this:

1. The full employment target, which initially had been somewhat pessimistic (between 3 and 8 per cent unemployment, with Keynes reckoning towards the higher bound), came to be interpreted very tightly (1.5 per cent ± 0.5 percentage points), so much so that during the 1960s and 1970s the *NIER* would report it to two decimal places (Hutchison 1977a, ch. VI). For Johnson (1975b) the proposition that '"full employment" is an exclusive definition of social well-being, and as such to be pursued at virtually any cost, became one of his five determining characteristics of English economics (pp. 23–4). By focusing concern for social justice on low unemployment targets it thus became inevitable that incomes policies would emerge as the favoured policy instrument once the Phillips curve began to crumble.
2. Were the continuance of economic growth or full employment to be threatened political debate would quickly refocus on the legitimacy of the market-determined distribution of income. Responses to social market failure have, together with war, provided the foundations of government growth this century, while the issue of consent for the market, equality and social justice have all been more fraught in Britain than in most other OECD states (Middleton 1996, chs 2–3). In such circumstances economics and economists were always potentially politicised, with there being the widespread accusation by opponents of the Keynesian orthodoxy that the majority of the British economics profession were to a greater or lesser extent committed to egalitarian principles of distributive justice which imposed a heavy welfare cost through a wide range of efficiency losses. This view is particularly associated with the IEA (for

example, Walters 1978), in effect the first British agency (established 1955) to be formed in opposition to core theory,[14] but was also of course argued by Harry Johnson (1973b) who was scathing about the 'infantile anthropomorphism' which underlay much egalitarian thought, that 'naïve public-school-cum-socialist belief that in economics as elsewhere everyone ought to do equally well, and that if they do not they should be levelled up at public expense' (1968, p. 51).

6.3 A 'MID-ATLANTIC HYBRID' OR A VERY BRITISH COMPROMISE

What's different about British (European) economics?

In a recent *Kyklos* symposium on the future of European-style economics,[15] Baumol (1995, p. 187) characterised the British profession as distinctly mid-Atlantic in character, mid-way academically, if not geographically, between Europe and America. Backhouse (1999a) identifies eight key characteristics of American in relation to European-style economics:

1. Greater proneness to fashion and intolerance of heterodox ideas.
2. Greater homogeneity across departments, at least in research-oriented universities.
3. More competitive labour markets and higher mobility.
4. Greater emphasis on technique and less emphasis on applied theory.
5. Less hierarchical organisation of departments, with individuals free to pursue independent research at a much earlier age.
6. Less involvement in public policy debates.
7. Lower social status of academics.
8. More highly-developed graduate programmes.

Accepting Baumol's label for the present these characteristics translate into five trends in postwar British economics (Backhouse 1997a, pp. 31–2):

1. That of undergraduates using the same textbooks and learning substantially the same theory as their counterparts in other countries.
2. That of graduate coursework as a precondition for research in economics, with the doctorate becoming essential to gain employment as an academic economist.

---

[14] On this avowedly 'anti-Fabian' think-tank, see Cockett (1994) and Muller (1996) and the self-examination of one of its founders, **Arthur Seldon** (1989).

[15] 'Is there a European economics?', ed. R.L. and B.S. Frey, *Kyklos*, 48 (1995), pp.185–311.

3. That of the imperative of frequent publication to secure professional advancement, and with the medium being the journal article, these being organised in a hierarchy of prestige and attracting an international cast of editors and contributors.
4. The development of conferences and pre-publication networks for the coterie, together with the exchange of staff between British and American institutions.
5. A growing emphasis on mathematical theory and econometric technique.

Such has been the strength of these trends that some economists have argued that, with so many economists taking their professional standards and views of what constitutes an interesting problem from the US, and with publications, citations and Nobel prizes also so dominated, 'It is perfectly reasonable to ask whether there is now any economics outside and independent of the United States' (Portes 1987, p. 1330). Many European economists have found this argument deeply objectionable (most notably Kolm 1988), and it has been widely and publicly discussed with a recent *Kyklos* symposium and the working party which produced Coats (1999). Unsurprisingly, stress has been placed on the role of language barriers in sustaining European national styles in economics teaching and research. This also operated in the British case where there was a positive production externality for British economists of sharing the language, or at least an approximation to a language (what Microsoft rather quaintly define as English (International) as against English (American), of the dominant economics producer.

Britain: a dual system

Differences in culture and institutions, both academic and political, and the ways in which they impact on incentive structures, have also been identified as sustaining different national styles (Frey and Eichenberger 1993), a result observable in other professions which have been examined on a cross-country basis.[16] Here also they are relevant to the British case and we posit that what developed in Britain resembled a dual economy, in part differentiated by institutions but also within institutions, some of which (notably Oxbridge) retained a traditional core and developing elements of the new professionalism, and that the delay in developing mass (American-style) higher education allowed British economists to maintain a world presence which would not otherwise have been possible.

---

[16] See the forthcoming Harvard Ph.D. of Marion Fourcade-Gourinchas, 'The social organization of economic knowledge: the US, Britain, France and Germany in comparative perspective'.

To test this hypothesis it would be desirable to have some cross-country quantitative data on publications, citations and departments for the 1950s and 1960s.[17] However, such data does not exist but we do have the results of a much more recent enquiry (1987–91) into the output of European research institutes (Kirman and Dahl 1994, tables 4–5), here measured by the exacting international standard of the Social Science Citation Index (SSCI), in effect a proxy for American-style economics.[18] From this it is clear that British economists were exceptionally productive by EC standards, and especially relative to the big nation states. Thus, against the British figure of 7.7 articles (co)authored by UK economists per million inhabitants, the Germans managed 2.0, the French 1.9 and the Italians 0.9. The British dominance is even more pronounced at the institutional level, with the LSE and Oxbridge pre-eminent by a very large margin and with a total of six out of the top ten institutions (or nine if the league table is extended to fifteen places).

These results, of course, relate to a period in which British academics were undergoing an accelerated catch-up to a system of mass higher education that had occurred in north America in the 1950s and 1960s. This, however, also enables us to argue that this result can be extrapolated backwards to the less pressurised elite system which prevailed around the time of the Robbins report (HMSO 1963a) and for a good many years thereafter. Taking the opportunity cost of undergraduate teaching as research activity foregone, it is apparent that British universities provided a more favourable environment for research than had been the case before the Second World War. Thus the Robbins committee (1963b, table 4) estimated that the average student:staff ratio (SSR, excluding Oxbridge) was 7.5 in 1961/2 as against 10.2 in 1938/9. Admittedly, this was set against a background of a huge absolute growth in undergraduate numbers: from approximately 20,000 full-time students in 1900, to 50,000 in 1938/9 and 118,000 in 1962/3 (1963a, table 3). Nonetheless, as is clear from comparative data compiled by UNESCO (1975, pp. 58, 66, 87), the British higher education system catered for a much smaller proportion of the potential student population than in North America, although this was also the case elsewhere in Europe and thus no simple case can be made about the opportunities for research enjoyed by British economists. The Robbins

---

[17] Such comparative data as exists was surveyed in the Robbins report (HMSO 1963a) and published as an appendix (HMSO 1963c), one incidentally compiled by **Richard Layard**, the committee's senior research officer. Pre-Robbins data is also discussed in Halsey and Trow (1971), with cross-country tables and country studies in OECD (1970) and UNESCO (1975).

[18] See also Hall (1987; 1990), the focus of which is econometrics and from which the dominance of the LSE is even more apparent, with a world ranking of third for all econometric publications between 1980–8 (Cambridge 21st, Oxford 34th, Southampton 42nd, Manchester 51st, Warwick 54th, Essex 57th, Bristol 61st, York 70th, Birmingham 75th and Birkbeck 90th).

committee did, however, collect some data which suggested that relative to the continental universities British higher education was more generously funded by government and secured an above average share of the total education budget. It also collected evidence of relative British efficiency in producing graduates, as measured by public funding per student completing higher education (HMSO 1963c, tables 15, 17).

American-style professionalisation had firm roots in Britain even before the expansion of higher education which followed acceptance of the Robbins report, but as yet little has been published on the postwar organisation of economic studies and research at the principal centres. Thus there is almost nothing on Cambridge, although the Cambridge Growth Project, which was established in 1960 at the Department of Applied Economics (DAE) and directed by Richard Stone (Nobel laureate, 1984), has been well documented (Epstein 1987, pp. 141–50). For Oxford economics we have Young and Lee's (1993, ch. 7) account of the early postwar years, during which time there were important developments, especially in postgraduate education, and a little later, during the years in which Klein (Nobel laureate, 1980) was at the Oxford Institute of Statistics, there was created the first large-scale quarterly macroeconometric model of the British economy (Ball and Holly 1991). Clearly, within both universities there was a predominance of world-class economists, and most took an active part in postgraduate supervision and research seminars, but many of the great, as well as the not so great, found themselves snowed under by an immense volume of undergraduate teaching for the colleges. As a consequence in Oxbridge there was a premium on generalist skills and breadth in economics; indeed, it was an important part of Johnson's (1968, p. 52) concerns about English economics that the Oxbridge tutorial system militated against specialisation, the foundation of progress in other sciences, a concern which was shared by Roy Harrod (cited in Blake 1970, p. 18) and other leading Oxbridge economists.

The LSE and empirical economics

The scope for specialisation and for the development of postgraduate education was, however, somewhat greater at the LSE where there took place between the late 1950s and early 1960s a major battle, the results of which helped determine the scope and style of economics elsewhere. As De Marchi (1988, p. 141) describes it, on the one side was Robbins, representing a non-quantitative and logically unfalsifiable economic theory, and on the other a 'palace guard' (led by Richard Lipsey (b. 1928) and Chris Archibald (b. 1926) which 'sought to recast economic knowledge in falsifiable form and proclaim their independence from the dogma, in which they had been schooled, that quantification is not only difficult but unnecessary'. Once more the specific target was Robbins's *Essay*; once more personalities (particularly Lipsey, himself influenced by Popper, the LSE philosopher) and social geography would be critical to the outcome.

The momentum for a more empirical economics had been gathering pace for some time with developments in econometrics (Morgan 1990; De Marchi and Gilbert 1989) and Friedman's (1953) methodological essay propounding a positive economic science, with the LSE the natural British focus in the early 1950s for what was about to occur. At the LSE there was a unique institutional relationship between teaching/research in economics and statistics (Gilbert 1989, p. 108) and such hybrid characters as Jim Durbin and Bill Phillips (1914–75), the latter now chiefly known as the originator of the Phillips curve (1958), but at that time held in high regard not for his published work but for his hydraulic model of the Keynesian system which, Bergstrom *et al.* (1978, p. xii) argue, 'was just what was required to popularize econometric model-building, then in its infancy'.

De Marchi's (1988) account of the triumph of empirical economics at the LSE, a process largely completed by 1964, when Lipsey left to become the founding professor of economics at Essex, makes compelling reading, not least for the political undertone that while Robbins had eventually embraced Keynesian macroeconomic theory his approach towards economic methodology underpinned his long-standing aversion to government intervention. De Marchi (1988, p. 143) describes the status quo ante at Robbins's research seminar:

> Models were examined for the realism of their assumptions and for internal consistency. Results might be tested for robustness (to assumption changes) but were rarely subjected to quantification using actual numbers. Overall assessment was made by an economic-linguistic test – is it economically meaningful? – or according to a largely undefined notion of relevance: Has light been shed?

The limitations this approach imposed on the application of economic theory to policy problems was, of course, not new but becoming more pressing as postwar governments more actively intervened, and more particularly once faster economic growth became a policy objective. As Ronald Tress (1964, p. vii) observed at the famous Colston Symposium, for which Sargan (1964) produced his path-breaking paper on econometric methodology (Gilbert 1989, pp. 114–18):

> The claims of economics to be a science still lie where Marshall placed them, in its power to appeal to definite external tests and in its internal homogeneity. As the materials for testing multiply, however, and theories themselves grow more complex, the disciplined imagination on which Marshall placed his main reliance becomes less trustworthy; the need grows for 'an external standard of measurement to steady the judgement'.

What Lipsey, Archibald and their young colleagues did was to establish a professional norm that empirical measurements are critical to the application of economic theory; that economists have to generate testable hypotheses if they are to discriminate scientifically between competing theories and thereby establish theory of policy relevance. How they did this it is somewhat beyond this study, and we here concentrate on the process of diffusion and its implications for economics and for policy. First and foremost we need to emphasis that Lipsey's now famous textbook (1963) communicated to generations of British 'A' level students and undergraduates a vision of economics as a quantitative social science. Secondly, it is argued by Gilbert (1989) that there has developed a very British approach to econometrics which is particularly associated with the LSE and David Hendry, one very different from prevailing American methodologies. Thirdly, most of the palace guard went on to other universities: Archibald joining Lipsey at Essex, Maurice Peston having a long career as an official adviser (including a spell at the Treasury, 1962–4) before returning to academic life at Queen Mary College, and so on.

Economics and the new (pre-1992) universities

This brings us directly to the most important of all postwar developments for British economics: the creation of the new universities, a process which begins well before the Robbins report and is sustained thereafter.[19] In Table 6.2 we list leading British economics departments on the basis of the RAEs carried out since the middle-1980s.[20] This confirms the dominance of Oxbridge and the LSE, but also shows that a number of universities founded in the middle-1960s attained distinction very quickly, most notably Essex, York and Warwick. It is noteworthy also that none of what are now called 1992 universities (the former polytechnics, created by the Robbins report) feature in this listing.[21]

---

[19] See Stewart (1989) for a history of postwar higher education which covers all sectors before the abolition in 1992 of the binary divide.

[20] Research performance is, of course, but one element of a university's contribution to social welfare, and its assessment has become highly contestable as the distribution of public funds to institutions has incorporated an ever stronger element of such assessment within the context of a squeeze on the global sum available for research. See Johnes (1992) on the economic problems of applying performance indicators in higher education, and Johnes and Johnes (1993) on the sensitivity of bibliometric studies of research performance to the staffing levels of departments and their research strategy.

[21] In the 1996 RAE the highest ranking new universities (East London and Manchester Metropolitan) were graded 3A (defined as 'national excellence in a substantial majority of sub-areas') but they only returned between 40–59 per cent of their staff as research active. Some (for example, Portsmouth) could only attain such a grade by excluding 61–80 per cent of their staff.

Table 6.2   Leading British university economics departments and summary of RAEs, 1986, 1989, 1992 and 1996

Department[a]	1986 Out-standing	1986 Above average	1989 Grade 5[c]	1989 Grade 4[c]	1992[b] Grade 5[c]	1992[b] Grade 4[c]	1992[b] Grade 5*[c]	1996[b] Grade 5[c]	1996[b] Grade 4[c]	Research active staff
Aberdeen (1495)									A	16.2
Birkbeck (1926)*		•	•		B			B		18.5
Birmingham (1900)		•				B			B	20.3
Bristol (1909)	•			•	A			B		19.5
Cambridge (C13th)	•			•	A			A		57.0
Dundee (1967)									B	11.0
East Anglia (1964)						A			B	13.0
Edinburgh (1583)									B	10.3
Essex (1961)			•		A			B		28.0
Exeter (1955)		•						C		9.9
Glasgow (1451)		•				B			C	13.2
Hull (1954)		•								12.0
Keele (1962)									B	14.0
Kent (1964)									A	15.0
Liverpool (1903)						B			B	12.0
LSE (1895)*	•		•		A		A			53.8
Loughborough (1966)									A	18.7
Manchester (1880)									B	32.2
Newcastle upon Tyne (1963)						B		C		15.4
Nottingham (1948)						A		A		23.0
Oxford (C12th)	•				A		B			52.5
Queen Mary Westfield (1915)*						A			A	19.8

University					
Reading (1926)	•		A	B	13.0
Southampton (1952)	•	A		A	34.0
St Andrews (1410)	•			B	14.0
Stirling (1967)				B	10.0
Strathclyde (1964)			B	B	23.0
Surrey (1966)				A	14.1
Sussex (1961)	•		A	A	20.0
Swansea (1920)			A	B	13.0
UCL (1907)*	•	A	A		24.1
Warwick (1965)	•	A		A	36.4
York (1963)	•	A		A	35.6

Notes:

a   Date of establishment of university in modern form (* for schools of the University of London).

b   Proportion of academic staff included in submissions: A 95–100%; B 80–94%; C 60-79%.

c   1996 RAE grades: 5* International excellence in a majority of sub-areas and of at least national excellence in all others; 5 International excellence in some sub-areas and national excellence in virtually all others; 4 National excellence in virtually all sub-areas.

Sources: Universities: Commonwealth universities yearbook; RAEs: Times Higher Education Supplement; RES Newsletter, 80 (January 1993), p. 3; 97 (April 1997), p.7.

The 1960s, as with the 1870s and 1880s and the creation of the civic universities, have rightly been seen as a watershed in British higher education (Sanderson 1972, p. 360), but it was a typically British revolution: one which left untouched the core institutions or existing disparities in funding between institutions. Thus those institutions which attained university status, whether entirely new (Warwick and York) or upgraded Colleges of Advanced Technology (Bath and Loughborough), fared very much better in terms of public funding than those technical colleges which became polytechnics. Thus was created the binary divide and, in this disparity, the possibility that British economics could sustain itself by concentrating resources upon the few with a large residual 'cheap and cheerful' tail which undertook much of the undergraduate teaching.[22]

The expansion of economics education, both undergraduate but particularly postgraduate, acted as a spur to a more empirical economics. The creation of entirely new institutions, which 'served no period of tutelage to a parent university, but were allowed the privilege of devising their own courses and granting their own degrees from the beginning' (Sanderson 1972, p. 368), undoubtedly encouraged innovation. Some new departments experimented with their undergraduate teaching, including writing their own textbooks (for example, at Lancaster and Liverpool); others went on to develop particular research specialisms: health economics (York), money and banking and industrial economics (Nottingham) or public sector economics (Leicester and Bath). During this period of rapid expansion of institutions and student numbers (200,000 undergraduates by 1967/8 and 244,000 by 1973/4, of which approximately 5,100 were economics students variously defined),[23] British economists maintained their traditional disdain for accountancy, resisting nearly all attempts to incorporate accounting into the economics curriculum, and remaining aloof from the two business schools (LBS and Manchester) established following the Robbins report.[24] There is a certain irony that the one major British economist in the twentieth century who came closest to integrating economics and accounting, namely Ronald Coase (an LSE graduate and Nobel laureate, 1991), spent the greater

---

[22] There appears not to be any published comparative cost data for the two sides of the binary divide in the 1960s, but for 1980 it has been estimated that recurrent costs per student in polytechnics were 84 per cent those in universities (Weale 1992, table 3).

[23] Department of Education and Science, *Statistics of education 1974*, Vol. 6: *Universities*, tables A, 9(9). Additionally, in November 1974 there were 54,000 full-time registered students for Council for National Academic Awards (CNAA) degrees in the polytechnics, with 310 economics degrees awarded that year (*Statistics of education 1974*, Vol. 3: *Further education*, tables 2, (60)). For details of the first polytechnics to offer economics degrees, see CNAA (1991, app. 2).

[24] See Locke's (1989, esp. pp. 177–98) important comparative history of why Britain lagged the US and Japan in management education and Napier (1996a; b) on the academic relations between economics, accountancy/accounting and business.

part of his career in the US, while both the Treasury and the Bank of England became heavily dependent upon LBS expertise in developing their forecasting models (Ball and Holly 1991, pp. 203–4).

There is a further irony that much of the justification for the expansion of higher education was thoroughly utilitarian. Implicit in the Robbins report, but argued with gusto by others and particularly government agencies like NEDO, was the belief that faster economic growth could only be secured if there was greater investment in human capital. The contemporary economic evidence for such claims was tendentious at best, but one widely cited study (Kaser 1966) suggested a strong inverse relationship between GNP growth rates and the number of university students per 1,000 primary school pupils. In truth economists were not much interested in the economics of education at this time, not least in the RES as the *EJ* carried no article, note or indeed review of the Robbins report.[25] This omission seems not to have been the subject of comment, no doubt because of the general enthusiasm for expansion and its coinciding with the flood of economists into Whitehall upon election of the first Wilson government, but it is significant that the participation of economists in the educational debate was limited to the bank reviews and to the IEA which was promoting vouchers and student loans.

The impression that academic economists were growing less interested in current and real-world concerns, with their research increasingly theoretical, formalistic and mathematical in style would appear to be confirmed by analysis of contemporary *EJ* papers (Table 6.1 and Figure 6.1). In terms of subjects within the *JEL* classification there would appear to have been great variability at the one-digit level, but it is probable that the sampling at ten year intervals is not satisfactory here, as instanced by there being no 200 class paper in 1970 whereas an enumeration for 1969 or 1971 would have registered such professional activity in quantitative economics. Notwithstanding the limitations of DISMAL as currently constructed, there is clear evidence that *EJ* publications exhibited the American-style predisposition to fashion (subject) and fad (technique). Most particularly we observe clusters of publications in 1960 and 1970 in class 111 (economic growth theory and models), and the emerging prominence of classes 022 (microeconomic theory) and 023 (macroeconomic theory). During the 1960s some topics became extremely fashionable, with, in Blaug's (1992a, p. 204; 1990, p. 6) assessment, the profession 'hopelessly enamoured' with the Phillips curve and 'drunk on Harrod-Domar growth theory'.

---

[25] Cf. its contribution to the more recent Dearing report where the policy forum section of the May 1997 issue contained three papers on the economics of higher education. Noteworthy also was the activities of economists before the establishment of the Dearing commission, as for example in *Oxford Review of Economic Policy*, vol. 8 (2) (1992) on higher education, eds. M. Cave and M.R. Weale.

Figure 6.1 Economic Journal: *papers by* Journal of Economic Literature *(1983) classification, 1940, 1950, 1960 and 1970*

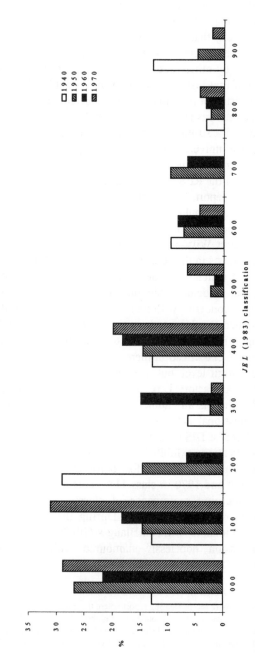

Note: JEL (1983) classification: **000** General Economics; Theory; History; Systems; **100** Economic Growth; Development; Planning; Fluctuations; **200** Quantitative Economic Methods and Data; **300** Domestic Monetary and Fiscal Theory and Institutions; **400** International Economics; **500** Administration; Business Finance; Marketing; Accounting; **600** Industrial Organisation; Technological Change; Industry Studies; **700** Agriculture; Natural Resources; **800** Manpower; Labour; Population; **900** Welfare Programmes; Consumer Economics; Urban and Regional Economics

The Cambridge capital controversies

To its critics the growing unworldliness of mainstream British (and American) economics, its arcane practices and propensity to disputatiousness, all reached their apotheosis with the Cambridge capital controversy of the 1960s.[26] This was to be a more protracted, wider-ranging and in many ways less intellectually coherent episode than that of the original Cambridge fault line developed during the 1930s with the concurrent revolutions in microeconomics of Joan Robinson and Chamberlin. There was some overlap of personnel, not least Robinson (1954; 1956) whose attack on neo-classical production functions initiated proceedings, but the other Cambridge was this time MIT (home to Samuelson, Solow and Modigliani) and not Harvard, although as before social geography was important. Thus even to talk of a Cambridge (England) position is potentially misleading as there were at least three variants of the complaint against growth theory in the NCS: that of Robinson; that of Kaldor (1957), whose voice was becoming increasingly important in Labour Party circles, and whose diagnosis of Britain's economic decline (1966) proved decisive in shaping Labour's policy when it attained government (Thirlwall 1989); and that other residuum of the 1930s, Sraffa (1960) whose neo-Ricardian revival would eventually lead some Cambridge economists to abandon the *EJ* and to establish their own radical *Cambridge Journal of Economics*.[27] Moreover, many Cambridge economists, especially those based in the DAE, remained aloof from this controversy although some (for example, **Godley** and Cripps) are seen as developing an important strand of post-Keynesian thought.

Capital theory has always been a controversial area. The notion of capital is central to the theory of both value and distribution, and thus impinges upon all areas of economics, not least as it holds the key to explaining profits, always a difficult topic in British economics and politics. What happened in the 1960s, apart from demonstrating that in the original Cambridge all semblance of deference to Marshall's aversion to controversy had finally been abandoned, appears in retrospect to have produced more

---

[26] For a broadly supportive assessment of the original Cambridges' position(s), see Harcourt (1972); for a critical review of all positions, wherever located, see Blaug (1975). Unsurprisingly, the *New Palgrave* gives much attention to these controversies, especially to Sraffa, for which it was much criticised by Blaug (1988), but the editors were unfortunate that the dictionary was being produced just as Romer, Lucas and others were developing endogenous growth theory (see Romer 1994).

[27] The initial editorial board included Cripps, Eatwell, Nuti, Rowthorn, Singh, Tarling, Wells and Wilkinson. The *Journal of Post-Keynesian Economics* was established the following year (1978), with *Contributions to Political Economy* established in 1982 and with Eatwell, Milgate and De Vivo as first editors.

heat than light on growth theory although arguably a valuable 'post-Keynesian' research agenda would eventually emerge.[28] What was sought, however, was altogether more radical and compelling: a second Keynesian revolution. Neutrality between the competing claims of the Cambridges is difficult when the political agendas of the main protagonists differed so violently, and especially when one of the protagonists proclaimed that in economics one could and should keep separate the scientific and ideological levels of analysis (Robinson 1962a). Ostensibly, the outcome of the Cambridge controversies was that MIT and the NCS were triumphant. Indeed, neo-classical analysis and rational calculation models of human behaviour went on to a new phase of colonisation within the social sciences. There were to be Nobel prizes for these new areas (Buchanan and public choice; Becker and the family/crime), as well as for the MIT trio who had defended the NCS against the nascent post-Keynesian challenge (see appendix II). By contrast, Joan Robinson received little official peer group regard, indeed did not even become a professor until the post was vacated by her estranged husband in 1965, while Kaldor, with Harrod, is the most notable British economists to have been denied the supreme professional honour. Moreover, Cambridge UK did successfully demonstrate that there is a circularity in the NCS, one built around the dichotomy of capital as finance and as physical product, and yet Samuelson *et al.* carried on regardless. Such was the dominance of the Americans and of American-style economics by the 1970s; such was the fate of a critique originating outside of America, notwithstanding its Cambridge pedigree.[29]

Stepping carefully then in this minefield we can conclude that then, as now, neither Cambridge was producing testable hypotheses about why growth rates differed between countries, this increasingly the central policy issue in Britain at least. It must be admitted that the esoterics of double-switching and capital-reversing proved an interesting and amusing diversion for some, and the very best of trainings in mental gymnastics for graduate students, while the combativeness of the participants produced new vituperative delights, especially when Robinson (1962b) coined her phrase 'bastard Keynesianism' and used it with such relish on its first outing against Johnson who, unusually, was not as active – or as hyperactive a – participant in this particular controversy.[30]

---

[28] Hamouda and Harcourt (1988, pp. 14–16, 20–1, 25) and Harcourt (1996).

[29] Hodgson (1997, p. 104); see also Katouzian (1980, ch. 5) for a discussion of this episode in relation to broader issues of professionalisation.

[30] Johnson was equally complimentary: 'Thus Joan Robinson writes the most arid of technical capital theory in the belief that, contrary to all the empirical evidence, capitalism cannot possibly work, because she can to her own satisfaction make a nonsense of the concept of the production function and of distribution by marginal productivity; and Nicholas Kaldor goes one better than her by admitting that capitalism does work, but maintaining that it cannot possibly work

A crisis of abstraction and challenges to core theory

Neither Phelps Brown (1972) nor Worswick (1972a) specifically implicated the capital controversy in the crisis of abstraction they identified as undermining the authority of contemporary economics, but others were less inhibited (Hutchison 1981a, pp. 87–96; 1984, p. 2). Concerns about such a crisis were certainly expressed in surprising quarters, as for example in Hahn's (1970, p. 1) presidential address to the Econometric Society which referred to 'something scandalous in the spectacle of so many people refining the analyses of economic states which they give no reason to suppose will ever, or have ever, come about.'[31] The growing formalism and unworldliness of economics also in part motivated the formation in 1969 of the Conference of Socialist Economists (CSE), in effect the British institutional New Left response to the stirrings of radical economics in the US and the very particular concurrent British troubles (Radice 1980).

For the dominant Cambridge economists, therefore, the NCS and bastardised Keynesianism led to a theoretical and policy cul-de-sac,[32] with this revolt against orthodoxy intensifying as Friedman came to propagate the monetarist counter-revolution. For the more orthodox British economist, however, whether theoreticians who broadly subscribed to the NCS or those with applied interests who were unmoved by theoretical games, the capital controversy was a dangerous diversion at a time when it was necessary to defend the citadel of Keynesian demand management against the twin challenges of the monetarist infidel and supporters of supply-side solutions to Britain's economic difficulties.

Both causes were championed by the IEA which, by the later 1960s, had become the leading institutional focus of resistance to core British theory and policy, with a less public and more international role being played by the Mont Pèlerin Society. This latter, rather shadowy, body had been formed in 1947 with an initial membership which included four future Nobel Laureates (Allais, Hayek, Friedman and Stigler), other leading European and American economists, with additional British involvement by Peter Bauer, Stanley Dennison, Jewkes and Robbins.[33] These four, together with Ely Devons,[34] formed an informal network of dissident economists who,

---

according to orthodox theories of how it works, proper understanding of it requiring acceptance of revolutionary new but unverified theories of his own devising' (1975a, p. 118).

[31] See, however, Hahn (1973) for his defence of general equilibrium and his limited sympathy for some of the critics of contemporary economics, Phelps Brown included.

[32] Kaldor (1972; 1975), a position also adopted by many Oxford Keynesians, Balogh (1982).

[33] Cockett (1994, app. I). Subsequently, a number of other LSE economists became members, including A. Plant, F.W. Paish and Hutt.

[34] Cockett (1994) makes no mention of Devons (1950; 1961) whose wartime experience in the Ministry of Aircraft Production led him to write a series of sceptical, but very illuminating, post-

some less publicly than others, continued to champion the cause of classical liberalism and, through their connections, teaching and publications, helped create the environment in which the New Right would eventually flourish.[35]

The image of a discipline in disarray was to be much promulgated by the serious and not so serious press, with television providing an additional medium through which economists' shortcomings could be advertised. The magnification (attenuation) of the extent of theoretical disagreement (agreement) came largely from the activities of economic journalists and not professional economists, although obviously Friedman is a notable exception, even to the extent of using *Playboy* magazine as a forum to distil his monetarist, pro-market wisdom.[36] In Britain the bank journals were to be an important outlet for those attacking, and those defending, core theory and the profession's reputation (Roberts 1995). But even here, as Knapp (1973) revealed, there was a problem: whatever the real measure of agreement about theory, senior mainstream economists (here represented as Phelps Brown and Worswick) now judged economics as unable to provide clear answers to pressing policy questions.

We report in Table 6.3 Knapp's enumeration of the situation, one which contrasted this anomie with the self-assured position of the NCS (here represented by Johnson) and the emphatic eclecticism of the ultra-Keynesian stronghold (Harrod), and in Table 6.4 the macroeconomic background. At this stage our point is simply to record that for the ultra-Keynesians, and in particular those 'insiders' to the Keynesian revolution, macroeconomic turbulence, and the trend deterioration of both inflation and unemployment, were to be a cause of immense disappointment. Thus Harrod (1971b, ch. 3), in his Chichele lectures of 1970, given at a time when demonstrably whatever certainties the Phillips curve had provided now lay in the past, and when high employment and output were being foregone to right the balance of payments, expressed the gravest of concerns that economists and politicians were losing sight of Keynesian fundamentals, not least that unemployment should not be deliberately increased to secure external balance. For this ultra-Keynesian, as for Meade (1971b), who shared with

---

mortems on government's capacity to plan and how such experience, far from buttressing the case for big government in peacetime, reinforced the case for the market (Cairncross 1991b).

[35] Jewkes, like Devons, used his wartime experience to campaign against the early postwar fashion for planning, with his *Ordeal by planning* (1948) being widely read and having a successor volume (1968) which put the failure of the 1960s' planning experiment in historical context. He also wrote or co-authored four IEA pamphlets and a further volume of critical essays on government's economic competency. Robbins wrote or contributed towards nine IEA pamphlets.

[36] Parsons (1989, p. 137). Just as Keynes had used a new medium, the radio, to advance radical ideas, Friedman was one of the first to use television. His series *Free to choose*, itself a spin-off from two earlier books (Friedman and Friedman 1962; 1980), were broadcast in the UK at exactly the time the Thatcher government launched their monetarist policy experiment. See Stewart (1980) for the horrified reaction of the British economics establishment.

Table 6.3   UK disciplinary agreement in the early 1970s

Allegedly unsettled questions	Phelps Brown (1972)	Worswick (1972a)	Johnson	Harrod
1. Do we know what is the proper scope for the free market and government intervention, if economic welfare is to be maximized?	?	...	Yes	No
2. a) Can economic theory explain why the growth rate in the UK and the US has been so much slower than elsewhere? b) And, more generally, do we know how to foster growth in poor countries and how to improve the performance of the industrial economies?	?	?	Yes	No
3. Do we know that free trade helps and does not hinder economic development?	...	?	Yes	No
4. Do we really know whether devaluation improves the balance of payments, and for how long, and do we know on what principles balance of payments adjustments should be managed?	?	?	Yes	No
5. Do we know why inefficiency exists and persists in British industry and what determines the rate at which technical innovations already understood will be adopted?	?	?	...	...
6. Do we know how to check cost inflation while maintaining full employment?	?	?	Nonsense question	No

Note: ... means question not posed, or not answered.

Source: Knapp (1973, table 1).

him an increasing preoccupation with how to build a workable incomes policy that would counter stagflation and thereby salvage the Keynesian inheritance, the profession's responsibilities were clear:

> Beneath all this fumbling and pathetic confusion, the real fault lies at a deeper level, namely in the unsatisfactory condition of economic dynamics itself. Until we economists can get that subject into better order, so that it can yield clearer and more valid maxims of policy, we must not blame the policy-makers too much.   (Harrod 1971b, p. 83)

We will reject absolutely this conclusion in sections 4 and 5, for

Table 6.4   Macroeconomic indicators (%), 1964–74

	Real GDP growth rate (on previous year	Current account balance of payments (% of GDP)	Change in consumer prices	Unemployment rate
1964	5.4	(1.1)	3.2	2.6
1965	2.3	(0.2)	4.8	1.5
1966	2.0	0.3	4.0	1.6
1967	2.3	(0.7)	2.5	2.5
1968	4.1	(0.6)	4.7	2.5
1969	1.8	1.0	5.5	2.5
1970	2.3	1.6	6.4	2.7
1971	2.1	1.9	9.4	2.7
1972	2.9	0.3	7.4	3.5
1973	7.2	(1.3)	8.8	3.8
1974	(1.6)	(3.8)	16.2	2.7

Source: CSO databank.

stagflation in Britain was a consequence much more of politics and politicians than of theory and economists, but here record that it was not just the Keynesian old guard who were contemplating economics' shortcomings:

> Following forty years of unprecedented critical inquiry, both at the theoretical and at the empirical levels, economics is currently in a state of flux, with controversy raging in almost all of its branches, and with the monism of the neoclassical message effectively replaced by a pluralism of competing viewpoints.   (Rowley and Peacock 1975, p. 1)

The difference, of course, is that these two British economists, who in the 1970s and 1980s did much – again through the IEA[37] – to revive a liberal political economy in Britain, welcomed such pluralism 'as a healthy indication of a vigorous and open profession still at the genesis of its potential' whereas for the old guard there was an increasing sense of a professional position to be defended against a plethora of challenges. We have then the hallmark of a crisis of the economics establishment, a particularly Oxbridge (and within that Cambridge-focused) crisis since the LSE maintained a political and theoretical diversity as well as having powerful figures (not least Harry Johnson) who were part of the growing

[37]   According to the IEA's catalogue of publications for 1957–82, Peacock wrote or contributed to seven IEA pamphlets and Rowley six. Of these, Peacock's (1977b) Wincott lecture and IEA (1978), to which they both contributed, were to prove particularly influential. Both were also prominent contributors to the bank reviews.

confrontation.[38] We consider in chapter 7 the full-blown crisis of Keynesian economics that ensued, but it is relevant here because explaining what later transpired is impossible without appreciating that the expansion of British economics in the 1950s and 1960s, with the attendant processes of professionalisation and Americanisation, created the institutions (rival departments) and incentives (professional advancement through publication) to challenge the Oxbridge dominance of British economics. We have already observed this process at the level of *EJ* publications, but we should also note that in the broader market for economic ideas it would be academics and policy entrepreneurs from 'peripheral' universities who would eventually acquire influence. For the 1980s we would highlight the influence of St Andrews' graduates, notably Eamonn Butler and Madsen Pirie, the founders of the Adam Smith Institute (ASI, established 1976), in 'thinking the unthinkable' about the proper role of government (Cockett 1994), whereas for the 1970s it is arguable that some of the most policy-oriented economic research was being conducted in Manchester at the SSRC-sponsored Inflation Workshop. This must rank as one of the most productive research projects ever funded by the SSRC,[39] and we must await the opening of the Treasury papers for the 1970s to assess the extent to which the Heath government was influenced by the policy advice being proffered by the project's leaders (David Laidler and Michael Parkin).

Economics research

The case of the Manchester Inflation Workshop leads us to consider more generally public funding of research in relation to the professionalisation and Americanisation of British economics. The Clapham committee (HMSO 1946) had pressed the case for greater social science funding just after the war but had rejected the proposal that there be a SSRC or similar body. Nearly twenty years later the perceived scarcity of public funds was more pressing, particularly within the economics profession where it was no longer possible to rely upon the benevolence of the Rockefeller Foundation as had been the case in the 1930s (RES 1963). The eventual establishment of the SSRC in 1965, some forty years after its American equivalent, came with acceptance of the Heyworth committee's report (HMSO 1965a, ch. VIII). This was to be vested with a budget that was minute by comparison

---

[38] In 1973, and in addition to Johnson, its economics professors included a significant number of IEA contributors (notably Bauer, Prest, Walters and Yamey) but also many who did not take part in the growing public debate or can be characterised as mainstream Keynesians (A.C.L. Day, M. Morishima, Denis Sargan and A.K. Sen).

[39] Established in 1971 as an inter-disciplinary group of twenty economists, econometricians and accountants it published six volumes in its *Studies in inflation* series between 1972–8. The foreword and preface to its last volume (Parkin and Sumner 1978) details their objectives.

with those disbursed by the comparable research councils for science and medicine, but it shared with these agencies a bureaucratic model which shielded social scientists from political manipulation of their research.[40] Economics soon acquired the second largest share of its funding in terms of project research and postgraduate studentships, the latter becoming increasingly important as at least a master's degree, if not yet the Ph.D., became a precondition for an academic post. In addition the SSRC proved an important source of funds for the macroeconomic model-building undertaken at Cambridge, the National Institute, the LBS, Southampton and elsewhere (SSRC 1981), although reservations remained amongst many senior policy-oriented economists– not least from the government's chief economic adviser[41] – about such funding relative to the other calls on the SSRC's limited budget.

We lack cross-country historical data on public funding of research with which to assess whether British economists were disadvantaged relative to their American and European counterparts, but a recent study (Kirman and Dahl 1994, p. 508) indicates that total provision for European economists compares favourably with that for Americans and the British appeared to enjoy a high degree of autonomy in how funds are distributed to university research. Certainly, relative to the more severe funding environment prevailing after OPEC I, the 1960s and the early 1970s were halcyon days for British universities. SSRs fell in the five years after the Robbins report, current expenditure per full-time student (at constant prices) rose and there was even a temporary halt to the longer-term erosion of academic salaries, although British salaries compared unfavourably with those in America.[42] It was during this period that significant numbers of British economists began to take leave to visit the US and, together with a return flow of US-trained economists who clustered at the LSE and some of the new departments (Essex and Warwick), but not Oxbridge or the older provincial universities, this was an important transmission mechanism for American professional values. Indeed, Sargent's (1963) observations about the profession, which heads this chapter, followed a year spent in the US. The hierarchical and conservative nature of British universities and the strict limits on occupational and geographical mobility made the US an attractive proposition for the more adventurous and ambitious, while the reduced real cost of transatlantic travel greatly assisted such migration.[43]

---

[40] Halsey (1992, pp. 179–80). See also SSRC (1975) for a brief account of the first ten years of the SSRC by its four chairmen during these years: the sociologist Michael Young and the economists Andrew Shonfield, Robin Matthews and Derek Robinson.

[41] From Cairncross (1969); see Worswick and Blackaby (1974) on the state of the art at the same time, with contributions from all of the leading modellers.

[42] Layard *et al.* (1969, ch. 10), Halsey and Trow (1971, table 9.1) and Backhouse (1997a, p. 47).

[43] Coats (1980, p. 600) and Backhouse (1997a, pp. 36–7).

Two further comparative points suggest themselves. First, given the disparity in resources between leading American and British universities, and the larger scale of the former, it seems probable that US economics departments gained earlier access to computing facilities and that this influenced the subsequent development of empirical economics. Whether British economists found themselves unable to compete with their better-resourced American counterparts, or whether they did not take full advantage of what was available in the 1950s and 1960s, has yet to be explored. An SSRC (1974) survey revealed that, within the social sciences, economics departments made the greatest call upon university computing facilities but that so far it could tell the social sciences were not clamouring for additional computer funding. However, it was undoubtedly the case that, relative to the US, British economists continued to be handicapped by the underdeveloped nature of official economic statistics (Peden 1990, p. 233). Famously, Harold Macmillan, when Chancellor, had complained that 'There are too many unknowns and too many variables ... [while] some of our statistics are too late to be as useful as they ought to be. We are always, as it were, looking up a train in last year's Bradshaw' (Hansard 1956, col. 867). Shortly thereafter, many economists used the opportunity of their giving evidence before the Radcliffe committee on the working of the monetary system to voice their concerns about official statistics.[44] This empowered Campion, the director of the CSO, to secure a greater Treasury commitment to funding the collection and dissemination of data, one early consequence of which was *Financial Statistics*, launched in 1962, just after the Bank issued its first quarterly bulletin. Subsequent development work under Campion and his successor, Claus Moser, allowed British economists to catch up with empirical work in the 1970s, although complaints about data deficiencies remained ubiquitous amongst economists and policy-makers.[45]

Our second observation is that the most penetrating assessments of the British economy at this time were made by outsiders, which raises questions about British capabilities in applied economics and the willingness of British economists to voice simple but hard truths about low productivity and policy errors. Two studies by outsiders are particularly noteworthy: that by Caves and his Brookings Institution associates, *Britain's economic*

---

[44] Its report, largely written by Richard Sayers (with Cairncross the other economist member), devoted a whole chapter to its recommendations for economic statistics (HMSO 1959, ch. X). In addition, it issued four volumes of evidence and memoranda which detail the submissions from almost every economist of note at this time. This valuable source has not yet been used by historians; yet, as Walters (1970) argued in criticism of Radcliffe, the lack of empirical testing in the report was indicative of the style of economics at that time. The Bank Rate Tribunal of 1957–8 has suffered similar neglect; see Devons (1959a) for its potential.

[45] See HMSO (1966) for a progress report on the CSO with proposals for further developments in the government's statistical capabilities; see also Peden (1999, ch. 9).

prospects (1968), and Hansen's (1969) more tightly focused study of fiscal policy for the OECD. Such was the furore generated by the former that when Caves came to organise a follow-up study 'British critics were brought in from the outset rather than left to fire their volleys after the ... book appeared' (Caves and Krause 1980, p. vii), a reference to the Cairncross (1971b) volume which contained a number of very critical responses but also – now that we have a longer historical perspective – some very astute concluding reflections (Cairncross 1971c, pp. 235–6):

> It seems to be characteristic of discussions in this country that it should be intermittent, lacking in follow-through, and not based on continuing professional enquiry. A debate starts up, work is done in various places and in various ways, and then the whole matter is allowed to drop.
> ... we badly need some way of sustaining discussion more systematically and at greater depth. It is impressive to compare the resources available in the United States – most conspicuously in the Brookings Institution – for continuous and comprehensive analysis of longer-term economic and social problems with the meagre resources available for this purpose in Britain. What resources are available are widely diffused and the few centres of research such as the National Institute do not compare in the range and calibre of their staff with Brookings. If we want to organize debate in Britain in a more satisfactory way we might well begin by seeking to build up an institution of comparable standing.

Cairncross's observations about the policy debate are capable of broader generalisation to the state of British economics on the eve of OPEC I. Possessed of some world-class economists and departments, and exhibiting a definite comparative advantage in important fields of research, one which reflected economic conditions (international economics and the openness of the British economy) and/or ideological predispositions (strength in public economics and the measurement of inequality), the British profession had in many ways an enviable record. But, and here mirroring some of the complaints levelled against British economic policy and enterprise performance, there was also grounds for concern: thus management was widely viewed as amateurish, research activities uncoordinated and with a bias towards pure rather than applied science. There was considerable dissatisfaction with the conservative policies and leadership of the RES, such as to bring about a revival of the AUTE, and the beginnings of concerns by senior economists and employers that university economics graduates, schooled in the new American-style, were not equipped for a working life of real-world concerns.[46] The remodelling of the curriculum brought about by the growing formalism of economic theory was not only at

---

[46] See in particular the debate in the *Lloyds Bank Review* initiated by the former DAE economist, Dudley Jackson (1980), and the concerns of Rybczynski (1972), a hybrid economist who kept a foot in both camps, academia and business; see also *The Economist*, 15 June 1974, p. 16.

the cost of students' understanding of the contemporary economy, but of their knowledge of the history of economic thought and of economic history.[47] Marshall would have recognised as a 'well-rounded economist' the typical product of a leading British department in 1939 or 1949, even perhaps 1959, but not by 1969. By then, and accelerating into the 1970s, professionalisation and particularly Americanisation were transforming economics education. As yet there were no adverse effects on the demand for economists or indeed university degrees in economics; indeed, economics was beginning to become a popular 'O' and 'A' level subject, having been actively promoted by the RES acting in concert with the AUTE and the Economics Association.[48] Given the initial opposition to such a development by many senior economists, most notably Robbins (1955), the discipline can be said to have acquired a stage of maturity by the eve of OPEC I.

6.4 ECONOMICS, ECONOMISTS, POLICY AND THE GOLDEN AGE

Britain did have a golden age!

The record of British economic performance and policy from the end of the Second World War until OPEC I has attracted such opprobrium that the label 'golden age', which economists apply routinely to this epoch for the other OECD states, might appear wholly inappropriate. That it is has to be defended at all, and that academics now have to remind each successive cohort of students studying the British economy that during these years the British people enjoyed full employment, no major recessions and the fastest rate of economic growth ever experienced on a sustained basis (not to mention its most egalitarian distribution), is a measure of how far the British policy debate has internalised the Thatcherite message of this era as one of generalised failure. We begin, therefore, with the facts, here represented in relation to the goal of simultaneous attainment of internal and external balance via the four central golden age macroeconomic objectives: high growth, full employment, gently rising prices and a current account balance of payments surplus sufficient to fund overseas investment:[49]

---

[47]　See Winch (1962) for early concerns about the history of economic thought, and Schwartz (1975) for the deliberations of a symposium held in Bristol, one conclusion of which was that student disillusionment with the new curriculum did not lead to a constructive interest in history. On the state of economic history, see Coleman (1987).

[48]　Booth and Coats (1978), Lumsden *et al.* (1980, ch. 2) and Robinson and Wilson (1977).

[49]　Averages for the original six EC member states and US in parentheses The measurement period is 1950–73, with the sources as for Table 6.4, supplemented by Maddison (1991, tables C-4, E4; 1995, table B-10a).

- real GDP growth averaged 3 per cent (5.1 and 3.9 per cent), approximately a 50 per cent improvement on the interwar period and sufficient to more than double the standard of living each quarter century;
- unemployment (on the ILO definition) averaged 2.8 per cent (3.1 and 4.6 per cent), approximately one-fifth of the interwar rate and, while still exhibiting regional disparities, nonetheless constituting a transformation of the labour market compared with the social tragedy (and costs) generated by the depressed areas of outer Britain;
- consumer price inflation averaged 4.7 per cent (3.7 and 2.7 per cent), this sufficient to halve the real value of money every fifteen years or so, and again in complete contrast to the years between the wars when the price trend was downwards; and
- even the current account balance of payments registered a small surplus on average (0.3 per cent of GDP), but was critically weak during boom years (1951, 1955, 1960, 1964, 1968 and 1973) and a source of constant concern to policy-makers, as indeed was the capital account because of the overseas investment programmes of Britain's multinational companies. Current account weakness was inevitable given Britain's low rate of export growth and high import propensities; yet, weakness was also self-imposed as the private sector balance of payments was, bar one exceptional year (1951), always in surplus (Middleton 1996, figure 12.1). It was the deficit on the government account which pushed the overall balance into deficit, with the principal debit item defence expenditures overseas. Had successive governments a more realistic conception of Britain's sustainable geo-political posture then much of the balance of payments problems would have been avoided, and this even before one thinks of the macroeconomic costs of key currency concerns and the other paraphernalia of Britain's great power delusion.

In relation to the interwar period then this record is deserving, if not of gold, than certainly of silver; even more so given the pessimistic forecasts, made during the war and immediate postwar planning phase, about the prospects for achieving high employment and a sustainable economic recovery. There are, of course, no shortage of possible objections to this attempted rehabilitation of this epoch. At one extreme we have the Barnett-Thatcherite view of a victory squandered in pursuit of a New Jerusalem, of a welfare state and substantial nationalised sector which burdened production through high taxes and entrenched X-inefficiency by sanctioning dysfunctional labour-capital relations; on the other, that such was the catch-up potential and scarcity of labour relative to capital that historically high growth and full employment are really not that difficult to explain, either in Britain or elsewhere in the OECD.

Unsurprisingly, most academic economists are disdainful of the former's arguments, but their enduring appeal requires that we take seriously popular perceptions of economic processes and events, for it is these, as much as specialist opinion, which impact on political choice and thus politicians' behaviour. At the other extreme we are offered the possibility that golden age growth, to a greater or lesser extent, was independent of government behaviour. Most famously, in Britain Matthews (1968, pp. 555–6) confronted the profession with:

> When the question is asked, *why* have we had full employment since the war? most people tend to reply, without thinking very much, that it is because we have had a full-employment policy – we have had the Keynesian revolution. Now supposing this were the right answer, it would be a remarkable thing. It would mean the most important single feature of the post-war British economy has been due to an advance in economic theory. It would be a most striking vindication of Keynes' celebrated dictum about the ultimate primacy of abstract thought in the world of affairs.

Government, economic knowledge and the golden age

Matthews's question came as something of a bombshell for a profession who believed in the efficacy of discretionary economic management, such that the quest for a viable escape route from the confines of the Stop-Go cycle absorbed many of the best talents. Having posed the question he then went on to demonstrate that full employment since the war owed more to the high spending propensities of the private sector at home and abroad than to Keynesian deficit-financing, although an indirect Keynesian expectations effect was acknowledged through the commitment to full employment underpinning a high marginal efficiency of capital.

His model was much criticised at the time but the conclusion has endured.[50] One reason for this is that greater historical perspective emphasises the buoyancy of aggregate demand before OPEC I, such that many considered seriously the obsolescence of the business cycle. That these were not years of substantial public sector budget deficits is confirmed by the long-term public finance dataset compiled for my earlier study (Middleton 1996, p. 111), while recent revisionist histories have revealed that in later life Keynes's advocacy of deficit-finance was heavily qualified, and that official acceptance of functional finance in peacetime had only been attained by the late 1950s. In any case, as the examples of Japan and Italy attest, golden age growth can be explained quite independently of Keynesianism.

---

[50] See Broadberry (1994) for a recent discussion; see also Tomlinson (1981a) for whom Matthews is an important building block in the argument that no meaningful Keynesian revolution in policy ever occurred in Britain.

In these two countries Keynesian ideas made little headway before the 1960s, whereas there was a pre-existing economic-political orthodoxy that economic growth required activist public policy, while in France and Germany Keynesianism was interpreted quite differently from in Britain (Hall 1989a, chs 7, 8, 11), with the French pursuing a neo-collectivist strategy of national economic reconstruction and the Germans a neo-liberal social market model. Moreover, when British policy is examined closely in terms of what was done, rather than what was said was being done, on every occasion bar the Heath U-turn of 1972, which was only possible because the fixed exchange rate regime had been abandoned, maintenance of sterling's value, the foreign exchange reserves and the balance of payments were all accorded higher priority than the full employment objective.

The distinguishing characteristic of this era was accordingly, less the commitment to full employment, than the fact that this commitment was never seriously tested, and when it was in Britain in the early 1970s it became quickly evident that government lacked the capability to deliver on its commitment. Government does, however, re-enter the equation in terms of policies which were growth-enhancing. Maddison (1991, pp. 168–77) identifies the following system characteristics of the golden age for the OECD as a whole:

1. Managed liberalism in international transactions.
2. Government promotion of domestic demand buoyancy.
3. Policies and circumstances which moderated inflation.
4. A backlog of growth possibilities which made the supply response very sensitive to high levels of demand.

These entailed a combination of domestic and international economic policies for the OECD member states, ones in which Britain had been a junior partner to the US in shaping the Bretton Woods system and had, through its 1944 employment policy white paper, established a lead for others to follow in setting domestic economic policy objectives. Two points are particularly important here. First, for all of the OECD, indeed all participants in the boom, this was an epoch in which nation states enjoyed unparalleled autonomy in macroeconomic policy. Indeed, limited international capital mobility, combined with national capital controls, created unique circumstances in which most governments – notably, Britain excepted – were able to reconcile the maintenance of the fixed exchange rates required by Bretton Woods with the domestic policy objective of high employment dictated by their national politics (Eichengreen 1996). A globalisation of trade and payments was developing and when it reached a critical mass it contributed to the collapse of the Bretton Woods system in

1971, exacerbated the supply shock of OPEC I in 1973–4, and thereafter progressively undermined this national macroeconomic autonomy and with it the especial role that economists had been able to play in policy. Before then, however, government was aided in its economic management by there being a nationalised (but far from docile) Bank of England, a balance between collectivism and individualism which favoured big government, the underdevelopment of consumer choices about public services and a relatively well-behaved labour market in that there was a strong demand for unskilled labour and government could target male, full-time employment.

Secondly, while Britain set the pace in establishing policy objectives favourable to demand buoyancy, its geo-political aspirations and its postwar settlement were uniquely unhelpful in securing this project. As was recognised from the time of Kalecki (1943) onwards it was clear that there was a wage-inflation timebomb ticking away in the relations between government, capital and labour in a fully employed economy and, in retrospect, the marvel is that it took so long before it was detonated. Similar reservations can be made about supply responsiveness to aggregate demand in Britain, where there were particular difficulties which exacerbated Stop-Go. But, as a NEDO (1976) study revealed, quantitatively business cycle fluctuations in Britain were actually smaller than in the more successful OECD economies (cf. Pollard 1984), while of course the breakdown of the Phillips curve in the late 1960s affected all of the OECD. Phelps Brown's (1983, pp. 164–5) 'hinge', whereby wage expectations and bargaining strategies were increasingly fuelled by younger workers who had no collective memory of the insecurities characteristic of interwar labour markets, has been invoked to explain European-US developments, but a more localised explanation is also necessary for Britain. This has been provided by Worswick (1992, esp. pp. 69–71), and has been supported by the recollections of the Chancellor (Jenkins) of the time and of his chief economic adviser (MacDougall), namely that the acceleration of wage inflation in Britain in 1969–70 might have been much less affected by the hinge had the Wilson government not belatedly and abortively attempted trade union reform (with *In place of strife*) instead of persevering with its incomes policy. The importance of this explanation, and indeed of the fate of the 1964–70 Wilson governments, is that it marries longer-term concerns about economic decline with shorter-term issues of stabilising demand in a manner which acknowledges the new politics of economic policy in two very important senses: that Labour was compelled finally to confront the culpability of organised labour in low productivity and to bear the fallout from unrealised expectations of real wage advancement generated by the political contest itself.

If we take 1954, the year of Butler's speech committing government to a doubling of the standard of living over the next quarter century, as the point at which government adopted an explicit growth objective we can say that within fifteen years, and whether in their incarnation as wage-bargainers or as the electorate, the British people came to judge governments primarily by the economy's performance (Mosley 1984, ch. 2). Early quantitative studies of political business cycles identified statistically significant relationships between political popularity and economic performance, while surveys conducted by political scientists distinguished between two channels through which the economy impacted on voters: perceptions of individual well-being and perceptions of the general state of the economy, with neither formed in a manner which economists wedded to rational calculation models of human behaviour would find reassuring. Arguably, Macmillan and Wilson had come to similar conclusions much earlier, and without the benefit of econometrics, one consequence of which was they sought to manage more actively the presentation of economic events and policy. The resulting politicisation of economic policy in the late 1950s-early 1960s thus created the conditions for a substantial increase in demand for economists, both in government and in financial and other market-sensitive institutions which came to require greater analytical capacity in order to fathom what government was actually doing.

Professional economic expertise and the policy pyramid

Whilst October 1964 was to be the watershed for the employment of economists in government, the rightwards shift in demand for their expertise predates the first Wilson administration, with the Plowden report (HMSO 1961) and the establishment of NEDO particularly significant. Moreover, there has perhaps been too much focus on the small numbers of economists in post hitherto, with insufficient attention paid to the efforts made to improve the post-entry training of the generalist, administrative class civil servants. A number of internal reviews in 1962 identified the need for more training in economics and statistics for those who administered in 'economic' departments, and in 1963 there was established the Treasury's Centre for Administrative Studies. In its first year this provided a fourteen week course for Assistant Principals, the entry grade for the predominantly graduate administrative class, which covered basic economic concepts supplemented by a seven week course which focused on the application of such concepts to government problems (Keeling 1971, p. 54). However, since nothing was done concurrently to alter recruitment to incorporate more economic specialists, the contemporary verdict, later amplified by the Fulton committee (HMSO 1968), was that Britain's civil service remained amateurish relative to that trained by the Ecole Nationale d'Administration.

This latter body, indeed all things French in economic affairs, was fast becoming the example to be emulated by those clamouring for modernisation, with the enthusiasm for planning, reignited during the last years of Macmillan's administration, its clearest manifestation.[51] Economists were amongst the most vocal of those calling for civil service reform as a precondition for remedying Britain's economic difficulties. For many, most notably Shonfield (1958) and Brittan (1964) in their radical popularising works, the civil service was still largely wedded to economic liberalism and this must be remedied for government to become more effective. For others, and especially the anonymous Fabian Society report (1964), the emphasis was that recruitment needed to be widened to embrace the talents available from all of the universities and academic disciplines, not just Oxbridge arts degrees; to encourage movement into and out of the service; a battery of measures to counter the prevailing cult of the amateur; and to eradicate the 'segregation, patronising attitudes, lack of responsibility and power, rule by supercilious amateurs and so on' to which specialist groups in the civil service, not least the economists, were then subjected (1964, p. 36). Particular criticism was reserved for the Treasury, with the group deeply unimpressed by the reorganisation of that department in 1962 (pp. 32–3). Of course, two of the members of this group were themselves economists (Balogh and Neild); both would subsequently serve as senior economic advisers to the Wilson governments, with the latter also a member of the Fulton committee. Balogh had long-established views about the British civil service (1959; 1963, pp. 30–5) but had never before been an insider, whereas Neild had. He had been in the ES between 1951–6, and as he latter recounted in interview to Fry (1993, pp. 18–19):

> By then the squeeze on the economists was on. With decontrol, out went the economists, and it was back to the Old School. I had a fixed term contract and I was told that if I wanted to become permanent I would have to take a late entry examination, even though I had passed the Administrative Class examination before. So I went into university life.

With its dual responsibilities for civil service and economic management the Treasury was a natural and compelling target. Dissatisfaction with the Treasury would reach a head with the deliberations of the Fulton committee between 1966–8 (Fry 1993), the very time when the Wilson administration in effect came to terms with the failure of its great planning experiment. However, as the committee's secretary, himself a former Treasury official, later recounts:

---

[51] See Leruez (1975) for a French assessment of British experience with planning, Hackett and Hackett (1963) for an unusually cosmopolitan British assessment of French experience, and **Budd** (1978) for a British 'insiders' account.

the Committee's common ground, the underlying assumptions on which they based their line in taking evidence and later in writing their report, were in part surprisingly naive. Throughout they showed a marked tendency to ignore, or at least underrate, the impact of political constraints upon the rationality of administration. There was an underlying assumption that if a carefully selected and well-trained civil service, using up-to-date techniques, produced rational solutions to the problems of central government, those solutions would normally prevail; and that Ministers, recognising a greater expert knowledge than their own, would be content to see civil service planners develop long-term policy proposals even if they appeared inconsistent with present policies or were likely to be unpopular with the government's own backbenchers. . . . In the more highly-charged political polarisation of the 1980s and 1990s, these assumptions, sadly, have a rather quaint, old-world air. It is not perhaps surprising that they partly sprang from a Fabian origin.   (Wilding 1995, p. 400)

At this stage, as we come to the events surrounding the huge influx of economists into Whitehall of 1964 and after, we need briefly to step back twenty years or so and be reminded of how economists had proved their worth during the war. Thus those who served in the ES during this period have all emphasised the premium placed on economists working within existing networks and to civil service norms of conduct, of having a personality that fitted.[52] Indeed, from my soundings of those who served at this time, only one economist has emerged as detracting seriously from the economists' reputation in Whitehall, and this because he was unable to wrench himself away from high theory to apply himself to the humdrum, routine character of wartime economic administration. There was a to be an enduring significance to the way in which economists were incorporated into the wartime bureaucracy and the skills that were sought by established civil servants. Thus, as Cairncross (1994) recollects, and as is attested by much documentary testimony by others who served in the ES, the distinctive skills that economists brought to bear were as much to do with their facility with numbers as with theory, both of which were pretty basic but required great ingenuity in application if value-added was to be provided. The economists' comparative advantage over peacetime administrators was in

---

[52] Chester (1951b); Robbins (1971, ch. VIII); Cairncross and Watts (1989); and Cairncross (1994). The case of Balogh, who as an alien did not serve in the wartime ES, comes immediately to mind when considering the role of personality. Robert Hall, who latter dubbed Balogh 'Wilson's spy', well conveys the problem in a February 1958 diary entry: 'Balogh talked to me over the weekend. He has been asked to submit a paper to the Radcliffe Committee and was very pleased – I am glad as he has some very good ideas which I only hope they take seriously. He also talked very wildly about the need to change key officials when and if the Labour Government came in – he . . . actually asked me if I would prefer to be Governor of the Bank or Joint Perm. Sec. of the Treasury. He hasn't got much idea of how these things are or can be done if he thinks it is going to be as easy as that' (Cairncross 1991a, pp. 147–8). In annotating his diaries, Cairncross (1997, p. 1) repeats with evident relish Keynes's judgement, 'the trouble with Tommy is that he never went to Winchester'.

their vision of what a war economy might look like, an application of their economic theory to the construction of a centrally planned economy in which both markets and politics were in abeyance. Whilst macroeconomic issues were clearly relevant, few actually spent their time on such glamorous concerns as the size of the inflationary gap. On the contrary, most were concerned with microeconomic issues, marrying supply to demand without benefit of the price mechanism in industries about which the majority knew little before the war. All of this, of course, is also consistent with our knowledge of what business economists were employed to do in the 1950s and 1960s (Alexander *et al.* 1967). Given this group's complaint that formalism was resulting in the broader profession failing to keep abreast of industrial, commercial or financial issues, or indeed to be interested in them in many cases, and that it was this which was contributing to macroeconomic policy failures (Rybczynski 1972), the question naturally arises of whether wartime successes with macroeconomic policy owed something to the orientation of most economists to microeconomic concerns.

After the war there undoubtedly developed a hierarchy of policy problems so far as the profession was concerned, one which approximated to Ward's (1972) ladder of prestige in economic theory. For Walters (1978), as for others academic economists who contributed towards the developing IEA critique of the British economics establishment,[53] this zeitgeist might be encapsulated as: the market is more prone to technical failures than is government; demand is more important than supply; and the distribution of wealth is more interesting than its generation.[54] Whether this constituted a professional bias against the market is unknowable, but it was the case that economists exhibited a much lower propensity to research and/or advise government on competition policy as against say macroeconomic policy. Indeed, we can invoke Andrews once more as an example both of this hierarchy in action and of the dominance of Oxbridge-LSE in the public policy role of the profession. The case of Andrews demonstrates that expert knowledge and Oxbridge credentials provided no guarantee of being incorporated into the policy community, for his dissidence ensured that his immense knowledge of industrial issues found no higher public application than as an occasional adviser to the Restrictive Practices Court. Indeed, there is sufficient circumstantial evidence to suggest that the micro-macroeconomic policy divide in effect reproduced the traditional Whitehall pecking order of the Treasury *primus inter pares* and the other economic department (principally the Ministry of Labour and the Board of Trade)

---

[53] The IEA catalogue, 1957–82, lists 330 authors or contributors to IEA publications, although clearly a significant number in the latter category were IEA critics, not least Collard (1968; 1981a) who coined the phrase the New Right in one of the earliest attacks upon this think-tank.

[54] For example, Hutchison (1981b) and O'Brien (1981b).

consigned to the less glamorous end of (microeconomic) policy.

Although no systematic analysis of the public service activities of postwar economists has been attempted, casual empiricism suggests that Oxbridge-London economists dominated appointments to the plethora of public agencies established as a consequence of the state's greatly expanded economic role. This was true at the highest level with the directors of the ES (later, heads of the GES) until **Burns** (Manchester, appointed by Thatcher in 1980), all of the senior advisers (whether unofficial in the 1950s as in Harrod, Paish and Robbins or official in the 1960s as in Balogh, Cairncross, Kaldor, MacDougall and Neild), and for appointments to important government enquiries (notably the Radcliffe committee) and to high-profile and politically-sensitive commissions (for example, the Council on Prices, Productivity and Incomes of 1957–61 which included amongst its 'Three Wise Men' such relics from a previous policy era as Dennis Robertson). Even at the less glamorous end of the policy spectrum, the economics establishment dominated, with for example George Allen's long tenure at the Monopolies and Restrictive Practices Commission. Indeed, his experience may be a further example of the policy pyramid in operation, for his Establishment reward for nearly twenty years of British public service (CBE) was more than matched by the Japanese government's award of the Order of the Rising Sun for his efforts to educate westerners in Japanese economy and society. But there again Allen was an IEA author and trustee.

The 1964 watershed: a triumph of numbers not influence

Focusing more specifically now on Whitehall and on economists actually employed in government service, Coats (1981c, pp. 370–1) has argued that 'One of the most unexpected features of the British case is the fact that the economists' acknowledged success in wartime and the conscious adoption of full employment as a major postwar policy objective did not automatically generate a substantial demand for professional economists in the peacetime civil service'; rather there was to be a lag of nearly twenty years before economists entered Whitehall in substantial numbers, this roughly coinciding with the first Wilson government although it was also a 'transformation [which] cannot be explained simply in political terms'. Booth and Coats (1978, table 5) estimate that in 1945 there were only 10 professional economists in Whitehall (excluding agricultural economists, who were separately graded until 1975, and statisticians), 18 some ten years later and 21.5 by 1964. In 1970, on these figures, there were 236, an elevenfold rise over the Wilson years. In Table 6.5 we detail the growth in numbers of the civil service economist class between 1964–75 and its distribution across the departments.

Table 6.5   Civil service: economist class, 1964 and 1975

Department/Ministry	1964	1975
Cabinet Office	0	7
Civil Service Department	0	3
Customs and Excise	0	2
Defence	0	3
Education and Science	0	5
Employment	0	14
Energy	0	18
Environment	0	84
Fair Trading	0	7
Foreign and Commonwealth Office	3	12
Health and Social Security	0	16
Home	0	3
Overseas Development	0	34
Scottish Office	1	9
Trade, Industry, Prices & Consumer Protection	0	45
Treasury	17	53
Welsh Office	0	1
Other	0	1
Total	21	317

Source: *The Times*, 24 November 1975, p. 1.

This development was to be a cause of much excitement both for Establishment critics like Sampson (1965, pp. 310–14), author of the influential *Anatomy of Britain* (1964), and for self-appointed guardians of that Establishment like Aims of Industry, a shadowy right-wing organisation which would come to prominence in the 1970s with its monitoring of trade unionists and other 'disruptive' elements (Grant and Marsh 1977, pp. 72, 169–70, 215). At this time, however, the focus for both was Buda and Pest – aka Balogh and Kaldor – who acquired a celebrity status not seen since Keynes's day. For Sampson they were the subject of warm-hearted amusement; for Aims of Industry, however, they were the source of all sorts of mischief, both 'actual', in the damage they had supposedly done to the LDCs whose governments they had advised, and potential were Labour to win the 1964 election: 'It is quite clear where the important influences of Messrs Kaldor and Balogh would lead: to punitive taxation; to nationalization; to a plethora of planning and licences and controls' (George and Bewlay 1964, p. 8). These representatives of organised capital were expressing the very real concerns of much of industry as it contemplated the prospect of a Labour victory. Fortunately, for them, the economists' triumph was to be one of numbers not of real influence.

Our explanation for this dissonance between expectations and outcome begins with the combination of demand and supply-side factors which Coats (1981c, pp. 371–2) identifies as having delayed the triumph of numbers in the first place. First, the initial enthusiasm for planning during Labour's first postwar administrations (1945–51) did not translate into a demand for government economists because of a combination of:

- personalities, with Meade and then Hall envisaging a small ES;
- the extreme difficulties of recruiting economists as salaries and conditions of service were unfavourable relative to academia and business; and
- the belief, born of war experience, that peacetime demand management could be exercised at a very high-level through judicious use of a few key macroeconomic policy instruments, whilst the conduct of microeconomic and supply-side policies need not entail the large administration that had been built up during the war.

Subsequently, the enthusiasm for planning would wane as Labour faced, and chose not to surmount, the considerable opposition to supply-side management which developed within both organised capital and labour. Moreover, there were two further constraints in operation during the years of the Labour and early postwar Conservative administrations. First, there was Dalton, the first and only Chancellor in British history to have come equipped to the post with a Ph.D. in economics,[55] but who by 1945 was both uninterested in economics, having wanted to be Foreign Secretary, and sufficiently confident of his own economic expertise as not to require expert advice from other economists (Pimlott 1985, pp. 423, 470). This unhappy situation contributed to Meade's resignation as ES director, and Hall's early conclusion that the ES had better make itself useful by developing its membership of key interdepartmental committees and consolidating good relations with ministers' advisers, the key to influence (Jones 1994, p. 77).

Secondly, there was both a power struggle and an inchoate intellectual debate about where the locus of power in economic policy formulation and coordination ought to reside in Whitehall. To begin with, Herbert Morrison as Lord President had responsibility for policy coordination (with the ES under his wing) and immense authority through taking charge of the nationalisation programme; Cripps was at the Board of Trade, where he was equipped with the potentially very powerful Distribution of Industry Act, 1945; with Dalton at the Treasury which, after having been downgraded by losing its seat in the War Cabinet, was anxious to re-establish its authority

---

[55] The next economists would be Nigel Lawson (1983–9); the next Chancellor with a Ph.D. would be Gordon Brown (1997–), though he does not use the title.

in Whitehall. The ES would finally come under Treasury authority in 1953, but meantime departmental and personal rivalries prevailed and, shaken by the fuel crisis in 1947, Labour even experimented with a central planning agency, the Central Economic Planning Staff (CEPS). This was led by a dynamic young industrialist (Edwin Plowden) who had wartime experience of Whitehall, such that he was able to secure appointment at twice the salary of the Treasury's permanent secretary, and was briefly the largest employer of economists within Whitehall.[56] It was terminated in 1953 as the ending of the Korean war provided opportunities to resume the policy of decontrols and disengagement, but its history is instructive for those wishing to understand why the next potential challenger to the Treasury, the DEA established in 1964, came to little.

With the return of the Conservatives to power in 1951 the demand for economists by government was, as Robert Neild experienced it, further squeezed. The new administration was committed to decontrol, lessened intervention and a reduction in the size of the public sector and its activities, that is at least initially for public expenditure growth was only contained until the crisis of 1958, while the contraction in the size of the civil service administrative class was sustained until 1960.[57] Thus beginning in the late 1950s, and strengthening quickly, a number of trends combined to increase both the demand for and supply of economists to government.

First, the expansion of higher education lessened the supply constraint, while by the time Hall retired in 1961 he was of the opinion that 'the original prejudice in the Treasury against economists was much less than it was when he arrived but there was still some prejudice in the Establishment Division and also in the First Division Association (the trade union of top civil servants) against improving the tenure or pay of economists and against giving them posts which would block promotion for the administrative grade' (Jones 1994, p. 173). His successor, Cairncross, was to be more assertive and ultimately more successful in pressing the case for economists in Whitehall, and indeed much of the triumph of numbers can be

---

[56] Plowden's (1989) memoirs recount its history, as do Cairncross and Watts (1989). Austin Robinson was an early member, although forced to return to academic life in 1948 when Dennis Robertson told him he had to choose between Whitehall or Cambridge; as was **Berrill** and **Douglas Allen** (later Lord Croham). Both LSE-trained economists Allen was to be instrumental in Berrill's appointment to head the GES, but his period in office was to be cut short by Labour's return to power because Kaldor, who would accompany **Healey** to the Treasury, and Berrill were long-standing Cambridge adversaries (Hennessy 1990, p. 249).

[57] From an establishment of 2,100 in 1939 the administrative class had grown to a peak in 1944–5 of 4,900. It then fell back to 4,000 by 1950, averaged 3,200 between 1958–60 and had grown again to 3,300 by 1964 and to 4,000 by 1970 (*Annual Abstract of Statistics*, various). Treasury establishment rose from 344 in 1938 to 1,396 in 1950, then fell to 1,322 in 1960 and to 1,012 in 1970, but, of course, after 1968 Treasury responsibilities for civil service management were transferred to the Civil Service Department (Butler and Butler 1994, pp. 287–8).

ascribed to his quiet but effective lobbying. But the idea of the GES was Hall's and the environment of the 1960s was different. Even so, recruitment literature betrayed a certain desperation when, just as Americanisation and particularly American incentive structures were becoming consolidated, it continued to claim that 'a spell in the Government Economic Service grappling with practical issues is an invaluable step towards becoming a fully trained and experienced professional economist' (HMSO 1970, p. 1).

Secondly, after 1958 all public sector indicators registered rapid expansion, and indeed the British economy was seriously over-heating in the run up to the 1964 election with what MacDougall (1987, p. 147) has called the 'Keeler' boom after the Profumo scandal which delayed the election by a year during which, and against NEDO advice, the government boosted public expenditure significantly above trend. Concurrently, and motivating the Plowden report (HMSO 1961) and much of the Treasury reorganisation of 1961–2, there were deepening concerns about the efficiency of resource allocation in the public sector.[58] These, together with the developing tools of CBA,[59] gave many more opportunities for economists to contribute to economic decision-making at all levels of government. CBA was to come to prominence with a number of substantial public sector transportation projects, starting with the Victoria Line and including the long debate over the site for London's third airport. Nonetheless, just as economists were developing CBA as a flexible analytical tool, capable of application to a wide range of private and public sector activities, there were areas of growing public involvement in which economists were not able to contribute as they ought. Foremost here was the revival of interest in regional issues in the 1960s, which in Britain were to be dominated by geographers and town and country planners, not by economists (Parsons 1986, pp. 171–3). Although there were notable exceptions, such as the commitment of universities like Manchester and Glasgow to providing economic studies of their regions, work at the National Institute which culminated in Brown (1972), and some debate in the bank journals, it is nonetheless the case that British economists were not much interested in regional analysis until the late-1960s. Indeed, measured by publications, they were hardly represented at all, as instanced by the dominance of American authors and journals in the AEA-RES survey of regional economics (Meyer 1963, but cf. Brown 1969). Parsons (1986, p. 171) argues that as a consequence the economic evaluation of regional policies was neglected, such that the House of Commons expenditure committee complained 'Much has been spent and

---

[58] See Clarke (1978) and Pliatzky (1984) 'insider' accounts, also Heclo and Wildavsky (1981).

[59] On the state of theory, see Prest and Turvey's 1965 *EJ* survey; on applications in government, see Williams's (1967) civil service paper on the contribution of CBA and microeconomics to efficiency in government and the later academic assessments of Self (1975) and Colvin (1985).

much may well have been wasted. Regional policy has been empiricism run mad, a game of hit-and-miss, played with more enthusiasm than success' (HMSO 1973, p. 72).' The early 1970s would see British economists respond to this criticism, in particular with continuing work at the National Institute and Moore and Rhodes (1973) at the DAE, but during the 1960s the impression was reinforced that economists were not always working on the topics that government needed there and now.

Finally, and initially operating more powerfully than any other influence, the new thinking about economic growth resulted in a substantial increase in demand for economists in government, and indeed perhaps supply as it gave to economics and official service a glamour and high profile which it had not really enjoyed since mass unemployment had stirred the ethical consciousness and technical inventiveness of the previous generation. This latter development was to prove decisive because its manifestations were so wide-ranging and enduring. Thus the quest for faster growth entailed:

- a radical revision of Britain's initial position on the EEC, with the first application for membership being made in 1960 (repeated in 1967 and 1970), and with this and all subsequent entry attempts justified domestically on economic not political grounds;
- new Whitehall departments, not least the DEA, but also the Ministry of Technology, the flagship for Wilson's 'white heat' revolution;
- new agencies embodying corporatist aspirations, such as the NEDC, the various prices/incomes boards/commissions which came and went from the 'Three Wise Men' onwards, and the Industrial Reorganisation Corporation, which acted as a merger broker on behalf of the government and whose operational philosophy of 'big is beautiful' provides a case study of the application of one interpretation of the economic theory of increasing returns in the context of British industrial politics;
- a willingness to innovate and to experiment with fiscal instruments to secure longer-term structural adjustments, with highlights including a corporation tax, designed to encourage investment through incentives to retain profits, and Kaldor's brainchild, the Selective Employment Tax, which sought to raise productivity by taxing the service sector to reduce the relative price of labour in manufacturing and thence, following Verdoorn's Law (as encapsulated in Kaldor's 1966 inaugural lecture), to increase the rate of growth of its output and productivity;
- yet greater efforts to improve demand management techniques, entailing increased investment in forecasting and in contracted-out research to the National Institute and leading universities; and
- a new policy activism with regional policy, including regional planning; and, of course, the National Plan itself.

'[C]onceived October 1964, born September 1965, died (possibly murdered) July 1966'. Such was the verdict of one of the plan's authors, Roger Opie (1972, p. 170), an 'irregular' Oxford economist brought in as Assistant Director of the DEA's Planning Division. Another irregular DEA economist, Brittan (1971, p. 317), who would also be much chastened by his experience of Whitehall, identified the strong political pressures to produce the published document as part of the problem for it meant that 'DEA officials, who should have been working on *policies* for faster growth, had to devote too much of their time to the arithmetic and presentation of a document which assumed that the policies had already been found and accepted.' In reality, the end product (HMSO 1965b) was more a feasibility study of what 4 per cent growth might look like than a plan of how to get to 4 per cent, and only on a most optimistic reading could it be viewed, as George Brown claimed, as 'a major advance in economic policy-making' (p. iii) when the growth strategy was flawed from the outset by the exchange rate choice. It was no wonder that the DEA's next, indeed last, public document was avowedly not a plan, but an economic assessment (HMSO 1969), evidence of a new realism but also of the thoroughly demoralised state of the DEA and of its economists (Opie 1972, p. 177). The experiment with a 'constructive tension' between the Treasury and the DEA, between the financial and real economies, between the short- and the long-term planning of policy, ended with the latter's abolition a few weeks later.

This is not the occasion to investigate why the Plan failed, nor to attempt to summarise the main policy episodes and problems from 1945 through to the end of the golden age. All of that has been ably done elsewhere, in so far as we yet have access to all of the required official papers to counter the much higher propensity of postwar ministers and senior officials to publish memoirs which offer a version of contemporary history which are often highly economical with the truth and which blur the already fuzzy distinction between history and the current policy agenda.[60] Rather, we now turn to our case study of exchange rate policy for here we have sufficient documentary record to observe closely the shifting currents of economic and political arguments in what notionally is presented as a technical choice in setting a policy instrument.

---

[60] Dell's (1996) history of the postwar Chancellors of the Exchequer well-illustrates this tendency and the dangers of attempting contemporary history on the basis of ministerial memoirs. Full access to the PRO papers is particularly important because as Cairncross (1985b, p. xiii) has found, although they 'supply some piquant details on the lines of argument ministers were prepared to entertain . . . they do not add a great deal to our knowledge of what they decided. What the papers do reveal more adequately is what went on at the official level, the techniques of analysis that were being developed, the possibilities of action that were being canvassed, the thinking and differences of opinion that underlay the ministerial pronouncements.' In short, exactly the sort of issues that concern us here.

6.5 THE 'UNMENTIONABLE': THE ECONOMICS AND POLITICS OF DEVALUATION, 1964–7

Cairncross's memo

In his memoirs Callaghan (1987, p. 218) records that on 1 November 1967 the Governor of the Bank of England was still advising Wilson that he 'did not intend to recommend devaluation, despite the effect of the apparently awful trade figures on sterling', but that the next day:

> a personal and 'top secret packet' was placed on my desk from Sir Alec Cairncross . . . Alec had been one of the staunchest of the praetorian guard determined to maintain sterling's parity, so it had a profound effect on me when I opened the packet and found it contained a personal and pessimistic typed memorandum on the outlook, together with a covering, handwritten letter from him for my eyes alone. In this, he said that, having started with the conviction that I was right to try as hard as possible to solve our problems without devaluing, he had after long consideration changed his mind and was now a 'convert to devaluation'. He continued by saying that world opinion would have condemned devaluation at an earlier date but would now be understanding because it was known how hard the Government had tried to avoid it. . . .
>
> I read this with emotion and then read it again in case I had missed an important meaning in trying to decipher Alec's spidery and difficult handwriting. But I found no qualification. His view was clear. . . . I folded the paper and placed it in my breast pocket, where it stayed, burning a hole, throughout the rest of the day, and long into the night.

Thus began the final chapter in Labour's efforts to sustain sterling at $2.80,[61] which ended sixteen days later when the pound was devalued by 14.3 per cent to $2.40, an occasion marked by Wilson's television broadcast, appropriately but hastily inserted into the slot usually reserved for 'Songs of Praise', in which he uttered the immortal phrase 'Devaluation does *not* mean that the value of the pound in the hands of the British consumer, the

---

[61] Cairncross's side of the story is covered in his published diary (1997, esp. pp. 239–42). Other sources which either cast light on Labour's exchange rate problems or on their authors include Wilson (1971, ch. 23), Douglas Jay (1980, chs. 12–13) and Jenkins (1991, chs 11–16) who, in succeeding Callaghan as Chancellor, had to make the devaluation effective. The contemporary mood is well-conveyed in Brandon (1966). Graham and Beckerman (1972) provide an economic assessment of Labour's exchange rate policy from the perspective of two irregulars who favoured an early devaluation, Stewart (1977), another insider, a broader economic history of the whole period, with Tew (1978, esp. pp. 354–6) and Cairncross and Eichengreen (1983, ch. 5) providing necessary balance and greater historical perspective. Labour's longer-run difficulties with the exchange rate are chronicled in Shipman (1991), while Hutchison (1968) documents in great detail economists' changing views on devaluation and other contemporary topics, this providing much grist to his mill that the profession was becoming corrupted by its growing involvement with politics (for responses by irregulars of this time who were outraged by his slurs against the economics establishment, see Opie 1968b and **Posner** 1970).

British housewife at her shopping, is cut correspondingly.' Such was the jauntiness of his delivery that, as one observer suggested, it was as if he 'had genuinely convinced himself that he had worked tirelessly for devaluation since October 1964 and had finally succeeded in overwhelming the resistance of all of his Cabinet colleagues, especially last-ditch obstruction by Callaghan and the Treasury' (cited in Pimlott 1992, p. 483).

The reality was that for three years Wilson and Callaghan had fought strenuously to avoid this outcome. They had sanctioned successive deflationary packages of fiscal and monetary measures to restrain aggregate demand and especially import growth. They had sacrificed the National Plan, public spending aspirations and hopes for industrial harmony as it became imperative to enforce wage restraint and to limit public borrowing. By not devaluing they were forced into palliatives which made them deeply unpopular at home (the overseas travel allowance) and abroad, especially with GATT and EFTA (the export rebate and import surcharge). Moreover, when the inevitable did come about in 1967, it required not the small adjustment that was thought sufficient in 1964 but that the authorities overshoot on both the exchange rate and on fiscal policy, to restore international financial confidence and to attempt a quick and substantial turnaround in the balance of payments. Arguably, the balance of payments did come good in the end, but, say the sternest critics, the medicine was so late in working that the ultimate consequence of the 1964 decision was, in effect, that Labour was robbed of the electoral victory it deserved in 1970.

The 'unmentionable'

Critics further contend that, by making devaluation the great 'unmentionable', Wilson and Callaghan generated a paranoia within Whitehall which, unprecedented in peacetime, was deeply unhealthy for the conduct of government. In fact, devaluation had become unmentionable somewhat earlier (MacDougall 1987, p. 140), but under Wilson an attempt was made to go far beyond the Treasury's natural reticence on foreign exchange matters: to create a climate in which there would be no discussion, no memoranda, no policy analysis of devaluation, not as an act of denial but as one of faith in the new government, in its modernising mission and in the unspecified, hypothetical world that lay between devaluation and deflation.

The initial decision to persevere with $2.80 was taken by the Triumvirate (Wilson, Callaghan and Brown) on Saturday 17 October,[62] the day after the

---

[62] MacDougall's (1987, p. 152) account begins with his attending a meeting – convened by Callaghan – of Brown, William Armstrong and Roll, in which only MacDougall expressed a pro-devaluation line at this stage. Callaghan and Brown then reported these proceedings to Wilson, at which point the decision was made (see also Roll 1985, p. 158).

election result was announced. This decision was confirmed in late November-early December 1964, in face of renewed pressure against the pound stemming from market assessments that the 11 November budget was insufficiently deflationary, and re-examined once more in 1966 when Brown tried to salvage something of Labour's growth strategy. Thus, not only did the argument against devaluation prevail, but there developed a self-denying ordnance of sorts on discussion within Whitehall, the City and, displaying a 'patriotism' which is unimaginable today, even within the press where 'open advocacy of devaluation was still ... the next worse thing to publishing obscene literature' (cited in Browning 1986, p. 5).

Indeed, such was the intellectual censorship of Wilson's office that Crossman (1975–7, vol. II, pp. 41–2), not a man prone to self-denial in argument, found himself unable to complete as he would have wished a speech on contemporary economic problems in September 1966 because his occasional economic adviser, Stewart, at that time number two to Balogh, refused point-blank to put on paper 'what would happen if instead of deflating we decided on economic growth plus devaluation.' When provoked by invoking his profession and position as an official adviser, Stewart would only reply lamely 'Tommy and I wouldn't dare do that now since it might get round to Harold.'[63] It may well be that this conspiracy of silence affected also economists who had no involvement with government, for the academic economics journals carried little on the topic (with Coppock 1965, which pressed for devaluation, a rare and detailed exception),[64] while the National Institute's *Economic Review* (*NIER*), which first raised devaluation as a possibility in 1961, was always very guarded.[65] Such was the profession's hesitancy to state fully the case for devaluation, lest it not only bring about that result but in a most uncontrolled manner, that 'opinion formed itself without professional debate and enormous speculative positions were taken on assessments that rested on simple probabilities rather than economic diagnoses' (Cairncross and Eichengreen 1983, p. 160).

The recent efforts of historians and biographers to rehabilitate Wilson and the 1964–70 governments have not extended to the devaluation issue or indeed to assessments of Labour's economic record (Table 6.4 details the

[63] The Crossman diaries also provide much material on Balogh, Kaldor and the other economists, senior and junior, who served between 1964–70, with frequent references to the efforts made by the pro-devaluation economists to remind Wilson and Callaghan of the deflationary costs of exchange rate policy. The entry for 6 April 1967 (1975–7, vol. II, p. 304) provides the background to why Balogh returned to Oxford and full-time academic duties; that for 26 September 1968 (vol. III, p. 201) how Balogh remained indispensable to Wilson long after.

[64] The bank reviews were similarly silent, although in the 1950s exchange rate policy had been debated there, with Meade (1955b) for one pressing the case for floating sterling.

[65] *NIER*, 13 (January 1961), p. 46. This was put initially in terms of an 'exchange realignment', with the emphasis on such periodic adjustments as normal to the Bretton Woods system and with there being no clear evidence as yet that Britain's situation merited such a course of action.

principal macroeconomic indicators). But so much has been loaded on exchange rate policy that, as one reassessment puts it, it 'has become a catch-all excuse, a fig-leaf for utopians' (Walker 1987, p. 207). A recent balanced economic assessment has been provided by Woodward (1993, p. 85): the 'failure to devalue and deflate at an early stage very probably did impair performance in the late 1960s. But it would probably be wrong to argue that the deteriorating or disappointing performance was due predominantly to this.'

At the time the pro-devaluation lobby argued that the technical Marshall-Lerner conditions for a successful devaluation were satisfied, although it is noteworthy that in presenting their case no reference was made to published estimates of the relevant price and income, export and import elasticities for Britain (not even in Coppock 1965), for in 1964 none existed,[66] although at the National Institute, and no doubt elsewhere, such estimates were being derived and employed as part of the routine process of economic forecasting. More than ten years later, when rival forecasting groups were set the task of running macroeconomic simulations which included modelling the effects of a hypothetical 1964 devaluation, there were very significant differences in the computed effects of such a counterfactual policy world (see Posner 1978). Admittedly, by then, economics was much more polarised, but the point remains that in the mid-1960s what economists knew, and agreed upon, about the effects of exchange rate adjustments on the balance of payments was very limited.[67]

Whether such professional ignorance actually mattered in October 1964 is questionable. As Cairncross and Eichengreen (1983, p. 166) describe it:[68]

---

[66] In 1963 Maurice Scott was working on the import side and had just published a substantial National Institute volume, as had Maizels for exports. Moore (1964) was also working on the export side in Oxford, which at that time was still developing the Klein-Ball econometric model. Concurrently, each issue of the *NIER* carried export forecasts. The National Institute's first post-devaluation assessment made reference to a number of studies which had estimated price elasticities of demand for exports and imports but significantly, apart from Scott (1963), none referred to work based on recent economic trends – *NIER*, 42 (November 1967), p. 4 n.1 (see also, their later assessment, NIESR 1972). A slightly later assessment produced as part of the Brookings report (Cooper 1968, p. 188 n.83) again used the Scott study but no other source available in 1964. Other contemporary work on export and import functions, and on balance of payments adjustment mechanisms, is surveyed in Prais (1962) and Junz and Rhomberg (1965). It is noteworthy that one of the pro-devaluation advisers in 1964 could claim some special expertise in international economics, but in his memoirs (MacDougall 1987, pp. 152–4) he makes clear that on 17 October and thereafter it was political calculation that prevailed.

[67] See also Thirlwall and Gibson (1992, p. 234) who express reservations about the manner in which many economists were thinking about balance of payments problems and remedies at this time; and Hutchison (1968, pp. 219ff; 1977a, ch. 5).

[68] Balogh would soon accept the case for devaluation, while Cairncross (1997, p. 1) had been convinced since 1961 'that the pound would have to be devalued at some stage in the 1960s. But I saw no point in devaluing in an overheated economy without the support of stringent deflationary measures which there was no likelihood that the Labour government would adopt.'

The decision taken in October 1964, and on all subsequent occasions when devaluation was mooted, owed little or nothing to official advice. When the Labour Government took office, ministers were presented with extensive briefs prepared in the Treasury and the Bank of England stating the case for and against devaluation. The Treasury, while less strongly opposed to devaluation than the Bank, saw it as having no compelling advantages and some considerable disadvantages. The government's incoming advisers initially were divided, with Dr Balogh opposed to devaluation and Professor Kaldor, Sir Donald MacDougall and Mr Neild in favour. But not much notice was taken of the arguments submitted by officials and advisers. The three ministers primarily concerned – Harold Wilson, George Brown and James Callaghan – had already made up their minds, and a firm decision was taken against devaluation on the first day after the election results were announced.

Thus the first significance of this episode, and the prime justification for choosing it as our case study, concerns the manner in which a new government arrived at a decision which, say critics and supporters alike, effectively negated the ambitious economic strategy which had been the centrepiece of its electoral campaign. Nor would its significance be diminished if a less hardline position was taken about the implications of the exchange rate decision, for what it reveals about economic decision-making is of importance whatever value is placed on the technical 'correctness' of the decision itself. Our ambition here is not to analyse exchange rate policy between 1964–7 in any depth, but to look at the role of the economists in decision-making and to highlight the informational weaknesses experienced by all of the participants and the process of learning – or being bloodied by economic reality – that the new government had to endure. The broader story of events cannot yet be written as the Bank records remain closed after 1960 or so and historians have not yet taken advantage of the official records for this period now becoming available in the PRO. Even so, enough is known about the unmentionable for our purposes, and perhaps this endeavour will prompt some to revisit this topic, both through the archives and through econometric reassessment.

Contemporary economic statistics

We begin with the inadequacies of the data available to the new government and its advisers, but start a few months before the election with Ross's (1964, p. 1) complaint, voiced in the *Oxford Bulletin*, that the CSO was not producing national income data of sufficient reliability for economists to address such basic questions as 'whether output rose or fell between 1961 and 1962, and whether or not there had been any acceleration in the overall rate of growth since the mid-1950s.' His particular target was the discrepancies between the three output measures of GDP (E, O and I), and

while his tone was measured the message was clear: inadequate data made
'the interpretation of economic developments and the formulation of
economic policy uncomfortably difficult,' and this at a time when the rate of
growth was fast becoming the focus of current discussion. In fact, at the
CSO and at the National Institute there was much activity directed towards
improving the main series (for example, Godley and Gillion 1964). But a
raw nerve had been touched, and whatever the objective quality of CSO
statistics by contemporary standards their utility in decision-making at this
time is highly questionable. We reproduce in Table 6.6 successive National
Institute estimates, revisions and forecasts for the key GDP and current
account series (together with their current incarnation in the CSO's
databank), beginning with the first that was available to the new
government. (We include also the unemployment and inflation rates, taking
these from a later *NIER* as they were hardly subject to revision.) Obviously,
care is required in such an 'at the time' and 'with hindsight' exercise, but it
is abundantly clear that with each successive *NIER* views about the
immediate past, the present and the future were all in a state of flux.
Boreham (1978, pp. 140–1), who undertook such an exercise for the rival
forecasting groups mentioned above and who was Chief Statistician
(Population) in the General Register Office at the time, provided the
following reconstruction:

> On 26 October 1964 the new government published a White Paper on the
> Economic Situation which forecast a balance of payments deficit of £700 million
> at least for 1964 and said that there was no undue pressure on resources calling
> for action. In October there was no quarterly index of GDP (Output). There was
> no seasonally adjusted monthly index of average earnings. Seasonally adjusted
> unemployment was not officially published as such, although normal seasonal
> changes were. The argument was that people who were only skilled enough to
> read figures from tables could not be trusted to make sensible use of seasonally
> adjusted figures whereas people who were skilled enough to add together figures
> taken from different tables could. The same was true for vacancies. Monthly
> figures of imports, f.o.b. and on a balance of payments basis, were not available.
> No figures of money supply were published. Nor, needless to say, was the
> exchange rate.

The balance of payments statistics were notoriously unreliable and
consequently subject to frequent and large revisions, as is clear from Table
6.6. The National Institute at this time routinely operated with a rule-of-
thumb that the first estimates undervalued credit items by £100 million per
annum or so, and, as has become well-known, such have been the later
revisions that had contemporaries access to these revised GDP and balance
of payments series certain policy actions might not have taken place.
Foremost here are the July 1966 deflationary measures, the final nail in the

Table 6.6 Macroeconomic indicators: contemporary NIER estimates and forecasts and revised ONS (1996) series, 1963.II–1965.IV[a]

	1963.II	1963.III	1963.IV	1964.I	1964.II	1964.III	1964.IV	1965.I	1965.II	1965.III	1965.IV
A. GDP (seasonally, adjusted, 1958=100)											
1. *NIER:* August 1964	116.3	117.9	120.5	122.2	123.2	124.1	125.1	126.4	127.8	128.8	129.7
November 1964(I)[b]	116.9	118.6	121.9	122.7	123.6	124.4	125.3	126.2	127.9	129.0	129.7
November 1964(II)[b]	116.9	118.6	121.9	122.7	123.6	124.4	125.4	126.3	127.3	128.3	129.1
February 1965	116.8	118.7	121.6	122.7	123.6	124.2	126.1	127.1	128.7	129.7	130.5
May 1965	116.9	118.2	121.1	123.1	123.7	124.0	125.6	127.7	128.4	129.5	130.3
2. CSO (1996) estimate (1990 prices)	119.4	120.2	122.2	124.3	125.6	125.5	127.5	128.3	128.9	129.5	130.9
B. Identified current account balance of payments, seasonally adjusted, £m											
1. *NIER:* August 1964	30	14	6	(62)	(95)	(72)	(72)	(31)	(31)	(31)	(31)
November 1964	34	2	(5)	(69)	(113)	..	(42)	(13)	(13)	(25)	(25)
February 1965	34	2	(5)	(70)	(109)	(127)	(85)	(10)	(10)	(10)	(10)
May 1965	28	(1)	(1)	(77)	(102)	(110)	(138)	(6)	(21)	(40)	(10)
2. CSO (1996) estimate	30	21	7	(67)	(53)	(114)	1.4	1.3	1.3	1.4	1.3
C. Unemployment rate	2.4	2.3	2.0	1.7	1.6	1.6	1.4	1.3	1.3	1.4	1.3
D. RPI, 1958=100	112.0	111.3	112.1	113.1	115.2	116.1	117.1	118.2	121.2	121.7	122.5

Notes:

[a] Central (medium) forecasts in shaded areas; estimates in italics.

[b] November 1964 forecast I=with allowance for policy effects; II=without allowance for policy effects.

Sources: *NIER*, 29–33 (August 1964-August 1965); ONS (1996, tables 1.2, 1.17).

259

coffin of the National Plan, which were precipitated by forecasts that there would be a substantial current account deficit by the end of the year whereas by 1969 revisions were showing a surplus and the latest CSO estimate is of a surplus approaching £130 million.[69] Mosley (1984, app. V) has estimated that during the 1960s and 1970s the average range of revisions to the GDP and current account balance series has been 1.2 per cent for the former and £268 million for the latter, with the revisions upwards for the former in seventeen out of the twenty years enumerated and improvements in the latter in eighteen years. In other words, 'there is a tendency for revisions in the statistics to make our view of the economy look rosier with hindsight than it looked at the time' (p. 243). He has also estimated that on average between 1951–84 the Treasury underestimated the public sector financial deficit by 0.5 per cent of GDP, about half the average amount by which Chancellors sought to fine tune demand through the budget, and with no tendency for the accuracy of forecasting to improve through time (Mosley 1985). No wonder that Croham (1992, p. 92), when asked to recollect on this period, observed:

> Anyone trying to recount the history of a period in which he was active, relying on memory and the material available at the time, would be totally astounded to find that most of the figures for the same period produced . . . twenty or thirty years later were quite unrecognizable. The most important instrument lacking was a position-finder to tell us exactly where we were at any given moment.

Appeals to data deficiencies run both ways, however, and whatever the subsequent revisions to both the quarterly GDP and current account series there has been no alteration to the basic story that by October 1964 the economy was at full capacity and with a payments deficit, now estimated at £372 million for the full year, about one half larger than at the previous business cycle peak in 1960. Admittedly, the industrial production index appeared stuck, and this argument was used by some to delay action (and even later by George Brown to warn of massive unemployment if Labour deflated), but labour market, foreign transactions and such consumer's expenditure indicators as there were all indicated a booming economy. That the boom could not be sustained was widely acknowledged in the City, where talk about raising interest rates was pretty general by February, and in the Treasury where Cairncross and others were pressing for a monetary and fiscal tightening. With well less than six months between the budget and when the election must be held Maudling not surprisingly chose the path of least political resistance, and nothing substantive was done to hobble the

---

[69] In sequence, between February and November 1966, the National Institute forecasts for the current balance for 1966 were -£80 million, -£55 million, -£40 million and -£173 million, with the last two incorporating the effects of the July measures – *NIER*, 35 (February 1966), table 3; 36 (May 1966), table 2; 37 (August 1966), table 4; 38 (November 1966), table 3.

dash for growth (Blackaby 1978b, pp. 23–8; Cairncross 1996, ch. 4). As summer turned to autumn and the election neared the prospective size of the balance of payments deficit became headline news, but it was all taken very calmly by the markets which were somewhat diverted by pressing geopolitical matters but were also, judges Cairncross (1996, p. 91), assuming that there would be early action by whichever party won in this closely fought contest. *The Economist* even backed Labour as, on the 'nicest balance', the riskier but better choice (Anon. 1964, p. 115).

The politics of exchange rate policy

Amongst critics of the decision not to devalue immediately there is a general view that a political as well as economic opportunity was missed: Wilson and Callaghan could have said simply that, having inspected the books, and found the situation much worse than had been admitted, thirteen years of Conservative mismanagement left no alternative. In 1964, just as in 1925, the political constraints were not ineluctable, just very difficult. That the markets did not expect Labour to devalue or indeed to float sterling, and that no such actions were in prospect had the Conservatives been reelected, sets the parameters of political possibilities. Had Labour secured a much larger majority, so that there was no need for another election within the next eighteen months; had they not been in power when sterling had been devalued on the previous occasion (in 1949 from \$4.03); had Gaitskell (like Wilson an economist before becoming a politician) lived and the new government not been led by Wilson, and it might all have been very different. In his memoirs Wilson (1971, p. 6) hints that the 'political temptations' were considered at the meeting on 17 October, 'But I was convinced, and my colleagues agreed, that to devalue could have the most dangerous consequences.' He cited three explanations for their decision:

1. The 1949 precedent and the likely consequences for the government's future credibility with the foreign exchange markets, for at that time 'the true facts of Britain's deficit were not known and politics, rather than economic necessity, would have been blamed';
2. 'We might well have started off an orgy of competitive beggar-my-neighbour currency devaluations – similar to those of the 1930s – which would have plunged the world into monetary anarchy'; and
3. '[S]trong reasons in terms of the domestic, economic and political scene', such that devaluation 'was not an easy way out' because, to be made effective, it would 'require a severe and rapid transfer of resources from home consumption, public and private, to meet the needs of overseas markets.'

Wilson provides no further depth to his economic thinking, but Stewart (1977, p. 28), combining insider knowledge with an interpretation of the public record, has argued that 'the ultimate reason for Wilson's almost pathological opposition to devaluation does not seem to have lain in his fear of the domestic or international consequences,' but that he:

> had no faith in the ability of the price mechanism to allocate resources in the efficient way postulated by classical economics. If resources were to flow to where they were most needed – to exports and industrial investment – they had to be pushed there or cajoled there by 'direct intervention' – by physical controls or official and unofficial arm-twisting. What was needed, if British industry was to be modernized and to compete in the world, were improvements in management, more industrial training, the development of new techniques and their embodiment in new investment. Compared with these much-needed structural reforms, tinkering with the price mechanism – such as a change in the exchange rate – were an irrelevance . . .

Wilson had long been preaching such a supply-side approach to relative economic decline, with much of the detail common ground between the Conservatives, Labour and agencies like NEDC. There was support also from academic economists who combined such a structuralist approach with being anti-devaluation, and not just Balogh. Indeed, for too long the myth has been perpetrated that there was a pro-devaluation consensus amongst academic economists which was opposed only by obstinate politicians (Thirlwall and Gibson 1992, p. 236). At one extreme there was Hawtrey (1961), now long retired from the Treasury but still active in public debate, who maintained that the problem was an under- not an overvaluation of sterling, with excess demand the consequences. A more mainstream view was that of Harrod, a long-standing 'elasticity pessimist', the contemporary term for those unconvinced by the price competitiveness arguments for devaluation. In 1965–6 others would join this camp, and from very different political standpoints (Robbins through Ball and Hicks to Joan Robinson).

Stewart (1977, p. 28) is undoubtedly right to press the point that 'Getting the demand side right was essential too', as a Conservative government would find in the 1980s, but what he and others have all evaded is the simple truth: had there been a devaluation in the circumstances of a (more than) fully employed economy there would have had to be deflationary measures to release capacity to provide for any increase in export demand that ensued. For Cairncross and for the Treasury the advice not to devalue was framed, at least in part, on the political judgement that Labour could not yet be expected to have the political will to enforce such restrictive measures. For advisers, whether generalist Treasury mandarins or professional economists, to be thus constrained is hardly novel, nor is there any novelty in attempting and failing to persuade ministers to take difficult decisions in the aftermath of an election.

There are, however, strong reasons for supposing that the political constraints were particularly pressing and that the new government was not as receptive to advice as it ought to have been. After thirteen years in opposition, during which Labour had berated the Treasury for a myriad of policy mistakes, and with a long-standing ideological ambivalence about capitalism, the new government were not well equipped to meet the challenge of an immediate sterling crisis. Stewart (1977, p. 29) suggests that part of the problem was that Callaghan lacked the self-confidence to challenge Wilson on the issue, while William Armstrong, mindful of Labour criticisms of the Treasury for supposedly railroading governments in the past, maintained a strict neutrality which on this occasion was ill-warranted. Certainly, as Cairncross has indicated, of the Triumvirate Callaghan was the most determined opponent of devaluation, but this was hardly because of a character defect. In his memoirs, Callaghan (1987, p. 160) presented an economic and a moral case for the parity, with his reference to the potential losses for Commonwealth countries that voluntarily maintained their reserves in London having the hallmark of sincerity more than political calculation. The problem for the advisers was that the moral commitment to $2.80 became such that 'to recommend devaluation to him was tantamount to calling for his resignation' (Cairncross 1996, p. 100).

There are further difficulties which are relevant here. The 1964 election campaign was the first conducted under the Douglas-Home rules, whereby the Opposition were able to discuss their planned changes with the permanent secretaries before the election, and to receive feedback (Hennessy 1990, p. 183), and yet the first few days of the new administration were chaotic, especially at the DEA (where Brittan's disillusionment with government started on day one of his new life as an irregular). Meanwhile, over in the Treasury there was an initial jockeying for position between Cairncross and Neild, with the new Chancellor unaware of what exactly Cairncross had been doing for the previous three years as Chief Economic Adviser and why a political appointment (Neild) might be a cause of consternation as it would entail a profound change in the system under which professional economists had hitherto worked in Whitehall without regard to the political complexion of government. Later the two found a happy working relationship which entailed joint supervision of the ES, with Neild adviser to the Chancellor, not the Treasury, and Cairncross the head of the newly established GES (Cairncross 1997, pp. 7–13, 211). Yet, all of this indicates a lack of preparedness by the politicians. While the Nuffield College seminars may well have inducted Callaghan in economics before assuming office (p. 102), why did the Triumvirate not do more to anticipate likely problems and prepare a contingency plan? After all, common sense dictated that, after thirteen years of the Conservatives, the money and foreign exchange markets would almost immediately test the resolve of the new administration (see Stewart 1977, pp. 31–2 for early City reaction to Labour). Was it that the new ministers actually believed in the manifesto, that the supply-side measures would produce quick results which negated other actions; was it that they deluded themselves that import surcharges were actually a costless alternative; and to what extent were Wilson and Callaghan carried along by the charismatic but dipsomaniac Brown and his insistence that he could broker a sustainable deal on wage bargaining with the trade unions? We must await the full availability of the official records to provide answers but meantime the matter of the devaluation rests firmly with the politicians who, unfortunately for them, were not blessed with that essential instrument of the economists' toolbox, 20:20 hindsight.[70]

An assessment: economics, economists and the Labour government

At least one serious retrospective economic assessment has argued that 'The difficulties of 1964 were cyclical and were on the capital account; they were not the result of forces to be rectified by exchange rate depreciation'; that the deflationary measures of 1965–6 were effective in bringing the current balance back into surplus by 1966.II, although the size of long-term capital flows ensured that the balance for official financing (and thus the basic balance) was always sizeable; and that much of the pressures that eventually forced the devaluation in 1967 were speculative (reinforced by arbitrage) and external (initially, a slow-down in the growth of world trade and then the effects of the Middle East crisis) rather than relating to a sustained deterioration in the trading balance.[71] Accepting this for the moment and that subsequently – after the J-curve effect – the current account did move back strongly into surplus by 1970, and one is left wondering whether too often economists and other critics have merely extrapolated backwards in the efficacy they imputed to devaluation. This has added force when one acknowledges that the devaluation did not initially release the pressure on the pound and that subsequently the price effects of the devaluation have themselves been questioned relative to the income effects of the renewed growth of world trade on British exports.

In such circumstances, and with an awareness of the risk of 20:20 hindsight at this point, it is legitimate to ask what might have happened if the pro-devaluation lobby had prevailed in 1964. Posing the question thus leads us to suggest that the Triumvirate might well have been right and the

---

[70] This is usually attributed to Walter Heller, chairman of the CEA, 1961–4.

[71] Thirlwall and Gibson (1992, pp. 235, 238), a view broadly supported by Cairncross and Eichengreen's (1983, p. 216) comparative study of the 1931, 1949 and 1967 devaluations.

devaluationists wrong, but each for contrary reasons. The politicians were deluded that this was a gladiatorial contest in which the markets would be defeated because morality was on the side of the democratically elected government. This was an enduring delusion in Labour thinking, given succour at this point by the nostalgia that Wilson and others clearly felt for the more highly regulated economy of their last period in power. Many of those economists, inside and outside of government, who in 1964 pressed for devaluation were also deluded about potential governmental capacity, with the claims made for the growth strategy the most evident symptom of this condition. One of their sternest critics, Hutchison (1977a, ch. 5), who has documented their utterances in such minute detail as to border on cruelty, cites two contemporary judgements (p. 131 n.50) which are appropriate here, the first from an Oxford economist who did not become an irregular and the second from a more popular work, the title of which – *Ninety-five per cent is crap* (1975) – might be taken to sanction less restraint:

> For the British economy, the sixties were years of bitter disappointment. The real failure of Governments lay not so much in their economic policies as in their extravagant claims of omnicompetence. A credulous public was led to expect El Dorado, found only plenty, and became understandably dissatisfied. . . .
>
> The decade opened in hope and closed in disillusion. Much vaunted economic expertise failed to bring home the goods that some Governments were foolish enough to predict. . . .
>
> The impression brilliantly conveyed to the electorate in 1964 was that some undefined negative attitude implicit in 'stop-go' and some unspecified kind of governmental amateurism were all that deprived Britain of rapid growth in the fifties and sixties. Purposive and dynamic government would suddenly restore her rightful rate of growth. (Sinclair 1972, pp. 94, 103)

> The professional politicians would dearly love the economists to tell them certain things. It is said that the way to a man's heart is through his stomach. But there is no surer way to a politician's heart than to tell him he can safely do things which are sure vote-winners. And when you've got to his heart, prestige, power, and if you're lucky, a knighthood, are not far away. (Arthur 1975, p. 184)

With greater historical perspective than that enjoyed by Hutchison the case for the former assessment is now undoubtedly strengthened, while the essence of the latter – the Johnson critique – is a common place of public choice theory. On the deeper charge of economists becoming corrupted by politics, itself hardly a new phenomenon by historical standards, there is no denying that public honours were bestowed on some who served as official advisers. Of the big five in 1964 MacDougall had already obtained his knighthood (1953) and Cairncross was similarly rewarded in 1967, but these were quite within the normal range of expectations for those who had distinguished senior positions in the civil service. Presumably, Johnson's initial (1968) target was more the other three, of whom two did receive life peerages (Balogh in 1968 and Kaldor in 1974) with only Neild unrewarded, although this was by his choice; some senior economists, who had previous government service but continued to operate behind the scenes (Harrod and Kahn's generation); and the more junior economists, many of whom had been politically active before becoming irregulars and then found it difficult to adapt to civil service conventions on party political conduct. Whether they were more political or partisan than earlier generations is a moot point. Much of the chorus against economists after 1964 was actually barely concealed opposition to Wilson's style of government and Labour policies, but within Whitehall the appointment of economists was undoubtedly more politicised, with Cairncross (1997, p. 2) detailing that he became Head of a 'phantom' GES 'while Ministers continued to assemble their own private armies of economists, sometimes with advice from Thomas Balogh, rarely with any reference to myself.'

At this point, as with his later (1975b) outburst against British economics, Johnson's lack of personal experience as a government adviser also begins to show. For we do have sufficient of a documentary record to demonstrate that, with the obvious exception of Balogh who, as even his friends admit, was 'unsystematic', 'impatient' and dissenting but as having had 'relatively little influence on economic policy' (Streeten 1970b, pp. ix–x), what distinguishes the big five is their commitment to keep ministers focused on the hard choices facing the government, their constant efforts to contain the politicians' expectations of what was economically possible, above all their professionalism. In any case, there was very little scope for them to corrupt their 'scientific economics' in pursuit of mere forensics when their role was very rarely that of fermenting economic policies. Balogh and Kaldor, the terrible twins, were obviously something of an exception in this respect, but here also the record, ranging from Cairncross (1997) to Crossman's diaries, is that in practice Kaldor could be relied upon to be as deflationary – the appropriate litmus test – as Cairncross or indeed Neild. Crossman (1975–7, vol. III, p. 568), something of a Balogh-Kaldor devotee who had use of the former as a outside consultant, made the following illuminating comparison between the two Hungarians in 1969:

> Harold [Wilson] and Roy [Jenkins] don't want him [Balogh] back in circulation
> . . . But I'd rather like to have him back. I have a different but parallel problem
> with Nicky Kaldor, whom I tried to get as Thomas's replacement. Nicky has a
> much better reputation in Whitehall and, on the whole, he is liked in the Treasury
> and the Inland Revenue. He is not thought of as a malicious Whitehall-
> manoeuvring politician, constantly fermenting ideas and launching attacks. . . . I
> can use him . . . but I can't lever him out of the Treasury. They won't let him go
> but they won't let him come across to me because Roy thinks S.E.T. damaged our
> image and is ashamed of Nicky as an adviser. . . . Roy and Harold . . . . don't

want the Government associated with Tommy and Nicky, who are in a way martyrs of the malicious gossip of the press.

For devotees of Yes Ministers this translates into the economists sans Balogh going native pretty quickly, but of course that was the essence of their effectiveness during the Second World War. If we take the extravagant claims of 1964 as the inevitable product of the process of adversary politics, with Labour quite desperate after thirteen years to oust the Conservatives, what remains of the charge that some economists behaved irresponsibly in fuelling the politicians' fantasies of what was possible through more energetic government? Certainly there is something in Hutchison's (1973, p. 223) additional charge, that some of the pro-devaluationists perpetrated a fictitious professional consensus to buttress the argument (and would do so again on the issue of the potential economic benefits of EEC membership). He ascribed this to 'a yearning for certainty and authority ... [which] leads to methodological oversimplification and misconceptions regarding the nature and extent of economic knowledge and ignorance which are unlikely to conduce towards the tendering of reliable policy advice.' But, and again greater perspective is helpful, 'professional consensus' deployed as rhetoric is hardly a new characteristic of economists' behaviour. What was new was the much higher quality of economic journalism which, relative to Keynes's time, made the market for economic ideas very much more competitive. In part, the problem for the ultra-empiricists and for the Johnson critique is that, as Neild's' successor at the Treasury has described:

> there is *no* natural consensus about what constitutes fair shares, *no* natural consensus that the 'national interest' exists or should be pre-eminent, *no* natural consensus about the direction which economic growth should take or the uses to which its fruits should be put. An incomes policy is only the most blatant of examples: in *all* its policies a government must struggle to create and preserve that most delicate of plants – a sense of common purpose, of social cohesion, of general will. Economic problems continue to dominate our national debates, partly, no doubt, because economic advisers and politicians still get into 'frightful and unnecessary muddles,' for want of a Keynes to help us; but chiefly, I would argue, because the economic problem is a problem of political economy.
>
> (Posner 1973, p. 118)

In Britain, as had occurred a little earlier in the US with the flood of economists into Washington during the Kennedy administration, the triumph of numbers coincided with that point at which politicians felt compelled to reassess the strategic direction of economic policy (delayed 'Keynesianism' in the US and nascent supply-side economics in Britain). With so many more economists in Whitehall after 1964, with more senior permanent officials better grounded in economics and statistics and with the financial press much improved in coverage and quality, the incentives for the irregulars to make their economic advice credible were greatly enhanced and we would thus expect quality improvements in advice. To sceptical and increasingly hostile outsiders the notion of 'quality' in British economic policy advice was laughable, but it is important to emphasise here that in the 1960s there was a massive cultural shift which resulted in a less deferential, more critical press, with the economists – and not just the terrible twins – a natural target. A comparison of *The Economist's* warm response to Cairncross's appointment in 1961 with the chilliness accorded his successor, MacDougall in 1968, is sufficient to make the point (Anon 1961; 1968). Finally, on the Johnson critique, Whitehall was very different from Washington, as were the characteristics of the British economy in terms of its openness and the size of the public sector. In Britain, as Peacock (1992b, p. 1217) recounts, economists who adopt 'a position of "highbrow agnosticism" in formulating policies are not likely to be listened to.'

Finally, on the devaluation issue itself, such have been the myths created about the Wilson administrations by disappointed irregulars and others that there is a risk that we forget the advantages of $2.80. In a rare reminder of these, Tew (1978, p. 313) has observed:

> To those economists, inside as well as outside the government, whose views on the British economy came to be broadly in line with Paish's, the $2.80 peg, at any rate up to mid-1966, was never an undesirable constraint on demand management, since from the end of the war up to that time demand had almost never been inadequate . . .

The great unmentionable, as with the prewar parity in 1925, provided financial discipline, a strait-jacket, at a time when politicians and advisers recognised the risks that the new government could succumb to the ambitions of spending ministers and the natural desire of trade union leaders to maintain free collective bargaining. Expectations of what Labour could deliver in 1964 were very high, impossibly inflated; had there been a devaluation or a free float of sterling the risks for the exchange rate, public borrowing and a wage-price spiral were immense. Possibly the worst could have been avoided, although what later transpired during the Heath years does not make for optimism. In retrospect, the really interesting question about Labour's exchange rate policy was not the 1964 decision but that of 1966, when George Brown raised the unmentionable once more and the economic fundamentals were more clearly commensurate with exchange rate realignment.[72] But this really is with the benefit of 20:20 hindsight.

[72] Brown's own account (1971, p. 114), which is possibly at variance with that of MacDougall (1987, p. 157), raises a number of fascinating issues which need exploring.

6.6 CONCLUSIONS

When the Heath government collapsed in February 1974 relative economic decline had brought Britain to the brink of political disaster, as had the gold standard with the General Strike in 1926. For the emerging New Right the coincidence of a quickening in the pace of decline with the period of greater macroeconomic, and increasingly microeconomic, policy activism under the Wilson and Heath governments proved a heaven-sent opportunity to secure a political and economic leverage sufficient to undermine fatally the Keynesian era. The conclusion that economists were in part responsible for this crisis also proved impossible to resist, although this would require a rather delicate balancing act on the part of some professional economists who were early converts to the monetarist cause. As in the 1930s, with the charge of policy inconstancy levelled against Keynes, the denigration of the profession was a key tactic adopted by the dissidents, especially by the non-academic economists seeking to re-establish their influence. The terrible twins would provide superb copy for journalists, while the growing practice of British economists advising other governments provided new opportunities for derision: that having brought the British economy to its knees Buda and Pest had now turned their hand to the Commonwealth (where they had quickly established a reputation for their advice getting governments overthrown).[73] More mundanely, the profession's public standing became more sensitive to media coverage as greater use was made of economists in high-profile public discussions of controversial infrastructure projects with significant environmental impacts. Even so, the press still hankered for a new Keynes (Knapp 1973), while the Keynesian old guard continued to muse on what Keynes would have done.

Keynes's (1930b, p. 332) oft quoted remark, that it would be 'splendid' if 'economists could manage to get themselves thought of as humble,

---

[73] The opportunities for economists to work in international agencies, which had begun in the 1920s with the ILO and the League of Nations (whence Meade had served 1937–40), were greatly expanded after the Second World War with the creation of the IMF and the IBRD (Coats 1986). For economists to provide advice to overseas governments was not unknown before 1939, but was an underdeveloped market and one in which non-academics predominated (for example, Niemeyer's mission to Australia in 1930). Henceforth, many senior British figures did develop such consultancy as part of their routine professional activities. Thus, apart from Balogh and Kaldor, Harrod, the Hicks, Meade, the Robinsons and many of the younger generation (Bauer, David Henderson, Little, Mirrlees, Seers, Stewart and Streeten) all participated in this growing market. Although there is now something of a literature on why visiting economists fail, one initiated by Seers (1962), and one of relevance to why they might also fail at home, the consultancy activities of British economists have not been studied from the standpoint of professionalisation. The contrary question, of why failed economists visit (suggested by Streeten, cited in Abbott 1976), has alas also not been pursued, although their espousal of a dirigistic development economics, and the damage this supposedly did to developing economies, attracted much attention within the IEA and elsewhere (Lal 1983).

competent people, on a level with dentists', in effect linked the fate of the economics profession to that of the new economics. By the early 1970s the risks associated with that strategy were only too apparent, but it is important to stress that the growing disillusionment with economists was part of a broader process of reassessing whether the faith in science, technology and investment in higher education were still warranted. Within a decade the optimism that greeted the Robbins report was transformed into hostility towards the universities and deepening retrenchment. The Keynesian era was, of course, always as much a political as an economic construct, but its dual character was not transparent until the troubles of the 1970s when stagflation ignited a full-bloodied distributional struggle. We discuss this in chapter 7 and here conclude this part of our assessment by casting our net across the whole period to, first, identify the areas of continuity and those of change in policy; and, secondly, to highlight episodes in which economic reasoning was able to triumph over political calculation, and *vice versa*.

In respect of the former, our starting point must be the underlying credo shared by all but a minority: that of a trust in the benevolence, effectiveness and reliability of government, even when in need of reform and even when, according to taste, the wrong political party was in power. Born of the war, and of the immense moral authority that victory against the odds gave the British state, this credo underpinned the great collectivist actions of the 1940s (nationalisation and NHS) and provided unique conditions of authority and, initially capability, for government to attempt a far-reaching policy activism which would have been impossible earlier. It also privileged economists, not indeed as much as many would have liked in terms of economics overriding politics in decision-making, but sufficient to admit greater numbers of academically-trained practitioners to Whitehall and for the Establishment to take more seriously their opinions. For a generation or more the profession could bask in the reflected glory of Keynes, Meade and the others who in their conduct of the war economy enabled their successors to help manage the peace. Moreover, at least initially, the very smallness and exclusivity of the ES, together with the absence of formal training in economics amongst the permanent civil servants, gave the economists an intellectual authority which could not endure. With the creation of the GES in 1964 and its subsequent growth, the development of post-recruitment in-house training in economics and statistics, but above all the generational shift of Treasury personnel towards those with degrees in economics (with Allen the first to become permanent secretary in 1968) and other social sciences, much of this authority was lost.[74] In a way it endured as long as it

---

[74] However, as Little (1957 , p. 35–6) observed from his time at the ES, a little economic theory in the wrong non-professional economist hands could be dangerous, leading to naive *post hoc ergo propter hoc* interpretations of the past and questionable applications of theory to the present.

did because, and without invoking Butskellism here, a much disputed construct amongst historians,[75] relative to the interwar period the parameters of golden age debate were narrow, with general agreement about ends and debate largely limited to means.

One long-standing Treasury official, Geoffrey Littler (Second Permanent Secretary by 1983), has provided the following account of economists' influence over his thirty years in Great George Street, one set against the backdrop of the profession's ability to present a common front:

> Outsiders like myself – I was not trained as an economist – and those who were in those days at the top of the Treasury were induced to believe the consensus amongst economists, and in the absence of respectable argument to the contrary, to assume that what they indicated was the right basis for policy, and the only problem was 'could you do it?' . . .
>
> If you look around now, it is true that there are more professionally-trained economists in the Treasury, and more people, either professionally trained or very substantially experienced, at the top of the Treasury who are experienced to discuss economic arguments with good intelligence among groups of economists. The striking feature is the very considerable range of economic philosophies, and the differences in those philosophies are certainly reflected in this building. So that if you think of the diffident non-professional looking at the range of economic advice he may get, he is less inclined to rely totally on what he may be told by anyone, he's less inclined to believe that whatever he's told and accepts is bound to be right. Consequently, there is a good deal more difficulty for us all in reaching judgements of what we ought to be doing, let alone what we can actually do.   (interview cited in Young and Sloman 1984, p.34)

These observations need, of course, to be seen in the context of ministers traditionally also taking advice from external sources; of officials themselves soliciting the views of the City, financial journalists and others with economic expertise; and of the Treasury, whatever its outside reputation, actually being one of the most democratic, intellectual and least hierarchical of departments when it comes to argument (Heclo and Wildavsky 1981). It seems also that Marshall might have been right about the conditions necessary for economists to exercise their maximum influence, but he would not have predicted that the advance of economics into this mature phase of professionalisation would roughly coincide with the decline in the capacity of governments, in Britain as elsewhere, to actually influence the economy and indeed all aspects of private and community behaviour.

This brings us to the transformation of the economic landscape between the Second World War and OPEC I. In 1945 the British economy was technically bankrupt and the central economic question was one of avoiding

---

[75] See Rollings (1994) for a balanced revisionist assessment which is also relevant to why official acceptance of peacetime deficit-finance was so long delayed.

a postwar slump and of day-to-day survival. Without undue exaggeration there was almost a Third World urgency and intensity about the economic problem (Cairncross 1985b), truly an age of austerity. Travel forward ten years or so to that interval between the end of the Korean War and the Suez debacle and we are in, if not quite the age of affluence, than at least the age of aspiration: 'the economically most blissful years (though, of course, ignorantly blissful) in many decades' with the British economy having weathered many crises, including an American slump which did not imperil full employment, and with no league tables of growth rates yet available 'to mar complacency'(Hutchison 1968, p. 93). In 1958 the UN published the first set of GNP growth statistics for OECD-Europe on a standardised basis (such standards being set by a committee chaired by Stone), with the UK ranking fifteenth of seventeen nations. Thereafter, the growth statistics were studied 'eagerly, not to say morbidly' by successive governments (Arndt 1978, p. 51). Another decade on from the 'blissful years' brings us, of course, to the 1964 election, in retrospect a conflict less between competing ideologies than between rival claims of managerial expertise, and with both parties seemingly intoxicated with the logic of compound interest and with the rhetoric of governmental dynamism. Indeed, as Croham (1992, p. 91) and other advisers and officials of this time have recollected, 'Growth rates ... were something politicians were extremely naive about. Whatever the achieved growth rate, they wanted a target significantly better and that was liable to mean bigger by more than 1 per cent.'

Massive hopes for what might be achieved by faster economic growth were thus entertained by all parties, although at least two of the economists (Cairncross and MacDougall) who came as close to real influence as any did always counselled caution about growth targets, with their memoirs/diaries making clear that they expended too much energy drafting documents setting targets and not enough framing and monitoring policies which might actually deliver higher growth. Hereafter, disappointment with economic performance and dissatisfaction with politicians and their advisers would move in tandem, and whilst some economists had very definitely avoided publicity and the public stage those who had not been so controlled and circumspect in effect exposed all of the profession to the much greater risks of the political marketplace. Economists were thus inevitably, and in many cases very willingly, participants in the process of adversary politics and governmental overload which many commentators now invoke to explain subsequent developments in British politics and policy and, increasingly, economic performance as the crisis intensified in the early 1970s. There are many variants of the adversary politics thesis (Gamble and Walkland 1984, ch. 2), but all provide considerable scope for the economist, whether insider or outsider, as supplier of ideas, as interpreter of competing claims upon the state and, ultimately, as whipping boy in a system in which politicians need to divert responsibility for policy failures because what they can actually achieve is so limited.

Our purpose in invoking adversary politics and governmental overload explanations of economic failure at this stage is most decidedly not to exonerate politicians or their advisers from their fair share of responsibility for policy failures and thence the underperformance of the British economy. That policy effectiveness was limited by the quality of official statistics and forecasting techniques was hardly news to the Treasury or markets, although, as Claus Moser (1973, p. 4) has observed, whatever progress was made with the former 'our policy customers are often less content now than in the old days. Somehow we are aiming at a moving target, with users always needing and thirsting for more accuracy than we are providing. The better we become, the more is expected of us.' Rising expectations leads naturally also to the view, advanced by many leading economists (Dow 1964 and Caves *et al.* 1968) and quickly established as orthodoxy within the City, that demand management could have been more effective ('Stop-Go' less disruptive) if the Treasury had been more skilful in the timing and magnitude of its fine tuning of demand. Moreover, in their different ways, Kalecki (1943) and Friedman (1948) had warned of this possibility long ago, and there was growing awareness that the politicians' efforts to synchronise the economic and electoral cycles were destabilizing and potentially growth-inhibiting. However, for other economists the problem was specified rather differently:

> It is as though we have been playing a game of musical chairs among our policy objectives of full employment, growth, stable prices, and so on; stop the music in any year you like from 1952 to 1967 and you will find one and sometimes two of the objectives without a chair. The mistake of the authorities was that instead of fetching more chairs, they simply started the music again, selecting a different tune.   (Worswick 1969, pp. 58–9)

What Worswick and many others, particularly those at the National Institute at this time (for example, Blackaby 1972), had in mind was a permanent incomes policy, an additional policy instrument (others such as Kahn and Harrod had long been campaigning for another, import controls). From 1957, and the 'Three Wise Men', through to 1978–9, and the winter of discontent, the cycle of experimenting with and then being forced to abandon incomes policies politicised economic policy in a manner which had not been seen since government had sanctioned nominal wage cuts in the 1920s as an unemployment remedy. It also, of course, somewhat negated the function of the growth target whose purpose was at least partially to lessen the distributional struggle between capital and labour. The adequacy of the available policy instruments was a long-standing question within the Treasury, as was that of how they might be augmented. But so also was the issue of governmental overload; that there were too many objectives in relation to Britain's sustainable go-political position. This was the line taken by the Brookings report, combined with identifying pervasive microeconomic inefficiencies (Caves *et al*. 1968). It was also the position of senior Treasury officials, and was typically expressed in terms of the excess load of public expenditure, on defence and other overseas commitments and of the growing costs of welfare programmes (Croham 1992, p. 88).

The emphasis upon adversary politics and governmental overload contained in the published recollections of past policy-makers is to be expected, but should not be dismissed as merely attempts to massage the historical record for posterity. The best of these memoirs are vindicated by the efforts of governments since 1979 to downplay their macroeconomic capabilities, reorder their responsibilities and policy objectives and reduce the size and scope of the public sector: in short, to try and contain voter expectations of what government can deliver. In fact, most 1960s officials were pretty cynical about the efficacy of incomes policies, but there appeared no alternative until Thatcher in 1979 sanctioned substantially higher unemployment to contain inflation. Clearly, it was competition in the political marketplace which led politicians to generate expectations of governmental competency which would not, indeed could not, be fulfilled, but the past also cast a heavy shadow over the policy space.

An Anglo-American comparison is instructive here, for during the 1940s and 1950s unemployment was perceived as bringing forth greater potential political penalties in Britain than in America, with the consequence that British (American) policy makers took more risks with inflation (unemployment) than with employment (prices). Thus the Okun discomfort index (inflation plus unemployment rates) for 1950–73 was almost identical for both, but in terms of the inflation-unemployment trade-off they were at different ends of the long-run Phillips curve. The political incentives to take greater risks with the goods market than with the labour market was, of course, always tempered by the weakness of the balance of payments and the foreign exchange reserves. However, the extraordinarily low rate of unemployment achieved in the 1950s, which surpassed all expectations, not least those of Keynes and Beveridge, not only reinforced these perceptions of potential penalties but created a climate in which over-optimistic growth targets could flourish (Croham 1992, p. 86). Such was the consent for the resulting excess demand amongst politicians of both parties and the mass of professional economists that those few academics (for example, Paish 1962; 1965) who argued for a larger margin of productive potential were vilified as reactionaries, as the modern day incarnation of those who had favoured wage cuts and opposed public works before the war.

Yet, theoretically and practically, in a world in which a *permanent* incomes policy proved politically and economically elusive, the Paish plan was the only means of relieving inflationary and balance of payments pressures, smoothing the output path and, through the more intense competition in the goods market that would result, promoting growth through greater efficiency. Nor was the margin of spare capacity sought very large, about one half a point on the unemployment rate according to Paish, but the association of this disinflationary school with the LSE and the IEA ensured its fate. Such were the political sensitivities of the early 1960s that MacDougall (1987, p. 140) found himself walking on eggshells about unemployment targets, when drafting the two key NEDC pre-National Plan documents (NEDC 1963a; b), because the general secretary of Britain's largest trade union 'could not be a party to a report which admitted that a single person should ever be out of a job.' This political problem would then be exacerbated as doubts grew, amongst those who were having second thoughts about full employment (Brittan 1975), about the appropriateness of the British unemployment statistics as a measure of pressure of demand in the labour market, but again this was initiated by the IEA and the mass of the profession were initially not much interested.[76]

Many of those economists who would later campaign for a back to basics in economic policy were greatly disillusioned by their experiences as irregulars during the Wilson (1964–70) and Heath administrations. But a greater number were not, at least in the sense that they proved willing to serve government once more, formally or informally, and did not abandon Keynesianism, with not surprisingly the strength of party allegiance the critical determinant (as shown for example in the characteristics of the signatories of the 364 economists letter of 1981, the one professional outburst against Thatcherism). Those on the political right who, for example, were early associates of the IEA, are actually of less interest in this respect than the turncoats, the erstwhile Keynesians. In the next chapter we identify two as particularly important in the 1970s: Brittan, whose spell in the DEA and assessment of the Treasury's management of the economy (1971) have already been discussed, and Peter Jay who left the Treasury in 1967 to pursue a career as economic journalist and broadcaster.

---

[76] Wood (1972). In November 1972, in a 'Memorial to the Prime Minister', a group calling themselves the Economic Radicals, and including academic and City economists, argued that 'real' unemployment amounted to only 300,000, about half a million less than on the unemployment count. A little later preliminary analysis of the 1971 census suggested that the count itself underestimated unemployment by half a million. The Heath government established a working party to investigate this variance of views, as did a little later the RES which, on Brittan's prompting, ran a conference on the concept and measurement of involuntary unemployment (Worswick 1976).

The question naturally arises whether economic policy and performance might have been very different if the formation and expansion of the GES had not taken place. Such a counterfactual might be seen as a subset of the Hennessy's (1990, p. 120) thesis, that 'The reform Hitler forced on Whitehall was undone by the peace because neither the politicians nor the senior Civil Service tried or cared to devise its peacetime equivalent ... [with this] probably *the* greatest lost opportunity in the history of British public administration.' Certainly, for one senior Labour ex-minister who had experience of both the war and the 1964–70 administration, and who would have been counted as a professional economist between the wars, fewer economists and other experts in government would actually have lessened the number of policy mistakes, with the 'intelligent expert ... [no] more disinterested than the ignorant and stupid' (Jay 1968, p. 144).

The exact contribution of defects in the machinery of government to explanations for the failure of the 1964–70 Labour governments is a hotly contested, deeply ideological topic. After losing power in 1970 Labour Party post-mortems were to make much of the failure to reform the civil service and tame the Treasury. Yet, looking back over the long-term, there is a continuity to economic policy mistakes, with a dominance of political calculation over economic reasoning which appears invariant to the party in power and the numbers and position of economic advisers. The following seem particularly pertinent to any verdict, and while each requires further study they bring us back to the politicians.

We have first the complications that ensue when prime ministers challenge their Chancellor's authority by maintaining their own economic advisers. Attlee resisted the temptation to interfere in economic matters; Churchill, an ex-Chancellor of course, did not. Indeed, his initial distrust of Butler was such that he told his new Chancellor that he was giving him the 'the best economist since Jesus Christ' as his aide, one Arthur Salter who was appointed Minister of State for Economic Affairs. Butler's memoirs (1971, p. 156) duly record – with gentlemanly reserve – his appreciation; Plowden (1989, p. 135) is more forthright that Salter was well past his intellectual peak and out of touch with developments in economic thinking. Churchill also brought back Lindemann (now Lord Cherwell), the Prof from the previous Prime Minister's Statistical Branch (p. 86). Eden, however, would be more Attlee than Churchill in such matters, although an endless meddler, while Harold Macmillan maintained a veritable harem of economists whose advice he typically played off against the Treasury,[77] a

---

[77] Horne (1989, p. 470) reproduces Macmillan's 1963 list of economic advisers: two financial journalists (Schwartz and Wincott), two academics (Harrod and Kaldor) and a close confidant, Juliet Rhys-Williams (1898–1964). The latter's inclusion is testimony to the continuing role of the interested amateur in economics and politics.

practice which began when he was Chancellor. Wilson, of course, was blessed with Balogh and, to a lesser extent, Kaldor, while Heath, whose managerial approach to government might be expected to value expertise tended to import businessmen into Whitehall and to seek advice from the Central Policy Review Staff (CPRS) which he established in 1970 as an independent Cabinet-office based think-tank. This would come to be seen by insider economists as a potential ally in conflicts with other departments, notably the Treasury (Blackstone and Plowden 1990, p. 65).

Secondly, we highlight the importance of relations between the Bank and the Treasury. From the time of nationalisation in 1946 the Bank was subordinate in statute but rarely attitude, this having been largely a technical shift of ownership which left the Bank notionally one of the least politically autonomous but in practice one of the most economically independent by European standards. As a consequence, although not uniformly, some Governors (particularly Cobbold and Cromer) were to be very assertive about the operational independence of the Bank, but on the whole relations between the Bank and the Treasury seem to have the same sorts of cyclical pattern that was characteristic of the interwar period. Some Chancellors came to rely heavily on the Governors for advice, to the extent that Robert Hall was worried that Butler used Cobbald as his principal adviser on exchange and monetary issues (Jones 1994, p. 131), while others like Roy Jenkins, more confident and/or economically literate, did not.

Postwar Bank-Treasury relations have not been much explored,[78] save one episode: that of operation Robot.[79] This 1952 plan for a limited convertibility of sterling, within a floating rate regime and with much of the sterling balances blocked, was originally conceived by Bolton in the Bank and Otto Clarke in the Treasury. It then gathered support from the Bank's Governor and from the head of the Treasury's Overseas Finance Division, a sufficient groundswell to persuade Butler, and initially Churchill and much of the Cabinet, that it offered an inventive means of escape from the worst of the external constraint. Butler (1971, pp. 158–9) would later write that had Robot been accepted 'Conservatives would have been saved some of the uncertainties and indignities of "stop-go" economics and Socialists the traumatic experience of a second formal devaluation.' That it was not accepted, and that the opposition came from the professional economists, with an alliance of Salter, Plowden, Hall, MacDougall and Lionel Robbins led by Cherwell, might be taken as demonstrating that, in exceptional circumstances, expert opinion could prevail, but now that the official papers have become available it is possible to see that ultimately the decision was

---

[78] See Howson (1993) for 1945–51, and also Cairncross (1987) and Fforde (1992).
[79] See MacDougall (1987, ch. 5), Plowden (1989, ch. 14) and Proctor (1993).

determined as much by foreign policy concerns while the Bank's underlying motive was to preserve sterling's international status. Clarke maintained to the end of his life that Robot's rejection was one of the greatest policy errors of the postwar era. Whether the case or not, it is clear 'this great battle cannot be said to have been decided on its merits ... It was a typical gladiatorial contest for the ear of those with ultimate power to decide, who are more often than not the ones least versed in the substance of the argument' (Roll 1995, p. 27).

Thirdly, we have the importance of relations between the Treasury and other economic departments at ministerial and official level. So much could be said about this topic, and has been elsewhere, that we will go no further than to repeat George Brown's (1971, p. 121) verdict, that 'Some Government, some day, will re-create a department on the lines of the D.E.A. and limit the out-dated authority of the Treasury. When that happens – and it is bound to happen – the thinking that went into the D.E.A. will be acclaimed', and to observe that for modern-day critics of the Treasury (for example, Hutton 1995; 1997) the DEA continues to fascinate.

Fourthly and finally, we have the imperative to act and the power of the past to misguide current policies. Neither were new characteristics of policy, but they did have a new emphasis after the Second World War with perhaps Macmillan embodying both to the greatest degree. Thus the reactivation of regional policy in 1963, one element of which was the appointment of a minister with special responsibility for the north east, followed naturally from Macmillan's oft-repeated and undoubtedly heartfelt concern for Stockton, his interwar constituency, which had suffered so badly from unemployment. But this was combined with a much more private conviction that no great expectations should be entertained for any of the policy innovations of this period. For Harold Wilson, the first economist to become British prime minister, a cynicism about what was possible and how to obtain it appeared to reach new heights, while, as we have seen with the embargo placed upon devaluation, he could prove most energetic in invoking the past in defence of current policy. In turn, his successor, in many ways the most unideological of postwar prime ministers, would in effect destroy his government and bring British politics to the precipice by an interpretation of the past which seriously misjudged the potential penalty for higher unemployment relative to the risk of hyperinflation and the possibility of industrial relations reform without the discipline of mass unemployment.

7. 'Back to basics': monetarism and the market

On the largest and most important question facing the governments of the industrial countries [the maintenance of internal balance] the economic profession – I choose my words with care – is intellectually bankrupt. It might as well not exist. (Galbraith 1975b)

[O]rthodox economics is in many ways an empty box. Its understanding of the world is similar to that of the physical sciences in the Middle Ages. A few insights have been obtained which will stand the test of time, but they are very few indeed, and the whole basis of conventional economics is deeply flawed.
. . . Good economists know . . . that the foundations of their subject are virtually non-existent. (Ormerod 1994, p. ix)

7.1 INTRODUCTION

For economists the golden age of economic growth ended in the autumn of 1973 with OPEC I, the quadrupling of the dollar price of oil which constituted a massive negative supply shock for the western industrialised economies. However, for Britain, which at this stage was still some years away from being a net oil exporter, OPEC I magnified a pre-existing economic and political crisis which reached a crescendo with the Heath government's attempts to combine a short-term demand stimulus (the famous U-turn which, later, would so obsess Thatcher) with efforts to stem long-term economic decline through industrial relations reform. With economists, professional and amateur, inside and outside of Whitehall, deeply implicated in these policies we can, unsurprisingly, date the end of the golden age for economists in Britain somewhat earlier than OPEC I.

In this second chapter on the postwar period we consider the subsequent travails of the British economy and of its economics profession through to the mid-1990s. The former story is comparatively well known, being covered in great detail in a number of academic and more popular studies conveying greater or lesser scepticism about the Thatcherite project, the centrepiece of these years. The latter story, however, is as yet largely unwritten, although there is now a growing literature on the role played by think-tanks such as the IEA and the ASI in influencing policy. In Britain, as in the US, such agencies provide an important outlet for academic economists to publish on current policy issues, that is providing they are prepared to bear the political and professional disapproval of many of their university colleagues.[1] That greater numbers have been prepared to do so since the 1960s forms an important element in this final chapter on the development of the British economics profession and on the relationship between economic ideas and economic policy. However, in contrast to this literature on think-tanks and those thinking the unthinkable, we also devote attention to university economics and economists, to those who did not abandon Keynesianism and big government, as well as to those who did pursue what we have here termed a back to basics in theory and policy.

The phrase 'back to basics' was, of course, invoked by John Major in a very different context from that of economics. Nonetheless, it has a deep resonance here for what, in the supreme triumph of ideology over economics, was to become the orthodoxy for the New Right by the late 1970s. In this story, clever Keynesian economists (aka the British economics establishment) had, together with an overmighty trade union movement, brought the British economy to its knees, and it could only be rescued by the reassertion and application of universal economic truths: of sound finance, through monetary rectitude, in macroeconomics; and of market incentives and disciplines, all supposedly deriving from core neo-classical theory, in microeconomics. A back to basics in theory and policy has a further significance. Thus, just as the phrase was invoked as a rhetorical device in education and social policy, where its purpose was to obscure the reality that public policy is limited in its capacity to actually alter educational or social outcomes, so also was this the case in economic policy.

Accordingly, back to basics was born of concerns about overload and governability, and while in economic policy the beginning of the Thatcherite project saw much anti-Keynesian triumphalism, the period of monetary fundamentalism was in fact only short lived. By the mid-1980s a form of pragmatic macroeconomic management prevailed. This has since been sustained, and in reality it would be familiar – if deeply disappointing – to those managing the economy in the 1960s, for the stated macroeconomic objectives are no longer fourfold but unidimensional, the minimisation or elimination of inflation. In practice, however, governments have been much preoccupied with the other three objectives of the golden age (low unemployment, high growth and balance of payments equilibrium), and

---

[1] Cockett (1994) and Stone (1996); see also Muller (1996) on the IEA and the accompanying studies of other British think-tanks (ASI, CPS, Demos, Fabian Society, Institute of Public Policy Research (IPPR) and the Social Market Foundation (SMF)) commissioned by the Institute of Contemporary British History and published in two parts in 1996 in *Contemporary British History*, vol. 10 (1 and 2), eds. M.D. Kandiah and Anthony Seldon.

acutely conscious of the political cycle (hence, the Lawson boom, 1986–8 and the Clark boomlet, 1996–7). While the emphasis upon controlling inflation accords with the new balance between government and market sought by the New Right, ascribing pre-eminence to abstract market forces does not remove the necessity for demand management. Indeed, between 1979 and 1997 the British economy experienced two deep recessions and at least one unsustainable boom, making it one of the most unstable of the OECD economies, in fact more unstable than during the classic 'Stop-Go' era of the 1950s and 1960s (Middleton 1996, pp. 631, 634).

In microeconomics, where supply-side policies were hailed as the structural means of reversing economic decline, it is arguable that back to basics had more substance and longer-term positive effects. However, a dispassionate examination of the data yields at best the conclusion that the Thatcher-Major years produced a much belated catch-up exercise, and thence a slowing of the pace of relative economic decline, but that relative to comparators the UK remains a low growth, high inflation and high unemployment economy. Nonetheless an economic renaissance was claimed, and at times brilliantly propagandised, with important implications for the conduct of economic policy. In the following discussion we make much of why some economists choose to support the Thatcherite project, why others resisted and whether two decades later, with the election of the New Labour, there might finally be a workable alternative. In the process we also complete our account of the professionalisation of British economics, thereby concluding our chronicle of the fate of Marshall's mission.

The organisation of this chapter follows our treatment of earlier developments, save that we do not attempt a case study. There is no possible shortage of topics; far from it. The years since OPEC I provide a rich store of policy episodes overflowing with controversy: from the 1976 public expenditure/sterling crisis, which prompted Callaghan's famous Labour Party conference speech which many see as inaugurating monetarism, through to September 1992 and Black Wednesday, when sterling fell out of the ERM and, with its macroeconomic policy in tatters, the last Conservative government inadvertently established the conditions for the current business cycle recovery. In some of these episodes economists played roles of high drama, as for example in the matter of Lawson's resignation in 1989. This was ascribed by him to a prime minister 'preferr[ing] the advice of an academic economist observing the British economy from 3,000 miles away to that of her Chancellor of the Exchequer' (1992, p. 796), a reference to the activities of her personal economic adviser, Alan Walters,[2] an early convert

---

[2] Cf. Lawson's account of events immediately preceding his resignation (1992, pp. 961–5) with Thatcher's (1993, pp. 707–9, 713–18). The former's obvious delight (p. 965) that the money and foreign exchange markets reacted badly to news of the resignation is deeply significant.

to monetarism and later an implacable opponent of the European project.[3]

Our proximity to these events, and the unsatisfactory, self-serving nature of much of the documentary record upon which contemporary history inevitably draws, must frustrate the ambition to include a case study for sake of completeness. The thirty year rule on the release of official papers provides an additional impediment, although in practice Whitehall, including the Treasury, was becoming more open to academic and journalistic enquiries some time before the last administration's so-called 'open government' initiative. We have thus Young and Sloman's BBC radio series and book (1984) which opened up the Treasury, allowing its officials to speak about their jobs and their assessment of their own performance in managing the economy, together with more heavyweight academic studies, such as Thain and Wright (1995) on the planning and control of public expenditure since cash limits were introduced in 1976, Campbell and Wilson's (1995) examination of the Whitehall model of governance, which draws heavily on interviews with officials, and Chapman's (1997) postwar history of the Treasury. Arguably, therefore, the omission of a case study is none too serious and will eventually be rectified once the records become available and due perspective is provided by greater distance from events.

What perhaps is more difficult to accommodate, and especially for those in the universities, is the enormous changes wrought by Thatcher's project for the policy community and the market for ideas. For economics and academic economists it is highly significant that Thatcher was a very intellectual prime minister in the sense that she delighted in ideas, but saw deference to the traditional intellectual authority of academics as producers of ideas (economists included) as part of the British disease. She was, as Harrison (1994, p. 206) has observed, a figure upon whom few can be neutral, and for the tax-funded British intelligentsia, in essence the university community, she was a figure both hated and feared, for in their dependency upon public funds was a cruel vulnerability. With economic reform central to her mission, and with deep structural changes in the economic policy community a precondition of policy success, there were inevitably going to be tensions between Britain's university economists and government. What we have to explain is why, after the 1981 economists' letter (pp. 34–5), there was actually so little protest. Why had British economics reached such a state by the 1980s that it could not more

---

[3] Walters (1990). Walters also resigned that day, the final crisis of this long-running conflict being precipitated by the *Financial Times*'s publication of extracts from his forthcoming autobiographical essay in *The American Economist*, one in a series of the life philosophies of eminent economists which had been solicited long before his return to government service. The editor of this latter journal (Szenberg 1990) has written a reflective paper on what this episode illustrates about the gulf between the world of the scholar and that of the mass media.

effectively confront the New Right, and why when credible alternatives to the Thatcherite project were being developed in the 1990s did these derive less from academics than from economist-journalists and others?

We proceed as follows. In section 2 we ask whether economics has now recovered from the crisis of the 1970s, using this as a springboard to introduce the various challenges to contemporary mainstream economics which have developed over the past quarter century. We then focus in section 3 on the crisis of Keynesian economics, the end of the Keynesian era in Britain and the search for a new theoretical consensus. Section 4 then completes our account of the professionalisation of British economics, while section 5 briefly surveys the economic policy debate since OPEC I and the contribution made by economists, whatever their persuasion or job description. Finally, some preliminary conclusions are drawn in section 6, with reflections upon the current state of Britain's economy and economics profession deferred until chapter 8.

7.2 CRISIS! WHAT CRISIS?

A cooling of controversy

In a recent guide to modern economics, edited by three British economists and specifically designed to be comprehensive and 'student-friendly', the introductory essay opens with the statement: 'One of the characteristics – perhaps in retrospect it will be viewed as the chief characteristic – of theoretical economics over the past decade has been the cooling of controversy and a gradual re-establishment of some form of consensus in the profession for the first time since the mid-1960s' (Bleaney 1996, pp. 3–4). The author then went on to describe today's economists as operating in an environment which was 'more placid, more assured and more reminiscent of recovery from trauma than of trauma itself,' with the process of theoretical discovery such that a new synthesis might now be possible. Three explanations were offered for why the crisis in economics that seemed so pressing in the 1970s and early 1980s might now have passed:

> Theoretical progress may have left the old disputes behind and redefined them as alternative special cases of a more general theory. Alternatively, practical experience might have shown that one side was right and the other wrong. . . . A further possibility is that the 'crisis' had more to do with the public perception of economics than its actual content, and that with the return to some degree of normality in the macroeconomy the reputation of economists has recovered and with it their self-assurance.

Whilst careful not to favour one above another of these explanations, Bleaney did point out that with hindsight this crisis of economics was bound to be temporary. Thus mainstream theory, the neo-classical synthesis (NCS) of the 1950s and 1960s, in combining a Keynesian economics oriented towards remedying short-term demand shocks with a neo-classical microeconomic theory predicated on long-run market efficiency, was always potentially vulnerable to a supply-side shock, with the Phillips curve the obvious weakest point. The appearance of stagflation, followed by OPEC I, was thus bound to wreak havoc. The Keynesians were revealed as having no effective policy prescriptions, such that they were forced to fall back on incomes policies, a strategy which magnified the dysfunctional bargain struck between capital and labour in postwar Britain; while those of the neo-classical tradition, in reiterating their faith in the resilience of market clearing, appeared but true disciples of Keynes's (1923, p. 65) famous dictum that 'the *long run* is a misleading guide to current affairs. *In the long run* we are all dead. Economists set themselves too easy, too useless a task if in tempestuous seasons they can tell us that when the storm is long past the ocean is flat again.'

As Bleaney puts it: 'As in ... 1929–33, a lacuna in economic theory that had previously lain hidden was brutally exposed by events [with] Theoretical weaknesses ... dramatically brought home to economists and public alike.' But, he continues, as supply shocks waned after OPEC II (1979), and progressive disinflation became characteristic of Britain and other western economies in the 1980s, 'publicly expressed dissatisfaction with economists' policy prescriptions became less frequent.' Moreover, after a period of confusion and disorientation, and after relaxation of certain extreme assumptions that had characterised the NCS (especially on the completeness of information), mainstream economics was once more able to regain the high ground of theoretical consistency and policy competence by 'remedying the weaknesses of existing theory, and particularly in bridging the chasm that seemed to have opened up between microeconomics and macroeconomics' (pp. 4–5). In reality, he contends, 'The old theoretical argument was not really won by either side'; rather:

1. The crisis spawned new theoretical tools (especially rational expectations and game theory) 'which have given economists the power to grapple with issues that had previously seemed intractable';
2. The recovery of all western economies from stagflation 'have removed some of the pressure that contemporary developments exerted on the economics profession during the 1970s'; and
3. It is also probable 'that the public now has lower expectations of what economic science can deliver' (p. 5).

In short, mainstream economics has emerged stronger than ever from the crisis, in the process seeing off the challenges posed by the radical right and the radical left, the latter of course fatally compromised by the collapse of the socialist economies. Bleaney's short history of economic theory since the late 1960s no doubt rings true for many if not most theoretical economists, very much in accord with the celebration of theory argued by Hahn in his Jevons memorial lecture, 'In praise of economic theory' (1985). Indeed, such optimistic sentiments are echoed in a number of other recent surveys, both by American and by European economists.[4]

Ugly currents in modern economics

While Bleaney's account also contains the germ of the story when told as political economy, it is a very internal history and – perhaps unconsciously – rather American, a reflection of the Americanisation of large parts of British economics. It also open to a number of other objections:

1. It ignores the continued flood of articles and books, originating from academic economists and economist-journalists, which berate economics for its lack of relevance to real world issues and which continue to talk of a crisis far from being resolved.[5]
2. The verdict that mainstream economics has triumphed over the challenges posed by the radical left and right might also been seen as premature, one born of a very narrow reading of disciplinary activity and one which does not acknowledge that outside of academe there are green, new age and feminist challenges to economics' authority.
3. Bleaney makes no mention, even indirectly, of those who advocate an 'imperialistic expansion of economics into the traditional domains of

---

[4] See, for example, and with varying degrees of emphasis, Barber (1997a), Kreps (1997) and Solow's (1997) contributions to a recent symposium on American academic culture; Blinder (1997a) and Tobin's (1997) *Challenge* papers on the future of macroeconomics; a number of upbeat contributions to the centenary issue of the *EJ*, especially Buchanan (1991) and Hahn (1991), but cf. Stiglitz (1991); and much of the literature on the vitality and distinctiveness of European- as against American-style economics (Frey and Eichenberger 1993). Even in macroeconometric forecasting, a traditional 'disaster' area for economics' public and policy reputation, there are those prepared to plough an optimistic furrow (for example, Wallis 1989).

[5] For example, from Ormerod (1994), a British academic economist turned economic consultant; from Heilbroner and Milberg (1995), two American academic economists, the former of whom has long been a merchant of doom about the profession; from Vickrey (1993), the 1996 Nobel laureate; from Cassidy (1996), an American journalist who used the Nobel awards for Mirrlees and Vickrey as a springboard to survey the decline of economics; and from *The Economist* (Anon 1997b), which in a recent piece on the 'puzzling failure' of economics prompted by the payment of an advance in excess of a million dollars to Gregory Mankiw for a new introductory economics volume set to rival Samuelson. Finally, although now dated, Kuttner's (1985) survey for the *Atlantic Monthly* is a classic in the crisis literature.

sociology, political science, anthropology, law and social biology'
(Hirshleifer 1985, p. 53), or that this might be a source of widespread
concern, both inside and outside of economics.[6] That economics might
actually benefit from the other social sciences as currently constituted
does not feature in Bleaney's account.[7]

4. Neither would his story satisfy economic methodologists. Indeed, it may
be significant that neither rhetoric nor methodology feature in this
volume:[8] a reflection no doubt that economics continues to be an
unreflective social science where the 'absence of methodological self-
consciousness is considered a virtue'[9] and where leading senior British
figures can advise seriously the young economist 'to ignore cries of
"economics is in crisis", to avoid discussions of "mathematics in
economics" like the plague, and to give no thought at all to
"methodology".'[10]

5. Finally, Bleaney is silent on the sorts of issues about the future of the
economics profession and economic studies that we introduced in chapter
1: thus concerns about the postgraduate education of economists, debate
on the appropriateness of the undergraduate economics curriculum and,
most recent of all, the problem of how university economists should
respond to the current decline in applications to read for economics
bachelor degrees. All are matters in which the AEA has been more active
than the RES, and whilst British trends might lag those in the US,[11] they
are still sufficiently well-established as not to be ignored.

An alternative formulation of the state of economics, here put by Blaug
(1997b) in reviewing Heilbroner and Milberg's (1995) widely-read book on

[6] For example, Demsetz (1997, p. 1) has recently argued that 'The strong export surplus
economics maintains in its trade in ideas and methods with the other social sciences is an
important indicator of the success of economics.' He omitted to mention the fear that his
'Economics Expeditionary Forces' (Commander-in-Chief, Gary Becker) might instil in their
potential subjects – see, for example, Fine's (1997) strictures from the perspective of British
socialist economics; and Ingham (1996) and Dogan (1996, esp. pp. 113–15) respectively on
economics and its relations with sociology and political science.

[7] Whilst rarely admitted as a possibility by economists, the most recent RES presidential address
is of particular interest because, after berating the profession for being uninterested in the subject
of income distribution, Atkinson (1997, p. 318) argues that the only grounds for optimism about
economics he could find were: first, 'an upsurge of interest in the recent past', and second a new
receptiveness to ideas from other social sciences, the 'sign of a discipline in good health.'

[8] They do, however, feature in the larger volume from which this is derived (Greenaway *et al.*
1991).

[9] Caldwell, cited in T. Mayer (1995, p. 1).

[10] As in Hahn's (1992a) reflections for the RES upon his retirement; see also Backhouse's (1992)
response, Hahn's (1992b) rejoinder and Backhouse's (1997b, ch. 2) more developed case for
methodological enquiry in economics.

[11] As for example in applications to read for bachelor degrees, upon which see Margo and
Siegfried's (1996) illuminating long-term study of US trends.

the crisis,[12] runs as follows:

> modern economics is sick; the discipline has increasingly become an intellectual game played for its own sake and not for its practical consequences in understanding the economic world; economists have converted the subject into a sort of social mathematics in which rigour is everything and relevance is nothing; to pick up a copy of *The American Economic Review* or *The Economic Journal* is to wonder whether one has landed on a strange planet in which tedium is the deliberate objective of professional publication. Economics was once condemned as the 'dismal science', but the dismal science of yesterday was infinitely preferable to the soporific scholasticism of today.

This is, of course, from the pen of an economic methodologist cum historian of economic thought, two sub-fields where there is an abundance of quantitative evidence that attests to their low status within the economics profession (for example, Diamond and Haurin 1995), populated as they are by 'the dolts who work the libraries instead of the bright lads at the blackboards', or so McCloskey (1980, p. 213) tells us. Thus amongst the bright lads the refrain is frequently heard that talk of a crisis by those within the profession comes only from those aged over 60 who are no longer able to play the game, and/or those not able to cut the mustard mathematically ('maths wimps')[13] and thus inhabiting the less arduous foothills of the subject, or even having decamped to sociology, political science or economic history. And, as for those outside of the academe ...? Interestingly, given these propositions, no one has yet sought to test them empirically, and while we do not attempt a detailed review here of the crisis literature we have established sufficient of a case that there is now a dissonance between the public face of a self-confident mainstream economics and the disquiet of many other producers and consumers of economic knowledge, eminent and less so, about the state of the discipline. We explore this dissonance in two stages: first, in section 3 through an examination of the trauma to which economists were subjected in the 1970s and early-1980s, and how the mainstream resolved that crisis; and then in section 4 through our study of the latest stage of professionalisation of British economics.

---

[12] Blaug (1997c) extends this and dates the onset of the illness (the 'ugly currents') as Arrow and Debreu (1954), the foundation stone of modern general equilibrium theory.

[13] This phrase comes from some illuminating traffic on the History of Economics Society list which was prompted by an 'innocent' enquiry by Neil Buchanan (posted for him by Mary Schweitzer on 16 September 1997) for references to economists who were prepared to be critical in print of the mainstream. The storm that then erupted can be read in the HES archive at <**http://cs.muohlo.edu/Archives/hes/**>

7.3 THE END OF THE KEYNESIAN ERA AND THE QUEST FOR A NEW CONSENSUS

The New Classical Macroeconomics (NCM)

At the annual meeting of the AEA in 1986, the year of the half centenary of the publication of the *General theory*, a session was organised on Keynes's contribution to modern economics. Amongst those presenting papers was Alan Blinder (b. 1945), a leading American applied economist and vocal opponent of the NCM which,[14] he maintained (in a slightly later paper developing his critique), had so supplanted Keynesian macroeconomics that by 1980 'it was hard to find an American academic macroeconomist under the age of 40 who professed to be a Keynesian' (1988, p. 278). In developing his opposition to the NCM in his AEA paper, the ascendancy of which he later ascribed to the 'triumph of *a priori* theorizing over empiricism, of intellectual aesthetics over observation and, in some measure, of conservative ideology over liberalism'- in short, not a Kuhnian paradigm shift (p. 296) – Blinder employed a cheap but effective rhetorical device which made use of a standard economists' joke: that in economics one can use the same examination paper each year with one's students, merely changing one's model answers.

Blinder's (1987) examination paper contained eight obligatory questions, and took the form of a comparison of the answers which would be provided by a hypothetical Robert Lucas (b. 1937; Nobel laureate, 1995), the chief expositor of the NCM, and a hypothetical Keynes. It should be observed that the argument is couched in terms of the NCM, not monetarism. The latter is a portmanteau term[15] which combined a number of hypotheses and was later to be picked up by politicians and the press, with in most cases an imperfect understanding of how it connected to the broader challenge to Keynesian macroeconomics and, indeed, the prevailing consensus constituting the NCS. Whilst monetarists and exponents of the NCM share many policy positions, so much so that the NCM was known as Monetarism Mark II by many of its opponents, monetarism is primarily an empirical doctrine while the NCM is essentially a theoretical construct. Moreover, in formal terms the former is distinguished from the latter by its preparedness to accept disequilibrium in the labour market and the slow adjustment of expectations;

---

[14] Later a member of the CEA and then Vice-Chairman of the Federal Reserve Board. In respect of the latter, much valuable material on what central bankers can learn from academic economists and *vice versa* is contained in Blinder (1997b) while, in the British context, **Goodhart** (1994) instructs the Governor of the Bank of England on how game theory can lend credibility to his monetary policy announcements.

[15] Invented by Brunner (1968), not by Friedman, who disliked the term and did not use it in his famous AEA presidential address on monetary policy (1968).

Table 7.1   Blinder's (1987) examination of Keynes and Lucas's
            macroeconomics

No	Question	Keynes	Lucas
1	Are expectations rational?	No	Yes
2	Is there involuntary unemployment?	Yes	No
3	Do wage movements quickly clear the labour market?	No	Yes
4	Is the natural rate of unemployment a strong attractor for the actual rate of unemployment?	No	Yes
5	Is there a reliable short-run Phillips curve?	Yes	No
6	Does a change in the money supply have real effects?	Yes	No
7	Does social welfare rise when business cycles are limited?	Yes	No
8	Must macroeconomics be built up from neoclassical first principles?	No	Yes

such that from the perspective of purist exponents of the NCM, monetarism and Keynesianism share unacceptable common characteristics in the crudeness of the empirical and theoretical (especially microeconomic) underpinnings of their macroeconomics. Our focus upon the NCM is thus appropriate, particularly when our concern is both economists and policy.[16]

We record in Table 7.1 the questions Blinder posed for the two candidates together with the Yes/No answers provided by those so examined. Discounting for the obvious charge of anachronism (Keynes had been dead a decade before the Phillips curve's invention), for the predisposition of many Keynesian economists to expound Keynes's thought with greater clarity than he apparently found possible, and with the qualifications removed (for example, Lucas's hypothetical answer to question 7 only tended towards No, depending upon the preferences of his infinitely lived consumer living under perfect capital markets), we are left nonetheless with the NCM a perfect mirror image of the paradigm it sought to supplant, with the policy implications clear enough for a managed-mixed economy such as Britain had been during the golden age.

The NCM posed both an empirical and a theoretical challenge: the former manifest as the phenomenon of stagflation; the latter, in turn, for what was then revealed about the weak microeconomic foundations of macroeconomic theory and policy, a matter upon which there had been long-standing concerns about the logical consistency of the NCS. Binding these together was the breakdown of the Phillips curve and the theoretical expositions – deriving from *micro*- not macroeconomic reasoning – of

[16]   See Hoover (1988, ch. 9) for a survey of the NCM which draws out these differences and relates the them to Kuhnian paradigm shifts, Blaug (1992a, ch. 12) who favours Lakatos's apparatus, and Beaud and Dostaler's (1997, esp. chs 7–8) history of very recent economic thought.

Friedman (1968) and Phelps (1968) that, once expectations were incorporated, there was no stable long-run trade-off between unemployment and inflation. Indeed, for Friedman and Phelps, the Phillips curve became largely useless as soon as policy-makers sought to exploit it by trading off price stability for lower unemployment for this would engender expectations of a yet higher rate of wage inflation (the perpetually rightwards-shifting expectations-augmented Phillips curve which, if unchecked, led onwards to political and economic disaster). The reassertion of the microeconomics of labour markets (of demand, supply, search time, trade union restrictive practices and the other explanatory variables in the natural rate of unemployment hypothesis proffered by Friedman 1968) opened up a rich research agenda for economists, but posed immediate and significant problems for policy-makers. While the simultaneous rise in unemployment and inflation that Friedman and others had predicted did indeed transpire, and arguably spectacularly so in Britain (Table 7.2 records the four main macroeconomic indicators), the long-run vertical Phillips curve offered no policy menu, with the natural rate defined tautologically as the rate of unemployment which would prevent inflation from increasing explosively.[17]

Friedman and Phelps's papers were the opening shots in what was to develop into a much more comprehensive attack on the Keynesian system,[18] but already they had got to the heart of two questions which

[17]   See, for example, Marin's (1972) attempt to explain to a lay audience why the Phillips curve
       was now 'out of action' and what the implications might be.

[18]   Much of this was conducted through the bank reviews, especially that issued by Lloyds which
       Kaldor (1970a) used to launch his counter-attack on the new doctrine. Thereafter, and in a series
       of waves over the next decade or so, there were more than twenty five articles defending or
       attacking Keynesianism. For example, on the defence team, after Kaldor's initial exchange with
       Friedman, there was Hicks (1975); Kahn (1976); Worswick (1977); and Kaldor and Trevithick
       (1981); and, for the prosecution, Friedman (1970b); Brunner (1971), Parkin (1975); Johnson
       (1976); Laidler (1976); Eltis (1976); and Brunner (1981). This 'debate' was conducted solely
       in terms of a Keynesian-monetarist discourse with the broader challenge of the NCM much less
       evident. Whilst there were parallel exchanges in the other bank reviews, some journals were
       probably more partisan than others. Thus, for example, that published by the *National
       Westminster Bank* provided a vehicle for the views of important British opinion-formers (for
       example, Laidler 1972; Congdon 1973; and Parkin 1974) without their being immediately
       subjected to replies from the Keynesian defence bench. With the theoretical impetus for the
       NCM originating in the US Klamer's (1984) volume of interviews with the main protagonists
       (Lucas, Sargent, Townsend for the NCM; Brunner for monetarism) and their opponents
       (Blinder, Modigliani, Solow, Tobin, for the neo-Keynesians; Gordon for the Marxists) is an
       invaluable source for all but those implacably opposed to the rhetoric debate, of which he is an
       active member. A companion volume on British economists would be most useful. Also, from
       the British perspective, we have the following historical assessments of the fall of Keynesianism
       and the subsequent rise and fall of monetarism: Bleaney (1985), Smith (1987), Argy (1988),
       Britton (1991, pt. 2) and Oliver (1997). Given his role as an exponent of monetary disciplines in
       the 1970s Laidler's (1981) contribution to the 1980 RES conference, 'Monetarism - an
       appraisal', is also of more than passing interest, while Cobham (1984) is unusual in focusing on
       British academic participants in the monetarism debate.

Table 7.2   Macroeconomic indicators (%), 1973–95

	Real GDP growth rate (on previous year)	Current account balance of payments (% of GDP)	Change in consumer prices	Unemployment rate
1973	7.2	(1.3)	8.8	3.8
1974	(1.6)	(3.8)	16.2	2.7
1975	(0.8)	(1.4)	24.4	2.6
1976	2.9	(0.6)	16.4	4.2
1977	1.9	0.0	15.8	5.7
1978	3.9	0.7	8.3	6.2
1979	2.8	(0.2)	13.4	6.1
1980	(2.1)	1.2	17.9	5.7
1981	(1.2)	2.6	11.9	7.4
1982	1.7	1.7	8.6	11.4
1983	3.7	1.2	4.6	13.0
1984	1.9	0.6	5.0	12.2
1985	3.9	0.8	6.1	11.5
1986	3.9	(0.0)	3.3	11.7
1987	4.8	(1.0)	4.2	11.8
1988	4.3	(3.2)	5.0	10.5
1989	2.3	(3.7)	7.8	8.3
1990	0.9	(3.4)	9.4	6.3
1991	(2.0)	(1.4)	5.9	5.8
1992	(0.5)	(1.7)	3.7	8.0
1993	2.1	(1.7)	1.5	9.8
1994	3.8	(0.4)	2.5	10.3
1995	2.4	(0.4)	3.4	9.4

Source: CSO databank.

macroeconomists thought had settled answers: what causes output and employment to fluctuate? and what is the correct policy response to those fluctuations?

Milton Friedman

Had Friedman been an obscure monetary economist his restatement of the quantity theory (1956), one which derived in large measure from his historical assessment of monetary trends, would have been much more easily dismissed, especially in Britain, as part of the continued marginalia of a Chicago school which – perversely – had never accepted Keynes. In fact, such a tactic was actually attempted, especially by the Keynesian-Cambridge old guard,[19] but of course Friedman was anything but obscure.[20] He first entered our story for his controversial essay on methodology (1953), but he had been working on monetary topics for a good two decades before his championing that money mattered, including an important paper on the difficulties of stabilisation policy (1948). He was also, of course, active in consumption theory, such research being cited in the award of the Nobel prize in 1976,[21] but what really gave bite to his monetary economics was his simultaneous espousal of an assertive free market economics, one not atypical of Chicago economics but pursued with unusual verve and vigour.

His *Capitalism and freedom* (1962) made him one of the most visible members of the Mont Pèlerin Society. In America he used his *Newsweek* column (1966–84) to promote a vision of economic freedom in a manner which would have been admired, if largely abhorred, by Keynes, whilst in Britain he targeted the IEA as the appropriate medium for influencing opinion. Thus his 1968 *AER* paper was quickly distilled into a Wincott memorial lecture for the IEA, and this was then followed by a flood of pamphlets and other contributions on the need for monetary discipline, the breakdown of the Phillips curve and the urgency of curtailing big government.[22] The culmination of this proselytising was, at one level, his follow-up book, *Free to choose* (1980), written jointly with his wife Rose, and televised by the PBS and BBC that year; and, on the other, his invitation to give evidence before the Treasury and Civil Service select committee in the very early days of the Thatcher government's period of monetary fundamentalism (1980), that of a new policy era ascribed in no little part to

---

[19]   For example, from Joan Robinson (1971, p. 87): there 'is an unearthly, mystical element in Friedman's thought'. See also Johnson's (1976, p. 15) delicious lambasting of 'sherry-party sophisticates who see contemporary inflation as a proof of the failure of what they think is economics, rather than proof of the predictive success of the actual monetary theory of inflation; and who seek to resolve the alleged failure of economics by invoking the *force majeure* of an incomes policy, under the erroneous impression that appealing to the loyalty of the citizen to the state to clean up a mess that the state's own irresponsibility to its citizens has created is a procedure with no short- or long-run social or political cost.'

[20]   We lack a full-scale intellectual biography of Friedman but the groundwork has been done by Hirsch and De Marchi (1990) which can be supplemented by Hammond's (1996) investigation of Friedman's methodology and Butler's (1985b) brief guide to his economic thought, the latter containing much pertinent material on the British case. Whilst written by a founder member of the ASI it manages to rise above hagiography, as does the companion volume on Hayek (Butler 1985a).

[21]   See appendix II; and Thygesen (1977) for the official Nobel assessment.

[22]   Beginning with his pamphlet on the monetarist challenge (1970a), and including his 1975 evaluation of the Phillips curve (with contained a commentary on the British situation by Laidler), his 1976 Nobel lecture (1977b) and his attack on Galbraith (1977a).

the success of his activities. Our argument is not that stagflation, or as the monetarists would put it, the 'great' inflation of monetary excess fuelled by high government borrowing, would have not caused some sort of crisis for economics, but that personality mattered in how that crisis evolved within economics and was perceived by politicians and other opinion-formers. For his supporters, as for his more considered opponents, Friedman was the one economist of the twentieth century who could rival Keynes for the effectiveness, breadth and scope of his economics and of its marketing.[23] It was the combination of monetarism and market optimism which made his message so potentially powerful, but because in Britain the initial focus was almost exclusively on the former there was a tendency to underestimate the force of the challenges to the Keynesian system until it was too late.

Policy ineffectiveness

Friedman and Phelps's prescience about the Phillips curve prepared the ground amongst macroeconomists for the much more comprehensive challenge of Lucas's (1976) critique of mainstream policy evaluation which 'became the rallying cry for those Young Turks intent on destroying the consensus' (Mankiw 1988, pp. 438–9). At one level the Lucas critique concerned a highly technical matter of econometric practice, that the parameters of an econometric model are derived under certain assumptions about policy behaviour, but that if these assumptions are sensitive to the policies pursued to influence the trajectory of policy targets (e.g. unemployment), the parameters cannot be thus specified and any forecasts or policy simulations are nullified.[24] Now known as the 'Lucas critique', this was merely a logical extension of the groundswell that was developing amongst the younger generation of rational expectations economists that hitherto macroeconomists had treated expectations in too cavalier a fashion. Whilst it had long been acknowledged that policy forecasts affect outcomes, Lucas cut the ground from under those who subscribed to the possibility of active stabilization policies by demonstrating that, as Bleaney (1985, p. 152) summarises it:

---

[23] Cf. Walters's (1987) assessment for the *New Palgrave* and Tobin (1981). Such has been his stature that he has even inspired the creation of a fictional character, one Professor Henry Spearman, the heroic economist-sleuth of the mystery novel *Murder at the margin*, penned by the aptly named Marshall Jevons (see Breit 1984, p. 19).

[24] This preoccupation with structural autonomy in econometric models was followed shortly by Sims (1980) on the inherent problems of large-scale structural models, Hendry's (1980) championing of alternative methods for estimating time-series models and Leamer's (1983) (Bayesian) challenge that existing econometric techniques provided limited assistance to policy-makers. For a wide-ranging survey of these developments, see Darnell and Evans (1990).

an econometric relationship observed by the government when it is pursuing macroeconomic policy X will not necessarily hold if it then tries to exploit that relationship and switches to macroeconomic policy Y, because the private sector, once having observed the switch in policy, will form its expectations differently and the econometric relationship which the government is seeking to exploit will either be modified or disappear altogether.

This policy-ineffectiveness proposition, which rapidly became the hallmark of the NCM, followed swiftly upon another nail in the coffin of the consensus, that of Barro's (1974) revival of the Ricardian theorem of the equivalence of public borrowing and taxation, itself a further application of rational expectations theory. Whether in practice voters do misperceive their tax burden, and whether they are as forward-looking as Ricardian equivalence requires, continues to be debated (Cullis and Jones 1992, pp. 341–2). But Ricardian equivalence provided, as Tobin (1981, pp. 40–1) describes it, 'an intellectually tight, if empirically implausible, rationale for monetarist dismissals of the macroeconomic importance of fiscal policies.' That it contradicted another strand of monetarist thinking which had by then entered the public debate over Keynesianism, that of government borrowing crowding-out private investment (Brunner and Meltzer 1976), was something of a problem, but it provided the means also to leap from issues of stabilisation to concurrent concerns about economic growth via the excess burden of the expanded public sector which had been generated by pursuit of a Keynesian managed-mixed economy. Whilst, in Britain, a very special role would here be played by Bacon and Eltis's (1976) influential book, it was but a short step from Friedman, Lucas and Barro to the critique of government economic policies being developed by the burgeoning (largely American) public choice school of economists and political scientists.

In his intellectual history of this exciting era Mankiw has argued that neither the empirical (the breakdown of the Phillips curve) nor the theoretical (Lucas critique) challenge were sufficient to destroy the NCS. To support this he posed two counterfactuals:

Suppose the macroeconometric models had failed to explain the events of the 1970s, but macroeconomists had felt confident in the theoretical underpinning of these models. Undoubtedly the events could have been explained away. As defenders of the consensus view often emphasize, much of the stagflationary 1970s can be attributed to the OPEC supply shock. The remainder could always have been attributed to a few large residuals. Heteroskedasticity has never been a reason to throw out an otherwise good model.

Alternatively, suppose the macroeconometric models had performed wonderfully in the 1970s, but that Friedman, Phelps, and Lucas had correctly pointed out the inadequate microeconomic foundations of these models. In this case, the absence of microfoundations would have disturbed only the theoretically obsessive. The prediction of Friedman and Phelps would have been forgotten, even if it had never been put to the test. The correct response to the Lucas critique would have been, 'If it ain't broke, don't fix it.'

The sociology and politics of monetarism marks I and II

Clearly, what distinguishes this period was the simultaneous revelation of empirical and theoretical deficiencies in the macroeconomics of the NCS. But, were these sufficient in themselves to generate the crisis that erupted, and were the theoretical responses to that crisis such as to constitute a counter-revolution as the protagonists, monetarist and NCM, were to claim? Blinder (1987; 1988) thought not, as indeed did Johnson (1971a; b). Indeed, the latter directed attention to the sociology of doctrinal dispute, and more particularly sought to explain monetarism's success in the very terms that could be used to model the initial revolutionary achievements of Keynesianism, such success, of course, being the precondition for its becoming the orthodoxy for the next generation to challenge. These conditions were:

> on the one hand, the existence of an important social and economic problem with which the prevailing orthodoxy was unable to cope; on the other hand, a variety of characteristics that appealed to the young generation of that period – notably the claim of the new theory to superior social relevance, and intellectual distinction, its incorporation in a novel and confusing fashion of the valid elements of traditional theory, the opportunity it offered to bypass the system of academic seniority by challenging senior colleagues with a new and self-announcedly superior scientific approach, the presentation of new methodology that made general-equilibrium theory both manageable and socially relevant, and the advancement of a new empirical relationship challenging for econometricians to estimate.   (1971b, pp 5–6)

Given the subsequent short-lived and unsuccessful nature of monetarism as policy in practice in the two chief OECD laboratory sites (the UK and US) this was remarkable prescience on Johnson's part, and needs also to be seen in the context of an economist who was developing his own 'monetarist' approach, albeit with the focus the balance of payments and world inflationary pressures (Frenkel and Johnson 1976). What, however, is so far missing from his and our account is that unlike the Keynesian challenge in the 1930s, this counter-revolution was much more broadly based and potentially more significant in its policy implications. This might be thought a very strong claim, but is actually a logical extension of our earlier arguments that Keynes's ambitions were extremely moderate and that, as it transpired, Keynesianism was implemented in Britain to a limited degree. By contrast, the agenda of those seeking to dissolve the consensus was exceedingly ambitious, with implications as strongly political, if typically unpublicised, as economic. Thus, for its critics, the professional face of the NCM – faith in the neo-classical theory of price, the conviction that markets are allocatively superior to all alternatives and fundamental scepticism about all activities of government – is a mask behind which the long-standing Chicago view of the world operates in Pavlovian fashion, blind to the distributional justice of capitalism and imperiously colonising all other fields of social enquiry for which rational calculation models, deriving from *Homo economicus*, might have possible application.

Bringing microeconomics in from the cold

A quarter century ago, or so it was claimed by those developing the NCM, 'mainstream economists were in the position of teaching on Tuesday and Thursday a macroeconomics that was fundamentally incompatible with the microeconomics taught on Monday and Wednesday' (cited – with reservations – by Solow 1997, p. 51). While, as we shall see, the original NCM failed empirically and has since been superseded by devotees of real business cycles, concerns about the dissonance between micro- and macroeconomics are no longer widely expressed; indeed, many now express the hope that they are finally reunified 'after decades of division under opposing ideological regimes' (Maloney 1992, p. vii). This attempted reconciliation has a number of important characteristics.

First, and foremost, the market stands pre-eminent, with greed, rationality and equilibrium the trinity of maintained canonical hypotheses uniting almost all branches of economics (Solow 1997; Kreps 1997, p. 59). Secondly, with victory for the market as politics, and as analytical apparatus, has come two changes of emphasis:

- the one that cardinal choice is neither between perfect markets and imperfect governments, nor between imperfect markets and perfect government, but between imperfect markets and imperfect governments in various combinations which cannot be derived *a priori*; [25] and
- the other, which was additionally conditioned by the post-OPEC I productivity slowdown and the subsequent explosion of welfare budgets, that the traditional treatment of the equity-efficiency trade-off (for example, Okun 1975) was not sufficiently attuned to the hard realities that a preference for equity was now impacting adversely on the quantity of funds for investment and on work incentives. Accordingly, there needed to be much more rigour in selecting policy instruments if lessened

---

[25] Wolf (1993); see also Solow (1980) on the conflicting pressures – 'scientific' and otherwise – economists confronted in judging between market failure and market efficiency.

inequality was to be obtained through non-market processes. In short, much of the social market intervention, which had been the mainstay of government growth during the golden age, would have to be reassessed.

Thirdly, although the micro-macro divide is now less of an organising framework than it used to be in teaching and almost meaningless in research terms, the case can be put that microeconomics is no longer the poor relation of macroeconomics. Indeed, in a world where governments profess more restricted macroeconomic capabilities, either through learning-by-doing or as the consequence of globalization, and the emphasis is upon supply-side measures, it could be said that the principal action is at the microeconomic level anyway. Certainly, we detect a new self-confidence amongst microeconomists, one reflected in publication trends and in the transformation of the teaching of this branch of economics.

Pick up any microeconomic text directed at more advanced undergraduates and the transformation of the analytical apparatus now employed is striking:[26] in optimisation theory, in the economics of uncertainty, in the application of game theory, principal-agent theory and transaction costs theory and, in possibly one of the most fruitful of all intellectual exports from the natural sciences, chaos theory.[27] In a recent survey Kreps (1997, p. 69) has argued that the whole body of economics has been enriched by 'the vocabulary and grammatical form of information economics and noncooperative game theory', and that from this richer understanding of individuals and groups has come a widening of the scope and policy relevance of economics once more. There have been many processes at work here. Some have involved partial rediscoveries (the revival of Austrian approaches, especially in respect of entrepreneurship and process competition); fads and fashions have been more evident than ever (especially in game theory); and, serving as a counterpoise to the renaissance of economists as practical problem-solvers, there has been a quantum leap in the use of mathematics, and thus in the potential barriers to entry for the non-professional economist.

For the profession's mainstream the current position now approaches one in which most economists, operating in most fields, draw upon a common core of microeconomic theory. Such an outcome was, of course, part of Marshall's mission, and arguably the years in which such a situation did not

[26] For example, Kreps (1990) or Varian (1996) which are used in my own institution.
[27] Unsurprisingly, such has been the Balkanisation of economics it would now be anachronistic to even attempt a full survey of the research frontiers of microeconomics. Feiwel (1985) and Hey (1989) are two of the last explicitly to do so, while volume 2 of the most recent RES surveys (Oswald 1991b) covers some topics. For a useful popular exposition of the pertinence of chaos theory for economics and management, see Parker and Stacey (1994).

pertain owed much to the interpretation of the (Keynesian) macroeconomics of one of his favoured pupils. Certainly, as we have seen, there were important centres of resistance to the NCS during the golden age. Whilst much of this resistance has endured, it is now much more the case that the British economics profession no longer lags its American counterpart in subscribing to a largely common core of micro- and macroeconomic theory, a result we ascribe to the latest phase in the diffusion of American-style professional economics and one which, incidentally, served to legitimate think-tanks such as the IEA whose championing of markets and microeconomics was now vindicated by economics as well as by politics.

Resolving the crisis?

In retrospect, it is now striking how quickly the profession's mood turned. If we take as our barometer of that mood AEA-RES presidential addresses, the doom and gloom so evident in the early 1970s quite quickly evaporated. In Britain, we first detect this turnaround in MacDougall (1974), and, in the US, in Heller's (1975) celebration of 'What's right with economics', and especially what's right with economics as a guide to public policy. While it is noteworthy that both these economists had enjoyed professional careers divided between academe and government service as senior policy advisers, we can observe this process amongst the slightly younger and more heavyweight theoreticians at approximately the same time.

Thus, for example, Modigliani (b. 1918), used his AEA address to argue for a new synthesis: that while monetarism had made valuable contributions in highlighting the weakness of Keynesian theory *vis-à-vis* the inherent stability of the private sector, the importance of money and the very real possibility that stabilization policies were often in practice destabilizing, there was no longer a crisis now that it was recognised that the post-OPEC I stagflation was due to the novelty of a supply shock which initially economists had not been able to accommodate within an adequate conceptual framework (1977). Unsurprisingly, and almost concurrently, Kaldor (1976, pp. 215–16) was maintaining in his RES address that it was novel circumstances which presented the greatest intellectual challenge, and that in that quest for understanding it would be 'futile to look for a single basic cause ... and ... wrong to suppose that the great acceleration of inflation of the last few years was the inevitable sequel of the long creeping inflation which preceded it.' While his successor, Arthur Brown (1979, p. 11), ascribed a greater role to historical processes, including *inter alia* the dysfunctional bargain struck between capital and labour, he also argued that 'there is no royal road ... out of our particular problem, and that our chief danger is of throwing away much hard-earned experience in the false hope that the untried is better than what we have tried, but found difficult.' The coincidence of this address with the efforts of the Callaghan government to enforce a final phase IV in its incomes policy, and what then transpired when that collapsed, makes Brown's message particularly prophetic.

Bringing on parade the Keynesian old guard to demonstrate that talk of a theoretical crisis was now overdone should convince no one, and certainly did not convince all of the old guard themselves, not least Meade who, after receiving his Nobel prize in 1977, embarked upon a quest to salvage the possibility of full employment, one which would occupy him to the end of his life (Meade 1978; 1982; 1995 and Vines *et al.* 1983). Nonetheless, in Britain subsequent events, more particularly the credit squeeze of 1979–81 and the revelation that it was in practice impossible to control the money stock with any precision, then made life rather easier for the old guard. Of course, British Keynesianism had always been more hardline, more extreme, than that prevalent in the US, this deriving from characteristics which Cobham (1984, pp. 160–1) decomposes as:

1. A long tradition of deep scepticism about the stability of the demand for money function, this mainly an oral tradition but having some documentary authority in Kahn and Kaldor's evidence before the Radcliffe committee on the working of the monetary system.[28]
2. Doubts over the existence of any transmission mechanism from the money stock to nominal income, this usually argued – *pace* the OERG studies of business behaviour of the 1930s – in terms of the interest inelasticity of investment demand.
3. A presumption 'that the growth of the money supply was endogenous to economic activity and inflation, an argument which came to be put more strongly (e.g. Kaldor, 1970[a]) as empirical evidence supporting the stability of the demand for money began to accumulate.'
4. A predisposition to explain the breakdown of the Phillips curve in terms of cost-push factors.
5. A majority that favoured fixed over floating exchange rates, because of the volatility of foreign exchange markets, and who were elasticity pessimists.

Rival camps: British monetarists and Keynesians

In Britain the early monetarists, if such a term can usefully be applied to British academic economists, were undoubtedly intellectual dependents of

---

[28] Reprinted in HMSO (1960, pp. 138–53). The list of those individuals giving evidence – all contained in this third volume – reads like a who's who of British economics at this time.

Friedman.[29] However, from the early 1970s a more independent British strand of monetary research was developing at the LSE (the International Monetary Economics Research Programme of Johnson and Swoboda), at Manchester (the Inflation Workshop of Laidler and Parkin) and, somewhat later, at the City University (with Griffiths and Wood in the Centre for Banking and International Finance). These research programmes were more appropriate to British conditions as an open economy with, by US standards, a comparatively large public sector and a central bank under greater political control.[30] From these centres, and from other professional and semi-professional activities such as W. Greenwell & Co.'s influential *Monetary Bulletin* (first issued in 1972 and edited by Gordon Pepper) and **Congdon's** writings from his new base in the stockbroker's L. Messel & Co. (after having worked with Peter Jay on the economics staff of *The Times*),[31] there emerged a set of characteristics of British monetarism which corresponded, albeit in mirror image, to those of the Keynesians. Whilst initially themselves hardline – stability in the demand for money function and exogeneity to the money supply, making control of its growth possible if the authorities had the courage to do so – as the proselytising of the 1970s turned into the monetary experiment (and disappointment) of the early 1980s there was in practice a convergence between the two positions in Britain (Cobham 1984), one which moved in parallel with, and possibly in advance of, the revival of Keynesianism in north America.[32]

Here, as in the early 1930s, when politicians unduly magnified the differences between economists over the efficacy of proto-Keynesian and existing classical solutions for unemployment, we can observe a dissonance between the convergence of economics as theory and its divergence in face of the monetarist juggernaut as political economy. In respect of the former, the circumstances appeared propitious for the British Keynesians, so much so that being 'unreconstructed' – a term that entered the economist's lexicon in the late 1970s – was worn as a badge of pride by many.[33] They could, for example, claim that Friedman and his disciples were pursuing a counter-revolution based on an entirely false reading of Keynes, who had never

---

[29] For example, see the contribution to Harris and Sewill (1975) by the former, the General Director of the IEA, who makes no reference to academic work in support of his monetarist approach which does not derive from Friedman and/or IEA publications.

[30] See Congdon (1989) on the differences between US and UK monetarism, and T. Mayer's (1990, esp. ch. 2 and 4) historical exploration of the fundamental monetarist propositions.

[31] Other City channels for monetarist propagation are detailed in Hall (1992b, p. 102).

[32] For example, Howitt (1986a; b), Blinder (1988), Mankiw (1988) and Thirlwall (1993).

[33] See, for example, Thirlwall's (1997) autobiographical essay on the British resistance to monetarism marks I and II. In his opposition to the macroeconomics of the Thatcherite project he was one of the most prolific and effective of British economists, in particular in his various pieces for the bank reviews (for example, Thirlwall 1981; 1982) and in his widely cited NIESR pamphlet on deindustrialisation (Bazen and Thirlwall 1989).

denied a role for money or that the supply-side mattered. Those Keynesians enjoying a sound knowledge of the history of economic thought, and an understanding of how Samuelson's version of the *General theory* came to the fore in the NCS, might then be deemed to have won the theoretical battle, albeit that in declaring their purity from the taint of bastardised Keynesianism this was at the expense of losing the subsequent policy war.

Subsequent developments are perhaps best understood in terms of a heightening of the tension between economic theory and economic experience to a point which had not been seen since the 1930s, when mass unemployment became the searing influence for the younger generation of economists. This time, of course, the searing influence was inflation and we hypothesise that individual economists' unemployment-inflation trade-offs were to an important extent age-related, and indeed have continued to be so. Thus many of the Keynesian old guard still hold that the costs of securing lower inflation – higher unemployment and output foregone – have been socially unwarranted and theoretically ill-founded when we still lack robust empirical evidence that low or zero inflation is a precondition for high and stable economic growth,[34] while the youngest generation are not much interested in OPEC I and the inflation of the 1970s.[35] Thus as inflation abated in the 1980s, and as a trend of gently rising prices became established in the 1990s, to the point that some now talk seriously of the death of inflation (Bootle 1996), we would expect the forces propelling convergence in mainstream theory to be strengthened. Nonetheless, the point remains that part of the theoretical significance of inflation in the 1970s was that, with economists unable to explain it as a purely economic phenomenon, the profession's competence was then challenged by political scientists and sociologists ever ready to model inflation on a scale running from Marxism through extreme neo-liberalism.[36]

A further consequence was that those economists who nonetheless tried to confine their exposition to economic factors, and who took to the public stage to do so, not infrequently found themselves embroiled in debates which were quasi-theological in intensity and about as useful, easy prey to the mass media who saw a good story in the titanic battle of Keynesians versus monetarists, of Cambridge versus Chicago (more rarely Vienna) and, at its

[34] For example, Reddaway (1997) and, in this tradition, Stanners (1993).

[35] While Ricketts and Shoesmith's (1990, figure 10) survey of 1,000 British economists' opinion found the age variable to be statistically insignificant for the question 'The prime concern of macro economic policy should be to eliminate inflation,' this survey was conducted in 1989 and was thus some 15–20 years after inflation became the central policy issue (see also p. 63).

[36] See Hirsch and Goldthorpe (1978) for a rare attempt to bring together social scientists of many disciplines and persuasions to provide a political economy of inflation. This was sponsored by the SSRC and centred on the Money Study Group (Johnson's brainchild and the intellectual powerhouse of academic monetarist thinking) and International Political Economy Group.

height, Cambridge versus Cambridge. This reached its apogee during 1976–7 when the correspondence columns of *The Times* became the forum for rival bands of economists to press their claims and counter-claims, many of whom in their desire to persuade resorted to reporting the detail of their econometric modelling of the money transmission mechanism. Needless to say the parading of R^2 values and the significance or otherwise of coefficients, not to mention talk of the infamous 'lag', that of inflation on money supply growth, may have brought economists to public attention but, as we detailed in our treatment of an earlier episode, the tariff reform controversy in 1903, it did not do much for their professional standing. On a lighter note, that it was all good fun was not lost upon at least one group of economics graduate students who inspired by the quality of public debate compiled a checklist of good econometric practice (here reproduced in Table 7.3) which displayed both cynicism about their elders and a prescience about the 'con' in econometrics identified by Hendry, Leamer, Sims and others, and so well-expressed in Orcutt's quip that 'Doing econometrics is like trying to learn the laws of electricity by playing the radio'.[37]

What was achieved?

In Britain, trial by correspondence column was but a brief episode, and as we now pass into the 1980s and through the short-lived monetarist policy experiment the mainstream of the profession, as with their colleagues in the US, returned to something resembling disciplinary agreement on fundamentals. In particular, macroeconomics returned to trying to explain the failure of the labour market to clear, in other words 'to give new theoretical answers to the old Keynesian question' (Blaug 1997a, p. 651); indeed, so strong was the resurgence of Keynesian economics by the latter 1980s that some spoke of Keynesianism as a permanent revolution (Shaw 1988). To examine how this came about, what was then achieved and what now pertains, we first ask of the protagonists, both monetarists Mark I and II, what they consider to be their achievements.

A natural starting point is with Friedman, but here unfortunately we are handicapped somewhat by his reticence of recent years, particularly with respect to theoretical issues.[38] However, his disappointment with the

---

[37] Cited in Leamer (1983, p. 31). This checklist was on the notice board of the common room used by Cambridge economics graduate students and younger staff by the time I began my Ph.D. there in October 1976. No author was identified and no one of my acquaintance professed to have any knowledge of the document's provenance but we all agreed that it represented the contemporary mood. The value of the Durbin-Watson statistic in point 6 of the checklist suggests that the author may not have excelled at econometrics.

[38] Although see his long entry on the quantity theory for the *New Palgrave* (1987) where one can detect a receptiveness to his monetary policy critics.

Table 7.3   How to slay 'em with science

---

1. After scrupulous scrutiny of the work of others, or by taking a pure punt, form a firm view about what causes the thing you're interested in to do what it does.
2. Collect the data, remembering never to quote the sources, because someone might check it; and making sure to smooth out all the erratic fluctuations and discernible movements that might prove a nuisance to the hypothesis.
3. Pile in observations on every conceivable variable that might help the explanation.
4. Express your hypothesis as a linear function of the variables you have assembled. This has the advantage that it can be estimated easily, you don't have to go up any nasty gradients, and the typist can put it all on the one line. And, after all, the world behaves almost linearly anyway, doesn't it?
5. Hand the job over to some bright guy who understands the computer and then cross your fingers. Instruct him to run every possible combination and transformation of the variables, and to perform every conceivable fancy trick in the package.
6. Scan the myriad of results, for there's bound to be some specification that confirms your hypothesis. Pull it out, remembering to say that the coefficients are of the 'right' sign and that all the coefficients suggested by competing hypotheses are of the 'wrong' sign. This makes the description purely scientific. If the time-series regressions are handled properly, both the R^2 and the Durbin Watson statistic are close to one. Having satisfied yourself of success, there is little need to report what these things are. And don't report the method of estimation used either. After all, that was someone else's concern; and although it was probably OLS, better let the reader think it was something fancier.
7. At this stage, your hypothesis is clearly right, and you should have no hesitation whatever in moving to your policy implications. Obviously the government or industry or unions are doing it all wrong, and you can now feel elated by the strength and importance of your discovery.
8. There is just one final point - it still might not have worked out. But all is not lost - add more variables, shift discretely the data period, throw in dummy variables, artificial variables, instrumental variables and if necessary even false variables. And then if everything to that stage has failed miserably for you, a drastic step will have to be taken - you'll just have to start cheating.

Thatcher and Reagan monetary policy experiments is a matter of public record, as is his pessimism about the short-term prospects for escaping from *The tyranny of the status quo*, this pithy phrase the title of another popular book written jointly with his wife (1984). Indeed, at mid-decade, and in a specifically British context, he concluded 'It is hard not to be discouraged by the [sic] miniscule changes in policy that have so far been produced by a major change in public opinion' (Friedman 1986, p. 139). Nonetheless, in the long-run, he remained optimistic about the public's ability to tame big government, even, in a neat twist, invoking Keynes's *General theory* and the argument of the eventual triumph of ideas over vested interests. Whether his enduring impact on economics will lie more with his neo-liberalism than with his monetary economics, and thus with the long-term implications of government than with stabilisation policies, remains an open question.

The chief exponent of monetarism Mark II has been more forthcoming about theory and controversy. Thus in his Yrjö Jahnsson lectures, Lucas (1987) was typically upbeat that the NCM had led to the reinvigoration of economics by making it genuinely dynamic, such that:

It is now entirely routine to analyze economic decision-making as operating through time in a complex, probabilistic environment, trading in a rich array of contingent-claim securities, and to study agents situated in economics with a wide variety of possible technologies, information structures, and stochastic disturbances. While Keynes and the other founders of what we now call macroeconomics were obliged to rely on Marshallian ingenuity to tease some useful dynamics out of purely static theory, the modern theorist is much better equipped to state *exactly* the problem he wants to study and then to study it.

This new ability to incorporate dynamic and probabilistic elements into economic theory, at the same level of rigor on which we study the problem of a single decision-maker making a one-time choice at given prices, has already had a deep, permanent influence on virtually every branch of applied economics. What people refer to as the 'rational expectations revolution' in macroeconomics is mainly the manifestation, in one field of application, of a development that is affecting *all* fields of application.   (pp. 2–3)

For Lucas and those others proclaiming the revolutionary status of the NCM it is important that these developments were marketed by their progenitors neither as a reaction to Keynes and Keynesianism, nor as a palace revolution amongst the monetarists, but as a reassertion both of classical macroeconomic theory and of the research programme of business cycle theoreticians of a pre-Keynesian generation (most notably Wesley Mitchell and Hayek). Lucas's purpose, therefore, was to transform economics so that it:

reincorporated aggregative problems such as inflation and the business cycle within the general framework of 'microeconomic' theory . . . [such that] If these developments succeed, the term 'macroeconomic' will simply disappear from use and the modifier 'micro' will become superfluous. We will simply speak, as did Smith, Ricardo, Marshall and Walras, of *economic theory*.   (pp. 108–9)

The realism and potential realisation of such grand ambitions needs, however, to be seen in the context of the doubts entertained by economic methodologists about the rhetoric of Lucas and his followers, in particular Klamer's (1984) strongly argued case that:

1. The initial success of the NCM owed less to its objective scientific merits than to the vast array and sophistication of rhetorical devices used to persuade others of their point of view; and
2. When subjected to close scrutiny, this aided by a series of candid interviews of Lucas and other leading new classical economists, the real theoretical core of the NCM is seen to be neither rational expectations nor even substantive issues such as the policy-ineffectiveness proposition but matters of style and rigour. Thus Klamer (1984, pp. 239–40) made much of Sargent's admission, that 'the key thing about the new classical

economics is the commitment to some notion of general equilibrium and some notion of optimizing, strategic behaviour,' and used this to argue that the core of the NCM was restricted to using a 'a new language that dictate[d] precision of expression, in strict adherence to the principles of microeconomics.' Moreover, and as developed by Howitt (1986b, p. 634), the NCM was able with 'amazing speed to displace Keynesian economics as the main source of new ideas in macro' because this rhetoric 'permitted young people the thrill of exhibiting their raw technical skills, uninhibited by the literary conventions that clothe their elders' flabby equipment.'

For these critics of the NCM, therefore, rational expectations and the assumption of market-clearing prices, two central strands in the neo-classical postulates of maximising behaviour, are being deployed less as theoretical advances than as intellectual straitjackets, as rhetoric designed not to expand the conversation between economists but to construct barriers between economists. In summing up all of the interviews he conducted with leading economists, Klamer (1984, p. 243) wrote:

> If the conversations make one thing clear, it is that no model, no single argument, is unexceptional and problem-free. When economists talk about their models, they do not pretend that the model in its current state gives *the* answer to the pressing economic questions of our time. They speculate about its possibilities and indicate which direction they want to follow in the future. In other words, they embark on a 'journey of discovery', or they involve themselves in a research program. New classical economists believe in the potential of combining rationality and the equilibrium postulates and are in the process of exploring the implications of this judgement. Neo-Keynesians and monetarists consider the new classical results unconvincing, and follow different research programs. The Keynesians admit their program has problems, but continue to believe in its possibilities. Accordingly, theoretical arguments are uncertain and their acceptability relies on a judgement which is made plausible with a variety of other arguments.

As we have seen, for many leading economists such an approach is not science and they will have no truck with such arguments, and even amongst those that do admit that methodology matters there is considerable debate about economics as conversation, especially in its more post-modern manifestation where the role of community and the context-dependency of knowledge (so-called reflexivity) have been elevated to the status of a fixation which threatens the possibility of any truth or progress in economics.[39] This as may be, both monetarism and the NCM are additionally

---

[39] Cf. the approaches of Solow and McCloskey in Klamer *et al.* (1988, esp. pp. 32–3); also McCloskey's (1994) and Backhouse's (1997b) most recent work on methodology.

vulnerable, or so different critics maintain, to the empirical scrutiny to which they have been subjected over the last quarter century. Here also, of course, we have a problem but from a different strand of economic methodologists, principally, but not exclusively, those favourably disposed towards Popper, Lakatos and falsification.[40] They are highly critical of the weak propensity of contemporary economists to commit to the empirical progress of the subject, and, *pace* McCloskey and the rhetoric project, continue to uphold economics as prescriptive, as depending *ex post facto* on empirical data. For them, and for many others, including some who profess to be uninterested in methodology, monetarism and the NCM have endured longer than they might have if there had not been a dissonance between what economists preach about the importance of submitting theories to empirical testing and what they practise, a dissonance explicable, Blaug (1992a, pp. 243–4) maintains, in terms of a professional incentive structure whereby:[41]

> Analytical elegance, economy of theoretical means, and the widest possible scope obtained by ever more heroic simplification have been too often prized above predictability and significance for policy questions.

Contemporary economics: convergence or tower of Babel?

In Blaug's (1992a, p. 192) judgement there has been 'an unending series of efforts to produce a decisive empirical test of the Keynesian and monetarist view of the causes of economic fluctuations', and whilst no decisive test has resulted monetarism's poor track record, especially with respect to the quantity theory and the monetary growth rule, did eventually result in a considerable narrowing of the gap between economists (pp. 193, 199).

Cobham's (1984) specifically British study documents this convergence, although it also predates the Lawson boom which breathed temporary new life into the monetarist cause.[42] Blaug is equally emphatic about the weaknesses of the NCM, emphasising its poor empirical track record, and that of its derivative (real business cycle theories), rather than following the easier route of highlighting the implausibility of much of the NCM's operational optimising assumptions. Nonetheless, by self-designation as well as by the denigration of others, monetarists and new classical economists endure in significant numbers, and this notwithstanding that, whatever their

---

[40] Most visibly Blaug (1992a), more restrictedly, Backhouse (1997b); see also Caldwell's (1982) rejection of falsification.

[41] See also Leontief (1971), one of the doom and gloom AEA presidential addresses which specifically identified weak professional incentives for economists to undertake empirical work as contributing to the crisis of economics.

[42] For example, Pepper (1990) and Congdon (1992); and, on this latter episode, Cobham (1997).

status as 'good' economists, their economics sits uneasily with the realities of contemporary politics: strangely, voters do not like to be told that mass unemployment is because of economic agents' misperceptions, while politicians feel distinctly queasy when informed that business cycles are optimal responses to uncertainty in circumstances of technical change, and where any attempt at stabilisation policy is welfare-reducing! For economists and policy-makers confronting rival theories there is a further difficulty: economists can't agree on the main empirical relations, with econometric results swinging one way and then the other, thereby exhibiting a sort of life cycle which Goldfarb (1997) labels emerging recalcitrant results (for example, from the NCM, first Barro's 1978 demonstration that only unanticipated changes in money affect output; then later, Mishkin's 1982 contrary result that anticipated changes can also have such effects).

Where does this leave us? In the view of another of the early challengers to the NCS, Edmund Phelps (1990), a quarter century of theoretical dispute had undoubtedly resulted in the creation once more of distinctive schools of economics – seven in all for macroeconomics – but that such diversity is evidence of the discipline's good health rather than of continuing crisis through a fracturing of the (Lakatosian hard) core. His seven are extant schools, with some not making it to the grand list, including the post-Keynesians. Those that do include the Keynesians, the monetarists and the NCM (now enumerated as two schools, as new classical and as neo-neo-classical real business cycle theorists), with additionally the new Keynesians, supply-side macroeconomists and, finally, a structuralist school of non-monetary theories of unemployment fluctuations.

Phelps's organising principle, that these are schools because of their distinctive approaches to price-wage setting and the role of expectations, would be objectionable to some, and particularly to post-Keynesians who are excluded from his version of modern macroeconomics. In the British context, where there has been a long-standing opposition to the mainstream and the NCS (now institutionalised for economists in the *Cambridge Journal of Economics* and the *Review of Political Economy* and, for a broader dissenting social science constituency, in *Economy and Society* and *Capital & Class*), this omission is particularly important. Whilst the post-Keynesians might have been dismissed by the mainstream as lacking sufficient theoretical coherence to be credible,[43] and famously so in Solow's remark that they are 'not so much a school of thought, more a state of mind' (cited in Chick 1995, p. 20), the survival of a strong dissenting tradition to the mainstream must raise uncomfortable questions for that mainstream, or would do if economists thought more about how they appraise economic

---

[43]   Cf. Walters and Young (1997) and Chick (1995); see also Dow (1997).

theories. This, of course, brings us back to notions of truth and progress in economics and about how ignoring methodology does not invalidate its significance for how economists practise their craft.[44]

For those not of the mainstream, far from economics having recovered from the crisis of the 1970s it now resembles a kind of tower of Babel where, with the global explosion in the numbers of economists and their publications, there are multiple schools, a plurality of objectives and approaches and a myriad of conceptions of the relationship between economic theory and reality (Beaud and Dostaler 1997, ch. 9). A brief focus on the production side of the economics literature supports the notion of overload in the discipline. Using Borchardt's iron law of important articles, which postulates that the number of scientifically significant papers increases to the extent of the square root of the total number of papers published, we here highlight Holub *et al.* (1991) which validates this hypothesis against the growth theory literature since Harrod (1939), and provides the depressing statistic that an economist, intending only to keep abreast of growth theory and reading just 12 papers per year in this field, will find at least one important article only every third to fifth year.

In short, a century ago when Marshall published his *Principles* he could read everything significant in economics, and absolutely everything if language had been no barrier, whereas today an economist can read but a minute fraction of the output of a small part (by field) of the whole. Twenty years ago, when the stock of economics literature was expanding at about 5 per cent per year (comprising some 800 books and 5,000 papers, to a total stock of approximately 100,000 papers),[45] George Stigler observed (1978, p. 185) 'It is a literature that no one person could possibly read – the limits imposed by sanity are stricter than those imposed by time'. More detailed research reveals an even bleaker situation: that between 1965–9 the leading 41 economics journals published 7,939 papers, representing 86,578 pages of scholarly literature, whereas the comparable figures for 1985–9 are 9,790 papers and 130,182 pages (Laband and Piette 1994, p. 643). Figures for the 1990s are not yet available, but they would not offer any relief to the overloaded economist, and this data relates only to the leading journals. With a total stock of economics journal literature now exceeding 250,000 papers (equivalent to say 3.5 million pages), and with current annual additions of say 13,000 papers (another 180,000 pages or so) being published in some 200 economics journals worldwide, there is now enormous congestion on the supply side of the economics literature and this

---

[44] Themes recently explored in Backhouse (1997b).
[45] Stigler (1978) did not give a stock figure, but the estimate of 5 per cent growth (a doubling every fourteen years) probably derives from Lovell (1973) whose estimates we have extrapolated. See also Stigler *et al.* (1995), p. 335 for more recent production trends.

without considering books which, admittedly, are of diminishing professional importance for economists.

At one level such overload is undoubtedly indicative of economists being the victims of their own intellectual success. But, whilst informational overload is the experience of all contemporary academics, whatever their discipline, the current production levels of the journal literature, and the flood of new journals since the early 1970s, might also indicate that one way in which economists responded to the crisis of Keynesian economics and the breakdown of the NCS was to develop alternative publication outlets to the general-interest journals, the *JPE*, *AER*, *QJE* and *EJ*. Clearly, with the proliferation of academic economists more publication capacity was required to service the enlarged supply of potential papers, and indeed the general-interest journals did expand in response. Thus this year's *EJ* has six issues and some 1,900 pages, whereas a quarter century earlier (1972) it was in four issues amounting to 1,380 pages (and, a further quarter century back, the 1947 journal was a slender 560 pages over four issues). Even so this greater capacity was inadequate in face of the surge in potential papers of quality. In such circumstances, and given the very strict hierarchy of journal prestige and the strong professional discipline enforcing research skill standardisation in economics (Whitley 1991), economists who wanted to explore new areas felt compelled to establish their own journals. As the ever-growing listings in the *JEL* attest, the discipline now has not only an enormous range of fields but numerous journals within fields, testimony to new interdisciplinary combinations and the strong presence of an ever more mathematical and formalistic economics.

This latter characteristic of models without data was, of course, what motivated Leontief's complaint (pp. 19–21), one which is still made although the empirical evidence is that total output is now less dominated by such work (Fels 1992). Even so, there is clear evidence that empirical work is less well-represented in the top tier general-interest journals (the Diamond core),[46] this indicative of its lower professional prestige.[47] If the crisis of the 1970s was a spur to create new journals and fields of enquiry, and from this has come about the explosion in the volume and variety of the literature, it is also the case that overload sustains those who have always been dissidents from the mainstream (the radical economists and the post-Keynesians) and has nurtured whole new groups emerging with environmental, gender, developmental and other agendas associated with the New Age. At the onset of the crisis a few economists were reasonably optimistic about the future for the discipline, but notably they were mainly those with experience as

---

[46]   A reference to Diamond's (1989) influential – but controversial (Burton and Phimister 1995) – listing of 27 journals as the 'core' of modern economics publishing. This includes the *EJ*.

[47]   Figlio (1994); see also T. Mayer (1993).

business economists and/or as students of the history of economic thought. Thus, and representing this first group, as well as being a long-standing Council member of the RES, Rybczynski (1972, p. 125) felt certain that since the crisis could be attributed to the hitherto 'inadequate effort[s] made by the profession to ... learn more about and understand the functioning of industry, commerce and finance and the changes which are taking place in these fields', the remedy was fairly apparent. Similarly, Eric Roll (1971, p. 44), whose expertise spanned academe, Whitehall and the City, thought monetarism would soon peter out and that providing the ideological extremes could be avoided, and that economists were chastened by experience into acknowledging their limitations in policy, the discipline would emerge strengthened from this experience.

What began with attempts to provide more realistic microeconomic foundations to macroeconomic theory and policy, and then evolved through experiments in monetary fundamentalism which, in their failure, led inevitably to some sort of neo-Keynesian regime of coarse as against fine tuning in the 1990s, would appear therefore wholly in keeping with the best professional expectations of economics' ability to grow out of crisis. But what also occurred was an opportunity, intellectual space so-to-speak, for pre-existing dissident traditions to grow to maturity and even newer critiques to flourish: a sort of economics of separate spheres in which some economists, academic and semi-professional, inhabit worlds of theorising and practice whilst maintaining only the most tenuous of links to the mainstream and their institutions of journals, conferences and other networks. Thus, for example, in the US there is a long-standing 'institutional' critique of both the neo-classical mainstream and Marxist or radical political economy alternative. This takes as its inspiration the founding fathers of American institutional economics (Veblen, J.M. Clark, Commons and Mitchell); it has its own Association for Evolutionary Economics (AFEE), producing since 1967 its own journal, the *Journal of Economic Issues*, one which unsurprisingly is not in the Diamond core; and, although somewhat of a loose union, the modern American institutionalists can field a very public figure (Galbraith) and some very senior and hitherto respectable professional economists (Boulding). That which broadly unites them also provides a longevity to the historical tension between Marshall and the German Historical School:

1. Concern about the mathematical and formalistic nature of contemporary neo-classical theory;
2. A demand that economics become a genuine inter-disciplinary subject rather than a coloniser of the other social sciences; and
3. Dissatisfaction with the casual empiricism of the mainstream.

The existence of separate spheres in American economics has been explored in Copp's (1992) study of the membership characteristics of a sample of the AEA with that of the Union for Radical Political Economists (URPE, publisher of the *Review of Radical Political Economy*) and, at the opposite end of the political spectrum, the AFEE. Unsurprisingly, what emerges are very different cultural belief systems and thus attitudes towards economic theory and policy, although there is also common ground in that many URPE and AFEE members also belong to the AEA, indicative that the pattern of professional separation is more pronounced at the level of theory than it is at the level of organisation. There is also an overlap in attendance at the annual AEA conference, but since this operates as the academic labour market for economists too much should not be read into this characteristic. Even so, at both ends of the political-philosophical spectrum, marked divergence in theory and value systems coincides with some organisational integration. In short, there are shared values in being an economist which, after a century of professionalisation, do transcend the long-standing divergences in theory and politics. Thus American institutionalists do not on the whole publish in the *AER*, while the current *JEL* subject classification scheme for publications does not even distinguish a radical/Marxist literature. Accordingly, as in Marshall's time, when economists like Hobson were excluded (or excluded themselves) from the mainstream, there are parallel conversations which do not have to communicate outside of their separate spheres. However, as we now turn to consider the most recent stage of professionalisation in Britain, it may well be that the onward march of American style economics in British universities is acting to undermine such diversity.

7.4 FROM ROBBINS TO DEARING: BRITISH ECONOMICS AND MASS HIGHER EDUCATION

The recent history of the British economics profession is one of great extremes and apparent contradictions. Internally, it can be represented as a success story, at least for those approving of the continued Americanisation of the mainstream: of greater professionalisation through the adoption of American-style graduate education programmes and stronger incentives on academics to publish; of an apparent healing of the theoretical breaches of the 1970s; of the development of new fields and the colonisation of others in the social sciences; and of the expansion of the profession both within the universities (staff, postgraduates and undergraduates) and outside in terms of the strong demand for economists by private businesses and government.

When viewed in wider public context, however, an external, outsider's history would be far less upbeat: of endemic crisis in the universities, deriving from a catch-up exercise from an elite to a mass higher education system in the context of a remorseless squeeze on resources; of the collapse of the intellectual authority of the academic, in particular those claiming scientific expertise; and of a trend towards the proletarianisation of hitherto secure middle-class professionals by an emerging 'Super class',[48] this at the very time when, ostensibly, wealth-creation is ever more dependent upon the knowledge base provided by academics. This generalised decline of donnish dominion, Halsey's (1992) aptly entitled update of his earlier report on British universities, was of especial significance for economists who, with the Thatcherite project, had not only to endure the appearance of eviction from the policy community but also found that the traditional complaint levelled against them, that in their pursuit of rigour they had abandoned real world relevance, was now buttressed by the accusation made against all academics (but with economists apparently particularly vulnerable) that the pursuit of scholarship was resulting in academics neglecting their core mission, that of teaching undergraduates and of providing them with relevant skills for the graduate labour market.[49]

The Americanisation of British economics

We begin with this internal version, and with a progress report on the Americanisation of British economics. In chapter 6 we noted that the first professional indications of concern about Americanisation began in the 1980s as part of a wider debate over the future of distinctive European economics traditions, ones which hitherto had contained the pressures for internationalisation/Americanisation through:

- the dominance of the European states in controlling and financing higher education institutions; and
- the maintenance – mainly through language barriers – of separate national professions and academic literatures.

The most vocal defenders of European-style economics have been Frey and Eichenberger (1993), with their defence founded on good economic

---

[48] Perkin (1996, p. 189) and Adonis and Pollard (1997).
[49] This functionalist view of higher education is particularly evident in the questionnaire responses on employment skills made by employers to the Dearing committee (HMSO 1997, app. 4), and it is noteworthy that while the committee's report endorsed the earlier Robbins 'liberal' principles on the purpose of a higher education it made much more of the employment skills component and in efforts to raise the status of university teaching vis-à-vis research (HMSO 1997, paras 5.7–5.10, ch. 8). The Towse-Blaug (1988; 1990) report also contains much on the inadequacies of British economics education.

principles: namely, that economists, as market agents, respond to incentives and operate with a welfare function which might be specified as combining the maximisation of the present value of their lifetime income with certain culturally-determined non-pecuniary goals. The American academic market is large and competitive, whereas European markets are segmented and thin. This conditions the propensity of an economist to invest in acquiring local knowledge of markets and institutions, resulting in Americans maximising journal publications and Europeans seeking a more balanced portfolio which includes participation in local and national affairs. Similarly, American economists concentrate on postgraduate teaching, while Europeans are largely preoccupied with undergraduate education. These differences between the US and European markets are then invoked to explain why European research is more policy-oriented, less prone to fads and, until very recently, quiet uninterested in league tables.[50] Indeed, in Frey and Eichenberger's (1993, p. 192) formulation, European-style economics is superior because 'economic knowledge is transformed more effectively into policy' in Europe than in the US, with the American preoccupation with league tables of publications indicative of an economics poor in health, reduced to a scientific game focusing on abstract issues, defined within the profession itself, rather with the direct improvement of human welfare through economists' contributions to policy.

Having made a powerful case that American-style economics wrongly specifies publications as outputs rather than as inputs in the economists' production function, where outputs are properly measured by the effects of economists on policy, they then proceed to acknowledge that the moves towards European integration and the internationalisation (Americanisation) of economics were now threatening the incentives which underpinned these distinctive European production functions. From this follows the pessimistic conclusion that 'the future of economics as a relevant social science seems rather gloomy'. In our earlier discussion we concurred with Baumol's (1995) judgement that Britain could be represented in this process as a mid-Atlantic hybrid, having by the eve of OPEC I a sort of dual economy, in part differentiated by institutions (with the LSE, Warwick and Essex the most highly Americanised) but also within institutions, some of which (notably Oxbridge) retained a traditional core and developing elements of the new professionalism, and that the delay in developing mass (American-style) higher education allowed British economists to maintain a world presence which would not otherwise have been possible.

---

[50] See Backhouse et al. (1997) for the US profession's love affair with league tables and the beginnings of an audit culture in Britain.

British academic economists and postgraduate economics education

Subsequent trends in the characteristics of academic staff and of their publications confirms the further growth of American-style economics in Britain. Thus, as Backhouse (1997a; 1999a; *et al.* 1997) shows, the proportion of staff with doctorates rose steadily from the 1970s onwards, reaching approximately 80 per cent for the LSE by 1995, 65 per cent for a sample of 'new' (pre-1992) universities (Essex and Warwick), 50 per cent for Oxbridge and 45 per cent for a sample of 'redbrick' universities (Birmingham, Bristol and Manchester). Of significance also, in some of these departments (most notably the LSE) there were leading figures from North America together with a substantial proportion of British staff who had earned their doctorates from a US Ph.D. programme, this indicative perhaps of the extent to which the younger generation came to appreciate that in many fields the discipline's agenda was now being set outside of Britain, that reputational leadership now lay with America and that being 'badged' with a US doctorate would improve one's standing in the academic labour market. Indeed, in the US, where the production of economics Ph.D.s is heavily concentrated upon leading institutions, with a four firm concentration ratio of 0.17 in 1990–1 (Harvard, Minnesota, Michigan and Stanford), where one's Ph.D. was minted has an enormous effect upon subsequent employment and publishing prospects.[51]

Americanisation has not yet proceeded to the point that possession of a Ph.D. – or of the state of near grace known as ABD, all but dissertation – is the precondition for securing an academic job, but the last quarter century, and in particular the last decade, has seen much greater emphasis on postgraduate education in Britain. In part, this was driven by financial need: on the one hand, cost pressures, with the ESRC blacklisting institutions which had low completion rates for Ph.D.s; and, on the other, revenue maximisation through attracting more graduate students to taught masters degrees, increasingly a prior requirement for admission to a Ph.D. programme, and the Ph.D. itself. As Table 7.4 shows the output of economics Ph.D.s by British universities nearly doubled between the early 1970s and the mid-1990s, but the total output of those with research degrees increased much less as students substituted the Ph.D. for the lower level research degree. It is noteworthy also that there was no change in the rankings of the top three producers and little change in the four firm concentration ratio, which incidentally suggests an even greater emphasis on institutional reputation than in the US where the four firm ratio is less than half the British figure and has halved over the postwar period (Barber

---

[51] Barber (1997b, table 3); see also Whitley (1984, p. 248) and Coats (1992b).

Table 7.4 Top ten British universities by production of economics research degrees, 3-year averages, 1970s and 1990s

| | 1971/2-early 1974/5: | | | | | 1993/4-early 1996/7: | | | | |
| | No. of degrees awarded | | Total | Share of total degrees (%) | Rank[c] | No. of degrees awarded | | Total | Share of total degrees (%) | Rank[c] |
	Masters[a]	Ph.D.[b]				Masters[a]	Ph.D.[b]			
Oxford	4	14	19	11.6	1	2	24	26	12.4	1
LSE	2	15	17	10.6	2	0	19	19	9.1	2
Cambridge	0	13	14	8.5	3	0	17	17	8.2	3
Strathclyde	8	3	11	6.8	4	1	5	5	2.5	12
Exeter	5	3	8	5.2	5	0	2	2	0.9	30
Sussex	0	6	6	3.9	6	1	2	2	1.1	28
York	3	4	6	3.9	7	1	7	8	3.8	6
Manchester	2	4	6	3.7	8	0	14	14	6.5	4
Leeds	3	3	6	3.7	9	0	5	5	2.2	13
Birmingham	0	5	5	2.9	10	0	0	1	0.3	54
Warwick	1	1	2	1.2	26	0	9	9	4.3	5
QMW	0	1	1	0.4	37=	0	6	6	2.8	8
LBS	0	0	0	0.2	40=	0	8	8	3.6	7
Loughborough	0	0	0	0.0	50=	1	5	6	2.8	9
UCL	0	0	0	0.0	50=	0	5	6	2.7	10
UK Total Degrees	53	108	161	100.0		12	200	212	100.0	
4 firm concentration ratio	0.26	0.43	0.37			0.17	0.37	0.36		
20 firm concentration ratio	0.78	0.85	0.82			0.61	0.76	0.75		

Notes:

[a] Includes so-called batchelor research degrees (B.Litt/B.Phil.).

[b] For 1990s includes DBAs.

[c] Determined by a score of 2 for a masters and three for a doctorate, these being proxies for the years of human capital acquired on the basis of the usual full-time study for these degrees.

Sources: Annual returns: *EJ*, 1973, pp. 239–45; 1974, pp. 183–8; 1975, pp. 178–85; 1995, pp. 834–44; 1996, pp. 804–13; 1997, pp. 918–29.

1997b, tables 1–3). There was, however, a change in the 20 firm concentration ratio and as is evident there was movement in and out of this league table, and in particular some of the currently highest ranking departments as measured by the RAE (see Table 6.2) are conspicuous by their absence in the early 1970s (most notably UCL and Warwick), with some also minority producers in both periods. Thus, although some of these departments were important in developing a more American-style economics, the building up of a strong postgraduate community has not proved necessary for a successful research culture for this discipline, while the departments that are significant producers of postgraduate economists do not necessarily coincide with those universities having the largest postgraduate communities across all disciplines.[52] This weak relationship at the institutional level between postgraduate education in economics and national/international eminence in economics research suggests that British economics is still different from US economics in some important respects.

Both financial needs also served the discipline's professional agenda, with master's coursework the vehicle for a more technical economics, increasing mathematical and econometric. This, of course, connects to concerns about what sort of economist results from postgraduate training (Coats 1984, pp. 27–9). These originate in the 1970s, and unsurprisingly with Johnson (1973a; 1974a; c; 1977b) a major participant in the debate over whether the narrowing of training in the Ph.D. programme, whereby mathematics and econometrics crowded-out economic history, the history of economic thought and, for most, any consideration of contemporary relevance, was impeding the scientific progress of the discipline and resulting in Ph.D. theses which were often trivial, the mere display of technical prowess.[53] His concerns, of course, stretched beyond graduate education to the state of theory, but in the following it is clear that he considered tenured economists to be setting their students a bad example:

> an increasing proportion of the profession has been concerned with acquiring expert knowledge about a small piece of a system assumed to be in broad outline a well-known and going concern (and therefore is inevitably driven back into *ceteris paribus* assumptions), and that specialist theories have to demonstrate their worth either by the armoured might of capture of exceptional cases and the clever trapping of tiny specimens of behavior hitherto considered too unnourishing or sufficiently pestilential to be worth worrying about, or else by the use of ever more elegant mathematics to arrive at ever more economical statements of general equilibrium results.   (Johnson 1974c, p. 323)

---

[52] Cf. Table 7.4 and the recent Harris report (HEFCE 1996, app. D).
[53] Johnson had, of course, been instrumental in raising the technical level of LSE postgraduate education. The fate of economic history in Britain is detailed in Coleman (1987) and, more optimistically, in Crafts (1991); that of the history of economic thought in Cardoso (1995).

Johnson's complaint that economics' incentive structures had resulted in a situation in which 'the value of a theoretical contribution [to a journal] is closely inversely correlated with its accessibility to the applied economist, and by the fact that ... professional status can be more quickly and lastingly established by a theoretical article than by a piece of applied research' was not lost on the next generation of economists. Indeed, the widely-publicised survey by Colander and Klamer (1987) found that 68 per cent of the profession's future leaders considered a thorough knowledge of the economy quite unimportant for career success, as against 57 per cent who thought excellence in mathematics very important. In the US this prompted a new round of disciplinary introspection, including an AEA commission on graduate education which was much discussed but then resulted in no structural changes of any significance.[54] There has been no equivalent investigation in Britain, and while concerns about the undergraduate curriculum surface from time to time they also have received nothing like the attention that the AEA devotes to these aspects of the profession.

Undergraduate economics education

It is routine for the AEA annual meeting to include a session of three or four papers on teaching issues,[55] and there is now quite a substantial literature on this area (*JEL* classification A2), albeit one dominated by American economists.[56] By contrast, interest by the RES has been sporadic and much lower in profile, a reflection undoubtedly of the very different roles that the two bodies have played since their inception in representing the profession to the outside world and in providing services to the membership. While there have been occasional sessions on economics education at the annual RES conference (which, of course, were taken over from the AUTE), none of these papers have been published in the *EJ*, and such discussions that have taken place within the profession have largely been confined to the twice-annual meetings of CHUDE, the Conference of Heads of University Departments of Economics. Reports of these meetings are circulated, and often reported in the *RES Newsletter*,[57] but it is significant that this body

---

[54] Hansen (1991); Krueger *et al.* (1991) and Kasper *et al.* (1991).

[55] For example, Becker and Watts (1996), a report on a recent large-scale survey of undergraduate teachers of economics.

[56] For example, the *JEL* A2 listing records 66 items in its four issues published between September 1996 and June 1997, none of which relates to British conditions or was produced by a British economist. A majority of the items listed were published in the *Journal of Economic Education*, which is largely the preserve of American writers.

[57] For example, issue 83 (October 1993), pp. 4–5 provided a summary of a CHUDE survey of teaching loads across the binary divide, thereby revealing that economists in pre-1992 universities enjoyed not only more favourable SSRs but annual teaching obligations of approximately half those of their colleagues in 1992 universities.

(initially run in parallel with a separate committee representing the polytechnic sector until 1992 when integration was made in name, if not in funding, across all of higher education) was established in 1987 in the wake of the first RAE and as another round of cuts in public funding of universities were in prospect, and thus its concerns are more to do with defending economics in an age of financial stringency and more exacting audit of its activities.

Until very recently the formal evaluation of teaching techniques and curriculum design excited little interest in British universities, economics departments included, but this is now changing as an audit culture is established in higher education, as it is has been elsewhere in the public sector (Power 1997, pp. 98–104). While economics departments in England and Wales have not yet been assessed under the Higher Education Funding Council's (HEFC) rolling programme of teaching quality assessments, and may indeed – post-Dearing and with the new government – not be so under the present arrangements, such issues have acquired a much higher profile because in economics more than in the other social sciences there have been great efforts made to promote information technology in the curriculum (Hobbs and Judge 1992). These efforts are associated principally with the work done by CTI Economics (the Computer Teaching Initiative Centre for Economics, established in 1986) and the CALECO Research Group (Computer Assisted Learning in Higher Education Economics, Portsmouth, 1987),[58] from which – through another government educational technology initiative, the TLTP – came the award-winning WINECON software.

Some 80 per cent of British HEIs now have a site licence for WINECON, while it is also being marketed abroad, including the US for which a customised version has been prepared. WINECON is most-decidedly not the sort of drill-and-practice software that is common in the US, and which is the subject of much derision by British academics who hitherto have been able to resist the financial and pedagogic logic of mass higher education. Indeed, with its use of multimedia and its approach to economic principles, WINECON is evidence of a synergy between economists and software engineers which has given Britain something of a comparative advantage in economics software, this also evident in econometrics packages with Hendry's PCGIVE and MICROFIT from the Persaran brothers. All of these developments provide considerable grounds for optimism that, at least at the undergraduate level, economics is being taught with greater sensitivity to real world issues and with more hands-on-practice with real data. The transformation in textbooks, where there are now many British competitors

---

[58] These bodies issue a twice-yearly journal, *Computers in Higher Education Economics Review* (*CHEER*), which is edited by Guy Judge, the *EJ*'s software review editor. They also operate a web site: <**http://www.ilrt.bristol.ac.uk/citecon/**>

to the American staple products, and even the beginnings of a pan-European market, is also encouraging and further evidence of the limits to Americanisation. That the works of such well-established traditional sub-degree textbook writers as Stanlake and Harvey have endured, and have such significant overseas sales, is also a testimony to the ability of British economists to service a global market.

Economics' research culture and the mathematisation project

For the median British academic economist, however, research is of very much more personal and professional significance than undergraduate teaching, and in this respect the British profession is undoubtedly a mid-Atlantic hybrid. Unlike continental Europe, where Frey and Eichenberger (1993, p. 190) identify strong incentives for academics to concentrate their resources on good undergraduate instruction, in Britain, and particularly in the pre-1992 universities, promotion and professional standing are almost exclusively research-dependent, although for Oxbridge-London academics the nurturing of contacts with past high-flying students is a traditional means of entryism into the wider policy community. While the Dearing committee has made recommendations directed at raising the status of teaching *vis-à-vis* research, without pecuniary incentives these are unlikely to influence the behaviour of the median academic. The fact that those departments rated as excellent in the HEFC's teaching quality audit subsequently received no additional resources in reward, and that economics departments were some of the first to use postgraduate students for a very high proportion of initial undergraduate teaching in research universities, suggests that this mid-Atlantic status will endure for some time yet.

This brings us to research and publications and thus to complete our reporting of DISMAL, our database of *EJ* papers and their authors. Beginning with publications we first observe in Table 7.5 how the *EJ*, in common with other general-interest and almost all specialist journals, became increasingly mathematical in style,[59] a representative agent in what Debreu (1991, pp. 1, 4) has described as a 'phase of intensive mathematisation that profoundly transformed our profession.' For its supporters, this mathematisation of economics underlay the increasing axiomatisation of economic theory, provided logical tools of such rigour that economists need no longer suffer physics envy and, *pace* the Leontief complaint, now made economists members of 'the group of applied mathematicians, whose values [they] espouse'. Indeed, for McCloskey and others, what is striking over the longer-run is not just the increased 'use of

---

[59] See Grubel and Boland (1986), Debreu (1986) and Weintraub and Mirowski (1994).

Table 7.5 Economic Journal: *classification of papers by rhetoric type (%
of total) and mode (Y=presence of style; N=absence), 1970,
1980 and 1990*

Year	Alg-ebra	Cal-culus	Dia-grams	Econo-metrics	Stat-istics	Wholly literary
1970						
Total (%)	66.7	33.3	26.7	11.1	35.6	11.1
Mode (15.6%)	Y	Y	N	N	N	
1980						
Total (%)	80.0	72.0	26.0	40.0	32.0	18.0
Mode (20.0%)	Y	Y	N	N	N	
1990						
Total (%)	72.6	68.2	20.9	47.3	52.8	17.6
Mode (30.8%)	Y	Y	N	Y	Y	

Note: Component parts do not sum to 100 per cent because each *EJ* paper can exhibit more than one style.

mathematics, but the way standards have changed [such that] ... economists have adopted the values of the maths department' (Backhouse 1997b, p. 22). In 1970 the modal *EJ* paper already incorporated algebra and calculus; by 1990 its rhetoric extended to econometrics and statistics. In 1970 66.7 per cent of papers made use of algebra and/or calculus, whereas by 1990 it was 72.6 per cent, with the most pronounced shift occurring in the 1970s rather than the 1980s.

The formidable mathematics now required to comprehend the average *EJ* paper, let alone have a paper accepted for publication in the *EJ*, places a considerable barrier to entry upon the non-academic economist who wants to eavesdrop on the professionals' conversation (Szenberg 1990). For the opponents of mathematisation this project is both undesirable and evidence of a retreat of economics from its core purpose into mere games-playing and mathematical aesthetics (for example, Hutchison 1993, p. 296). In this respect Britain is undoubtedly closer to America than to continental European economics, for in the latter the propensity to mathematisation in national conversations has been constrained intellectually, and in terms of teaching, by the maintenance of connections with the law, political science and business (Coats 1997a; 1999). This difference also extends to the other methodological characteristic of the transformation of modern economics: that of econometrics which, as is also clear from Table 7.5, has become much more prevalent in the *EJ* as elsewhere. Here also, of course, there have been complaints from the founding fathers like Frisch, who condemned much current work as 'playometrics' (Hutchison 1977a, p. 71), through to now leading-edge econometric practitioners, that econometrics is something of a failed project, and certainly that part of Leontief's complaint, that reputations in economics are highest in those branches not subject to empirical uncertainties, still prevails (Earl 1983; Whitley 1984, p. 154).

At the core of the mathematisation project has been general equilibrium analysis, and it is this which has attracted the most ire and some of the staunchest defences of contemporary mainstream economics, most notably in Britain from Hahn. The charge sheet is long and involved: that general equilibrium models produce abstract theory which is empirically empty and that typically these are based on unrealistic assumptions, ones even inconsistent with the known facts of the real world. Arguably, it is now game theory which is the mainstay of this project, but for its detractors the methodological effect upon economics and the possibility of truth and progress is comparable (Backhouse 1997b, pp. 22–3).

The consequences of this project are evident in terms of American-style fad and fashion in techniques and in the subjects economist select for study. Figure 7.1, which completes our enumeration of *EJ* papers by *JEL* one-digit classification, shows continued variability in topics but no discernible overall trend. At the three-digit level, however, we can detect continuity in the clustering of papers in the 022 (microeconomic theory) and 023 (macroeconomic theory) classes, together with continued interest in a long-standing British topic (431, balance of payments), and a certain topicality in the number of papers in the 052 (in effect, now transitional economics) and 824 (labour market studies) classes. These last two classes of papers certainly invalidate the gross charge that formalism has resulted in contemporary economists being not much interested in current and real-world concerns, although it should be noted that for the *EJ* what we are observing is the policy forum section introduced in 1990, one of the innovations which derive from Hahn's reforming period as RES president between 1986–9.

The structure of production of economic knowledge

Turning now to the profession when viewed at the institutional level we first observe that the Oxbridge, and in particular Cambridge, dominance of the *EJ* has ended. Secondly, and contrary to the internationalisation of economics, the *EJ* has actually the appearance of being a more British journal than at any time since the 1950s, with over 60 per cent of authors in 1990 claiming a UK institutional affiliation. This is not an aberrant result produced by DISMAL being a one in ten sample. Rather, it is probably the

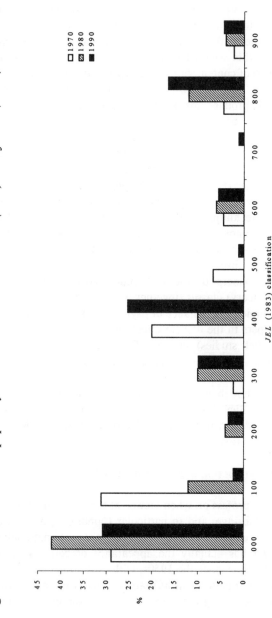

Figure 7.1 Economic Journal: *papers by Journal of Economic Literature (1983) classification, 1970, 1980 and 1990*

Note: JEL (1983) classification: **000** General Economics; Theory; History; Systems; **100** Economic Growth; Development; Planning; Fluctuations; **200** Quantitative Economic Methods and Data; **300** Domestic Monetary and Fiscal Theory and Institutions; **400** International Economics; **500** Administration; Business Finance; Marketing; Accounting; **600** Industrial Organisation; Technological Change; Industry Studies; **700** Agriculture; Natural Resources; **800** Manpower; Labour; Population; **900** Welfare Programmes; Consumer Economics; Urban and Regional Economics

consequence of three developments: first, the *EJ's* declining world status, one which particularly affects the publication strategies of US economists; secondly, the pressures generated by the RAEs on non-Oxbridge British economists to publish within the Diamond core; and thirdly, an important recent trend in economics towards group research resulting in multiple authorship and the reporting of multiple institutional affiliations of which some are cross-national. In 1950 two out of the forty three papers published were joint-authored; in 1970 it was eight out of forty four; and in 1990 it was forty two out of ninety one (some 46 per cent), with no less than nine papers having three authors.[60] Of this 1990 cohort some 16 per cent of authors reported more than one affiliation, with some reporting as many as three: typically a university together with a NGO, such as the World Bank, or a research agency, this latter group being one or more of the following – an independent body, such as the National Institute or the Institute for Fiscal Studies (IFS), a specialist unit within a university department, such as Cambridge's DAE or the LSE's Centre for Economic Performance, and/or research networks like the CEPR.

These developments indicate a structural shift in the production of economic knowledge, with these new institutions also noteworthy as evidence of how many economists responded to the crisis of the 1970s by developing more policy-oriented research bodies. Of these, the foremost is now the IFS which has developed an enviable reputation amongst practising economists, informed commentators and policy-makers for combining the production and dissemination of applied research of the highest professional standard and topicality to the widest possible policy constituency. Inspired initially by a desire to improve the quality of public debate about the public finances, the IFS was established in 1969 by amongst others Dick Taverne (1984), a former Treasury minister in the second Wilson government. It first came to prominence with its sponsorship of the Meade report on taxation (IFS 1978), and the year after it launched its journal, *Fiscal Studies*, which has since taken a very broad interpretation of its topic: from the economics of training and savings behaviour, through privatisation and regulation, to tax law, tax incidence, the benefits system and public expenditure control. Above all, during the long years of Conservative rule, the IFS kept in public view the issue of the distributional consequences of the Thatcherite project, often to the extreme discomfort of ministers (as, for example, in the widely discussed paper by Jenkins and Cowell 1994 which revived Pen's striking visual image of the income distribution as a parade of a few giants and many, many dwarfs). In its latest annual report its current director,[61] Andrew

---

[60] See Chung *et al.* (1993, pp. 40–1) on multiple authorship as a research strategy for economists within the context of an investigation of the most prolific authors in world economics.
[61] *IFS annual report, 1996–97*, p. 17.

Dilnot, records that his staff made 123 radio broadcasts and 81 television appearances and that their press cuttings file of the mentions of IFS research runs to 562 items. Dilnot is too modest for he made most of those public appearances, and indeed he and the IFS have over the last fifteen years or so done much through their straightforward presentation of the facts, and of the hard choices that must be made by politicians, and therefore by voters, to repair the damage done by the monetarists-Keynesians debate to the public's perception of economists. The contrast with the other, more frequent, television image of economics and economists – that of loud, brash, sharp-suited City dealing-room types whose propensity for instant comment has done so much to generate a public perception of capitalism's casino nature – could not be more striking.

The development of agencies like the IFS is further testimony to a new stage of professionalisation, as is, for example, the creation of research centres, such as Warwick's Macroeconomic Modelling Bureau, which was established by the ESRC in 1983 (director Kenneth Wallis), and the LSE's Centre for Economic Performance, another ESRC funded project which, under Richard Layard's direction, is charged with studying the reasons for economic success amongst firms and nations. Another notable British located, but pan-European, development is the CEPR which was established in 1983 to 'promote independent, objective analysis and public discussion of open economies and relations among them' (director Richard Portes). This has since grown into a major network of 300 or so European and US economists working on a wide variety of projects, many of which have attracted ESRC, EU and other funding, and which produces approximately 250 discussion papers per year and the journal *Economic Policy: A European Forum* to provide 'timely and authoritative analyses of the choices which confront policy-makers.' This, as with the IFS, has sought corporate contributions as well as public funding, and accordingly maintains a pluralist and non-partisan approach to policy-making in the tradition pioneered by the Brookings Institution. Its journal is, if anything, even more topical than *Fiscal Studies* with, for example, the most recent issue to hand containing a cross-country paper on public finance solutions to the European unemployment problem (Sørensen 1997), a topic dear to the heart of Maastricht convergence criteria minded policy-makers. Another notable British publishing development has been the *Oxford Review of Economic Policy* which quickly established a reputation for high-quality topical applied analysis which emphasises, in a largely non-technical style, how developments in economic theory can be applied to illuminate policy problems.

The growth of economic consultancies (such as Congdon's Lombard Street Research and **Bill Robinson's** London Economics) and independent forecasters (from the large and long-established Henley Centre for Economic Forecasting through to the smaller and more recent Oxford Economic Forecasting and Cambridge Econometrics) are also indicative of a new stage of professionalisation. The now general practice in most large-scale industrial-financial-commercial concerns of employing economists as economists is a further manifestation of the profession's maturity, as indeed is the number of economists now sustaining hybrid careers straddling academe, business consultancy and government service, with **Gavyn Davies** and Bill Robinson two notable contemporary examples.[62]

The subjugation of British universities

Whilst there is undoubtedly a process of catch-up on American economics evident in many of these developments, there is also a difference of enormous significance: the subjugation of Britain's universities to the will of the state acting as monopsonist, this part of a broader process – a counterpoise to the privatisations of the Thatcherite project – in which leading institutions are subjected to a more active and impositional style of government (Richardson 1994; Gamble 1994b). Hitherto, state control of the universities had been light (Shattock 1994), with generous, arm's-length Treasury control through the University Grants Committee, a body dominated by academics and operating with the freedom provided by quinquennial budgets, sustainable so long as the higher education system served but an elite and that this elite were not compelled to question whether the universities provided value for money and met national policy objectives.

Unsurprisingly, all of this changed in the 1970s: first, following the 1960s expansion, substantial public funds were now entailed, and yet the universities were still manifestly serving an elite (albeit that the age participation rate had doubled from 7.2 to 14.2 per cent between 1962/3–72/3 – Halsey 1992, table 4.3); secondly, with the universities having taken advantage of the Robbins report they had inadvertently tied themselves to the politicians' agenda of raising economic growth through greater investment in human capital, such that the economic troubles of the 1970s then provided considerable scope for questioning both their achievements and influence; and with thirdly, student unrest and the New Right's targeting of criticism on the social sciences (later manifest in Keith Joseph's insistence that the SSRC become the ESRC) all completing the process of disillusionment with the traditional relations between state and academe. In short, as Sanderson (1991, p. 417) puts it, there was a slide from 'benign

---

[62] Evidence for these hybrid careers, of the growth of economic consultancies and of the demand for business economists is provided in the twenty fifth anniversary issue of the SBE's journal, *The Business Economist*, vol. 26 no. 3 (1995), esp. pp. 6–37.

indulgence to scepticism and [then] hostility.'

Beginning thus in the mid-1970s as financial stringency born of the general fiscal stress which followed OPEC I, and developing in the early 1980s as the new Conservative government subjected universities to even greater pressures on resources and a new culture of directing them on what to do and how to do it, the system was then transformed in the late 1980s by the decision to sanction but not to fund a mass higher education system. From this has followed *inter alia* the end of academic tenure; an end also to the binary divide between universities and polytechnics, such that there are now 115 university institutions; a developing culture of audit of all university activities, and particularly teaching quality and research output; and, of course, a huge explosion in student numbers. Indeed, the quantitative dimension is quite extraordinary when consideration is given to the very brief time over which there has been a transformation in the environment in which British academics now work.

In 1973/4 there were 244,000 undergraduates, of which about 5,100 were economics students variously defined;[63] by 1995/6 the numbers for the unified system had grown to a total undergraduate (full- and part-time) population of 1.35m, of which 16,460 were economics students.[64] With an age participation rate now approaching 35 per cent, as against under 20 per cent in 1989 when the decision was made to sanction a doubling of student numbers over the next quarter century (quickly raised in a 1991 white paper to a target participation rate of one third by 2000), Britain has in under a decade acquired a system which in terms of sheer numbers is mass higher education, but it is not a mass system in the US sense of mass access or indeed one that is underpinned by a viable mass funding structure.[65] Moreover, it is a system which sustains a number of fictions: most obviously, of the comparability and equality of degrees between institutions and over time; of the possibility, let alone desirability, that all institutions and thus all academics can be adequately funded from taxation to undertake research; and, above all, of an economic case for mass higher education when the quality problems associated with schools education have not been tackled.

Thus, if the situation has been transformed for students, so also has it been for staff. In the 1960s in the pre-1992 universities SSRs of well less than 10:1 generally prevailed, and rather greater in what are now 1992 universities. In 1972/3 the SSR for universities actually averages 8.0, rising very gently to 8.8 by 1979/80 and then more steeply to 10.2 in 1983/4 (Stewart 1989, p. 285). In 1995/6 the figure for the combined system was

[63] With perhaps another 1,000 economics students in the then polytechnics.
[64] With a further 5,860 economics postgraduates, divided between 1,940 taking research degrees and the remainder taught masters – HESA (1997, pp. 7, 59, 63, 67, 71).
[65] Walden (1996, ch. 9); Dolton *et al.* (1997) and Williams (1997).

17.5, and while this was subject to considerable institutional and subject variations the biggest gulf remained that between the pre-1992 and 1992 universities. The background to this has been a combination of a sixfold rise in the number of students since OPEC I and remorseless squeeze on resources, more particularly on the unit of resource per full time equivalent student through so-called efficiency savings. Thus between 1989/90 and 1996/7, during which the age participation rate doubled, there were efficiency savings of 40 per cent in real terms, this an acceleration of a trend which had actually been in place since quinquennial budgets were abandoned in 1975. Although long-run data are not available it is probable that in real terms the unit of resource is now 60–70 per cent lower than at the time of the Robbins report, and while this is manifest in pressure on libraries, buildings and equipment it is most obvious in terms of the deterioration in the wage-effort bargain for academics who now work some of the longest hours in the British economy and whose salaries,[66] being one of the few professions in the public sector not offered some degree of protection by a pay review body, have fallen massively behind groups hitherto considered comparators. Mass higher education was achieved by some reduction in public funding of student maintenance, some deterioration in the quality of the educational experience for students, but above all by academics delivering massive 'productivity' gains and foregoing lifetime income on a scale quite unprecedented in modern history.

Thus, as part of its campaign for resources, the academics' trade union, the Association of University Teachers (AUT), has made much of the fact that in 1981/2 the earnings (at current prices) of an MP at £13,950, a civil service principal at £13,191 and a lecturer on the top of their salary scale at £12,860 were all broadly comparable, whereas by 1994/5 (real rises in parentheses) the MP had advanced to £31,637 (16.5 per cent) and the civil servant to £31,507 (22.7 per cent) while the academic was on £25,735 (2.8 per cent), since which time MPs have, of course, voted themselves a significant rise to £43,000.[67] That MPs and civil servants, but not academics, have been permitted to share in the growth of the British economy is a matter of considerable significance, not to mention grief for those directly affected. Many commentators have referred to this, together with the casualisation of much of the academic labour force and other wage-effort bargain trends, as evidence of the proletarianisation of intellectual labour (Halsey 1992, p. 174), but what seems to have been missed by most

---

[66] See Court (1996) for an AUT survey of academics' time budgets which found that in 1994 the average hours worked in term-time were 54.8 as against – calculated on a different basis for the Robbins report – 40.5 in 1962. This result should be set against the 1994 whole-economy New Earnings Survey which found that for male non-manual workers the average was 38.9 hours.

[67] Data from AUT (1996, figure 2).

commentators – the AUT included – is that budget-makers were merely taking advantage of the known ethos of academics, which would be to try and protect students from the efficiency gains and to pursue scholarship at all cost, and that if they are prepared to do this with fewer resources in year t they will do it in year t+1, t+2 etc. with yet smaller budgets.

What of the implications for academic economics? Whilst it is the case that fewer graduates with first class degrees now consider an academic or indeed civil service career compared with the early postwar years (Hannah 1993, figure 9.1) there is no general shortage of candidates for academic posts, economics included. A 1991 CHUDE survey of recruitment found evidence on the demand side of considerable competition for academic economists, both by universities and other agencies, resulting in the prevalence of devices (additional pay and accelerated promotion) to attract and retain high-quality staff, while on the supply-side there was general agreement that 'the majority of applicants for most posts were of low calibre' as 'good British graduates were less and less inclined to pursue academic posts and those coming through the Ph.D. route were diminishing in number'.[68] This survey did not relate the experience of economics to other disciplines, and its findings present something of a contrast to the Towse-Blaug report on the overall market for economists, which controversially identified over-supply. None the less, the longer-term context and the probable future for academic economics is perhaps better indicated by the data reported in Table 7.6 for the median salaries of members of the SBE together with the first point on the salary scale for a lecturer in an old university and the professorial minimum salary point for that sector. In both cases these understate median initial and terminal career salaries, but only by 10 per cent or so, and the general impression is clear: that of a relative deterioration in university economist salaries beginning in the 1970s and accelerating from the late 1980s onwards as significant numbers of those in the private sector shared in the growing gap between professional-Super Class salaries and other non-manual workers' remuneration,[69] this gap also being evident in the public sector between those who managed to secure a pay review body (physicians, the police, nurses and school teachers) in the 1980s and those that did not (notably academics). Academic economists, in common with other social scientists (Rudd 1990), have long known that the private rate of return on their Ph.D.s was negative, but this has now acquired such a magnitude that, when taken in conjunction with the loss of status for academics and deteriorating working conditions relative to the opportunities

[68] *RES Newsletter*, no. 76 (January 1992), p. 5
[69] See Leyland (1997) for a survey of the employment characteristics of SBE members, of which the most significant group were in consultancy, media, research and information services (17 per cent) with education and academic research (13 per cent) the second most significant group.

Table 7.6   SBE survey of members' median salaries by sector and
            university comparators at current prices (£'000s), selected
            years, 1973–95

	1973	1980	1987	1995
A. SBE survey (median salaries):				
Banking	4.2	12.0	25.1	55.0
Consultancy	5.3	12.3	27.7	45.0
Private industry	4.9	12.7	24.9	45.0
Government (including universities)	5.9	10.6	19.4	34.8
B. Universities:				
Lecturer, first salary point	1.9	5.1	9.0	15.2
Professor, minimum	5.4	12.8	22.7	32.0

Sources: Milligan (1995, table 1); AUT (1996).

for research careers in business, it is difficult to avoid the conclusion that
were present trends to continue the academic world might very well become,
as the church has, a career attractive only to those with private means or a
devotion so strong as to massively override pecuniary disincentives.[70]

Research assessment

For the present the full implications of these trends have been somewhat
muted by, first, the system-wide 'waiting for Dearing', and then waiting for
government to do something sensible with Dearing (HMSO 1997); and,
second, the treadmill of university audit, especially the periodic RAEs. This
latter audit of so-called research productivity now preoccupies all in the
universities and, in the case of economics, has a particular significance as a
decisive factor in promoting the further Americanisation of the mainstream
in the principal research departments, now defined, of course, in terms of
their RAE rankings (Table 6.2). The RAE is another brilliant invention
which taps directly into the academic ethos and collective psychology, and
which, whilst deeply controversial, has nonetheless proved both compulsory
and compulsive, unlocking frenetic energies, if not perhaps lasting
creativity.[71] For academics as a whole, and for the institutions to which they

[70] Backhouse's (1997a, figures 5–6) comparison of UK-US academic salaries confirms this
      deterioration; see also Elliott and Duffus's (1996) survey of British public sector pay trends,
      from which it is evident how academics have been displaced from the top of the pay pyramid;
      and Keep and Sisson's (1992) exploration of the personnel implications of academics' treatment.
[71] See McNay's (1997) investigation of the impact of the 1992 exercise on institutional and
      individual behaviour.

belong, the RAEs have magnified the weaknesses, vacillations and divisions which allowed governments to target the universities in the first place, and they now provide the unedifying spectacle of hitherto rational, highly intelligent people competing for funds (the hallowed QR) in a negative sum game in which, first, they had to maximise output (the 1986 and, to a lesser extent, 1989 exercises) and, now, to maximise the quality of that output and the quantity of some input measures, most notably research grants.

The general arguments against the RAEs are many: from the diversion of energies brought about by audit, with consequent opportunity costs for teaching and indeed research; through accusations of the corruption of academic incentives structures, because of the inherent difficulties of peer group review and, in particular, of the problematic nature of quality scores for the humanities and social sciences; to resistance to contemporary higher education managerialism, based on performance indicators and hierarchical control, which has fast superseded collegiate control through peer groups vested with consent for their authority. But, whatever the cultural resistance, the financial pressures dictating selective funding are ineluctable, as consequently has been the quest to establish what Halsey (1992, p. 188) calls the 'geography of excellence': the raw material for league tables, long a feature of American university competition and increasingly prevalent in Britain. Moreover, although almost never admitted by academics in low ranking departments, the logic that with diminishing global resources there has to be some means of distinguishing between those departments that are excellent in research, and those which underperform in relation to the resources they have historically enjoyed, has become more widely accepted.[72]

The RAE remains acutely controversial in all disciplines, and were the Dearing committee's recommendations to be accepted (HMSO 1997) the next exercise could be very different, not least in offering hitherto low ranking departments a means of escape from the audit treadmill (which, given the distribution for economics in Table 6.2, would have significant effects for the discipline in 1992 universities). That the present Secretary of State for Education has, citing the experience of his undergraduate son, deep misgivings about academics so preoccupied with research as to see undergraduates as a chore and diversion, suggests that the RAE in its present form and the current balance between teaching and research will not endure. Arguably, however, academic economics has been permanently affected by the four RAEs already completed. The most developed critique has been made by Lee and Harley (1998a; b).[73] This builds upon the anxieties expressed by many during the session at the 1994 RES conference

---

[72] For example, O'Brien's (1994) balanced observations about the third, 1992 RAE.
[73] See also the anxieties expressed in mimeograph by Geof Hodgson and by Tony Culyer in the *RES Newsletter*, no. 87 (October 1994), pp. 16–17.

in which the chairman of the 1992 RAE economics panel (Tony Atkinson) answered questions from the floor about the panel's criteria, manner of operation and the effects that the RAE might be having on the discipline. The argument advanced is comprehensive and acutely controversial, as can be judged from the non-mainstream status of the journals which have accepted it for publication:

1. Economics, as a paradigm bound subject, split between two opposing but unequal camps (of a dominant neo-classical mainstream and of a number of heterodox dissenting traditions), presents particular problems under any system of assessment of publications and professional activities.
2. The four RAE economics panels have not been appointed in an open, democratic manner resulting in the under-representation of these heterodox traditions and some panel members who are neither eminent and/or currently active in research. Indeed, Lee and Harley argue, those administering the RES have used the opportunities offered by the RAEs to strengthen the RES as the professional body representing all economists and that, for university economists, authority is exercised by the unequal rewards granted to the mainstream, their publications and their institutions.
3. Whatever the intellectual shortcomings of bibliometric measures of research activity, and since Stigler's (1964) pioneering work citation counts have become more deeply established in economics than in other social sciences, it is maintained that their use in practice as the basis of informed peer review by the economics panels has worked to the detriment of the non-mainstream. The initial focus for complaint was the Diamond (1989) list of core (exclusively mainstream) journals which it was presumed had guided the panels in rating each economist's publications. This was subsequently denied and the focus then became the augmented Diamond list which had emerged from the work of Johnes and Sloane, commissioned by the RES and CHUDE and which still excluded non-mainstream journals, including the *Cambridge Journal of Economics*, the *Journal of Post-Keynesian Economics* (both journals for which citation counts are possible) and the *British Review of Economic Issues*, the in-house journal of those located in the 1992 universities. It is this they contend, combined with the reality that core journals are in effect closed referencing systems, reporting only work contained within the core and ignoring all else, which produced the subsequent clustering at RAE grades 2–3 of those departments with a significant number of publications in non-core journals.
4. In economics, as elsewhere, there have been accusations that the panels have suffered from moral hazard, such that, for example, the grades

awarded were not invariant to panel membership. Very wisely, Lee and
Harley do not pursue this argument for economics.
5. The RAEs have worked to privilege the journal paper above all other
types of publication and professional activity. The chairman of the 1996
panel of assessors (Hendry 1997) has certainly admitted that time
constraints 'meant that books could not be read in the detail and depth
given to papers', but strongly defended the position that common values
of excellence were demanded and applied to all activities which were
being audited. Whilst the Lee-Harley survey of British economists did not
ask about books in its questions about publishing strategies, the strong
responses on targeting papers on the core journals implies that this
medium is now more favoured with obvious implications for the writing
of textbooks, the production of innovative courseware and other activities.

Whether the Lee-Harley critique is accepted in whole or in part it is
undoubtedly the case that the mainstream have been strengthened in recent
years and will continue to prosper at the expense of heterodox traditions so
long as there is a RAE which is taken as justifying recruitment practices
which now frequently emphasise that only mainstream, highly research-
productive candidates need apply for lectureships. If, as is assumed but not
reported in Lee-Harley, the average age of the heterodox cohort is higher
than that of the mainstream, the passage of time will undoubtedly bring a
further erosion of the former in British economics. But, in a finding from the
1992 RAE, made available just before submissions for the 1996 exercise, it
is clear that the most important explanatory variable for an economics
department's ranking was academic journal articles per capita (Taylor and
Izadi 1996, p. 20). Thus whatever was said by the assessors, quantity as well
as assumed quality mattered, and this brings us back to the old problem of
differential resources across the old binary divide.[74] The Lee-Harley view is
vulnerable also with respect to the charges levelled against the RES and the
manner of appointment to the panels, for the heterodox are not well
represented anywhere in the peak associations of British academic life, while
in any case nominations to the panel came from CHUDE not the RES. The
panels merely reproduce the reality of the ESRC or the British Academy,
and the question has to be asked whether the triumph of the market might
pose a more serious threat to the continued health of heterodox traditions.
Moreover, given the dual funding structure for research in Britain, of QR
determined by the RAE and of open competition for grants from the research
councils, these dissenting economists are offered a future through access to

[74] Admittedly, the 1996 exercise was the first not to require that departments return full
quantitative details of all their research 'output', but even casual empiricism of the results
(Table 6.2) demonstrates the association between RAE ranking and department size.

the ESRC, but perhaps it would be argued that the cards are stacked against them here as well. That the Lee-Harvey critique also derives from the less well-funded side of the old binary divide, and that both authors are located in some of the highest ranking of the 1992 university departments, unfortunately also lessens its impact.

The frustrations of dissenting traditions so well-expressed in Lee and Harley need also to be seen in the broader context of the RAEs and financial stringency undermining the market conditions that Frey and Eichenberger identify as distinguishing European from American-style economics. This extends not only to the shift in emphasis from undergraduate to postgraduate education, from teaching to research, but to all of those extra-mural elements in economists' time budgets which were integral to Marshall's mission: consultancy, service on government committees, participation in local through national debate, etc. There is no hard, but much anecdotal, evidence that university economists have become more focused on research as against all other activities, but so far as extra-mural activities are concerned this may reflect a shift in demand rather than supply fundamentals. Thus, for example, the market for economic consultancy is now very much more competitive with academics no longer enjoying unchallenged claims to technical expertise, and indeed for many regulatory activities it is the lawyer who is emerging with the comparative advantage. Similarly, concerns that the RAE is undermining interdisciplinary work would not seem to be borne out by the profusion of new journals on the borders of traditionally distinct, separate fields, nor by the imperialism of *Homo economicus* elsewhere in the social sciences.

Still British after all this time

The question of whether 'there is now any economics outside and independent of the United States', one first posed by Portes (1987, p. 1330) before the culture of audit became firmly established, but now having added significance after a decade of RAEs, is easier to answer for Britain than for other European economics professions. While the RAE has undoubtedly accelerated the process of Americanisation, and it is significant that amongst the criteria by which departments are assessed for the highest grades (5* and 5) 'international excellence' is prominent, British economics none the less remains distinctive in a number of ways.

First, as cross-country surveys of economists' opinions attest (pp. 30–1), relative to American economists the British profession are more sceptical about the market as against government in the cardinal choice between allocative systems, and in the distributional justice of their outcomes; more Keynesian in their short-term policy prescriptions; and still more likely to support wage-price controls in an anti-inflationary policy menu (Ricketts and Shoesmith 1990; 1992). Secondly, survey evidence designed to test Grubel-Boland (1986) hypotheses about the efficient use of mathematics in economics find that British economists share with their American and Canadian peers the opinion 'that the proportion of journal space devoted to mathematical articles is excessive; that mathematical specialists can publish more easily than non-mathematical specialists; and can obtain jobs more easily, thereby implying a perception that mathematical competence ... is used as a screening device for entry into the profession' (Greenaway 1990, p. 1351). Thus American economics is not all it seems, or is made out to be by certain interest groups within the profession.

Thirdly, while British economists no longer feature in the global output and prestige league tables,[75] they have maintained eminence in certain fields which connect either to the distinctive normative positions that characterise the British profession or to policy problems that have preoccupied them. Thus, for example, British economists worked with a different market order and stylised facts (big government, open economy) than their American counterparts: slow growth kept distributional issues to the fore (Atkinson and Sen on inequality); big government raised challenges for public economics (with Atkinson, Coase, Mirrlees and Lipsey attaining distinction);[76] while the open economy, balance of payments and exchange rate problems all encouraged a strong presence in international economics. Finally, while there is perhaps now less of a self-conscious British tradition as reaction to American economics, and nothing comparable to the Cambridge capital controversy, there is a deep-seated scepticism about American educational techniques and the insularity of American economists. This, combined with the appeal of the European project, seems likely therefore to keep the British profession a mid-Atlantic hybrid.

7.5 ECONOMICS, ECONOMISTS, POLICY AND THE THATCHERITE PROJECT

The evolution of economic policy

Between 1972 and 1975–7 the number of newspaper articles on economic policy issues in the British broadsheets jumped from under 200 per annum to over 3,000 (Blyth 1997, p. 248 n. 32), thereby giving a prominence to the economy in British politics not attained hitherto and not since abated.

---

[75]   The latest (Chung *et al.* 1993) enumerates the most prolific authors in the top twenty economics journals between 1963–88 and records only one British economist, E.J. Mishan.
[76]   See, for example, Atkinson (1990) who considers public economics a European speciality.

Indeed, a leading American observer of modern British politics has described the 1970s as a period of 'revolution' in British economic policy, for in 1970 Britain was the 'paradigmatic case of ... the Keynesian era', whereas by the 1980s Britain was 'again leading but in a different direction' as 'monetarist modes of economic policy-making replaced their Keynesian antecedents' (Hall 1992b, p. 90). In fact, and more specifically, we should distinguish three phases in British economic policy since OPEC I:

*   1974–9: beginning as a combination of last-ditch Keynesianism with a twist of high corporatism and socialist rhetoric, and punctuated by the flirtation with New Cambridge economics and then the 1976 crisis which polarised debate within the Labour Party for a decade or more, producing on the one hand the left's Alternative Economic Strategy (AES) and on the other – via Callaghan's 'We used to think that you could spend your way out of recession ...' Labour Party conference speech – the antecedents of monetarism, this era then culminated in a period of macroeconomic pragmatism (of Keynesian objectives moderated by soothing proto-monetarist language) through to the 1979 election;[77]
*   1979–83: a short-lived era of monetary fundamentalism, of conscious and strident experimentation which introduced a new policy framework (the Medium Term Financial Strategy, MTFS) designed to engineer a monetary and fiscal disinflation, to downgrade expectations of government, by educating workers and managers about market disciplines through higher unemployment and bankruptcy (non-accommodation of wage and other cost-push pressures), and to prepare the ground for supply-side policies (privatisation, industrial relations and tax-benefit reforms) calculated to counter Britain's long-run decline.[78]
*   1983-present: a progressive retreat from monetarist rhetoric and monetary policy restraint resulting, after the Lawson boom and subsequent ERM debacle, in the current policy environment which might be described as combining pragmatic macroeconomic management, more coarse- than fine-tuning, of closet Keynesianism within a disciplinary framework provided or often not – by monetary policy credibility, with a continued commitment to longer-run supply-side reforms directed at securing stable output and employment growth without reawakening inflationary pressures.

[77] On 1976, see Burk and Cairncross (1992); on the AES and Labour Party, Wickham-Jones (1996); and, for a revisionist economic assessment of this phase, Artis and Cobham (1991).
[78] Although Howe was Chancellor during the experiment, Lawson's (1992) memoirs provide the most upbeat politicians' assessment. This can be usefully contrasted with Gilmour (1992), the most articulate of the 'wets'. Academic perspective and balance is provided by, on the one hand, Maynard (1988), an economist with Whitehall experience and broad sympathy for the project's aims, and on the other, much more critically on aims and outcomes, N.M. Healey (1993).

Policy learning

If the Keynesian policy era had, as **Minford** (1982) portrays it, been something of an age of innocence followed by a dialogue with the serpent (inflation) and a fall from grace, the years since can be characterised as the quest for wisdom through two processes. First, there was a belated recognition that policy-makers, and those seeking to influence them, needed to operate with richer models of policy learning through policy transfer and lesson-drawing. For economists this was initiated by Matthews (1968), who questioned the 'success' of Keynesianism in delivering full employment since the war, and was then developed by Coddington (1974), who asked more formally why economists and policy-makers tended only to address why a particular theory or policy failed, and rarely what the conditions for theoretical and policy success might be. Subsequently, the running has been made by political scientists and other public policy specialists, and as we saw in chapter 2 there are now many different theoretical approaches which seek to understand the policy-formulation-evaluation process. Of these, social learning (pp. 60–1) is currently in vogue (for example, Oliver's 1997 account of the rise and fall of monetarism), and particularly suitable for our purpose in its classification of learning as proceeding through three ascending stages: from shifts in policy instruments, through alterations to the hierarchy of instruments, to transformations of the policy regime itself.

Secondly, there was a reordering of the balance between demand and supply-side management, one which was as much political as economic. That economic growth was supply not demand constrained was a long-standing concern, but one given added force by the failure of the monetary policy experiment to provide an alternative demand route to a national economic renaissance. This can, of course, be variously explained: as evidence of Goodhart's (1984, p. 96) law, that 'any observed statistical regularity will tend to collapse once pressure is placed upon it for control purposes' (and hence the performance of M1 and £M3 once elevated into intermediate targets); or, as some maintain, because the Bank and the Treasury were hostile to monetarism and stymied the development of effective monetary control (N.M. Healey 1987, p. 480); or perhaps more routinely because, even in the best of policy worlds, Britain's financial system – of rapid financial innovation and globalisation – was quite simply unsuited to the experiment, thereby resulting in Lawson's decision to shift attention from interest rates to the exchange rate by shadowing the deutschmark. This would, of course, eventually precipitate his resignation and lead to the ill-fated ERM experiment under his next two successors, with in-between a recession which demonstrated that, whilst the electorate would now tolerate permanently higher unemployment, they were acutely sensitive to interest rates and, ultimately, intolerant of politicians who reneged on promises not to raise taxation and who were insensitive to middle-class concerns about economic insecurity.

The politics of the macroeconomic learning process follows on from the disappointments experienced by academic economists, other policy entrepreneurs and above all the politicians that the period of monetary fundamentalism provided no decisive empirical test of the competing claims of the rival camps of economists. As N.M. Healey (1987, p. 496) observes:

> Amongst supporters and opponents alike, there was a general air of expectancy and a feeling that this experience would answer important theoretical questions about the design of macroeconomic policy.
>
> In the event, the experiment has proved, or rather disproved, nothing. Monetarists have denied that an experiment ever took place; they have developed new theories to explain the behaviour of the income velocity of circulation or blamed external shocks for structural shifts in the demand for money and the natural rate of unemployment. Non-monetarists, in contrast, have interpreted the Government's failure to execute its strategy as planned as evidence that the money supply cannot be controlled; the gyrations in the velocity of circulation have been taken as further proof that the demand for money is inherently unstable and the coincidence of mass unemployment and stable inflation has been used to attack the natural rate hypothesis.
>
> In a political sense, the 1979–82 experiment certainly did provide test of practical monetarism and, if nothing else, it established that rigid monetary rules are not the panacea for inflation-free growth in a dynamic, open economy that the Government originally hoped. But in the economic sense of testing key macroeconomic theories, the experiment has merely served to illustrate once again the limitations of empiricism and to highlight the fact that the sources of controversy in economics runs far deeper than many of its practitioners would like to believe.

One manifestation of these disappointments was that after the 364 non-monetarist economists' letter in 1981, the entirely negative stance of which played straight into the hands of politicians itching for the academic economics establishment to validate the experiment by trumpeting their opposition to the Thatcherite project (pp. 34–5), progressively less and less is heard of monetarism as the emphasis shifts to other elements of the project, some equally experimental (privatisation, quasi-markets in the public sector), but where the results might be more visible, more empirically decisive and thus more effective in meeting the ultimate objectives of policy. This is not to say that macroeconomics and demand management have taken a back seat, nor that they are no longer controversial. Far from it. The allocative, distributional and stabilisation issues associated with the public sector remain at the forefront of political and technical economic debate, while EMU raises macroeconomic issues of enormous importance. But, after two very public macroeconomic gambles which went seriously awry, that of monetary fundamentalism in the early 1980s and the ERM in the early 1990s, all mainstream politicians have retreated from the sorts of political games that were typical of the Keynesian-Monetarists contest, with macroeconomic ambitions accordingly downgraded.

The search for policy credibility

Since September 1992, when sterling was forced to abandon the ERM, the emphasis has thus been on the long-term and on policy credibility. Indeed, the Treasury now has a mission statement, designed according to its (economist) permanent secretary (Burns 1996, p. 21) to 'be relatively unchanging and [to] avoid political differences', to the effect that it is:

- required to 'maintain a stable macroeconomic environment', entailing the 'objectives of low inflation, sound public finance, affordable public expenditure and an efficient and effective tax policy'; and
- to 'help strengthen the long-term performance of the economy and the outlook for jobs, in strategic partnership for others', this associated 'with a range of supply-side policies including efficient public expenditure management, efficient markets, privatisation and the Private Finance Initiative' but also with intangibles (predictability and stability) in reality deriving from the effect of macroeconomic policies on the general economic climate.

The counterpart to this very quiet revolution in British economic policy as seen from the Treasury are the developments at the Bank of England since the ERM debacle forced government into designing a new framework in the hope of finally attaining monetary policy credibility. Thus, beginning in October 1992 and continuing to-date, an explicit domestic inflation target was set by government (initially 0–2 per cent per annum, currently less than 2.5 per cent) and a process of institutional reform was set in train which, by giving greater influence (and, in May 1997, operational responsibility) to the Bank, provided transparency and openness to the setting of interest rates directed at meeting that target.[79] The Bank now publishes both a quarterly inflation report and the proceedings of its new Monetary Policy Committee (MPC) which is charged with setting rates and is currently constituted with a membership of the Governor and Deputy Governor, two Bank executive directors (one of whom is **Mervyn King**) and four 'recognised experts'

---

[79] King (1994; 1997); see also the Bank's web site: <**http://www.bankofengland.co.uk/**> and Treasury news releases available at <**http://www.hm-treasury.gov.uk/pub/html/press97/**>

appointed by the Chancellor – Willem Buiter (Cambridge), Goodhart, Budd and a City economist. This latter arrangement replaces the monthly meetings between the Governor and Chancellor which set interests rates, again with some transparency but – immortalised in the press as the Ken and Eddie show – not perhaps with the gravitas that those who favour rules over discretion might wish for.

The monetarist policy experiment

In looking back at the years since the monetarist experiment it is important to remind ourselves why monetarism was initially appealing. First, and as was acknowledged by proponent and opponent alike, monetarism appeared to depersonalise the economic problem. Imposition of a monetary growth rule, combined with a view of the private sector as inherently stabilising, led directly to a minimal short-term role for government. As Balogh (1982, p. 160) thundered: 'What more comfort could be derived from any doctrine? It absolves everyone of all direct responsibility.' Secondly, monetarism and the elevation of price stability above all other macroeconomic objectives was a veil behind which other neo-liberal agendas could be pursued: the contraction of the public sector, with reduced public borrowing justified in terms of monetary disinflation; labour market reforms to reduce the NAIRU so that such disinflation did not result in permanently higher unemployment once agents accepted the credibility of the MTFS; and tax and benefit reforms which, in strengthening incentives rejuvenated the supply-side and thus eased the public finances on both the receipts and expenditure side.

What caused incredulity amongst monetarism's critics, however, was not just the deceit but the wishful thinking that was implicit in the project. Thus, in an early attack on the experiment, one coinciding with the broadcast of Friedman's television adaptation of *Free to choose*, Michael Stewart (1980, p. 12) took the monetarists to task for trying to retreat from the democratic and economic complexities of the real world and for tapping into the fantasies of policy-makers that there might after all be a painless means of achieving disinflationary growth, for 'elevating them from agreeable daydreams to the epitome of wisdom and statesmanship'.[80] While the key Conservative ministers have in their memoirs all, by commission or omission, denied that in 1979–80 they believed in rational expectations, in effect the precondition for pursuing a disinflation which would not generate mass unemployment,[81] or at the other extreme that they deliberately sought a slump to break inflationary expectations, the fact remains that between the

---

[80]   See also Kaldor (1983) on the economic consequences of Mrs Thatcher.
[81]   For example, Lawson (1992, p. 69).

peak of 1979.II and the trough of 1981.II the unemployment rate rose from 5.1 to 9.7 per cent while at constant prices industrial production and GDP fell by 13.2 and 6.4 per cent respectively,[82] making this depression the second most serious business cycle reaction of the twentieth century (more serious than even 1929–32 but less serious than 1920–1). Moreover, not-withstanding the subsequent recovery in output, unemployment continued to rise for a further five years to levels which, if not quite comparable to those of the 1930s, were none the less of such national, and particularly regional, significance that the social and economic costs of the disinflation thereafter remained acutely controversial and, through their impact on social behaviour and thence the public finances, of enduring significance.

That the lower turning-point of the cycle almost exactly coincided with the 1981 budget and thus the 364 economists' letter, and that there then ensued one of the longest business cycle recoveries of the century (to 1990.II), presented exactly the sort of public relations coup rarely offered all but the luckiest of Chancellors. Few opportunities were then missed to score debating points over the 364, with the crowing still in progress a decade later (Howe 1991), but what is of enduring significance about this episode is that Britain's economics establishment were then marginalised by events. Perhaps then the key to understanding monetarism is not with the academic debate; it is with the rhetorical strategies of its proponents and in the limited capabilities that a lay audience (the voters) have in reasoning on economic issues as presented them by economists as against politicians. Thus, for example, the subsequent majority professional view that the post-1980 deceleration in inflation derived from the OPEC II induced fall in commodity prices, as against the effects of higher unemployment on the labour market, would not appeal to lay reasoning about inflation or unemployment.[83]

Monetarism won the popular argument in the sense that politicians were able to mobilise a coalition of opinion formers and thence voters who accepted that there had to be a disinflation (Wickham-Jones 1992). Galbraith was probably right, that if monetarism was to be put to the test 'what better people to try it on than the British, whose famous phlegm will put up with anything' (cited in Keegan 1984, p. 183), but his usual perspicacity about the British failed him when he did not recognise that monetarism enjoyed such wide support because it was a means of punishing those deemed responsible for the trauma of the 1970s, whether the Labour Party, the trade unions (the members of which voted overwhelmingly for Thatcher) or the British economics establishment who were seen as offering either no alternative or only a gentler disinflation (for example, that offered

---

[82] HMSO (1985a, pp. 6, 86, 109).

[83] For example, Beckerman and Jenkinson (1986); cf. the survey evidence reported in Lewis *et al.* (1995, pp. 183–7).

by Hopkin *et al* 1982) which lacked political-market credibility. If there was to be an experiment there were also to be scapegoats; if the experiment was to be based on a theory this should be provided by an economist from another apparently much more successful economy who was preaching a message of 'commonsense'. If that message then had not only lay appeal but fitted with the dominant views of the newly empowered money and foreign exchange markets so much the better. If Thatcherism was in part about making Britain more American in character, Friedman the guru Nobel prize winning American economist could not have better fitted the bill.

This provides a clue to why the experiment's failure did not vindicate the economics establishments' stance on monetarism. Indeed, a useful parallel can be drawn here between the 1981 and 1933 budgets. Thus in 1981, *pace* the 364, Howe stuck to the MTFS targets (of reducing the PSBR from 4¾ per cent of GDP in 1979/80 to 1½ per cent by 1983/4) at a time of rising unemployment, while in 1933, and confounding Keynes and a powerful expansionist lobby led by *The Times*, Neville Chamberlain refused to deviate from the path of fiscal orthodoxy, again at a time of (seasonally unadjusted) rising unemployment. First, in both instances tough-talking Chancellors generated policy credibility with the markets which gave more room for manoeuvre in practice. Thus 1981 was the high-water mark of the monetarist policy experiment, as indeed was 1933 for the public face of the Treasury view. Secondly, what matters in economic policy is not the intellectual coherence of a strategy *ex post* but the results in meeting *ex ante* objectives enjoying the consent of the dominant market agents. That inflation abated in 1981, that the rate of growth of unemployment slowed and that economic growth resumed were powerful demonstrations that whatever had happened had transpired if not because of government action than at least because policy had not made matters worse; similarly, that economic recovery began in 1933 and the worst was past for unemployment were convenient but powerful reinforcements of the *status quo ante*. In the 1980s, more so than the 1930s, the economists were outmanoeuvred by the politicians but in both episodes circumstances provided considerable latitude for interpretations more or less unfavourable to dissident opinion.

As the Thatcherite project progressed, and as the Conservatives demonstrated in successive general elections that their version of economic reality could be sustained, the 364 sensibly withdrew and attempted no further mass protest. There have been economists' letters since, even from erstwhile government supporters, most notably that orchestrated by Minford and Walters in protest about the value at which sterling entered the ERM.[84]

---

[84] *The Times*, 13 February 1991, pp. 1, 13. The other signatories were all City economists: Congdon, Pepper, Bill Martin and Peter Warburton. In a reference to this letter and to the 364 economists, *The Economist* could perhaps be forgiven for its observation 'The last time

Teenage and other scribblers

Whilst it would be convenient to see the low profile of academic economists in public debate since 1981 as part and parcel of the 'dumbing down' of British politics, of rhetoric, soundbites, xenophobia, taxation Dutch auction and other assaults on the intelligence, to do so would be to miss the changes that have affected the various markets in which economists of all job descriptions operate. Parsons (1989, p. 203) has labelled the mid-1970s as a golden age of 'scholarly campaigning journalism' in both the UK and the US, with Brittan and Jay the counterparts of Jude Wanniski, a leader writer on the *Wall Street Journal* who perhaps more than anyone else was responsible for propagating supply-side ideas (notably the famous but flawed Laffer curve) and ensuring that they entered into the 'Republican Congressional bloodstream' (Stein 1994, p. 246) from which they might then progress onward to the Conservative Party. With the collapse of the Bretton Woods system, the resulting shift in exchange rate regime and the onset of substantial public sector borrowing, there occurred in Britain (and America) a 'quantum jump in the financial markets' influence between the 1960s and 1970s'.[85] Contemporaneously, there developed a greater role for opinion in the foreign exchange and money markets, and with the traditional preoccupation of the newspapers and television with conflict, drama and novelty the stage was set for the economic policy debate to be opened up to much greater scrutiny. The near monopoly of elite debate behind largely closed Whitehall/Washington doors was over. As Graham, who was an economic adviser to the first Wilson government, has put it:

> One of the things I would say that has changed dramatically . . . is that at the time, in the late 1960s, although politicians would have been reading the press, the economic [sic] com-mentators were not taken anything like as seriously. Of course, politicians were watching the press for headlines that could cause trouble in the House of Commons or whatever, but I did not have the impression of the press and television running the agenda of debate in the way they do now.
>
> (Seldon and Graham 1996, p. 159)

As early as 1977–8, and reputedly emanating from the then Chancellor of the Exchequer, the refrain was often heard that 'A few young men in stockbrokers' offices are now virtually in charge of economic policy'.[86] These changes were subsequently immortalised in the complaint, by an ex-*Financial Times* journalist turned Chancellor, that it was inadvisable 'to

economic policy was similarly criticised . . . the attack virtually coincided with the beginning of the upturn' ('Still in chains', 16 February 1991, p. 33).

[85] Keegan and Pennant-Rea (1979, p. 132).

[86] Ibid. p. 133.

take too much notice of the teenage scribblers in the City who jump up and down in the effort to get press attention.' In his memoirs Lawson (1992, pp. 841–2) qualified his off-the cuff – 'as accurate as it was unwise' – remarks by reference to the 'very small number of economists of distinction and perception who work for various City firms', but then rather spoilt the effect with his reference to this 'self-important tribe of City analysts' and how, after the teenage jibe, 'they were determined to get even and were unremitting in their hostility'. This Chancellor's fate was, of course, settled a little over a year later when the Thatcher-Lawson-Walters ménage à trois in economic policy-making could no longer be sustained.

In Britain, economist-financial journalists have always been potentially influential, and since the 1970s conditions have been particularly propitious for them as the conduit between the less esoteric developments in economic theory and economic reality as experienced by market operators. For the latter, and especially for the young and impressionable, there was both a susceptibility to academic fad and fashion and an attitude that the greater part of the British academic establishment were unreliable, not so much because they were Keynesian, but because they still subscribed to a view of government as benevolent. At issue then, and here was the IEA's campaigning genius in the 1970s, was less the respective merits of Keynesianism and monetarism as approaches to demand management, and more the deeper problem of what – in a world of floating exchange rates, growing capital mobility and the demonstrable fiscal imprudence of western governments and bureaucracies – should now be the appropriate economic functions of government. As the IEA proclaimed in its pamphlets, *The taming of government* (1979), even *The end of government ...?* (Harris 1980), was the objective, not its reform. And monetarism offered the greatest prospect of securing a reduction in the size and scope of government. In a sense, therefore, the neo-liberalism of Friedman and Hayek merely provided ideological icing on a monetarist cake already sufficient for the purpose of challenging big government.

Twenty years on, however, and few now talk of Keynesians and monetarists as anything other than a distant memory,[87] one fading fast even from undergraduate textbooks. Meanwhile, the policy agenda has also progressed, and not just in western states, from the essential pessimism of the 1970s about government capacity to a more optimistic stance that big

---

[87] It is still, however, routinely invoked in business education where the economics that is taught as part of professional examinations is often appallingly stereotypical, as for example in that for the conversion course for the Institute of Chartered Accountants in England and Wales (AfP Ltd 1997, ch. 6). This lower level economics education, the means whereby a significant proportion of the business class – for example, there are 100,000 accountants in Britain – believe they acquire economic understanding, ought to be examined in the context of lay reasoning of economic phenomena.

government will endure but is capable of reform. The spur here has been threefold: the 1980s LDC debt crisis, and especially the responses of certain Latin American states; the challenges posed by the former eastern European (transitional) economies once a simplistic triumphalism of the market had been overcome; and the western experience, in which Britain shared, that while it has not been possible to much reduce the size of public sectors the relations between government and market can be transformed through privatisations, labour market, tax and regulatory reforms.[88]

The Washington economics consensus

The economic theory and social learning underlying this contemporary policy agenda have become known as the 'Washington Consensus', a term coined by John Williamson, which in turn builds upon the concept of a 'technopol', a sort of modern-day economic technocrat with attitude who acquires a position of political responsibility – typically in a transitional economy or LDC, but occasionally in Europe – and 'who dispenses advice intended to influence the course of public policy along the lines suggested by normative economics'.[89] Williamson (1994b, p. 18) defines the Washington consensus 'as embodying the common core of wisdom embraced by all serious economists, whose implementation provides the minimum conditions that will give a developing country the chance to start down the road to the sort of prosperity enjoyed by the industrialized countries'.

This wisdom is distilled in Table 7.7, and can be thought of as active government to eradicate microeconomic distortions and to establish macroeconomic stability. Whilst both concepts remain acutely controversial, and Williamson has subsequently suggested the phrase 'universal convergence' as more appropriate than that of 'consensus',[90] the broad arguments have endured. We detect this convergence at a number of levels. First, the old division between one body of economic principles and policies for developed economies, and another for LDCs (a largely self-standing development economics), no longer holds, and especially so in the principal international agencies, the World Bank and the IMF. Secondly, a convergence of opinion about policy reform in the OECD states was assisted by the fresh look at the LDCs forced by the debt crisis followed by the

---

[88] Richardson (1994) and Rodrik (1996).

[89] Williamson (1994b, p. 15); see also Harberger (1993).

[90] Williamson (1994b, p. 17 n. 9); see also Toye's (1994) comments on this paper and the various discussions in Coats (ed.) (1997a, pp. 345–6, 351–2, 361, 366, 381, 396). A very clear example of Williamson's original concept and of current international economic thinking on government capacity is IBRD (1997), the latest World Bank development report which focuses on the state in a changing world.

Table 7.7   The Washington economics consensus

Fiscal discipline
Budget deficits, properly measured to include those of provincial governments, state enterprises, and the central bank, should be small enough to be financed without recourse to the inflation tax. This typically implies a primary surplus (i.e., before adding debt service to expenditure) of several per cent of GDP, and an operational deficit (i.e., disregarding that part of the interest bill that simply compensates for inflation) of no more than about 2 per cent of GDP.

Public expenditure priorities
Policy reform consists in redirecting expenditure from politically sensitive areas, which typically receive more resources than their economic return can justify, such as administration, defense, indiscriminate subsidies, and white elephants, toward neglected fields with high economic returns and the potential to improve income distribution, such as primary health and education, and infrastructure.

Tax reform
Tax reform involves broadening the tax base and cutting marginal tax rates. The aim is to sharpen incentives and improve horizontal equity without lowering realized progressivity. Improved tax administration (including subjecting interest income on assets held abroad - flight capital - to taxation) is an important aspect of broadening the base in the Latin context.

Financial liberalization
The ultimate objective of financial liberalization is market-determined interest rates, but experience has shown that, under conditions of a chronic lack of confidence, market-determined rates can be so high as to threaten the financial solvency of productive enterprises and government. Under that circumstance a sensible interim objective is the abolition of preferential interest rates for privileged borrowers and achievement of a moderately positive real interest rate.

Exchange rates
Countries need a unified (at least for trade transactions) exchange rate set at a level sufficiently competitive to induce a rapid growth in non-traditional exports, and managed so as to assure exporters that this competitiveness can be maintained in the future.

Trade liberalization
Quantitative trade restrictions should be replaced rapidly by tariffs, and these should be progressively reduced until a uniform low tariff in the range of 10 percent (or at most around 20 percent) is achieved. There is, however, some disagreement about the speed with which tariffs should be reduced (with recommendations falling in the band between 3 and 10 years), and about whether it is advisable to slow down the process of liberalization when macroeconomic conditions are adverse (recession and payments deficit).

Foreign direct investment
Barriers impeding the entry of foreign firms should be abolished; foreign and domestic firms should be allowed to compete on equal terms.

Privatization
State enterprises should be privatized.

Deregulation
Governments should abolish regulations that impede the entry of new firms or restrict competition, and ensure that all regulations are justified by such criteria as safety, environmental protection, or prudential supervision of financial institutions.

Property right
The legal system should provide secure property rights without excessive costs, and make these available to the informal sector.

Source: Williamson (1994b, pp. 26–8).

emergence of the transitional economies, both of which then led economists to think for the first time about the political preconditions for successful economic policies. Thirdly, there is a broad accord here with the reunification of micro- and macroeconomics that we identified in section 4, but it is within the context that whilst the insights provided by public choice theory and the new political economy cannot be jettisoned a means must be found whereby economics can once more assist politicians and bureaucrats to pursue the public good rather than their self-interest. Fourthly, and finally, with the triumph of the market there has resulted the possibility of de-coupling economic policies from ideological orientation, such that some left-of-centre OECD governments (for example, Australia, New Zealand and Spain) have pursued major policy reforms to the point that 'left' and 'right' have themselves become somewhat meaningless positions on the ideological spectrum when applied to economic policy.

This convergence is not, therefore, simply neo-conservative economics in a modern guise although it is tantamount to a more advanced stage in the internationalisation of economics prosecuted through the triumph of mainstream economic theory. In a recent conference volume on internationalisation, Williamson (1997, p. 365) has reaffirmed his thesis that the international convergence of economists has now proceeded to the point that national origin, professional training and residence are no longer significant explanatory variables for differences in the techniques employed and policy positions held by economists. There was a consensus at this conference that this internationalisation derived from the massive falls in transport costs, making possible the international conferences which have come to dominate economics at least as practised by its elite academics and policy-makers; the decline in the cost of communications and the growth of new media; the establishment of English as the economists' lingua franca (there was no French economist at this conference!); and the growth of mathematics and formalism which have reduced the barriers to entry for those whose first language is not English. Moreover, whilst Williamson acknowledged that the other conference participants had, through their individual country studies, demonstrated that the homogenisation of economics had proceeded less far than its internationalisation, he took solace that the homogenisation was now so well advanced that there could be optimism that economics was after all a 'science' capable of truth and progress. The relevance of these broader developments to the British case are both political and economic, this of course in addition to the participation of many British economists in policy reform in both the transitional economies and the LDCs,[91] as well as their more anonymous

---

[91] For example, with respect to the former, economists at the LSE's Centre for Economic Performance and the London-based European Bank for Reconstruction and Development; and, for the latter, those associated with, for example, Oxford's Centre for the Study of African Economies or engaged in such World Bank projects as produced Little *et al.* (1993).

work in a range of EU and international agencies beyond the IBRD-IMF nexus, which forms the core of the Washington consensus, most notably the ILO, GATT, OECD and the myriad of UN agencies.[92]

Towards New Labour and a 'new' role for the state

The politics and economics of these developments concerns the revival of belief in the possibility of government reform, and thus escape from the Austrian-Chicago induced nihilism about inherent government (in)capacity which underpins the triumphalism of the market. Undoubtedly in Britain there was an excess of pro-market rhetoric between 1979–97 to the point that, as two Oxford economists have judged, Conservative governments 'Fearful of the risks of "government failure" ... apparently bec[a]me oblivious to the well documented risks of "market failure"' (Boltho and Graham 1992, p. 286). This clearly made life difficult for those professional economists in Whitehall, regulars and irregulars, who tried to maintain a balance between government and market which was contrary to the 'one of us' bunker mentality that prevailed for much of the 1980s.[93] The retreat from the extremes of neo-liberalism that occurred in Britain in the 1990s takes us beyond our brief but it is relevant here to report that amongst leading political scientists (for example, Marquand 1992, p. 224) there has been general support for Hirschman's (1982) thesis that the relative popularity of individualistic and collectivist ideas and policy solutions conforms to a cycle in which first the one and then the other arouse expectations which, given the human condition and political competition, could never be satisfied and as the disappointments with one are amassed, so are the attractions of the other, until in turn a new body of disappointments is generated and the cycle moves into its alternate phase. The appeal of this model for the British case is its marriage of empiricism with evolving ideas, although it has to be modified somewhat by what is perhaps the most significant long-term political effect of the Thatcherite project: that of the transformation of the Labour Party into New Labour, its rejection of the AES and its adoption of a version of supply-side socialism which deploys the language of market optimists on allocation tinged with traditional left-of-centre concerns for distributional justice (Thompson 1996, ch. 18).

---

[92] See Pechman (1989, chs. 12–15) and Coats (1986; 1997a, pt. 3). These, together with central banks and, in the US, the federal reserve banks, are also important centres of economic research. For a long-term study of IMF research, see the papers commissioned to celebrate its fiftieth anniversary in 1995 (*IMF Staff Papers*, 42 (4), pp. 707–835); for an attempt to assess the professional value of federal research bank research departments, see Jansen (1991).

[93] For example, C.R. Bean, now a Professor of Economics at the LSE and a confidant of the current Chancellor, was in the Treasury 1975–9 and 1981–2 but left 'fed up' because the government were not interested in disinterested advice (interview in Swain 1997).

The conditions for policy reform success which have emerged from the Washington consensus are also of relevance to the British case, notwithstanding their origins in observations of what 'worked' in Latin America. They are here presented, some in the form of competing hypotheses, by Williamson (1994b, pp. 25–6) in a manner which quite accidentally strikes chords for both the Thatcherite project and for its inheritor, New Labour:

- the 'crisis hypothesis' (that public perception of a crisis is needed to create the conditions under which it is politically possible to undertake extensive policy reforms) versus the 'mandate hypothesis' (that a government may be able to introduce reforms if it campaigned on a program of reform in the preceding election)
- the 'honeymoon hypothesis' (that extensive reforms have to be implemented immediately after a government takes office) and its relation to the length of time before economic benefits begin to materialize
- the presence of a fragmented and demoralized opposition
- the existence in government of a team of economists (headed by a technopol? did it matter?) with a common, coherent view of what needed to be done and commanding the instruments of concentrated executive authority
- the presence at the top of a political leader with a vision of history, who is not unduly concerned about being reelected
- the existence of a comprehensive program for transformation of the economy and a rapid timetable for implementation
- the will and ability to appeal directly to the public and bypass vested interests.

In this Washington consensus, and in New Labour's supply-side socialism, the state is represented as umpire, rather than as favour-granting mechanism, with this new role clearly informed, but not made impotent by, the insights provided by public choice and the new political economy. The economic functions of the state are thus being redesigned in light of the known hazards of both government and market, and to the above list we would add for the British case that policy reforms should:

- so shift the policy agenda that were the reforming government to lose office the reforms would be entrenched and would thus endure; and
- so change the political contest that opposition parties are either permanently consigned to opposition or have to adopt the reform programmes to make themselves credible.

Whether contemporary economic policy wisdom is portrayed as consensus or as convergence, it is clear however that in the west it has been bought at the expense of economists, in effect, downgrading unemployment and income distribution issues. This can be viewed in part as a further example of Americanisation. Thus, from OPEC I until very recently, America's labour market was viewed as more successful in generating employment growth than that of Britain's, or other European economies, whilst there is a longer history to the higher levels of income inequality in the US than in the UK and elsewhere in western Europe.[94] Since OPEC I income inequality has widened in most OECD states, and spectacularly so in Britain through a combination of the Thatcherite project working on the tax-benefit systems and deeper structural forces operating to erode the demand for unskilled labour. Indeed, quite possibly British and American economists have on the whole been less preoccupied with unemployment because the personal characteristics of those without work (the young and old, and those poor in human capital) mesh with contemporary Anglo-American political prejudices of an underclass and of what Galbraith (1993) calls the 'culture of contentment': that of the dominance of the political agenda by the economically successful, or, in the British case, of the top portion of the 40:30:30 society analysed in Hutton's hugely influential *The state we're in.*[95]

This latter book has been something of a catalyst for the centre-left to reawaken to the possibility of convincing the economically successful of the centre-right (the location of the median voter) that the triumph of the market in Britain has been at the expense of damage to the social fabric which is borne by all classes as the spill-over costs of crime, health, unemployment, environmental degradation and so on which require higher taxes as the economically disadvantaged rebound on the public finances. Of course, the mechanisms underlying this 'new optimism' would be utterly familiar to the Edwardian generation, the first to be persuaded of the existence of social market failure, but it is of interest that unlike this earlier time academic economists have played but a background role in shaping opinion. There are no equivalents of Keynes or Beveridge today, nor an expectation that there could or should be. We are fortunate also that, outside of the business schools, the 1970s-early 1980s appeared to have been the high point for economist gurus. We are thus back to the mid-late Victorian world in which financial journalists command large audiences and more than most influence the agenda of informed opinion. They are, of course, now much more dependent on the research conducted by professional economists, but as is clear from the authorities cited in Hutton (1995) these economists are attached to a variety of agencies, and economists are but one group within the public policy community.

There is a further reason why in Britain unemployment does not generate the same professional interest as it once did: that it confronts the rump of the Keynesian old guard and other contemporary dissidents with an uncomfortable question – what was the alternative to the Thatcherite

---

[94] Layard *et al.* (1991), Atkinson (1997) and Nickell and Bell (1996).

[95] Indeed, sufficiently threatening to merit an IEA symposium, more particularly on ideas of stakeholding – Hutton *et al.* (1997)

project? Economists and policy specialists since 1979 have provided countless studies that document the project against its stated objectives but we have precious few attempts to assess whether the benefits would have been greater or the costs smaller under alternative policy regimes or, indeed, to specify what those alternatives might have been (Bean and Symons 1989, pp. 13, 54). This is particularly so with respect to macroeconomic objectives. Thus, if as successive Chancellors have maintained, inflation is the 'judge and jury' of a government's record we cannot but be negative about the project. The failure to meet stated objectives for reducing the size of the public sector and the average PSBR compel a similar conclusion, while the coincidence of the project with the heyday of North Sea oil and gas invites myriad counterfactuals that there might have been an alternative (Middleton 1996, ch. 13). But, if the project is judged by its direct and indirect effects in remedying long-standing X-inefficiency in the private and public sectors, and in downgrading expectations of what government can reasonably deliver, back to basics in economic policy acquires considerably more status as the broadly appropriate strategy given Britain's economic and political circumstances. Indeed, herein lies the problem for its continuing opponents.

Back to basics has so transformed the political contest that New Labour have been unwilling to countenance the resumption of any of the neo-corporatist baggage of the 1970s, nor to repeal the labour market 'reforms' of the Thatcher years or to adjust the tax-benefit systems to claw back some of the ground lost by low income groups. Moreover, it has also so changed the climate of ideas that many who were in the vanguard attacking Keynesianism in the 1970s have by the 1990s begun to argue that the supply-side reforms had made finer rather than coarse demand management workable once more and that a revival of more Keynesian policies would aid macroeconomic performance and stability (for example, Skidelsky 1997). However, this sits rather uneasily with one of the longer-term lessons of British economic policy, that governments are too often deluded that they have 'themselves improved the underlying performance of the supply-side sufficiently for the economy to be able to respond to greater increases in demand' (Cobham 1997, p. 90).

Moreover, whilst unemployment – even talk of full employment – has come back on to the politicians' agenda, the driving force has been the urgency of reducing the welfare component of public expenditure, this even within New Labour where the party's principal professional economic adviser on unemployment has been Layard, an important contributor to the new government's plans for welfare-to-work (see Patel 1997). Indeed the impasse on the public finances, with the expenditure side swelled by dependency and the tax side limited by a perception of voters' preferences, has created something of a stasis for economic – particularly fiscal – policy generally, resulting *inter alia* in monetary policy through adjustment of interest rates taking the greater part of the strain for macroeconomic management. Such has been New Labour's transformation that in opposition they even committed themselves to public finance targets stricter than those in the Maastricht Treaty, but with there still being no professional consensus about the price versus real effects of monetary policy it is argued by many that given British structural conditions the interest rate remains a blunt instrument which, before impacting on domestic components of demand, works first on the exchange rate and thus the competitiveness of internationally traded goods and services.[96] Such is the consequence of according price stability primacy over other objectives.

The initial reaction against Keynesianism, as Eltis (1992, p. 53) explains it, 'caused great distress to the British economics profession ... because most academic economists could not understand why it was right to sacrifice output and employment in order to reduce inflation' nor appreciated the potential benefits in the political market place of doing so. Whether the subsequent disinflation was too steep and sustained too long will no doubt always excite controversy, but those seeking a more robust verdict on the Thatcher years are entitled to ask whether, comparing the mid-1990s with 1979, the British economy is now more capable of achieving simultaneous internal and external balance in the short-run and as rapid a growth of living standards as possible in the long-run (Wells 1993, pp. 107–8).

For many the continuance of Stop-Go since 1979, with two deep depressions and a massive deterioration in the current account balance of payments, especially that in manufactures, provides decisive evidence of the project's failure. Even admitting a once and for all catch-up exercise in manufacturing sector productivity, critics thus point to continued deindustrialisation as a consequence of low investment in physical and human capital. For Wells, as for many other Cambridge economists, the current low priority accorded to reducing unemployment was unacceptable; there had been no economic miracle since 1979, because the market was and is insufficient for the task of modernising the British economy; and such limited policy activism on unemployment as had been attempted was now being undermined by inflated notions and loose talk that globalisation removed any remaining macroeconomic policy autonomy.[97] Nor was this simply Cambridge of its wilderness years, of no longer dominating the RES

---

[96] See, for example, C.P. Mayer (1994) and Bean's recent evidence to the Treasury and Civil Service select committee; cf. the recent *Journal of Economic Perspectives* (vol. 9, Fall 1995, pp. 3–96) symposium on the channels of the money transmission mechanism, about which there is broad US agreement.

[97] For example, Coutts *et al.* (1990) prepared for the IPPR, Kitson and Michie's contribution to an 1996 *EJ* debate on deindustrialisation, and Michie and Grieve Smith's (1996; 1997) edited volumes which bring together other Cambridge colleagues and sympathetic financial journalists.

and *EJ* and of the very public humiliation in 1982 of having SSRC funding terminated for the Cambridge Economic Policy Group (CEPG) which had been the vehicle, first, for New Cambridge economics and then for the opposition to monetarism that produced the 364 economists' letter.[98] There are plenty who subscribe to this negative view of the Thatcherite project, but much of their opposition is evident not in the economics journals or the press but in New Labour policy networks – stalwartly the Fabian Society, more recently augmented by the IPPR and other new entrants – or elsewhere in the social sciences, as for example in Kenworthy (1995), a US sociologist who has done interesting empirical work on the relationship between economic inequality and economic efficiency for the postwar OECD states which contradicts the mainstream view of this trade-off.

7.6 CONCLUSIONS

The eclipse of Cambridge economics, evident first in terms of diminished peer group status in the 1970s and then as eviction from the wider economic policy community in the 1980s, has now ended with the New Labour government. But its return to favour in Whitehall owes less to renewed claims for technical and theoretical eminence than for its sustaining a political economy of credible alternative policies. While the wilderness years may be over, intellectual debate is now diffused over a much wider range of think-tanks than ever before. Thus, for example, the new government's minister (Frank Field) charged with 'thinking the unthinkable' on welfare has promoted his case not just in Labour circles but within the IEA.

This 'informational pluralism', argues Parsons (1989, p. 204), 'mirrors and informs the absence of an ideological fixity which pertains in the world of politics', with its logic clear for all economists aspiring to contribute to the public debate. Mere academic authority is insufficient to command attention, however eminent that authority be. Politicians now delight in brushing aside professors and presidents of royal societies as merely self-serving or unworldly or both. But, by stint of compelling economic logic, academic economists can still exercise comparative advantage over financial journalists in illuminating current policy problems,[99] while those who can combine economics and business expertise – a career pattern more common in the US than the UK – and thus make longer-term sense of short-term market behaviours are also much in demand.[100]

---

[98] On New Cambridge, see Stewart (1977, pp. 194–8); on the CEPG's loss of funding, see Weir (1982).

[99] For example, Eltis (1997) on EMU.

[100] For example, John Kay, ex IFS, author of a well regarded 1993 study on corporate success.

Both the dumbing down of politics and concerns about short-termism of markets can also be turned to economists' advantage. While presentation acquires a premium, so also does clarity and coherence, traditionally areas in which literate economists excel. Thus, as King (1994, p. 110) observes in the context of British monetary policy, with the death of deference and the triumph of the market 'central banks must rely more on a willingness and ability to explain and convince, and less on the power of mystique' with the 'winning [of] the intellectual argument [the] means of acquiring and maintaining credibility'. Indeed, the demand for economic analysis and the numbers of economists employed has if anything grown faster in the Bank than within government where there has been no increase in the total size of the GES since its peak in 1976, although there has been some hidden growth through the development of think-tanks within Whitehall, notably the CPRS (1970–83) and the Prime Minister's Policy Unit (created in 1974). Thus while the GES now has 500 members, the Bank currently employs about 200 economists in a wide variety of functions, including its Conjunctural Assessment and Projects Division which, supporting the MPC, its inflation report and other activities, provides high level policy research with, for example, recent published studies of the money transmission mechanism and macroeconomic models.[101]

In the Bank, as in Whitehall, there is no longer a clear distinction between economists and administrators,[102] and in both it is now usual for new recruits, if they do not already possess an economics education at least to masters level, to be sent off to the LSE for a part-time M.Sc. At the Treasury, where the greater part of GES members continue to be situated, there have been significant changes also. After a series of GES Heads/Chief Economic Advisers who were in post for only a few years the appointment in 1980 of Terrence Burns ushered in a period of stability, as he remained in post until 1991, longer than anyone since Robert Hall, and then innovation as he was promoted to Permanent Secretary at the Treasury, the first professional economist to attain this position. His successor at the GES, his former LBS colleague and another with expertise in forecasting, Alan Budd, was then appointed after a further innovation, that of the post being advertised. Relative to twenty, let alone fifty years ago, the Treasury does not now want for high-level economic expertise, although arguably the GES does not contain as much experience and real-worldliness as it might because of the comparatively low average age of its members, this partly because it is no longer the practice for mid-career academic economists to take leave of absence from their universities to become an irregular.

---

[101] Britton and Whitley (1997) and Whitley (1997).
[102] See Young and Sloman (1984, pp. 31–2) on the convergence in the Treasury.

The scrutiny to which these government economic advisers, if not always their ministers, are now routinely subjected has increased greatly since OPEC I. First, and following the intervention in 1975 of Jeremy Bray, formerly an ICI technocrat turned Labour MP, the Treasury are now required to publish their forecasts twice-yearly and to make their forecasting model publicly available for others to test its properties and to simulate alternative policy choices. This development should, of course, also be seen in the context of the transformation of macroeconomic modelling and forecasting which has taken place over the last two decades.[103] Secondly, since the 1979 reform of the Parliamentary select committee system the House of Commons Treasury and Civil Service Committee (TCSC) has been charged with monitoring economic policy, and while constrained by a number of factors, including that these select committees are chaired by a senior backbencher of the governing party, this one none the less quickly came to prominence with a highly critical report on the new Conservative government's monetary policy (HMSO 1981). At their most effective these select committees are potentially formidable. As Hennessy (1990, p. 332) remarks of the TCSC:

> the knowledge that some difficult but gifted MP on this committee, like Dr Jeremy Bray . . . , might embark upon a series of desperately difficult questions one twilight afternoon in Committee Room 15 was enough to keep the lamps in the Treasury burning late, thinking through the nuances of departmental policy, to avoid the Chancellor, the permanent secretary, or even a deputy or under secretary, being slowly pinned to the wall in front of appreciative eyes on the press bench conveniently placed between interrogator and interrogated. . . .

Parliamentary scrutiny of economic policy and performance is exercised on a number of occasions, not least the budget and subsequent debates, and through a variety of agencies, some long-standing (the Public Accounts Committee) and some which have recently become more significant (notably the National Audit Office). However, while there can be occasional surprises in Whitehall, such as when a report from the House of Lords select committee on overseas trade suddenly reignited the deindustrialisation debate (HMSO 1985b), the emasculation of Parliament relative to the power of the executive in the contemporary British constitution provides few safeguards (Dunleavy *et al.* 1997, chs. 7–10). In this sense it is markets that now monitor British governments, with politicians providing the raw material for market agents to form their judgements amidst the noise of Whitehall. Arguably, in opposition New Labour learnt this lesson in the

---

[103] See Hall (1995). Bray, an example of a contemporary hybrid economist-politician, has extensive expertise in economic forecasting and its contribution to economic policy-making (1994; 1996); he has also contributed to an *EJ* symposium on the topic (Bray *et al.* 1995).

1990s rather faster than the Conservatives in government (Sanders 1996).

One interesting by-product, however, of the select committee system has been in providing new opportunities for academic economists to serve as special advisers and as a consequence to gain new insights into the policy process. Atkinson (1984) for one has written most illuminatingly on this, with his experience of the TCSC's sub-committee on taxation and social security reform providing a fascinating case study of an economist's learning how economic analysis can best be distilled for policy-makers' consumption.[104] Another who has provided vital insights on this process, but from the perspective of a consumer of economists' wares, is Denis Healey (1989, pp. 383, 391) who, looking back on his period as Chancellor, described himself as an 'eclectic pragmatist' with 'Karl Popper play[ing] a far more important role in my thinking than Karl Marx – or Maynard Keynes, or Milton Friedman.' That this was so was partly circumstance, that of being in the Treasury when the hitherto stable macroeconomic relations all appeared to collapse, but also as he describes it of 'Odium academicum [being] quite as virulent a disease as odium theologicum', at least as practised by his senior special adviser Kaldor,[105] and so much so that 'in despair at finding a really first-class British economist as chief adviser' he was tempted to offer the job to Arthur Okun, then at the Brookings Institution. While a different adviser, first-class or otherwise, would not have made much difference to British economic policy, and it was Healey's political instincts that saved him from giving way to temptation, his predicament shows how over thirty years after the creation of the ES Chancellors still felt dissatisfied in their quest for technically able but politically sure-footed senior economists of the first rank.

Healey's difficulties presage an important shift in the 1980s in Whitehall and the wider policy community which has since endured. One close to the centre for some of the Thatcher years, Pirie (1988), president of the ASI, has reflected on a new micropolitics which resulted in the balance of power amongst policy entrepreneurs shifting from the more theoretical end of the spectrum to that in which 'policy engineers, coming in the wake of the pure scientists of political and economic theory, ... made the machines which changed events.' In this new world 'success in practice preceded the victory in theory and helped to bring it about'; indeed, such 'events were determined by men and women of action doing things that worked, and

---

[104] See also Hills (1983) on relations between the TCSC and the Treasury as viewed from the research staff of the former; Atkinson (1990) on the Stephen Hawking principle of science books as applied to economics, that each equation included halves the potential policy impact/sales; and Aaron (1989) for a US perspective which also uses public economics.

[105] See, however, Thirlwall (1989, pp. 134–6) for a sympathetic assessment of Kaldor's difficulties when Healey preferred the advice of orthodox economists.

towing theory in their wake' (pp. 267, 272). This sense of mission, almost of wartime urgency, is attested by numerous sources and comes through strongly in the memoirs of those most committed to the Thatcherite project.

Economists can flourish in such a world, but not perhaps those in the mode of Keynes or Kaldor who, however ingenuous their advice in face of intractable policy problems, however much their intuition ran ahead of their theoretical explanations, are not suited for the new demands for policy engineers as able with the presentation of policy as with its substance. Fortunately, there is perhaps a countervailing force here in that during the 1990s, and most explicitly so since the 1995 launch of the thematic priorities programme, the ESRC has been funding research which is as mindful of the priorities of the 'user' community of business and government as of the traditional academic 'producer' community (Rappert 1997). The emphasis on cross-disciplinary themes (for example, economic beliefs and behaviour, crime and social order) goes some way to address the long-standing complaint that much research lacks real world relevance, and that it reinforces the Balkanisation of the social sciences, while the joint ESRC-RES Economists in the Media Initiative also marks a new stage for the public face of the British economics profession. The media consultant appointed under this initiative has recently identified the characteristics of economists' work that attracts the most media attention. This forms a suitable epitaph to the state of economists after the first century of Marshall's mission:

> it covers subjects high on the domestic economic policy agenda, such as job security and fat cats; it comes up with distinct and easily quantifiable results; it has clear implications for government and/or the private sector; it provides novel perspectives on industries of general public interest, such as Hollywood and horse racing; or it offers an over-arching theory on matters of broad *fin de siècle* concern, such as the impact of globalisation and new technology.
>
> (Vaitilingam 1997, p. 8)

8. Conclusions

We need a new, fresh, buoyant, forward-looking economics, to replace the tired old economics telling us we can't do the things we want to do – the things we have to do.   (Hubert Humphrey, cited in Ackley 1982, p. 201)

Would the story of Britain's relative economic decline have turned out very differently if there had been more, fewer, or indeed perhaps no, professional economists advising successive British governments in the century since Marshall initiated his mission for the professionalisation of the discipline? Might the size and scope of Britain's public sector, and of its economic policies, have been very different had certain economists not lived or not acquired eminence? Or would we still, in the absence of Keynes and Beveridge, have had a managed-mixed economy and welfare state during the golden age and then, in a hypothetical world bereft of Hayek, Friedman, Lucas and the supply-siders, a reaction, a back to basics which underpinned the eventual triumph of the market? That these are unanswerable questions does not lessen their pertinence, for they bring us to the heart of the matter: of the relationship between ideas and actions and of the very British obsession with decline. Indeed, as has been observed in a major revisionist account of modern British history: as the century draws to a close all confidence has evaporated that in Britain's twentieth-century history there might be anything to celebrate and instead it 'threatens to become a history of decline, centred on the question: where did it go wrong?' (Clarke 1996, p. 3). Accordingly, whether as charlatans, saviours or as largely innocent bystanders, economists are inevitably an integral part of this story.

Such concerns, of course, conditioned Postan's complaint about the plague of British economists (pp. 21–2), one formulated at the very time that the majority of OECD countries were enjoying full employment and super-normal economic growth without obvious benefit of world class theoreticians and advisers within their national economics professions. Subsequently, this would be encapsulated in Allen's (1979) extrapolation from the British disease that 'a country's economic progress is in inverse proportion to the distinction of its economists!' Whether this be a robust empirical relationship or not, many critics consider it validated by the emergence of the newly industrialising countries and the renaissance of the British economy since the rout of the 364 economists and the re-establishment of orthodox economics, while for others it is evidence of the 'ugly currents' that infect contemporary academic economics.

We have throughout this study maintained that the peculiarities of the British case conditioned uniquely the relationship between economics and policy. In now drawing our conclusions about the current and prospective state of economics, economists and the British economy, we do so within parameters set by an unusual degree of uncertainty about the immediate future and the need for a view about the recent past. Thus, at the time of writing (late March 1998), it is probable that the British economy is entering recession as a consequence of the tightening of monetary policy (operating through an appreciation of the exchange rate), while simultaneously the global implications of the Asian economic crisis are unknown, but potentially perilous. As regards the recent past, and whatever the Conservative propaganda since 1979, we have argued that there was no economic renaissance. Indeed, the National Audit Office recently set the sustainable non-inflationary growth rate for the British economy at 2¼ per cent, one quarter percentage point above the rate attained during the crisis years of 1973–9 and the 'renaissance' of 1979–97, but three quarters of a point below the average for the golden age, 1951–73. Thus the achievement of the Thatcher project lies less with the growth record since 1979 and more with their supply-side reforms improving the British economy's capacity to take advantage of growth potential in a more competitive, global market.

There is a further significance to these years. New Labour's conversion to the market guards against at least an early resumption of the Jekyll and Hyde policies characteristic of the 1960s and 1970s. Whilst party political competition is far from being in abeyance, and economic issues – notably EMU and welfare-to-work – contain enormous potential to generate conflict, a combination of globalisation and social learning about governmental overload has led both major parties to depress voter expectations of government's capacity. As N.M. Healey (1993, p. xiv) observes:

> Whichever party governs in the future . . . [t]he electorate now appears to accept that government has no business running productive enterprises or fixing prices and wages for the private sector; that government cannot permanently hold down unemployment by pumping demand into the economy; and that the primary role of government is to control inflation.

New Labour's accommodation of capital can be understood as social learning about how globalisation restricts the policy space for national governments; of how, as Blair told a conference of US businessmen, 'Errors in macroeconomic policy will be published rapidly and without mercy' by markets (cited in Wickham-Jones 1997, p. 257). Given the long history of conflict between old Labour and capital, both domestic and international, this is a development of momentous significance. Its most transparent manifestation has been the appeasement of the City, one begun in opposition and promoted spectacularly in the early days of the new government with the granting of operational independence in monetary policy to the Bank of England. This has the hallmark of New Labour having studied 'sequencing' in the policy reform literature, and of being mindful of how the probability of re-election can be maximised by pursuing a rigorous anti-inflation policy to buy initial policy credibility, thereby widening the policy space later in this and any subsequent Parliament. In the words of one close to the centre, 'New Labour's post-election macroeconomic strategy should reflect the efforts of a Government that is seeking to do a small number of things very well' (Sanders 1996, p. 301). A precondition for exploring the contribution that economists might make to these policies is to consider the health of the discipline and the activities of its practitioners.

'At best, it's of minor significance in terms of human welfare'

Thus observed Vickrey 'of the obscure mathematical theory', 'one of my digressions into abstract economics', that underlay his 1996 Nobel prize (shared with Mirrlees) for contributions to the economic theory of incentives under asymmetric information (cited in Cassidy 1996, p. 50). To economics' many critics, when even a Nobel laureate denigrates his work in so public a manner, and when one of the most publicly visible of the rising generation (Mankiw) goes on record that economic research and Ph.D. production is over-funded by government, the professions' commitment to rigour over relevance has finally yielded its bitter harvest. According to Cassidy's widely-reported *New Yorker* article, this decline of economics was manifest at three levels, all of which bode ill for the discipline's future:

- a precipitous drop in undergraduate demand, especially as a major subject;
- employer resistance to those with economics Ph.D.s, that is unless – in the words of one Wall Street recruiter – they have 'at least a three-to-four-year cleansing experience to neutralize the brainwashing that takes place in these graduate programs' (pp. 51–2); and
- clear evidence that the Clinton administration had turned to non-economists as advisers because of the profession's inability to contribute much of value to the health care and welfare reform debates, this to the detriment of the attention given to incentives and efficiency in the proposals that subsequently emerged from the policy process.

Cassidy's portrayal of an introverted discipline obsessed with minor technical problems is hardly new, nor is there anything novel in the attention it then commanded in the US, and to a lesser extent UK, media. What perhaps was new was the connection now drawn between the failure of the project to turn economics into a relevant policy science and the aversion to economics now being exhibited by students and employers. Moreover, given the strong influence of American-style economics in Britain, and the opportunities afforded by the new government, the question naturally arises whether in a few years' time a journalist might undertake a similar critical exercise on the failure of British economics.[1] What then are the prospects?

British economics after Dearing

First, it is significant that one cannot find a major British economist over the last two years who has published an upbeat assessment of the discipline in a national newspaper.[2] That few have sought a public stage in recent years is no doubt a rational response to the indifference of the serious press to academic economics. However, over the last year or so editors have found academics' research much more newsworthy, with recent papers in the *EJ* now quite regularly reported.[3] This most encouraging development reflects both the efforts of the ESRC-RES media consultant and the new salience of social science research assumed with the advent of a Labour government.

Secondly, as meetings of CHUDE, RES conferences and reports in its Newsletter attest, there are grave concerns about the falloff in applications to read for economics degrees together with the poor prospects for maintaining quality in the new mass higher education system.[4] There is also a dearth of British candidates for Ph.D.s in economics, such that many doctoral programmes are only viable because of overseas students.[5] This, of course, bodes ill for the future supply of professionally qualified economics researchers in all sectors of the British economy, as well as increasing the vulnerability of British universities to shifts in demand in what is increasingly a global market.

Thirdly, there are very grave concerns over the equity and efficiency of the financial squeeze on university economics, and more so in England than in Scotland. Thus it appears that the HEFCE's current funding formula

---

[1] For a foretaste, see Anon (1997b).
[2] We specifically exclude the debate in the *Financial Times* which coincided with the 1995 RES conference because economists did not initiate the exchange.
[3] For example, the business section of *The Observer*, 18 January 1998, p. 4 carried a full page on the prospects for full employment, with Arestis and Sawyer's January 1998 policy forum paper given much prominence.
[4] *RES Newsletter*, 98 (July 1997), pp. 13–14.
[5] *The Guardian*, Guardian Higher, 17 March 1998, p. xxxiii.

disadvantages economics and econometrics relative to disciplines (pure mathematics or statistics and operational research) deemed comparable in terms of research methods and techniques, resulting in the perverse situation that the quantum of funding is independent of the discipline's quality (as measured by the RAE).[6]

These disciplinary concerns must, of course, be seen within the context of the rapid transition to mass higher education, the financial constraints under which this has been achieved and the growing frustration that, after having waited so long for government to undertake a strategic review of higher education, the resulting Dearing report, and even more so its partial implementation, will in practice further undermine research excellence and the provision of high-quality undergraduate education. Ranged against this essentially elitist 'Dearing disappointment' is the argument that growing state control of the universities will compel academics to acquire teaching qualifications and to redirect more of their time budgets to teaching, resulting in a lower output of essentially trivial research, much of it produced solely to satisfy the audit needs of the RAEs.

This leads to the broader context for the state of the discipline. There is first the debate about the future of the universities as the principal producers of knowledge and skilled personnel relative to potential competitor organisations (Levine 1997). Secondly, there are worldwide concerns about all of the social sciences, with for example the recent Gulbenkian commission report (1996, p. 98) arguing that the Balkanisation and disciplinary boundaries must be overcome, that:

> Economic issues are not the exclusive purview of economists. Economic questions are central to any and all social scientific analyses. Nor is it absolutely sure that professional historians necessarily know more about historical explanations, sociologists more about social issues, economists more about economic fluctuations than other working social scientists. In short, we do not believe that there are monopolies of wisdom, nor zones of knowledge reserved to persons with particular university degrees.

Such a prospect is in effect the antithesis of Marshall's mission, although no doubt he would not be surprised that academics, by not exercising restraint in public controversy, have accordingly seen their intellectual authority eroded and challenged. This development is undoubtedly one reason why those who are especially entrepreneurial and/or policy advocates have in the main sought employment in think-tanks rather than universities in recent years (Stone 1996), but according to a major social survey of

---

[6]   Analyses conducted by the chairman of CHUDE (John Beath) and reported in *RES Newsletter*, 100 (January 1998), pp. 20–2.

political culture the British public are now inclined to 'trust their own experience and intuition more than that of professional experts', while politicians also express an unwillingness to allow expert opinion to override public opinion formed in such a manner (Miller *et al.* 1996, pp. 50, 71). The recent BSE experience also provides a chilling foretaste of the difficulties government faces in conveying information about a complex situation to a public sceptical of experts, while the reaction by both the political left and right against publicly-funded educational research may also be an indication of economics' future unless it presents itself as more immediately relevant.[7]

The new prominence of central bankers, the propensity of the New Labour government to use businessmen and women as advisers on high-profile policy reforms, and the global ambitions of accountancy and management consultancy firms, together with their deepening involvement in managing Leviathan, all presage a profound shift in the demand for economic expertise.[8] University economists are likely to be marginalised even more by these developments, and particularly so in Britain where the traditional strength of economic journalism will continue to dominate the interpretation of the discipline for mass consumption. Moreover, as John Kay (1991, p. 57) observed in his contribution to the issue of the *EJ* celebrating the RES centenary:

> If you ask most businessmen what they think economics is about, their answer will be economic forecasting. They do not think very much of economic forecasting – although they go on thinking they need it – and so they do not think very much of economists. Every day they are concerned to analyse their costs – which is done by their accountants. They determine their prices – this is the responsibility of their marketing department. They need to interpret the business environment they face – the task of their corporate planners and strategic advisers. The economic input into any of these functions is minimal. Yet costs, prices, industries and markets are the very lifeblood of microeconomics . . .

The continued identification in the public and business mind of forecasting as the principal activity of economists has caused immense harm to the discipline's reputation. Yet, to fulfil the ambitions for social relevance that was central to Marshall's mission, economics must be able to 'predict and not merely to understand' (Blaug 1992a, p. 246). Economic forecasting is viewed by its critics as another failed project, one moreover which has absorbed enormous intellectual effort and financial resources. However, in a world in which there is a growing call for all economic agents to anticipate and manage the multiple and unpredictable risks to which society is perceived to be subjected, the demand for the services of those prepared to

---

[7]   See, for example, McKinstry's (1997) robust assessment.
[8]   See Luttwak (1996), Strange (1996, ch. 10) and Micklethwait and Wooldridge 1996, ch. 13).

offer a view of the future is unlikely to diminish.[9] This market has always been served by gurus, especially management gurus, the witch doctors of the contemporary age. Whilst the fads and fashions of management theory, as economic theory, are an easy target for criticism there is a deeper point here, developed by Kay (1996) and others, that economists must examine corporate behaviour more closely for the current dissonance between the business world's understanding of their activities and that of mainstream microeconomic theory's rendering of business is unhelpful to both. It seems, however, that it is only those rare economists whose careers straddle academe and business who can truly appreciate the extent of this cultural and theoretical divide, and for many of them the project to expound the deficiencies of mainstream theory is also a vehicle for promoting an alternative vision of economics. For Kay this is stakeholding, and for Ormerod, whose book *The death of economics* (1994) has attained such fame as to be serialised as a cartoon strip in Indonesia, non-linear systems. That economists are not all practitioners of a dismal science, but have a sense of humour, is however confirmed by the existence of the Society of Lapsed Economists (see Gilchrist 1994).

Hitherto, we have equated professional economics with university economics; but will this endure? In a forthcoming study of British economics between 1860–1970, Keith Tribe concludes that the discipline is the creation of the modern university structure; that initially neo-classical economics was arcane and had to be taught rather than imbibed from semi-popular books, but that now the university is no longer so important for the development or the application of economic knowledge the dynamic in economics lies elsewhere.[10] The advent of mass higher education, and in particular greater state and managerial control over the academic labour process, are part cause and part consequence of this development. In such a higher education system the majority of institutions will on the one hand focus on transmitting textbook knowledge and on the other on production of largely pointless research, the prime function of which is as a device for the accreditation of individuals. The shambles that has been New Labour policy towards the universities, and the nonsense of a supposedly social democratic government devising a funding system which is so regressive in its incidence, does not give grounds for optimism that this apocalyptic view of British universities, and therefore of university economics, will not ensue. It is axiomatic that the brightest students will not give a moment's thought to a university career, but in such a world this may not be to the detriment of the longer-term prospects of the discipline. Clearly, some elite institutions will

---

[9] See Reddy (1996) and Thompson (1997).
[10] See, for example, Brown (1996, esp. ch. 7) on economists and financial markets where he discusses why companies perceive and receive profit in developing their research capabilities.

endure, sustaining world-class teaching and research, but to do so they will have to break free of the yoke of government as monopsonist. This is inevitable, with the only question being when.

Economics and policy

In economics we would thus expect Oxbridge and the LSE to maintain their traditional dominance of the discipline. Indeed, to judge from that part of the LSE's strategic plan made public, their ambitions extend also to recovering the pivotal role in public debate and policy influence that its academics have been exercising variously since the time of Hewins and the Webbs. However, its new director, the sociologist Anthony Giddens, is adamant that this ambition can only be realised if academics guard against following any political agenda, but instead aim at being central to the intellectual and policy-maker's debate of 'how you survive in a global marketplace and construct a society that is reasonably cohesive and respects norms of social justice.'[11] Of course, the LSE's historical distinctiveness has been as a home for radical thought of both left and right, but in this renewal of its mission we detect:

- a caution lest its academics become so aligned with New Labour that they are perceived as politically committed, thereby repeating the mistakes of the Wilson years; and
- a reassertion perhaps that policy-oriented social scientists can, now that the Thatcherite project has worked through its stage of rampant individualism, make arguments once more which appeal to ethics.

The sub-field of economics and ethics is one in which British economists have always been prominent, but its recent higher profile is very significant for a number of reasons.[12] It allows us to look back towards Marshall's mission, as for example in Skidelsky's (1995) use of Keynes's life and age to illustrate the intellectual authority that economics can command when presented as applied ethics, and its lack of authority when economics was dominated by positivist methodology for much of the postwar period. It also reaches forward to the possibilities for a more humane capitalism in the context of the triumph of the market. Indeed, this was the theme of a recent section F meeting of BAAS, one given particular authority because of the status of that year's president, Samuel Brittan. As we have seen, he was a central figure in the promotion of a back to basics in economics and policy

---

[11]   *The Guardian*, Guardian Higher, 20 January 1998, pp. ii–iii.

[12]   Explored in Hausman and McPherson's (1993) *JEL* survey; see also any of the recent works by Amartya Sen, Britain's most distinguished contemporary practitioner of economics and ethics.

and we can, therefore, expect his current espousal of the market's potential to support altruism and fraternity to command attention (Brittan 1995a; b). His conclusions, that 'The idea of technocratic value-free economics has had its day' (1995a, p. 21), and that what went 'wrong with economics is the over-emphasis on technique as opposed to underlying ideas' (1995b, p. 17), are hardly novel but nonetheless most welcome for his attempt to empower economists once more in the spirit of Keynes's economists-as-dentists:

> Economists do not need to pose as *ersatz* physicists. Philosophers and literary critics know more about their subjects than lay outsiders without their being in a position to supply authoritative answers; and economists may be nearer to them than they are to hard scientists. (1995b, p. 17)

This leads us to consider economists' professional conduct and the public face of discipline *if* the modernist project of economics as science is accepted as a qualified failure. Within the sociology of economics there is now a developed literature on how to do and how not to do economics to attain professional success.[13] We have also McCloskey's writings (1994; 1996) on how economics cleansed of its vices might be reinvented as an interpretive discipline. However, there is little on how to improve the profession's public standing and the effectiveness of its policy advocacy,[14] although the recent efforts of the ESRC-RES media consultant demonstrate a sensitivity to presentational issues which is as effective as it is overdue. None the less, relative to Marshall or Keynes's generation, western economists now rarely interpret their professional functions as including the economics education of the public at large (Nelson 1989, p. 18); they do not advertise how the inventions of economists – for example, peak-load pricing, marginal analysis and numerous contributions to finance – are widely used by private industry and government (Faulhaber and Baumol 1988); and they rarely try to address public misunderstanding of economics by explaining, for example, that 'One of the functions of theoretical economics is to provide fully articulated, artificial economic systems that can serve as laboratories in which policies that would be prohibitively expensive to experiment with in actual economies can be tested out at much lower cost' (Lucas 1980, p. 696).

Economics' incomplete professionalisation relative to the law or medicine is frequently cited as one reason for the discipline's ineffectiveness,[15] but as we have seen in Britain the market for advice is intensely competitive and it

---

[13] See the contributions in Medema and Samuels (1996).

[14] See, however, Leman and Nelson's (1981) ten commandments for policy economists; and the 1992 *Journal of Economic Perspectives* (vol. 6 no. 3, pp. 59–67) symposium on economists as policy advocates.

[15] Higgins (1952), for example, is still worth consulting; see also Matthews' (1991) assessment of the economics of professional ethics.

is by no means clear that as 'unlicensed professionals' economists have been disadvantaged. The call for economic policy to be made more technocratically, by transferring from politicians to unelected economists responsibility for more key decisions on tax rates etc., is also often heard but has recently been put as an argument which would enhance the standing of politicians as well as the profession.[16] The recent granting of operational independence in monetary policy to the Bank of England suggests that such arguments are now being heard in Britain, but whether it is economists' technical expertise and their predisposition to longer-run time horizons that is being valued is unknown. The depoliticisation of economic policy in any meaningful sense does not look in prospect and arguably is not desirable.

The ugly currents in contemporary British politics, and in particular the disregard for official statistics as public good (Levitas 1996), certainly provides scope for economists (and statisticians) to act as guardians of the public interest, while the growing disadvantage of the legislature relative to the executive provides plenty of scope to offer critical scrutiny of government. Yet, as is clear from the political furore generated by the report of the Senate-appointed Boskin commission on the consumer price index, that a subject is technical, and that it is chaired by such an unimpeachable source as a former chairman of the CEA, does not take the politics out of economics (Madrick 1997). That there can ever be a Hippocratic Oath for economists thus remains a chimera. Similarly, economic policy advice will always be vulnerable to failure in the political market, whereby politicians have an incentive to espouse policies for electoral and ideological reasons, and to understate uncertainty for reasons of ex ante policy effectiveness. In the absence of constitutional constraints, there may actually be a premium on economists' disagreement if it alerts voters to the potential for government failure.[17]

What economists can do is perform their timeless function 'of vetting nonsensical arguments one way or the other' and 'of replac[ing] vague waffle or rhetoric with a clear judgement of what positive information is required and what value judgements may be important' (Beckerman 1986, p. 24). This applies very clearly in, for example, public finance decisions; it is also highly relevant, as Krugman (1996) has stressed with great effect, as a counter to the DIYE, or what he calls pop internationalism, which has created such confusion in political and popular discussions of US trade policy and the wider competitiveness debate. At one level then the value of economics is to avoid politicians and other economic agents making 'big' mistakes, as in the stock market crashes of 1987 when the example of policy

---

[16] For example, Blinder (1997c), this deriving from his experience at the Federal Reserve.
[17] Jones and Cullis (1993); cf. Peacock (1994).

errors in 1929 was used to good effect. At another, it consists of the debunking function and of acting as a constant reminder to politicians of the equity-efficiency trade-off. Indeed, so important is the last of these that, when called to account for the size of its budget ($3.4 million in 1995), Joseph Stiglitz, the outgoing chairman of the CEA, 'argued that the savings from just one of the policies it had prevented (e.g. subsidies for high-definition television) would be enough to finance a permanent endowment for its activities' (Anon 1997a, p. 84). It remains to be seen whether the new CEA in Britain, announced by Brown in August 1997 but about which little has since been heard, will be so cost-effective.[18]

Marshall's mission: retrospect and prospect

Marshall's mission, according to his nephew, himself a distinguished economist, was 'the furtherance of economics as a branch of knowledge to be used in the service of mankind' (Guillebaud 1971, p. 5). In Coats's (1990, p. 154) judgement, Marshall 'would surely have deplored the narrowing, fragmentation, excessive abstraction and mathematisation that has occurred in economics since his death, although he would have welcomed the growth of quantification, within limits.' Looking outward to the real world, to the ubiquity of economic inequality, instability and environmental degradation, and the conclusion beckons that economics has not made that desired contribution to improving the human condition.

The profession's response to this, of course, is that economic policy is made by politicians and not by economists. However, even this does not absolve economists of responsibility for the current malaise stems not from politicians being deaf to economists, but, as Eatwell (1994, p. 36) puts it, 'because economics today is built upon theoretical foundations which exclude the very substance of economic policy, namely the economic

---

[18] Treasury News Release 99/97. The CEA's terms of reference are 'To advise the Chancellor of the Exchequer on the design and implementation of policies for the achievement of the Government's economic objectives.' Its only two members announced to-date are Chris Wales (previously Tax Partner, Arthur Anderson) and Paul Gregg (previously NIESR, a labour economist who will remain part-time at the LSE's Centre for Economic Performance). (The other significant development under New Labour is that, on Alan Budd reaching the usual retirement age, Gus O'Donnell has been appointed Head of the GES and Chief Economic Adviser to HMG.) The CEA replaces the Panel of Independent Forecasters, established in 1993 as part of the post-ERM withdrawal quest for policy credibility, which had an evolving membership (at various times, Andrew Britton, Kate Barker, Tim Congdon, David Currie, Gavyn Davies, Wynne Godley, Patrick Minford, Bridget Rosewell, Andrew Sentance and Martin Weale). This, in turn, superseded the so-called Gooies, the group of outside independent economists, established in 1986 and comprising Alan Budd, Samuel Brittan, Walter Eltis, Mervyn King, Geoffrey Maynard, Patrick Minford, John Muellbauer, Gordon Pepper and Harold Rose (Oliver 1997, p. 140).

institutions through which economic life is lived.' Eatwell's well-known scepticism about the fundamental theorems of welfare economics, and his opposition to the New Right's project that equity is the enemy of efficiency, should not, however, lead those who are more optimistic about market efficiency to dismiss his arguments about institutions. After all, criticism of economics for its neglect of institutions, and for the poverty of its assumptions about the rationality of individuals, are not confined to the political left, whilst elsewhere in the social sciences it is a commonplace that the market is too important a social phenomenon to be left to economists. Indeed, as Lie (1997, p. 354) reminds us by citing Wicksteed, 'Economics must be the handmaid of sociology.'

A profession whose formal modelling of individual rationality seems based on a mythical figure of inexorable rationality, a sort of Mr Spock, the Vulcan brainbox of the Starship Enterprise, is a discipline in trouble, even if that apparatus does proffer insights into new areas such as the economics of crime or personnel economics. As Neil Kay (1984, p. 188) has observed, 'the individual intent on pursuing a career as economist has to be bright enough to understand the abstract ramifications of neoclassical theory and dumb enough to have faith in them.' This characteristic, together with the barriers to entry that mathematics now poses for the study of economics, undoubtedly underlie its diminished appeal relative to competitor disciplines, and in particular business studies. Moreover, in a system of mass higher education, one where students act as customers and are short on deference to established academic authority, economics as now taught will not prosper. Hopefully, and notwithstanding the charge of special pleading here, economists will reconsider the wisdom of providing undergraduate, and particularly postgraduate, education which excludes study of economic history and the history of economic thought and which limits exposure to the other social sciences. Were some then to rediscover the moral purpose that underlay Marshall's mission, so much the better.

In concluding his survey of economists' opinions Brittan (1973, pp.79–80) observed that 'A profession that spends so much time examining other people's markets might profitably devote a little time to examining its own.' Our study confirms this. It demonstrates that to understand economics' ugly currents requires study of the market for economists' pronouncements, and it makes clear that economists need to know about their profession and its history if they are to be effective. Proposals to reform the discipline have been made from inside and outside the profession. Within academe the call is often made for remedial action on professional incentive structures, with the proposal that the Nobel prize be abolished commanding wide support, even from some Nobel laureates. Non-economists, Mayer (1997, p. 21) argues, can also be of assistance: they should continue to criticise economists for their devotion to formalism, but they should do so in a much more informed manner lest economists retreat to 'circle the wagons'. As the sales of Galbraith's many books show, there exists a reading public hungry for 'literate, relevant economics in an age of intense formalism in the profession' (Stanfield 1996, p. ix), but few British academic economists are now prepared to supply that demand.

There seems no immediate prospect then of economists regaining that rigorous intellectuality and moral authority that was the hallmark of the best of British economics from Marshall to Meade. It is appropriate to end with the body with which we began, the RES, and with the economist, midway between Marshall and Meade, who inherited from the former and bequeathed to the latter, a very particular British ethical economics. In 1945, shortly before his death, and at the farewell dinner given by the RES to mark his thirty-three years as editor of the *EJ*, Keynes said: 'I give you the toast of the Royal Economic Society, of economics and economists, who are the trustees, not of civilisation, but of the possibility of civilisation.'[19] That such a toast was possible then was a measure of the progress made by Marshall's mission in its first half century; that it would now seem preposterous is a testimony to the fate of that mission when the presuppositions of Harvey Road (p. 45) were confronted first by the reality of adversary mass politics and then by the growing national obsession with decline. In an age of experts (Brint 1994), economists suffered a more pronounced erosion of their authority than comparable knowledge-based elites not because the market for their services was more contestable, nor through incomplete professionalisation, but simply because more than other social scientists they dared to try to make a difference.

[19] Cited in Harrod (1951, pp. 193–4).

Appendix I Dramatis personae

The form of address relates to their standing when first introduced into the narrative. Full details of ministerial, official and/or academic/professional careers are not given, with the following limited to highlights, economic experience and the periods in office when reference is made in the main body of the text. Where known a person's first degree and granting university is given as are any subsequent academic appointments.

Allen, Douglas (later Lord Croham) (b. 1917): economics, LSE, 1938; entered Treasury 1948, Under-Secretary, 1960–2; Third Secretary, 1962–4; Deputy Under–Secretary, DEA, 1964–6; Second, then Permanent Under–Secretary, 1966–8; Permanent Secretary, Treasury, 1968–74.

Andrews, Philip W.S. (1914–71): economics, Southampton, 1934; Secretary, OERG, 1938; Fellow, Nuffield College, Oxford, 1946–67; Founding Editor, *Journal of Industrial Economics*; Professor of Economics, Lancaster, 1968–71.

Armstrong, Sir William (later Lord) (1915–80): entered civil service, 1938; Principal Private Secretary to successive Chancellors of the Exchequer, 1949–53; Under-Secretary, 1953–8; Third Secretary, 1958–62; Joint Permanent Secretary, Treasury, 1962–8; Permanent Secretary, Civil Service Department and Official Head of Home Civil Service, 1968–74.

Ashley, William J. (later Sir) (1860–1927): history, Balliol College, Oxford, 1881; Fellow, Lincoln College, Oxford, 1885–8; Professor of Political Economy and Constitutional History, Toronto, 1888–92; Professor of Economic History, Harvard, 1892–1901; Professor of Commerce, Birmingham, 1901–25.

Atkinson, Sir Fred (b. 1919): Lecturer in Economics, Oxford, 1947–9; ES, 1949–51; Treasury, 1955–69; Chief Economic Adviser to Department of Trade and Industry, 1970–3; to Department of Energy, 1975–7; and to Treasury and Head of GES, 1977–9.

Balogh, Thomas (later Lord) (1905–85): economist in the City, 1931–9; NIESR, 1938–42; Oxford Institute of Statistics, 1940–55; Fellow, Balliol College, Oxford, 1945–73; Reader in Economics, Oxford, 1960–73; Economic Adviser, Cabinet, 1964–7; Consultant to Prime Minister, 1968; Minister of State, Department of Energy, 1974–5.

Berrill, Kenneth (later Sir) (b. 1920): economics, LSE; Lecturer in Economics, Cambridge, 1949–69; Treasury Special Adviser, 1967–9; Head, GES and Chief Economic Adviser, 1972–4; Head, CPRS, 1974–80.

Beveridge, Sir William (later Lord) (1879–1963): mathematics and classics, Balliol College, Oxford, 1902; Director of Labour Exchanges, 1909–16; Ministry of Munitions and Food, 1915–18; Director, LSE, 1919–37; Master, University College, Oxford, 1937–45.

Bowley, Arthur Lyon (later Sir Arthur) (1869–1957): mathematics, Trinity College,

Cambridge; Lecturer in Statistics, 1898–1908, Reader, 1908–19, Professor, LSE, 1919–36; Director, Oxford Institute of Statistics, 1940–4.

Bradbury, Sir John (1872–1950): Joint Permanent Secretary, Treasury, 1913–19; Principal British Delegate to Reparations Commission, Paris, 1919–25.

Bridges, Sir Edward (later Lord) (1892–1969): Treasury, 1919–38; Secretary to the Cabinet, 1938–45; Permanent Secretary, Treasury, 1945–56.

Brittan, Samuel (later Sir) (b. 1933): economics, Jesus College, Cambridge, 1955; *Financial Times*, 1955–61; Economics Editor, *Observer*, 1961–4; advisor, DEA, 1965; Principal Economic Commentator, since 1966, and Assistant Editor, since 1978, *Financial Times*.

Brown, Arthur J. (b. 1914): PPE, 1936, D.Phil., Oxford, 1939; Lecturer in Economics, Hertford College, Oxford, 1937–40; ES, 1945–7; Professor of Economics, Leeds, 1947–65; NIESR, 1966–72.

Budd, Sir Alan (b. 1937): economics, LSE; Ph.D., Cambridge; Lecturer in Economics, Southampton, 1966–9; Senior Economic Adviser, Treasury, 1970–4; Senior Research Fellow, 1974–8, Director, Centre for Economic Forecasting, 1980–8; Professor of Economics, LBS, 1981–91; Chief Economic Adviser to the Treasury and Head, GES, 1991–7.

Burns, Sir Terence (b. 1944): economics, Manchester; research posts, then Lecturer, Senior Lecturer, Professor of Economics, LBS, 1965–79; Director, LBS Centre for Economic Forecasting, 1976–9; member, Treasury Academic Panel, 1976–9; Chief Economic Adviser to the Treasury and Head, GES, 1980–91; Permanent Secretary, Treasury, 1991–.

Cairncross, Sir Alec (b. 1911): economics, Glasgow; Ph.D., Trinity College, Cambridge; member ES, 1940–1; Economic Adviser, Board of Trade, 1946–9; Head, Economic Division, OEEC, 1950; Professor of Applied Economics, Glasgow, 1951–61; Economic Adviser to HM Government, 1961–4; Head, GES, 1964–9; Master, St Peter's College, Oxford, 1969–78.

Campion, Harry (later Sir Harry) (b. 1905): Reader in Statistics, Manchester, 1933–9; member, CEIS, 1939–40; Director, CSO, 1941–67.

Cannan, Edwin (1861–1935): Lecturer in Economics, 1897–1907; Professor of Economics, LSE, 1907–26.

Chapman, Sir Sydney J. (1871–1953): Stanley Jevons Professor of Political Economy, Manchester, 1901–18; entered Board of Trade, 1915; Permanent Secretary, 1919–27; Chief Economic Adviser to HMG, 1927–32.

Clark, Colin G. (1905–89): chemistry, Oxford, 1931; staff, EAC, 1930–1; Lecturer in Statistics, Cambridge, 1931–7; Director, Institute for Research in Agricultural Economics, Oxford, 1953–69.

Clarke, Otto (R.W.B.) (later Sir Richard) (1910–75): mathematics, Cambridge, 1931; staff, *Financial News*, 1931–9; entered Treasury 1945; Second Secretary, 1962–6; Permanent Secretary, Ministry of Aviation, 1966; Ministry of Technology, 1966–70.

Clay, Sir Henry (1883–1954): Ministry of Labour, 1917–19; Stanley Jevons Professor of Political Economy, Manchester, 1927–30; Economic Adviser, Bank of England, 1930–44; Warden, Nuffield College, Oxford, 1944–9.

Congdon, Timothy G. (b. 1951): history and economics, Oxford; economics staff, *The Times*, 1973–6; Chief Economist, L. Messel & Co., 1976–86; Director, Lombard Street Research; member, Treasury Panel of Independent Forecasters, 1993–7.

Crowther, Geoffrey (later Baron) (1907–72): modern languages and economics,

Clare College, Cambridge; postgraduate studies, Yale and Columbia, 1929–31; Editor, *The Economist*, 1938–56; temporary civil servant, 1939–45; business career, 1956–72, including chairman, Trust House.

Dalton, E. Hugh J. (later Lord) (1887–1962): mathematics and economics, King's College, Cambridge, 1910; economics D.Sc., LSE, 1921; Lecturer in Economics, LSE, 1919–21; Cassel Reader in Commerce, 1920–5, then Reader in Economics, 1925–36, London; Labour MP, 1924–9, 1935–59; Minister of Economic Warfare, 1940–2; President, Board of Trade, 1942–5; Chancellor of the Exchequer, 1945–7.

Davies, Gavyn (b. 1950): Economic Adviser, No. 10 Policy Unit, 1974–9; economist, Phillips and Drew, 1979–81; Chief UK Economist, Simon & Coates, 1981–6; Chief UK Economist, 1986–93, then Chief International Economist, Goldman Sachs, 1993–; Visiting Professor, LSE, 1988–; member, Treasury Panel of Independent Forecasters, 1993–7; Economic Advisor to Gordon Brown.

Devons, Ely (1913–67): economics, Manchester; Economic Assistant, Joint Committee of Cotton Trade Organisations, Manchester, 1935–1939; ES, 1940–1; Ministry of Aircraft Production, 1941–5; Reader in Applied Economics, 1945–59; Professor of Commerce (with special reference to international trade), LSE, 1959–65.

Durbin, Evan F.M. (1906–48): zoology and PPE; Lecturer in Economics, LSE, 1930–40; ES, 1940–2; Personal Assistant to Clement Attlee, 1943–5; Labour MP, 1945–8; Parliamentary Secretary, Ministry of Works, 1947–8.

Edgeworth, Francis Ysidro (1845–1926): classics, Balliol College, Oxford; Tooke Professorship of Economic Science and Statistics, King's College, London, 1888–91; Drummond Professor of Political Economy, University of Oxford, 1891–1922: Editor, *EJ*, 1890–1911.

Einzig, Paul (1897–1973): university education, Hungary and, Ph.D., Paris; Paris correspondent and then Political Editor, *Financial News* (later *Financial Times*), 1921–56.

Flux, Alfred W. (later Sir) (1867–1942): mathematics, St John's College, Cambridge; Lecturer in Political Economy, 1893–8; Professor of Political Economy, Manchester, 1898–1901; Professor of Economics, McGill, 1901–8; Statistical Adviser, Board of Trade, 1908–32.

Foxwell, Herbert Somerton (1849–1936): moral sciences, St. John's College, Cambridge; Professor of Political Economy, UCL, 1881–1928.

Friedman, Milton (b. 1912): economics, Rutgers; AM, Chicago; Ph.D., Columbia; NBER, 1937–45, 1948–82; Professor of Economics, Chicago, 1948–82; Economic Columnist, *Newsweek*, 1966–84; Senior Research Fellow, Hoover Institution, Stanford, 1976–; Nobel Laureate, 1977.

Gaitskell, Hugh T.N. (1906–63): Lecturer in Economics, 1928–38; Reader in Political Economy, London, 1938; Labour MP, 1945–63; Minister of Fuel and Power, 1947–50; Chancellor of the Exchequer, 1950–1; leader, Labour Party, 1955–63.

Giffen, Sir Robert (1837–1910): statistician and journalist; Assistant Editor, *The Economist*, 1868–76; head, Statistical Department, Board of Trade, 1876–82; Assistant Secretary, Board of Trade, 1882–97.

Godley, Wynne A.H. (b. 1926): entered ES, 1956; Deputy Director, 1967–70; Official Adviser, Select Committee on Public Expenditure, 1971–3; Economic Consultant to Treasury, 1975; Director, 1970–85, Acting Director, 1985–7, DAE; Professor of Applied Economics, Cambridge, 1980–93; member, Treasury Panel of Independent Forecasters, 1993–7.

Goodhart, Charles A.E. (b. 1936): economics, Cambridge; Ph.D., Harvard, 1963; Assistant Lecturer in Economics, Cambridge, 1963–4; Economic Adviser, DEA, 1965–7; Lecturer in Economics, LSE, 1967–9; Bank of England Adviser (monetary policy), 1969–80; Chief Adviser, 1980–5; member, Monetary Policy Committee, 1997–.

Goschen, George J. (later Lord) (1831–1907): MP, 1863–1900; Chancellor of the Exchequer, 1887–92.

Hahn, Frank H. (b. 1925): economics, Cambridge; Ph.D., LSE; Lecturer, then Reader in Mathematical Economics, Birmingham, 1948–60; Fellow, Churchill College, Cambridge, 1960–; University Lecturer in Economics, Cambridge, 1960–7; Professor of Economics, LSE, 1967–72; Professor of Economics, Cambridge, 1972–92.

Hall, Robert L. (later Lord Roberthall) (1901–88): engineering, Queensland, and modern greats, 1926; Lecturer in Economics, Trinity College, Oxford, 1926–47; Ministry of Supply, 1939–46; Adviser, Board of Trade, 1946–7; Director, ES, 1947–53; Economic Adviser to HMG, 1953–61.

Harrod, Roy Forbes (later Sir Roy) (1900–78): history, New College, Oxford, 1922; Student, Christ Church, Oxford, 1923–67; Lecturer in Economics, Oxford, 1929– 37, 1946–52; Prime Minister's Statistical Branch, 1940; Prime Minister's Office, 1940–2; Statistical Adviser to Admiralty, 1943–5; Fellow, Nuffield College, Oxford, 1938–47, 1954–8; Nuffield Reader in Economics, 1952–67; Editor, *EJ*, 1945–61.

Hawtrey, Ralph G. (later Sir) (1879–1975): mathematics, Trinity College, Cambridge; Second, then First Clerk, 1904–19; Director of Financial Enquiries, Treasury, 1919–45; Visiting Professor of Economics, Harvard University, 1928– 9; Price Professor of International Economics, RIIA, 1947–52.

von Hayek, Friedrich August (1899–1992): economics D.Sc., Vienna; Director, Austrian Institute for Economic Research, 1927–31; Lecturer in Economics, Vienna, 1929–31; Tooke Professor of Economic Science and Statistics, London, 1931–50; Professor of Social and Moral Science, Chicago, 1950–62; Professor of Economics, Freiburg i.Brg., 1962–9; Nobel Laureate, 1974.

Healey, Denis W. (later Lord) (b. 1917): Labour MP, 1952–92; Chancellor of the Exchequer, 1974–9.

Henderson, Hubert Douglas (later Sir Hubert) (1890–1952): economics, Clare College, Cambridge; Fellow, Clare College and Lecturer in Economics, Cambridge, 1919–23; Editor, *The Nation & Athenaeum*, 1923–30; Joint Secretary, EAC, 1930–4; member, CEI, 1931–9; Fellow, All Souls, Oxford, 1934–51; member, Stamp Survey, 1939–40; Economic Adviser, Treasury, 1939– 44; Drummond Professor of Political Economy, Oxford, 1945–51.

Henderson, P. David (b. 1927): PPE, Corpus Christi College, Oxford; Fellow and Tutor in Economics, Lincoln College, Oxford, 1948–65; University Lecturer in Economics, Oxford, 1950–65; member, ES, 1957–8; Chief Economist, Ministry of Aviation, 1965–7; Economist, World Bank, 1969–75; Professor of Political Economy, UCL, 1975–83; Head, Economics and Statistics Division, OECD, 1984–92.

Hewins, W.A.S. (1865–1931): Professor of Economics and Director, LSE, 1895– 1903; Professor of Economics and Statistics, King's, London, 1897–1903; Secretary, Tariff Commission, 1903–17; MP, 1912–18; Under-Secretary of State for Colonies, 1917–19.

Hicks, John R. (later Sir John) (1904–89): Lecturer in Economics, LSE, 1926–35; Fellow, Gonville and Caius College, Cambridge, 1935–8; Professor of Political Economy, Manchester, 1938–46; Fellow, Nuffield College, Oxford, 1946–52; Drummond Professor of Political Economy, Oxford, 1952–65; Nobel Laureate, 1972.

Hirst, Francis W. (1873–1953): classics, Wadham College, Oxford; postgraduate study, principally in law, LSE, 1896–9; Editor, *The Economist*, 1907–16.

Hobson, John A. (1858–1940): classics, Lincoln College, Oxford, 1880; schoolteacher; Lecturer in English Literature and Economics, Oxford University Extension Delegacy and the London Society for Extension of University Teaching, 1887–1897.

Hobson, Oscar R. (later Sir Oscar) (1886–1961): classics and mathematics, King's College, Cambridge; banker; Financial Editor, *Manchester Guardian*, 1920–9; Editor–in–Chief, *Financial News*, 1929–34; City Editor, *News Chronicle*, 1935–59; business career.

Hopkin, Sir Bryan (b. 1914): economics, St John's College, Cambridge; Prime Minister's Statistical Branch, 1941–45; ES, 1945–8; Director, NIESR, 1952–7; Deputy Director, ES, 1958–65, Director and Head, GES, 1974–7; Professor of Economics, Cardiff, 1972–82.

Hopkins, Sir Richard V.N. (1880–1955): Inland Revenue, 1902; Chairman, Board of Inland Revenue, 1922–7; Controller of Finance and Supply Services, Treasury, 1927–32; Second Secretary, 1932–42; Permanent Secretary, 1942–5.

Howe, Geoffrey (later Lord) (b. 1926): lawyer; Conservative MP, 1964–6, 1970–92; Chancellor of the Exchequer, 1979–83.

Hutton, D. Graham (1904–88): economics, LSE; barrister; research fellow, LSE, 1929–33; Assistant Editor, *The Economist*, 1933–8; temporary civil servant, 1939–45; business career, including economic consultancy.

Hutton, Will (b. 1950): economics, Bristol; stockbroker; economics correspondent, BBC Newsnight, 1983–8; Economics Editor, the *Guardian*, 1990–6; Editor, the *Observer*, 1996–.

Jay, Douglas P.T. (later Lord) (b. 1907): classics, New College, Oxford; Fellow, All Souls, 1930–7, 1968–; staff, *The Times*, 1929–33; *The Economist*, 1933–7; City Editor, *Daily Herald*, 1937–41; Ministry of Supply, 1941–3; Board of Trade, 1943–5; PA to the Prime Minister, 1945–6; Labour MP, 1946–83; Economic Secretary, Treasury, 1947–50, Financial Secretary, 1950–1; President, Board of Trade, 1964–7.

Jay, Peter (b. 1937): PPE, Christ Church, Oxford, 1960; Assistant Principal, Treasury, 1961–4; Private Secretary to Joint Permanent Secretary, 1964; Principal, 1964–7; Economics Editor, *The Times*, 1967–77; Presenter, Weekend World (ITV), 1972–7; Ambassador to US, 1977–9; radio and TV financial journalism to present.

Jewkes, John (1902–88): Professor of Social Economics, Manchester, 1936–46; Director, CEIS and then ES, 1939–41; Professor of Economic Organisation, Oxford, 1948–69.

Johnson, Harry G. (1923–77): Fellow, Jesus College, then King's College, Cambridge, 1949–56; Professor of Economics, Manchester, 1956–9; Chicago, 1959–77; LSE, 1966–74; Geneva, 1976–7; Editor, *JPE*, 1960–6, 1969–77.

Kahn, Richard F. (later Lord) (1905–89): mathematics and physics, 1927, and economics, 1928, King's College, Cambridge; Fellow, King's College, Cambridge, 1930–89; wartime civil servant, mainly Board of Trade; Professor of

Economics, Cambridge, 1951–72.

Kaldor, Nicholas (later Lord) (1908–86): economics, LSE, 1930; Assistant Lecturer, Lecturer and Reader in Economics, LSE, 1932–47; NIESR, 1943–5; Fellow, King's College, Cambridge, 1949–86; Reader in Economics, Cambridge, 1952–65; Professor, 1968–75; Special Adviser to Chancellor of the Exchequer, 1964–8 and 1974–6.

Keynes, John Maynard (later Baron) (1883–1946): mathematics, King's College, Cambridge; entered India Office 1906; Lecturer in Economics, Cambridge, 1908–14; Fellow, King's College, Cambridge, 1909–46; Editor, *EJ*, 1912–44; Treasury, 1915–19, 1940–6; Principal Treasury Representative, Paris Peace Conference, 1919; member, Macmillan committee and EAC.

Keynes, John Neville (1852–1949): Fellow, Pembroke College, Cambridge, 1876–82; University Lecturer in Moral Science, Cambridge, 1884–1911; Secretary of the Local Examinations and Lectures Syndicate, 1892–1910; Registrary University of Cambridge, 1910–1925.

King, Mervyn (b. 1948): economics, King's College, Cambridge, 1969; Research Officer, DAE, 1969–76; Fellow, St. John's College, Cambridge, 1972–7; Esmée Fairbairn Professor of Investment, Birmingham, 1977–84; Professor of Economics, LSE, 1984–95; Director, since 1990, and Chief Economist, since 1991, Bank of England; member, Monetary Policy Committee, 1997–.

Lawson, Nigel (later Lord) (b. 1932): PPE, Christ Church, Oxford, 1954; staff, *Financial Times*, 1956–60; City Editor, *Sunday Telegraph*, 1961–63; Editor, the *Spectator*, 1966–70; Conservative MP, 1974–90; Financial Secretary to the Treasury, 1979–81; Chancellor of the Exchequer, 1983–9.

Layard, Richard (b. 1934): schoolteacher; Senior Research Officer, Robbins committee, 1961–3; Lecturer in Economics, 1968–75; Reader in the Economics of Labour, 1975–80; Professor of Economics, LSE, 1980–, and Director, Centre for Economic Performance, 1990–; Economic Consultant to Russian Government, 1991–.

Layton, Sir Walter T. (later Lord) (1884–1966): Fellow, Gonville and Caius, and Lecturer in Economics, Cambridge, 1908–19; Ministry of Munitions, 1916–18; Editor, *The Economist*, 1922–8; Ministry of Supply, 1940–2; Ministry of Production, 1942–3.

Leith–Ross, Sir Frederick W. (1887–1968): classics, Balliol College, Oxford; entered Treasury 1909, Private Secretary to Prime Minister, 1911–13; Deputy Controller of Finance, 1925–32; Chief Economic Adviser to HMG, 1932–46.

MacDougall, G.D.A. (later Sir Donald) (b. 1912): Lecturer in Economics, Leeds, 1936–9; Prime Minister's Statistical Branch, 1940–5; member, ES, 1945; Economic Director, OEEC, 1948–9; Fellow, Nuffield, Oxford, 1952–64; Director–General, DEA, 1964–8; Head, GES, 1969–73; Chief Economic Adviser, CBI, 1973–84.

Marshall, Alfred (1842–1924): mathematics, St John's College, Cambridge (Fellow, 1865–77, 1885–1908); Principal, University College, Bristol, 1877–83; Fellow, Balliol College, Oxford, 1883–4; Professor of Political Economy, Cambridge, 1885–1908.

Meade, James E. (1907–95): PPE, Oriel College, Oxford, 1930; Fellow, Hertford College, Oxford, 1931–7; Economic Section, League of Nations, 1937–40; member, ES, 1940–6; Director, ES, 1946–7; Professor of Commerce, LSE, 1947–57; Professor of Political Economy, Cambridge, 1957–67; Senior Research Fellow, Christ's College, Cambridge, 1967–74; Nobel Laureate, 1977.

Minford, Patrick (b. 1943): PPE, Balliol College, Oxford; M.Sc. and Ph.D., LSE; Economic Assistant, Ministry of Overseas Development, 1966; Treasury, 1971–4; NIESR, 1975–6; Gonner Professor of Applied Economics, Liverpool, 1976–; member, Treasury Panel of Independent Forecasters, 1993–7.

Neild, Robert R. (b. 1924): economics, Trinity College, Cambridge; Secretariat, UN Economic Commission for Europe, Geneva, 1947–51; member, ES, 1951–6; Deputy Director, NIESR, 1958–64; Economic Adviser, Treasury, 1964–7; Director, Stockholm International Peace Research Institute, 1967–71; Professor of Economics, Cambridge, 1971–84; Fellow, Trinity College, Cambridge, 1971–.

Nicholson, J. Shield (1850–1927): Professor of Political Economy and Mercantile Law, Edinburgh, 1880–1925.

Niemeyer, Sir Otto (1883–1972): entered Treasury, 1906; Controller of Finance, 1922–7; Bank of England, 1927; Director, 1938–1952.

Norman, Montagu C. (later Lord) (1871–1950): Deputy Governor, Bank of England, 1918–20; Governor, 1920–44.

Paish, Frank W. (1898–1988): economics, Trinity College, Cambridge; Standard Bank of South Africa, 1921–32. Lecturer in Economics, LSE, 1932–38; Reader, 1938–49; Professor of Economics, 1949–65; Secretary, LCES, 1932–41, 1945–49; Editor, 1947–49; Deputy-Director of Programmes, Ministry of Aircraft Production, 1941–45; Consultant on Economic Affairs, Lloyds Bank, 1965–70.

Paish, George (later Sir) (1867–1957): staff, then Editor, the *Statist*, 1881–1916; Adviser to the Chancellor of the Exchequer, 1914–16.

Peacock, Alan T. (later Sir Alan) (b. 1922): political economy, St Andrews; Lecturer in Economics, St Andrews, 1947–8; LSE, 1948–51; Reader, 1951–6; Professor of Economics, Edinburgh, 1957–62; York, 1962—78; Buckingham, 1978–80; Chief Economic Adviser, Department of Trade and Industry, 1973–6.

Phelps Brown, E. Henry (1906–94): PPE, Wadham College, Oxford, 1929; Fellow, New College, Oxford, 1930–47; Professor of the Economics of Labour, London, 1947–68.

Phillips, Sir Frederick (1884–1943): mathematics and natural sciences, Emmanuel College, Cambridge, 1907; entered Treasury 1908, Under–Secretary, 1932; Treasury representative in US, 1940–3.

Pigou, Arthur C. (1877–1959): history and moral sciences, King's College, Cambridge; then Fellow, 1902–59; Girdlers Lecturer in Economics, 1904–8; Professor of Political Economy, Cambridge, 1908–43.

Posner, Michael V. (b. 1931): PPE, Balliol College, Oxford; Research Officer, Oxford Institute of Statistics, 1953–7; Assistant Lecturer, Lecturer, Reader in Economics, 1958–79; Fellow and Director of Studies in Economics, Pembroke College, Cambridge, 1960–83; Director of Economics, Ministry of Power, 1966–7; Economic Adviser, Treasury, 1967–9; Economic Consultant, Treasury, 1969–71; Energy Adviser, NEDO, 1973–4; Economic Adviser, Department of Energy, 1974–5; Deputy Chief Economic Adviser, Treasury, 1975–6; Chairman, SSRC, 1979–83; Economic Director, NEDO, 1984–6.

Robbins, Lionel C. (1898–1984): Lecturer in Economics, LSE, 1925–7; Fellow and Lecturer, New College, Oxford, 1927–9; Professor of Economics, London, 1929–61; member, ES 1940–1; Director, ES, 1941–5.

Robertson, Dennis H. (later Sir) (1890–1963): economics, Trinity College, Cambridge, 1912; then Fellow, 1914–38, 1944–63; University Lecturer in Economics, 1924–8; Girdlers' Lecturer, 1928–30; Reader, 1930–8; member, CEI, 1936–9; Cassel Professor of Economics, LSE, 1938–44; Adviser, Treasury, 1939–

44; Professor of Political Economy, Cambridge, 1944–57.

Robinson, Bill (P.W.) (b. 1943): PPE; D.Phil., Sussex, 1969; Economic Assistant, 10 Downing Street, 1969–70; Cabinet Office, 1970–71; Economic Adviser, Treasury, 1971–4; Senior Research Fellow, LBS, 1979–86; Adviser, Treasury and Civil Service Committee, 1981–6; Director, IFS, 1986–91; economic columnist, the *Independent*, 1989–91; Special Adviser to Chancellor of Exchequer, 1991–3; Director, London Economics.

Robinson, E.A.G. (later Sir Austin) (1897–1993): economics, Christ's College, Cambridge; Fellow, Corpus Christi College, Cambridge, 1923–6; Sidney Sussex College, Cambridge, 1931–93; University Lecturer in Economics, Cambridge, 1929–50; Assistant Editor, *EJ*, 1934–44; Joint Editor, 1944–70; member, ES, 1939–42; Ministry of Production, 1942–5; Economic Adviser, Board of Trade, 1945–6; Professor of Economics, Cambridge, 1950–65; Secretary, RES, 1945–70; Chairman, NIESR, 1949–62.

Robinson, Joan (1903–83): economics, Girton College, Cambridge, 1925; Assistant Lecturer in Economics, Cambridge, 1931–7; Lecturer, 1937–49; Reader, 1949–65; Professor of Economics, 1965–71.

Roll, Sir Eric (b. 1907): B.Comm, Birmingham, 1928; Ph.D., 1930; Lecturer in Economics, then Professor, Hull, 1935–46; Member, later Deputy Head, British Food Mission to N America, 1941–6; CEPS, 1948; Economic Minister and Head of UK Treasury Delegation, Washington, 1963–4; Permanent Under-Secretary of State, DEA, 1964–6; merchant banker and company director.

Salter, Sir Arthur (later Lord) (1881–1975): classics, Brasenose College, Oxford; entered civil service, 1904; Chairman, Allied Maritime Transport Executive, 1918; Gladstone Professor of Political Theory and Institutions, Oxford, 1934–44; Independent MP, 1937–50; Conservative MP, 1951–3; Parliamentary Secretary, Ministry of Shipping, 1939–1941; Head, British Merchant Shipping Mission, Washington, 1941–1943; Minister of State for Economic Affairs, 1951–2.

Seldon, Arthur (b.1916): economics, LSE, 1937; industrial economist, 1949–59; Editorial Director, IEA, 1957–88.

Shonfield, Andrew (later Sir Andrew) (1917–81): PPE, Magdalen College, Oxford; staff, *Financial Times*, 1947–57; Foreign, then Economics Editor, *The Observer*, 1957–61; Director of Studies, Research Fellow and then Director, RIIA, 1961–77; Professor of Economics, EUI, Florence, 1978–81. KW: 1958; 1965.

Sidgwick, Henry (1838–1900): Trinity College, Cambridge; Fellow, 1859–69, 1885–1900; Knightbridge Professor of Moral Philosophy, Cambridge, 1883–1900.

Smith, Sir Hubert Llewellyn (1864–1945): mathematics, Corpus Christi College, Oxford, 1886; Lecturer in Political Economy to Oxford University Extension and Toynbee Trust, 1887–8; Commissioner for Labour, Labour Department, Board of Trade, 1893–1907; Permanent Secretary, 1907–19; Chief Economic Adviser to HMG, 1919–27; Director of New Survey of London Life and Labour, 1928–35.

Sraffa, Piero (1898–1983); law, Turin, 1920; Professor of Political Economy, Perugia, 1924; Cagliari, 1926; Lecturer in Economics, 1927–31, Assistant Director of Research in Economics and Marshall Librarian, 1935–63, Reader in Economics, Cambridge, 1963–5; Fellow, Trinity College, Cambridge, 1939–83.

Stamp, Sir Josiah C. (later Lord) (1880–1941): entered Inland Revenue 1896; B.Sc., London, 1912; Assistant Secretary, Board of Inland Revenue, 1916–19; President, LMS, 1926–41; Director, Bank of England, 1928–41; member, EAC, 1930–9; Chairman, Survey of Financial and Economic Plans, 1939–41.

Stone, J.R.N. (later Sir Richard) (1913–91): economics, Gonville and Caius College,

Cambridge; stockbroker, ES, 1940; CSO, 1940–5; Director, DAE, 1945–50; Fellow, King's College, Cambridge, 1945–91; P. D. Leake Professor of Finance and Accounting, University of Cambridge, 1955–80; Nobel Laureate, 1984.

Thatcher, Margaret H. (b. 1925): chemistry, Somerville College, Oxford; chemist, then lawyer; Conservative MP, 1959–92; Prime Minister, 1979–90.

Walters, Sir Alan A. (b. 1926): economics, Leicester; MA, Nuffield College, Oxford; Lecturer in Econometrics, then Professor, Birmingham, 1951–68; Cassel Professor of Economics, LSE, 1968–76; Professor of Economics, Johns Hopkins, 1976–91; Senior Fellow, American Enterprise Institute, 1983–; Economic Adviser to World Bank, 1976–80, 1984–88; Personal Economic Adviser to the Prime Minister, 1981–84, 1989.

Wilson, J. Harold (later Lord) (1916–95): PPE, Jesus College, Oxford; Lecturer in Economics, New College, Oxford, 1937; Fellow, 1938–45; member, ES, 1940–1; Labour MP, 1945–83; President, Board of Trade, 1947–51; Prime Minister, 1964–70, 1974–6.

Wincott, Harold E. (1906–69): *Financial News*, 1930–8; Editor, then Editor–in–Chief, *Investors Chronicle*, 1938–66; contributor, *Financial Times*, 1950–69; business career, mainly directorships.

Withers, Hartley (1867–1950): classics, Christ Church, Oxford; schoolteacher and then stockbroker; staff, *The Times*, 1894–1910; Director, Financial Enquiries, Treasury, 1915–16; editor, *The Economist*, 1916–21.

Sources: *Dictionary of National Biography*; *Who was who?*; *Who's who?*; Cairncross (1991a, app. 2; 1996, pp. 299–304); Eatwell *et al.* (eds) (1987); Howson and Winch (1977, app. 2); Moggridge (1992, pp. 859ff); and Whitaker (1996, vol. I, pp. xxvii–xlvii).

Appendix II Nobel memorial prizes in economics, 1969–97[a]

Year of award	Name	Institutional Affiliation	Nationality	Year of birth/death[b]	Prize citations[c]
1969	Tinbergen, Jan	Netherlands School of Economics	Dutch	1903/1994	'for having developed and applied dynamic models for the analysis of economic processes.'
	Frisch, Ragnar A.K	Oslo	Norwegian	1895/1973	
1970	Samuelson, Paul A.	MIT	American	1915	'for the scientific work through which he has developed static and dynamic economic theory and actively contributed to raising the level of analysis in economic science'
1971	Kuznets, Simon	Harvard	American	1901/1985 (Russia)	'for his empirically founded interpretation of economic growth which has led to new and deepened insight into the economic and social structure and process of development.'
1972	Arrow, Kenneth J.	Harvard	American	1921	'for their pioneering contributions to general economic equilibrium theory and welfare theory.'
	Hicks, John R.	Oxford	British	1904/1989	
1973	Leontief, Wassily	Harvard	American	1906 (Russia)	'for the development of the input-output method and for its application to important economic problems.'
1974	Hayek, Friedrich A. von	Friedburg	British	1899/1992 (Austria)	'for their pioneering work in the theory of money and economic fluctuations and for their penetrating analysis of the interdependence of economic, social and institutional phenomena.'
	Myrdal, Gunnar	Stockholm		1898/1987	
1975	Koopmans, Tjalling C.	Yale	American	1910/1986 (Netherlands)	'for their contributions to the theory of optimum allocation of resources.'
	Kantorovich, Leonid V.	Academy of Sciences, Moscow	Russian	1912/1986	
1976	Friedman, Milton	Chicago	American	1912	'for his achievements in the field of consumption analysis, monetary history and theory and for his demonstration of the complexity of stabilization policy.'

Year of award	Name	Institutional Affiliation	Nationality	Year of birth/death[b]	Prize citations[c]
1977	Meade, James E.	Cambridge	British	1907/1995	'for their pathbreaking contributions to the theory of international trade and international capital movements.'
	Ohlin, Bertil G.	Stockholm	Swedish	1899/1979	
1978	Simon, Herbert A.	Carnegie-Mellon	American	1916	'for his pioneering research into the decision-making process within economic organizations.'
1979	Lewis, W. Arthur	Princeton	British	1915/1991 (St. Lucia)	'for their pioneering research into development, with particular consideration of the problems of developing countries.'
	Schultz, Theodore	Chicago	American	1902	
1980	Klein, Lawrence R.	Pennsylvania	American	1920	'for the creation of econometric models and their application to the analysis of economic fluctuations and economic policies.'
1981	Tobin, James	Yale	American	1918	'for his analysis of financial markets and their relations to expenditure decisions, employment, production and prices.'
1982	Stigler, George J.	Chicago	American	1911/1991	'for his seminal studies of industrial structure, functioning of markets and causes and effects of public regulation.'
1983	Debreu, Gerard	California, Berkeley	American	1921 (France)	'for having incorporated new analytical methods into economic theory and for his rigorous reformulation of the theory of general equilibrium.'
1984	Stone, J. Richard N.	Cambridge	British	1913/1991	'for having made fundamental contributions to the development of systems of national accounts and hence greatly improved the basis for empirical economic analysis.'
1985	Modigliani, Franco	MIT	American	1918 (Italy)	'for his pioneering analysis of saving and of financial markets.'
1986	Buchanan, James M.	George Mason	American	1919	'for his development of the contractual and constitutional bases for the theory of economic and political decision-making.'
1987	Solow, Robert, M.	MIT	American	1924	'for his contributions to the theory of economic growth.'
1988	Allais, Maurice	Ecole Nationale Supérieure des Mines, Paris	French	1911	'for his pioneering contributions to the theory of markets and efficient utilization of resources.'
1989	Haavelmo, Trygve	Oslo	Norwegian	1911	'for his clarification of the probability theory foundations of econometrics and his analyses of simultaneous economic structures.'

Year of award	Name	Institutional Affiliation	Nationality	Year of birth/death[b]	Prize citations[c]
1990	Markowitz, Harry	City, New York	American	1927	'for their pioneering work in the theory of financial economics.'
	Miller, Merton	Chicago	American	1923	
	Sharpe, William	Stanford	American	1934	
1991	Coase, Ronald	Chicago	British	1910	'for his discovery and clarification of the significance of transaction costs and property rights for the institutional structure and functioning of the economy.'
1992	Becker, Gary S.	Chicago	American	1930	'for having extended the domain of micro-economic analysis to a wide range of human behavior and interaction, including non-market behavior.'
1993	Fogel, Robert W.	Chicago	American	1926	'for having renewed research in economic history by applying quantitative methods in order to explain economic and institutional change.'
	North, Douglass C.	Washington	American	1920	
1994	Harsanyi, John	California, Berkeley	American	1920 (Hungary)	'for their pioneering analysis of equilibria in the theory of non-cooperative games.'
	Nash, John	Princeton	American	1928	
	Selten, Reinhart	Bonn	German	1930	
1995	Lucas, Robert E.	Chicago	American	1937	'for having developed and applied the hypothesis of rational expectations, and thereby having transformed macroeconomic analysis and deepened our understanding of economic policy.'
1996	Mirrlees, James	Cambridge	British	1936	'for their fundamental contribution to the economic theory of incentives under asymmetric information.'
	Vickrey, William	Columbia	Canadian	1914/1996	
1997	Merton, Robert C.	Harvard	American	1944	'for a new method to determine the value of derivatives.'
	Scholes, Myron S.	Stanford	American	1941	

Notes:
[a] More exactly, the Bank of Sweden Prize in Economic Science in Honour of Alfred Nobel.
[b] And country of birth if different from nationality at time of prize being awarded.
[c] Full citations accompanying the official announcements of the prize were reported in the *Swedish Journal of Economics* (1969-74) and, since 1975, the *Scandinavian Journal of Economics*.

Sources: Adapted from Lindbeck (1985), Deane (1990b, app.) and Coats (1997b); biographical data from Blaug and Sturges (1983) and <http://www.nobel.se/cgi-bin/uncgi/laureate-search>

A guide to further reading

Introductory

There exists no comprehensive bibliography to all of the themes explored in this study, although Middleton (1996) contains a very full listing on many of the issues concerning economic performance and policy. On the latter, Tomlinson (1990; 1994) also introduces most of the main episodes and reports on the latest research, while Pollard (1992) performs the same service for economic performance and, for the prewar, interwar and postwar periods, should be supplemented by Pollard (1989), Solomou (1996) and Crafts and Woodward (1991) respectively. Floud and McCloskey (1994, vols 2–3) should also be consulted for the latest research, especially on economic performance. K. Robbins (1994) and P. Clarke (1996) provide general and reliable political histories of the period, with Gamble (1994a) combining economics and politics to produce a powerful account of Britain's decline.

Histories of economic thought

Amongst the numerous histories of economic thought Schumpeter (1954) still repays a close reading, while the following are either most appropriate to the British case or the most recent, reliable and comprehensive in their coverage: Backhouse (1985; 1988), Blaug (1997a) and Roll (1992); see also Blaug (1985; 1986) for brief biographical studies of leading economists, and O'Brien and Presley (1981) and Greenaway and Presley (1989) for more extended accounts of pioneers of modern economics in Britain.

For unrivalled snapshots of the state of economics and much associated material, see Palgrave's (1894–1908) original dictionary of political economy, the revised edition by Higgs (1923–6) and the mammoth latest edition by Eatwell *et al.* (1987) (which should be supplemented by Greenaway *et al.* 1991 and Newman *et al.* 1992), although the latest edition has come under much criticism for its partiality (see Blaug 1988).

Contemporary surveys of economic theory are also a useful source for charting developing professional concerns. Beginning with Ellis (1948), for the early postwar period, we highlight: AEA-RES (1965a; b; 1966), a collection – sponsored by the Rockefeller Foundation – of papers first published in the *AER* and *EJ* from the late 1950s onwards; the two further volumes on applied economics later issued by the RES-SSRC (1973; 1977), being reprints of specially commissioned *EJ* survey articles; and the latest collection of *EJ* survey articles edited by Oswald (1991b). In addition, both the International Economic Association (established 1950, and with Austin Robinson playing a central role in its activities from the outset) and the AEA were active in publishing surveys and books of readings from which one can sample at regular intervals the theoretical frontiers and economists of the moment.

The role of economics and economists in policy

This literature is now quite enormous, though less so for Britain than for America. It is also, again inevitably, biased towards the postwar period, and in the following selection we focus on Britain and attempt a broad historical coverage.

Beginning with academic studies of economists and public policy, Hutt (1936) was a pioneering effort to delineate the appropriate and actual roles of economists, while Walker (1943) was one of the first to attempt to bridge the gulf between theory and policy. One of the first manuals, offering advice on how to advise, was prepared by Jöhr and Singer (1955) and this can still be read with profit (see also Boulding 1958). Subsequently this market has become somewhat dominated either by manuals on project appraisal in developing countries, which explore the intricacies of CBA, or those that give guidance on how economists working in LDCs and international organisations can best tender advice, and the debate over their effectiveness. On the latter, see Seers's (1962) classic on why visiting economists fail and Coats (1986) on the experience of economists in international organisations. The locus classicus of manuals on project appraisal is Little and Mirrlees (1969), and for a current example of this genre, see HMSO (1988). The application of CBA, which is in effect applied welfare economics, and in practice the preoccupation of the greater number of economists now working in government broadly defined, in the context of British public policy has been surveyed by Colvin (1985), but see also Self (1975).

Studies of the role of economists include Pechman (1975), W.R. Allen (1977), Chester (1982), Rhoads (1985) and Nelson (1987). Of the historical studies, Winch (1969) provides an obvious starting point and has yet to be superseded for the prewar period. For the interwar period, the following all deal with specific policy areas but have much to say on the broader topic: Moggridge (1972) and Howson (1975) on monetary policy, Capie (1983) on tariffs and Middleton (1985) on fiscal policy. In addition, Howson and

Winch (1977) provide both a history of the EAC, the first formal agency for economists to advise government in Britain, and a more general treatment (see also G.C. Allen 1975).

For the Second World War and postwar period we have a mass of studies emanating from a number of sources. First, we have the accounts written by economists who have spent greater or lesser periods in government service. Foremost here is Alec Cairncross who has published more on this topic than anyone in Britain, or indeed, elsewhere (his US equivalent would be Herbert Stein). Unfortunately, Cairncross's papers (1955; 1968; 1970a; b; 1981; 1985a; 1986; 1989b; 1990; 1992; 1994; 1995; 1996; 1997; Cairncross and Watts 1989) have yet to be brought together in one collection. Within this category we should also include, for the war and early postwar years, Anderson (1947), Jewkes (1953; 1955; 1978), Chester (1951b), Devons (1959b; 1965) and the diaries of James Meade and Lionel Robbins (Howson and Moggridge 1990a; b); for the 1950s, the early works of Cairncross already cited together with Marris (1954), Robert Hall (1955; 1959), his diaries (Cairncross 1989c; 1991a) and K. Jones's (1994) biography, Ian Little (1957) and P.D. Henderson (1961; 1986); for the 1960s, Hallett (1967), Opie (1968a), Roll (1968b), Brittan (1969; 1971), Shanks (1970) and Seldon and Graham (1996); for the 1970s, Coddington (1973; 1974) and Peacock (1977a; 1991; 1992b); and for the 1980s to the present, Bray (1994; 1996), Budd (1994), Burns (1994), Eltis (1993) and Walters (1981).

Secondly, we can make use of biographical essays and memoirs from and about leading economists. Apart from Cairncross's works above we include here his biography of Austin Robinson (Cairncross 1993a), O'Brien's (1988) life of Robbins (together with Robbins's 1971 memoirs and Howson's introduction to Robbins 1997), Thirlwall (1987; 1989) on Kaldor, Eric Rolls's memoirs and musings (1978; 1985; 1995; Seldon and Roll 1996); interviews conducted by the journal *Econometric Theory* with Denis Sargan, Jim Durbin and Richard Stone (respectively Phillips 1985; 1988 and Pesaran 1991); and the following, commissioned by the *Banca Nazionale del Lavoro Quarterly Review* (many of which are reprinted in Kregel 1988–9): Hicks (1979), Phelps Brown (1980a), Shackle (1983), Kaldor (1986), Hahn (1994), Reddaway (1995) and Harcourt (1995). The introductory biographical essays to the series of *Economists of the Twentieth Century* (published by Edward Elgar, eds M. Perlman and M. Blaug) are also a fruitful source (for example, Thirlwall 1997 and Lipsey 1997). These two essays, together with thirty others from the series, are reproduced in Backhouse and Middleton (1999).

The third useful source is that of career civil servants, usually Treasury mandarins, governors of the Bank of England and politicians who held economic posts. In respect of the former, we have very little published material for the prewar years and First World War, but see Heath (1927), McFadyean (1964), Grigg (1948) and Hubback's (1985, esp. ch. 3) life of Walter Layton; for the interwar and early postwar period, Bridges (1950) is invaluable and can be supplemented by Leith-Ross (1968). There is also a study of Hawtrey, the one economist in the Treasury before the Second World War, but Deutscher (1990) has little to say about his official career (see also Howson 1985). For the postwar period we have a much fuller record, including contributions from – in addition to the all important Hall diaries detailed earlier – Cairncross's successor at the GES (MacDougall 1974; 1978; 1987), Browning (1986) and Plowden (1989). The specific problems of economic management are considered in short studies by R.W.B. Clarke (1964; also 1978), Armstrong (1969), Wass (1978), P. Middleton (1989) and Burns (1996) and in greater depth by Pliatzky (1984). In the next category, unfortunately few Bank governors have been studied, save, of course, the notorious Montagu Norman, on which see Clay's (1957) life; see also Sayers's (1976) study of the Bank for the early part of our period, Fforde (1992) who continues the account through to 1958 and Green (1992) on the influence of the Bank and the City on economic policy. Of the politicians, and more particularly Chancellors of the Exchequer, we have Dell's (1996) analysis of the performance of incumbents from Dalton to Major and studies of the following significant earlier figures: Austen Chamberlain (Dutton 1985, chs 1, 5), Lloyd George (Emy 1973, ch. 6), Snowden (Cross 1966, chs 12–16), Churchill (Clarke 1993), Neville Chamberlain (Middleton 1985, ch. 6). Others holding economic posts who have illuminated the policy process include Boyle (1979), Douglas Jay (1980), Barnett (1982), Dell (1991), and of course Crossman (1975–7).

Finally, the literature on economists and policy in the US provides useful benchmarks for assessing British developments. Stein (1986; 1994), a former chairman of the Council of Economic Advisers (CEA), the federal government agency of senior economists reporting directly to the president, provides a useful starting point (for an assessment of the CEA, see Feldstein 1992 and *Journal of Economic Perspectives*, vol. 10 (3) 1996, pp. 3–53). See also, for international surveys, Coats (1981a; 1997a; 1999), Pechman (1989) and Markoff and Montecinos (1993).

References

For reasons of economy, and to minimize repetition, the abbreviation **q.v.** has been used to refer the reader to the full entry for edited volumes; and the place and publisher of all CSO, HMSO and ONS entries is London: HMSO unless otherwise indicated.

Aaron, H.J. (1989) 'Politics and the professors revisited', *American Economic Review*, 79 (2, Papers & Proceedings), pp. 1–15.

Abbott, G.C. (1976) 'Why visiting economists fail: an alternative interpretation', *Public Administration*, 54 (1), pp. 31–43.

Ackley, G. (1982) 'Providing economic advice to government', in J.A. Pechman and N.J. Simler (eds) (1982) *Economics in the public service: papers in honor of Walter W. Heller.* New York: W.W. Norton, pp. 200–34.

Adonis, A. and Pollard, S. (1997) *A class act: the myth of Britain's classless society.* London: Hamish Hamilton.

AEA-RES (1965a; b; 1966) *Surveys of economic theory.* Vols I: *Money, interest and welfare*; II: *Growth and development*; III: *Resource allocation.* London: Macmillan.

AfP (1997) *Fast track study system: conversion examination – economics.* London: AfP Ltd.

Alexander, K.J.W. and Kemp, A.G. (1967) 'The economist in business: a survey', in K.J.W. Alexander *et al.* (eds) (1967) **q.v.**, pp. 1–58.

____, ____ and Rybczynski, T.M. (1967) *The economist in business.* Oxford: Basil Blackwell.

Allen, G.C. (1975) 'Advice from economists – forty-five years ago', *Three Banks Review*, 106 (June), pp. 35–50.

____ (1979) *The British disease: a short essay on the nature and causes of the nation's lagging wealth*, 2nd edn. London: IEA.

Allen, W.R. (1977) 'Economics, economists and economic policy: modern American experiences', *History of Political Economy*, 9 (1), pp. 48–88.

Alston, R.M., Kearl, J.R. and Vaughan, M.B. (1992) 'Is there a consensus among economists in the 1990s?', *American Economic Review*, 82 (2, Papers & Proceedings), pp. 203–9.

Anderson, J. (1947) *The organization of economic studies in relation to the problems of government.* London: Oxford University Press.

Andrews, P.W.S. (1949) *Manufacturing business.* London: Macmillan.

____ (1964) *On competition in economic theory.* London: Macmillan.

____ and Brunner, E. (1975) *Studies in pricing.* London: Macmillan.

Anon. (1895) 'Dinner of the British Economic Association', *Economic Journal*, 5 (2), pp. 301–2.

____ (1961) 'Professor for Whitehall', *The Economist*, 14 January, p. 117.

____ (1964) 'A vote of no confidence?', *The Economist*, 10 October, pp. 113–

15.
_____ (1968) 'Too many Treasury knights?', *The Economist*, 9 November, pp. 74–7.

_____ (1971) 'The flag flies for Europe', *The Economist*, 30 October, pp. 11–12.

_____ (1976) 'The work of the Economic Intelligence Department', *Bank of England Quarterly Bulletin*, 16 (4), pp. 436–46.

_____ (1997a) 'Economic policy advice: department of debunkery', *The Economist*, 18 January, pp. 83–4.

_____ (1997b) 'The puzzling failure of economics', *The Economist*, 23 August, p. 11.

Anyadike-Danes, M.K. (1985) 'Dennis Robertson and Keynes's *General Theory*', in G.C. Harcourt (ed.) (1985) q.v., pp. 105–23.

Arestis, P., Palma, J.G. and Sawyer, M.C. (eds) (1997) *Capital controversy, post-Keynesian economics and the history of economic thought: essays in honour of Geoff Harcourt*. London: Routledge.

_____ and Sawyer, M.C. (1998) 'Keynesian economic policies for the new millenium', *Economic Journal*, 108 (1), pp. 181–95.

Argy, V. (1988) 'A post-war history of the rules vs discretion debate', *Banca Nazionale del Lavoro Quarterly Review*, 41 (2), pp. 147–77.

Armstrong, W. (1969) *Some practical problems in demand management*. London: Athlone Press.

Arndt, H.W. (1978) *The rise and fall of economic growth: a study in contemporary thought*. Melbourne: Longman Cheshire.

Arrow, K.J. (1967) 'Samuelson collected', *Journal of Political Economy*, 75 (5), pp. 730–7.

_____ and Debreu, G. (1954) 'Existence of an equilibrium for a competitive economy', *Econometrica*, 22 (3), pp. 265–90.

Arthur, T. (1975) *Ninety-five per cent is crap: a plain man's guide to British politics*. Wharley End, Bedford: Libertarian Books.

Artis, M.J. and Cobham, D. (eds) (1991) *Labour's economic policies, 1974–1979*. Manchester: Manchester University Press.

Ashley, W.J. (1907) 'The present position of political economy', *Economic Journal*, 17 (4), pp. 467–89.

_____ (1908) 'The enlargement of economics', *Economic Journal*, 18 (2), pp. 181–204.

Atkinson, A.B. (1984) 'Taxation and social security reform: reflections on advising a House of Commons select committee', *Policy and Politics*, 12 (2), pp. 107–18.

_____ (1990) 'Public economics and the economic public', *European Economic Review*, 34 (2–3), pp. 225–48.

_____ (ed.) (1993) *Alternatives to capitalism: the economics of partnership*. London: Macmillan.

_____ (1997) 'Bringing income distribution in from the cold', *Economic Journal*, 107 (2), pp. 297–321.

AUT (1996) *Professional pay in universities: the problem and the solutions*. London: AUT.

Backhouse, R.E. (1985) *A history of modern economic analysis*. Oxford: Basil Blackwell.

_____ (1988) *Economists and the economy: the evolution of economic ideas, 1600 to the present day*. Oxford: Basil Blackwell.

_____ (1992) 'Should we ignore methodology?', *RES Newsletter*, 78 (July), pp. 4–5.

_____ (ed.) (1994) *New directions in economic methodology*. London: Routledge.

_____ (1995) *Interpreting macroeconomics: explorations in the history of macroeconomic thought*. London: Routledge.

_____ (1997a) 'The changing character of British economics', in A.W. Coats (ed.) (1997a) q.v., pp. 33–60.

_____ (1997b) *Truth and progress in economic knowledge.* Cheltenham: Edward Elgar.

_____ (1999a) 'Economics in mid-Atlantic: British economics, 1945–95', in A.W. Coats (ed.) (1999) q.v., forthcoming.

_____ (1999b) 'The transformation of US economics, 1920–1960', in M.S. Morgan and M. Rutherford (eds) (1999) *On the transformation of American economics: from interwar pluralism to postwar neoclassicism.* Duke: Duke University Press, forthcoming.

_____ and Middleton, R. (eds) (1999) *Exemplary economists*, 2 vols. Cheltenham: Edward Elgar, forthcoming.

_____, _____ and Tribe, K. (1997) '"Economics is what economists do", but what do the numbers tell us?', paper presented to History of Economic Thought Conference, Bristol.

Bacon, R.W. and Eltis, W.A. (1976) *Britain's economic problem: too few producers.* London: Macmillan.

Bagehot, W. (1873) *Lombard Street: a description of the money market.* London: C. Kegan Paul & Co.

Baldassarri, M. (ed.) (1992) *Keynes and the economic policies of the 1980s.* London: Macmillan.

Ball, R.J. and Holly, S. (1991) 'Macro-econometric model-building in the United Kingdom', in R.G. Bodkin, L.R. Klein and K. Marwah (eds) (1991) *A history of macroeconometric model-building.* Aldershot: Edward Elgar, pp. 195–230.

Balogh, T. (1959) 'The apotheosis of the dilettante: the establishment of mandarins', in H. Thomas (ed.) (1959) q.v., pp. 83–126.

_____ (1963) *Planning for progress: a strategy for Labour.* London: Fabian Society.

_____ (1979) 'Post-Keynesian international economics', *Challenge*, 22 (4), pp. 67–8.

_____ (1982) *The irrelevance of con-ventional economics.* London: Weidenfeld & Nicolson.

Barber, W.J. (1996) *Designs within disorder: Franklin D. Roosevelt, the economists and the shaping of American economic policy, 1933–1945.* Cambridge: Cambridge University Press.

_____ (1997a) 'Reconfigurations in American academic economics: a general practitioner's perspective', *Daedalus*, 126 (1), pp. 87–103.

_____ (1997b) 'Postwar changes in American graduate education in economics', in A.W. Coats (ed.) (1997a) q.v., pp. 12–30.

Barkai, H. (1993) 'Productivity patterns, exchange rates and the gold standard restoration debate of the 1920s', *History of Political Economy*, 25 (1), pp. 1–37.

Barnett, J. (1982) *Inside the Treasury.* London: André Deutsch.

Barro, R.J. (1974) 'Are government bonds net wealth?', *Journal of Political Economy*, 82 (6), pp. 1095–1117.

_____ (1978) 'Unanticipated money, output and the price level in the United States', *Journal of Political Economy*, 86 (4), pp. 549–80.

Baumol, W.J. (1995) 'What's different about European economics?', *Kyklos*, 48 (2), pp. 187–92.

Bazen, S. and Thirlwall, A.P. (1989) *Deindustrialization.* Oxford: Heinemann.

Bean, C.R. and Symons, J.S.V. (1989) 'Ten years of Mrs T', in O.J. Blanchard and S. Fischer (eds) (1989) *NBER macroeconomics annual, 1989.* Cambridge, MA: MIT Press, pp. 13–61.

Beaud, M. and Dostaler, G. (1997) *Economic thought since Keynes: a history and dictionary of major economists.* London: Routledge.

Becker, W.E. and Watts, M. (1996) 'Chalk and talk: a national survey on teaching undergraduate economics',

American Economic Review, 86 (2, Papers & Proceedings), pp. 448–53.

Beckerman, W. (ed.) (1972) *The Labour government's economic record, 1964–1970*. London: Duckworth.

_____ (1986) 'How large a public sector?', *Oxford Review of Economic Policy*, 2 (2), pp. 7–24.

_____ and Jenkinson, T.J. (1986) 'What stopped inflation?: unemployment or commodity prices?', *Economic Journal*, 96 (1), pp. 39–54.

Bell, D. and Kristol, I. (eds) (1981) *The crisis in economic theory*. New York: Basic Books.

Benn, T. (1989) *Against the tide: diaries, 1973–76*. London: Hutchinson.

Bergstrom, A.R., Catt, A.J.L., Peston, M.H. and Silverstone, B.D.J. (eds) (1978) *Stability and inflation: a volume of essays to honour the memory of A.W.H. Phillips*. Chichester: John Wiley.

Bharadwaj, K. (1972) 'Marshall on Pigou's *Wealth and welfare*', *Economica*, n.s. 39 (1), pp. 32–46.

Blackaby, F.T. (ed.) (1972) *An incomes policy for Britain*. London: Heinemann.

_____ (ed.) (1978a) *British economic policy, 1960–74*. Cambridge: Cambridge University Press.

_____ (1978b) 'Narrative, 1960–74', in F.T. Blackaby (ed.) (1978a) q.v., pp. 11–76.

Blackstone, T. and Plowden, W. (1990) *Inside the think tank: advising the Cabinet, 1971–1983*. London: Heinemann.

Blake, R. (1970) 'A personal memoir', in W.A. Eltis *et al.* (eds) (1970) q.v., pp. 1–19.

Blaug, M. (1975) *The Cambridge revolution – success or failure?: a critical analysis of Cambridge theories of value and distribution*, rev. edn. London: IEA.

_____ (1985) *Great economists since Keynes: an introduction to the lives*

and works of one hundred modern economists*. Brighton: Wheatsheaf.

_____ (1986) *Great economists before Keynes: an introduction to the lives and works of one hundred great economists of the past*. Brighton: Wheatsheaf.

_____ (1988) *Economics through the looking glass: the distorted perspective of the new Palgrave dictionary of economics*. London: IEA.

_____ (1990) Review of Young (1989), *History of Economic Thought Newsletter*, 44 (Spring), pp. 4–6.

_____ (1991) 'Second thoughts on the Keynesian revolution', *History of Political Economy*, 23 (2), pp. 171–92.

_____ (1992a) *The methodology of economics or how economists explain*, 2nd edn. Cambridge: Cambridge University Press.

_____ (ed.) (1992b) *Arthur Pigou (1877–1959)*. Aldershot: Edward Elgar.

_____ (1997a) *Economic theory in retrospect*, 5th edn. Cambridge: Cambridge University Press.

_____ (1997b) Review of Heilbroner and Milberg (1995), *Times Higher Education Supplement*, 23 May, p. 23.

_____ (1997c) 'Ugly currents in modern economics', *Policy Options*, 18 (7), pp. 3–8.

_____ and Sturges, R.P. (eds) (1983) *Who's who in economics: a biographical dictionary of major economists, 1700–1981*. Brighton: Wheatsheaf.

Bleaney, M.F. (1985) *The rise and fall of Keynesian economics: an investigation of its contribution to capitalist development*. London: Macmillan.

_____ (1996) 'An overview of emerging theory', in D. Greenaway, M.F. Bleaney and I.M.T. Stewart (eds) (1996) *A guide to modern economics*. Vol. I. London: Routledge, pp. 1–18.

Blinder, A.S. (1987) 'Keynes, Lucas and scientific progress', *American Eco-*

nomic Review, 77 (2, Papers & Proceedings), pp. 130–6.

_____ (1988) 'The fall and rise of Keynesian economics', *Economic Record*, 64 (4), pp. 278–94.

_____ (1997a) 'A core of macroeconomic beliefs?', *Challenge*, 40 (4), pp. 36–44.

_____ (1997b) *Central banking in theory and practice*. Cambridge, MA: MIT Press.

_____ (1997c) 'Is government too political?', *Foreign Affairs*, 76 (6), pp. 115–26.

Bliss, C. (1987) 'John Richard Hicks', in J. Eatwell *et al.* (eds) (1987) q.v., vol. II, pp. 641–6.

Bloom, A. (1987) *The closing of the American mind: how higher education has failed democracy and impoverished the souls of today's students*. New York: Simon and Schuster.

Blyth, M.M. (1997) '"Any more bright ideas?": the ideational turn of comparative political economy', *Comparative Politics*, 29 (2), pp. 229–50.

Boltho, A. and Graham, A.W.M. (1992) 'Has Mrs Thatcher changed the British economy?', in M. Baldassarri (ed.) (1992) q.v., pp. 259–89.

Booth, A.E. (1985) 'Economists and points rationing in the Second World War', *Journal of European Economic History*, 14 (2), pp. 297–317.

_____ (1986) 'Economic advice at the centre of British government, 1939–1941', *Historical Journal*, 29 (3), pp. 655–75.

_____ (1989) *British economic policy, 1931–49: was there a Keynesian revolution?* London: Harvester Wheatsheaf.

_____ and Coats, A.W. (1978) 'The market for economists in Britain, 1945–75: a preliminary survey', *Economic Journal*, 88 (3), pp. 436–54.

_____ and _____ (1980) 'Some wartime observations on the role of the economist in government', *Oxford Economic Papers*, n.s. 32 (2), pp. 177–99.

Bootle, R.P. (1996) *The death of inflation: surviving and thriving in the zero era*. London: Nicholas Brealey.

Bordo, M.D. and Landau, D. (1979) 'The pattern of citations in economic theory, 1945–68: an exploration towards a quantitative history of thought', *History of Political Economy*, 11 (2), pp. 240–53.

Boreham, A.J. (1978) 'A statistician's view', in M.V. Posner (ed.) (1978) q.v., pp. 139–50.

Boulding, K.E. (1958) *The skills of the economist*. London: Hamish Hamilton.

Bowley, A.L. (1921) *Official statistics: what they contain and how to use them*. London: Oxford University Press.

Boyce, R.W.D. (1988) 'Creating the myth of consensus: public opinion and Britain's return to the gold standard in 1925', in P.L. Cottrell and D.E. Moggridge (eds) (1988) *Money and power: essays in honour of L.S. Pressnell*. London: Macmillan, pp. 173–97.

Boyle, C. (1979) 'The economist in government', in J.K. Bowers (ed.) (1979) *Inflation, development and integration: essays in honour of A.J. Brown*. Leeds: Leeds University Press, pp. 1–23.

Brandon, H. (1966) *In the red: the struggle for sterling, 1964–1966*. London: André Deutsch.

Bray, J. (1994) 'The game of managing the economy', in S. Holly (ed.) (1994) q.v., pp. 3–25.

_____ (1996) 'Making economic policy', *Political Quarterly*, 67 (4), pp. 325–33.

_____, Hall, S.G., Kuleshov, A., Nixon, J. and Westaway, P. (1995) 'The interfaces between policy makers, markets and modellers in the design of economic policy: an intermodel comparison', *Economic Journal*, 105

(4), pp. 989–1000.

Breit, W. (1984) 'Galbraith and Friedman: two versions of economic reality', *Journal of Post-Keynesian Economics*, 7 (1), pp. 18–29.

Bridges, E.E. (1950) *Portrait of a profession: the civil service tradition.* Cambridge: Cambridge University Press.

Brint, S. (1994) *In an age of experts: the changing role of professionals in politics and public life.* Princeton, NJ: Princeton University Press.

British Association (1935) *Britain in depression: a record of British industries since 1929.* London: Isaac Pitman.

____ (1938) *Britain in recovery.* London: Isaac Pitman.

Brittan, S. (1964) *The Treasury under the Tories, 1951–1964.* Harmondsworth: Penguin.

____ (1969) 'The irregulars', in R. Rose (ed.) (1969) *Policy-making in Britain: a reader in government.* London: Macmillan, pp. 329–39.

____ (1971) *Steering the economy: the role of the Treasury*, rev. edn. Harmondsworth: Penguin.

____ (1973) *Is there an economic consensus?: an attitude survey.* London: Macmillan.

____ (1975) *Second thoughts on full employment.* London: CPS.

____ (1995a) 'Economics and ethics', in S. Brittan and A. Hamlin (eds) (1995) **q.v.**, pp. 1–22.

____ (1995b) 'Introduction: footfalls in the memory', in S. Brittan (1995) *Capitalism with a human face.* Aldershot: Edward Elgar, pp. 1–25.

____ and Hamlin, A. (eds) (1995) *Market capitalism and moral values.* Aldershot: Edward Elgar.

Britton, A.J.C. (1991) *Macroeconomic policy in Britain, 1974–87.* Cambridge: Cambridge University Press.

Britton, E. and Whitley, J.D. (1997) 'Comparing the monetary transmission mechanism in France, Germany and the United Kingdom: some issues and results', *Bank of England Quarterly Bulletin*, 37 (2), pp. 152–62.

Broadberry, S.N. (1994) 'Why was unemployment in postwar Britain so low?', *Bulletin of Economic Research*, 46 (3), pp. 241–61.

____ and Crafts, N.F.R. (1990) 'Explaining Anglo-American productivity differences in the mid-twentieth century', *Oxford Bulletin of Economics and Statistics*, 52 (4), pp. 375–402.

____ and ____ (1996) 'British economic policy and industrial performance in the early post-war period', *Business History*, 38 (4), pp. 65–91.

Bronfenbrenner, M. (1970) 'Radical economics in America: a 1970 survey', *Journal of Economic Literature*, 8 (3), pp. 747–66.

Brown, A.J. (1969) 'Surveys of applied economics: regional economics, with special reference to the United Kingdom', *Economic Journal*, 79 (4), pp. 759–96. Rep. in RES-SSRC (1973) **q.v.**, pp. 1–44.

____ (1972) *The framework of regional economics in the United Kingdom.* Cambridge: Cambridge University Press.

____ (1979) 'Inflation and the British sickness', *Economic Journal*, 89 (1), pp. 1–12.

____ (1987) 'A worm's eye view of the Keynesian revolution', in J. Hillard (ed.) (1987) *J.M. Keynes in retrospect: the legacy of the Keynesian revolution.* Aldershot: Edward Elgar, pp. 18–44.

Brown, B. (1996) *Economists and the financial markets.* London: Routledge.

Brown, G. (1971) *In my way.* London: Victor Gollancz.

Browning, P. (1986) *The Treasury and economic policy, 1964–1985.* London: Longman.

Brunner, K. (1968) 'The role of money

and monetary policy', *Federal Re-serve Bank of St Louis Review*, 50 (7), pp. 9–24. Rep. in K.A. Chrystal (ed.) (1990) **q.v.**, vol. 2, pp. 391–406.

____ (1971) 'The monetarist view of Keynesian ideas', *Lloyds Bank Review*, 102 (October), pp. 35–49.

____ (1981) 'The case against monetary activism', *Lloyds Bank Review*, 139 (January), pp. 20–39.

____ and Meltzer, A.H. (1976) 'Government, the private sector and "crowding out"', *The Banker*, 126 (July), pp. 765–9.

Buchanan, J.M. (1991) 'Economics in the post-socialist century', *Economic Journal*, 101 (1), pp. 15–21.

____, Burton, J. and Wagner, R.E. (1978) *The consequences of Mr Keynes: an analysis of the misuse of economic theory for political pro-fiteering with proposals for con-stitutional disciplines*. London: IEA.

Budd, A. (1978) *The politics of economic planning*. Glasgow: Collins/Fontana.

____ (1994) *Economic policy: too important to be left to economists?* Second Hilton Memorial Lecture. Southampton: University of Southampton.

Burk, K. (ed.) (1982a) *War and the state: the transformation of British government, 1914–1919*. London: George Allen & Unwin.

____ (1982b) 'The Treasury: from impotence to power', in K. Burk (ed.) (1982a) **q.v.**, pp. 84–107.

____ and Cairncross, A.K. (1992) *'Goodbye, Great Britain': the 1976 IMF crisis*. New Haven: Yale University Press.

Burns, T. (1994) 'Some reflections on the Treasury', in S. Holly (ed.) (1994) **q.v.**, pp. 39–61.

____ (1996) 'Managing the nation's economy: the conduct of monetary and fiscal policy', *Economic Trends*, 509 (March), pp. 21–6.

Burton, M.P. and Phimister, E. (1995) 'Core journals: a reappraisal of the Diamond list', *Economic Journal*, 105 (2), pp. 361–73.

Butler, D. and Butler, G. (1994) *British political facts, 1900–1994*, 7th edn. London: Macmillan.

Butler, E. (1985a) *Hayek: his con-tribution to the political and eco-nomic thought of our time*. New York: Universe Books.

____ (1985b) *Milton Friedman: a guide to his economic thought*. Aldershot: Gower.

Butler, R.A. (1971) *The art of the possible*. London: Hamish Hamilton.

Cain, P.J. (1979) 'Political economy in Edwardian England: the tariff-reform controversy', in A. O'Day (ed.) (1979) *The Edwardian age: conflict and stability, 1900–1914*. London: Macmillan, pp. 35–59.

Cairncross, A.K. (1955) 'On being an economic adviser', *Scottish Journal of Political Economy*, 2 (3), pp. 181–97.

____ (1968) 'The work of an economic adviser', *Public Administration*, 46 (1), pp. 1–11.

____ (1969) 'Economic forecasting', *Economic Journal*, 79 (4), pp. 797–812. Rep. in A.K. Cairncross (1971a) **q.v.**, pp. 139–58.

____ (1970a) 'Economists in government', *Lloyds Bank Review*, 95 (January), pp. 1–18. Rep. in A.K. Cairncross (1971a) **q.v.**, pp. 197–216.

____ (ed.) (1970b) *The managed economy*. Oxford: Basil Blackwell.

____ (1970c) 'The managed economy', in A.K. Cairncross (ed.) (1970b) **q.v.**, pp. 3–22.

____ (1970d) 'Writing the history of recent economic policy', unpublished paper.

____ (1971a) *Essays in economic management*. London: George Allen & Unwin.

____ (ed.) (1971b) *Britain's economic prospects reconsidered*. London:

George Allen & Unwin.

____ (1971c) 'Concluding reflections', in A.K. Cairncross (ed.) (1971b) **q.v.**, pp. 217–36.

____ (1981) 'Academics and policy makers', in F. Cairncross (ed.) (1981) *Changing perceptions of economic policy*. London: Methuen, pp. 5–22.

____ (1985a) 'Economics in theory and practice', *American Economic Review*, 75 (2, Papers & Proceedings), pp. 1–14.

____ (1985b) *Years of recovery: British economic policy, 1945–51*. London: Methuen.

____ (1986) *Economics and economic policy*. Oxford: Basil Blackwell.

____ (1987) 'Prelude to Radcliffe: monetary policy in the United Kingdom, 1948–57', *Rivista di Storia Economica*, 2nd ser. 4 (1), pp. 1–20.

____ (1988) 'The development of economic statistics as an influence on theory and policy', in D. Ironmonger, J.O.N. Perkins and T. Van Hoa (eds) (1988) *National income and economic progress: essays in honour of Colin Clark*. London: Macmillan, pp. 10–25.

____ (1989a) 'In praise of economic history', *Economic History Review*, 2nd ser. 42 (2), pp. 173–85.

____ (1989b) 'The United Kingdom', in J.A. Pechman (ed.) (1989) **q.v.**, pp. 25–46.

____ (ed.) (1989c) *The Robert Hall diaries*. Vol. I: *1947–53*. London: Unwin Hyman.

____ (1990) 'Reflections on economic ideas and government policy, 1939 and after', *Twentieth Century British History*, 1 (3), pp. 318–40.

____ (ed.) (1991a) *The Robert Hall diaries*. Vol. II: *1954–61*. London: Routledge.

____ (1991b) 'Reflections: how British aircraft production was planned in the Second World War', *Twentieth Century British History*, 2 (3), pp.

344–59.

____ (1992) 'From theory to policy making: economics as a profession', *Banca Nazionale del Lavoro Quarterly Review*, 45 (1), pp. 3–20.

____ (1993a) *Austin Robinson: the life of an economic adviser*. London: Macmillan.

____ (1993b) 'James Meade', in A.B. Atkinson (ed.) (1993) **q.v.**, pp. 1–6.

____ (1994) 'Economists in wartime', *Contemporary European History*, 4 (1), pp. 19–36.

____ (1995) 'Economic advisers in the United Kingdom', unpublished paper.

____ (1996) *Managing the British economy in the 1960s: a Treasury perspective*. London: Macmillan.

____ (1997) *The Wilson years: a Treasury diary, 1964–1969*. London: Historian's Press.

____ (1998) 'A century of economics', *Scottish Journal of Political Economy*, forthcoming.

____ and Eichengreen, B.J. (1983) *Sterling in decline: the devaluations of 1931, 1949 and 1967*. Oxford: Basil Blackwell.

____ and Watts, N. (1989) *The Economic Section, 1939–1961: a study in economic advising*. London: Routledge.

Cairncross, F. and Cairncross, A.K. (eds) (1992) *The legacy of the golden age: the 1960s and their economic consequences*. London: Routledge.

Caldwell, B.J. (1982) *Beyond positivism: economic methodology in the twentieth century*. London: Allen & Unwin.

____ (ed.) (1995a) *Collected works of F.A. Hayek*. Vol. IX: *Contra Keynes and Cambridge: essays, correspondence*. London: Routledge.

____ (1995b) 'Introduction', in B.J. Caldwell (ed.) (1995a) **q.v.**, pp. 1–48.

Callaghan, J. (1987) *Time and chance*. London: Collins.

Campbell, C. and Wilson, C.K. (1995) *The end of Whitehall: death of a paradigm?* Oxford: Basil Blackwell.

Cannan, E. (1927) *An economist's protest.* London: P.S. King.

____ (1932) Review of Robbins (1932), *Economic Journal*, 42 (3), pp. 424–7.

____ (1933) 'The need for a simpler economics', *Economic Journal*, 43 (3), pp. 367–78.

Capie, F.H. (1983) *Depression and protectionism: Britain between the wars.* London: George Allen & Unwin.

____ (1994) *Tariffs and growth: some illustrations from the world economy, 1850–1940.* Manchester: Manchester University Press.

Cardoso, J.L. (1995) 'Teaching the history of economic thought', *European Journal of the History of Economic Thought*, 2 (1), pp. 197–241.

Cassidy, J. (1996) 'The decline of economics', *New Yorker*, 2 December, pp. 50–60.

Caves, R.E. and Associates (1968) *Britain's economic prospects.* London: George Allen & Unwin.

____ and Krause, L.B. (eds) (1980) *Britain's economic performance.* London: George Allen & Unwin.

Chamberlin, E.H. (1933) *The theory of monopolistic competition: a reorientation of the theory of value.* Cambridge, MA: Harvard University Press.

Champernowne, D.G., Deane, P.M. and Reddaway, W.B. (1973) 'The Economic Journal: note by the editors', *Economic Journal*, 83 (2), pp. 495–504.

Chapman, R.A. (1997) *The Treasury in public policy-making.* London: Routledge.

Chester, D.N. (ed.) (1951a) *Lessons of the British war economy.* Cambridge: Cambridge University Press.

____ (1951b) 'The central machinery for economic policy', in D.N. Chester (ed.) (1951a) q.v., pp. 5–33.

____ (1982) 'The role of economic advisers in government', in A.P. Thirlwall (ed.) (1982) *Keynes as a policy adviser.* London: Macmillan, pp. 126–59.

____ (1986) *Economics, politics and social studies in Oxford, 1900–85.* London: Macmillan.

Chick, V. (1995) 'Is there a case for post-Keynesian economics?', *Scottish Journal of Political Economy*, 42 (1), pp. 20–36.

Chipman, J.S. and Moore, J.C. (1978) 'The new welfare economics, 1939–1974', *International Economic Review*, 19 (3), pp. 547–84.

Chrystal, K.A. (ed.) (1990) *Monetarism*, 2 vols. Aldershot: Edward Elgar.

Chung, K.H., Cox, A.K. and Okunade, A.A. (1993) 'Publishing behaviour of individuals and most prolific authors in the economics literature', *Quarterly Journal of Business and Economics*, 32 (3), pp. 32–42.

Clark, C.G. (1977) 'The "golden" age of the great economists: Keynes, Robbins et al. in 1930', *Encounter*, 48 (6), pp. 80–90.

Clarke, P.F. (1988) *The Keynesian revolution in the making, 1924–1936.* Oxford: Clarendon Press.

____ (1990a) 'The Treasury's analytical model of the British economy between the wars', in M.O. Furner and B.E. Supple (eds) (1990) q.v., pp. 171–207.

____ (1990b) 'The twentieth-century revolution in government: the case of the British Treasury', in F.B. Smith (ed.) (1990) *Ireland, England and Australia: essays in honour of Oliver MacDonagh.* Cork: Cork University Press, pp. 159–79.

____ (1993) 'Churchill's economic ideas, 1900–1930', in R. Blake and W.M. Louis (eds) (1993) *Churchill.* Oxford: Oxford University Press, pp. 79–95.

____ (1996) *The Penguin history of Britain. Vol. 9: Hope and glory.*

Britain, 1900–1990. London: Allen Lane.

Clarke, R.W.B. (1964) *The management of the public sector of the national economy.* London: Athlone Press. Rep. in R.W.B. Clarke (1978) **q.v.**, app. B.

_____ (1978) *Public expenditure, management and control: the development of the Public Expenditure Survey Committee (PESC),* ed. A.K. Cairncross. London: Macmillan.

Clay, H. (ed.) (1955) *The inter-war years and other papers: a selection from the writings of Hubert Douglas Henderson.* Oxford: Clarendon Press.

_____ (1957) *Lord Norman.* London: Macmillan.

Clifford, C. and McMillan, A. (1997) 'Witness seminar: the Department of Economic Affairs', *Contemporary British History,* 11 (2), pp. 117–42.

CNAA (1991) *Economics in the polytechnics and colleges.* London: CNAA.

Coats, A.W. (1964) 'The role of authority in the development of British economics', *Journal of Law and Economics,* 7 (1), pp. 85–106.

_____ (1967) 'Sociological aspects of British economic thought (ca.1880–1930)', *Journal of Political Economy,* 75 (5), pp. 706–29.

_____ (1968a) 'Political economy and the tariff reform campaign of 1903', *Journal of Law and Economics,* 11 (1), pp. 181–229.

_____ (1968b) 'The origins and early development of the Royal Economic Society', *Economic Journal,* 78 (2), pp. 349–71.

_____ (1969) 'The American Economic Association's publications: an historical perspective', *Journal of Economic Literature,* 7 (1), pp. 57–68.

_____ (1971) 'The role of scholarly journals in the history of economics: an essay', *Journal of Economic Literature,* 9 (1), pp. 29–44.

_____ (1975) 'The development of the economics profession in England: a preliminary review', in L. Houmanidis (ed.) (1975) *International congress of economic history and history of economic theories.* Piraeus: Piraeus Graduate School of Industrial Studies, pp. 277–90.

_____ (1976) 'The development of the agricultural economics profession in England', *Journal of Agricultural Economics,* 27 (3), pp. 381–92.

_____ (1977) 'The current "crisis" in economics in historical perspective', *Nebraska Journal of Economics and Business,* 16 (Summer), pp. 3–16. Rep. in A.W. Coats (1992a) **q.v.**, pp. 459–471.

_____ (1980) 'The culture and the economists: some reflections on Anglo-American differences', *History of Political Economy,* 12 (4), pp. 588–609.

_____ (ed.) (1981a) *Economists in government: an international comparative study.* Durham, NC: Duke University Press.

_____ (1981b) 'Introduction', *History of Political Economy,* 13 (3), pp. 341–64.

_____ (1981c) 'Britain, the rise of the specialists', *History of Political Economy,* 13 (3), pp. 365–404.

_____ (1982) 'The distinctive LSE ethos in the inter-war years', *Atlantic Economic Journal,* 10 (1), pp. 18–30. Rep. in A.W. Coats (1993) **q.v.**, pp. 372–392.

_____ (1984) 'The sociology of knowledge and the history of economics', in W.J. Samuels (ed.) (1984) *Research in the history of economic thought and methodology,* Vol. 2. Greenwich, CT: JAI Press, pp. 211–34. Rep. in A.W. Coats (1993) **q.v.**, pp. 11–36.

_____ (ed.) (1986) *Economists in international agencies: an exploratory study.* New York: Praeger.

_____ (1987a) 'Richard Theodore Ely', in J. Eatwell *et al.* (eds) (1987) **q.v.**, vol. II, pp. 129–30.

____ (1987b) 'Royal Economic Society', in J. Eatwell *et al.* (eds) (1987) **q.v.**, vol. IV, pp. 227–8.

____ (1987c) 'Mercantilism: economic ideas, history, policy', University of Newcastle, NSW, Australia Occasional Paper, 139. Rep. in A.W. Coats (1992a) **q.v.**, pp. 43–62.

____ (1988) 'Economics and psychology: a resurrection story', in P.E. Earl (ed.) (1988) *Psychological economics: development, tensions, prospects*. Boston, MA: Kluwer Academic, pp. 211–25.

____ (1990) 'Marshall and ethics', in R. McWilliams Tullberg (ed.) (1990) **q.v.**, pp. 153–77.

____ (1991a) 'Economics as a profession', in D. Greenaway *et al.* (eds) (1991) **q.v.**, pp. 119–42.

____ (1991b) 'The learned journals in the development of economics and the economics profession: the British case', *Economic Notes*, 20 (1), pp. 89–116.

____ (1992a) *British and American economic essays*. Vol. I: *On the history of economic thought*. London: Routledge.

____ (1992b) 'Changing perceptions of American graduate education in economics, 1953–1991', *Journal of Economic Education*, 23 (4), pp. 341–52.

____ (1993) *British and American economic essays*. Vol. II: *Sociology and professionalization of economics*. London: Routledge.

____ (1996) 'Memoirs of an economist watcher', *Journal of the History of Economic Thought*, 18 (2), pp. 250–70.

____ (1997a) *The post-1945 internationalization of economics*. Durham, NC: Duke University Press.

____ (1997b) 'The Nobel prize in economics', in P. Arestis *et al.* **q.v.**, vol. I, pp. 339–51.

____ (ed.) (1999) *The post-1945 de-velopment of economics in Europe*. London: Routledge, forthcoming.

____ and Coats, S.E. (1970) 'The social composition of the Royal Economic Society and the beginnings of the British economics "profession", 1890–1915', *British Journal of Sociology*, 21 (1), pp. 75–85.

____ and ____ (1973) 'The changing social composition of the Royal Economic Society 1890–1960 and the professionalization of British economics', *British Journal of Sociology*, 24 (2), pp. 165–87.

____ and Colander, D.C. (1989) 'An introduction to the spread of economic ideas', in D.C. Colander and A.W. Coats (eds) (1989) **q.v.**, pp. 1–19.

Cobham, D. (1984) 'Convergence, divergence and realignment in British macroeconomics', *Banca Nazionale del Lavoro Quarterly Review*, 37 (2), pp. 159–76.

____ (1997) 'The Lawson boom: excessive depreciation versus financial liberalisation', *Financial History Review*, 4 (1), pp. 69–90.

Cockett, R. (1994) *Thinking the unthinkable: think-tanks and the economic counter-revolution, 1931–1983*. London: Harper Collins.

Coddington, A. (1973) 'Economists and policy', *National Westminster Bank Quarterly Review*, (February), pp. 59–68.

____ (1974) 'Re-thinking economic policy', *Political Quarterly*, 45 (4), pp. 426–38.

____ (1983) *Keynesian economics: the search for first principles*. London: George Allen & Unwin.

Colander, D.C. (1994) 'The art of economics by the numbers', in R.E. Backhouse (ed.) (1994) **q.v.**, pp. 35–49.

____ and Coats, A.W. (eds) (1989) *The spread of economic ideas*. Cambridge: Cambridge University Press.

____ and Klamer, A. (1987) 'The

making of an economist', *Journal of Economic Perspectives*, 1 (2), pp. 95–111.

Cole, G.D.H. (ed.) (1933) *What everybody wants to know about money: a planned outline of monetary problems by nine economists from Oxford*. London: Victor Gollancz.

Coleman, D.C. (1987) *History and the economic past: an account of the rise and decline of economic history in Britain*. Oxford: Clarendon Press.

Collard, D.A. (1968) *The New Right: a critique*. London: Fabian Society.

—— (1981a) 'Market failure and government failure', in Arthur Seldon (ed.) (1981) q.v., pp. 123–46.

—— (1981b) 'A.C. Pigou, 1877–1959', in D.P. O'Brien and J.R. Presley (eds) (1981) q.v., pp. 105–39.

—— (1990) 'Cambridge after Marshall', in J.K. Whitaker (ed.) (1990a) q.v., pp. 164–92.

—— (1996) 'Pigou and modern business cycle theory', *Economic Journal*, 106 (4), pp. 912–24.

Colvin, P. (1985) *The economic ideal in British government: calculating costs and benefits in the 1970s*. Manchester: Manchester University Press.

Congdon, T.G. (1973) 'Why has inflation accelerated?', *National Westminster Bank Quarterly Review*, (February), pp. 6–19.

—— (1989) 'British and American monetarism compared', in R. Hill (ed.) (1989) *Keynes, money and monetarism*. London: Macmillan, pp. 38–72.

—— (1992) *Reflections on monetarism: Britain's vain search for a successful economic strategy*. Aldershot: Edward Elgar/IEA.

Cooper, R.N. (1968) 'The balance of payments', in R.E. Caves *et al.* (1968) q.v., pp. 147–97.

Coopey, R., Fielding, S. and Tiratsoo, N. (eds) (1993) *The Wilson governments, 1964–70*. London: Pinter.

Cooter, R. and Rappoport, P. (1984) 'Were the ordinalists wrong about welfare economics?', *Journal of Economic Literature*, 22 (2), pp. 507–30.

Copeland, M.A. (1941) 'Economic research in the federal government', *American Economic Review*, 31 (3), pp. 526–36.

Copp, C. (1992) 'Three kinds of economists: memberships and characteristics', *American Journal of Economics and Sociology*, 51 (1), pp. 43–55.

Coppock, D.J. (1965) 'The alleged case against devaluation', *The Manchester School*, 33 (3), pp. 285–312.

Corner, J. (1996) *The art of record: a critical introduction to documentary*. Manchester: Manchester University Press.

Coughlin, P.J. (1989) 'Economic policy advice and political preferences', *Public Choice*, 61 (3), pp. 201–16.

Court, S. (1996) 'The use of time by academic and related staff', *Higher Education Quarterly*, 50 (4), pp. 237–60.

Coutts, K., Godley, W.A.H., Rowthorn, R.E. and Zezza, G. (1990) *Britain's economic problems and policies in the 1990s*. London: IPPR.

Covick, O.E. (1974) 'The quantity theory of drink: a restatement', *Australian Economic Papers*, 13 (2), pp. 171–7.

Crafts, N.F.R. (1991) 'Economics and history', in D. Greenaway *et al.* (eds) (1991) q.v., pp. 812–29.

—— and Woodward, N.W.C. (eds) (1991) *The British economy since 1945*. Oxford: Clarendon Press.

Croham, Lord (1992) 'Were the instruments of control for domestic economic policy adequate?', in F. Cairncross and A.K. Cairncross (eds) (1992) q.v., pp. 81–93.

Croome, D.R. and Johnson, H.G. (eds) (1970) *Money in Britain, 1959–1969*. Oxford: Oxford University Press.

Cross, C. (1966) *Philip Snowden.* London: Barrie & Rockliff.

Crossman, R.H.S. (1975–7) *The diaries of a cabinet minister,* 3 vols. London: Hamish Hamilton/Jonathan Cape.

Crowther, G. (1940) *An outline of money.* London: Thomas Nelson.

Cullis, J.G. and Jones, P.R. (1992) *Public finance and public choice: analytical perspectives.* London: McGraw-Hill.

Dahrendorf, R. (1995) *LSE: a history of the London School of Economics and Political Science, 1895–1995.* Oxford: Oxford University Press.

Dale, H.E. (1941) *The higher civil service of Great Britain.* Oxford: Oxford University Press.

Darnell, A.C. and Evans, J.L. (1990) *The limits of econometrics.* Aldershot: Edward Elgar.

David, P.A. (1993) 'Historical economics in the longrun: some implications of path-dependence', in G.D. Snooks (ed.) (1993) **q.v.**, pp. 29–40.

Davidson, R. (1985) *Whitehall and the labour problem in late-Victorian and Edwardian Britain: a study in official statistics and social control.* London: Croom Helm.

____ (1993) 'The state and social investigation in Britain, 1880–1914', in M.J. Lacey and M.O. Furner (eds) (1993) *The state and social investigation in Britain and the United States.* Cambridge: Cambridge University Press, pp. 242–75.

Deane, P.M. (ed.) (1990a) *Frontiers of economic research.* London: Macmillan.

____ (1990b) 'A view from the frontiers of economic research', in P.M. Deane (ed.) (1990a) **q.v.**, pp. 1–19.

Debreu, G. (1986) 'Theoretic models: mathematical form and economic content', *Econometrica,* 54 (6), pp. 1259–70.

____ (1991) 'The mathematization of economic theory', *American Economic Review,* 81 (1), pp. 1–7.

Dell, E. (1991) *A hard pounding: politics and economic crisis, 1974–1976.* Oxford: Oxford University Press.

____ (1996) *The Chancellors: a history of the Chancellors of the Exchequer, 1945–90.* London: Harper Collins.

De Marchi, N.B. (1988) 'Popper and the LSE economists', in N.B. De Marchi (ed.) (1988) *The Popperian legacy in economics.* Cambridge: Cambridge University Press, pp. 139–66.

____ and Blaug, M. (eds) (1991) *Appraising economic theories: studies in the methodology of research programs.* Aldershot: Edward Elgar.

____ and Gilbert, C.L. (eds) (1989) *History and methodology of econometrics.* Oxford: Clarendon Press.

Demsetz, H. (1997) 'The primacy of economics: an explanation of the comparative success of economics in the social sciences', *Economic Inquiry,* 35 (1), pp. 1–11.

Desai, M. (1991) 'The underworld of economics: heresy and heterodoxy in economic thought', in G.K. Shaw (ed.) (1991) *Economics, culture and education: essays in honour of Mark Blaug.* Aldershot: Edward Elgar, pp. 53–63.

____ (1997) 'Foreword', in P. Arestis *et al.* (eds) (1997) **q.v.**, vol. I, pp. xvii–xx.

Deutscher, P. (1990) *R.G. Hawtrey and the development of macroeconomics.* London: Macmillan.

Devons, E. (1950) *Planning in practice: essays in aircraft planning in wartime.* Cambridge: Cambridge University Press.

____ (1959a) 'The economist's view of the Bank Rate Tribunal evidence', *The Manchester School,* 27 (1), pp. 1–16.

____ (1959b) 'The rôle of the economist in public affairs', *Lloyds Bank Review,* 53 (July 1959), pp. 26–38. Rep in E. Devons (1970) **q.v.**, pp. 33–46.

_____ (1961) *Essays in economics*. London: George Allen & Unwin.

_____ (1965) 'Economists and the public', *Lloyds Bank Review*, 77 (July), pp. 19–29. Rep. in E. Devons (1970) **q.v.**, pp. 174–85.

_____ (1970) *Papers on planning and economic management*, ed. A.K. Cairncross. Manchester: Manchester University Press.

Dewald, W.G., Thursby, J.G. and Anderson, R.G. (1986) 'Replication in empirical economics: the *Journal of Money, Credit and Banking* project', *American Economic Review*, 76 (4), pp. 587–603.

Diamond, A.M. (1989) 'The core journals of economics', *Current Contents*, 21 (January), pp. 4–11.

_____ and Haurin, D.R. (1995) 'Changing patterns of subfield specialization among cohorts of economists from 1927–1988', *Research in the History of Economic Thought and Methodology*, 13, pp. 103–23.

Dixit, A.K. (1996) *The making of economic policy: a transaction-cost politics perspective*. Cambridge, MA: MIT Press.

Dobb, M.H. (1978) 'Random biographical notes', *Cambridge Journal of Economics*, 2 (2), pp. 115–20.

Dogan, M. (1996) 'Political science and the other social sciences', in R.E. Goodin and H.-D. Klingemann (eds) (1996) *A new handbook of political science*. Oxford: Oxford University Press, pp. 97–130.

Dolton, P.J. and Makepeace, G.H. (1990) 'The earnings of economics graduates', *Economic Journal*, 100 (1), pp. 237–50.

_____, Greenaway, D. and Vignoles, A. (1997) '"Wither higher education"?: an economic perspective for the Dearing committee of inquiry', *Economic Journal*, 107 (3), pp. 710–26.

Dow, J.C.R. (1964) *The management of the British economy, 1945–60*. Cambridge: Cambridge University Press.

Dow, S.C. (1997) 'Mainstream economic methodology', *Cambridge Journal of Economics*, 21 (1), pp. 73–93.

Dunleavy, P., Gamble, A.M., Holliday, I. and Peele, G. (eds) (1997) *Developments in British politics 5*. London: Mamcillan.

Durbin, E.F. (1985) *New Jerusalems: the Labour Party and the economics of democratic socialism*. London: Routledge & Kegan Paul.

Durbin, E.F.M. (1938) 'Methods of research: a plea for co-operation in the social sciences', *Economic Journal*, 48 (2), pp. 183–95.

_____ (1943) 'Economists and the future functions of the state', *Political Quarterly*, 14 (3), pp. 256–69.

Dutton, D. (1985) *Austen Chamberlain, gentleman in politics*. Bolton: Ross Anderson.

Earl, P.E. (1983) 'A behavioral theory of economists' behavior', in A.S. Eichner (ed.) (1983) **q.v.**, pp. 90–125.

_____ (1993) 'Epilogue: whatever happened to P.W.S. Andrews's industrial economics?', in F.S. Lee and P.E. Earl (eds) (1993) **q.v.**, pp. 402–27.

Eatwell, J. (1994) 'Institutions, efficiency and the theory of economic policy', *Social Research*, 61 (1), pp. 35–53.

_____, Milgate, M. and Newman, P. (eds) (1987) *The new Palgrave: a dictionary of economics*, 4 vols. London: Macmillan.

Edgeworth, F.Y. (1891) 'The British Economic Association', *Economic Journal*, 1 (1), pp. 1–14.

Edwards, R.D. (1993) *The pursuit of reason: the Economist, 1843–1993*. London: Hamish Hamilton.

Eichengreen, B.J. (1992) *Golden fetters: the gold standard and the great depression, 1919–1939*. New York: Oxford University Press.

_____ (1996) *Globalizing capital: a history of the international monetary system*. Princeton, NJ: Princeton University Press.

Eichner, A.S. (1978) Review of

Andrews and Brunner (1975), *Journal of Economic Literature*, 16 (4), pp. 1436–8.

____ (ed.) (1983) *Why economics is not yet a science*. New York: M.E. Sharpe.

Einzig, P. (1960) *In the centre of things: an autobiography*. London: Hutchinson.

Elbaum, B. and Lazonick, W.H. (eds) (1986a) *The decline of the British economy*. Oxford: Clarendon Press.

____ and ____ (1986b) 'An institutional perspective on British decline', in B. Elbaum and W.H. Lazonick (eds) (1986a) **q.v.**, pp. 1–17.

Elliott, R.F. and Duffus, K. (1996) 'What has been happening to pay in the public sector of the British economy?: developments over the period 1970–1992', *British Journal of Industrial Relations*, 34 (1), pp. 51–85.

Ellis, H.S. (ed.) (1948) *A survey of contemporary economics*. Philadelphia: Blakiston Co.

Eltis, W.A. (1976) 'The failure of the Keynesian conventional wisdom', *Lloyds Bank Review*, 122 (October), pp. 1–18.

____ (1992) 'Has the reaction against Keynesian policy gone too far?', in M. Baldassarri (ed.) (1992) **q.v.**, pp. 51–64.

____ (1993) 'Introduction: how my economics evolved', in W.A. Eltis (1993) *Classical economics, public expenditure and growth*. Aldershot: Edward Elgar, pp. ix–xxxi.

____ (1997) *The creation and destruction of EMU*. London: CPS.

____, Scott, M.FG., and Wolfe, J.N. (eds) (1970) *Induction, growth and trade: essays in honour of Sir Roy Harrod*. Oxford: Clarendon Press.

Emmison, M. (1983) '"The economy": its emergence in media discourse', in H. Davis and P. Walton (eds) (1983) *Language, image, media*. Oxford: Basil Blackwell, pp. 139–55.

Emy, H.V. (1973) *Liberals, radicals and social politics, 1892–1914*. Cambridge: Cambridge University Press.

Epstein, R.J. (1987) *A history of econometrics*. Amsterdam: North–Holland.

Fabian Society (1964) *The administrators: the reform of the civil service*. London: Fabian Society.

Faulhaber, G.R. and Baumol, W.J. (1988) 'Economists as innovators: practical products of theoretical research', *Journal of Economic Literature*, 26 (2), pp. 577–600.

Feiwel, G.R. (ed.) (1985) *Issues in contemporary microeconomics and welfare*. London: Macmillan.

Feldstein, M.S. (1992) 'The Council of Economic Advisers and economic advising in the United States', *Economic Journal*, 102 (5), pp. 1223–34.

Fels, R. (1992) 'An update on Leontief's complaint', *Journal of Economic Perspectives*, 6 (1), pp. 201–4.

Fforde, J.S. (1992) *The Bank of England and public policy, 1941–1958*. Cambridge: Cambridge University Press.

Figlio, D. (1994) 'Trends in the publication of empirical economics', *Journal of Economic Perspectives*, 8 (3), pp. 179–87.

Fine, B. (1997) 'The new revolution in economics', *Capital & Class*, 61 (Spring), pp. 143–8.

Floud, R.C. and McCloskey, D.N. (eds) (1994) *The economic history of Britain since 1700*, 2nd edn. 3 vols. Cambridge: Cambridge University Press.

Forte, F. (1995) 'European economics: a tiny creature under tutorship', *Kyklos*, 48 (2), pp. 211–17.

Foxwell, H.S. (1887) 'The economic movement in England', *Quarterly Journal of Economics*, 2 (1), pp. 84–103.

Fraser, L.M. (1938) 'Economists and their critics', *Economic Journal*, 48 (2), pp. 196–210.

Freeden, M. (ed.) (1990) *Reappraising*

J.A. Hobson: humanism and welfare. London: Unwin Hyman.

Frenkel, J.A. (1987) 'Harry Gordon Johnson', in J. Eatwell *et al.* (eds) (1987) **q.v.**, vol. II, pp. 1022–6.

___ and Johnson, H.G. (eds) (1976) *The monetary approach to the balance of payments.* London: Allen & Unwin.

Frey, B.S. and Eichenberger, R. (1993) 'American and European economics and economists', *Journal of Economic Perspectives*, 7 (4), pp. 185–93.

___, Pommerehne, W.W., Schneider, F. and Gilbert, G. (1984) 'Consensus and dissension among economists: an empirical inquiry', *American Economic Review*, 74 (5), pp. 986–94.

Friedman, M. (1948) 'A monetary and fiscal framework for economic stability', *American Economic Review*, 38 (3), pp. 245–64.

___ (1953) *Essays in positive economics.* Chicago: University of Chicago Press.

___ (1956) 'The quantity theory of money: a restatement', in M. Friedman (ed.) (1956) *Studies in the quantity theory of money.* Chicago: University of Chicago Press, pp. 3–21.

___ (1968) 'The role of monetary policy', *American Economic Review*, 58 (1), pp. 1–17. Rep. in K.A. Chrystal (ed.) (1990) **q.v.**, vol. 2, pp. 374–90.

___ (1970a) *The counter-revolution in monetary theory.* London: IEA.

___ (1970b) 'The new monetarism: comment', *Lloyds Bank Review*, 98 (October), pp. 52–3. Rep. in N. Kaldor (1978b) **q.v.**, pp. 23–5.

___ (1972) 'Have monetary policies failed?', *American Economic Review*, 62 (2, Papers & Proceedings), pp. 11–18.

___ (1975) *Unemployment versus inflation: an evaluation of the Phillips curve.* London: IEA.

___ (1977a) *From Galbraith to economic freedom.* London: IEA.

___ (1977b) *Inflation and unemployment: the new dimension of politics.* London: IEA.

___ (1980) 'Memorandum', in HMSO (1980) House of Commons Treasury and civil service committee, *Memoranda on monetary policy*, HC 720 (1979–80), pp. 55–61.

___ (1986) 'Has liberalism failed?', in IEA (ed.) (1986) *The unfinished agenda: essays on the political economy of government policy in honour of Arthur Seldon.* London: IEA, pp. 125–39.

___ (1987) 'Quantity theory of money', in J. Eatwell *et al.* (eds) (1987) **q.v.**, vol. 4, pp. 3–20.

___ (1991) 'Old wine in new bottles', *Economic Journal*, 101 (1), pp. 33–40.

___ and Friedman, R.D. (1962) *Capitalism and freedom.* Chicago: University of Chicago Press.

___ and ___ (1980) *Free to choose: a personal statement.* London: Secker & Warburg.

___ and ___ (1984) *The tyranny of the status quo.* London: Secker & Warburg.

Fry, G.K. (1976) 'The Marshallian school and the role of the state', *Bulletin of Economic Research*, 28 (1), pp. 23–35.

___ (1993) *Reforming the civil service: the Fulton committee on the British home civil service of 1966–1968.* Edinburgh: Edinburgh University Press.

Furner, M.O. and Supple, B.E. (eds) (1990) *The state and economic knowledge: the American and British experiences.* Cambridge: Cambridge University Press.

Galbraith, J.K. (1958) *The affluent society.* London: Hamish Hamilton.

___ (1975a) 'How Keynes came to America', in M. Keynes (ed.) (1975) **q.v.**, pp. 132–41.

___ (1975b) Letter, *The Times*, 16 July, p. 12.

____ (1993) *The culture of contentment*. Harmondsworth: Penguin.

Gamble, A.M. (1989) 'Ideas and interests in British economic policy', in IEA (ed.) (1989) **q.v.**, pp. 1–21.

____ (1994a) *Britain in decline: economic policy, political strategy and the British state*, 4th edn. London: Macmillan.

____ (1994b) *The free economy and the strong state: the politics of Thatcherism*, 2nd edn. London: Macmillan.

____ and Walkland, S.A. (1984) *The British party system and economic policy, 1945–1983: studies in adversary politics*. Oxford: Clarendon Press.

Garside, W.R. (1980) *The measurement of unemployment: methods and sources in Great Britain, 1850–1979*. Oxford: Basil Blackwell.

George, C. and Bewlay, S. (1964) *Two men of influence: a new look at Professor Kaldor and Professor Balogh*. London: Aims of Industry.

Gilbert, C.L. (1989) 'LSE and the British approach to time series econometrics', *Oxford Economic Papers*, n.s. 41 (1), pp. 108–28. Rep. in N.B. De Marchi and C.L. Gilbert (eds) (1989) **q.v.**, pp. 108–28.

Gilchrist, P. (1994) *Economic realism*. Adelaide: Society of Lapsed Economists.

Gilmour, I. (1992) *Dancing with dogma: Britain under Thatcherism*. London: Simon & Schuster.

Godley, W.A.H. and Gillion, C. (1964) 'Measuring national product', *National Institute Economic Review*, 27 (February), pp. 61–7.

Goldfarb, R.S. (1997) 'Now you see it, now you don't: emerging contrary results in economics', *Journal of Economic Methodology*, 4 (2), pp. 221–44.

Goodhart, C.A.E. (1984) *Monetary theory and practice: the UK experience*. London: Macmillan.

____ (1994) 'Game theory for central bankers: a report to the Governor of the Bank of England', *Journal of Economic Literature*, 32 (1), pp. 101–14.

Gordon, H.S. (1971) 'The ideology of laissez-faire', in A.W. Coats (ed.) (1971) *The classical economists and economic policy*. London: Methuen, pp. 180–205.

Graham, A.W.M. (1992) 'Thomas Balogh (1905–1985)', *Contemporary Record*, 6 (1), pp. 194–207.

____ and Beckerman, W. (1972) 'Introduction: economic performance and the foreign balance', in W. Beckerman (ed.) (1972) **q.v.**, pp. 11–27.

Grant, W.P. and Marsh, D. (1977) *The Confederation of British Industry*. London: Hodder & Stoughton.

Green, E.H.H. (1992) 'The influence of the City over British economic policy, c.1880–1960', in Y. Cassis (ed.) (1992) *Finance and financiers in European history, 1880–1960*. Cambridge: Cambridge University Press, pp. 193–218.

Green, S.J.D. and Whiting, R.C. (eds) (1996) *The boundaries of the state in modern Britain*. Cambridge: Cambridge University Press.

Greenaway, D. (1989) 'James Meade, 1907–', in D. Greenaway and J.R. Presley (eds) (1989) **q.v.**, pp. 120–43.

____ (1990) 'On the efficient use of mathematics in economics: results of an attitude survey of British economists', *European Economic Review*, 34 (7), pp. 1339–51.

____, Bleaney, M.F. and Stewart, I.M.T. (eds) (1991) *Companion to contemporary economic thought*. London: Routledge.

____ and Presley, J.R. (eds) (1989) *Pioneers of modern economics in Britain*. Vol. 2. London: Macmillan.

Greenleaf, W.H. (1983) *The British political tradition. Vol. I: The rise of collectivism*. London: Methuen.

Gregory, T.E. and Dalton, H. (eds)

(1927) *London essays in economics: essays in honour of Edwin Cannan.* London: George Routledge & Sons.

Grigg, J. (1993) *The History of The Times.* Vol. VI: *The Thompson years, 1966–1981.* London: Times Books.

Grigg, P.J. (1948) *Prejudice and judgement.* London: Jonathan Cape.

Groenewegen, P.D. (1995) *Soaring eagle: Alfred Marshall, 1842–1924.* Aldershot: Edward Elgar.

____ (1996) *Official papers of Alfred Marshall: a supplement.* Cambridge: Cambridge University Press.

Grubel, H.G. and Boland, L. (1986) 'On the efficient use of mathematics in economics: some theory, facts and results of an opinion survey', *Kyklos*, 39 (3), pp. 412–42.

Guillebaud, C.W. (1971) 'Some personal reminiscences of Alfred Marshall', *History of Political Economy*, 3 (1), pp. 1–8.

Gulbenkian Commission (1996) *Report of the commission on the restructuring of the social sciences.* Stanford, CA: Stanford University Press.

Hackett, J. and Hackett, A.-M. (1963) *Economic planning in France.* London: George Allen & Unwin.

Hahn, F.H. (1970) 'Some adjustment problems', *Econometrica*, 38 (1), pp. 1–17.

____ (1973) 'The winter of our discontent', *Economica*, n.s. 40 (3), pp. 322–30.

____ (1985) *In praise of economic theory.* London: University College London.

____ (1990) 'John Hicks the theorist', *Economic Journal*, 100 (3), pp. 539–49.

____ (1991) 'The next hundred years', *Economic Journal*, 101 (1), pp. 47–50.

____ (1992a) 'Reflections', *RES Newsletter*, 77 (April), p. 5.

____ (1992b) 'Answer to Backhouse: Yes', *RES Newsletter*, 78 (July), p. 5.

____ (1993) 'James Meade and benevolence', in A.B. Atkinson (ed.) (1993) **q.v.**, pp. 251–62.

____ (1994) 'An intellectual retrospect', *Banca Nazionale del Lavoro Quarterly Review*, 47 (3), pp. 245–58.

____ and Weale, M.R. (1988) 'Were the 364 wrong?', *The Times*, 12 September, p. 12.

Hall, A.D. (1987) 'Worldwide rankings of research activity in econometrics, 1980–1985', *Econometric Theory*, 3 (2), pp. 171–94.

____ (1990) 'Worldwide rankings of research activity in econometrics: an update, 1980–1988', *Econometric Theory*, 6 (1), pp. 1–16.

Hall, P.A. (1986a) *Governing the economy: the politics of state intervention in Britain and France.* Cambridge: Polity Press.

____ (1986b) 'The state and economic decline', in B. Elbaum and W.H. Lazonick (eds) (1986a) **q.v.** pp. 266–302.

____ (ed.) (1989a) *The political power of economic ideas: Keynesianism across nations.* Princeton, NJ: Princeton University Press.

____ (1989b) 'Introduction', in P.A. Hall (ed.) (1989a) **q.v.**, pp. 3–26.

____ (1992a) 'Economics and the modern state', *Twentieth Century British History*, 3 (1), pp. 84–91.

____ (1992b) 'The movement from Keynesianism to monetarism: institutional analysis and British economic policy in the 1970s', in S. Steinmo, K. Thelen and F.H. Longstreth (eds) (1992) *Structuring politics: historical institutionalism in comparative analysis.* Cambridge: Cambridge University Press, pp. 90–113.

____ (1993) 'Policy paradigms, social learning and the state: the case of economic policymaking in Britain', *Comparative Politics*, 25 (3), pp. 275–96.

Hall, R.L. (1955) 'The place of the economist in government', *Oxford Economic Papers*, n.s. 7 (2), pp.

119–35.

___ (1959) 'Reflections on the practical application of economics', *Economic Journal*, 69 (4), pp. 639–52.

___ and Hitch, C.J. (1939) 'Price theory and business behaviour', *Oxford Economic Papers*, old ser. 2 (1), pp. 12–45. Rep. in Wilson and Andrews (eds) (1951) q.v., pp. 107–38.

Hall, S.G. (1995) 'Macroeconomics and a bit more reality', *Economic Journal*, 105 (4), pp. 974–88.

Hallett, G. (1967) 'The rôle of economists as government advisers', *Westminster Bank Review*, (May), pp. 2–20.

Halsey, A.H. (1992) *Decline of donnish dominion: the British academic professions in the twentieth century*. Oxford: Clarendon Press.

___ and Trow, M.A. (1971) *The British academics*. London: Faber & Faber.

Ham, A. (1981) *Treasury rules: recurrent themes in British economic policy*. London: Quartet Books.

Hammond, J.D. (1996) *Theory and measurement: causality issues in Milton Friedman's monetary economics*. Cambridge: Cambridge University Press.

Hamouda, O.F. and Harcourt, G.C. (1988) 'Post-Keynesianism: from criticism to coherence?', *Bulletin of Economic Research*, 40 (1), pp. 1–33.

Hancock, W.K. and Gowing, M.M. (1949) *British war economy*. London: HMSO.

Hannah, L. (1983) *The rise of the corporate economy*, 2nd edn. London: Methuen.

___ (1993) 'Cultural determinants of economic performance: an experiment in measuring human capital flows', in G.D. Snooks (ed.) (1993) q.v., pp. 158–71.

Hansard (1956) Budget speech, *Parliamentary Debates* (House of Commons), 5th ser. 551 (17 April), cols. 852–889.

___ (1981) Prime minister's questions, *Parliamentary Debates* (House of Commons), 6th ser. 2 (31 March), cols. 147–52.

Hansen, B. (1969) *Fiscal policy in seven countries, 1955–1965: Belgium, France, Germany, Italy, Sweden, United Kingdom, United States*. Paris: OECD.

Hansen, W.L. (1991) 'The education and training of economics doctorates: major findings of the executive secretary of the American Economic Association's commission on graduate education in economics', *Journal of Economic Literature*, 29 (3), pp. 1054–87.

Harberger, A.C. (1993) 'Secrets of success: a handful of heroes', *American Economic Review*, 83 (2, Papers & Proceedings), pp. 343–50.

Harcourt, G.C. (1972) *Some Cambridge controversies in the theory of capital*. Cambridge: Cambridge University Press.

___ (ed.) (1985) *Keynes and his contemporaries*. London: Macmillan.

___ (1995) 'Recollections and reflections of an Australian patriot and a Cambridge economist', *Banca Nazionale del Lavoro Quarterly Review*, 48 (3), pp. 225–54.

___ (1996) 'Some reflections on Joan Robinson's changes of mind and their relationship to post-Keynesianism and the economics profession', in M.C. Marcuzzo, L.L. Pasinetti and A. Roncaglia (eds) (1996) *The economics of Joan Robinson*. London: Routledge, pp. 317–29.

Hargrove, E.C. (1972) *Professional roles in society and government: the English case*. Beverly Hills, CA: Sage.

Harris, J. (1972) *Unemployment and politics: a study in English social policy, 1886–1914*. Oxford: Clarendon Press.

____ (1977) *William Beveridge: a biography*. Oxford: Clarendon Press.

____ (1990a) 'Society and state in twentieth-century Britain', in F.M.L. Thompson (ed.) (1990) *The Cambridge social history of Britain, 1750–1950*. Vol. 3: *Social agencies and institutions*. Cambridge: Cambridge University Press, pp. 63–117.

____ (1990b) 'Economic knowledge and British social policy', in M.O. Furner and B.E. Supple (eds) (1990) **q.v.**, pp. 379–400.

Harris, R. (1980) *The end of government ...?* London: IEA.

____ and Sewill, B. (1975) *British economic policy, 1970–74: two views*. London: IEA.

Harrison, B. (1994) 'Mrs Thatcher and the intellectuals', *Twentieth Century British History*, 5 (2), pp. 206–45.

Harrod, R.F. (1936) *The trade cycle: an essay*. Oxford: Clarendon Press.

____ (1938) 'Scope and method of economics', *Economic Journal*, 48 (3), pp. 383–412.

____ (1939) 'An essay in dynamic theory', *Economic Journal*, 49 (1), pp. 14–33.

____ (1948) *Towards a dynamic economics: some recent developments of economic theory and their application to policy*. London: Macmillan.

____ (1951) *The life of John Maynard Keynes*. London: Macmillan.

____ (1963) 'Themes in dynamic theory', *Economic Journal*, 73 (3), pp. 401–21.

____ (1969) 'Keynes: the arrested revolution', *New Statesman*, 78 (5 December), pp. 808–10.

____ (1971a) 'Philip Andrews and the Oxford Economists' Research Group', *Journal of Industrial Economics*, 20 (1), pp. 6–7.

____ (1971b) *Sociology, morals and mystery*. London: Macmillan.

Hart, P.E., Mills, G. and Whitaker, J.K. (1964) *Econometric analysis for national economic planning*. London: Butterworths.

Hausman, D.M. and McPherson, M.S. (1993) 'Taking ethics seriously: economics and contemporary moral philosophy', *Journal of Economic Literature*, 31 (2), pp. 671–731.

Hawkins, R.G., Ritter, L.S. and Walter, I. (1973) 'What economists think of their journals', *Journal of Political Economy*, 81 (4), pp. 1017–32.

Hawtrey, R.G. (1913) *Good and bad trade: an inquiry into the causes of trade fluctuations*. London: Constable.

____ (1927) *The gold standard in theory and practice*. London: Longmans, Green & Co.

____ (1931) *Trade depression and the way out*. London: Longmans, Green & Co.

____ (1937) *Capital and employment*. London: Longmans, Green & Co.

____ (1961) *The pound at home and abroad*. London: Longmans.

von Hayek, F.A. (1931) *Prices and production*. London: Routledge.

____ (1933a) 'The trend of economic thinking', *Economica*, 13 (2), pp. 121–37.

____ (1933b) *Monetary theory and the trade cycle*. Trans. N. Kaldor and H.M. Croome. London: Jonathan Cape.

____ (1944) *The road to serfdom*. London: Routledge & Kegan Paul.

____ (1963) 'The economics of the 1930s as seen from London', unpublished lecture, University of Chicago. Rep. in B.J. Caldwell (ed.) (1995a) **q.v.**, pp. 49–73.

____ (1966) 'Personal recollections of Keynes and the "Keynesian revolution"'. Rep. in S.R. Shenoy (ed.) (1978) *A tiger by the tail: a 40-years' running commentary on Keynesianism by Hayek*, 2nd edn. London: IEA, pp. 99–106.

Heald, D. (1983) *Public expenditure: its defence and reform*. Oxford: Basil Blackwell.

Healey, D. (1989) *The time of my life*. London: Michael Joseph.

Healey, N.M. (1987) 'The UK 1979–82 "monetarist experiment": why economists still disagree', *Banca Nazionale del Lavoro Quarterly Review*, 40 (4), pp. 471–99.

—— (ed.) (1993) *Britain's economic miracle: myth or reality?* London: Routledge.

Heath, T.L. (1927) *The Treasury*. London: Putnam.

Heclo, H. and Wildavsky, A. (1981) *The private government of public money: community and policy inside British politics*, 2nd edn. London: Macmillan.

HEFCE (1996) *Review of postgraduate education* (Harris report). Bristol: HEFCE/CVCP/SCOP.

Heilbroner, R.L. and Milberg, W.S. (1995) *The crisis of vision in modern economic thought*. Cambridge: Cambridge University Press.

Heller, W.W. (1975) 'What's right with economics?', *American Economic Review*, 65 (1), pp. 1–26.

Henderson, H.D. (1922) *Supply and demand*. London: Nisbet & Co.

—— (1931) 'The state of economics', in H. Clay (ed.) (1955) q.v., pp. 78–80.

—— (1936) 'Mr Keynes's theories', in H. Clay (ed.) (1955) q.v., pp. 161–77.

Henderson, P.D. (1961) 'The use of economists in British administration', *Oxford Economic Papers*, n.s. 13 (1), pp. 5–26.

—— (ed.) (1966) *Economic growth in Britain*. London: Weidenfeld & Nicolson.

—— (1986) *Innocence and design: the influence of economic ideas on policy*. Oxford: Basil Blackwell.

Henderson, W., Dudley-Evans, T. and Backhouse, R.E. (eds) (1993) *Economics and language*. London: Routledge.

Hendry, D.F. (1980) 'Economtrics: alchemy or science?', *Economica*, n.s. 47 (4), pp. 387–406.

—— (1997) 'Research assessment exercise – revisited', *RES Newsletter*, 99 (October), p. 6.

Hennessy, P. (1975) 'Economists multiply and thrive', *The Times*, 24 November, p. 1.

—— (1990) *Whitehall*, rev. edn. London: Fontana.

HESA (1997) *Students in higher education institutions, 1995/6*. Cheltenham: Higher Education Statistics Agency.

Hey, J.D. (ed.) (1989) *Current issues in microeconomics*. London: Macmillan.

—— and Winch, D.N. (eds) (1990) *A century of economics: 100 years of the Royal Economic Society and the Economic Journal*. Oxford: Basil Blackwell.

Hicks, J.R. (1937) 'Mr Keynes and the classics: a suggested interpretation', *Econometrica*, 5 (2), pp. 147–59. Rep. in J.R. Hicks (1967) *Critical essays in monetary theory*. Oxford: Clarendon Press, pp. 126–42.

—— (1939) *Value and capital: an inquiry into some fundamental principles of economic theory*. Oxford: Clarendon Press.

—— (1963) *The theory of wages*, 2nd edn. London: Macmillan.

—— (1973) 'Recollections and documents', *Economica*, n.s. 40 (1), pp. 2–11.

—— (1975) 'What is wrong with monetarism', *Lloyds Bank Review*, 118 (October), pp. 1–13.

—— (1979) 'The formation of an economist', *Banca Nazionale del Lavoro Quarterly Review*, 32 (3), pp. 195–204.

Higgins, B. (1952) *What do economists know?* Cambridge: Cambridge University Press.

Higgs, E. (1988) 'The struggle for the occupational census, 1841–1911', in R.M. MacLeod (ed.) (1988a) q.v., pp. 73–86.

Higgs, H. (ed.) (1923–6) *Palgrave's dictionary of political economy*, 3 vols. London: Macmillan.

Hills, J. (1983) 'A co-operative and constructive relationship?: the Treasury response to its select committee, 1979–82', *Fiscal Studies*, 4 (1), pp. 1–13.

Hirsch, A. and De Marchi, N.B. (1990) *Milton Friedman: economics in theory and practice*. Hemel Hempstead: Harvester Wheatsheaf.

Hirsch, F. and Goldthorpe, J.H. (eds) (1978) *The political economy of inflation*. Oxford: Martin Robertson.

Hirshleifer, J. (1985) 'The expanding domain of economics', *American Economic Review*, 75 (6), pp. 53–68.

Hirschman, A.O. (1982) *Shifting involvements: private interest and public action*. Oxford: Martin Robertson.

Hirst, F.W. (1947) *In the golden days*. London: Frederick Muller.

HMSO (1918) Committee on currency and foreign exchanges after the war (Cunliffe committee), *First interim report*, BPP 1918 (9182), vii, 853.

____(1919) Committee on currency and foreign exchanges after the war (Cunliffe committee), *Final report*, BPP 1919 (464), xiii, 593.

____ (1927) Committee on national debt and taxation (Colwyn committee), *Report*, BPP 1927 (2800), xi, 371.

____ (1929) Committee on industry and trade (Balfour committee), *Final report*, BPP 1928–9 (3282), vii, 413.

____ (1931) Committee on finance and industry (Macmillan committee), *Report*, BPP 1930–1 (3897), xiii, 219.

____ (1944) Ministry of Reconstruction, *Employment policy after the war*, BPP 1943–4 (6527), viii, 119.

____ (1946) Committee on the provision for social and economic research (Clapham committee), *Report*, BPP 1945–6 (6868), xiv, 655.

____ (1959) Committee on the working of the monetary system (Radcliffe committee), *Report*, BPP 1958–9 (827), xvii.

____ (1960) *Principal memoranda of evidence submitted to the Committee on the working of the monetary system* (Radcliffe committee), Vol. 3.

____ (1961) Control of public expenditure (Plowden committee), *Report*, BPP 1960–1 (1432), xxi, 713.

____ (1963a) Committee on higher education (Robbins committee), *Report*, BPP 1962–3 (2154), xi.

____ (1963b) Committee on higher education (Robbins committee), Appendix III: *Teachers in higher education*, BPP 1962–3 (2154-III), xii.

____ (1963c) Committee on higher education (Robbins committee), Appendix 5: *Higher education in other countries*, BPP 1962–3 (2154-V), xiii.

____ (1965a) Committee on social studies (Heyworth committee), *Report*, BPP 1964–5 (2660), xxii.

____ (1965b) Department of Economic Affairs, *The national plan*, BPP 1964–5 (2764), xxx.

____ (1966) Estimates committee, *Fourth report: government statistical services*, HC 246 (1966–7).

____ (1968) Committee on the civil service (Fulton committee), *Report*, BPP 1967–8 (3638), xviii.

____ (1969) Department of Economic Affairs, *The task ahead: economic assessment to 1972*.

____ (1970) Civil Service Commission, *Economists in government service*.

____ (1973) House of Commons expenditure committee, *Second report together with the minutes of evidence taken before the trade and industry sub-committee, Regional development incentives: report*, HC 85 (1973/4).

____ (1974) *Report of the Social Sciences Research Council, April 1973-March 1974*, HC 177 (1974).

____ (1981) House of Commons, *Third report from the Treasury and civil service committee, Monetary policy*, HC 163-I (1980–1).

_____ (1985a) *Economic trends, annual supplement.*

_____ (1985b) House of Lords, *Report from the select committee on overseas trade*, HL 238-I (1984–5).

_____ (1988) Overseas Development Administration, *Appraisal of projects in developing countries: a guide for economists.*

_____ (1994) Office of Population Censuses and Surveys and General Register Office for Scotland, *1991 census: qualified manpower, Great Britain*, 2 vols.

_____ (1997) National committee of enquiry into higher education (Dearing committee), *Report: higher education in the learning society*, HC 70 (1996–7).

Hobbs, P. and Judge, G. (1992) 'Computers as a tool for teaching economics', *Computers and Education*, 19 (1/2), pp. 67–72.

Hobson, J.A. (1938) *Confessions of an economic heretic*. London: George Allen & Unwin.

Hobson, O.R. (1938) *How the city works*. London: News Chronicle.

Hodgson, G.M. (1997) 'The fate of the Cambridge capital controversy', in P. Arestis *et al.* (eds) (1997) **q.v.**, vol. I, pp. 95–110.

Hogwood, B.W. and Gunn, L.A. (1984) *Policy analysis for the real world*. Oxford: Oxford University Press.

Holly, S. (ed.) (1994) *Money, inflation and employment: essays in honour of James Ball*. Aldershot: Edward Elgar.

Holmes, C.J. (1976) 'Laissez-faire in theory and practice: Britain, 1800–1875', *Journal of European Economic History*, 5 (3), pp. 671–88.

Holub, H.W., Tappeiner, G. and Eberharter, V. (1991) 'The iron law of important articles', *Southern Economic Journal*, 58 (2), pp. 317–28.

Hoover, K.D. (1988) *The new classical macroeconomics: a sceptical inquiry*. Oxford: Basil Blackwell.

Hopkin, W.A.B., Miller, M.H. and Reddaway, W.B. (1982) 'An alternative economic strategy – a message of hope', *Cambridge Journal of Economics*, 6 (1), pp. 85–103.

Horne, A. (1989) *Macmillan*. Vol. II: *1957–1986*. London: Macmillan.

Howe, G. (1991) 'The 364 economists: ten years on', *Fiscal Studies*, 12 (4), pp. 92–107.

Howitt, P. (1986a) 'Conversations with economists: a review article', *Journal of Monetary Economics*, 18 (1), pp. 103–18.

_____ (1986b) 'The Keynesian recovery', *Canadian Journal of Economics*, 19 (4), pp. 626–41.

Howson, S.K. (1975) *Domestic monetary management in Britain, 1919–38*. Cambridge: Cambridge University Press.

_____ (1985) 'Hawtrey and the real world', in G.C. Harcourt (ed.) (1985) **q.v.**, pp. 142–88.

_____ (ed.) (1988) *The collected papers of James Meade*. Vol. I: *Employment and inflation*. London: Unwin Hyman.

_____ (1993) *British monetary policy, 1945–51*. Oxford: Clarendon Press.

_____ and Moggridge, D.E. (eds) (1990a) *The wartime diaries of Lionel Robbins and James Meade, 1943–45*. London: Macmillan.

_____ and _____ (eds) (1990b) *The collected papers of James Meade*. Vol. IV: *The Cabinet Office diary, 1944–46*. London: Unwin Hyman.

_____ and Winch, D.N. (1977) *The Economic Advisory Council, 1930–1939: a study in economic advice during depression and recovery*. Cambridge: Cambridge University Press.

Hubback, D. (1985) *No ordinary press baron: a life of Walter Layton*. London: Weidenfeld & Nicolson.

_____ (1988) 'Sir Richard Clarke, 1910–

1975: a most unusual civil servant', *Public Administration Review*, 3 (1), pp. 19–34.

Hume, L.J. (1963) 'The gold standard and deflation: issues and attitudes in the 1920s', *Economica*, n.s. 30 (3), pp. 225–42. Rep. in S. Pollard (ed.) (1970a) **q.v.**, pp. 122–45.

Hutchison, T.W. (1938) *The significance and basic postulates of economic theory*. London: Macmillan.

_____ (1953) *A review of economic doctrines, 1870–1929*. Oxford: Clarendon Press.

_____ (1955) 'Insularity and cosmopolitanism in economic ideas, 1870–1914', *American Economic Review*, 45 (2, Papers & Proceedings), pp. 1–16.

_____ (1968) *Economics and economic policy in Britain, 1946–1966: some aspects of their interrelations*. London: George Allen & Unwin.

_____ (1973) Review of Beckerman (1972), *Economica*, n.s. 40 (2), pp. 222–3.

_____ (1977a) *Knowledge and ignorance in economics*. Oxford: Basil Blackwell.

_____ (1977b) *Keynes versus the 'Keynesians' ...? An essay in the thinking of J.M. Keynes and the accuracy of its interpretation by his followers*. London: IEA.

_____ (1978a) Review of Howson and Winch (1977), *Economic History Review*, 2nd ser. 31 (1), pp. 155–6.

_____ (1978b) *On revolution and progress in economic knowledge*. Cambridge: Cambridge University Press.

_____ (1981a) *The politics and philosophy of economics: Marxians, Keynesians and Austrians*. Oxford: Basil Blackwell.

_____ (1981b) 'The changing intellectual climate in economics', in Arthur Seldon (ed.) (1981) **q.v.**, pp. 21–49.

_____ (1984) 'Our methodological crisis', in P.J.D. Wiles and G. Routh (eds) (1984) **q.v.**, pp. 1–21.

_____ (1992) *Changing aims in economics*. Oxford: Basil Blackwell.

_____ (1993) 'The uses and abuses of academic economics'. Rep. in T.W. Hutchison (1994a) **q.v.**, pp. 282–306.

_____ (1994a) *The uses and abuses of economics: contentious essays on history and method*. London: Routledge.

_____ (1994b) 'Ends and means in the methodology of economics', in R.E. Backhouse (ed.) (1994) **q.v.**, pp. 27–34.

Hutt, W.H. (1936) *Economists and the public: a study of competition and opinion*. London: Jonathan Cape.

Hutton, W. (1995) *The state we're in*. London: Jonathan Cape.

_____ (1997) 'Can the Treasury culture change?', *Political Quarterly*, 68 (1), pp. 85–7.

_____, Congdon, T.G., Green, D.G., Kalms, S., Ricketts, M. and Sternberg, E. (1997) *Stateholding and its critics*. London: IEA.

IBRD (1997) *World development report, 1997*. Oxford: Oxford University Press.

IEA (ed.) (1978) *The economics of politics*. London: IEA.

_____ (ed.) (1979) *The taming of government: micro/macro disciplines on Whitehall and town hall*. London: IEA.

_____ (1986) *Keynes's General theory: fifty years on. Its relevance and irrelevance to modern times*. London: IEA.

_____ (ed.) (1989) *Ideas, interests and consequences*. London: IEA.

IFS (1978) *The structure and reform of direct taxation: report of a committee chaired by Professor J.E. Meade*. London: George Allen & Unwin.

Ingham, B. (1992) 'Shaping opinion on development policy: economists at the Colonial Office during World War II', *History of Political Economy*, 24 (3), pp. 689–710.

Ingham, G. (1996) 'Some recent changes in the relationship between economics and sociology', *Cambridge Journal of Economics*, 20 (2), pp. 243–75.

Jackson, D. (1980) 'Economics education and the real world', *Lloyds Bank Review*, 138 (October), pp. 42–54.

Jacobsson, E.E. (1979) *A life for sound money: Per Jacobsson, his biography*. Oxford: Clarendon Press.

Jansen, D.W. (1991) 'Ranking Federal Reserve System research departments by publications in professional journals', *Journal of Macroeconomics*, 13 (4), pp. 733–42.

Jay, D.P.T. (1937) *The socialist case*. London: Faber & Faber.

_____ (1968) 'Government control of the economy: defects in the machinery', *Political Quarterly*, 39 (2), pp. 134–44.

_____ (1980) *Change and fortune: a political record*. London: Hutchinson.

Jenkins, R. (1991) *A life at the centre*. London: Macmillan.

Jenkins, S.P. and Cowell, F.A. (1994) 'Dwarfs and giants in the 1980s: trends in the UK income distribution', *Fiscal Studies*, 15 (1), pp. 99–118.

Jewkes, J. (1948) *Ordeal by planning*. London: Macmillan.

_____ (1953) 'The economist and public policy', *Lloyds Bank Review*, 28 (April), pp. 18–32.

_____ (1955) 'The economist and economic change', in A. Smithies *et al.* (ed.) (1955) *Economics and public policy*. Washington, DC: Brookings Institution, pp. 81–99.

_____ (1968) *The new ordeal by planning: the experience of the forties and the sixties*, 2nd edn. London: Macmillan.

_____ (1978) *A return to free market economics?: critical essays on government intervention*. London: Macmillan.

Jha, N. (1973) *The age of Marshall: aspects of British economic thought, 1890–1915*, 2nd edn. London: Frank Cass.

Johnes, G. (1992) 'Performance indicators in higher education: a survey of recent work', *Oxford Review of Economic Policy*, 8 (2), pp. 19–34.

_____ and Johnes, J. (1993) 'Measuring the research performance of UK economics departments: an application of data envelopment analysis', *Oxford Economic Papers*, n.s. 45 (2), pp. 332–47.

Johnson, C. (1996) *In with the Euro, out with the pound: the single currency for Britain*. Harmondsworth: Penguin.

Johnson, H.G. (1960) 'Arthur Cecil Pigou, 1877–1959', *Canadian Journal of Economics and Political Science*, 26 (2), pp. 150–5.

_____ (1962) *Money, trade and economic growth*. London: George Allen & Unwin.

_____ (1968) 'A catarrh of economists?: from Keynes to Postan', *Encounter*, 30 (5), pp. 50–4.

_____ (1970) 'Monetary theory and monetary policy', *Euromoney*, 2 (7), pp. 16–20. Rep. in H.G. Johnson (1972a) **q.v.**, pp. 77–87.

_____ (1971a) 'Revolution & counter-revolution in economics: from Lord Keynes to Milton Friedman', *Encounter*, 36 (4), pp. 23–33.

_____ (1971b) 'The Keynesian revolution and the monetarist counter-revolution', *American Economic Review*, 61 (2, Papers & Proceedings), pp. 1–14. Rep. in H.G. Johnson (1972a) **q.v.**, pp. 50–69.

_____ (1972a) *Further essays in monetary economics*. London: George Allen & Unwin.

_____ (1972b) Review of Robbins (1971), *Journal of Political Economy*, 80 (4), pp. 835–6.

_____ (1972c) 'Individual and collective choice', in W.A. Robson (ed.) (1972) *Man and the social sciences*. London: George Allen & Unwin, pp. 1–22.

_____ (1973a) 'National styles in economic research: the United States, the United Kingdom, Canada and various European countries', *Daedalus*, 102 (2), pp. 65–74.

_____ (1973b) 'Some micro-economic reflections on income and wealth inequalities', *Annals of the American Academy of Political and Social Science*, 409 (5), pp. 53–60.

_____ (1974a) 'The current and prospective state of economics', *Australian Economic Papers*, 13 (2), pp. 1–27.

_____ (1974b) 'Major issues in monetary economics', *Oxford Economic Papers*, n.s. 26 (2), pp. 212–25.

_____ (1974c) 'The state of theory', *American Economic Review*, 64 (2, Papers & Proceedings), pp. 323–4.

_____ (1975a) 'Keynes and British economics', in M. Keynes (ed.) (1975) q.v., pp. 108–22.

_____ (1975b) 'What passes for economics in the English establishment', *The Banker*, 125 (October), pp. 1159–61. Rep. in E.S. Johnson and H.G. Johnson (eds) (1978) *The shadow of Keynes: Keynes, Cambridge and Keynesian economics*. Oxford: Basil Blackwell, pp. 221–6.

_____ (1976) 'What is right with monetarism', *Lloyds Bank Review*, 120 (April), pp. 13–17.

_____ (1977a) 'Cambridge as an academic environment in the early 1930s: a reconstruction from the late 1940s', in D. Patinkin and J.C. Leith (eds) (1977) q.v., pp. 98–114.

_____ (1977b) 'The American tradition in economics', *Nebraska Journal of Economics and Business*, 16 (Summer), pp. 17–26.

_____ (1978) 'James Meade's contribution to economics', *Scandinavian Journal of Economics*, 80 (1), pp. 64–85.

Jöhr, W.A. and Singer, H.W. (1955) *The role of the economist as official adviser*. Trans. J. Degras and S. Frowein. London: George Allen & Unwin.

Jones, K. (1988) 'Fifty years of economic research: a brief history of the National Institute of Economic and Social Research, 1938–88', *National Institute Economic Review*, 124 (May), pp. 36–62.

_____ (1994) *An economist among mandarins: a biography of Robert Hall (1901–1988)*. Cambridge: Cambridge University Press.

Jones, P.R. and Cullis, J.G. (1993) 'Public choice and public policy: the vulnerability of economic advice to the interpretation of politicians', *Public Choice*, 75 (1), pp. 63–77.

Jones, T. (1954) *A diary with letters, 1931–1950*. London: Oxford University Press.

Jordan, G. and Richardson, J.J. (1982) 'The British policy style or the logic of negotiation?', in J.J. Richardson (ed.) (1982) *Policy styles in western Europe*. London: George Allen & Unwin, pp. 80–110.

Junz, H.B. and Rhomberg, R.R. (1965) 'Prices and export performance of industrial countries, 1953–63', *IMF Staff Papers*, 12 (3), pp. 224–69.

Kadish, A. (1982) *The Oxford economists in the late nineteenth century*. Oxford: Oxford University Press.

_____ (1989) *Historians, economists and economic history*. New York: Routledge.

_____ (1991) 'The foundation of Birmingham's faculty of commerce as a statement on the nature of economics', *The Manchester School*, 59 (2), pp. 160–72.

_____ and Freeman, R.D. (1990) 'Foundation and early years', in J.D. Hey and D.N. Winch (eds) (1990) q.v., pp. 22–48.

_____ and Tribe, K. (eds) (1993a) *The market for political economy: the advent of economics in British university culture, 1850–1905*. London: Routledge.

——— and ——— (1993b) 'Introduction: the supply of and demand for economics in late Victorian Britain', in A. Kadish and K. Tribe (eds) (1993a) **q.v.**, pp. 1–19.

Kahn, R.F. (1931) 'The relation of home investment to unemployment', *Economic Journal*, 41 (2), pp. 173–98.

——— (1976) 'Thoughts on the behaviour of wages and monetarism', *Lloyds Bank Review*, 119 (January), pp. 1–11.

——— (1984) *The making of Keynes' General theory*. Cambridge: Cambridge University Press.

Kaldor, N. (1957) 'A model of economic growth', *Economic Journal*, 67 (4), pp. 591–624. Rep. in N. Kaldor (1960) *Collected economic essays*. Vol. II: *Essays on economic stability and growth*. London: Duckworth, pp. 259–300.

——— (1966) *Causes of the slow rate of economic growth in the United Kingdom*. Cambridge: Cambridge University Press. Rep. in N. Kaldor (1978a) **q.v.**, pp. 100–38.

——— (1970a) 'The new monetarism', *Lloyds Bank Review*, 97 (July), pp. 1–18. Rep. in N. Kaldor (1978b) **q.v.**, pp. 1–23.

——— (1970b) 'The new monetarism: reply', *Lloyds Bank Review*, 98 (October), pp. 54–5. Rep. in N. Kaldor (1978b) **q.v.**, pp. 25–7.

——— (1972) 'The irrelevance of equilibrium economics', *Economic Journal*, 82 (4), pp. 1237–55. Rep. in N. Kaldor (1978a) **q.v.**, pp. 176–201.

——— (1975) 'What is wrong with economic theory', *Quarterly Journal of Economics*, 89 (3), pp. 347–57. Rep. in N. Kaldor (1978a) **q.v.**, pp. 202–213.

——— (1976) 'Inflation and recession in the world economy', *Economic Journal*, 86 (4), pp. 703–14. Rep. in N. Kaldor (1978a) **q.v.**, pp. 214–30.

——— (1978a) *Collected economic essays*. Vol. 5: *Further essays on economic theory*. London: Duckworth.

——— (1978b) *Collected economic essays*. Vol. 6: *Further essays on applied economics*. London: Duckworth.

——— (1983) *The economic consequences of Mrs Thatcher*. London: Duckworth.

——— (1986) 'Recollections of an economist', *Banca Nazionale del Lavoro Quarterly Review*, 39 (1), pp. 3–26.

——— and Trevithick, J. (1981) 'A Keynesian perspective on money', *Lloyds Bank Review*, 139 (January), pp. 1–19.

Kalecki, M. (1943) 'Political aspects of full employment', *Political Quarterly*, 14 (4), pp. 322–31.

Kaser, M.C. (1966) 'Education and economic progress: experience in industrialized market economics. A preliminary approach to a statistical examination', in E.A.G. Robinson and J. Vaizey (eds) (1966) *The economics of education*. London: Macmillan, pp. 89–173.

Kasper, H. *et al.* (1991) 'The education of economists: from undergraduate to graduate study', *Journal of Economic Literature*, 29 (3), pp. 1088–1109.

Katouzian, M.A.H. (1980) *Ideology and method in economics*. London: Macmillan.

Kay, J.A. (1991) 'Economics and business', *Economic Journal*, 101 (1), pp. 57–63.

——— (1993) *Foundations of corporate success: how business strategies add value*. Oxford: Oxford University Press.

——— (1996) *The business of economics*. Oxford: Oxford University Press.

Kay, N.M. (1984) *The emergent firm: knowledge, ignorance and surprise in economic organisation*. London: Macmillan.

Kearl, J.R., Pope, C.L., Whiting, G.C. and Wimmer, L.T. (1979) 'A confusion of economists?', *American Economic Review*, 69 (2, Papers & Proceedings), pp. 28–37.

Keegan, W. (1984) *Mrs Thatcher's economic experiment*. Harmondsworth: Penguin.

____ and Pennant-Rea, R. (1979) *Who runs the economy?: control and influence in British economic policy*. London: Temple Smith.

Keeling, D. (1971) 'The development of central training in the civil service, 1963–70', *Public Administration*, 49 (1), pp. 51–71.

Keep, E. and Sisson, K. (1992) 'Owning the problem: personnel issues in higher education policy-making in the 1990s', *Oxford Review of Economic Policy*, 8 (2), pp. 67–78.

Kendrick, J.W. (1970) 'The historical development of national-income accounts', *History of Political Economy*, 2 (2), pp. 284–315.

Kenworthy, L. (1995) *In search of national economic success: balancing competition and cooperation*. London: Sage.

Keynes, J.M. (1919) *The economic consequences of the peace*. JMK, Vol. II (1971). London: Macmillan.

____ (1923) *A tract on monetary reform*. JMK, Vol. IV (1971). London: Macmillan.

____ (1924a) 'A comment on Professor Cannan's article', *Economic Journal*, 34 (1), pp. 65–8. Rep. in JMK, Vol. XI (1983), pp. 415–19.

____ (1924b) 'Alfred Marshall, 1842–1924', *Economic Journal*, 34 (3), pp. 311–72. Rep. in JMK, Vol. X (1972), pp. 161–231.

____ (1925) *The economic consequences of Mr Churchill*. London: Hogarth Press. Rep. in JMK, Vol. IX (1972), pp. 207–30.

____ (ed.) (1926a) *Official papers of Alfred Marshall*. London: Macmillan.

____ (1926b) *The end of laissez-faire*. London: Hogarth Press. Rep. in JMK, Vol. IX (1972), pp. 272–94.

____ (1930a) *A treatise on money*, 2 vols. JMK, Vols V–VI (1971). London: Macmillan.

____ (1930b) 'Economic possibilities for our grandchildren', *The Nation and Athenaeum*, 48 (11 and 18 October), pp. 36–7, 96–8. Rep. in JMK, Vol. IX (1972), pp. 321–32.

____ (1931) *Essays in persuasion*. JMK, Vol. IX (1972). London: Macmillan.

____ (1933) 'The means to prosperity', *The Times*, 13–16 March. Rep. in JMK, Vol. IX (1972), pp. 335–66.

____ (1936) *The general theory of employment, interest and money*. JMK, Vol. VII (1973). London: Macmillan.

____ (1940a) *How to pay for the war*. London: Macmillan. Rep in JMK, Vol. IX (1972), pp. 367–439.

____ (1940b) 'The Society's jubilee, 1890–1940', *Economic Journal*, 50 (4), pp. 401–9. Rep. in JMK, Vol. XII (1983), pp. 846–55.

Keynes, J.N. (1891) *The scope and method of political economy*. London: Macmillan.

Keynes, M. (ed.) (1975) *Essays on John Maynard Keynes*. Cambridge: Cambridge University Press.

Khan, M.S. and Johnson, H.G. (1972) 'The common market questionnaire, October 1971', *Economica*, n.s. 39 (3), pp. 316–24.

King, J.E. (ed.) (1988) *Economic exiles*. London: Macmillan.

King, M.A. (1994) 'Monetary policy in the UK', *Fiscal Studies*, 15 (3), pp. 109–28.

____ (1997) 'Changes in UK monetary policy: rules and discretion in practice', *Journal of Monetary Economics*, 39 (1), pp. 81–97.

Kirman, A. and Dahl, M. (1994) 'Economic research in Europe', *European Economic Review*, 38 (3), pp. 505–22.

Kitson, M. and Michie, J. (1996) 'Britain's industrial performance since 1960: underinvestment and relative economic decline', *Economic Journal*, 106 (1), pp. 196–212.

Klamer, A. (1984) *Conversations with economists: new classical economists and their opponents speak out on the current controversy in macroeconomics.* Totowa, NJ: Rowman & Allanheld.

____ and Colander, D.C. (1990) *The making of an economist.* Boulder, CO: Westview Press.

____, McCloskey, D.N. and Solow, R.M. (eds) (1988) *The consequences of economic rhetoric.* Cambridge: Cambridge University Press.

Knapp, J. (1973) 'Economics or political economy?', *Lloyds Bank Review*, 107 (January), pp. 19–43.

Kolm, S.-C. (1988) 'Economics in Europe and the US', *European Economic Review*, 32 (1), pp. 207–12.

Koot, G.M. (1987) *English historical economics, 1870–1926: the rise of economic history and neomercantilism.* Cambridge: Cambridge University Press.

Kotlikoff, L.J., Razin, A. and Rosenthal, R.W. (1990) 'A strategic altruism model in which Ricardian equivalence does not hold', *Economic Journal*, 100 (5), pp. 1261–8.

Kregel, J.A. (ed.) (1988–9) *Recollections of eminent economists*, 2 vols. London: Macmillan.

Kreps, D.M. (1990) *A course in microeconomic theory.* Hemel Hempstead: Harvester Wheatsheaf.

____ (1997) 'Economics: the current position', *Daedalus*, 126 (1), pp. 59–85.

Krueger, A.O. *et al.* (1991) 'Report of the commission on graduate education in economics', *Journal of Economic Literature*, 29 (3), pp. 1035–53.

Krugman, P.R. (1994) *Peddling prosperity: economic sense and nonsense in the age of diminished expectations.* New York: W.W. Norton.

____ (1996) *Pop internationalism.* Cambridge, MA: MIT Press.

Kuttner, R. (1985) 'The poverty of economics', *Atlantic Monthly*, (February), pp. 74–84.

Kynaston, D. (1988) *The Financial Times: a centenary history.* London: Viking.

Laband, D.N. and Piette, M.J. (1994) 'The relative impacts of economics journals, 1970–1990', *Journal of Economic Literature*, 32 (2), pp. 640–66.

Laidler, D.E.W. (1972) 'The current inflation: explanations and policies', *National Westminster Bank Quarterly Review*, (November), pp. 6–21.

____ (1976) 'Lord Kahn on monetarism', *Lloyds Bank Review*, 120 (April), pp. 47–8.

____ (1981) 'Monetarism: an interpretation and an assessment', *Economic Journal*, 91 (1), pp. 1–28.

____ (1984) 'Harry Johnson as a macroeconomist', *Journal of Political Economy*, 92 (4), pp. 592–615.

Lal, D. (1983) *The poverty of 'development economics'.* London: IEA.

Lane, R.E. (1991) *The market experience.* Cambridge: Cambridge University Press.

Laski, H.J. (1931) *The limitations of the expert.* London: Fabian Society.

Lawson, C.W. (1990) 'The current state of undergraduate economics in the United Kingdom', *Economic Journal*, 100 (5), pp. 1280–5.

Lawson, N. (1992) *The view from no. 11: memoirs of a Tory radical.* London: Bantam Press.

Layard, P.R.G., King, J. and Moser, C.A. (1969) *The impact of Robbins.* Harmondsworth: Penguin.

____, Nickell, S.J. and Jackman, R. (1991) *Unemployment: macroeconomic performance and the labour market.* Oxford: Oxford University Press.

Leamer, E.E. (1983) 'Let's take the con out of econometrics', *American Economic Review*, 73 (1), pp. 31–43.

Lee, F.S. (1993) 'Introduction: Philip Walter Sawford Andrews, 1914–1971', in F.S. Lee and P.E. Earl (eds) (1993) q.v., pp. 1–34.

_____ and Earl, P.E. (eds) (1993) *The economics of competitive enterprise: selected essays of P.W.S. Andrews*. Edward Elgar: Aldershot.

_____ and Harley, S. (1998a) 'Economics divided: the limitations of peer review in a paradigm bound social science', *Cambridge Journal of Economics*, forthcoming.

_____ and _____ (1998b) 'Research selectivity, managerialism and the academic labour process: the future of mainstream economics in UK universities', *Human Relations*, forthcoming.

_____ and Irving-Lessmann, J. (1992) 'The fate of an errant hypothesis: the doctrine of normal cost price', *History of Political Economy*, 24 (2), pp. 273–309.

Leijonhufvud, A. (1968) *On Keynesian economics and the economics of Keynes: a study in monetary theory*. London: Oxford University Press.

_____ (1973) 'Life among the Econ', *Western Economic Journal*, 11 (3), pp. 327–37.

_____ (1984) 'Hicks on time and money', *Oxford Economic Papers*, n.s. 36 (4, Supplement), pp. 26–46.

Leith-Ross, F. (1968) *Money talks: fifty years of international finance*. London: Hutchinson.

Lekachman, R. (1977) 'The radical Keynes', in R.J. Skidelsky (ed.) (1977) q.v., pp. 59–66.

Leman, C.K. and Nelson, R.H. (1981) 'Ten commandments for policy economists', *Journal of Policy Analysis and Management*, 1 (1), pp. 97–117.

Leontief, W.W. (1971) 'Theoretical assumptions and nonobserved facts', *American Economic Review*, 61 (1),

pp. 1–7.

_____ (1982) 'Academic economists', *Science*, 217 (9 July), pp. 104–7.

Leruez, J. (1975) *Economic planning and politics in Britain*. Trans. M. Harrison. Oxford: Martin Robertson.

Levine, A. (1997) 'How the academic profession is changing', *Daedalus*, 126 (4), pp. 1–20.

Levitas, R. (1996) 'The legacy of Rayner', in R. Levitas and W. Guy (eds) (1996) *Interpreting official statistics*. London: Routledge, pp. 7–25.

Lewis, A., Webley, P. and Furnham, A. (1995) *The new economic mind: the social psychology of economic behaviour*. London: Harvester Wheatsheaf.

Leyland, J. (1997) 'Where do economists work and what do they do?: a survey of SBE members', *Business Economist*, 28 (1), pp. 6–13.

Lie, J. (1997) 'Sociology of markets', *Annual Review of Sociology*, 23, pp. 341–60.

Lindbeck, A. (1970) 'Paul Anthony Samuelson's contribution to economics', *Swedish Journal of Economics*, 72 (3), pp. 342–54.

_____ (1985) 'The prize in economic science in memory of Alfred Nobel', *Journal of Economic Literature*, 23 (1), pp. 37–56.

Linder, M. and Sensat, J. (1977) *The anti-Samuelson*, 2 vols. New York: Urizen Books.

Lipsey, R.G. (1963) *An introduction to positive economics*. London: Weidenfeld & Nicolson.

_____ (1997) 'Introduction: an intellectual autobiography', in R.G. Lipsey (ed.) (1997) *The selected essays of Richard G. Lipsey*, Vol. I: *Microeconomics, growth and political economy*. Cheltenham: Edward Elgar, pp. ix–xxxvii.

Little, I.M.D. (1950) *A critique of welfare economics*. Oxford: Clarendon Press.

_____ (1957) 'The economist in Whitehall', *Lloyds Bank Review*, 44 (April), pp. 29–40.

____, Cooper, R.N., Corden, W.M. and Rajapatirana, S. (1993) *Boom, crisis and adjustment: the macreoconomic experience of developing countries.* Oxford: Oxford University Press.

____ and Mirrlees, J.A. (1969) *Manual of industrial project analysis in developing countries.* Vol. 2: *Social cost benefit analysis.* Paris: OECD.

Locke, R.R. (1989) *Management and higher education since 1940: the influence of America and Japan on West Germany, Great Britain and France.* Cambridge: Cambridge University Press.

Lovell, M.C. (1973) 'The production of economic literature: an interpretation', *Journal of Economic Literature*, 11 (1), pp. 27–55.

____ and Selover, D.D. (1994) 'Econometric software accidents', *Economic Journal*, 104 (3), pp. 713–25.

Lucas, R.E. (1976) 'Econometric policy evaluation: a critique', in K. Brunner and A.H. Meltzer (eds) (1976) *The Phillips curve and labor markets*, Vol. 1. Amsterdam: North-Holland, pp. 19–46.

____ (1980) 'Methods and problems in business cycle theory', *Journal of Money, Credit and Banking*, 12 (4, pt. 2), pp. 696–715.

____ (1987) *Models of business cycles.* Oxford: Basil Blackwell.

____ and Sargent, T.J. (1978) 'After Keynesian macroeconomics', in Federal Reserve Bank of Boston (ed.) (1978) *After the Phillips curve: persistence of high inflation and high unemployment.* Boston, MA: Federal Reserve Bank of Boston, pp. 49–72.

Lumsden, K.G., Attiyeh, R. and Scott, A. (1980) *Economics education in the United Kingdom.* London: Heinemann.

Luttwak, E. (1996) 'Central bankism', *London Review of Books*, 14 November, pp. 3–7.

McCloskey, D.N. (1980) 'Scattering in open fields: a comment', *Journal of European Economic History*, 9 (1), pp. 209–14.

____ (1983) 'The rhetoric of economics', *Journal of Economic Literature*, 21 (2), pp. 481–517.

____ (1994) *Knowledge and persuasion in economics.* Cambridge: Cambridge University Press.

____ (1996) *The vices of economists – the virtues of the bourgeoisie.* Amsterdam: Amsterdam University Press.

McCormick, B.J. (1992) *Hayek and the Keynesian avalanche.* New York: Harvester Wheatsheaf.

MacDougall, G.D.A. (1938) 'General survey, 1929–37', in British Association (ed.) (1938) **q.v.**, pp. 1–83. Rep. in G.D.A. MacDougall (1975) **q.v.**, vol. I, pp. 3–77.

____ (1951) 'The Prime Minister's Statistical Section', in D.N. Chester (ed.) (1951a) **q.v.**, pp. 58–68.

____ (1974) 'In praise of economics', *Economic Journal*, 84 (4), pp. 773–86.

____ (1975) *Studies in political economy*, 2 vols. London: Macmillan.

____ (1978) 'The machinery of economic government: some personal reflections', in D. Butler and A.H. Halsey (eds) (1978) *Policy and politics: essays in honour of Norman Chester.* London: Macmillan, pp. 169–81.

____ (1987) *Don and mandarin: memoirs of an economist.* London: John Murray.

McFadyean, A. (1964) *Recollected in tranquillity.* London: Pall Mall Press.

MacKenzie, D.A. (1981) *Statistics in Britain, 1865–1930: the social construction of scientific knowledge.* Edinburgh: Edinburgh University Press.

McKinstry, L. (1997) 'Sending out research parties, *The Spectator*, 279 (20 September), pp. 24–5.

MacLeod, R.M. (ed.) (1988a) *Government and expertise: specialists, ad-*

ministrators and professionals, 1860–1919. Cambridge: Cambridge University Press.

____ (1988b) 'Introduction', in R.M. MacLeod (ed.) (1988a) **q.v.**, pp. 1–24.

McNay, I. (1997) *The impact of the 1992 RAE on institutional and individual behaviour in English higher education: the evidence from a research project.* Bristol: HEFCE.

McWilliams Tullberg, R. (ed.) (1990) *Alfred Marshall in retrospect.* Aldershot: Edward Elgar.

Maddison, A. (1991) *Dynamic forces in capitalist development: a long-run comparative view.* Oxford: Oxford University Press.

____ (1995) *Monitoring the world economy, 1820–1992.* Paris: OECD.

Madrick, J. (1997) 'The cost of living: a new myth', *New York Review of Books,* 19 (4), pp. 19–24.

Malabre, A.L. (1994) *Lost prophets: an insider's history of the modern economists.* Boston, MA: Harvard Business School Press.

Maloney, J. (1985) *Marshall, orthodoxy and the professionalisation of economics.* Cambridge: Cambridge University Press.

____ (1990) 'Gentlemen versus players, 1891–1914', in J.D. Hey and D.N. Winch (eds) (1990) **q.v.**, pp. 49–64.

____ (ed.) (1992) *What's new in economics?* Manchester: Manchester University Press.

Mankiw, N.G. (1988) 'Recent developments in macroeconomics: a very quick refresher course', *Journal of Money, Credit and Banking,* 20 (3, pt. II), pp. 436–49.

Margo, R.A. and Siegfried, J.J. (1996) 'Long-run trends in economics bachelor's degrees', *Journal of Economic Education,* 27 (4), pp. 326–36.

Marin, A. (1972) 'The Phillips curve (born 1958– died ?)', *Three Banks Review,* 96 (December), pp. 28–42.

Markoff, J. and Montecinos, V. (1993)

'The ubiquitous rise of economists', *Journal of Public Policy,* 13 (1), pp. 37–68.

Marquand, D. (1988) *The unprincipled society: new demands and old politics.* London: Fontana.

____ (1992) *The progressive dilemma,* rev edn. London: Heinemann.

Marris, R.L. (1954) 'The position of economics and economists in the government machine: a comparative critique of the United Kingdom and the Netherlands', *Economic Journal,* 64 (4), pp. 759–83.

Marrison, A.J. (1996) *British business and protection, 1903–1932.* Oxford: Clarendon Press.

Marshall, A. (1885) 'The present position of economics', inaugural lecture. Rep. in A.C. Pigou (ed.) (1925) **q.v.**, pp. 152–74.

____ (1890) *Principles of economics: an introductory volume,* 8th edn. (1920). London: Macmillan.

____ (1897a) 'The old generation of economists and the new', *Quarterly Journal of Economics,* 11 (2), pp. 115–35. Rep. in A.C. Pigou (ed.) (1925) **q.v.**, pp. 295–311.

____ (1897b) Letter to Lord Acton, 13 November, in J.K. Whitaker (ed.) (1996) **q.v.**, vol. II, pp. 206–7.

____ (1901) Letter to the editor, *The Echo,* 27 June. Rep. in J.K. Whitaker (ed.) (1996) **q.v.**, vol. II, pp. 333–4.

____ (1907) 'The social possibilities of economic chivalry', *Economic Journal,* 17 (1), pp. 7–29. Rep. in A.C. Pigou (ed.) (1925) **q.v.**, pp. 323–46.

____ (1919) *Industry and trade: a study of industrial technique and business organization; and of their influences on the conditions of various classes and nations,* 4th edn. (1923). London: Macmillan.

____ (1923) *Money credit and commerce.* London: Macmillan.

Marwick, A. (1964) 'Middle opinion in the thirties: planning, progress and political "agreement"', *English Hist-*

orical Review, 79 (2), pp. 285–98.

Mason, R. (1996) 'Robert Giffen and the tariff reform campaign, 1865–1910', *Journal of European Economic History*, 25 (1), pp. 171–88.

Matthews, R.C.O. (1968) 'Why has Britain had full employment since the war?', *Economic Journal*, 78 (3), pp. 555–69.

_____ (1991) 'The economics of professional ethics: should the profession be more like business?', *Economic Journal*, 101 (4), pp. 737–50.

May, A.M. (1996) 'The challenge of feminist economics', in C.J. Whalen (ed.) (1996) *Political economy for the 21st century: contemporary views on the trend of economics*. London: M.E. Sharpe, pp. 65–83.

Mayer, C.P. (1994) 'The assessment: money and banking – theory and evidence', *Oxford Review of Economic Policy*, 10 (4), pp. 1–13.

Mayer, T. (1990) *Monetarism and macroeconomic policy*. Aldershot: Edward Elgar.

_____ (1993) *Truth versus precision in economics*. Aldershot: Edward Elgar.

_____ (1995) *Doing economic research: essays on the applied methodology of economics*. Aldershot: Edward Elgar.

_____ (1997) 'On the usefulness of economics', *Policy Options*, 18 (7), pp. 19–21.

Maynard, G.W. (1988) *The economy under Mrs Thatcher*. Oxford: Basil Blackwell.

Meade, J.E. (1936) *An introduction to economic analysis and policy*. Oxford: Clarendon Press.

_____ (1948) 'Financial policy and the balance of payments', *Economica*, n.s. 15. (2), pp. 101–15.

_____ (1951; 1955a) *The theory of international economic policy*. Vol. I: *The balance of payments.*; Vol. II: *Trade and welfare*. London: Oxford University Press.

_____ (1955b) 'The case for variable exchange rates', *Three Banks Review*, 27 (September), pp. 3–27.

_____ (1964) *Efficiency, equality and the ownership of property*. London: George Allen & Unwin.

_____ (1965; 1968; 1971a; 1976) *Principles of political economy*. Vols I: *The stationary economy*; II: *The growing economy*; III: *The controlled economy*; IV: *The just economy*. London: George Allen & Unwin.

_____ (1971b) *Wages and prices in a mixed economy*. London: IEA.

_____ (1975a) *The intelligent radical's guide to economic policy: the mixed economy*. London: George Allen & Unwin.

_____ (1975b) 'An effective social contract', in IEA (ed.) (1975) *Crisis '75..?* London: IEA, pp. 28–33.

_____ (1978) 'The meaning of "internal balance"', *Economic Journal*, 88 (3), pp. 423–35.

_____ (1982) *Stagflation*, Vol. I: *Wage-fixing*. London: George Allen & Unwin.

_____ (1983) 'Impressions of Maynard Keynes', in G.D.N. Worswick and J. Trevithick (eds) (1983) **q.v.**, pp. 263–6.

_____ (1995) *Full employment regained?: an Agathotopian dream*. Cambridge: Cambridge University Press.

_____ and Andrews, P.W.S. (1938) 'Summary of replies to questions on effects of interest rates', *Oxford Economic Papers*, old ser. 1 (1), pp. 14–31.

_____ and Stone, J.R.N. (1941) 'The construction of tables of national income, expenditure, savings and investment', *Economic Journal*, 51 (2/3), pp. 216–33.

Meadows, D.H., Meadows, D.L., Randers, J. and Behrens, W.W. (1972) *The limits to growth: a report for the Club of Rome's project on the predicament of mankind*. London: Pan Books.

Medema, S.G. and Samuels, W.J. (eds) (1996) *Foundations of research in economics: how do economists do economics?* Cheltenham: Edward Elgar.

Meyer, J.R. (1963) 'Regional economics: a survey', *American Economic Review*, 53 (1), pp. 19–54. Rep. in AEA-RES (1965b) q.v., pp. 240–71.

Michie, J. and Grieve Smith, J. (eds) (1996) *Creating industrial capacity: towards full employment.* Oxford: Oxford University Press.

____ and ____ (eds) (1997) *Employment and economic performance: jobs, inflation, and growth.* Oxford: Oxford University Press.

Micklethwait, J. and Wooldridge, A. (1996) *The witch doctors: what the management gurus are saying, why it matters and how to make sense of it.* London: Heinemann.

Middleton, P. (1989) 'Economic policy formulation in the Treasury in the post-war period', *National Institute Economic Review*, 127 (February), pp. 46–51.

Middleton, R. (1985) *Towards the managed economy: Keynes, the Treasury and the fiscal policy debate of the 1930s.* London: Methuen.

____ (1989) 'Keynes's legacy for post-war economic management', in A. Gorst, L. Johnman and W.S. Lucas (eds) (1989) *Post-war Britain, 1945–64: themes and perspectives.* London: Pinter, pp. 22–42.

____ (1996) *Government versus the market: the growth of the public sector, economic management and British economic performance, c.1890–1979.* Cheltenham: Edward Elgar.

Miller, W.L., Timpson, A.M. and Lessnoff, M. (1996) *Political culture in contemporary Britain: people and politicians, principles and practice.* Oxford: Clarendon Press.

Milligan, A. (1995) 'Don't put your daughter on the stage, Mrs Worthington: the Society of Business Economists' salary survey, 1964–95', *Business Economist*, 26 (3), pp. 15–24.

Minford, A.P.L. (1982) 'The four-ages of post-war British policy debate', *National Institute Economic Review*, 100 (May), pp. 21–4.

Mirowski, P. (1989) *More heat than light: economics as social physics; physics as nature's economics.* Cambridge: Cambridge University Press.

Mishan, E.J. (1967) *The costs of economic growth.* London: Staples Press.

Mishkin, F.S. (1982) 'Does anticipated monetary policy matter?: an econometric investigation', *Journal of Political Economy*, 90 (1), pp. 22–51.

Modigliani, F. (1977) 'The monetarist controversy or, should we foresake stabilization policies?', *American Economic Review*, 67 (2), pp. 1–19.

Moggridge, D.E. (1972) *British monetary policy, 1924–1931: the Norman conquest of $4.86.* Cambridge: Cambridge University Press.

____ (1992) *Maynard Keynes: an economist's biography.* London: Routledge.

Moore, B. and Rhodes, J. (1973) 'Evaluating the effects of British regional economic policy', *Economic Journal*, 83 (1), pp. 87–110.

Moore, L. (1964) 'Factors affecting the demand for British exports', *Bulletin of the Oxford University Institute of Economics and Statistics*, 26 (4), pp. 343–59.

Morgan, E.V. (1970) 'The Radcliffe report in the tradition of official British monetary documents', in D.R. Croome and H.G. Johnson (eds) (1970) q.v., pp. 3–21.

Morgan, M.S. (1990) *The history of econometric ideas.* Cambridge: Cambridge University Press.

Morgan, T. (1988) 'Theory versus empiricism in academic economics: update and comparisons', *Journal of Economic Perspectives*, 2 (4), pp. 159–64.

Moser, C.A. (1973) *Statistics and econ-*

omic policy. Mercantile Credit Lecture. Reading: University of Reading.

Mosley, P. (1984) *The making of economic policy: theory and evidence from Britain and the United States since 1945.* Brighton: Wheatsheaf.

___ (1985) 'When is a policy instrument not an instrument?: fiscal marksmanship in Britain, 1951–84', *Journal of Public Policy*, 6 (1), pp. 69–86.

Mueller, D.C. (1989) *Public choice II: a revised edition of Public choice.* Cambridge: Cambridge University Press.

Muller, C. (1996) 'The Institute of Economic Affairs: undermining the post-war consensus', *Contemporary British History*, 10 (1), pp. 88–110.

Napier, C.J. (1996a) 'Accounting and the absence of a business economics tradition in the UK', *European Accounting Review*, 5 (3), pp. 449–81.

___ (1996b) 'Academic disdain?: economists and accounting in Britain, 1850–1950', *Accounting, Business and Financial History*, 6 (3), pp. 427–50.

NEDC (1963a) *Growth of the United Kingdom economy to 1966.* London: HMSO.

___ (1963b) *Conditions favourable to faster growth.* London: HMSO.

NEDO (1976) 'Cyclical fluctuations in the United Kingdom economy', *NEDO Discussion Paper* no. 3.

Nelson, R.H. (1987) 'The economics profession and the making of public policy', *Journal of Economic Literature*, 25 (1), pp. 49–91.

___ (1989) 'Introduction and summary', in J.A. Pechman (ed.) (1989) q.v., pp. 1–22.

Nevin, E.T. (1972) 'Europe and the regions', *Three Banks Review*, 94 (June), pp. 54–78.

Newman, P., Milgate, M. and Eatwell, J. (eds) (1992) *The new Palgrave dictionary of money and finance*, 3 vols. London: Macmillan.

Nicholson, J.S. (1896) *Strikes and social problems.* London: A. & C. Black.

___ (1893–1901) *Principles of political economy*, 3 vols. London: A. & C. Black.

___ (1903) *Elements of political economy.* London: A. & C. Black.

Nickell, S.J. and Bell, B. (1996) 'Changes in the distribution of wages and unemployment in OECD countries', *American Economic Review*, 86 (2, Papers & Proceedings), pp. 302–8.

NIESR (1972) 'The effects of the devaluation of 1967 on the current balance of payments', *Economic Journal*, 82 (1), pp. 442–64.

Norton, H.S. (1969) *The role of the economist in government: a study of economic advice since 1900.* Berkeley, CA: McCuthan Publishing.

O'Brien, D.P. (1975) *The classical economists.* Oxford: Clarendon Press.

___ (1981a) 'A. Marshall, 1842–1924', in D.P. O'Brien and J.R. Presley (eds) (1981) q.v., pp. 36–71.

___ (1981b) 'The emphasis on market economics', in Arthur Seldon (ed.) (1981) q.v., pp. 51–77.

___ (1988) *Lionel Robbins.* London: Macmillan.

___ and Presley, J.R. (eds) (1981) *Pioneers of modern economics in Britain.* London: Macmillan.

O'Brien, P.K. (1994) 'Research selectivity exercises: a sceptical but positive note', *Higher Education Review*, 26 (3), pp. 7–17.

OECD (1970) *Development of higher education, 1950–1967.* Paris: OECD.

Offer, A. (1983) 'Empire and social reform: British overseas investment and domestic politics, 1908–1914', *Historical Journal*, 26 (1), pp. 119–38.

Okun, A.M. (1975) *Equality and efficiency: the big tradeoff.* Washington, DC: Brookings Institution.

Oliver, M.J. (1997) *Whatever happened*

to monetarism?: economic policy-making and social learning in the United Kingdom since 1979. Aldershot: Ashgate.

ONS (1996) *Economic trends, annual supplement, 1996/97 edn.*

Opie, R.G. (1968a) 'The making of economic policy', in H. Thomas (ed.) (1968) *Crisis in the civil service.* London: Anthony Blond, pp. 53–82.

_____ (1968b) Review of Hutchison (1968), *New Statesman*, 76 (1 November), p. 586.

_____ (1972) 'Economic planning and growth', in W. Beckerman (ed.) (1972) q.v., pp. 157–77.

Ormerod, P.A. (1994) *The death of economics.* London: Faber & Faber.

Oswald, A.J. (1991a) 'Progress and microeconomic data', *Economic Journal*, 101 (1), pp. 75–80.

_____ (ed.) (1991b) *Surveys in economics*, 2 vols. Oxford: Blackwell.

Paish, F.W. (1962) *Studies in an inflationary economy: the United Kingdom, 1948–1961.* London: Macmillan.

_____ (1965) 'The management of the British economy', *Lloyds Bank Review*, 76 (April), pp. 1–17.

Palgrave, R.H.I. (ed.) (1894–1908) *Dictionary of political economy*, 3 vols. London: Macmillan.

Parker, D. and Stacey, R. (1994) *Chaos, management and economics: the implications of non-linear thinking.* London: IEA.

Parkin, J.M. (1974) 'United Kingdom inflation: the policy alternatives', *National Westminster Bank Quarterly Review*, (May), pp. 32–47.

_____ (1975) 'Where is Britain's inflation going?', *Lloyds Bank Review*, 117 (July), pp. 1–13.

_____ and Sumner, M.T. (eds) (1978) *Inflation in the United Kingdom.* Manchester: Manchester University Press.

Parsons, D.W. (1986) *The political economy of British regional policy.* London: Croom Helm.

_____ (1989) *The power of the financial press: journalism and economic opinion in Britain and America.* Aldershot: Edward Elgar.

_____ (1995) *Public policy: an introduction to the theory and practice of policy analysis.* Aldershot: Edward Elgar.

Patel, K. (1997) 'Patron of the skills arsenal', *Times Higher Education Supplement*, 27 June, p. 17.

Patinkin, D. (1976) 'Keynes and econometrics: on the interaction between the macroeconomic revolutions of the interwar period', *Econometrica*, 44 (6), pp. 1091–123.

_____ (1981) *Essays on and in the Chicago tradition.* Durham, NC: Duke University Press.

_____ and Leith, J.C. (eds) (1977) *Keynes, Cambridge and the General theory.* London: Macmillan.

Peacock, A.T. (1977a) 'Giving economic advice in difficult times', *Three Banks Review*, 113 (March), pp. 3–23.

_____ (1977b) *The credibility of liberal economics.* London: IEA.

_____ (1979) *The economic analysis of government and related themes.* Oxford: Martin Robertson.

_____ (1989) 'Introduction', in D. Greenaway and J.R. Presley (eds) (1989) q.v., pp. 1–10.

_____ (1991) 'Economic advice and economic policy', in D. Greenaway *et al.* (eds) (1991) q.v., pp. 713–26.

_____ (1992a) *Public choice analysis in historical perspective.* Cambridge: Cambridge University Press.

_____ (1992b) 'The credibility of economic advice to government', *Economic Journal*, 102 (5), pp. 1213–22.

_____ (1994) 'The utility maximizing government economic adviser: a comment', *Public Choice*, 80 (1), pp. 191–7.

_____ (1995) 'Professional "Gleich-

schaltung": a historical perspective',
Kyklos, 48 (2), pp. 267–71.

Pechman, J.A. (1975) 'Making economic policy: the role of the economist', in F.I. Greenstein and N.W. Polsby (eds) (1975) *Handbook of political science*. Vol. 6: *Policies and policymakers*. Reading, MA: Addison–Wesley, pp. 23–78.

_____ (ed.) (1989) *The role of the economist in government: an international perspective*. London: Harvester Wheatsheaf.

Peden, G.C. (1983) 'Sir Richard Hopkins and the "Keynesian revolution" in employment policy, 1929–1945', *Economic History Review*, 2nd ser. 36 (2), pp. 281–96.

_____ (1990) 'Old dogs and new tricks: the British Treasury and Keynesian economics in the 1940s and 1950s', in M.O. Furner and B.E. Supple (eds) (1990) **q.v.**, pp. 208–38.

_____ (1996) 'Economic knowledge and the state in modern Britain', in S.J.D. Green and R.C. Whiting (eds) (1996) **q.v.**, pp. 170–87.

_____ (1999) *Politics and economics: the Treasury and public policy, 1905–59*. Oxford: Clarendon Press, forthcoming.

Pepper, G.T. (1990) *Money, credit and inflation: an historical indictment of UK monetary policy and a proposal for change*. London: IEA.

Perelman, M. (1996) *The end of economics*. London: Routledge.

Perkin, H. (1989) *The rise of professional society: England since 1880*. London: Routledge.

_____ (1996) *The third revolution: professional elites in the modern world*. London: Routledge.

Pesaran, M.H. (1991) 'Professor Sir Richard Stone', *Econometric Theory*, 7 (1), pp. 85–123.

Phelps, E.S. (1968) 'Money-wage dynamics and labor-market equilibrium', *Journal of Political Economy*, 78 (4, pt. II), pp. 678–711.

_____ (1990) *Seven schools of macroeconomic thought*. Oxford: Clarendon Press.

Phelps Brown, E.H. (1959) *The growth of British industrial relations: a study from the standpoint of 1906–14*. London: Macmillan.

_____ (1972) 'The underdevelopment of economics', *Economic Journal*, 82 (1), pp. 1–10.

_____ (1980a) 'The radical reflections of an applied economist', *Banca Nazionale del Lavoro Quarterly Review*, 33 (1), pp. 3–14.

_____ (1980b) 'Sir Roy Harrod: a biographical memoir', *Economic Journal*, 90 (1), pp. 1–33.

_____ (1983) *The origins of trade union power*, rev. edn (1986). Oxford: Oxford University Press.

Phillips, A.W.H. (1958) 'The relationship between unemployment and the rate of change of money wage rates in the United Kingdom, 1861–1957', *Economica*, n.s. 25 (4), pp. 283–99.

Phillips, P.C.B. (1985) 'Professor J.D. Sargan', *Econometric Theory*, 1 (1), pp. 119–39.

_____ (1988) 'Professor James Durbin', *Econometric Theory*, 4 (1), pp. 125–57.

Pigou, A.C. (1903) *The riddle of the tariff*. London: R.B. Johnson.

_____ (1912) *Wealth and welfare*. London: Macmillan.

_____ (1920) *The economics of welfare*. London: Macmillan.

_____ (ed.) (1925) *Memorials of Alfred Marshall*. London: Macmillan.

_____ (1927) *Industrial fluctuations*. London: Macmillan.

_____ (1928) *A study in public finance*. London: Macmillan.

_____ (1933) *Theory of unemployment*. London: Macmillan.

_____ (1936) 'Mr J.M. Keynes' General theory of employment, interest and money', *Economica*, n.s. 3 (2), pp. 115–32.

_____ (1939) 'Presidential address', *Eco-

nomic Journal, 49 (2), pp. 215–21.

____ (1941) 'Newspaper reviewers, economics and mathematics', *Economic Journal*, 51 (2/3), pp. 276–80.

____ (1950) *Keynes's General theory: a retrospective review*. London: Macmillan.

____ (1953) *Alfred Marshall and current thought*. London: Macmillan.

Pimlott, B. (1985) *Hugh Dalton*. London: Jonathan Cape.

____ (1992) *Harold Wilson*. London: Harper Collins.

Pirie, M. (1988) *Micropolitics*. Aldershot: Wildwood House.

____ (ed.) (1989) *A decade of revolution: the Thatcher years*. London: ASI.

Platt, D.C.M. (1989) *Mickey Mouse numbers in world history: the short view*. London: Macmillan.

Pliatzky, L. (1984) *Getting and spending: public expenditure, employment and inflation*, 2nd edn. Oxford: Basil Blackwell.

Plowden, E. (1989) *An industrialist in the Treasury: the post–war years*. London: André Deutsch.

Pollard, S. (ed.) (1970a) *The gold standard and employment policies between the wars*. London: Methuen.

____ (1970b) 'Introduction', in S. Pollard (ed.) (1970a) **q.v.**, pp. 1–26.

____ (1984) *The wasting of the British economy: British economic policy 1945 to the present*, 2nd edn. London: Croom Helm.

____ (1989) *Britain's prime and Britain's decline: the British economy, 1870–1914*. London: Edward Arnold.

____ (1992) *The development of the British economy, 1914–1990*, 4th edn. London: Edward Arnold.

Porter, T.M. (1986) *The rise of statistical thinking, 1820–1900*. Princeton, NJ: Princeton University Press.

Portes, R. (1987) 'Economics in Europe', *European Economic Review*, 31 (6), pp. 1329–40.

____ (1990) 'Priorities for economic policy research', in P.M. Deane (ed.) (1990a) **q.v.**, pp. 148–65.

Posner, M.V. (1970) Review of Hutchison (1968), *Economic Journal*, 80 (1), pp. 107–9.

____ (1973) 'Making economic policy', *Economic Journal*, 83 (1), pp. 111–19.

____ (ed.) (1978) *Demand management*. London: Heinemann.

Postan, M.M. (1968) 'A plague of economists?: on some current myths, errors and fallacies', *Encounter*, 30 (1), pp. 42–7.

Power, M. (1997) *The audit society: rituals of verification*. Oxford: Oxford University Press.

Prais, S.J. (1962) 'Econometric research in international trade: a review', *Kyklos*, 15 (3), pp. 560–78.

Presley, J.R. (ed.) (1992) *Essays on Robertsonian economics*. London: Macmillan.

Prest, A.R. (1983) 'Letter to a young economist', *Journal of Economic Affairs*, 3 (1), pp. 130–4.

____ and Turvey, R. (1965) 'Cost-benefit analysis: a survey, *Economic Journal*, 75 (4), pp. 683–735. Rep. in AEA–RES (1966) **q.v.**, pp. 155–207.

PRO (1932) T175/70, pt. I, R.V.N. Hopkins to Chancellor, 20 October.

____ (1935) T188/117, F. Leith-Ross, 'The New Deal and British trade', 6 February.

____ (1943) CAB 87/72, MGO 1, Memorandum by Professor Robbins, 25 January.

Proctor, S.J. (1993) 'Floating convertibility: the emergence of the Robot plan, 1951–52', *Contemporary Record*, 7 (1), pp. 24–43.

Radice, H. (1980) 'A short history of the CSE', *Capital & Class*, 10 (Spring), pp. 43–9.

Rappert, B. (1997) 'Irreconcilable differences?: the business of social science research and users', *Higher Education Quarterly*, 51 (3), pp. 239–50.

Reddaway, W.B. (1970) 'Was $4.86 inevitable in 1925?', *Lloyds Bank Review*, 96 (April), pp. 15–28.

___ (1995) 'Recollections of a lucky economist', *Banca Nazionale del Lavoro Quarterly Review*, 48 (1), pp. 3–16.

___ (1997) 'The changing significance of inflation', in G.C. Harcourt and P.A. Riach (eds) (1997) *A 'second edition' of The general theory.* Vol. 2. London: Routledge, pp. 28–40.

Reddy, S.G. (1996) 'Claims to expert knowledge and the subversion of democracy: the triumph of risk over uncertainty', *Economy and Society*, 25 (2), pp. 222–54.

Reder, M.W. (1982) 'Chicago economics: permanence and change', *Journal of Economic Literature*, 20 (1), pp. 1–38.

Reisman, D. (1990) *Alfred Marshall's mission.* London: Macmillan.

RES (1963) *Report on the finance of economic research.* London: RES.

___ (1983) *The Economic Journal: cumulative index of articles and book reviews, volumes 41–90 (1931–1980).* Cambridge: Cambridge University Press.

RES–SSRC (1973; 1977) *Surveys of applied economics*, 2 vols. London: Macmillan.

Rhoads, S.E. (1985) *The economist's view of the world: governments, markets and public policy.* Cambridge: Cambridge University Press.

Richardson, J.J. (1994) 'Doing less by doing more: British government, 1979–1993', *West European Politics*, 17 (3), pp. 178–97.

Ricketts, M. and Shoesmith, E. (1990) *British economic opinion: a survey of a thousand economists.* London: IEA.

___ and ___ (1992) 'British economic opinion: positive science or normative judgement?', *American Economic Review*, 82 (2, Papers & Proceedings), pp. 210–5.

Robbins, K. (1994) *The eclipse of a great power: Modern Britain, 1870–1992.* London: Longman.

Robbins, L.C. (1930) 'The present position of economic science', *Economica*, 10 (1), pp. 14–24.

___ (1932) *An essay on the nature and significance of economic science*, 2nd edn (1935). London: Macmillan.

___ (1934) *The great depression.* London: Macmillan.

___ (1952) *The theory of economic policy in English classical political economy*, 2nd edn. (1978). London: Macmillan.

___ (1955) 'The teaching of economics in schools and universities', *Economic Journal*, 65 (4), pp. 579–93.

___ (1971) *Autobiography of an economist.* London: Macmillan.

___ (1997) *Economic science and political economy: selected articles*, ed. S.K. Howson. London: Mac-millan.

Roberts, R. (1995) '"A special place in contemporary economic literature": the rise and fall of the British bank review, 1914–93', *Financial History Review*, 2 (1), pp. 41–60.

Robertson, D.H. (1936) 'Some notes on Mr Keynes' General theory of employment', *Quarterly Journal of Economics*, 51 (1), pp. 168–91.

___ (1938) 'A survey of modern monetary controversy', *The Manchester School*, 9 (1), pp. 1–19.

___ (1940) *Essays in monetary theory.* London: P.S. King.

___ (1951) 'Utility and all that', *The Manchester School*, 19 (2), pp. 111–42.

Robinson, E.A.G. (1947) 'John Maynard Keynes, 1883–1946', *Economic Journal*, 57 (1), pp. 1–68.

___ (1951) 'The overall allocation of resources', in D.N. Chester (ed.) (1951a) **q.v.**, pp. 34–57.

___ (1968) 'Arthur Cecil Pigou', in D.L. Sills (ed.) (1968) *International encyclopedia of the social sciences.* Vol. 12. New York: Macmillan and

Free Press, pp. 90–7.

____ (1977) 'Keynes and his Cambridge colleagues', in D. Patinkin and J.C. Leith (eds) (1977) q.v., pp. 25–38.

____ (1978) 'The London and Cambridge Economic Service: an historical outline', *Kraus Bibliographical Bulletin*, 26 (June), pp. 217–22.

____ (1987) 'Hubert Douglas Henderson', in J. Eatwell *et al.* (eds) (1987) q.v., vol. II, pp. 638–9.

____ (1988) 'The National Institute: the early years', *National Institute Economic Review*, 124 (May), pp. 63–5.

____ (1990a) 'Fifty-five years on the Royal Economic Society Council', in J.D. Hey and D.N. Winch (eds) (1990) q.v., pp. 161–92.

____ (1990b) 'Cambridge economics in the post-Marshallian period', in R. McWilliams Tullberg (ed.) (1990) q.v., pp. 1–7.

____ (1992) 'My apprenticeship as an economist', in M. Szenberg (ed.) (1992) *Eminent economists: their life philosophies*. Cambridge: Cambridge University Press, pp. 203–21.

Robinson, J. (1932) *Economics is a serious subject: the apologia of an economist to the mathematician, the scientist and the plain man*. Cambridge: W. Heffer & Sons.

____ (1933) *The economics of imperfect competition*. London: Macmillan.

____ (1954) 'The production function and the theory of capital', *Review of Economic Studies*, 21 (2), pp. 81–106. Rep in J. Robinson (1964) *Collected economic papers*. Vol II. Oxford: Basil Blackwell, pp. 114–31.

____ (1956) *The accumulation of capital*. London: Macmillan.

____ (1962a) *Economic philosophy*. London: C.A. Watts.

____ (1962b) Review of Johnson (1962), *Economic Journal*, 72 (3), pp. 690–2.

____ (1971) *Economic heresies: some old-fashioned questions in economic theory*. London: Macmillan.

Robinson, K. and Wilson, R. (eds) (1977) *Extending economics within the curriculum*. London: Routledge & Kegan Paul.

Rodrik, D. (1996) 'Understanding economic policy reform', *Journal of Economic Literature*, 34 (1), pp. 9–41.

Roll, E. (1968a) *The world after Keynes: an examination of the economic order*. London: Pall Mall Press.

____ (1968b) 'The uses and abuses of economics', *Oxford Economic Papers*, n.s. 20 (3), pp. 289–302. Rep. in E. Roll (1978) q.v., pp. 15–29.

____ (1971) *Economics and economic policy since Keynes*. O'Brien lecture. Rep. in E. Roll (1978) q.v., pp. 30–45.

____ (1978) *The uses and abuses of economics and other essays*. London: Faber & Faber.

____ (1985) *Crowded hours*. London: Faber & Faber.

____ (1992) *A history of economic thought*, 5th rev. edn. London: Faber & Faber.

____ (1995) *Where did we go wrong?: from the gold standard to Europe*. London: Faber & Faber.

Rollings, N. (1994) '"Poor Mr Butskell: a short life wrecked by schizophrenia"?', *Twentieth Century British History*, 5 (2), pp. 183–205.

Romer, P.M. (1994) 'The origins of endogenous growth', *Journal of Economic Perspectives*, 8 (1), pp. 3–22.

Rose, R. and Karran, T.J. (1984) 'Inertia or incrementalism?: a long-term view of the growth of government', in A.J. Groth and L.L. Wade (eds) (1984) *Comparative resource allocation: politics, performance and policy priorities*. London: Sage, pp. 43–71.

Rosenberg, A. (1979) 'Can economic theory explain everything?', *Philosophy of the Social Sciences*, 9 (4), pp. 509–29.

Roseveare, H. (1969) *The Treasury: the*

evolution of a British institution. London: Allen Lane.

Ross, C.R. (1964) 'What has really happened to output?: a note on the statistical discrepancies in the UK national income estimates', *Bulletin of the Oxford University Institute of Economics and Statistics*, 26 (1), pp. 1–20.

Rowley, C.K. and Peacock, A.T. (1975) *Welfare economics: a liberal restatement*. London: Martin Robertson.

Rudd, E. (1990) 'The early careers of social science graduates and the value of a PhD', *Journal of the Royal Statistical Society*, ser. A. 153 (2), pp. 203–32.

Rybczynski, T.M. (1972) 'Economics, economists and industry', in G.D.N. Worswick (ed.) (1972b) **q.v.**, pp. 124–33.

Salter, A. (1967) *Slave of the lamp: a public servant's notebook*. London: Weidenfeld & Nicolson.

Sampson, A. (1965) *Anatomy of Britain today*. London: Hodder & Stoughton.

Samuelson, P.A. (1946) 'Lord Keynes and the *General theory*', *Econometrica*, 14 (3), pp. 187–200.

____ (1947) *Foundations of economic analysis*. Cambridge, MA: Harvard University Press.

____ (1948) *Economics: an introductory analysis*. New York: McGraw-Hill.

____ (1959) 'What economists know', in D. Lerner (ed.) (1959) *The human meaning of the social sciences*. New York: Meridian Books, pp. 183–213.

____ (1972) 'Economics in a golden age: a personal memoir', in G. Holton (ed.) (1972) *The twentieth-century sciences: studies in the biography of ideas*. New York: W.W. Norton, pp. 155–70.

Sanders, D. (1996) 'New Labour, new Machiavelli: a cynic's guide to economic policy', *Political Quarterly*, 67 (4), pp. 290–302.

Sanderson, M. (1972) *The universities and British industry, 1850–1970*. London: Routledge & Kegan Paul.

____ (1991) 'Higher education in the post-war years', *Contemporary Record*, 5 (3), pp. 417–31.

Sargan, J.D. (1964) 'Wages and prices in the United Kingdom: a study in econometric methodology', in P.E. Hart *et al.* (eds) (1964) **q.v.**, pp. 25–54.

Sargent, J.R. (1963) 'Are American economists better?', *Oxford Economic Papers*, n.s. 15 (1), pp. 1–7.

Sayers, R.S. (1956) *Financial policy, 1939–45*. London: HMSO/Longman.

____ (1960) 'The return to gold, 1925', in L.S. Pressnell (ed.) (1960) *Studies in the industrial revolution*. London: Athlone Press, pp. 313–27. Rep. in S.Pollard (ed.) (1970a) **q.v.**, pp. 85–98.

____ (1976) *The Bank of England, 1891–1944*, 3 vols. Cambridge: Cambridge University Press.

Schumpeter, J.A. (1954) *History of economic analysis*. Oxford: Oxford University Press.

Schwartz, P. (1975) 'Teaching the history of economic thought: report of a symposium at Bristol, 1973', *History of Political Economy*, 7 (1), pp. 112–15.

Scott, M.FG. (1963) *A study of United Kingdom imports*. Cambridge: Cambridge University Press.

Seers, D. (1962) 'Why visiting economists fail', *Journal of Political Economy*, 70 (4), pp. 325–38.

Seldon, Anthony and Graham, A.W.M. (1996) 'The influences on economic policy', *Contemporary British History*, 10 (1), pp. 152–67.

____ and Roll, E. (1996) 'The influence of ideas on economic policy (I)', *Contemporary British History*, 10 (1), pp. 186–98.

Seldon, Arthur (ed.) (1981) *The emerging consensus?: essays on the interplay between ideas, interests and circumstances in the first 25 years of the IEA*. London: IEA.

_____ (1989) 'Economic scholarship and political interest: IEA thinking and government policies', in IEA (ed.) (1989) q.v., pp. 75–98.

Self, P. (1975) *Econocrats and the policy process: the politics and philosophy of cost–benefit analysis*. London: Macmillan.

_____ (1993) *Government by the market?: the politics of public choice*. London: Macmillan.

Sen, A.K. (1985) 'The moral standing of the market', in E.F. Paul, J. Paul and F.D. Miller (eds) (1985) *Ethics and economics*. Oxford: Basil Blackwell, pp. 1–19.

Shackle, G.L.S. (1967) *The years of high theory: invention and tradition in economic thought, 1926–1939*. Cambridge: Cambridge University Press.

_____ (1983) 'A student's pilgrimage', *Banca Nazionale del Lavoro Quarterly Review*, 36 (2), pp. 107–16.

Shanks, M. (1970) 'The "irregular" in Whitehall', in P. Streeten (ed.) (1970a) q.v., pp. 244–62.

Shattock, M. (1994) *The UGC and the management of British universities*. Buckingham: Society for Research into Higher Education/Open University Press.

Shaw, G.K. (1988) *Keynesian economics: the permanent revolution*. Aldershot: Edward Elgar.

Shipman, A. (1991) 'Falling with the pound: the Labour Party's exchange rate problems, 1947–76', *Contemporary Record*, 5 (1), pp. 105–14.

Shonfield, A. (1958) *British economic policy since the war*. Harmondsworth: Penguin.

_____ (1965) *Modern capitalism: the changing balance of public and private power*. Oxford: Oxford University Press.

Simpson, D. (1988) 'What economists need to know', *Royal Bank of Scotland Review*, 160 (December), pp. 3–

11.

Sims, C.A. (1980) 'Macroeconomics and reality', *Econometrica*, 48 (1), pp. 1–48.

Sinclair, P.J.N. (1972) 'The economy: a study in failure', in D. McKie and C. Cook (eds) (1972) *The decade of disillusion: British politics in the sixties*. London: Macmillan, pp. 94–121.

Skidelsky, R.J. (ed.) (1977) *The end of the Keynesian era: essays on the disintegration of the Keynesian political economy*. London: Macmillan.

_____ (1983) *John Maynard Keynes*. Vol. I: *Hopes betrayed, 1883–1920*. London: Macmillan.

_____ (1992) *John Maynard Keynes*. Vol. II: *The economist as saviour, 1921–1937*. London: Macmillan.

_____ (1995) 'The role of ethics in Keynes's economics', in S. Brittan and A. Hamlin (eds) (1995) q.v., pp. 88–100.

_____ (1996) 'Thinking about the state and the economy', in S.J.D. Green and R.C. Whiting (eds) (1996) q.v., pp. 70–86.

_____ (1997) 'Bring back Keynes', *Prospect*, 19 (May), pp. 30–5.

Skousen, M. (1997) 'The perseverance of Paul Samuelson's *Economics*', *Journal of Economic Perspectives*, 11 (2), pp. 137–52.

Smith, D. (1987) *The rise and fall of monetarism*. Harmondsworth: Penguin.

Smyth, R.L. (1971) 'The history of section F of the British Association, 1835–1970', in N. Kaldor (ed.) (1971) *Conflicts in policy objectives*. Oxford: Basil Blackwell, pp. 156–75.

Snooks, G.D. (ed.) (1993) *Historical analysis in economics*. London: Routledge.

Solomou, S.N. (1996) *Themes in macroeconomic history: the UK economy, 1919–1939*. Cambridge: Cambridge University Press.

Solow, R.M. (1980) 'On theories of unemployment', *American Economic Review*, 70 (1), pp. 1–10.

____ (1997) 'How did economics get that way and what way did it get?', *Daedalus*, 126 (1), pp. 39–58. ;

Sørensen, P.B. (1997) 'Public finance solutions to the European unemployment problem?', *Economic Policy*, 25 (October), pp. 223–64.

Sraffa, P. (1926) 'The laws of returns under competitive conditions', *Economic Journal*, 36 (4), pp. 535–50.

____ (1960) *Production of commodities by means of commodities: prelude to a critique of economic theory*. Cambridge: Cambridge University Press.

SSRC (1974) *Computing and the social sciences*. London: SSRC.

____ (1975) *SSRC Newsletter*, 29 (November).

____ (1981) *Macro-economic research in the United Kingdom*. London: SSRC.

Stamp, J.C. (1916) *British incomes and property: the application of official statistics to economic problems*. London: P.S. King.

Stanfield, J.R. (1996) *John Kenneth Galbraith*. London: Macmillan.

Stanners, W. (1993) 'Is low inflation an important condition for high growth?', *Cambridge Journal of Economics*, 17 (1), pp. 79–107.

Stein, H. (1986) 'The Washington economics industry', *American Economic Review*, 76 (2, Papers & Proceedings), pp. 1–9.

____ (1994) *Presidential economics: the making of economic policy from Roosevelt to Clinton*. 3rd edn. Washington, DC: AEI Press.

Stewart, M. (1972) *Keynes and after*, 2nd edn. Harmondsworth: Penguin.

____ (1977) *The Jekyll and Hyde years: politics and economic policy since 1964*. London: J.M. Dent.

____ (1980) 'This Milton's paradise spells nothing but loss', *Times Higher Education Supplement*, 27 June, pp. 11–12.

Stewart, W.A.C. (1989) *Higher education in postwar Britain*. London: Macmillan.

Stigler, G.J. (1949) 'A survey of contemporary economics', *Journal of Political Economy*, 57 (2), pp. 93–105.

____ (1964) 'Statistical studies in the history of economic thought'. Rep. in G.J. Stigler (1965) *Essays in the history of economics*. Chicago: University of Chicago Press, pp. 31–50.

____ (1978) 'The literature of economics: the case of the kinked oligopoly demand curve', *Economic Inquiry*, 16 (2), pp. 185–204.

____ (1990) 'The place of Marshall's *Principles* in the development of economics', in J.K. Whitaker (ed.) (1990a) q.v., pp. 1–13.

____, Stigler, S.M. and Friedland, C. (1995) 'The journals of economics', *Journal of Political Economy*, 103 (2), pp. 331–59.

Stiglitz, J.E. (1991) 'Another century of economic science', *Economic Journal*, 101 (1), pp. 134–41.

Stone, D. (1996) 'From the margins of politics: the influence of think-tanks in Britain', *West European Politics*, 19 (4), pp. 675–92.

Stone, J.R.N. (1951) 'The use and development of national income and expenditure estimates', in D.N. Chester (ed.) (1951a) q.v., pp. 83–101.

____ (1977) *Inland Revenue report on national income, 1929*. Cambridge: University of Cambridge, Department of Applied Economics.

Strange, S. (1996) *The retreat of the state: the diffusion of power in the world economy*. Cambridge University Press: Cambridge.

Streeten, P. (ed.) (1970a) *Unfashionable economics: essays in honour of Lord Balogh*. London: Weidenfeld & Nicolson.

____ (1970b) 'Thomas Balogh', in P. Streeten (ed.) (1970a) q.v., pp. ix–

xviii.

Supple, B.E. (1990) 'Official economic inquiry and Britain's industrial decline: the first fifty years', in M.O. Furner and B.E. Supple (eds) (1990) **q.v.**, pp. 325–53.

Swain, H. (1997) 'Eminences grises' eminence grise', *Times Higher Education Supplement*, 7 November, p. 17.

Szenberg, M. (1990) 'The Walters-Lawson affair and the two worlds of communication: a collision course', *American Journal of Economics and Sociology*, 49 (3), pp. 293–6.

Taverne, D. (1983) 'Looking back', *Fiscal Studies*, 4 (3), pp. 1–6.

Taylor, J. and Izadi, H. (1996) 'The 1992 Research Assessment Exercise: outcome, outputs and inputs in economics and econometrics', *Bulletin of Economic Research*, 48 (1), pp. 1–26.

Tew, J.H.B. (1978) 'Policies aimed at improving the balance of payments', in F.T. Blackaby (ed.) (1978) **q.v.**, pp. 304–59.

Thain, C. and Wright, M.W. (1995) *The Treasury and Whitehall: the planning and control of public expenditure, 1976–1993*. Oxford: Clarendon Press.

Thatcher, M. (1993) *The Downing Street years*. London: Harper Collins.

Thirlwall, A.P. (1981) 'Keynesian employment theory is not defunct', *Three Banks Review*, 131 (September), pp. 14–29.

—— (1982) 'De-industrialisation in the United Kingdom', *Lloyds Bank Review*, 144 (April), pp. 22–37.

—— (1987) *Nicholas Kaldor*. Brighton: Wheatsheaf.

—— (1989) 'Kaldor as a policy adviser', in T. Lawson, J.G. Palma and J. Sender (eds) (1989) *Kaldor's political economy*. London: Academic Press, pp. 121–39.

—— (1993) 'The renaissance of Keynesian economics', *Banca Nazionale*

del Lavoro Quarterly Review*, 46 (3), pp. 327–37.

—— (1997) *Selected essays*. Vol. 2: *Macroeconomic issues from a Keynesian perspective*. Cheltenham: Edward Elgar.

—— and Gibson, H.D. (1992) *Balance-of-payments theory and the United Kingdom experience*, 4th edn. London: Macmillan.

Thomas, H. (ed.) (1959) *The establishment*. London: Anthony Blond.

Thompson, G.F. (1997) 'Where goes economics and the economies?', *Economy and Society*, 26 (4), pp. 599–610.

Thompson, N. (1996) *Political economy and the Labour Party: the economics of democratic socialism, 1884–1995*. London: UCL Press.

Thurow, L.C. (1983) *Dangerous currents: the state of economics*. Oxford: Oxford University Press.

Thygesen, N. (1977) 'The scientific contributions of Milton Friedman', *Scandinavian Journal of Economics*, 79 (1), pp. 56–98.

Tobin, J. (1978) 'Harry Gordon Johnson, 1923–1977', *Proceedings of the British Academy*, 64, pp. 443–58.

—— (1981) 'The monetarist counter-revolution today: an appraisal', *Economic Journal*, 91 (1), pp. 29–42.

—— (1983) 'Macroeconomics and fiscal policy', in E.C. Brown and R.M. Solow (eds) (1983) *Paul Samuelson and modern economic theory*. New York: McGraw-Hill, pp. 189–201.

—— (1997) 'Macroeconomics in the conservative era', *Challenge*, 40 (4), pp. 27–35.

Tolles, N.A. (1968) 'Who are the economists?: number, mean salary and mean income in 1964 of "economists" under eight definitions of the profession', *American Economic Review*, 58 (5, Pt. II, Supplement), pp. 123–53.

Tomlinson, J.D. (1981a) 'Why was there never a "Keynesian revolution" in economic policy?', *Economy and Society*, 10 (1), pp. 72–87.

—— (1981b) *Problems of British economic policy, 1870–1945*. London: Methuen.

—— (1987) *Employment policy: the crucial years, 1939–1955*. Oxford: Oxford University Press.

—— (1990) *Public policy and the economy since 1900*. Oxford: Clarendon Press.

—— (1994) *Government and the enterprise since 1900: the changing problem of efficiency*. Oxford: Oxford University Press.

Towse, R. and Blaug, M. (1988) *The current state of the British economics profession*. London: RES.

—— and —— (1990) 'The current state of the British economics profession', *Economic Journal*, 100 (1), pp. 227–36.

Toye, J. (1994) 'Comment', in J. Williamson (ed.) (1994a) **q.v.**, pp. 35–43.

Tress, R.C. (1964) 'Preface', in P.E. Hart *et al.* (eds) (1964) **q.v.**, pp. vii–viii.

Tribe, K. (1992) 'The *Economic Journal* and British economics, 1891–1940', *History of the Human Sciences*, 5 (1), pp. 33–58.

—— (1993) 'Political economy in the northern civic universities', in A. Kadish and K. Tribe (eds) (1993a) **q.v.**, pp. 184–226.

—— (1997) *Economic careers: economics and economists in Britain, 1930–1970*. London: Routledge.

Turner, J. (1988) '"Experts" and interests: David Lloyd George and the dilemmas of the expanding state, 1906–19', in R.M. MacLeod (ed.) (1988a) **q.v.**, pp. 203–23.

Turvey, R. (1963) 'Present value *versus* internal rate of return: an essay in the theory of the third best', *Economic Journal*, 73 (1), pp. 93–8.

Tutton, T. (1976) 'Intellectual conceptions of economic justice', in A. Jones (ed.) (1976) *Economics and equality*. Oxford: Philip Allan, pp. 149–62.

UNESCO (1975) *Higher education: international trends, 1960–1970*. Paris: UNESCO.

Vaitilingam, R. (1997) 'Economists in the media', *Social Sciences: news from the ESRC*, 34 (March), p. 8.

Varian, H.R. (1996) *Intermediate microeconomics: a modern approach*. New York: W.W. Norton.

Vickrey, W. (1993) 'Today's task for economists', *American Economic Review*, 83 (1), pp. 1–10.

Viner, J. (1941) 'Marshall's economics, in relation to the man and to his times', *American Economic Review*, 31 (2), pp. 223–35.

Vines, D., Maciejowski, J.M. and Meade, J.E. (1983) *Stagflation*, Vol. II: *Demand management*. London: George Allen & Unwin.

Walden, G. (1996) *We should know better: solving the education crisis*. London: Fourth Estate.

Walker, D. (1987) 'The first Wilson governments, 1964–1970', in P. Hennessy and A. Seldon (eds) (1987) *Ruling performance: British governments from Attlee to Thatcher*. Oxford: Basil Blackwell, pp. 186–215.

Walker, E.R. (1943) *From economic theory to policy*. Chicago: University of Chicago Press.

Wallis, K.F. (1989) 'Macroeconomic forecasting: a survey', *Economic Journal*, 99 (1), pp. 28–61.

Walters, A.A. (1970) 'The Radcliffe report – ten years after: a survey of empirical evidence', in D.R. Croome and H.G. Johnson (eds) (1970) **q.v.**, pp. 39–68.

—— (1978) *Economists and the British economy*. London: IEA.

—— (1981) *The economic adviser's role: scope and limitations*. London: CPS.

—— (1987) 'Milton Friedman', in J. Eatwell *et al.* (eds) (1987) **q.v.**, pp. 422–7.

_____ (1990) *Sterling in danger: the economic consequences of pegged exchange rates*. London: Fontana.

Walters, B. and Young, D. (1997) 'On the coherence of post-Keynesian economics', *Scottish Journal of Political Economy*, 44 (3), pp. 329–49.

Ward, B. (1972) *What's wrong with economics?* New York: Basic Books.

Ward, R. and Doggett, T. (1991) *Keeping score: the first fifty years of the Central Statistical Office*. London: HMSO.

Wass, D. (1978) 'The changing problem of economic management', *Economic Trends*, 293 (March), pp. 97–104.

_____ (1987) Foreword to Thirlwall (1987) q.v., pp. xi–xiv.

Weale, M.R. (1992) 'The benefits of higher education: a comparison of universities and polytechnics', *Oxford Review of Economic Policy*, 8 (2), pp. 35–47.

Weintraub, E.R. (1975) '"Uncertainty" and the Keynesian revolution', *History of Political Economy*, 7 (4), pp. 530–48.

_____ (1979) *Microfoundations: the compatibility of microeconomics and macroeconomics*. Cambridge: Cambridge University Press.

_____ (1991) *Stabilizing dynamics: constructing economic knowledge*. Cambridge: Cambridge University Press.

_____ and Mirowski, P. (1994) 'The pure and applied Bourbakism comes to mathematical economics', *Science in Context*, 7 (2), pp. 245–72.

Weir, S. (1982) 'The model that crashed', *New Society*, 61 (12 August), pp. 251–3.

Wells, J.R. (1993) 'The economy after ten years: stronger or weaker?', in N.M. Healey (ed.) (1993) q.v., pp. 91–108.

Whitaker, J.K. (1986) 'The continuing relevance of Alfred Marshall', in R.D.C. Black (ed.) (1986) *Ideas in economics*. London: Macmillan, pp. 176–90.

_____ (ed.) (1990a) *Centenary essays on Alfred Marshall*. Cambridge: Cambridge University Press.

_____ (1990b) 'What happened to the second volume of the *Principles*?: the thorny path to Marshall's last books', in J.K. Whitaker (ed.) (1990a) q.v., pp. 193–222.

_____ (1996) *The correspondence of Alfred Marshall, economist*, 3 vols. Cambridge: Cambridge University Press.

Whitley, J.D. (1997) 'Economic models and policy–making', *Bank of England Quarterly Bulletin*, 37 (2), pp. 163–73.

Whitley, R. (1984) *The intellectual and social organization of the sciences*. Oxford: Clarendon Press.

_____ (1991) 'The organisation and role of journals in economics and other scientific fields', *Economic Notes*, 20 (1), pp. 6–32.

Wickham–Jones, M. (1992) 'Monetarism and its critics: the university economists' protest of 1981', *Political Quarterly*, 63 (2), pp. 171–85.

_____ (1996) *Economic strategy and the Labour Party: politics and policy-making, 1970–83*. London: Macmillan.

_____ (1997) 'Social democracy and structural dependency: the British case – a note on Hay', *Politics and Society*, 25 (2), pp. 257–65.

Wilding, R. (1995) 'The Fulton report in retrospect', *Contemporary Record*, 9 (2), pp. 394–408.

Wiles, P.J.D. and Routh, G. (eds) (1984) *Economics in disarray*. Oxford: Basil Blackwell.

Williams, A. (1967) 'Output budgeting and the contribution of microeconomics to efficiency in government', Civil Service Department CAS Occasional Paper no. 4.

Williams, G. (1997) 'The market route to mass higher education: British experience, 1979–1996', *Higher Education Policy*, 10 (3/4), pp. 276–89.

Williamson, J. (ed.) (1994a) *The political economy of policy reform*. Washington, DC: Institute for International Economics.

_____ (1994b) 'In search of a manual for technopols', in J. Williamson (ed.) (1994a) **q.v.**, pp. 11–28.

_____ (1997) 'Comments', in A.W. Coats (ed.) (1997a) **q.v.**, pp. 364–8.

Wilson, J.H. (1971) *The Labour government, 1964–1970: a personal record*. London: Weidenfeld & Nicolson.

Wilson, T. (1995) *Churchill and the prof*. London: Cassell.

_____ and Andrews, P.W.S. (eds) (1951) *Oxford studies in the price mechanism*. Oxford: Clarendon Press.

Winch, D.N. (1962) 'What price the history of economic thought?', *Scottish Journal of Political Economy*, 9 (3), pp. 193–204.

_____ (1969) *Economics and policy: a historical study*. London: Hodder & Stoughton.

_____ (1990a) 'A century of economics', in J.D. Hey and D.N. Winch (eds) (1990) **q.v.**, pp. 3–21.

_____ (1990b) 'Economic knowledge and government in Britain: some historical and comparative reflections', in M.O. Furner and B.E. Supple (eds) (1990) **q.v.**, pp. 40–70.

Withers, H. (1909) *The meaning of money*. London: Smith, Elder & Co.

Wolf, C. (1993) *Markets or governments: choosing between imperfect alternatives*, 2nd edn. Cambridge, MA: MIT Press.

Wood, J.B. (1972) *How much unemployment?: the methods and measures dissected*. London: IEA.

Wood, J.C. (1983) *British economists and the empire*. London: Croom Helm.

Woodward, N.W.C. (1993) 'Labour's economic performance, 1964–70', in R. Coopey *et al.* (eds) (1993) **q.v.**, pp. 72–101.

Wootton, B. (1938) *Lament for economics*. London: George Allen & Unwin.

Worswick, G.D.N. (1969) 'Fiscal policy and stabilization in Britain', *Journal of Money, Credit and Banking*, 1 (1), pp. 36–60. Rep. in A.K. Cairncross (ed.) (1971b) **q.v.**, pp. 36–60.

_____ (1972a) 'Is progress in economic science possible?', *Economic Journal*, 82 (1), pp. 73–86. Rep. in G.D.N. Worswick (ed.) (1972b) **q.v.**, pp. 21–38.

_____ (ed.) (1972b) *Uses of economics*. Oxford: Basil Blackwell.

_____ (ed.) (1976) *The concept and measurement of involuntary unemployment*. London: George Allen & Unwin.

_____ (1977) 'The end of demand management?', *Lloyds Bank Review*, 123 (January), pp. 1–18.

_____ (1992) 'How was it possible to run economies at such high pressure without accelerating wage rates?', in F. Cairncross and A.K. Cairncross (eds) (1992) **q.v.**, pp. 45–66 (and discussion, pp. 66–80).

_____ and Blackaby, F.T. (eds) (1974) *The medium term: models of the British economy*. London: Heinemann.

_____ and Trevithick, J. (eds) (1983) *Keynes and the modern world*. Cambridge: Cambridge University Press.

Wright, H. (1927) 'Frederick Lavington', *Economic Journal*, 37 (3), pp. 503–4.

Wright, R. (1989) 'Robbins as a political economist: a response to O'Brien', *Economic Journal*, 99 (2), pp. 471–8.

Young, H. and Sloman, A. (1984) *But, Chancellor: an inquiry into the Treasury*. London: BBC.

Young, W.L. (1989) *Harrod and his trade cycle group: the origins and development of the growth research programme*. London: Macmillan.

_____ and Lee, F.S. (1993) *Oxford economics and Oxford economists*. London: Macmillan.

Index

Page numbers in heavy type refer to biographical details in Appendix I.